MOON

ISTANBUL
& THE TURKISH COAST

LEEANN MURPHY

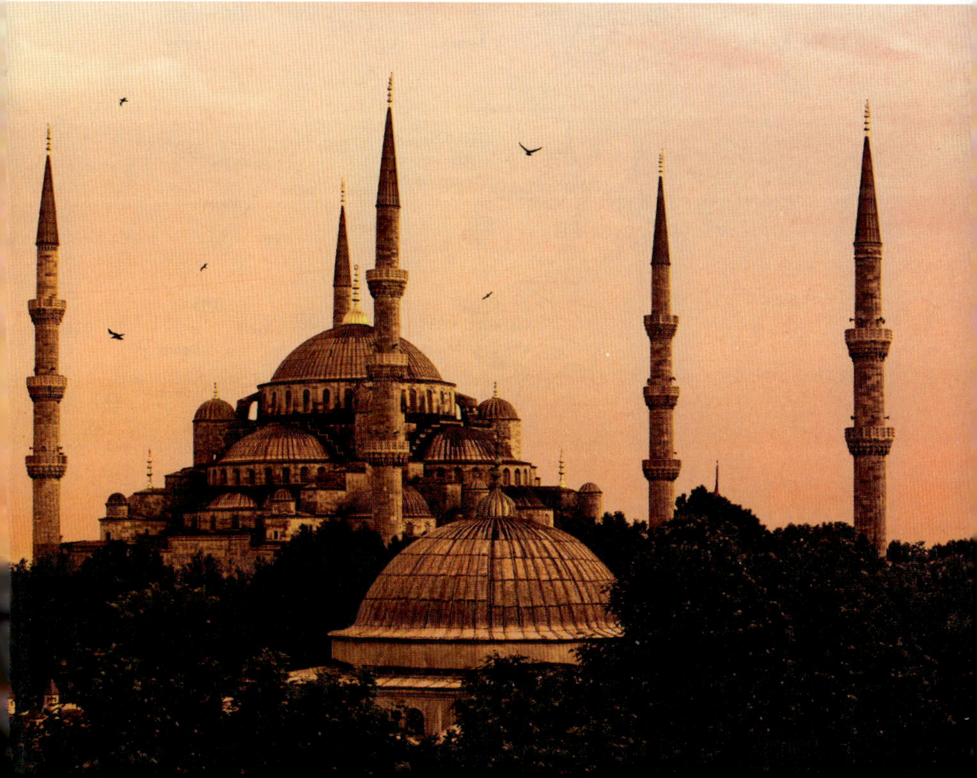

Contents

Discover Istanbul & the Turkish Coast 8
Planning Your Trip 12
- If You Have 14

The Best of Istanbul............... 15
- Turkish Delight 16

Ancient Cities and the Blue Cruise.... 18
- Best Photo-Ops 19
- Best Beaches 20
- Top Outdoor Adventures 22
- Unique Places to Stay 24

Cappadocia's Lunar Landscape...... 25
The Seven Churches of the Revelation 27

Istanbul...................... 29
Sights 34
Entertainment and Events......... 81
Shopping 85
Sports and Recreation............ 90
Accommodations 94
Food 101
Information and Services 109
Getting There 110
Getting Around................. 113

Thrace and the Sea of Marmara 116
Marmara Denizi (Sea of Marmara).... 120
Edirne 140
Gelibolu Yarımadası (Gallipoli Peninsula)............ 147

The Northern Aegean Coast................ 154
Çanakkale and Truva (Troy) 159
Bergama (Pergamum)............ 184
İzmir 191

The Southern Aegean Coast................ 210
The Ephesus Region 214
Pamukkale.................... 238

The Turquoise Coast 246
Bodrum....................... 249
Marmaris 265
Dalyan....................... 274
Fethiye 280
Kalkan 297
Kaş.......................... 301
Olympos, Çıralı, and Chimera 309
Antalya 312

Cappadocia and Central Anatolia **328**
Cappadocia..................... 332
Konya 356
Ankara........................ 365
Hattuşaş (Boğazkale)............... 377

Background.................. **381**
The Land 382
Flora and Fauna.................. 385
History........................ 387
Government 403
Economy....................... 406
People and Culture 409

Essentials **414**
Getting There 415
Getting Around.................. 416
Visas and Officialdom 421
Accommodations 423
Food and Drink 424
Travel Tips 427
Health and Safety 432
Information and Services 437

Resources **442**
Glossary....................... 442
Turkish Phrasebook............... 443
Suggested Reading............... 450
Internet Resources 452

Index........................ **454**
List of Maps **471**

DISCOVER
Istanbul & the Turkish Coast

Istanbul not only delineates the continental divide between Asia and Europe, it serves as a lively meeting point of the modern and traditional, and of Western, Eastern, and Middle Eastern cultures. Turkey's crown jewel won the hearts of the emperors and sultans of four empires who fought to claim the city as their capital. Even Napoleon thought it should be the capital of the world.

The magic of Istanbul lies in its many contradictions. Five times a day the *müezzinler* call the faithful to prayer from minarets, some atop former basilicas that were built by early Christians. In the streets, female fashionistas don designer dresses in the bars lining the Bosphorus while the more religious color-coordinate their *hijabs* with conservative overcoats adorned with gold buttons and trim. Nowhere is the synergy more apparent than on dining tables, where spice-infused kebabs are served alongside mezes (appetizers) and the ubiquitous Western cola.

This rich historical, cultural, and spiritual melting pot extends to the coastal lands just beyond Istanbul as well. Spanning over 10 millennia, the history of this fertile land is as layered as baklava. More than a dozen distinct empires have risen and fallen here, each fighting to gain or retain their wedge of this unique landscape. In

Clockwise from top left: the Rüstem Paşa Mosque; the Galata District at sunset; camels at Kayaköy; Blue Cruise on the Mediterranean; spices for sale; caves of Cappadocia.

Turkey's interior, between the sun-kissed rambling Aegean coast in the west and the glistening waters of the Turkish Riviera in the south, there are hundreds of thousands of kilometers of rugged mountain ranges and cultivated plains, peppered with innumerable remnants of past civilizations.

Perhaps the most surreal geography in the country is in Cappadocia. The region is home to centuries-old cave dwellings and chapels carved inside majestic fairy chimneys, eroded from volcanic tuff accumulation. Explore this intense and unbelievable landscape from above in a hot-air balloon, the preferred method of sightseeing. Rides almost dip low enough for passengers to pick lusciously ripe apricots from high branches.

Sail the dreamy Blue Voyage along the Turquoise Coast, see giant loggerhead turtles glide in the waters off Dalyan, trek the 509-kilometer Lycian Way along the pine-clad mountains that jut into the Mediterranean, and whirl into mysticism at the Mevlânâ Museum in Konya. As dazzling and mysterious as its landscape and history are, Turkey's people are just as amazing. Meet the locals and experience Turkish hospitality for yourself.

Clockwise from top left: colorful Ottoman homes of Balat, Istanbul; Ortaköy Mosque and the Bosphorus Bridge, Istanbul; market outside the Ayasofya, Istanbul; Lycian tombs of Myra.

Planning Your Trip

Where to Go

ISTANBUL
Istanbul offers an intimate view of civilizations past and quickens the heart with its fast-paced metropolitan beat. Old Istanbul's **Sultanahmet** sights include **Topkapı Palace,** the 1,500-year-old Byzantine basilica **Ayasofya,** the scintillating **Blue Mosque,** and the original enclosed mall, the **Grand Bazaar.** Cross the Golden Horn for **Taksim**'s belle epoque architecture, cruise the Bosphorus into **Asia,** or sail to the **Princes' Islands.**

THRACE AND THE SEA OF MARMARA
This little-known slice of Turkey is gaining popularity due to its scenery and proximity to Istanbul for day trips. The **Dardanelles Strait,** gateway to inland Anatolia, bears the scars of lengthy battles at **Gallipoli National Park.** Other highlights of the region are the Selimiye Mosque in **Edirne,** Ottoman landmarks in **Bursa,** and **Iznik,** where Christianity's First Ecumenical Council met in AD 325.

THE NORTHERN AEGEAN COAST
At the tip of Anatolia, this region unfurls like an archaeological dig in progress, heightened by history's major capitals **Pergamum** and King Croesus's **Sardis.** Catapult back 5,000 years by visiting **Troy.** Sample Turkey's best vintages in the rustic B&Bs on the island of **Bozcaada.** Visit **İzmir**'s metropolitan and Levantine haunts and explore **Alaçatı**'s windsurfing and spa-hopping potential in **Çeşme.**

THE SOUTHERN AEGEAN COAST
Hugged by gorgeous beaches and the ruins of 17 historic cities, this coast lures sun worshippers and history buffs. **Ephesus,** once home to the **Temple of Artemis,** is Turkey's largest ancient city. Another crowd-pleaser, **Meryemana** is said to be the final resting place of the Virgin

carpets for sale in Cappadocia

Cities bloom with color in April for the Tulip Festival.

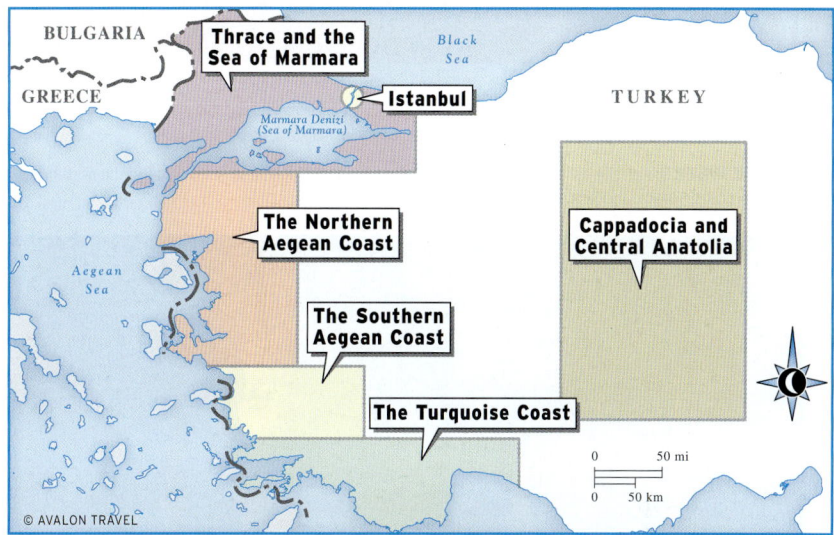

Mary. **Kuşadası** entices with modern hotels, sandy beaches, and water sports, while **Selçuk** offers fine antiquities scattered around a laid-back rural town. Turkey's interior beckons with dizzying petrified waterfalls, terraced basins at **Pamukkale,** and Greco-Roman ruins at the 2,300-year-old spa **Hierapolis.**

THE TURQUOISE COAST

The idyllic **Blue Cruise** putters along 1,000 kilometers of coastline, set against vertiginous cliffs, luxuriant forests, ancient cities, and the azure Mediterranean Sea. The region features hedonist resort **Bodrum; Fethiye**'s ghost town, **Kayaköy;** the natural Blue Lagoon near **Ölüdeniz;** and **Dalyan**'s river-hugging mountains. Coastal resorts **Kaş** and **Kalkan** give way to **Kaleköy,** with its Crusader fortress and sunken city. En route to historical and modern **Antalya** is **Demre**'s Byzantine church of Santa Claus.

CAPPADOCIA AND CENTRAL ANATOLIA

The Turkish capital, **Ankara,** was settled over 3,000 years ago. Its **Citadel** district boasts the **Museum of Anatolian Civilizations.** To the west, **Konya** awaits with spectacular Selçuk mosques, the **Mevlânâ Shrine,** and its whirling dervish order. East of Ankara lies **Hattuşaş,** whose 4,000-year-old Lion's Gate is impressive. Inland, **fairy chimneys, underground cities,** rock-hewn chapels, and five-star cave hotels and restaurants make up **Cappadocia**'s global appeal.

When to Go

The country's most visited destinations remain the coastal provinces, with a tourist high season in **June-early September.** Istanbul's humidity and long lines can be overwhelming in July and August. The western and southern coasts benefit from a seasonal Mediterranean climate, with hot summers and chilly winters, while Turkey's Anatolian plateau is dry and cold in winter.

The shoulder seasons, **early March-late May** and **mid-September-mid-November,** offer milder weather, sparser crowds, and better deals on airfares and hotels. Spring heralds Istanbul's annual tulip celebration and the city's world-renowned arts festivals. Wine aesthetes uncork their passion in Thrace, Çeşme, or Cappadocia at the end of September, just in time for the grape harvest.

Ramadan, the month of Islamic fasting between sunrise and sunset, is based on the lunar

If You Have . . .

- **ONE WEEK:** Visit Istanbul and Cappadocia.
- **TWO WEEKS:** Add a cruise through the Turquoise Coast's half-dozen resorts.
- **THREE WEEKS:** Add the southern Aegean cities of Kuşadası, Pamukkale, and Selçuk. Or add the northern Aegean coast, Ankara, and Konya.

Blue Mosque and fountain in Istanbul

calendar and will fall during summer for at least the next decade. Ramadan affects tourists in a minor way. The practice translates into low-energy staff and cranky cabbies but also presents occasion to partake in festivities including the breaking of bread over a hearty Iftar (breaking the fast) meal proffered by many eateries throughout the country.

Before You Go

To visit Turkey for tourism or commerce, you need a **valid passport** and an **e-visa** (www.evisa.gov.tr). Visas for work or study are obtained through embassies and consulates. Obtaining visas when you enter the country is no longer possible as of 2014. There are no medical requirements to enter Turkey.

The Best of Istanbul

Plan for three days in Istanbul, and you'll wish you stayed longer. A five-day itinerary will show you the best of the city that straddles two continents. Start in old Istanbul, but don't forget the abundance of attractions outside the old city walls in Eyüp and across the Golden Horn in Beyoğlu. Asia is also a five-minute undersea train ride away on the Marmaray. For the quintessential Istanbul experience, board the intercontinental Bosphorus ferry instead.

From Istanbul, you can easily extend your trip along the coast to experience ancient Ephesus, the snowy white travertines of Pamukkale, and sun-kissed Antalya (page 18). The must-see moonscape of Cappadocia and spiritual Konya (page 25) are the perfect end to your journey. *Iyi tatiller!* (Have a nice holiday!)

Old Istanbul
DAY 1
Hoşgeldiniz (welcome) to Istanbul! To acclimate to the beat of this modern city, head to **Sultanahmet,** where the underground **Basilica Cistern** and **Ayasofya** beckon. Take an hour or more to visit the latter, which has withstood the whim of several empires over nearly 1,500 years. Then turn your sights to the **Blue Mosque,** 100 meters away, and stop by the dancing fountain of **Sultanahmet Park** for a photo opportunity with Istanbul's greatest monuments in the background. Once inside the 17th-century mosque, gaze at the blue tiles that give it its name before stepping out to the **Hippodrome** that once hosted Roman chariot races. Finally, work up an appetite for dinner by wandering up to Beyazıt to browse the 4,000 shops of the **Grand Bazaar.** When you're shopped out, head back to Sultanahmet to feast on Ottoman cuisine.

DAY 2
Head to **Topkapı Palace,** Istanbul's top tourist draw, for a long stroll through the harem, treasury, and Seraglio Point. Refuel and revive in the

Dolmabahçe Palace on the Bosphorus, Istanbul

Turkish Delight

The specialties that make Turkey's tables unique are easily found in culinary-rich Istanbul, but foodies should also bring their appetites to western and central Turkey's inner realms. *Afiyet olsun* (bon appétit)!

ANATOLIAN CUISINE

A mix of cuisines either indigenous to the steppe region or derived from Turkey's neighbors, Anatolian cuisine rarely gets the praise it deserves. Check out anthropologist Musa Dağdeviren's **Çiya Sofrası** restaurant in Kadıköy for soups, herbed pilafs, tender kebabs, veggie stews, ambrosial sherbets, and exotic desserts concocted daily in the open kitchen. The day's specialties are created from long-lost recipes the master chef retrieved through decades of research. Dağdeviren's feasts have even garnered international accolades from food critics. Try dishes like *alinazık*—grilled morsels of lamb or chicken atop roasted eggplant pureed with garlic and yogurt—and piping hot portions of *künefe* (a sweet cheesy shredded pastry dish). Çiya also boasts one of the meanest *lahmacun* (thin-crust meaty pizza) in town.

BAKLAVA AND TURKISH DELIGHT

Head to the original **Karaköy Güllüoğlu** café in Istanbul's Karaköy neighborhood for layers of flaky phyllo dough stuffed with toasted nut morsels and sweetened to perfection. Of the many contenders for Baklava mastery, this one remains the top.

The other sweet indigenous to Istanbul is *lokum* (Turkish delight), a nougat-like confection created by Ali Muhiddin Hacı Bekir in 1777 for the fickle tastes of Topkapı Palace's concubines. **Ali Muhiddin Hacı Bekir** boasts 27 varieties of *lokum* from its original location in Istanbul's Bahçekapı quarter, but the twice-roasted pistachio *lokum* remains the best seller at its other branches in Eminönü and Kadıköy.

ÇAY

Çay (black tea), grown in the eastern Black Sea region, is ubiquitous in Turkey. Brewed samovar-style until it's crimson, like the color of the Turkish flag, *çay* is served in a small tulip-shaped glass and is best enjoyed with others and with a dash of *keyfi* (the art of idle relaxation). Just add a lump or two of sugar to subdue the bitter flavor.

FISH

Wherever you stay along the coast, chances are a great fish restaurant is nearby. Try **Çengelköy Iskele Restaurant,** in Istanbul's Çengelköy neighborhood, for grilled *levrek* (sea bass) and the dish called Atom—a stew of seafood plucked from the waters of the Bosphorus just outside.

Along the Aegean coast, among the best is **Deniz Restaurant.** Try any of its lauded calamari dishes or the grilled *çipura* (gilthead sea bream).

OTTOMAN CUISINE

The culinary tradition of the ancient Ottomans is alive throughout Turkey with dishes like dolmas and *imam bayıldı*, a concoction of onion, garlic, and tomato stuffed inside an eggplant and cooked to such perfection it made an "imam swoon" (the literal translation) centuries ago. To experience firsthand the mortar-and-pestle ateliers of the Ottoman sultans' master chefs, one must head to the grand kitchens of Topkapı Palace and taste their handed-down artistry on-site at the regally decorated **Konyalı Topkapı Sarayı Lokantası.**

TURKISH COFFEE

The number of custom coffeehouses has eclipsed that of traditional Turkish coffee joints in Turkey's largest metropolises, but the café culture still remains. Join the Turks in one of their favorite pastimes—*kahve muhabbeti* (coffee chat)—at **Pierre Loti Café** in Fatih for supreme views of the Golden Horn.

Istanbul's illuminated Basilica Cistern

palace grounds with Ottoman *şerbet* drinks and Bosphorus views at **Konyalı Topkapı Sarayı Lokantası** before launching into shopping in the **Egyptian Spice Bazaar.** Sample some Turkish delight, then walk to Eminönü port to locate the Şehir Hatları ferry and board a two-hour **Bosphorus Cruise.** If there's still energy in them bones, board a public ferry to Asia's Kadıköy district. Spend the early evening exploring the streets of the **open-air bazaar** around Güneşli Bahçe Sokak, and don't return to Europe before dining at **Çiya Sofrası.** Finish the day by cruising back to Europe and finding a café to smoke a fruity narghile.

Beyoğlu
DAY 3

Today, turn your back on the history of old Istanbul to take in the lifestyles of modern day *Istanbullus* (Istanbul residents). Take the guided tour of the 19th-century **Dolmabahçe Palace,** stopping briefly to pay homage to the father of modern day Turkey, Mustafa Kemal Atatürk, who took his last breath here in 1938. Make your way to **Taksim Square** and onto the famous **Istiklal Caddesi**—one of Europe's busiest pedestrian avenues—for two kilometers of shopping, dining, and sightseeing. At the end of Istiklal, stroll the cobbled Galip Dede Caddesi that brims with musical instruments and boutiques to find your way to the medieval **Galata Tower.** Time your visit for sunset and climb to the top for stunning 360-degree views of the city and the calming waters of the Bosphorus. Get here early—there's often a wait to go up for sunset. With those postcard-perfect photos captured, follow the maze of streets downhill to **Galata Bridge,** order a freshly cooked fish sandwich by the water's edge, and people-watch as dusk settles over the city.

Greater Istanbul
DAY 4

Plan a day to venture to the sights lining one of the world's best natural harbors—the Haliç (Golden Horn). Don't miss the impressive golden mosaic frescoes of **Chora Museum,** about one kilometer from the harbor's southern shores. Afterward, make your way to the iconic **Eyüp Mosque** before taking the **cable car** nearby up to **Pierre Loti Café** to savor lunch at the panoramic lookout made popular by the author of the same name. Walk back downhill through the cemetery to Eyüp port to cruise across to **Miniatürk** to roam the miniature models of the Ottoman Empire's and Turkey's greatest architectural feats and natural wonders. If time allows, continue the day on the Golden Horn's northern shores at **Rahmi M. Koç Museum** to have a hands-on experience exploring submarines, steam trains, and a planetarium. Cap the day with a **Turkish Night** of authentic folkloric dancing, belly dancing, and other musical surprises.

Princes' Islands
DAY 5

Say good-bye to Istanbul by visiting the **Princes' Islands** on a relaxing 95-minute cruise of the Bosphorus and Marmara Sea aboard an Istanbul

Come summer, the Princes' Islands beaches lure a local or two.

slow ferry. Take in the sights and sounds of the city's waterways, order a tea from the vendor roaming the decks, and feed the seagulls with freshly baked bread sold on board before disembarking at **Büyükada** (big island). The islands are car-free, so rent a bicycle near the port or take the horse and cart to trot around the island, making sure to stop at Lunapark to climb to the hilltop **Aya Yorgi Monastery** for spectacular views of Istanbul. Try the island seafood, the *dondurma* (ice cream), and soak up the serene island vibe.

Ancient Cities and the Blue Cruise

Begin in the quaint town of Selçuk and tour the famed ancient city of Ephesus before continuing on to Pamukkale to laze on the white travertines. Cap off your coastal journey on the Turquoise Coast, exploring Kaş and Antalya or floating away on a Blue Cruise.

Selçuk and Ephesus
DAY 1
From Istanbul, fly early to İzmir Airport, where you can hire your own car or use the train to transfer to the sleepy rural town of **Selçuk.** Take an hour or two to see the **Basilica of St. John, Isabey Camii,** and the **Byzantine aqueducts** side-by-side on St. Jean Caddesi. If you have time, head to the bucolic wine bastion of **Şirince** for brunch in the village. Around 1pm, join the pilgrimage to Bülbül Dağı to the venerated **House of the Virgin Mary,** before finishing your day with a cooler three-hour tour of **Ephesus** and its terraced houses. In the evening, check out the low-key vibe of Selçuk town or take the *dolmuş* (communal taxi) to Kuşadası to party with a rowdy northern European set.

Best Photo-Ops

Pack an extra camera battery and charge up every evening because Turkey is packed with gorgeous photo opportunities. Pack a tripod as well: enchanting night shots all around the country are a sight to behold.

ISTANBUL

- Have the lens focused on the gilded mosaics, marble columns, and hanging chandeliers of the grand old **Ayasofya.** Lately it has nearly been upstaged by another attraction—the cross-eyed chubby-faced resident **Ayasofya cat,** so photogenic he's got his own blog and Twitter account.

- The **Egyptian Spice Bazaar,** full of sugar-powdered green, red, and yellow Turkish delight and the warm hues of saffron and red peppers, is a feast of visual temptations.

- Take a **Bosphorus cruise** at sunset to capture the quintessential shot of a mosque silhouetted against a glowing orange sky. At dusk, find a spot near the **Galata Bridge** in Eminönü to capture neon-lit boats bobbing against the docks.

THE COAST AND CAPPADOCIA

- The camera will get a workout on the haunting **rock-cut Lycian tombs** of Dalyan, Fethiye, and Myra.

- Capture the village life of the quaint whitewashed **Şirince** and the timber **tree houses of Olympos** set against lush green forests.

- Arrive in the morning to capture that shot of the **Library of Celsus** at Ephesus in perfect harmony with natural lighting, or contend with shadows in the late afternoon as the sun sets behind this majestic structure.

Library of Celsus in Ephesus

- Hike through the ghostly stone remains of **Kayaköy** or up through the cobble paths of **Assos** to photograph Turkey's remote pine-clad coastlines with nearby islands adorning azure seas.

- Ottoman homes with tons of character are best in Antalya's **Kaleiçi** and Ankara's **Citadel** districts, while the former homes of Greeks make for a nostalgic excursion in **Ayvalık** and **Bozcaada.**

- No photo album of Turkey should lack the moonscape lands of **Cappadocia,** painted with multicolored hot-air balloons hovering above the Rose Valley.

Best Beaches

With a coastline extending more than 6,700 kilometers, Turkey's sandy expanses are numerous, and finding the "best" stretch of beach mostly depends on your itinerary. Though there are popular beaches on the southern Aegean coast by the party town of Kuşadası, the sandy beaches of the northern Aegean and Turquoise Coast are less crowded and more picturesque.

NORTHERN AEGEAN

The sunshine and sparkling waters near İzmir are best embraced along the **Çeşme Peninsula** with the white sands of **Altınkum, Pırlanta,** and **Alaçati** offering a retreat for swimmers, sunbathers, kitesurfing, and windsurfing enthusiasts. **Ilıca** and **Sifne Bay** even have healing natural springs that seep through the seabed on Çeşme's northern coast to lures those with an interest in natural remedies.

THE TURQUOISE COAST

Where the southern Aegean coast meets the Mediterranean, the **Bodrum Peninsula** overflows with blue-flag beaches known to be the safest, cleanest, and most environmentally friendly in the world. Beach-loving families seeking shallow calm water can safely vacation here, reveling in the bays of **Bodrum, Gümüşlük, Bitez,** and **Akyarlar.**

Along the **Mediterranean coast,** the sunshine warms several shores worthy of a dip. Dalyan's **Iztuzu** is a four-kilometer stretch of pale sand popular among day-trippers and endangered loggerhead turtles.

windsurfing in Alaçati, Çeşme

Farther east, the pebbly lagoon of **Ölüdeniz** is touted nationally as the best seashore and bluest waters in the country. Sharing national top billing with Ölüdeniz, the 19-kilometer-long latte-colored sands of **Patara Beach** between Fethiye and Kalkan offers a little surf. Rounding off the best of the beaches in Turkey is the open-water **Kaputaş.** A path down a rocky gorge from the coastal D400 highway between Kalkan and Kaş leads to a small shingle cove that's popular for its secluded ambiance.

the ghost town of Kayaköy

nighttime dining in Kayaköy

Pamukkale
DAY 2

Visit Selçuk's **Ephesus Museum** early, then hit the road or rails to Denizli and onto the cotton castles of **Pamukkale.** After a three-hour journey, you'll be ready to walk barefoot up through the cool cascading waters of the **white travertines** to the ruins of the Roman city of **Hierapolis,** where Saint Philip the Apostle is said to be buried. Your reward for your efforts today is a long soak in Cleopatra's healing **Sacred Pool,** followed by a delicious home-cooked meal prepared by your friendly Anatolian hosts.

Fethiye, Kayaköy, and the Blue Lagoon
DAY 3

It's an early start again today as you travel for four hours south through the Taurus Mountains to the seaside resort town of **Fethiye.** Stroll along the town's port and through the **bazaar area** to be tempted to buy Turkish trinkets such as evil eyes, mosaic glassware, and painted ceramics. Keep walking southeast to find the **Tomb of King Amyntas** high on the cliff east of the **Crusader Fortress.** Locate the *dolmuş* station to board the minibus bound for the ghost town of **Kayaköy.** Here you'll visit the hauntingly surreal orthodox churches of a 17th-century Greek community that once resided in this picturesque valley. For dinner, linger in Kayaköy at one of the gourmet restaurants.

DAY 4

Today is your day off from the long intercity journeys. Take to a sun lounge by the **Blue Lagoon** of **Ölüdeniz** or board a day-long Mediterranean **12-Island Tour** to do nothing but swim, read, and chat over a fresh seafood lunch.

Day trips from Fethiye to **Dalyan** or **Saklıkent** are also possible either by private vehicle or with a tour. In Dalyan, stunning cliff-face **Lycian tombs, loggerhead turtles,** and a plunge in the riverbank **mud baths** await. East of Fethiye, the rushing waters of the Saklıkent give adventure seekers a chilly welcome to a one-hour hike in a 500-meter-deep crevasse. Lycia's oldest and most commanding city, **Tlos,** just 15 kilometers from

Top Outdoor Adventures

Adrenaline junkies and nature enthusiasts will find their share of adventures in Turkey. Contact the tour agencies listed in this guidebook in advance for itineraries and departure dates.

ON LAND
- **Biking:** Embark on a downhill mountain-biking expedition through the villages near **Demre.**
- **Hiking:** The 509-kilometer **Lycian Way** is the crème de la crème of Anatolian trails for beginners and experienced hikers. Venturing into the icy cascading waters of Ak Dağı (White Mountain) to walk **Saklıkent Gorge** should be on a hiking itinerary, as should the summer trails of **Uludağ** near **Bursa,** which has also becomes Turkey's premier **snow resort** four months a year.
- **Other activities:** Hiking the not-to-be-missed **valleys of Cappadocia** is an option, but **horseback rides** and **ATV tours** are also available. While you're close by, roam parts of the enchanting 14-kilometer Ihlara Valley.

ON THE WATER
- **Scuba diving:** The remains of World War I battleships near **Çanakkale** and **Gallipoli** are fascinating, as is the diversity of underwater landscapes and marine life off **Antalya, Bodrum,** and **Marmaris.** But most agree that **Kaş** is the best places for diving; it offers an unforgettable experience with over 19 locations and wrecks scattered around a Mediterranean cove brimming with creatures such as loggerhead turtles.
- **White-water rafting:** Rafters can try the **Dalaman River** with organized tours from any of the coastal towns between Bodrum and Fethiye.

IN THE AIR
- **Ballooning:** Jump into the basket of a hot-air balloon for a bird's-eye view of **Cappadocia's volcanic landscape.**
- **Paragliding:** Start from Babdagı (Father Mountain) for a 40-minute flight over the **Blue Lagoon of Ölüdeniz.**
- **Skydiving:** Take flight over the ancient city of **Ephesus.**

Ölüdeniz and the Blue Lagoon, as seen from the Lycian Way

enchanting Kaş

the canyon, is a magnificent reminder of Anatolia's rich history. End the day with a lively meal in Fethiye's open-air **fish markets,** where you can personally pick out the freshest catch of the day.

Blue Cruise or Kaş
DAY 5

If the 12-Island Tour left you hungry for more Mediterranean magic, set sail on an unforgettable three-night **Blue Cruise** to **Olympos,** which chugs along Turkey's rugged southern coastline, mooring by **Santa Claus Island, Ölüdeniz, Butterfly Valley, Kaş,** and **Kekova,** disembarking near Demre for a bus journey to Olympos. Spend a few days in the tree houses of Olympos before flying back to Istanbul from Antalya.

Alternatively, skip the cruise and travel by land today to the whitewashed town of **Kaş.** Explore the town's narrow lanes and boutiques before a mid-afternoon dip at a **beach club** lining the rocky bays. Trek west to the **amphitheater** on the edge of town to watch the sun set.

Kekova
DAY 6

Today is set aside for an organized tour, departing from your hotel, to cruise or kayak over the **sunken Lycian city** of Kekova Island. The tour also provide opportunities to venture up to the Byzantine **Fortress of the Knights of St. John** above the remote village of **Kaleköy.** Dinner at **Hayta Meyhane** in the evening will have you rubbing shoulders with the locals as traditional Turkish music plays in a cozy narrow laneway in Kaş.

Demre and Antalya
DAY 7

Drive for an hour on the D400 highway to reach Demre, where you can take a two-hour pit stop to see the rock-cut tombs and theater masks of **Myra** and pay respects to the legend of Santa Claus at the **Church of St. Nicholas.** From Demre, it's a picturesque three-hour drive to **Kaleiçi,** Antalya's old town, where you can spend the night in a restored Ottoman abode. If you arrive early, visit the **Antalya Museum** or wander the **ancient harbor** and **Kaleiçi Museum** to see how Ottoman architecture kept the locals cool in the summer swelter. Later, relax at the **Castle Bar & Restaurant** for a sunset drink while looking back on the Mediterranean coast as the sun dips behind the **Gulf of Antalya.**

Unique Places to Stay

From tree houses to Ottoman mansions to a cave complex that's also a UNESCO World Heritage site, Turkey offers unforgettable lodgings.

NORTHERN AEGEAN COAST

- **Hotel Armagrandi, Bozcaada:** Abandoned after 100 years in operation as the Aral **winery,** this stone building was refurbished and reopened in 2006 as a boutique hotel with elegant touches reminding guests of the factory's viticultural heritage.

- **Bonjour Pansiyon, Ayvalık:** Tucked away in cobbled lanes, this **former French consulate** preserves its European flair, albeit with a Turkish twist, with ornate antiques and century-old painted ceilings.

TURQUOISE COAST

- **Kadir's Treehouses, Olympos:** The tree house phenomenon of Olympos started in the 1980s when Kadir Kaya built his original Robinson Crusoe home for himself and his friends. Kadir's vision has since evolved into a fully functioning cedar-wood **tree house resort** in the lush forest and towering cliffs sheltering a secluded village near the Mediterranean.

Kadir's Treehouses, in the lush forest of Olympos

- **Aboard a *Gület*:** Blue Cruises on *gületler* (motorized wooden sailboats) are the chance to fall asleep under the stars on a balmy Mediterranean summer night. Cabins are available below deck, but take the opportunity to sleep above deck and snuggle in a blanket by the still waters lit by the moon.

- **Tuvana Hotel, Kaleici, Antalya:** Four classic **Ottoman mansions** once belonging to the officer Abdi Effendi welcome guest in the old town of Antalya. Gold-leafed ceilings and plush opulent drapery are just a few of things to expect in these abodes that hosted lavish parties for visiting dignitaries in the 18th century.

CAPPADOCIA

- **Kayakapı Premium Caves, Ürgüp, Cappadocia:** Check into the Mehmet Tokat Evi suite to have a plunge pool in the bedroom, in a UNESCO World Heritage Site, in a **complex of restored caves.** Perhaps a former inhabitant of the area, Saint John the Russian, a saint of miracles, had a hand in creating this hotel.

- **Divan Çukurhan, Ankara:** Once on the "Watch List of 100 Most Endangered Sites of the World," this **restored *han*** from the 16th and 17th centuries welcomed weary Ottoman traders descending on Ankara to flaunt their goods. It still retains its original charm.

stone columns in Love Valley near Göreme

Cappadocia's Lunar Landscape

Begin in Göreme, soaking in Cappadocia's moonscape as you explore underground cities and villages carved out of tufa. Make a pilgrimage to Konya, explore Turkey's capital city, Ankara, or end your trip in Göreme with an unforgettable hot-air balloon ride.

If continuing on to Cappadocia from Antalya on the Turquoise Coast, consider stopping in Konya (5 hours by car) first before traveling to Göreme (4 hours). It's a simply spectacular road trip for appreciating Anatolia's diverse topography.

Cappadocia
DAY 1

For the best airfares from Istanbul, take an 80-minute flight to Kayseri Erkilet International Airport, then transfer by minibus or car to Göreme, just an hour away. If you have time today, take the *dolmuş* to the **Open-Air Museum** and spend two to three hours marveling at the frescoes and religious remnants adorning this world-heritage national park. Make sure you're back in Göreme to finish the day with an ATV ride to **Çavuşin** and **Love Valley,** pausing at **Sunset Point** to watch dusk settle on **Pigeon Valley,** peppered with fairy chimneys, or saddle up for a sunset trot on horseback through **Rose and Honey Valleys.**

DAY 2

Rise early for the hot-air balloon parade of colors over the Cappadocian valleys before launching into a day of adventure. Take one of the highly recommended color-coded guided tours: the Green Tour for the **underground city** and the **Ihlara Valley,** or the Red Tour to roam Cappadocia's **Open-Air Museum** (if you didn't see it yesterday) and its northern rock formations and carved tufa villages.

Uçhisar Castle

Passing on the tour means an escapade with local *dolmuş* services to the UNESCO-protected **Zelve Open-Air Museum** and the nearby mushroom rock formations of **Paşabağları.** You then have the flexibility to board any of the *dolmuşlar* in the afternoon to head north for the pottery town of **Avanos,** or southeast to climb Temenni Hill in **Ürgüp.** Alternatively, transfer to the Uçhisar-bound *dolmuş* in Göreme to climb **Uçhisar Castle** for mind-blowing 360-degree views of Anatolia's diverse topography.

If your energy allows, the evening can be used to gain an appreciation for the *sema*—the ceremony of the whirling dervishes at the 13th-century **Saruhan**—perhaps the finest caravanserai in Turkey. The show starts at 6pm, with transfers from your hotel.

DAY 3

Wake up before sunrise to bid *hoşçakal* (farewell) to Cappadocia from the sky with a **hot-air balloon** tour—a one-hour, once-in-a-lifetime flight over the changing hues of the Cappadocian landscape. Back on solid ground, visit the sights you missed before packing to return to Istanbul, or continue on your journey to learn more about Turkey's legends—the father of modern day Turkey, Mustafa Kemal Ataturk, in Ankara or 13th-century poet and scholar, Rûmî (or Mevlânâ) in Konya. *Gürüşürüz* (see you again soon) Cappadocia.

Excursions
KONYA

Set aside a day for the city of **Konya,** which is an easy four-hour drive through the changing landscape of central Anatolia following the D300 highway from Nevşehir. First, pay respects to the tomb of Sufi mystic Rûmî and the legacies of the Mevlevi Order at the **Mevlânâ Museum.** After appreciating the origins of the **whirling dervish,** treat your taste buds at **Mevlevi Sofrası** with a menu straight from the kitchens of the Mevlevi Order. It's quite possibly the most innovative restaurant in the country. Afterward, travel to your next destination or work your way through the city's numerous museums and sights that pay homage to Konya's days as the capital of the Selçuk Empire, the center for the Mevlevi Order, and major city for the Ottoman dynasty. If you're visiting on a Saturday, complete the day with an authentic Sufi ceremony at the **Mevlânâ Culture Center** in the evening. Bed down for a night at the **Hich Hotel,** a historical mansion overlooking the rose garden of the Mevlâna Museum, and recite the words of the great poet who rests for eternity nearby.

ANKARA

A side trip to **Ankara** at the end of a Turkish adventure will benefit many travelers. To reach the capital, first travel to Aksaray from Göreme or Konya, then proceed north for three hours along the efficient E90 motorway. Spend two hours browsing the **Museum of Anatolian Civilizations,** which distills the eons of epochs of the country into an informative history lesson. From here, wander the **citadel area** nearby before taking a taxi to the **Ethnography Museum,** which once doubled as the resting place of Mustafa Kemal Atatürk and is a perfect segue to your next destination: **Anıtkabir**—Atatürk's Mausoleum. Take a taxi to the mausoleum to save time or use the metro, disembarking at Tandoğan station, and allow up to three hours to visit his tomb, explore the exhibits, and soak up the love for the man who modernized Turkey out of the rubble of the Ottoman Empire.

hot-air balloons above Cappadocia

The Seven Churches of the Revelation

For thematically and spiritually driven travelers, the proximity of the Seven Churches of the Revelation—discussed in the New Testament's Book of Revelation—offers a great opportunity to retrace Christianity's early footsteps in Asia Minor and discover the ruins along the sinuous Aegean Coast. The writer, John, believed to be Saint John the Apostle, received visions in which he was instructed to pen and send what would later be considered apocalyptic messages to the church of each of seven major cultural centers, famed for their commerce, trade, military, or hedonism. Allow two or three days to visit them all by private vehicle.

Smyrna

Just one hour's flight from Istanbul, the port city of İzmir has been an important trading center since time immemorial. Turkey's third largest city, with a population nearing three million, İzmir is known domestically as the "Pearl of the Aegean" and remains a Western-looking cultural melting pot, but the biblical message warned of "impending persecution" while encouraging "perseverance that will be rewarded."

Pergamum

Forget mincing words: In the Book of Revelation this materialistic city is encouraged to repent for preaching mixed doctrines. Just two hours north of İzmir, Pergamum was a major metropolis in Asia Minor since the 3rd century BC, and its temples and healing medical center became influential places of worship for Greeks and Romans. Today's Bergama is an increasingly influential city in terms of regional politics, mining, and agriculture.

the Agora of Smyrna

Thyatira

While the locals were commended for their increasing faith, the Book of Revelation reprimands Thyatira's church for also following the seductive prophetess Jezebel. The ruins of Thyatira, once known for its textile and dye trade, are about 65 kilometers from the Aegean Sea in the modern city of Akhisar, on the D565 highway, inland between Bergama and İzmir.

Sardis

An hour southeast from Akhisar, this "dead" church was told to wake up from its long sleep and that some of its parishioners were "worthy" for they had not yet "soiled their clothes." Sardis is strictly an archaeological site with spectacular temples and bathhouse complexes. Getting there is also possible with *dolmuşlar* from İzmir via Salihli.

Philadelphia

This church of fraternal love is applauded for its perseverance, but told of a pending judgment of the false Jews who represented the "Synagogue of Satan." Located about 45 kilometers southeast of Sardis in the modern city of Alaşehir, Philadelphia's scant remains are still one of Asia Minor's largest centers of temple worship.

Ephesus

Early Christianity's most important center was heralded in its time but is condemned in the Book of Revelation for "forsaking its first love." Ancient Ephesus was one of Asia Minor's prominent capitals; in fact, it was the Roman Empire's second largest city. Today, it's the world's best-preserved ancient site, replete with a hub of ancient streets, arches, temples, and monuments, including its spectacular funeral library and a whopping 25,000-seat amphitheater. Base yourself in Selçuk or Kuşadası to make the most of this site.

Laodicea

Criticized as a church of "lukewarm" faith, the Book of Revelation tells Laodicea's wealthy church to forgo adoration of worldly goods to focus on its spirituality. The ruins of Laodicea, once an important stop on the east-west trade route just north of modern-day Denizli, have slowly been excavated since 2003.

Istanbul

Sights 34	Food 101
Entertainment and Events 81	Information and Services 109
Shopping...................... 85	Getting There 110
Sports and Recreation 90	Getting Around.................113
Accommodations............... 94	

Highlights

Look for ★ to find recommended sights, activities, dining, and lodging.

★ **Ayasofya (Saint Sophia Church):** The grand Byzantine sanctuary is a UNESCO World Heritage Site that has welcomed worshippers of three religions since the 6th century (page 35).

★ **Sultanahmet Camii (Blue Mosque):** Light reflects through hundreds of glass windows onto blue tiles, casting a blue haze within the mosque's main hall (page 40).

★ **Topkapı Sarayı (Topkapı Palace):** As the vanguard of all imperial palaces, this royal residence houses one of the rarest collections of porcelain as well as the mythic 86-carat Spoonmaker's Diamond (page 41).

★ **Yerebatan Sarayı (Basilica Cistern):** Used as one of the film locations for James Bond's *From Russia with Love*, this surreal 6th-century underground cistern mystifies with hundreds of columns that lead to its innermost sanctum, the Medusa pillars (page 43).

★ **Kapalı Çarşı (Grand Bazaar):** Haggle like a pro, sip Turkish tea, or just take in the Grand Bazaar's historical splendor (page 46).

★ **Istiklal Caddesi:** This famous pedestrian avenue, packed with shops and restaurants, is the heart of Istanbul's most vibrant and contemporary neighborhood (page 58).

★ **Dolmabahçe Sarayı (Dolmabahçe Palace):** Offering a glimpse of Ottoman decadence at its best, this mid-19th-century imperial structure has a crystal staircase and a bed made of pure silver (page 61).

★ **Bosphorus Cruise:** Perhaps the pièce de résistance of a journey to Istanbul, this cruise boasts myriad historical sights that convey the value of these straits (page 64).

★ **Kariye Müzesi (Chora Museum):** So beautiful were its iconography, mosaics, and frescoes that even Constantinople's Islamic conquerors could not bring themselves to whitewash its gilded treasures (page 73).

Blending the lines between East and West, modernism and antiquity, secularism and piety, Istanbul brims with diversity, complexity, and some 8,000 years of history. Lulled only by the harmony of 1,000 *müezzinler* singing the call to prayer, vibrant Istanbul is abuzz with activity day and night. More than Constantinople, it's a sprawling city of 17 million residents where, within a five-kilometer radius, travelers can explore modern and traditional ways of life.

Sultanahmet, heart of the most visited area, is located on one of the city's seven hills. The tip of this historic peninsula and the Süleymaniye quarter, with its imperial mosque and bazaar quarters, are UNESCO World Heritage sites. The rails of a 21st-century T1 tramway bisect this area, leading to merchants selling textiles, ceramics, and jewelry, just as their predecessors did for centuries. Just beyond Sultanahmet in Fatih, Istanbul's oldest district, a simple village lifestyle plays out in a maze of cobblestone lanes lined with traditional Ottoman homes. Here, children play hopscotch while women in floral headscarves hand-clean goat-hair mattresses and carpets outside modest abodes.

Across the Golden Horn in Beyoğlu, residents live a more contemporary European existence among the fancy bars of Taksim, art galleries of Tophane, and brand-name shops of Nişantaşı and Istiklal Street. Beyoğlu's tree-lined boulevards are filled with posh eateries and fashionistas showing off their duds. Steps away, shoeshine boys and scarf-selling Anatolian women reside among the cacophony of street vendors, seagulls, and inescapable traffic.

The Bosphorus Strait and Marmara Sea are visible from almost any point in the greater city; the Black Sea to the north is within an hour's travel. More than just a pretty landscape, the city's geographic location and the abundance it brings have for millennia been Istanbul's claim to fame. It is at once the world's busiest maritime strait and home to nature's richest underwater bounty. Come winter, fish large and small are caught along

Previous: view from Galata Tower; the 6th-century Ayasofya. **Above:** the Egyptian Spice Bazaar.

these precious waters. The waters' edge also becomes a playground for well-to-do fun-seekers, who flock in droves to the many trendy hangouts.

As the only city in the world to spread over two continents, Istanbul also comprises a history-filled Anatolian (Asian) side just across the Bosphorus Strait. Its name was once Chalcedon, an Asian outpost that dates back to at least 3000 BC. The water-lapped quarter of Kuzguncuk near Üsküdar exemplifies this legacy with the centuries-old sanctuaries of three different religions dwelling uneventfully side-by-side. But if you expected sleepy villages, the diversity will surprise you. The district of Kadıköy boasts world class shopping and dining along the hectic thoroughfare of Bağdat Caddesi, whose highbrow destinations include Louis Vuitton and Burberry. With so much diversity, it's no surprise that Istanbul was recently chosen as the European Capital of Culture by the European Union Council.

PLANNING YOUR TIME

In three whirlwind days you can check out the charm of the city, learn to feast the Turkish way, motor along the Bosphorus, and click heels with *Istanbullus* at shopping and partying meccas around town. To get a real grasp of the city in all its contrasting beauty, plan to spend at least five days. This will allow for a couple of side trips: a cruise to the nearby Princes' Islands and a hop to the city's various Asian draws. With five days there's also time to explore the city at night, including its boisterous cabarets and posh waterside nightclubs near Ortaköy and Kuruçeşme.

The best time to visit Istanbul is April, when the city's tulip commemoration is in full bloom and the entire city is covered with the spectacular indigenous flower. Spring also announces the beginning of Istanbul's popular arts festival season. Summer is still the busiest tourist season countrywide. Istanbul's late spring and early fall now constitute shoulder seasons with lower prices than June-September. For some, winter is the best time of year, and the occasional snow flurry kisses historical sites, transforming the city into a winter wonderland.

HISTORY

The emergence of the land that straddles the strategic Bosphorus Strait is the stuff of legends. But a chance discovery of four human skeletons some six kilometers beneath Yenikapı in mid-2008 confirmed that the city was inhabited an estimated 8,000 years ago, during the Neolithic period. The first to actually colonize it was King Byzas, ruler of the Greek town of Megara who, after consulting with the Oracle at Delphi as to where to found a new city, was told to look "opposite the blind." Byzas reached the settlement of Chalcedon—today's Kadıköy—and thought that Chalcedonians must have been "blind" for not realizing that much finer land lay just across the Bosphorus Strait. Byzas settled the territory in the 7th century BC and called it Byzantion, after himself. Later the colony took on the Latin form of the name, Byzantium. It became a part of the Roman Empire in the 1st century BC, and by AD 306 it was assigned the status of capital by Emperor Constantine, who renamed the city Constantinople.

The 5th century proved tempestuous and fractious for the Roman Empire. The west was conquered by Barbarians, and the Eastern Roman Empire—a.k.a. the Byzantine Empire—remained centralized in Constantinople. In 532, the Nika Revolts fanned the flames of a brewing discord among the city's two political factions. After a week of fires and pillaging that reduced the Sultanahmet and its environs to rubble, some 30,000 rioters were slaughtered in the Hippodrome. But from the ruins, structures such as Ayasofya and the Great Palace of Constantinople were entirely rebuilt—the former to such grandeur that it still remains a symbol of the Byzantine Empire's architectural and cultural prowess.

What made the city so desirable—mainly its straits—continued to be the Achilles' heel for its occupiers, as Persians, Arabs, and nomadic tribes each tried to conquer the city.

Discount Cards

You won't always have to rely on your wit, charm, and bargaining power to save money in Istanbul. These passes are designed for savings on museum admission and public transportation:

MUSEUM PASS

Skip queues and gain "free" entry to major museums, including the Ayasofya and Topkapı Sarayı (Topkapı Palace), for a 72-hour period with the 85TL Museum Pass. The card also gives discounts on some tours, as well as discounts on entry to Pera Müzesi (Pera Museum) and Kız Kulesi (Maiden's Tower), to name a few. Purchase the card from the ticket booths of the Ayasofya, Topkapı Palace, and other locations listed at www.muze.gov.tr. Before purchase, check the entry fees in this guide against your itinerary and confirm that the pass is worth your while.

ISTANBULKART

Boarding the tram, ferry, or metro requires a 4TL pp *jeton*. Do what the locals do and purchase an IstanbulKart swipe card, which reduces the fare to 2.15TL pp per journey. These are sold at confectionery kiosks near public transportation stations for a non-refundable 10TL, and you can add value to the card at these kiosks as well. If you travel within a two-hour period, the subsequent fare is only 1.25TL. One card can be used by up to five people, and it conveniently fits in your wallet like a credit card.

Finally, during the Fourth Crusade, the Catholic Latin Empire replaced its Orthodox Byzantine namesake in 1204. Their rule would last slightly more than 50 years under various diminutive emperors until the previous Byzantine rulers recaptured Constantinople in 1261. By then, the city was in ruins and its population had dwindled to a mere 30,000—less than 10 percent of what it had been under Justinian, the Eastern Roman emperor. The advancing Ottoman Turks led by Sultan Fatih Mehmet II (The Conqueror) ascended the peninsula from the northeast, gained control of the city, and changed its name once again. Now it would be called Istanbul—the seat of the Islamic Caliphate, and the head of an empire that would become one of the largest in history.

In just six decades, Istanbul's multicultural population under the Turks exploded tenfold as the reigning sultan offered Istanbul as a refuge to Jews and Muslims fleeing the Iberian peninsula during the Spanish Inquisition. The city became a cultural, political, and commercial center under the Ottomans, with opulent palaces and spiritual sanctuaries. This lasted until their demise at the hands of the Allied forces during World War I.

After a bloody four-year war of independence, in 1923 Mustafa Kemal Atatürk—known nationally as the father of Turks—moved the newly formed Turkish nation's seat of government to Ankara. Despite its loss of status as the capital, Istanbul has always remained the cultural heart of Turkey.

Sights

Istanbul is bisected by the Bosphorus Strait, which serves as a natural continental divide between Europe and Asia. The major attractions in the "old town" of Sultanahmet and crowded Beyoğlu, as well as posh Nişantaşı and Ortaköy, are all located on the European flank. The old town and Beyoğlu are separated by the Golden Horn, an inlet of the Bosphorus that forms a natural harbor. Destinations lying on the periphery, like the working-class district of Kadıköy on the Asian side, the sleepy retreats of the Princes' Islands in the Marmara

The 6th-century Ayasofya bears the inscriptions of its Christian and Islamic past.

Sea, and the Rumeli and Anatolian Fortresses farther afield on the European side, are easily reached and can be explored on a half-day or full-day excursion. Don't be afraid to walk, ride the tramway, or get around the city by funicular (underground cable car), *dolmuş* (communal taxi), metro train, Bosphorus ferry, bus, or taxi. Armed with a map, this guide, and a couple of Turkish words, getting around Istanbul is a snap.

SULTANAHMET AND VICINITY

Containing by far the most popular sights, Sultanahmet Square and the Kapalı Çarşı (Grand Bazaar) precinct are the meat and potatoes of your journey. Along with Topkapı Palace and the Egyptian Spice Bazaar, a dozen sights virtually piled atop each other await the curious.

Classified as a UNESCO World Heritage site since 1985, the urban historical area of Sultanahmet boasts relics of bygone civilizations in a jumble of attractions jam-packed into an area that was once the glorious capital of the Roman, Byzantine, Latin, and Ottoman Empires. Jutting off from the central attractions are cobblestone streets with hotels, shops, and eateries that are ideal for absorbing the atmosphere of this virtual open-air museum, one of the world's top tourist destinations.

Conquering old Istanbul on foot is easy. It's relatively flat, with one incline between Eminönü and Sultanahmet, atop the first of Istanbul's seven hills. Frequent tram service can also whip you from one end of the peninsula to the heart of old Istanbul in less than 10 minutes. Most roads are designated pedestrian thoroughfares, so expect delays in taxis as they maneuver the few crowded alleyways.

Group your visits to the Ayasofya, Blue Mosque, Basilica Cistern, Hippodrome, and Grand Bazaar in one day followed by Topkapı Palace, the Spice Bazaar, and a two-hour Bosphorus cruise from Eminönü port on day two. Make sure you reserve another two hours for a scrub, wash down, and oil massage in a humid hamam (Turkish bath) at the end of a day. Plan these excursions around the days the major sites are closed.

★ Ayasofya (Saint Sophia Church)

The magnificent **Ayasofya** (Sultanahmet Square, 0212/522-1750, www.muze.gov.tr, 9am-7pm Tues.-Sun. Apr.-Oct., 9am-4:30pm Tues.-Sun. Nov.-Mar., 30TL, audio guide 15TL) was commissioned by Emperor Justinian I as a means to establish his claim to the imperial throne of Byzantium. This basilica remains one of the largest testaments of faith and architectural might on the globe. It was inaugurated by the Byzantines in 537 as the Great Church and later as Hagia Sophia—Greek for Holy Wisdom—and remained the largest Christian cathedral for more than 1,000 years. So enthralled was Justinian by its magnificence and opulent interior, replete with glittering mosaics and sleek marble pillars, that he proclaimed: "Solomon, I have surpassed thee."

Justinian employed the architect Antheius of Tralles and the mathematician Isidorus of

Sorry, We're Closed!

When planning your itinerary, keep in mind the closures for these top sites:

- **Closed Monday:** Archaeological Museums, Ayasofya, Dolmabahçe Palace, Great Palace Mosaics Museum
- **Closed Tuesday:** Topkapı Palace and Harem
- **Closed Wednesday:** Chora Museum, Rumeli Fortress
- **Closed Thursday:** Dolmabahçe Palace
- **Closed Sunday:** Grand Bazaar

Major attractions and shopping centers remain open for normal trading hours for the month of **Ramazan** (Ramadan, June 18-July 17, 2015; June 6-July 5, 2016; May 27-June 25, 2017), but they will close for half a day on the first day of religious holidays, with the indoor shops of the Grand Bazaar closing for the entire **Şeker Bayramı** (Sugar Holiday, three days immediately after Ramazan) and for the four days of **Kurban Bayramı** (Feast of Sacrifice, starting Sept. 23, 2015; Sept. 11, 2016; Sept. 1, 2017). It's business as usual on public holidays.

The other day to avoid travel is **May 1,** when Istanbul comes to a standstill with road closures and public transportation shutting down to prevent May Day demonstrations.

Miletus to design a plan to place a circular dome on a rectangular floor plan, a feat that had never been achieved before. With the empire's treasury at their disposal, the duo devised the basilica with a perimeter of 72 by 78 meters, topped by a gigantic dome with a height of 55.6 meters, supported by four pendentives—hollow triangular sections of stonework that transfer the dome's weight to the four pillars at each corner of the basilica. These pendentives were the first of their kind to be used in structural engineering. Half domes at both western and eastern ends also assisted in bearing the dome's weight, creating the oblong-ish interior. The dome today has a diameter of 31 to 32 meters and is decorated with 40 arched windows, imperfectly shaped due to several earthquakes and rebuilding efforts. Eight gigantic Corinthian columns imported from Lebanon support the structure's center. Using only the best materials mined from quarries throughout the empire, it took more than 10,000 workers five years to craft this truly extraordinary Great Church. Incidentally, today's structure is the third church on the site; the previous two were burned during rioting in 404 and 532.

A series of earthquakes shook Hagia Sophia's structure, causing the main dome to collapse twice (in 558 and 989), both times requiring immediate reconstruction. When the Fourth Crusaders took hold of the city in 1204 and created the Latin Empire, the church briefly became a place of worship for Roman Catholics, until 1261 when the Byzantines reclaimed Constantinople. By then decades of sieges and tremors had taken their toll on the basilica. A major retrofit was undertaken, with the addition of the four buttresses on its flank. The interior hall was in a state of disrepair by the time the Ottomans arrived in 1453. Sultan Mehmet II (The Conqueror) ordered the third major overhaul, which included its conversion into a mosque. A century later, Sultan Selim II commissioned the famed Ottoman architect Sinan to retrofit the building by adding buttresses to the dome and broader structure. He also commissioned the original sultan's loge (a private prayer mezzanine), two larger minarets located on the western flank, and the mausoleum of Selim II. In 1739, Sultan Mahmud I ordered yet more work, adding a *medrese* (Ottoman Islamic school), a library, a soup kitchen, and a fountain. In the mid-19th century, however, architectural aesthete Sultan Abdülmecid ordered the most complete renovation yet. Under the watchful eye of two Italian architects, it took more than two years to refurbish the structure. In 1935, Turkish President Mustafa Kemal Atatürk converted the sanctuary into a museum, an act that began the painstaking process of restoring the basilica to its original state, which continues to this day. Restoration has slowly uncovered the basilica's original mosaics and frescoes, a process that has been somewhat controversial since the sanctuary has served both as a mosque and a church since its inauguration. Removing the plaster and tiles to reveal the Christian iconography beneath would destroy significant Islamic art, such as the golden calligraphy that covers what is thought to be a mosaic of Christ Pantocrator on the dome.

From afar, the sheer size of the building is astounding. The inner grounds are filled with stone remains of the second church, which stood on the site before Ayasofya; marble blocks depicting 12 lambs representing the 12 Apostles are strewn below the path leading to the Ayasofya's **exonarthex,** a large hall once reserved for worshippers who were yet to be baptized. The next chamber is the marble **inner narthex** that reveals the mosaic of **Christ Pantocrator** with the Virgin Mary, Archangel Gabriel, and a prostrating emperor just above the massive Imperial Door. The open bible Christ holds says, "Peace be with you. I am the Light of the World." The imperial doorway, which was reserved for the Emperor, is the largest of three entrances. The calm interior with its seemingly floating chandeliers beckons. To the right is a 500-year-old **marble jar** carved from a single marble slab during the Hellenic period. The jar originates from Pergamum and was once filled with sherbet for religious ceremonies. Behind this are the purple **porphyry columns,** quarried from pits in central Egypt and thought to represent Roman royalty as well as the importance placed on those worshipped here.

Walking toward the apse, where the **mihrab** (niche indicating the direction of Mecca) can be found, you'll first pass the Byzantine **coronation square**—a collection of colored marble inlays where emperors were once crowned. Behind this, between the columns, are the imprints of where the Byzantine throne is presumed to have stood. The large platform between this and the apse is the 16th-century marble *müezzin mahfili*—a raised dais where the Koran was read during services. Ayasofya's three other smaller *mahfililer,* built to meet the size of the community, also date from the reign of Sultan Murat III (1574-1595). Before reaching the apse, look up to admire the **seraphim** (six-winged angels) on each of the pendentives, uncovered in excavation work in 2009. Thought to protect the Lord's throne in heaven, the two closest to the apse (east) are mosaics, whereas the western seraphim were renewed as frescoes. Hung along the walls below the dome are eight 7.5-meter-diameter **calligraphy slates,** the largest in the Islamic world. Each one dates to the 19th century and depicts a different figure, including Allah, Prophet Muhammad, four caliphs, and the grandsons of Muhammad, Hasan and Husayn.

The largest structure of the apse is the **minbar,** where the imam (worship leader of the mosque) would lead prayers and sermons. To the left of this is the *mihrab*, flanked by two candelabras brought from Hungary during the reign of Sultan Süleyman I (The Magnificent) in the 16th century. The **apse mosaic** above represents the Virgin and Child, which was the first post-iconoclastic work of its kind, in 867; she sits on a backless throne with Christ the Child sitting comfortably on her lap. To the right you can make out the remnants of a scene involving Archangels Michael and Gabriel, with only the latter visible today. The ornate mezzanine to the left of the apse was devised by Sultan Ahmet III as a semiprivate **sultan's loge** to use the sanctuary surreptitiously.

Upon exiting the ground floor, visit the

copper-covered marble **Stele of Saint Gregory Thaumaturgus**—the miracle worker. It's believed to bring good luck and is found to the north of the Imperial Door entrance. Also referred to as the wishing column, many legends exist about its spiritual and magical past. Just stick your thumb in the central recess, make a wish, and rotate it counterclockwise. If it comes out moist, the wish and good fortune will follow.

The second-floor horseshoe-shaped gallery, once reserved for the empress and her court and the Patriarch, gives another perspective of this gigantic structure and contains four more mosaics featuring Christ or the Virgin Mary with Byzantine emperors and empresses. The revered **Deësis mosaic,** with Mary and John the Baptist asking Christ to forgive all mankind, was created in 1261 to honor the return of the Church to the Byzantines and is the finest mosaic in the museum.

Upon exiting at ground level, turn around to see the most prominent **Sunu mosaic,** showing the Virgin Mary with Christ the Child, with Justinian I on her right offering the Ayasofya and Constantine I offering the city of Constantinople.

There is continuing pressure from Turkey's pious Muslim community to convert the museum back into a mosque, but Christians argue that the Hagia Sophia was built as a church and served as one for over 1,000 years—if conversion was possible, it should return to its Christian roots. What the Ayasofya will become in the future is anyone's guess, but as of today it remains a magnificent structure celebrating the Orthodox, Roman Catholic, and Islamic religions that were once worshipped here.

Behind the Ayasofya is a not-to-be-missed quaint side street, **Soğukçeşme Sokak.** It's part of a sweeping decades-long project undertaken by Turkey's Touring and Automobile Club to restore historical landmarks. Celik Gülersoy, the visionary at the helm of the club, saw a diamond in the rough when ambling along the string of greasy automotive repair shops between the Ayasofya and Topkapı

the Blue Mosque

Palace some 30 years ago. In a love-hate relationship with the municipality, Gülersoy labored to convince the city's leadership of his grand plan to erect a row of houses reminiscent of Istanbul's late-19th-century architectural wealth.

The eastern end of the street ends near the first church of Constantinople, the 4th-century **Hagia Eirene.** Today it's only open for concerts or with special permission, but it served as the church of the Patriarchate before the Hagia Sophia was completed. Much of the structure you see today, however, dates to the 8th century.

★ Sultanahmet Camii (Blue Mosque)

Completed in 1617, the **Sultanahmet Camii** (Sultanahmet Square, www.sultanahmetcami.com, daily, donation) was commissioned by Sultan Ahmet as a means to outdo what was at the time the most lavish sanctuary in the world—the Ayasofya. Ahmet, left raw from a peace deal with Persia and thus with no spoils of war, veered heavily from tradition by dipping into state coffers to fund his project.

The Sultanahmet Camii indeed towers alongside the Ayasofya, and in fact is the last grand mosque built in the classical style, widely considered to be the epitome of Byzantine and Ottoman mixed architecture. Its crown is a jumble of full and half domes topped by a massive central dome that soars to about 45 meters at its center and measures 23.5 meters in diameter. On completion, the mosque had six minarets, one of only two in the world that had so many. Ahmet's audacity for constructing an edifice with the same number of spires as Mecca's Sacred Mosque was criticized until a seventh minaret was added to the mosque at Mecca.

Today, light from the 260 glass windows still floods the cavernous, carpeted space and bounces off the more than 21,000 hand-painted blue Iznik tiles to create a bluish haze, hence its nickname, the Blue Mosque. Almost as large as the mosque, the forecourt is defined by a continuing archway on its perimeter, with a central fountain some consider too cautious in size for the sheer dimension of the courtyard.

Visiting the grounds shouldn't take more than 30 minutes. All mosques in the city are open daily except at prayer times. Entry is free to mosques, but donations are advised. Individuals baring too much skin are asked to cover their legs, and women are expected to cover their heads and shoulders with scarves provided at the entrance. Worshippers will visit throughout the day, so keep noise and flash photography to a minimum.

★ Topkapı Sarayı (Topkapı Palace)

Serving as the seat of the Ottoman government, the imperial residence, and the location of the Sultan's legendary harem, **Topkapı Sarayı** (Sultanahmet, 0212/522-1750, www.muze.gov.tr, 9am-7pm Wed.-Mon. Apr.-Oct., 9am-4:30pm Wed.-Mon. Nov.-Mar., 30TL) housed more than 4,000 people and regaled many a visiting dignitary in its heyday. Sultan Mehmet II (1432-1481) ordered its construction atop the ruins of the Acropolis of Byzantium. The New Palace opened its doors in 1465; its name changed to Topkapı Palace in the 19th century. Vastly improved from the Old Palace, the New Palace is situated atop Seraglio Point, overlooking the Sea of Marmara, the Golden Horn, and the Bosphorus Strait. The site's structures were originally built around a variety of ruins, including the Aya Eirene church, an underground Byzantine cistern, and four main courtyards. But subsequent sultans added their flair to create what resulted in an asymmetrical exterior layout. To the north and west of the palace is Gülhane Park, which faces the Bosphorus and the Sea of Marmara. Much larger than the 70-hectare complex seen today, the palace was once home to mosques, schools, dormitories, a mint, a treasury, the Ottoman archives, and even kiosks and pavilions. This palace deteriorated after Abdülmecid (1823-1861) decided to move his court to the opulent Dolmabahçe Palace in 1853. Converted by Atatürk into a museum in 1923, Topkapı remains the largest and oldest palace in the world.

The Imperial Gate, or Gate of the Sultan, was built along with the palace, but its marble overlay was added in the late 19th century. With gilded calligraphy and a Sultan's seal embellishing the upper portion, verses from the Koran appear on either side of the entrance. Only viziers and foreign diplomats were allowed to cross to the **First Courtyard.** This garden currently houses, among others structures, the former 15,800-square-meter imperial mint, the 6th-century Church of Aya Eirene, the Fountain of the Executioner, and the tiled Ceremonial Pavilion. Accessible through the Gate of Salutation, the **Second Courtyard** is the actual and sole entrance to the museum. It opens onto a square that was once the administrative center of the Ottoman government. Only citizens with official business, janissaries on payday, or foreign diplomats were allowed here. Ceremonies, sometimes attended by thousands, were held in the courtyard, with the sultan sitting atop his throne by the gate. Only accessible from the harem, the building's only tower—the Tower of Justice—is here. It's a high dungeon from which the city, the straits, and nearby Marmara could be seen.

Sprawling over 60 percent of the property and accessible via the Second Courtyard is the **harem** (0212/512-0480, www.muze.gov.tr, 9am-5pm Wed.-Mon. Apr.-Oct., 9am-4pm Wed.-Mon. Nov.-Mar., 15TL), which became the residence of the sultan and his court—his immediate family as well as concubines and the eunuchs, who were charged with their safety—by the mid-1500s. Enhanced and enlarged by various sultans, the 400 or so rooms are connected by narrow hallways. It's an area so secretive it became the stuff of legend for adulterous love affairs and murderous plots.

The separate guided tour of the harem starts through the 40 ornate rooms reserved for the Valide Sultan, followed by the spacious marbled hamam, and finally the sultan's domed grand hall. The tour leads visitors past lavish spaces adorned with ornate fireplaces and relaxing fountains to the large hall where an astounding tiled pool awaits. The tour ends with two 16th-century rooms, outfitted by large stained-glass windows, from which the sultan-in-waiting would gaze out, undoubtedly biding his time for the throne.

The surrounding structures offer an intimate view of the history, wealth, breadth, and power of the once mighty Ottoman rule. Particularly impressive is the **Armory and Council Hall,** housed in the former realm's Council of State, where viziers and secretaries would meet on affairs of state chaired by the Grand Vizier, as the Sultan watched from a window carved high in a wall. An extensive collection of weapons and fatigues are displayed chronologically. Long, curved gilded sabers give way to intricately inlaid 19th-century firearms, some used by sultans, others from conquered nations. The **Kitchen and Porcelain Collection** has, among others, a priceless array of some 12,000 gifted Chinese and Japanese pieces, including a

the Imperial Hall inside the harem of Topkapı Palace

large 15th-century Ming vase with Ottoman gold mounts displayed along with another 2,500 pieces in a separate room. The **Third Courtyard,** the private domain of the Sultan, was guarded by white eunuchs. The **Treasury** and the **Sacred Relics** building are here. Guarded by a handpicked selection of deaf and mute young men, the sultans heard foreign ambassadors and high officials in the throne room, also located in this square. In its center, the 18th-century **library** commissioned by Ahmet III defines the epoch's popular blend of baroque and Turkish architectural styles. Along the remaining buildings that boast the luxurious, ankle-length silk caftans of the sultans, perhaps the most remarkable is the Treasury Hall. A collection of thrones, including the golden throne used for coronations and holidays, and, of course, the 86-carat **Spoonmaker's Diamond,** one of the largest in the world, await among the world's largest—and most expensive—jewelry stashes. Beyond this third court is the Tulip Garden or **Imperial Courtyard,** with sweeping views of the Bosphorus and Golden Horn, that once served as the ultimate private domain for the sultan, hence its elegant pavilions and opulence.

To visit Topkapı, arrive early, as crowds start flocking by mid-morning. Start with the harem, obviously the most popular section, and plan at least half a day to view the palace. If you don't have that much time, do the 30-minute tour of the harem and move on to the Treasury. Cafés are located in the Imperial Courtyard to rest and rejuvenate halfway through your visit.

★ Yerebatan Sarayı (Basilica Cistern)

The largest underground structure of its kind, the **Yerebatan Sarayı** (Yerebatan Cd. 13, 0212/522-1259, www.yerebatan.com, 9am-6:30pm daily Apr.-Sept., 9am-5:30pm daily Oct.-Mar., 20TL), is a refreshing experience, particularly when the thermometer soars in summer. The cistern is a surreal, wide colonnaded space that is capable of holding over 80,000 cubic meters of water. The mid-6th-century cistern was another of Emperor Justinian I's schemes, and it bears the name of the grand basilica that preceded it.

The idea behind building the cistern was to collect water for local use via the Valens Aqueduct from the Belgrade Forest, some 20 kilometers away. The cistern was constructed with 5-meter-thick brick walls and 336 Doric and Corinthian columns standing 3 meters tall and just 5 meters apart. Seven thousand slaves are thought to have built the formidable structure, whose ceiling is entirely supported by the 12 rows of 28 marble and granite cylindrical columns. Be sure not to miss the two Medusa heads used as pedestals for two of the columns; one lies sideways and the other upside down in the cistern's northwest corner.

Today, the shallow waters of the cistern are home to koi fish bobbing above a veritable fortune in coins of various currencies. Strolling through Yerebatan takes about 30 minutes and is one of the most memorable sights Sultanahmet has to offer.

Ayasofya Hürrem Sultan Hamam (Baths of Roxelana)

Nestled between the Ayasofya and Blue Mosque is the historic **Ayasofya Hürrem Sultan Hamam** (Bab-ı Hümayun Cd. 1, 0212/517-3535, www.ayasofyahamami.com, 8am-10pm daily). With the motto *Some rituals never change,* the crème de la crème of Turkish baths is now housed in this stunning 16th-century hamam built by chief Ottoman architect Mimar Sinan. Rumors suggest that Sultan Süleyman the Magnificent commissioned the hamam after an assassination attempt on his beloved wife, Hürrem Sultan (Roxelana), while she bathed in Topkapı Palace. The site he selected was once home to the Statue of Zeus, one of the Seven Wonders of the Ancient World, until AD 462, and thereafter the ancient Baths of Zeuxippus. When commissioned in 1556, the hamam enabled the Ottoman elite to bathe privately until 1910. From then on, the function of the building varied from managing the overflow of prisoners of the nearby Sultanahmet Prison (now the Four Seasons Hotel) to a carpet emporium and exhibition space until 1997. From 2008 to 2011 the building was restored to its former classical Ottoman glory at a cost of US$11 million. Today, separate male and female sections built as mirror images with matching domes offer luxurious hamam packages. Although more expensive than other local hamams, the personalized service, tasty sherbet drinks, private change rooms, and massage rooms are worth the cost.

At Meydanı (Hippodrome)

What was once the Hippodrome is now a municipal concrete park and pedestrian thoroughfare known as **At Meydanı** (Horse Square, adjacent to the Blue Mosque). The ancient Hippodrome predates many of the top sights in the city, but it is buried 4 meters under the current promenade, with only its tall obelisks to mark its presence. In its heyday, 100,000 spectators would fill its stands, cheering for one of four chariot teams, each team bankrolled by different political parties.

Victory here led to power in politics some 1,800 years ago.

This site is where the Nika Revolt of AD 532 took place, as dissent between the two major chariot teams of the day—the Blues and the Greens—led to a tense six-day siege of the city. It ended when Emperor Justinian ordered the massacre of some 30,000 rioters in the Hippodrome.

The Hippodrome was built in AD 203 by Septimius Severus to echo Rome's Circus Maximus and was later enlarged and strengthened at its Sphendome by Constantine. The racetrack was abandoned as early as the 13th century with the arrival of the Fourth Crusade. It even served as a quarry under the Ottomans. Today, the Sphendome—the Hippodrome's 180-degree curve and retaining wall—is located at the southwestern end of the square, visible by following the westernmost road of the square downhill, veering to the right where the road forks.

The columns that once embellished the Hippodrome and marked its center were brought from the farthest reaches of the Roman Empire. One of the remaining columns is the original **Serpent Column** from the Temple of Apollo at Delphi, which Constantine had removed and transferred to the Hippodrome. The Serpent Column was placed at the dead center of the Hippodrome. Originally, the three entwining serpents peaked in three golden serpent heads that supported a golden bowl. The bowl was either destroyed or stolen by knights of the Fourth Crusade. The serpent heads have been separated, with one now in the Istanbul Archaeology Museum and another in the British Museum in London.

The second column, the **Obelisk of Theodosius,** was a gift from Theodosius the Great. In AD 390, Theodosius ordered the 60-ton pink granite obelisk, which had graced Luxor's Temple of Karnak since the late 15th century BC, to be cut into three pieces and shipped to Constantinople. Two of the pieces were lost in transit from Egypt, but the remaining piece was placed on a marble pedestal in the Hippodrome. The surviving piece is etched with depictions of Theodosius' clan, racing scenes, and hieroglyphics attesting to the greatness of the God Horus and the pharaoh, which run along the 20-meter height of the pillar's four surfaces.

A third surviving column is the **Walled Obelisk,** which was originally commissioned by Emperor Constantine Porphyrogenitus in the 10th century AD. The Walled Obelisk is located at the southwestern end of the Hippodrome near the Sphendome. The obelisk was used to secure a pulley system that would raise awnings to shade spectators from the sun. Its original gold-plated bronze plaques were removed by knights of the Fourth Crusade to be minted into coins.

At the opposite (northern) end of the square lies the octagonal, domed **Fountain of Kaiser Wilhelm II.** The initials of both Sultan Abdul Hamid (1842-1918) and Wilhelm II attest to a longstanding friendship between the two empires, a friendship that led to developments in trade such as the construction of the Berlin-Baghdad railroad. Constructed in Germany, the fountain was brought in pieces to Istanbul in 1898 and reassembled in the Hippodrome to commemorate Wilhelm II's second visit to the city.

Türk ve Islam Eserleri Müzesi (Museum of Turkish and Islamic Arts)

Inaugurated in 1984, **Türk ve Islam Eserleri Müzesi** (At Meydanı 46, Sultanahmet, 0212/518-1805, 9am-7pm Tues.-Sun. Apr.-Oct., 9am-5pm Tues.-Sun. Nov.-Mar., 20TL) lies on the Hippodrome's northwestern flank. A visit to view floor-to-ceiling Uşak carpets, the ethnographic collection, and the historical Korans are well worth a half-hour stroll. Its lesser-known tea garden in the former palace's lush central court is an ideal resting place on a hot summer day.

Also known as the Ibrahim Paşa Palace Museum, At Meydanı Palace, Mehterhane Summer Pavilion, and Hiyamite Summer Pavilion, the building has had as many incarnations as it has names. Its most renowned owner, Ibrahim Paşa, was a close friend and the brother-in-law of Süleyman the Magnificent. He was captured as a child in Greece and brought into the imperial court as a slave. He trained as a page, befriending the young Prince Süleyman. Ibrahim was appointed grand vizier when the latter became sultan and received this palace after accepting the hand of Süleyman's sister, Hadice. But Ibrahim's growing wealth and influence over state affairs riled many in the court, including the cunning Roxelana. After being accused of disloyalty by one of his peers, she convinced her husband Süleyman that his best friend could no longer be trusted. Ibrahim was strangled in 1536 and his assets reverted to the state. In the late 18th century, the palace, by then dilapidated, housed the official registry and functioned as the headquarters of the royal band. A mental hospital ensued, then a textile workshop, and finally slums before it was partially razed in 1939 to accommodate a modern courthouse. The museum today is the result of years of restoration that began in 1966.

Büyük Saray Mozaik Müzesi (Great Palace Mosaics Museum)

It wasn't until the late 1930s that the amazing mosaics of the peristyle courtyard (an open court with porticos) of Constantine's Great Palace were discovered. Led by a team of Scottish archaeologists from the University of St. Andrews, the dig took place right under the Arasta Bazaar, an early 17th-century row of shops built by Sultan Ahmet I (1590-1617) that ironically protected the ceramic mosaics from the elements. Returning two decades later, the British team excavated pavement consisting of hunting and mythological scenes near the rear of the Blue Mosque. By then, Turkish authorities realized the significance of the find and sacrificed the more than a dozen shops to open **Büyük Saray Mozaik Müzesi** (Torun Sk. Arasta Çarşısı, 0212/518-1205, 9am-7pm Tues.-Sun. Apr.-Oct., 9am-5pm Tues.-Sun. Nov.-Mar., 10TL) to the public. If you have an hour to spare, preferably in the morning, plan to stroll along this structure's galleries to look at the remains of what is perhaps the only Byzantine mosaic collection in the entire city sans religious depictions.

Vakıflar Halı ve Kilim Müzesi (Vakıflar Carpet Museum)

The collection of antique carpets and kilims that once graced the floors of mosques throughout the Ottoman Empire have found a home at the **Vakıflar Halı ve Kilim Müzesi** (Imperial Pavilion, Blue Mosque, 0212/518-1330, 9am-4pm Tues.-Sun., free). The former Imperial Pavilion—a place utilized by sultans during their prayer time at the Blue Mosque—is a fitting setting for the display of these 14th- to 20th-century rugs. The good half-hour tour shows carpets exhibited next to the sultan's loge and kilims in the vaulted galleries right beneath the mosque. Once short on funds, this museum lacked the proper lighting to display its then-threadbare assortment, but renewed efforts have remedied the situation, rendering this collection a must for carpet enthusiasts.

BAZAAR QUARTERS

Istanbul's bazaar quarters slopes from the Kapalı Çarşı (Grand Bazaar), which crowns the city's second hill, through a jumble of narrow streets down to the Mısır Çarşısı (Egyptian Spice Bazaar) and Yeni Cami near the large port of Eminönü. Along the massively populated squares and back alleys, you might get the sense that you're in for yet another history lesson, with the countless *hans* (inns) and historical buildings.

Just outside the Kapalı Çarşı is the historical Beyazıt Mosque and adjacent square, where Istanbul University's colossal gate looms. The road leading northeast slants toward Mimar Sinan territory, where two of his greatest architectural accomplishments—the mid-16th-century Mosques of Süleyman and Rüstem Paşa—are located. Also in the vicinity is the complex of the Armenian Orthodox

Patriarchate, a highly guarded, fully functioning complex unfortunately not open to the public. Beware; it is easy to get disoriented in the Spice Bazaar's web of backstreets full of tiny overstocked shops, relentless peddlers, and avid local shoppers. Pencil in half a day at least to explore this area, allowing an hour or so to get your bearings. Also beware of pickpockets in these areas. If you make it through the maze, you'll be rewarded with a glass of steaming *çay* (tea) at the waterside cafés along the Galata Bridge's lower level. If walking between the two bazaars sounds daunting, the Beyazıt and Eminönü tramway stations are right at the front of the Grand Bazaar and Spice Bazaar, respectively.

★ Kapalı Çarşı (Grand Bazaar)

A must on any visit to Istanbul, the **Kapalı Çarşı** (Beyazıt, www.grandbazaaristanbul.org, 9am-7pm Mon.-Sat.) is a mind-boggling collection of over 4,000 businesses that make up one of the oldest shopping malls in the world. Souvenirs, leather, jewelry, clothing, carpets, copper, and anything else that might interest visitors can be found here. Roughly 65 pedestrian streets traverse the bazaar, which is accessed through 22 gates. There are two enclosed *bedestens* (marketplaces) and also 24 *hans* that now function more as markets rather than the inns and stalls of old.

Kapalı Çarşı has been a place to bargain for centuries, though nowadays most salespeople won't budge on items they've marked up as much as 300 percent. A leather jacket priced at 900TL in one shop can be 300TL in another. Half the tactic of procuring a bargain here is to shop around and know what the locals are willing to pay. The rest is a game of patience as you talk the vendor down to a price you're willing to pay.

The shops' sky-high rates have become too steep for locals, except for the haunts of a select few who can afford the famed artisans' opulent, custom-made goods. Multilingual merchants have an innate ability to sniff out unseasoned shoppers by guessing "where you from." Prices fluctuate from shop to shop and from customer to customer, but most vendors are open to negotiation. Bargaining is easy once you get the hang of it. Offer liras in cash instead of dollars and the price will go down. The rules of engagement state that once a deal is reached, it's in bad taste to back out.

Entering from the **Çarşı Kapısı** (Bazaar Gate), 50 meters from Beyazıt tram station, is highly recommended for its convenience. Or,

Food is served from bobbing boats near the Yeni Cami (New Mosque) in Eminönü.

if walking from Sultanahmet, turn right at the Çemberlitaş tram station (where the **Column of Constantine** is), and after 150 meters, take a left and walk past the **Nuruosmaniye Mosque,** which is noted for being the prototype for Istanbul's baroque architectural era. The path leads to the **Nuruosmaniye Kapısı** (Nuruosmaniye Gate) of the Grand Bazaar. Once inside, the structure's largest street—**Kalpakçılar Caddesi**—unfolds before your eyes with astounding displays of gold and the heady smell emanating from the myriad leather shops. Head to the **İç Bedesten** (Inner Bazaar) by hanging a right on Kolancılar Caddesi. Exquisite copperware, intricate pipes, boxes of indigenous meerschaum, and rows of modern and antique-style jewelry are found here.

Historically, the Bedesten was Mehmet the Conqueror's first order of business to reinvigorate trade after conquering Constantinople. Mehmet commissioned the construction of the Iç Bedesten in the mid-15th century. But after burning down twice, prior to being rebuilt of block stone, the **Sandal Bedesten** (Silk Bazaar) near the Nuruosmaniye Gate was built and is now considered the oldest structure in the bazaar. Other markets, like the jewelry and carpet-focused **Zincirli Han**—a quaint open-air haven that featured in the 1963 James Bond film *From Russia with Love*—are more recent additions. You can spend days roaming through every cranny of this place, but do earmark at least three hours to roam the main streets. Download a map of the bazaar from the internet to your smartphone to help with navigation.

Beyazıt Meydanı (Beyazıt Square)

Officially called Freedom Square, **Beyazıt Meydanı** is flanked to the east by **Beyazıt Mosque** and to the north by **Istanbul University.** On weekend evenings the square is abuzz with a makeshift flea market. The monumental portal across the square from the mosque is the entrance to Istanbul University, which was built by Sultan Mehmet II in 1453 and is considered one of the oldest colleges in the world.

The paved, landscaped entrance of the university bears a few marble blocks of the triumphal arch that graced the former Byzantine plaza known as Forum of Theodosius, after the 4th-century emperor. It was the largest forum of antiquity and was patterned after Rome's Forum of Trajan, with a gigantic arch crowned by bull heads. Perhaps that's how it earned its other moniker, the Forum of Tauri (bulls). Another possibility is that Theodosius was paying homage to the Roman cattle market that had been here before this colossal architectural scheme.

Between the mosque and Grand Bazaar, just off Çadırcılar Caddesi, the **Sahaflar Çarşısı** (Old Book Bazaar) is the place to buy secondhand books, the Koran in most languages, and maps—even out-of-print English titles, if you look hard enough. The bazaar is rumored to be where the first book was printed in Turkey in 1729 by Ibrahim Müteferrika, an Ottoman diplomat whose statue can be found in the courtyard.

Süleymaniye Camii (Mosque of Süleyman the Magnificent)

By far the finest sanctuary of its kind in the city, the **Süleymaniye Camii** (Prof. Siddik Sami Onar Cd., free) towers over the Golden Horn, eclipsing all other structures peppering the peninsula's skyline. It not only crowns Istanbul's second hill; the complex's strategic placement seems to extend organically the promontory. Its intricate facade and interior attest to the immaculate and complex workmanship that propelled Mimar Sinan to be recognized as the ablest of all imperial architects.

It also symbolizes the military and reigning prowess of its benefactor Sultan Süleyman I (The Magnificent), under whose reign the Ottoman Empire expanded to encircle the Mediterranean, nearly as far as Vienna. Commissioned in 1550, the mosque is second in size to Sultan Ahmet, but its interior and exterior designs outshine those of the former.

The Genius of the Imperial Architects

Nearly five centuries of Ottoman rule gave Istanbul its dramatic cachet. From the grand spired mosques in the Sultanahmet quarter to the plush palaces lining the Bosphorus, ornate buildings attest to the grandeur of their imperial commissioners. This impressive architecture is the amalgam of a variety of styles, each stamped by a master builder handpicked from within the imperial realm or invited from Europe's capitals by the ruler himself. Brick-and-mortar testaments to spectacular (or not-so-memorable) reigns didn't start with the Ottomans—the Greeks, Romans, and Persians had built such testaments long before. But what makes Ottoman architecture unique is the almost unlimited creative autonomy of the architects, the variety of building styles typical of the era, and the sheer decadence of the structures' exteriors and interiors.

Ottoman architecture emerged in Bursa at the turn of the 14th century during the reign of the dynasty's founder, Osman I (1258-1324). From a base rooted deeply in Selçuk architecture, a mixture of Byzantine and Persian ornamentation was incorporated as the style evolved. Bursa's Ulu Cami exemplifies the budding movement. It's fashioned in the traditionally modest Selçukian architectural style, characterized by large, dark praying halls, forested with columns holding massive ceilings. But its exterior was later amended to portray the grander Ottoman style with the addition of domes and gilded calligraphy. Buildings grew bigger and more lavish when the Ottomans named Edirne (1365) and later Istanbul (1453) their capital. The many-domed Topkapı Palace (1465) reflects that era. More sweeping innovations were introduced with the construction of Istanbul's Fatih Camii (1470); the first of its kind to include a *külliye* (social-religious complex) on its grounds.

The **Classical Period** (1437-1703) was highlighted by the mastery of Mimar Sinan, who is lauded for greatly advancing world architecture during his lifetime. He conceived vast interiors enclosed by seemingly weightless yet massive domes, introduced harmony between inner and outer spaces, and played with light and shadow throughout his grand designs. During his time, mosques went from being somber and confined caverns embellished by Islamic calligraphy to artistically and technically complex sanctuaries. Süleymaniye Camii, in Istanbul, and Edirne's Selimiye are considered the movement's most exquisite examples.

By the turn of the 18th century, the **Westernization Period** was in full swing. Baroque and rococo styles found in France were introduced in the Ottoman Empire. During the **Tulip Period** (1730-1757), the introverted Ottoman elite began to explore the outdoors. Public places became focal points, and lavish fountains, waterside residences, and large outdoor recreational spaces were all the rage. The curved lines of the **Baroque Period** (1757-1808), exemplified by the Selimiye Barracks on Istanbul's Asian side, preceded the memorable **Empire Period** (1808-1876). Much as the Classical Period is synonymous with Mimar Sinan, the Balyan family of architects highlights the Empire Period. The spectacular Dolmabahçe and Beylerbeyi palaces as well as the petite yet fabulous Ortaköy Camii, highlight their achievements in Istanbul.

Finally, the **Late Period** (1876-1922) was shaped by eight master builders whose slants tended toward art nouveau, Vienna Secession, and revivalism. Two architects, Raimondo D'Aronco and Alexander Vallaury, in particular, impacted the imperial building trove. The former's greatest contributions are the massive Haydarpaşa School of Medicine campus (Marmara University, 1883) on Istanbul's Asian shore and the chalet-like compound of Yıldız Palace in Beşiktaş (1893). Vallaury, a Levantine of French parentage, is remembered as the founder of neo-Ottoman style best presented in buildings like the Istanbul Archaeological Museum and the famed Pera Palace Hotel.

What makes Süleymaniye's architecture unique for its time is the location of its minarets, in which the spires delineate the courtyard rather than the mosque. This innovative concept filled the negative space created by the low-lying complex adjacent to the towering building. Sinan followed the dome design of Ayasofya, adding buttresses to strengthen the building in an area he knew was prone to seismic activity.

The surrounding grounds were planned to function as a *külliye*, a semiautonomous complex with a *medrese*, infirmaries, caravanserais, hamams, and a hospital. The courtyard is filled with columns of fine crystalline rock known as porphyry as well as marble and granite. One towering minaret rises to the sky from each corner of the grounds to indicate that Süleyman was the fourth sultan to rule in Istanbul; the 10 balconies attest to his place in the Ottoman Dynasty. Sinan's tomb is in a walled plot north of the mosque, while Süleymaniye's southeastern corner is home to a cemetery where the elaborately tiled tomb of Süleyman I can be found, alongside that of his wife, Hürrem (Roxelana).

The mosque's interior is splendid in its simplicity. The light hue of its inner walls refracts sunlight flooding in from hundreds of windows, rendering Süleymaniye's inner sanctum bright and cheery, unlike the often cavernous feel of other mosques. Both the *minbar* and *mihrab* are crafted of a fine indigenous Proconnesian marble. Heralded imperial calligraphers Ahmet Karahısarı and Hasan Celebi also beautifully inscribed their creative involvement. Take an hour to linger in this complex, stopping to absorb its unique charm and sanctity in hidden tea gardens and restaurants along its perimeter.

Mısır Çarşısı (Egyptian Spice Bazaar)

A rambling expanse of back alleys, **Mısır Çarşısı** (0212/513-6597, www.misircarsisi.org, 8am-7:30pm Mon.-Sat.) is across from the Eminönü dock. You'll find the freshest condiments just beyond its gate. For the finest fabrics, school supplies, or anything else of interest, shop the side alleys. The spice bazaar is much smaller than the Grand Bazaar. It's where you'll rub shoulders with locals to snare a bargain in the laneways just outside the main building. It was built in 1660 to support the maintenance of Yeni Cami and as a sales point for exotic spices arriving from the then-newly conquered state of Egypt. The spectral colors of herb and spice stands as well as baskets of tea are simply mesmerizing; so is the sheer selection of Turkish delicacies such as *lokum* (Turkish delight), baklava, and dried fruits. Merchants braying to attract their next sale may appear intimidating, but most will gladly let you sample their offerings if you ask. *Kuruyemiş* (dry foodstuffs) stands make a great stop for caked olive soap as well as inexpensive bath accessories like loofahs and indigenous sea sponges. Try the reportedly aphrodisiac honey-soaked pistachios, olives of every color and size, succulent dried figs, and Turkey's reputable cheeses. Most of the stands sell loose spices, but ask about the possibility of vacuum-sealing your selections.

Rüstem Paşa Camii (Mosque of Rüstem Paşa)

Fresh from the architectural triumph of Süleymaniye Camii, Sinan went right to work on the rarely visited marvel of **Rüstem Paşa Camii** (Hasırcılar Cd., Eminönü, free). It may just be a fraction of its predecessor, but what this mosque lacks in size it oozes in prime Ottoman artistry. An octagonal thimble-size design gives rise to just one minaret, replete with doors crafted in three dimensions, *kündekâri* wood art that involves the mind-boggling, painstaking task of placing pieces of wood of various geometric shapes decorated with vegetal motifs side by side. The intricate interior boasts finely gilded minutiae high up on its entrance walls; its inner sanctum amazes with the finest of tile work. Iznik tile mastery is epitomized seen in the red-on-white primary colors, unlike the more typical easily blended tints of blue, green, and yellow prevalent in the 1560s, and the faience that depicts flowers throughout. These pricey decorative ceramics show yet again the power and wealth of its egotistical owner, Rüstem Paşa.

As Süleyman's Grand Vizier and son-in-law, Rüstem was a Bosnian who attained the highest seat in government through manipulation and greed. He fell in with Süleyman's wife, the pretty Roxelana, and the two schemed to convince the sultan that his son, Prince Mustafa, born by consort Mahidevran Sultan, was himself devising a military coup to dethrone him. Süleyman fell for the ruse, and Mustafa's beheading guaranteed Roxelana's son Selim's ascension to the throne.

Ironically, Selim was a womanizing drunkard who became known as Selim the Sot, and his pitiful reign signified the start of the empire's 200-year decline. The Rüstem Paşa Camii is located in the side streets west of the Egyptian Spice Bazaar.

Yeni Cami (New Mosque)

Only Turks, who live among some of the oldest monuments on the planet, would refer to a building erected over 300 years ago as *yeni* (new). The **Yeni Cami** (Yeni Cami Meydanı Sk., Eminönü, free) is actually the Mosque of Valide Sultan (Queen Mother), after Sultan Mehmet III's mom, Safiye. Commissioned in 1597, construction was halted for more than five decades after Safiye lost her power and royal funding when her son died. Incidentally, her ruthless son Mehmet is rumored to have ordered the strangulation of more than 36 of his siblings in order to secure his accession to the throne and her undivided love. The mosque was completed in 1657, thanks to its new benefactor, Turhan Hatice, the mother of Sultan Mehmet IV. Though large, Yeni Cami pales in comparison to Istanbul's other mosques. It's crafted in true Ottoman style with a series of domes crowned by a large dome; the sanctuary features a wealth of gold, meticulously crafted tiles, and carved marble. Turhan Hatice's tomb is located here; her son Mehmet and five other sultans are entombed alongside her.

Galata Köprüsü (Galata Bridge)

While only a fraction of the size of the two massive suspension bridges that span the Bosphorus, **Galata Köprüsü** is pure Istanbul—a successful mix of modern and old. Its center lane accommodates a rapid tramway that whooshes along past hundreds of anglers lazily lining the bridge's edge waiting for their next catch. Professionals and homemakers alike scurry across as peddlers push socks, fortune-telling rabbits, and poor-quality gadgets. About 20 waterside cafés, fish restaurants, and narghile (water pipe) joints line the bridge's lower terrace; it's an ideal spot to experience the city's rhythms, particularly when the call to prayer by a thousand *müezzinler* from the nearby mosques simultaneously beckons the faithful over a backdrop of screeching seagulls.

The bridge links the frantic ports of Karaköy and Eminönü and extends over the Golden Horn—the natural estuary that flows from the Bosphorus. Built in 1994, today's

Friday prayers at the 16th-century Rüstem Paşa Camii

Hidden Istanbul

Hidden caravanserais, secret doors, colorful abodes, and serene tea gardens are all on offer as you explore the cobbled back streets of old Istanbul. Even the major mosques listed in this book house gems such as tea gardens, mini bazaars, and artisanal shops where you can snare a good deal on Turkish handicrafts. Don't be afraid to wander a mosque's environs to find your own oasis in this expansive city.

Çorlulu Ali Paşa Medresesi (on the T1 tramline between Beyazıt and Çemberlitaş), an old Ottoman Islamic seminary, hosts a series of cafés where you can recline on continental wooden lounges and drift away with the wafting fruity aromas and bubbling sounds of the narghile. Another old seminary, the **Caferağa Medresesi,** is off Caferiye Sokak, which lines the northwestern perimeter of the Ayasofya. It is now home to the secluded Turkish Cultural Service Foundation, with art workshops and small artisanal galleries set in a 16th-century *medrese*, promoting the arts of marbling, tile-making, ceramic painting, and calligraphy.

Between the Spice Bazaar and Grand Bazaar is the 17th-century **Büyük Valide Han** (off Çakmakçılar Ykş 26-46). Over 350 years ago it operated as an Ottoman inn. In 2012 the James Bond flick *Skyfall* used the *han* as a "blink and you miss it" location for the motorcycle chase through Eminönü. Nowadays, the tiny abandoned rooms on the second floor host craftspeople repairing old Anatolian carpets or molding brassware for narghile pipes. Try to locate the caretaker, and gesture to go to the roof. With luck (and a small tip), he will unlock a door revealing a rickety stone staircase to the roof for magnificent views of Eminönü, Galata, and the Bosphorus. Stick to the main path, as there are no guardrails for stability.

Another off-the-beaten-track location for sweeping Bosphorus and Galata vistas is the tea gardens along the northern edge of **Gülhane Park.** From the tramline, follow the main path through the park and take a right before the exit. The cafés are uphill from there. This is a favorite spot for locals and a lovely place to escape the crowds at the nearby Topkapı Palace. Stop a while for tea and *keyfi* while watching the slow pace of nautical life on the Bosphorus.

Galata Bridge modernized a nostalgic pontoon bridge that seductively swayed along with the currents beneath it. Overpasses spanning the waterway have actually been around since Constantine's time, and previous constructions of this famous link can be walked along five kilometers up the Golden Horn by the old Fez factory in Eyüp.

SIRKECI AND VICINITY

A stroll downhill from Sultanahmet following the tramline snakes past facades of modern shops and boutique hotels interspersed with antique Ottoman buildings, leading to Sirkeci by the busy port of Eminönü. Just a 10-minute walk from Sultanahmet, the neighborhood of Gülhane offers a rambling park that was once part of Topkapı Palace. It's now home to picnickers and the entrance of the History of Science and Technology Museum and Istanbul's Museum of Archaeology, where more than one million relics are on display. Farther along the tramline is the Istanbul *gar* (train station)—the famed former Sirkeci Train Station and terminus for the *Orient Express*—just 50 meters from the water's edge.

Gülhane Parkı (Gülhane Park)

Once the gardens of sultans and concubines, today's sprawling 16-hectare park is by far Istanbul's largest and oldest. **Gülhane Parkı** (adjacent to Topkapı Palace) is a meticulously landscaped hangout for sunflower seed-gnawers, picnickers, and runners. Spreading along the rear of Topkapı Palace to Seraglio Point, panoramic terraces and benches are scattered throughout to offer visitors places to enjoy the park's lush atmosphere. Tea gardens set high up on a slope overlooking the Bosphorus afford fantastic views of the Maiden's Tower as well as Europe and Asia strung together by the Bosphorus Bridge. The park must be visited at least once during your stay. In April, stroll the park to view millions of tulips blooming color and life into springtime.

Historically, the space Gülhane occupies served as military depots during the Byzantine era. By the late 11th century it was home to the Mangana Palace, Hagios Georgios Monastery, and Sacred Panagia Fountain. When Mehmet the Conqueror claimed Sarayburnu (the tip of Seraglio Point) in 1453, he ordered the construction of lavish city walls around the land. A series of pavilions and mansions were later built by his successors in and around these lush gardens, of which the Sepetçiler Kasrı (Basket Weavers Palace)—a late 16th-century imperial dock and ceremonial pavilion—is the last remaining on the waterfront.

The fragrance of the millions of rosebushes once planted here during the sultanate was replaced by the stench and cacophony of dozens of animals during the park's short stint as a municipal zoo in the early 20th century. Today, whistles warning that the grass is off-limits and the passing of the occasional municipal vehicle break the serenity of this green enclave.

Getting past the vendors just outside the entrance 50 meters uphill from the Gülhane tram stop is always tricky, but walking past them without engaging in conversation is the best approach. Following the ample footpath will take you directly to the coastal road and tea gardens that border the Sea of Marmara, while the road on the right at the entrance leads to the Archaeology Museum and Topkapı Palace.

Istanbul Arkeoloji Müzesi (Istanbul Archaeological Museums)

The impressive artifact collections displayed at **Istanbul Arkeoloji Müzesi** (Gülhane Park, 0212/520-7740, www.istanbularkeoloji.gov.tr, 9am-7pm Tues.-Sun. Apr.-Oct., 9am-5pm Tues.-Sun. Nov.-Mar., 15TL) are among the most extensive in the world, with over one million pieces on display in three buildings—the Museum of Archaeology, the Ancient Orient Museum, and the Tiled Kiosk Museum.

In the Museum of Archaeology, a **lion statue** originating from the Mausoleum of Halicarnassus, one of the Seven Ancient Wonders of the World, indicates the magnitude of the museum's contents. In the halls on the left, a series of 4th century BC sarcophagi, found at the ancient city of Sidon in 1887 and 1888 in what is now Lebanon, are displayed. These were uncovered by Osman Hamdi Bey, a prominent figure in Ottoman archaeology and director of the Istanbul museums for 29 years from 1881. Demonstrating superb Roman stone artistry influenced by the ancient Mediterranean cultures, the jewel in the sarcophagi collection is the **Alexander Sarcophagus,** with carvings relating to the battles and life of Alexander the Great. Ironically, this tomb was long thought to be his, but later investigation revealed that it was actually that of Sidonian King Abdalonymos. The **Sarcophagus of the Mourning Women,** found in the same Sidonian necropolis, boasts 18 panels of complex carvings depicting women weeping. Incidentally, the facade of the museum, designed by imperial architect Alexandre Vallaury in the late 19th century, was inspired by the intricate carvings of both sarcophagi.

Next is a 14th-century **Galata Tower bell** and one of the three snake heads from the Hippodrome's **Serpentine Column.** Also on the ground floor is a **Children's Museum,** a hands-on exhibit complete with a Trojan horse for the little ones to climb into.

The museum's mezzanine level houses the **Istanbul through the Ages** exhibit, which received the Council of Europe Museum Award in 1993. Adeptly presented, this section's maps and diagrams effectively give a bird's-eye view into the city's past, from prehistoric remains found on Istanbul's Asian flank to mid-15th-century Byzantine artistry. Aside from a library that boasts more than 70,000 titles, the upper floor comprises smaller items like terra-cotta statuettes, cooking implements and a collection of 800,000

Ottoman coins, medals, and seals. A fascinating exhibit displaying the 8,000-year-old finds from the construction of the Marmaray are also on display. The upper floors are home to the **Anatolia and Troy through the Ages** exhibit as well as the halls containing Syrian and Palestinian sculptures.

Once a fine arts school, the building commissioned by Osman Hamdi Bey in 1883 now houses the **Ancient Orient Museum.** The museum displays an exceptionally abundant array of artifacts from the earliest civilizations of Anatolia, the Arabian Peninsula, Egypt, and Mesopotamia. Along with a small collection of Egyptian artifacts, pagan divinities originating from the Al-Ula temple are on display. Keep a look out for one of three known tablets of the **Treaty of Kadesh,** the first recorded peace treaty, signed between Ramses II and the Hittites and inscribed in Akkadian, the local vernacular of the time.

The third marvelous building, the **Tiled Kiosk,** is the oldest building in the museum complex, constructed in 1472 during the reign Fatih Mehmet II. It was the first museum on the site after the original museum, the Hagia Eirene, proved too small for the archaeological finds uncovered throughout the Ottoman lands. Today, the kiosk displays some 2,000 pieces of Islamic and Turkish ceramics and art from Iznik, Çanakkale, Miletus, and Kütahya dating to the 11th through 20th centuries.

History aesthetes can revel in the richness of the museum's buildings for days, but for the rest of us, three hours at opening time should suffice.

History of Science and Technology Museum

This little-known museum, officially called the **Istanbul Museum for History of Science and Technology in Islam** (0212/528-8065, 9am-7pm Tues.-Sun. Apr.-Oct., 9am-5pm Tues.-Sun. Nov.-Mar., 5TL), is housed in the former stables of Topkapı Palace on the western edge of Gülhane Park. The museum celebrates the inventions and advancements of the Islamic world from the 8th to 16th centuries, with replicas of gadgets in the fields of architecture, medicine, mathematics, physics, astronomy, navigation, and warfare. Lengthy technical explanations are available to visitors, but don't expect the interactive displays typical of science museums—it's a hands-off exhibition only.

Istanbul Gar (Istanbul Train Station)

The famed terminus of the *Orient Express* (opposite the Sirkeci tram station) is now the **Istanbul Gar and Sirkeci Marmaray Station.** The building's fusion of oriental architecture was once the terminus of the Simplon Line, which transported passengers to seductive Istanbul from Paris's Gare de l'Est in utter luxury. It shut down in 1977, although a similar service started to much fanfare in 2007. What that meant for Sirkeci was a renovation to highlight its early-20th-century mystique while modernizing its services and facilities to accommodate well-heeled travelers. Unfortunately, the red carpet is no longer rolled out for arrivals. These days the terminal is for daily commuters only, though it is still possible to relive the charm of the *Orient Express* once a year with **Venice Simplon Orient Express** (www.vsoe.com). A six-day journey from Paris to Istanbul via Budapest and Bucharest, or a journey from Istanbul to Venice, offers the VIP luxury of yesteryear with a price tag for the modern wealthy elite.

At 1,200 square meters, the terminal is pure European orientalism in architecture and worth a look. Stylishly bold at the time of its inauguration in 1890, its unique design was replicated across the continent. The building sprawls on either side of a soaring turreted entrance that boasts geometrical detail extending to a series of circular oriels and lofty bay windows.

The Orient Express Restaurant inside became a hub for elite members of the media and writers, such as Graham Greene and Agatha Christie, in the mid-20th century. Christie is said to have researched the classic *Murder on the Orient Express* here. A pint-size **Turkish Railroad Museum** (9am-5pm Tues.-Sat., free) displays memorabilia of the Turkish State Railways, and the splendidly renovated exhibition hall welcomes the traditional whirling dervish ceremony of the *sema* (7:30pm Mon.-Tues. and Fri.-Sat., 50TL). Five musicians and five dervishes perform for one hour with a ceremony that the UNESCO awarded as one of the "Masterpieces of the Oral and Intangible Heritage of Humanity" in 2005.

BEYOĞLU AND ŞİŞLİ

Across the Golden Horn from old Istanbul, the district of Beyoğlu winds vertiginously from the busy port of Karaköy, up to the tiny neighborhood of Galata with its looming Genoese tower, through cobbled backstreets of artisans, to the crowded pedestrian avenue of Istiklal Caddesi. Istiklal, meaning "independence," itself ends in Taksim Square—the heart of modern Istanbul. From here, Beyoğlu flows north into the Bosphorus-side district of Beşiktaş and the inner city district of Şişli, where the prized enclave of Nişantaşı—Istanbul's smaller version of New York City's 5th Avenue—draws the nation's elite.

Once called Péra, Beyoğlu was the financial and diplomatic center in the 19th and early 20th centuries. Furriers, cafés, and grand hotels catered to foreign attachés, the literati, and all the trade that went along with it. When Turkey's capital was moved to Ankara in the mid-1920s, foreign embassies followed suit, leaving their lavish townhouses to function as consular offices. Beyoğlu's mystique spiraled downward and it became known for back alleys where drug dealing and prostitution thrived. But by the early 1990s, the smaller neighborhoods of this district were reenergized with brand-name boutiques, rooftop bars, and swanky restaurants that beautified this modern face of Istanbul.

Beyoğlu is also renowned for its centuries-old Jewish synagogues and its Greek and Armenian Orthodox sanctuaries. In fact, Karaköy owes its name to a small, albeit still thriving, Jewish colony of Karaites, whose ancestors escaped the Spanish Inquisition in the late 15th century.

Moving quickly, these districts can be experienced in one day by riding the city's T1 tramway to Karaköy, climbing Galata's backstreets to Istiklal Caddesi, and ambling along the thoroughfare to Taksim Square. Once there, Şişli's Military Museum and Nişantaşı are both at an easy 15-minute walk from Taksim's famous Gezi Park.

Istanbul Gar once greeted guests of the *Orient Express*.

Karaköy

As recently as 2008, this run-down, forgotten neighborhood was home to gritty hardware stores, banks, and back-street businesses, and was unsafe in the evenings. But thanks to the fleet of international cruise ships that dock here most days in summer, **Karaköy** is transforming into an upscale hangout where you can drink European coffees on shady vine covered patios, shop in boutique stores, and chill out to house music in the upmarket bars and restaurants that are popping up all over this waterfront neighborhood. The greatest lure to this stretch of real estate are the crispy, juicy desserts that seep out of **Karaköy Güllüoğlu** (Kemankeş Sk., 0212/249-9680, www.karakoygulluoglu.com). Put simply, there is no better place to try baklava. The Güllüoğlu family has been rolling out layers upon layers of pastry and baking this delicate dessert, awash with butter and sugar syrup, since the 1800s. In business since 1949, this is one Istanbul's most iconic cafés. Before climbing the hill to Galata, do yourself a favor and stop here to refuel on this tasty dessert, best consumed with tulip-shaped glasses of black *çay*.

Galata

Galata's main claim to fame is the Galata Tower and the narrow cobbled lanes of vintage goods, musical instruments, and artisans' shops, but a wealth of Jewish sanctuaries also abound in this small neighborhood. The **Neve Shalom Synagogue** (Büyük Hendek Cd. 61), the largest Sephardic synagogue in the city, was built by Galata's conservative congregation in 1951. Just above Bankalar Caddesi, The **Ashkenazi Synagogue** (Yüksek Kaldırım 37) remains the only active Ashkenazi synagogue in Istanbul. The nearby **Italian Synagogue** (Laleli Çeşme Sk. 8) was founded in the late 19th century after turf disputes led Beyoğlu's Jewish population to seek protection from the Italian Embassy. Entering through the front reveals the sanctuary's Gothic facade and lovely marble staircase. The mid-17th-century **Zülfaris Synagogue**

Enjoy 360-degree views of the city from Galata Tower.

(Haracci Ali Sk.) houses the Museum of Turkish Jews, which covers Sephardic Jewish life in Turkey over the past 500 years. Visits to the synagogues can be organized by contacting the Chief Rabbinate (www.musevicemaati.com).

Galata Kulesi (Galata Tower)

For the ultimate 360-degree view of Istanbul, the **Galata Kulesi** (Galata Meydanı, 0212/293-8180, 9am-8pm daily, 19TL) can't be beaten. The 67-meter citadel's upper terrace is just a short ride by elevator, followed by a climb up a spiraling staircase. Opening up to a circular expanse pocked with watch windows, this was, and remains, the best vantage point to keep tabs on the sprawling city.

The tower was named the Tower of Christ in the mid-14th century by the Genoese. It was renamed Galata Kulesi after the Ottoman conquest of Istanbul. Looming over the walled enclave of Galata, sentries would utilize its lofty location until well after the mid-1950s to monitor the vulnerable straits and Sea of

Novel City Tours

HELICOPTER
A 20-minute helicopter sightseeing tour with **Arpanu Travel** (www.helicoptertoursinistanbul.com, €195 pp) features imperial Sultanahmet, the Golden Horn, the majestic Bosphorus, and the Black Sea. Tours are 3pm-5pm Saturday or Sunday and include transfers to and from the helipad at Miniatürk.

CAÏQUE (ROWBOAT)
For a regal tour of the Bosphorus or Golden Horn, try an imperial *caïque*. Ottoman sultans checked on their realm by traveling Istanbul's waterways aboard seaworthy, jewel-embellished elongated gondolas. Today, the pompous glitter is mostly gone, but the style remains: recent passengers include Naomi Campbell and Elizabeth Hurley, who celebrated a birthday on one. For bookings, contact **Sultan Kayıkları** (www.sultankayiklari.com).

DOUBLE-DECKER BUS
Big Bus Tours (www.bigbustours.com, adults €30, ages 5-15 €15, families €75) offers two "hop on, hop off" routes covering all the major sights, as well as free Wi-Fi and multilingual audio guides. The Red Tour (9 stops, uninterrupted tour 2.5 hours) travels through the major old town landmarks before crossing over to Beyoğlu, Taksim, and eventually Beylerbeyi Palace via the Bosphorus Bridge. Families will enjoy the Blue Tour (6 stops, uninterrupted tour 75 minutes) which loops the Golden Horn, stopping in Eyüp for the cable car to Pierre Loti, followed by Miniatürk, and Rahmi Koç Museum. Buses depart every 30 minutes from Sultanahmet Square, near the Ayasofya. Purchase tickets at hotels, via the website, or upon boarding.

VINTAGE CAR
These Buicks, Chevrolets, DeSotos, Plymouths, and Dodges were sent as part of the United States' post-World War II Marshall Plan, which aimed to boost local economies against the expanding Soviet Union. Operating as *dolmuşlar* (communal taxis) until the 1990s, these beauties are now owned by collectors who hire them for private tours of the city. For more information, contact **Turkey Tour Center** (www.turkeytourcenter.com, car and tour €650). To see more classic vehicles, visit the Ural Ataman Classic Car Museum (www.atamanmuseum.com) in Sariyer, 20 kilometers north of Taksim.

Marmara, as well as to get an early bead on the recurrent fires that then afflicted the city. Even a 17th-century aviator, Hezarfen Ahmet Çelebi, utilized the tower to launch the first intercontinental flight to Üsküdar using artificial wings.

Checking out the panorama that extends well beyond the Princes' Islands and the hilly Asian banks of the Bosphorus is well worth a half hour. The queue to get to the top for sunset can take much longer than the visit itself, so leave enough time to secure a spot atop the tower at the end of the day.

Galata Mevlevihanesi (Galata Mevlevi Monastery)
Experiencing a *sema*—or whirling dervish ceremony—is a must on any trip to Turkey; attending one in Istanbul rates second-best to actually visiting the lavish performance hall in Konya, where the ritual originated. The **Galata Mevlevihanesi** (Galip Dede Cd. 15, 0212/245-4141, 9:30am-4:30pm Wed.-Mon., free) was refurbished in 2007 and welcomes visitors for 5pm Sunday performances (40TL). While the new hall offers a cleaner look, the regularly sold-out shows tend to be uncomfortably packed.

The dervish hall was founded by an Ottoman aristocrat of Sultan Beyazıt II's court in the late 15th century. Its first leader was Sheikh Muhammad Semaî Sultan Divanî, a direct descendant of Mevlânâ Jelaleddin Rûmî. The street on which the structure lies was named after Galip Dede (Grandfather Galip), a respected leader of the order; his tomb is located to the left of the entrance. Kumbaracıbaşı Ahmet Paşa, a French count who converted to Islam and served in the imperial army, is also buried here alongside Ibrahim Müteferrika, who introduced the first printing press in the empire in the 17th century. Unless you're attending the show, the Galata Mevlevihanesi is a bit lackluster and truly doesn't warrant a special trip.

If tickets to the Galata show prove elusive, there are still one-hour evening performances (7:30pm Mon.-Tues. and Fri.-Sat., 50TL) at the quaint exhibition hall of Istanbul Gar in Sirkeci or three minutes south of here at Hodjapasha Cultural Center (Hocapaşa Hamam Sk., 3B, 0212/511-4626, www.hodjapasha.com, 60TL) starting at 7pm most days.

Tünel Funicular

Tünel is home to Istanbul's original underground cable car, the **Tünel Funicular** (4TL pp, 2.15TL with IstanbulKart, 6am-10pm daily). It connects Karaköy to Tünel, at Istiklal Caddesi's southern end, through a 460-meter-long, 90-second ride. Such a short hop may seem pointless, but it's ideal for those who don't want to scale or seesaw up the cobbled backstreets that link the two spots. Inaugurated in 1875, the single car was originally powered by horses. It wasn't until 1910 that the wooden cable cars were outfitted for electrical power. Tünel is the oldest subway in the world after the London Underground. Renovated in 1971 with spiffy metal cars, the connector was most recently upgraded with a silent car in 2007. The lower station's late-19th-century European orientalism, with multicolored tiles and yellow walls, was unfortunately replaced to accommodate modern tastes. Today, taking this easy ride up to Tünel is well worth the five-minute wait for the next car, particularly with children in tow.

★ Istiklal Caddesi

The hectic two kilometer long **Istiklal Caddesi** exudes old European flair and style. Apart from the arabesque or traditional *fasıl* music drifting from restaurants, you could be in any European capital. A contradiction here is that the tall buildings that line this avenue are categorized as historical by Turkish government standards, but the shops at street level are anything but antiquated. For decades, Istiklal has been the core and the muse for Beyoğlu's culture. From Tünel all the way to Taksim Square, this is where to find artists seeking inspiration and buskers entertaining shoppers who store-hop from one brand-name haunt to the next along the two-kilometer route. Some of Istiklal's side and backstreets, however, lead to interesting finds, such as the antiques shops in **Çukurcuma** (Turnacıbaşı Cd.), Turkish novelist Orhan Pamuk's **Museum of Innocence** (Dalgıç Sk. 2, Beyoğlu, 0212/252-9738, www.masumiyetmuzesi.org, 10am-6pm Tues.-Wed. and Fri.-Sun., 10am-9pm Thurs., closed Mon., 5TL), the art galleries of **Tophane** (Boğazkesen Cd.), traditional Turkish music venues (Hasnun Galip Sk.), highly reputable gourmet restaurants (Meşrutiyet Cd.), and even subcultures such as the transvestites of Tarlabaşı, whose lifestyles openly play out alongside the hustle of Beyoğlu's mosaic of beings. For a good sense of what lies ahead along this street, hop on the **nostalgic tram** that runs through the middle of the avenue linking Tünel to Taksim Square, and walk back.

Starting from Tünel, the **Tünel Pasajı** opposite the funicular station is a gallery of tiny cafés and shops selling nostalgic items and books. To the north of Tünel Square is the nighttime entertainment district of **Asmalı Mescit,** and beyond it the **Tepebaşı** neighborhood, home to the **Pera Palace Hotel** (Meşrutiyet Cd. 52, 0212/251-4560, www.jumeirah.com, from €196), the famed pied-à-terre of such notables as Agatha Christie, Ernest Hemingway, and the irresistible World War I spy Mata Hari.

Farther up the Meşrutiyet Caddesi is **Pera Müzesi** (Pera Museum, Meşrutiyet Cd. 141, Beyoğlu, 0212/334-9900, www.peramuzesi.org.tr, 10am-7pm Tues.-Sat., noon-6pm Sun.,

15TL). In 2005 the splendid colonnaded mansion opened as a museum of Turkish Arts, boasting extensive collections of priceless Kütahya tiles, some dating back to 1377; 18th- to 20th-century paintings of the Imperial Ottoman Court; and a vast array of Anatolian weights and measures, including bronze balance pans and a cylindrical seal impression used by Assyrian traders 4,000 years ago. Some outstanding temporary exhibitions are also on offer throughout the year. Visit 6pm-10pm Friday for free entry.

Almost a dozen Roman Catholic and Orthodox churches as well as synagogues can be found along Istiklal. A prime example is **Saint Antoine** (a.k.a. San Antonio di Padova, Istiklal Cd. 325, Beyoğlu, 0212/244-0635, Catholic Mass Sun., donation). Since its inauguration in 1912, Saint Antoine has remained Istanbul's largest church and congregation. The church is one of the few open to the public; others, like **Aya Triada** (Holy Trinity, Meşelik Sk. 11/1, Taksim, 0212/244-1358, donation), are more often than not closed. If the gates are closed, knock; the warm Turkish caretaker might indulge a gentle request. The Greek Orthodox Aya Triada is one of Beyoğlu's hidden jewels, with its adjoining school, founded in 1882. The inner sanctum reflects its wealthy congregation with massive crystal chandeliers, ornate walnut pews, and exquisite iconographical artwork on panels that open to secret loges.

The monumental gilded gate rising halfway down Istiklal Street is the entrance to **Galatasaray Lisesi,** a high school built by imperial edict in 1481; it remained the first of its kind in Istanbul until a transformation some four centuries later propelled it to exemplary status for its superb European Oriental architecture, a rigorous French curriculum, and its status as one of modern Turkey's most prestigious scholastic establishments.

Following the school's perimeter downhill leads to **Fransız Sokak** (French Street), Istanbul's tribute to Paris's belle epoque. In pure Toulouse-Lautrec fashion, the facades on either side of the back alley's steep flight of stairs are rose-colored, with blooming planters gracing their forged iron balconies. The sounds of Edith Piaf and the aroma of French-press coffee served at a handful of cafés fill the air. Enjoy lunch or dinner at one of the cafés along this colorful sloping street. This collaborative effort between the municipality and a group of creatives highlights centuries of French influence on Beyoğlu's architecture and arts, which included the area's first café in the 19th century and first movie theater.

Just north of Galatasaray on Istiklal is **Çiçek Pasajı** (Flower Passage), an arched, L-shaped arcade comprising lofty early-19th-century facades. This was the Cité de Péra—the hobnobbing center for fashionistas. It was refurbished in the early 1990s after decades of neglect. The mundane beer joints and *köfteciler* (eateries specializing in grilled meat patties) that lined its sides were transplanted to side streets to make way for more upscale yet reasonably priced *meyhaneler* (Turkish taverns). Just outside, the **Balık Pazarı** (Fish Market) is a noisy hodgepodge of fishmongers and delis interspersed with side streets replete with estate jewelry dealers and souvenir shops. Watch for **Nevizade Street,** a side alley where you'll find Taksim's busiest evening dining and drinking hubs full of *meyhaneler.* Pull up a chair or stool to drink beer and *rakı* (an aniseed-flavored aperitif) with the locals, as busking Turkish musicians earn their keep entertaining the masses with their *darbuka* (drum), clarinet, and violin.

Taksim Square

The transportation hub of the "new" city, **Taksim Square** signifies the end of bustling Istiklal Street. This is the heart of secular Turkey. Originating from the Arabic *taqṣīm,* meaning "division," Taksim Square was named by Sultan Mahmud I (1696-1754) for an underground stone reservoir that collected water from Istanbul's aqueducts. Today, on the east the square is flanked by grand hotels, banks, Western-style cafés, and the lofty **Atatürk Kültür Merkezi** (Atatürk Cultural Center), home of the State Symphony

Orchestra and Choir, Modern Folk Music Ensemble, and Classical Turkish Music Choir.

The 11-meter-high statue in the square is the **Republic Monument** depicting the father of modern Turkey, Mustafa Kemal Atatürk, and his comrades. Public monuments were forbidden under the religious law of the Ottomans, so Atatürk commissioned this statue in 1928 to symbolize Turkey's reinvention as a secular republic, where religion and government are separate entities. Almost every day of the week advocacy groups demonstrate peacefully on a range of issues affecting Turkish society. Taksim Square remains heavily guarded to deter political rallies and marches, like the Gezi Park protests of 2013 and the Taksim Square Massacre of 1977, where more than 30 left-wing protesters were shot by alleged right-wingers. Don't be surprised to see riot police stationed close by, ready to tame the passionate crowd that occasionally congregates. Generally, Taksim is a safe place to watch people and loiter, but avoid the square when political rallies are planned, usually in the afternoon on weekends. Excessive use of tear gas and water cannons throughout 2013 against antigovernment demonstrators did catch unsuspecting locals and visitors out on weekend jaunts.

Askeri Müze ve Kültür Sitesi Komutanlığı (Military Museum)

With conquests encompassing the Arabian Peninsula, Eastern Europe, North Africa, and a variety of Turkic states, the might of the Ottoman—and later Turkish—military and its more than 1,000-year history are proudly displayed at the celebrated **Askeri Müze ve Kültür Sitesi Komutanlığı** (Valı Konağı Sk., Harbiye-Şişli, 0212/233-2720, 9am-4:30pm Wed.-Sun., 5TL). This interesting museum displays some 9,000 pieces of an inventory of 55,000, ranging from massive cannons and mortars on the museum's extensive lawns to Ottoman uniforms and weapons in some 22 rooms. But the pièce de résistance has to be the chain the Byzantines stretched across the Golden Horn to block the sultan's navy from entering Constantinople. And so is the imperial *sayeban*—a jewel-encrusted campaign pavilion in which the sultan received foreign ambassadors. This military facility once housed the Ottoman Imperial Military Academy, similar to West Point in the United States. It also served as a military reserve until 1993, when the grounds opened as a museum.

Time a one-hour visit to the museum in the late afternoon so you can experience the performances (3pm-4pm) of the traditionally-garbed Janissary Band, the world's oldest military ensemble. The Ottomans were the first to integrate live music in military life and during campaigns. The soldiers fought to the tune of the janissaries. The band also joined the commander in a slow march in and around newly conquered lands to inform its populace of their victory. The museum is about a 15-minute walk due north from Taksim Square.

Nişantaşı

Just a few minutes' walk from the Military Museum, but an entire world away, at the intersection of Valı Konağı Sokak and Rumeli Caddesi heading toward the Bosphorus, is the shopping paradise of **Nişantaşı.** Foodies and the well-heeled rejoice in this old affluent neighborhood. Names like Dior and Valentino along Abdi İpekçi Caddesi cater to Istanbul's super-rich. Those looking for affordable apparel will love pounding the pavement here too, with plenty of stores and the mall **City's** (Teşvikiye Cd. 162, 0212/373-3300, www.citysnisantasi.com) creating a hot spot for brand names and swanky eateries. If you stay in Sultanahmet and wonder where all the modern dress shops are, you'll need to strut over to this side of the city, via the M2 metro, for a different perspective of Istanbul life.

TOPHANE THROUGH EMIRGAN

Stretching 13 kilometers along the European flank of the Bosphorus, this area simultaneously evokes the city's erstwhile splendor and its modern glitz, with opulent palaces and some of the world's most exclusive nightclubs and hotels. After spending an hour or two in Tophane's art and cultural neighborhood, you can easily go to Dolmabahçe Palace to witness the grandeur of the late Ottoman Empire's European digs. Brand new to this area is the revamped stretch of **Akaretler.** This row of houses was built in the 1870s at the order of Sultan Abdülaziz as housing for the staff of the nearby palace. Today, it's an über-exclusive thoroughfare that includes such names as the W Hotel as well as top-notch bars and eateries.

The next major stop along the coast is Beşiktaş, home to the country's splendid maritime museum and the famed mausoleum of Barbarossa—a privateer so feared that Süleyman the Magnificent thought it wise to install him at the head of the mighty Ottoman navy. Prior to reaching Bebek, the waterside enclave of Istanbul's upper crust, the often jam-packed seaside road passes Yıldız Park before slicing through the quaint Bosphorus-side haunt of Ortaköy.

In April, if you have a spare day, it's worthwhile to travel another five kilometers beyond Bebek, past the 15th-century **Rumeli Fortress** and the second Bosphorus Bridge, to **Emirgan Park** to see the city's best display of tulips for the International Tulip Festival. Also found in Emirgan is the **Sakıp Sabancı Museum** (Sakıp Sabancı Cd. 42; 0212/277-2200, www.muze.sabanciuniv.edu; 10am-6pm Tues., Thurs.-Sun., 15TL; 10am-8pm Wed., free; closed Mon.), with its collection of Ottoman fine arts and calligraphy from the 14th to the 20th centuries as well as temporary exhibits of equal charm.

Several ports serve this European stretch of land, but the well-connected hubs of Kabataş and Beşiktaş bear the brunt of commuter sea traffic originating from the Asian coast. There are a couple of transportation options along this coastline: the T1 tram that serves Sultanahmet stops at Tophane before terminating at Kabataş; and a modern funicular (F1) runs down also to Kabataş tram station from Taksim Square in less than three minutes. From here, hop on bus 25E to reach Beşiktaş, Ortaköy, and beyond from the bus station between the Kabataş tramline and the port. If buses, trams, and ferries sound too complicated, tour it by taxi at a higher cost. Be aware that traffic along this stretch is a nightmare at peak hours; expect a 20-minute ride to take twice as long or longer.

Tophane

Edging Beyoğlu on the shore of the Bosphorus and about one kilometer northeast of Galata Bridge, **Tophane** is home to the Istanbul Museum of Modern Art, art galleries, overpriced narghile cafés, the 19th-century Mimar Sinan University of Fine Arts, and the baroque late-19th-century Nusretiye Clock Tower and Tophane Mosque. Of all of these, the most popular location for visitors is the **Istanbul Modern Müzesi** (Istanbul Museum of Modern Art, Meclis-i Mebusan Cd. Liman İşletmeleri Sahası Antrepo 4, 0212/334-7300, www.istanbulmodern.org, 10am-6pm Tues.-Wed. and Fri.-Sun., 10am-8pm Thurs., 17TL). In 2004, this museum, right on the docks of the Bosphorus, opened its doors to international fanfare, blazing trails in modernism in a city known for its burgeoning art scene. Besides paintings, the basement houses carefully curated temporary exhibitions from international and Turkish masters as well as a massive art library, under a low ceiling, of books seemingly floating in midair. Plan about 90 minutes to visit this space, and if you've been bitten by the art bug, explore the neighborhood art galleries that line Boğazkesen Caddesi, uphill from the Tophane tram station.

★ Dolmabahçe Sarayı (Dolmabahçe Palace)

Decadent, to say the least, the **Dolmabahçe Sarayı** (between Beşiktaş and Kabataş ports, 0212/236-9000, www.dolmabahcepalace.com, 9am-4pm Tues.-Wed. and Fri.-Sun., 40TL) is the Ottomans' version of Versailles, with rococo detailing taken to the extreme. Some 285 rooms boast floor-to-ceiling gilded mirrors, nacre-inlaid furniture, wall-to-wall carpets of the sheerest silk, and the most extravagant collection of Bohemian and Baccarat crystal chandeliers—including one that weighs 4.5 tons and has some 750 light bulbs. The highlight, however, remains the view of the Bosphorus and the building's rear facade seen from the imperial *caïque* (rowboat) dock.

The palace is a signature piece of the Balyans, the Armenian family of imperial architects responsible for the construction of some of the most lavish 19th-century Ottoman structures, including the spectacular Ortaköy Mosque, as well as the Çırağan and Beylerbeyi palaces, also flanking the Bosphorus. Built on land reclaimed from the straits, Dolmabahçe (filled garden) bears meticulously landscaped flowerbeds and centuries-old oaks and plane trees. In another way to squander the empire's fortunes, Sultan Abdülmecid (1823-1861) called in Garabet Balyan and his son, Nikoğos, to design a regal mansion grander and bolder than any other ruler's in the world. It took nine years to create the 37,000-square-meter palace that stands on 4.5 hectares. Thanks to an unlimited budget, the pair utilized a reported dozen tons of gold to gild the expansive ceilings.

Dolmabahçe's *selamlık* (men's quarters) features a famed crystal staircase that leads to the gigantic Red Room, a hall where the sultan received visiting dignitaries. Twin bear rugs—heads and all—given by Czar Nicholas I of Russia have graced the room for more than 150 years. The harem (women's quarters) has the sultan's private quarters, including a collection of personal tomes in a small library, a bed of pure silver in his personal boudoir, and his private marble bathing rooms with a soaking tub made of sheer alabaster. Mustafa Kemal Atatürk, the Turkish Republic's founder, spent the last years of his life in Dolmabahçe Palace and died here in the room overlooking the Bosphorus. His small master suite has a bed covered with the Turkish flag and a set of toiletries in the adjoining bathroom.

Grand fountains, lofty trees, a spectacular

Dolmabahçe Palace's elaborate 19th-century facade

marble clock tower, and a flock of showy pheasants in an aviary fill this palace's grounds. The Dolmabahçe Camii, commissioned in 1853 by Abdülmecid's mother, is just outside the ticket office. The **Clock Room,** near the aviary, features some of the palace's timepieces. They read 9:05, the time of Atatürk's death on November 10, 1938. The **Crystal Palace** is lots of fun, free to visit, and features splendid chandeliers, candelabras, and even a crystal baby grand piano.

Allow at least two hours to view the palace's lavish interior and grounds. While you're free to photograph and roam the gardens, exploring the palace is only possible on guided tours that depart throughout the day, hence the higher entry fee. Photography is also prohibited inside the palace.

Deniz Müzesi (Museum of Naval History)

The new purpose-built **Deniz Müzesi** (Beşiktaş Cd. 6/1, Beşiktaş, 0212/327-4345, www.denizmuzeleri.tsk.tr, 9am-5pm

Tues.-Sun., 6TL) explores the might of the Ottoman and Turkish navies through large collections of ensigns, navy uniforms, early navigational instruments, barnacle-crusted amphorae, and an array of maps dating back to 1461. Guests will find the imperial *caïques* impressive. These gilded beauties would carry the Ottoman sultans up the Bosphorus as surrounding vessels came to a standstill in admiration.

The ornate mausoleum of Barbaros Hayrettin Paşa is adjacent to the museum's entrance. Responsible for several successful naval campaigns as a privateer—a legal pirate—for the Ottomans, Barbaros Hayrettin Paşa was installed as admiral-in-chief of the Ottoman Navy by Süleyman the Magnificent in 1534. He dominated the Mediterranean for decades; his successful campaigns enlarged the empire into North Africa and Western Europe. At his request, a tomb was built by Mimar Sinan near a *medrese* in Beşiktaş. The burial structure is crafted of ashlar (stacked stone) masonry on an octagonal base plan and topped with a dome. Seven sides each have twin windows; the eighth side has a portico and serves as the entrance. Next to Paşa lie the remains of his wife and son. The tomb is only open to the public on April 4 and July 1, in commemoration of the Naval Martyrs and National Cabotage Days, respectively. Visitors need about an hour to view the museum, best combined with a trip to Yıldız Park, Ortaköy, or farther afield.

Yıldız Parkı (Yıldız Park)

Yıldız Parkı (Çirağan Cd., 0212/261-8460, 9am-5:30pm daily) comprises the remains of Yıldız Palace and its gardens that are free to explore, along with some old pavilions, and a renowned imperial porcelain factory (5TL).

Yıldız Park has an interesting past. Until the 18th century the hill that rises from the traffic-congested Çirağan Caddesi was a popular imperial hunting ground and lush gardens with regal accommodations. When overly suspicious Sultan Abdul Hamid II took the throne in 1876, he chose to build his own palace along this part of town for added security, rather than reside in Dolmabahçe Palace down the road. This palace was commissioned to the Balyan family of architects and has five major structures that functioned as an autonomous, well-protected imperial city where Abdul Hamid II both conducted official business and had his harem—as well as hours of carpentry and porcelain art. He is remembered as the "Red Sultan" for the atrocities he ordered against minorities during his 33-year reign.

Several of the pavilions are open to the public. The meticulously kept gardens, alpine architecture, and priceless collection of antiques—including a large ceramic stove and grand carpets—make the **Şale Pavilion** particularly interesting, as it diverges slightly from the other garish monuments along the water. The rolling courtyards boast more pavilions, greenhouses, pools, aviaries, workshops, and servants quarters. There are also mosques outside the two main entrances.

While the property is connected to Cırağan Palace by a footbridge, the official entrance to Yıldız Parkı is along Cırağan Caddesi. Stroll down toward the **Çadır Köşkü** (Tent Pavilion), where a stop at a relaxing café serves as the perfect transition back to Istanbul's hectic rush. Hungry? Reasonable buffet lunches are available at the splendid neoclassic **Malta Köşkü** (Yıldız Parkı, 25TL).

Ortaköy

Ortaköy is a pleasure for sightseers, shore-lovers, trend-watchers, souvenir-seekers, and culinary aficionados. Whatever the appeal, the 15 extra liras to hire a taxi heading northbound from Beşiktaş is well worth it, especially in the evening when upmarket Bosphorus-side bars turn up the beat for late night groovers. Most days are busy because Ortaköy is a chic lunch and dinner destination, but Sunday features a fantastic **Farmers Market**. Stands filled with fresh produce attract the wealthy toting canvas bags. A favorite thing to do here any day of the week is to people-watch by the water while eating a make-your-own *kumpir* (baked potato), best shared with a friend.

Ortaköy, today a mix of ethnicities, expatriates, and artists of all genres, was known as Damianou, after a monastery built here in the 9th century. It became a holiday hot spot for the Ottoman aristocracy 600 years later. Sultan Abdülmecid I selected this appealing site for his personal mosque, which he commissioned to Nikoğos Balyan in the late 19th century. Perhaps the most beautiful and most photographed building in Istanbul is the **Ortaköy Camii** (Ortaköy Mosque, Ortaköy Pier Square), which seems to cower in the shadow of the colossal Bosphorus Bridge. Pint-size compared to the mosques on the other side of the Golden Horn, Ortaköy Camii was crafted in a style later called neo-baroque. The interior walls have wide, high bay windows that refract daylight and its reflections on the water. This translates into an inner sanctum filled with natural bright lighting. Also of note are several panels of calligraphy, produced by Sultan Abdülmecid himself.

pint-sized Ortaköy Mosque

★ BOSPHORUS CRUISE

One of the highlights of any trip to Istanbul are the Bosphorus cruises that depart from Eminönü port throughout the day. If you're short on time or budget-conscious, board a public ferry that crosses from Eminönü to Üsküdar or Kadıköy on the Asian side. On this "cruise," which is a standard commuting route for many locals, from the deck you can view the old Sultanahmet peninsula, Maiden's Tower, the Bosphorus Bridge, and the Marmara Sea. Plan a sunset journey and watch the sun drop behind the minarets of the old town, creating a magical Istanbul signature moment—a sunset skyline peppered with oriental silhouettes. In late spring to early fall, keep an eye on the water along the way for a glimpse of a playful dolphin.

Travel companies in Sultanahmet have short Bosphorus cruises for 25TL and up (check the size of the boat and whether they have English commentary aboard before you buy), and all along the Eminönü dock hawkers will peddle tickets for boats. Often these don't leave until they are full and are barely seaworthy. Skip these hawkers completely to avoid common scams, and instead opt for the short (12TL pp, 2 hours) or full (25TL pp) Bosphorus cruise with **Şehir Hatlari** (0212/313-8000, www.sehirhatlari.com.tr). Tickets and departures are available daily from their terminal at Eminönü port near the Galata Bridge. While the staff do not provide commentary about sites (consider the logistics of catering to the multitude of languages on board), you can rent audio guides (10TL) before boarding. The timetable for the short tour changes throughout the year depending on the season (check the website), but the itinerary involves a loop past both European and Asian shores as far north as the Fatih Sultan Mehmet Bridge.

The full tour is ideal for a day trip to the fishing village of Anadolu Kavağı on the Asian side near the Black Sea. The Şehir Hatları ferry departs daily from Eminönü (10:35am) and Beşiktaş (10:50am) before arriving at *Anadolu Kavağı* around noon. The return journey departs at 3pm, leaving enough time to enjoy a seafood lunch by the Bosphorus followed by a steep climb to Yoros Castle, settled by the Phoenicians and Greeks before the Byzantine period. A panoramic view of the Bosphorus meeting the Black Sea is the reward for the climb.

In summer, Şehir Hatları offer moonlight cruises (20TL) on the Bosphorus to see the Bosphorus Bridge and city lights by night.

Çırağan Palace

The cruise glides by Dolmabahçe Palace on the European side, then nears another regal residence: The 19th-century **Çırağan Palace** (Çırağan Cd. 32, 0212/326-4646, www.kempinski.com), commissioned to the illustrious imperial architect Nikoğos Balyan by Sultan Abdülaziz in 1863, was the last imperial residence to be built on the straits. The strength of the marble used in its facade proved little resistance to the fire that ravaged its interior wooden structure in 1910. It deteriorated until the 1990s, when the hotel conglomerate Kempinski purchased the land and reconstructed the palace to its former grandeur to serve as one of the world's finest five-star hotels.

Bosphorus Bridge

Just above the Ortaköy Mosque looms the majestic **Bosphorus Bridge** (First Bridge). Fifteen years of planning led to the 1973 inauguration of this 1,560-meter-long suspension connector that links Asia and Europe. The pylon structure was designed by the British civil engineer Gilbert Roberts and cost US$200 million, a fraction of the US$2.5 billion flagged for the new 2.1-kilometer third bridge due to open in 2015. At night, the connector is lit by an LED system that washes the structure, and water below, in a spectacular rainbow of colors.

Rumeli Hisarı (European Fortress)

The 15th-century **Rumeli Hisarı** (Tarabya Yeniköy Cd., north of Sarıyer, 0212/263-5305, 9am-4pm Thurs.-Tues., 5TL) faces Anadolu Hisarı (Anatolian Fortress), which was built 60 years earlier. The point between the two forts marks the Bosphorus's narrowest point, about 760 meters across. It took three Ottoman viziers, each tasked with supervising the construction of one tower, just 4.5 months to construct this massive structure. Mehmet the Conqueror's Ottoman troops controlled the strait's northern end from the forts and watchtowers, and thus isolated Byzantine Constantinople from any aid arriving from Genoese Black Sea ports. So strong are the fort's 7-meter-thick walls that they've withstood more than 500 years of considerable seismic activity and fires.

Fatih Sultan Mehmet Bridge

Istanbul's second intercontinental connector, the **Fatih Sultan Mehmet Bridge,** not only bears the name of Constantinople's conqueror but also the brunt of commercial traffic. It accommodates traffic from the Trans-European Motorway that links the Thracian peninsula and the capital, Ankara, and all traffic beyond those two points. Built in 1988, it's a mirror copy of the Bosphorus Bridge, minus the disco light show in the evening.

Yalılar (Waterside Residences)

The Bosphorus coast is strewn with some 600 elegant *yalılar* (waterside mansions). At the going rate of US$20-115 million, these wooden abodes are a restoration pastime for the very rich and constitute some of the most expensive real estate in the world. They're categorized according to their historical importance, and any renovation of the older structures must adhere to the original architectural and interior design plans. These summer homes were originally built by the Ottoman aristocracy, with some bearing names like Crazy Ali Fuat Pasha, Snake, or Cypriot Mansion to reflect the character of their owners or architectural originality. At the height of the empire, building a *yalı*, from the Greek *yialos* (shore), signaled societal class; the bigger the abode, the richer its owner. The trend for *yalılar* (plural of *yalı*) began in the late 17th century, as stark wooden blocks following traditional Turkic interior design—a central room, sometimes with a fountain in the middle, with side rooms of separate gender-specific living quarters. Some of the most pivotal viziers hosted foreign dignitaries in the abodes' central *sofa* (welcoming room), in which the fate of states and alliances were invariably discussed after lavish meals. Such was the case of Sait Halim Paşa, the grandson of a former Egyptian governor who rose to the post of minister of foreign affairs when he cemented a German-Ottoman alliance with German envoy Baron Wangenheim in his eponymous waterside residence in 1914, leading to the Ottoman involvement in World War I. Other mansions, such as today's popular Sakıp Sabancı Museum, which was transformed from a villa commissioned in 1928 by Egyptian Prince Mehmed Ali Hasan in Emirgan, later became exhibition spaces for their owners' extensive collections of Ottoman and Anatolian artifacts. But while quite a few serve as superior boutique hotels and lavish restaurants, the majority remain private residences, and when sold, the utmost confidentiality ensures secrecy about the assets of Istanbul's elite.

Kanlıca

One of the succulent surprises on this trip is a stop at **Kanlıca,** an Asian port village famous for its sumptuous, creamy yogurt. Luckily, there's no need to get off, as servers often come aboard to sell the dairy delicacy. The yogurt's uniqueness comes from its blend of cow, sheep, and goat milk that's slowly scalded, not boiled, for 20 minutes. When the final product is mixed with powdered sugar, it results in a unique, zesty creaminess. The Asian enclave of Kanlıca is also known for a small waterside mosque built by Sinan for Iskender Paşa and for its Mecca-style coffee served in large, handleless cups. Farther north are the outposts of Sarıyer and Rumeli Kavağı in Europe and Anadolu Kavağı in Asia, accessible on a longer cruise.

Kuleli Military High School

On the return trip, the mid-19th-century **Kuleli Military High School** soars over the water north of Çengelköy's shore. The double-turreted structure is soaked in history. In addition to being Turkey's first military academy and high school, it served as a hospital for injured British and Turkish soldiers when war broke between the Ottoman Empire and Russia in 1875, and again during the yearlong Balkan Wars of 1912. The Kuleli Barracks were crucial both as an armory and as an infirmary.

Küçüksu Kasrı (Küçüksu Palace)

Farther along the Anatolian shore, just south of the second bridge, lies the solitary imperial hunting lodge **Küçüksu Kasrı** (Küçüksu Cd., 0216/332-3303, 9:30am-4:30pm Tues.-Wed. and Fri.-Sun., 5TL). Its lush gardens along the tamer and warmer waters of Küçüksu were once the preferred haunt of royals who opted for this petite abode over the much more formal Topkapı Palace. This imperial playground and resting pavilion was commissioned by Sultan Abdülmecid in 1857, replacing an earlier 18th-century timber vacation abode of Mahmud I. Within this lodge's walls, Abdülmecid's successors rubbed elbows with their foreign contemporaries, particularly during the growing entente between the powerful German and Ottoman Empires. Designed by the prolific architectural master Nikoğos Balyan, the baroque three-story structure includes a basement filled with kitchens and storage rooms. Its charm is defined by its exquisite marble fireplaces throughout, wall-to-wall inlaid parquet, fine European period furnishings, and dozens of imperial crystal chandeliers. Noteworthy are the gigantic Hereke carpets, which were woven in an imperial rug workshop known to this day for some of the world's finest silk rugs.

Beylerbeyi Sarayı (Beylerbeyi Imperial Palace)

The **Beylerbeyi Sarayı** (Ağa Cd., 0216/321-9320, 9am-4pm Tues.-Wed. and Fri.-Sun., 20TL), just north of the Bosphorus Bridge, is another early-19th-century project taken on by the illustrious Balyan family of architects. Beylerbeyi is a favorite with Turks but not a big destination for foreign visitors. It has all the pomp and detailing of the grand palaces packed in a one-hour tour. The *selamlık* and harem display the usual palatial accoutrements, such as Hereke carpets, priceless crystal chandeliers, and Chinese Ming and Parisian Sèvres porcelain, as well as a fountain in the main hall. It was commissioned in 1829 by Sultan Mahmud II as a location to hold Topkapı's official affairs, and it is the first imperial structure with European-style architecture. Built entirely out of timber, a fire raged through it some four decades after its completion, requiring Sultan Abdülaziz to order it rebuilt out of marble. What distinguishes this palace from others is its furniture, all created by Sultan Abdülaziz himself. Also worth noting are the many royal figures who stayed at Beylerbeyi when it served as an imperial guesthouse. France's Empress Eugénie, the wife of Napoléon III, was so impressed with the windows of her guest room during her stay in 1869 that she had them duplicated at Paris' Tuileries Palace. Beylerbeyi served as Sultan Abdul Hamid II's final residence after he was deposed and placed under house arrest by the Young Turks in 1913. You can also reach the palace via bus 15 from Üsküdar bus station, opposite the port.

Kız Kulesi (Maiden's Tower)

Approaching Eminönü, the **Kız Kulesi** seems to float on the Bosphorus. The story goes that it once housed a beautiful princess whose overprotective father—an emperor who feared a curse that she would succumb to a snakebite on her 18th birthday—had her locked inside the tower until the end of her life. But the prophecy that a reptilian bite would cause her death came true, and she died in her father's arms. During Byzantine times, the tiny islet served as a tollbooth where traders paid to make their way across the Bosphorus. It was known as Leander's Tower during antiquity after the Greek tale of Leander and Hero, a priestess of Aphrodite. The tower was originally built by the Athenian general Alcibiades in the 5th century BC to keep an eye on Persian ships crossing the strait. Since the Ottoman ousting of the Byzantines, it has been used as a lighthouse, and today the tower is home to a restaurant downstairs and a café and bar five flights up atop the tower. Beautifully lit in the evenings, the Maiden's Tower is Istanbul's best location, bar none, to watch the sun set over Sultanahmet during late summer and early fall.

To visit during the day, take the small boat (20TL) either from Kabataş (hourly) or the continuous shuttle from Salacak (9am-6:45pm). The fare is high compared to other cruises, but consider it an entry fee to a classic historical site. In the evening, the restaurant has two three-course set menus (140-170TL) that include the shuttle from Salacak (continuous, 8:15pm-11:30pm), and Kabataş (8pm, 8:45pm, and 9:30pm, returning 11pm, 11:45pm, and 12:30am). The tiny port of Salacak is a 20-minute walk south of Üsküdar *iskele* (port) and Marmaray train station. Kabataş is the terminal station for the T1 tram that runs through Sultanahmet.

ASIAN SHORE

The city's Asian shore is within a 25-minute Bosphorus cruise from Europe, and at 4TL pp (2.15TL with IstanbulKart), it's the cheapest intercontinental journey you'll ever take. Istanbul's Anatolian neighborhoods march to a different beat from that of their European counterparts. The feeling is simultaneously more suburban and modern, and those who relish Old World charm may find themselves longing for the historical ambiance of Sultanahmet on arrival in Asia.

Plan a visit to the distinctive strait-side village near **Beylerbeyi Palace** and the artsy, ethnic enclave of **Kuzguncuk** by way of the ancient port of **Üsküdar,** and then walk south from the port to board a boat to spend an hour at **Maiden's Tower.** You could also jump in a taxi (10TL) from Üsküdar and commute up to **Camlica Hill** to drink *çay* with the locals while savoring a spectacular view of the Bosphorus and Europe.

Well worth a trip, the district of **Kadıköy** is the city's oldest known outpost and deserves at least half a day of exploration. From Kadıköy's feverish port, you may want to hop on the historical tram to the exclusive promontory of **Moda,** where tea gardens offer views of old Istanbul. To the southeast, the elite neighborhood of **Fenerbahçe** beckons, famed both for its soccer team and for its park, which boasts a large, meticulously landscaped expanse replete with tea gardens, beachfront restaurants, and waterside benches to enjoy a panorama of the Sea of Marmara and the Princes' Islands. And **Bağdat Caddesi**'s fashionable boutiques and pricey eateries rival those of any Western European capital.

To reach the Asian side, it's best to embark from either Üsküdar or Kadıköy ports, from the docks at Eminönü, or Beşiktaş with the half-hourly **Şehir Hatları** (www.sehirhatlari.com.tr) ferries, which also travel to Kadıköy from the port of Karaköy. **IDO** (www.ido.com.tr) ferries cross to Kadıköy from Kabataş and Beşiktaş ports, and both companies offer connections once daily to Kadıköy from Istinye (1 hour) and Sarıyer (1.5 hours) farther north of Beşiktaş.

The **Marmaray** train travels under the Bosphorus to Üsküdar from Istanbul Gar in Sirkeci in four minutes. You can stay on this line to Ayrılık Çeşmesi and transfer to the M4 metro to Kadıköy.

To travel by land to Kadıköy, hop on a *dolmuş* (5.50TL) from the eastern end of Taksim Square near Gezi Park to traverse the Bosphorus Bridge and arrive near the Kadıköy port. Taxis also do the crossing, but land-based travel involves traffic congestion. The ferry and Marmaray train are the fastest, most pleasant options for transportation to Asia. It's five kilometers between Üsküdar or Kadıköy ports, best reached via a *dolmuş*, municipal bus 12 or 12A, or the Marmaray and M4 metro.

Üsküdar and Kuzguncuk

So nostalgic is **Üsküdar** that Turks even sing about it in the folk song "Üsküdar'a Gider Iken" (When Going to Üsküdar) on regular occasions. Today, it's more a commercial zone and transportation hub, but home to 180 mosques, a reputable hamam, and waterside cafés where locals come to relax on weekends to enjoy the view. Just a 20-minute walk south of the Üsküdar is Salacak—the departure point for Maiden's Tower, and high above the port, the panoramic Camlica Hill park is ideal for a lazy hour or two in the sun.

Located less than two kilometers north of Üsküdar port, the sleepy multicultural village of **Kuzguncuk** always appealed to artists, but in the late 1990s galleries started popping up at street level in the enclave's historical wooden abodes, reviving the neighborhood and ratcheting up already steep real estate prices. The arrival of the suburban upper-middle class, along with diplomats and expatriates of all genres, revamped lackluster residences and the surrounding landscape. Today, the village is vibrant and upscale, yet rustic; its environs encapsulate the older Greek and Jewish neighborhood and serve as a background for many TV shows. The main Icadiye Caddesi unfurls from the Paşalimanı Caddesi coastal road from Üsküdar port and leads up through the village lined with bright facades that offer a colorful backdrop to the stalls of the lively farmers market on Thursday.

Along with Galata and Balat on the Golden Horn, tiny Kuzguncuk is home to Jewish synagogues—the 19th-century **Bet Yaakov Synagogue** (Icadiye Cd. 9) and **Bet Nissim Synagogue** (Yakup Sk. 8). Visits can be organized through www.musevicemaati.com. Kuzguncuk also boasts the **Üryanizade Mescid Camii** (Paşalimanı Cd.) which abuts the Armenian **Surp Krikor Kilesi** (Church of Saint Gregory, Çarşı Cd. 49), and the Greek Orthodox Church of **St. Panteleimon**

(Tuyan Sk. 28), all in just a few square kilometers. According to Surp Krikor's pastor, in 1860 the local Jewish minority proposed that a mosque be built on the sanctuary's large adjoining acreage to serve Kuzguncuk's growing Muslim population, a request to which the Armenians agreed by donating some of the church's land and assisting in the construction. Kuzguncuk's heights also boast one of the oldest Jewish cemeteries in the world, with tombstones dating to the 14th century.

Before leaving this area, point and select some *etli borek* (meat savory pastry) and cakes from the **Dilim Pastanesi** (Icadiye and Paşalimanı Cd., 0216/334-1260) to take out. Then cross busy Paşalimanı to find a seat in the park. Order a *çay* from the waiter who cruises this area, and *afiyet olsun* (bon appétit)! Savor your purchase on a park bench right on the Bosphorus, with views of the first bridge.

For an enjoyable afternoon of sightseeing, start from Üsküdar's port or Marmaray station. Travel to Kuzguncuk via a blue *dolmuş* (1TL) opposite Üsküdar port. The *dolmuş* travels up Paşalimanı Caddesi, stopping near Icadiye Caddesi, before continuing on toward Beylerbeyi. Afterward, head back to the Üsküdar port with the *dolmuş* and walk 20 minutes south, following the shore to Salacak to board the boat to Maiden's Tower.

Kadıköy

Lapped by the Sea of Marmara to the west, the port of **Kadıköy** is a transportation hub that connects to neighboring districts. It's also home to a busy open-air market where consumers and retailers jostle in crowded back alleys. Aside from staples like bread, fish, socks, computers, and saffron are products peddled in adjoining networks of related shops. Romany women in baggy floral *sharwal* pants hustle to sell flowers, adding a little color and attitude to these streets. Not for those seeking quiet, the port of Kadıköy and its environs are cosmopolitan Turkey at its best: an organic disharmony of vehicular traffic, braying trade, packed real estate and sublime food. As with everywhere else in the city, the district dates back to the eighth century BC.

This area was a trade center when the Megarians conquered it in the Chalcolithic period (5000-3500 BC); they renamed it Chalcedon. During the first five centuries of the Common Era, the by-then suburb of Constantinople was host to the Chalcedon Tribunal, where Emperor Julian the Apostate condemned many of his predecessor's

The Bosphorus ferry crosses to Europe from Kadıköy on Istanbul's Asian side, passing Haydarpaşa Train Station.

ministers to death. Chalcedon also hosted the Ecumenical Council of AD 451, in which the human and divine natures of Christ were defined—a concept that did not go over well with the Eastern Orthodox churches. By the time the Ottomans arrived in 1353, the city was still reeling from extensive damage caused during the Fourth Crusade (1204). The victorious Sultan Orhan Gazı renamed the outpost Kadıköy after selecting this area as the legal seat of his growing empire. Kadıköy's religious sanctuaries and monuments—mainly Marmara University, Selimiye Barracks, and the former Haydarpaşa Train Station—boast long traditions. Not far away, the neighborhoods of Fenerbahçe and Moda as well as the six-kilometer-long Bağdat Caddesi remain popular recreational destinations for Turks and expatriates alike.

AROUND KADIKÖY ÇARŞISI

Beyond the Kadıköy dock, south of the main Söğütlü Çeşme Caddesi and the 17th-century **Osmanağa Camii** (Mosque of Osman the Landowner), are the tiny arteries that make up the **Kadıköy Çarşısı** (open-air market). Wander the streets to find the refurbished copper steeple of the **Surp Takavor Ermeni Kilisesi** (Mühürdar Cd.), an Armenian Orthodox Church that begs to be photographed. From here the alleys slant up to the busy street of Güneşli Bahçe Sokak, where, in either direction, Kadıköy's version of the Spice Bazaar unfurls. Here you can taste mind-bending hors d'oeuvres and delicate pistachio baklava along with spices, dry fruits, fish, and cheese; if it relates to food, it's sold here. Continue browsing past the antiques shops on Tellalzade Sokak, winding uphill to reach Bahariye Caddesi, bisected by a tramline. This area is known as the **Altıyol** (the six-road intersection). To the left is a bull sculpture atop a small plaza where six roads intersect, or turn right, following the tramline, and continue to climb the avenue lined with stores, cafés, and restaurants. Eight hundred meters up Bahariye Caddesi, the refurbished **Süreyya Operası** (Süreyya Opera and Culture Center, Bahariye Cd. 29, 0216/336-0682, 10am-6pm daily) recalls the turn of the 20th century in a smart combination of art deco and Ottoman design styles. It opened its doors in the late 1920s as Kadıköy's first opera house; its design was heavily influenced by German architecture and the interior decor of Paris's Champs-Elysées, which its commissioner, Süreyya Paşa, so revered during his travels.

In front of the opera house is a stop on the historical tram that snakes along a two-kilometer route into Moda. Ride the tram or amble back down to the port to investigate its historical monuments. On Tuesday, Kuşdıllı Caddesi—the continuation of Soğutlu Çeşme that slants past the bull statue—welcomes **Salı Pazarı** (Tuesday Farmers Market). It's Istanbul's largest street market, where hundreds of merchants vie for space and customers and peddle everything from clothing to food.

HISTORICAL BUILDINGS

Just beyond Kadıköy's public bus and *dolmuş* terminuses by the port are a trio of significant **historical buildings** whose mundane interiors belie the majesty of their facades. Follow the busy Haydarpaşa Kadıköy Rhıtım Caddesi north to the former Haydarpaşa Train Station. Then wander off to the other structures of interest along this stretch, which include Marmara University and the Selimiye Barracks. Consider spending a couple of hours ambling along this route.

Jutting from the coastal road, the former **Haydarpaşa Train Station** is set atop more than 1,000 wooden pilasters, each 21 meters in height, driven into the seabed. It looks more like a neo-renaissance palatial residence than a transportation hub, but it was inaugurated in 1908 by the Anatolia-Baghdad Corporation as a gift to Sultan Abdul Hamid II from his ally, Kaiser Wilhelm II. Haydarpaşa served as the terminus of the railroads that linked Istanbul to eastern Ottoman provinces, including today's Iraqi capital of Baghdad and Saudi Arabia's holy city of Medina. A steep pitched roof and most of the fourth floor were largely destroyed in a 2010 fire, and rail services are currently suspended for construction of the new high-speed rail service to Ankara. There are community concerns that the upgrades will render the majestic station obsolete; rumors abound that the handsome building, whose refurbished baroque decor and balconies surely tantalize redevelopers, will go the way of Çırağan Palace and become a luxury hotel.

The Haydarpaşa campus of **Marmara University** (Göztepe Campus, 0216/414-0545, www.marmara.edu.tr/en) is on Tebbiye Caddesi. While the university has only been open since the mid-1980s, the locale was the first in Turkey to evolve from *medrese*-style medical training to the more modern medical education, on March 14, 1827—which is also the date of the annual celebration of *Tıp Bayramı* (Medicine Commemoration Day). The building has seen many firsts in the development of medicine in Turkey and it treated thousands of injured during World War I and during the National War of Independence (1919-1923). Costing 450,000 pieces of gold in 1895, the original school's buildings encompassed 21,000 square meters on three times as much land. Late-18th-century imperial architects Alexandre Vallaury and Raimondo d'Aronco were tasked with the construction, which included obtaining the best building materials from all over Europe, including windows and metal frames from Vienna. Today, more than 50,000 students attend the school, the only campus in Turkey to offer undergraduate and postgraduate classes in four languages: Turkish, French, English, and German.

The third major historical building in Kadıköy is **Selimiye Kislasi** (Selimiye Barracks, Haydarpaşa, 0216/343-7310, 9am-5pm Mon.-Fri., appointments must be made at least 48 hours prior to visit), a gigantic building that serves as the First Army Command Post. It's heavily guarded and requires ID to enter. The barracks were crucial as a military hospital, and within its halls walked such notables as Florence Nightingale. Along with other rooms in the building's northwest tower, Nightingale's room is now the **Florence Nightingale Museum.** During the mid-19th-century Crimean War, Nightingale and 38 other female volunteers took care of wounded soldiers. She returned to England three years later to a heroic welcome for having dramatically curtailed the high mortality rate and improved sanitary conditions in the facility. In 1857, some 6,000 British soldiers succumbed to a cholera epidemic and were interred in an adjoining plot, which later became known as the Haydarpaşa Cemetery. Another Balyan design, the buildings—an elongated square block with two soaring towers—were constructed in the 19th century by edict of Sultan Selim III.

MODA

With so many touristy neighborhoods to choose from, making the trip to **Moda** doesn't score highly in many travel guidebooks. But its laid-back vintage feel, along with a plethora of eateries and sidewalk cafés, make this neighborhood irresistible. Moda is just a stone's throw from Kadıköy's port, on foot via the southwest seaside promenade or by nostalgic tram along a rickety three-kilometer route through Bahariye. Get off at Moda Caddesi before the tram snakes back down to the port. From the tram stop, hang a left and walk about one kilometer to reach the enclave's center. Once there, take a right on Ferit Tek Sokak and go straight down to **Moda Çay Bahçe** (Moda Tea Garden, Ferit Tek Sk. 7, 0216/337-9986, 8am-midnight daily), just past the woodsy park on the left. Here, enjoy what is arguably one of the best views of Sultanahmet over a cup of the famous Turkish coffee; or stroll around the lush promontory's steep promenade to the century-old Moda dock.

Back up in Moda's center are 40 ice cream flavors peddled at **Ali Usta Dondurmacı** (Ali the Ice Cream Master, Moda Cd. 264, 0216/414-1880, 10am-midnight daily). It's a famous stop for many *Istanbullus* who enjoy partaking in the secret creamy recipe of one of Istanbul's oldest ice cream parlors.

FENERBAHÇE

Known for its lighthouse, football team, and enclaves of retired military brass, **Fenerbahçe** is arguably one of the most exclusive waterfronts on Istanbul's Sea of Marmara coast. During the week it is a quiet leisure seaport, but come weekends the main street is a showroom for the latest European sports cars. Just steps away from the waterfront is the serene **Fenerbahçe Parkı.** The park is dotted with marble kiosks and adjacent tables that combine into open-air makeshift cafés that afford perfect locations to rest, particularly during summer sunsets. The area also beckons early morning joggers, moonlight strollers, and antsy toddlers. The park's lush parterres, playgrounds, and glass pergolas unite with the grounds' lofty trees to create a truly scenic experience. Take a *dolmuş* (3TL) or taxi (15TL) to get to Fenerbahçe Park, south of the port of Kadıköy, five kilometers away.

BAĞDAT CADDESI

Revealing the disparities among Turkey's social classes, **Bağdat Caddesi**'s upmarket Suadiye stretch boasts stores like Burberry as errant hawk tissues and other goods nearby. On weekdays, homemakers congregate over coffee at the many java joints; on weekends, seats at the coffee places lining the clogged six-kilometer stretch are hard to come by. This shopping and chill-out haven is a magnet for teenagers and shoppers alike; it offers a good view of the shopping habits of Turkey's middle and upper classes. Just beware of the weekend traffic: The three-lane stretch is so congested that it becomes a polluted parking lot of frustrated drivers, which makes getting in and out a hassle. Other than shopping and people-watching at sidewalk cafés, the seaside Fenerbahçe-Bostancı promenade is parallel and just 150 meters to the west. The best way to get to this part of town is to hop on a *dolmuş* (4TL) from the port of Kadıköy or from the Bostancı dock, about two kilometers to the southeast. From Taksim Square, the Bostancı *dolmuş* (7TL) travels alongside the shopping strip but lets passengers off on a parallel avenue, a block to the south.

GREATER ISTANBUL

Istanbul is loaded with sights just outside its central hubs: the districts of Fatih, Eyüp, and Edirnekapı are not far from the Golden Horn; and don't forget the Princes' Islands that pepper the Sea of Marmara. All offer great day-trip destinations and are easily reached by public transportation. Fatih and Eyüp have incredible views, museums, and mosques. About 90 minutes away by boat, the five Princes' Islands are an ideal escape from Istanbul's hectic pace. If there is only time for one day trip, get an early start and visit the City Fortifications and neighboring Chora Museum in Fatih in the morning, and return to the nearby port of Eminönü to hop on the cruise to the islands.

Around Fatih

Fatih is one of the city's oldest and largest districts—so old, in fact, that the locals call it the "real" or "first" Istanbul since it was the Ottomans' earliest conquest near Constantinople. It's a conservative bastion of traditional lifestyles centered on several crucial religious sites as well as garrison remnants and massive walls that hark back to Byzantine times. Fevzi Paşa Caddesi is the main road that slices through this district. It originates in Beyazıt, near the Grand Bazaar, and stretches out past the ancient Valens Aqueduct to the city walls and the amazing Chora Museum near Edirnekapı. The views atop Istanbul's third, fourth, and fifth hills here are simply breathtaking and are probably the main reason why the Byzantine emperors erected palaces in the area, and why Ottoman sultans built their tombs here, forever above the city's chaos. Many sites have survived the passage of time, seismic activity, devastating fires, and conquests; others, like Constantine's memorial and the Byzantine Church of the

Holy Apostles, built by Justinian to commemorate the 12 disciples, did not.

You can easily spend a whole day in this western district visiting Chora Museum, the old Istanbul walls, Eyüp Mosque, and Pierre Loti Café before walking back to Eminönü along the rejuvenated Golden Horn or through the colorful old Jewish and Greek neighborhoods of Fener and Balat. Often walking the six kilometers back to Eminönü from Eyüp via the Golden Horn is much faster than waiting in traffic, but there is also a **Şehir Hatlari** (0212/313-8000, www.sehirhatlari.com.tr) ferry that leaves every hour from Eyüp, arriving in Eminönü in 35 minutes.

BOZDOĞAN KEMERI (VALENS AQUEDUCT)

How does one connect a city of hills and channel water to flow amply? The answer in the 4th century AD was to build the **Bozdoğan Kemeri** to link Istanbul's third and fourth hills. A marvel of early Roman engineering, for 1,500 years it transported water from the hills of Kağıthane and the Sea of Marmara into Sultanahmet. The original 971-meter-long aqueduct was only one of many endpoints in a water-collection system that spanned 260 kilometers through hilly Thracian country; the aqueduct was also the largest of its kind in antiquity. Runoff was stored in a series of cisterns, including the Basilica Cistern, that totaled an estimated capacity of more than 95,000 cubic meters. Beginning as Constantine's lofty project known as the "Arcade of the Gray Falcon," it was inaugurated in AD 373 by Emperor Valens. The Valens Aqueduct spans the busy Atatürk Boulevard, just up from the Golden Horn, en route to Taksim Square.

FATIH CAMII (FATIH MOSQUE)

The **Fatih Camii** (entrance on Fevzi Paşa Cd., Fatih) is both illustrious and larger than life, just like its namesake, Sultan Mehmet II. He callously ordered the destruction of Emperor Justinian I's Church of the Holy Apostles to erect this great monument, obliterating what was at the time perhaps Christianity's greatest monument.

The site was first built by Constantine the Great in AD 330 and renovated by Emperor Justinian in 550. It served as the burial place of Constantinople's greatest Byzantine emperors and Patriarchs in the 4th-11th centuries and also housed the remains of Christian saints Luke, Andrew, Timothy, Gregory the Theologian, and John Chrysostom.

The story goes that the sultan hacked off the hands of the architect who didn't quite carry out his orders to create a mosque that would outdo Ayasofya. The once great *külliye*, though, was impressively large for its time, comprising a caravanserai, a market, a hospital, many hamams, kitchens, and *medrese* for more than 1,000 students. The tombs of Mehmet II and his wife are located behind the eastern wall. Much like other 15th-century mosques, the structure has a large central dome supported by partial domes on four sides. The colors and tiles gracing the mosque's interior reflect the baroque influence of an 18th-century reconstruction, done after a fire ravaged the building in 1771. A busy farmers market fills the streets adjacent to the mosque on Wednesday.

1453 PANORAMA MUSEUM

Take the T1 tram to the suburb of Topkapı, 20 minutes from Sultanahmet, to see the **1453 Panorama Museum** (Topkapı Kultur Parkı, 0212/415-1453, http://panoramikmuze.com, 8am-6pm daily, 10TL, audio guide 5TL). The highlight of the museum is the massive 360-degree panorama mural of the famous battle for Constantinople in 1453 when Fatih Sultan Mehmet conquered the city. Rent the audio guide, as the information panels throughout the museum are only in Turkish.

★ KARIYE MÜZESI (CHORA MUSEUM)

The **Kariye Müzesi** (Camii Sk., Kariye Meydanı, Edirnekapı, 0212/631-9241, www.kariye.muze.gov.tr, 9am-7pm Thurs.-Tues.

Apr.-Oct., 9am-4:30pm Thurs.-Tues. Nov.-Mar., 15TL) boasts Istanbul's finest mosaics. Ayasofya's age and size may have earned the basilica its worldwide acclaim, but Saint Savior in Chora's array of 14th-century artwork and iconography is far more elaborate.

Just like its larger counterpart in Sultanahmet, Chora was not treated kindly through its history. Knights of the Fourth Crusade looted it in 1204, and some of its ornate frescoes were plastered over when Sultan Beyazit II's grand vizier ordered the sanctuary transformed into a mosque in 1511. But unlike Ayasofya's mosaics, the Ottomans barely touched the ones that had graced Chora's walls since 1310, perhaps out of respect for their sheer beauty and intricacy.

The unexciting brick facade belies the interior's astounding loftiness. There are over 50 mosaics; some are barely discernible, while others are astonishing in their detail. Upon entering the museum, the first mosaics encountered depict dedication scenes to Jesus and the Virgin Mary along with tableaux illustrating Jesus with wealthy patron and builder Theodore Metochites. Located in the nave are three mosaics: Jesus, the Virgin Mary as Teacher, and the Dormition of the Virgin. The inner narthex's two small domes portray several depictions of Jesus' ancestry, including Adam. Other sets sketch the stages in the Virgin Mary's life, Jesus' youth, and his teachings. Built to house the tombs of its benefactor, Metochites, and his family, the Paracclesion (mortuary chapel) aptly has death and resurrection frescoes.

Taking a taxi is by far the most convenient and direct way to access the Chora Museum; otherwise, take the T1 tram that runs through Sultanahmet to Topkapı, 20 minutes away, and switch to the T4 tram to Mescid-I Selam, disembarking in Edirnekapı. From here, walk northeast, winding through a couple of streets for 10 minutes following the brown tourist signs for the museum. Bus 55EB from the bus station adjacent to Beyazıt tram stop also runs to Edirnekapı, but traffic congestion makes it a slow journey—stick to the trams or a taxi.

FETHIYE CAMII (VICTORY MOSQUE)

Formerly the Church of Theotokos Pammakaristos, the **Fethiye Camii** (Fethiyekapısı Sk., 0212/522-1750, 9:30am-4:30pm Thurs.-Tues., 5TL) is a functioning mosque adjoined by a museum. The original church ranks third in the hierarchy of Istanbul's basilicas, after Ayasofya and Chora. Lavish mosaics and frescoes fill its inner sanctum. There is also a side chapel that contains the tomb of General Michael Glabas, a nephew of Byzantine emperor Michael VIII Palaeologos who bankrolled the basilica's renovation in the 13th century. The church served as a convent after the Ottoman invasion in 1453, and two years later became the seat of the Christian Orthodox Patriarchy. The church was converted into a mosque by Murat III, and to commemorate his successful campaigns in Azerbaijan and Georgia, he had it renamed *Fethiye* for victory. While the conversion meant taking down most of the inner walls to create a larger prayer hall, the sanctuary still boasts restored remnants of spectacular Byzantine mosaic panels. These include a depiction of Christ Pantocrator flanked by the 12 prophets; one of Christ Hyperagathosis beside the Virgin Mary and John the Baptist, in the apse; and the dazzling Baptism of Christ. It's easiest to reach Fethiye Camii from Chora Museum. Walk along Draman Caddesi, below Chora Museum; it becomes Fethiye Caddesi. Then, hang a left onto Fethiye Kapısı Sokak.

ISTANBUL SURLARI (ISTANBUL CITY WALLS)

Extending slightly more than six kilometers from the Golden Horn to the Sea of Marmara, the **Istanbul Surlari**—Constantinople's great fortifications—were virtually impregnable. That is, until the Fourth Crusade in 1204 when the Venetians, under Enrico Dandolo, successfully climbed the walls of the Phanar Gate. They were breached again by Ottoman troops in 1453, when gunpowder and Sultan Mehmet the Conqueror's cannons rendered them forever obsolete. Today, not much is left of what is perhaps one of the greatest fortification systems of antiquity.

Ever since the arrival of King Byzas in the 7th century BC, walls have delineated the perimeter of Byzantium, which was then just a trading outpost of little importance. But in time, as the city grew, new fortifications were built and expanded, first by Constantine the Great in AD 364, and some 40 years later by Theodosius II, who extended the city's limit by 1,500 meters, from the Sea of Marmara to the Golden Horn. The crenulated two-meter-thick Theodosian Walls were protected by moats at half of the 10 main gates, which can be seen along the structure. A few sections were restored in the 1980s thanks to UNESCO funding, but topical restoration may have caused the destruction of many relics. With the city's population boom, compounded with environmental pollution and the lack of a proper comprehensive restoration plan, the nonprofit World Monuments Fund panel was prompted to include this site on its 2008 Watch List of the world's 100 Most Endangered Sites. While minor works have maintained the walls, plans for a more comprehensive restoration program have yet to be developed.

TEKFUR SARAYI (PALACE OF PORPHYROGENITUS)

While only a wall or two of the last and only remaining Byzantine palace still stand, that's enough to convey the scale of the 13th-century sprawling imperial Byzantine structure. **Tekfur Sarayı** was built at the meeting point of the Theodosian Walls and the ancient holy suburbs of Blachernae in the city's northwest region. The name Tekfur Sarayı actually means "Palace of the Christian Ruler" in Turkish; for a long time it was thought to have been the 10th-century regal abode of Emperor Constantine VII Porphyrogenitus. But the palace was actually constructed at least 200 years later, and its commissioner was actually Constantine Palaiologos—not an emperor, but the son of one. Since the mid-15th century the locale has served as a brothel, a pottery atelier, and tenements under Ottoman rule. Tekfur Sarayı, along with the adjoining Theodosian Walls, was part of a four-year citywide reconstruction project done before 2010, when Istanbul was chosen as the European Capital of Culture. The remains of this palace are located just steps from Chora Museum and abut the city walls.

FENER RUM PATRIKHANESI (CHURCH OF SAINT GEORGE AND THE GREEK PATRIARCHATE)

Located in the Fener district, the **Fener Rum Patrikhanesi** (Sadrazam Ali Paşa Cd. 35, 0212/591-3670, www.ec-patr.org, 8:30am-4pm daily, free) has been home to the Greek Patriarchate—the seat of the Eastern Christian Church—since 1586. The present Ecumenical Patriarch of Constantinople, Patriarch Bartholomew, is recognized as the "first among equals" of all Orthodox spiritual leaders. This honor has been passed on continuously since Constantinople became the capital of the Roman Empire 1,600 years ago.

Refurbished in 1991, the architecture of the Church of Saint George pales in comparison to the city's more elaborate sanctuaries, although it's filled with the requisite ornate iconography. It does, however, contain impressive artifacts, including the Column of Flagellation, on which Jesus was purportedly tied to and flogged; an early-5th-century patriarchal throne; relics of Saints Gregory the Theologian and John Chrysostom; the tombs of three female saints; and three antique mosaics. As the magnificent churches of Constantinople slowly transformed into the grand mosques of Istanbul, the Orthodox Patriarchate complied with the change by moving from its first home of Ayasofya to the Church of the Holy Apostles, then to Theotokos Pammacaristos Church, before making this home. The adjoining buildings include the Patriarchate Library and its accounting and authorization offices. The Fener Rum Patrikhanesi is located just west of Abdülezelpaşa Caddesi, between Incebel Sokak and Yıldırım Caddesi, 1.5 kilometers northwest of Atatürk Bulvarı.

While you're in the neighborhood, take some time to wander through the backstreets of the **Fener** neighborhood, passing the former colorful Ottoman homes of Greek families, to the commanding red brick structure on the hill, known as **Kırmızı Okul** (Red School). From the 15th century until the fall of the Ottoman Empire, an Orthodox religious school existed on the site. The current structure dates to 1881 and is an active private primary and high school. Closer to the old city walls is the former Jewish quarter of **Balat**. All throughout Fener and Balat you can photograph Istanbul's raw beauty. Rows of colorful and abandoned Ottoman homes that once served wealthy families now shelter impoverished families in properties that are worth millions. It's perhaps Istanbul's next up-and-coming suburb for gentrification now the Golden Horn has been cleaned up.

The **Church of St Stephen of the Bulgars** (Mürsel Paşa Cd. 85) is on the shore of Golden Horn in this district. What sets this Gothic church apart is that it's made entirely from cast iron that was shipped from Vienna in 1871. It's rarely open to the public, so photos are only possible from the outside.

As Fener and Balat are still transforming, the Old World charm of the area makes it like a village within a big city. Keep your belongings safe and remember where the Golden Horn is—it's easy to lose your bearings in the maze of streets. If you're nervous about navigating it on your own, hire the local guides of **My Local Guide Istanbul** (www.mylocalguideistanbul.com); they run the Istanbul Heritage walking tour through Fener, Balat, and on to Eyüp and Pierre Loti Café. If you're a photographer, this area of Istanbul is not to be missed.

YEDIKULE (FORTRESS OF THE SEVEN TOWERS)

Over by the Sea of Marmara, **Yedikule** (Yedikule Meydanı Sk., 0212/585-8933, 8:30am-5pm daily, 10TL) was once the impressive Golden Gate of Constantinople. Flanked by four massive towers, the gates were covered in gold, hence the name, and provided a monumental portal for foreign dignitaries entering the city along the Roman road called Via Egnatia. Theodosius II inaugurated the gate in AD 450, and a millennium later Mehmet the Conqueror added three towers. The whole complex became known as the Heptapyrgion, Greek for "seven towers," or *yedikule* in Turkish. Its fate would change; first, it became the imperial treasury, and then a state prison complete with dungeons. The 18-year-old Sultan Osman II was executed by Janissaries here in 1622 after he was incarcerated for trying to reform what he thought was a corrupt Janissary court. Today, connected by thick Theodosian Walls, the eerie space serves as a concert venue. To get to Yedikule, take the Marmaray to Kazlıçeşme, then walk through the city walls following the brown tourism signs. Once past the enormous walls, follow the fortress perimeter to the entrance. The easy walk to the entrance from the Marmaray station takes about 10 minutes.

Around Eyüp

Farther down the Golden Horn, the district of **Eyüp** simultaneously induces reverence for the sacred sites and for the scenic beauty of the land. One of the most revered places in Islam, Eyüp features a namesake mosque and cemetery, both popular pilgrimage destinations for Muslims. Eyüp's quaint Friday bazaar is a jumble of traditional wares, trinkets, and souvenirs at a fraction of Grand Bazaar prices.

Accessible on foot or *teleferik* (cable car), high over Istanbul the scenic area known as Pierre Loti, a nod to the late-19th-century French writer, is truly mesmerizing.

The large red building on the Golden Horn 600 meters southeast of the port is Fezhane, an old fez (Ottoman felt hat) factory. It hosts the Festival of Somewhere most Sundays, showcasing cultures and cuisine from different regions of Turkey. It's a good excuse to try some regional cuisine and to see inside another historic building. Peppered along the Golden Horn is a plethora of family attractions—Miniaturk, Rahmi Koç Museum, Istanbul Dolphinarium, and Santralistanbul Museum all lie along this ancient natural harbor.

The hourly Üsküdar-Eyüp **Şehir Hatları** (www.sehirhatlari.com.tr) ferry travels down the Golden Horn, docking at Eminönü, Hasköy, and Sütlüce before terminating at Eyüp *iskelesi* (port). Municipal buses 399B or 399C from Eminönü bus station stop at Eyüp *iskelesi* or Teleferik Pierre Loti (where you can reach the mosque), before continuing to the bus stops at Çeltik and Sakarya Mahallesi, a five-minute walk from the Dolphinarium. Bus 55EB from outside Beyazıt Mosque also travels to Eyüp *iskelesi*, past Edirnekapı (for Chora Museum). Buses 47 from Eminönü or 54HT from Taksim serve the Hasköy Park stop for Rahmi Koç Museum and Sütlüce's Miniatürk, past the Haliç Bridge. Taxis to these venues are also recommended, but traffic can often be slower than walking.

EYÜP CAMII (MOSQUE OF EYÜP)

The oldest of its kind in Istanbul, **Eyüp Camii** (Eyüp Meydanı, off Camii Kebir Cd.) was erected by Mehmet the Conqueror in 1458 on a holy site he "located" during the 1453 Siege of Constantinople. Halid bin Zeyd Ebu Eyyûb (Eyüp Sultan), the standard-bearer of the Prophet Muhammad, was slain while commanding Arab troops during an earlier Siege of Constantinople AD 668. In accordance with a peace agreement struck between the Arabs and the Byzantines, this site was selected to bury his remains. While Mehmet claimed to have discovered Eyüp Sultan's tomb, the exact location of the site was discussed in texts some 300 years before his arrival. Nevertheless, the "miracle" helped rally his troops to victory during the dogged days of the Siege of Constantinople in 1453. The Mosque of Eyüp was the site of the enthronement of Ottoman princes in a ceremony celebrating the dynasty's progression and its dedication to promote Islam. So holy were the grounds, known as Eyüp Sultan Türbesi, that royals and the high Ottoman aristocracy sought to be buried alongside the revered remains as a way to ensure a peaceful afterlife. In fact, a pricey interment near Eyüp's grave became so popular that the few 15th-century tombs here became the large cemetery it is today.

The cemetery gives way to the famed **Pierre Loti Café** and scenic area atop Eyüp's rise. It can be accessed by a leisurely walk

Pierre Loti Café offers inspiring views.

Pierre Loti in Istanbul

Pierre Loti, the French naval officer turned novelist, was inspired to write his 1879 novel *Aziyadé* at a café situated uphill from Eyüp Camii, overlooking the Golden Horn. This breakthrough novel described trysts between a harem girl and a Spanish valet. It was reportedly based on personal diaries Loti kept during a three-month tour in Istanbul. Described by many as a consummate orientalist, Loti's exotic tales may have contributed to Istanbul's claim to fame in the late 1800s. His 1913 novel *La Turquie Agonisante* (Turkey in Agony) was so appreciated by people in the new Turkish Republic that they named the café and avenue on Eyüp hill after the author. When Loti died in 1923, Istanbul's flags flew at half-mast.

uphill through the cemetery or by riding the *teleferik* (4TL, 2.15TL with IstanbulKart) that conveniently hauls sightseers from near the mosque to the locale's lofty position over the Golden Horn.

RAHMI KOÇ MÜZESI (RAHMI KOÇ MUSEUM)

It's hard to believe that the **Rahmi Koç Müzesi** (Hasköy Cd. 27, 0212/369-6600, www.rmk-museum.org.tr, 10am-5pm Tues.-Fri., 10am-6pm Sat.-Sun., 12.50TL) was once the former Ottoman navy anchor foundry and the historic dockyard of the Ottoman Maritime Company. Call it serendipitous that both historical structures would not only be part of the museum's exhibits, but would also house an impressive museum featuring naval history and transportation in general. The main structure, called the *lengerhane* (anchor house), was erected atop the rubble of a 12th-century Byzantine building during the reign of Selim III. The second building, the Hasköy Dockyards, operated as a maintenance harbor for imperial ships. When the state put both dilapidated structures up for sale in the 1990s, the canny Rahmi Koç, one of Turkey's wealthiest industrialists, saw a potential exhibition space for his growing collection of exotic vehicles and transportation paraphernalia. The popular 9,300-square-meter museum displays an eclectic array of road, rail, marine, and aviation pieces as well as engineering, communications, and scientific instruments. The models, toys, and loads of hands-on activities are a huge attraction for local youths. Saturday is the ideal time to view—and play—with all of the exhibits and learn about environmentally friendly transportation and industry. The museum has snack bars, a bar, and best of all, a restaurant, Café du Levant, a stylish French brasserie whose *steak moutarde* is reason enough to check out the museum.

MINIATÜRK (MINIATURE PARK OF TURKEY)

The more than 46,000-square-meter open-air park **Miniatürk** (Imrahor Cd., 0212/222-2882, www.miniaturk.com.tr, 9am-6pm daily, 10TL) boasts the largest collection of miniatures in the world. While it does feature representations of some of Turkey's most renowned destinations, like Ephesus's Library of Celsus and Nemrut Dağı's venerated stone heads, the majority of the exhibits focus on the country's famed mosques, unsurprising since the concept was the brainchild of a conservative municipal government. Within Miniatürk, the Museum of Victory, inaugurated in 2003 to commemorate Turkey's 80th birthday, depicts the War of Independence through vignettes that feature light and sound. In a nod to Atatürk, the adjoining Zafer exhibit offers illustrative photos and famous quotes of the statesman. The museum is worth the trip if Istanbul is the only destination on your itinerary. Otherwise, you should see Turkey's grand destinations in person rather than miniature replicas.

İSTANBUL DOLPHINARIUM

In 2008, Europe's largest indoor dolphinarium opened near the shore of the Golden

Horn. The 8,700-square-meter **İstanbul Dolphinarium** (Silahtarağa Cd. 2/4, 0212/581-7878, www.istanbuldolphinarium.com, 35TL, 50TL VIP) offers more than just highly intelligent dolphins. Its seven interconnected pools also boast a singing white beluga whale, 950-kilogram walruses, and northern fur seals who line up alongside the star attractions—the dolphins—for the daily shows. The open hours for the park coincide with the one-hour show at 2pm Tuesday-Sunday. With advance bookings, dolphin therapy is possible for one to three people with basic interactions (100-300TL, 10 minutes), swimming with dolphins (180-300TL, 10 minutes), and dives (300-600TL, 20 minutes). It's a great excursion for families to combine with adventures to nearby kid-friendly locales.

SANTRALISTANBUL MUSEUM

If you have two hours to spare in Eyüp, you could visit the Ottoman Empire's first urban power plant, which has been converted into the Museum of Energy and is a hub for international cultural exhibitions and events. **Santralistanbul Museum** (Kazım Karabekir Cd. 2, 0212/311-7878, www.santralistanbul.org, 10am-6pm Mon.-Fri., 10am-8pm Sat.-Sun., 15-25TL) will keep the kids entertained with 22 interactive exhibits and a tour of the former control room and turbine engines. The highlight of the visit is the *reactable,* an electronic instrument that creates sounds when objects are moved over an illuminated tabletop. It was used by Björk on her 2007 Volta world tour to create psychedelic tunes.

Adalar (Princes' Islands)

Just 16 kilometers west of Istanbul in the Sea of Marmara, the **Adalar** have lured tourists and weekenders alike for centuries. Four of the eight islands are lush and filled with exquisite wooded villas, a good majority of them protected as historical structures. You'll also find relics of bygone empires, the occasional beach club, great fish restaurants, and no private vehicles.

The islands have been home to Jewish, Armenian, and Greek minorities as well as princes throughout history. What Turks call "minorities" were in fact the settlers of the archipelago in antiquity. Aristotle first spoke of these isles in the 4th century BC. Byzantine prince Justinus Kouropalates named the largest island, today's Büyükada (Big Island), Prinkipo (Greek for "Prince") in AD 569, a time when he was heir apparent to the

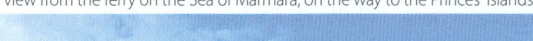
view from the ferry on the Sea of Marmara, on the way to the Princes' Islands

Byzantine throne. Eventually it did become the home of princes: Deposed Byzantine and Ottoman royalty were exiled to Aya Yorgi Monastery on the island.

If you are short on time, cruise to Büyükada on the 10:50am IDO fast ferry from Kabataş, then take in a sumptuous brunch by the water followed by a *fayton* (horse-drawn carriage) tour (30-79TL, 60-75 minutes) to see the monastery or rent a bicycle to tour the island's 15-kilometer perimeter in an hour or two. The whole journey will take about six hours including the boat trip.

Fayton rides, one of the islands' main attractions, are available on Büyükada, Heybeliada, and Burgazadası. Prices are set by the island's municipality (www.adalar.bel.tr), so there is no haggling.

KINALIADA

Known as "Henna Island" for its red tint due to now-defunct copper and iron mines, **Kınalıada** is the closest isle to Istanbul's European flank. Its proximity to Constantinople made the island the preferred location to exile unwanted Byzantine royalty. Romanos IV Diogenes spent his last days here, after his Byzantine troops were defeated in the Battle of Manzikert in AD 1071. Kınalıada's intrinsic lack of forestation—the archipelago's most protected commodity—has given free rein to developers, who've covered virtually every bit of the island with unimpressive housing. On the upside, its upstream location has somewhat cleaner waters.

BURGAZADA

At less than two kilometers in length, the archipelago's third-largest island, **Burgazada** (Fort Island), rises from a solitary hill. It was named Antigoni in classical times, after Antigonus I Monophthalmus, the father of Demetrius I of Macedon, a 4th-century-BC king who built the bastion. The isle's main claim to fame is the writer Sait Faik Abasiyanik, whose descriptive early-20th-century prose has been likened to Mark Twain's. His immaculately preserved summer abode has been transformed into the intriguing **Sait Faik Abasiyanik Müzesi** (Sait Faik Abasiyanik Museum, Burgaz Çayırı Sk. 15, 0216/381-2060, 10am-noon and 2pm-5pm Tues.-Fri., 10am-noon Sat., free), with displays of his personal and professional letters, photographs, and manuscripts.

HEYBELIADA

Translated as "Island of the Saddlebag," **Heybeliada** has an atmosphere that is both homey and academic. It's a lot less visited than Büyükada and is a holiday escape for thousands of *Istanbullus,* including 2007 Nobel laureate Orhan Pamuk. Fine sandy shores, Orhan Pamuk, and the noted sunbathing haven of Green Beach Club are helping the island gain popularity with a fashionable urban crowd thirsty for leisure, serenity, and *fayton* rides.

Heybeliada's most noted landmark is the **Aya Triada Manastırı** (Monastery of the Holy Trinity) on its northernmost hill. The complex is just 15 minutes' amble up from the jetty and consists of a repository for some 200,000 books, including significant Byzantine texts. The manicured grounds boast a small 13th-century chapel, whose interior reveals an intricately gilded iconostasis and timeworn dusty classrooms replete with antique desks on the periphery. Access to this literary trove is reserved to academics who can secure permission through the Greek Orthodox Patriarchate, and touring Aya Triada's complex is by appointment only (0212/531-9670, www.ec-patr.org).

Heybeliada is also home to the Turkish Naval Academy, the large white building to the left of the docks when you arrive.

BÜYÜKADA

It's easy to see why this island was the favored retreat of Constantinople's aristocracy from the first millennium. Rising steeply from the shore over two hills, each crested by celebrated monasteries, **Büyükada** welcomed Princess Zoe in AD 1012. Its most famous visitor, however, was Leon Trotsky, the Russian theorist who stylishly hobnobbed with pashas and financiers in the 1930s at the **Izzet Paşa Köşkü Mansion** (Çankaya Cd. 55) while penning the *History of the Russian Revolution*.

Büyükada's southern hill, Yüce Tepe, lays claim to **Aya Yorgi Kililesi ve Manastırı** (Aya Yorgi or St. George Monastery). It's a series of chapels built on three different levels. The chapel nearest the road, which is also the oldest, has a sacred spring where women have come seeking fertility for centuries. During Byzantine times, another chapel served as a mental asylum where patients were shackled with iron restraints bolted to the floor. To reach the monastery, the main road circling the island leads to Lunapark. Once here, climb uphill for 10 minutes to Aya Yorgi, or "borrow" one of the donkeys conveniently waiting by the roadside.

Getting around the island is easy. About 50 meters from the ferry terminal lies the town square, where most of the hotels, shops, and eateries are located. Bicycles (less than 5TL per hour, 20TL per day) can be rented virtually anywhere. Horse-drawn carriage tours from the clock tower can accommodate up to four people for a small tour (67TL, 1 hour) or long tour (79TL, 75 minutes). Both tours travel to Lunapark, but will not stop long enough or wait for you to walk the rest of the way to Aya Yorgi. Direct, one-way transfers to and from Lunapark via horse and carriage are best if you wish to trek up to Aya Yorgi (29TL per *fayton*).

GETTING THERE AND AROUND

The only way to reach the islands is from the European port of Kabataş or from Kadıköy and Bostancı on the Asian shore. The **IDO** (www.ido.com.tr) fast ferry departs from Kabataş (10TL, 7.80TL with IstanbulKart, twice daily summer, once daily winter, 25-60 minutes) and Bostancı (7TL, 4.25TL with IstanbulKart, once daily summer only, 25 minutes). The slower ferry with **Şehir Hatları** (www.sehirhatlari.com.tr, 5TL, 3.85TL with IstanbulKart, 90 minutes) also departs eight times daily from Kabataş and Kadıköy. All boats for the archipelago depart from quays called Adalar Iskelesi. Since timetables vary by season, confirm departure times on the ferry company websites. It's possible to visit more than one of the islands in a day with the schedule of ferries available.

Entertainment and Events

As one of the few still affordable metropolises in Europe, Istanbul brims with excitement and has plenty of places to get your groove on. Whether it's live jazz, dancing, performing arts, or world-class bars, Istanbul's party scene has it all. *Meyhaneler* (Turkish taverns), where the *rakı* flows freely, are popular, but jazz clubs are the new buzz among well-heeled hipsters, largely due to Istanbul's incredibly popular annual jazz festival. Also somewhat new to the scene are *şaraphaneler* (wine bars), with a new respect for domestic vintages. These after-dark pursuits may seem odd to visitors when you consider that Turkey is mostly Muslim, but most locals—particularly in Istanbul—are moderate in their beliefs and don't always strictly adhere to the religion's aversion to alcohol.

Time Out Istanbul (www.timeoutistanbul.com/en) lists the current hot spots as well as the up and coming events. The magazine version (7TL) is available monthly at newsstands throughout the city. Also check out The Guide (www.theguideistanbul.com) for a complete listing of events and venues.

NIGHTLIFE

Weekend nightlife revolves around Ortaköy's fancy all-in-one venues—with a bar, restaurant, and nightclub under one roof. Upscale

Reina, just beyond the Bosphorus Bridge, exemplifies this trend with sprawling terraces set along the Bosphorus beckoning starlets and wealthy wannabes. Another great nighttime destination is Beyoğlu with its popular raving bar scene set atop turn-of-the-20th-century houses and back alleys.

Bring your dancing shoes: Istanbul offers great venues to groove the night away to a variety of international sounds. Go glam for venues from Ortaköy to Kuruçeşme; in Beyoğlu, casual and comfortable is the way to go. Alcoholic drinks in Turkey tend to be pricey. Earmark at least 10-25TL per glass of wine, 10TL for beer, and 25TL or more for cocktails. Prices are around 1-5TL for nonalcoholic drinks and 20-30TL for premiere liqueurs.

Most bars open at sunset with food service, gravitate toward live entertainment around 9pm or 10pm, and throb well into the night. In more conservative corners of town, some locations (generally those near mosques) restrict the sale of alcohol, but these venues tend to be more lax in tourist season. A good example is Sultanahmet, where several Muslim sanctuaries reside alongside restaurants and one or two bars. By law, alcohol is off-limits to anyone under age 18.

Although legitimate party locations reside along shady nooks throughout the city (particularly along Beyoğlu), these venues are notorious for overcharging foreigners and attracting crooks that prey on visitors. Avoid shady Aksaray near Sultanahmet in particular. Use common sense, and if traveling alone, opt for taxis and don't use larger bank notes, such as 50s or 100s, to avoid getting counterfeit bills in return. Groups of men without women may be denied entry to bars in an attempt to balance the sexes in the venue.

Nightclubs and Bars

Still reigning supreme is **Reina** (Muallim Cd. 44, Kuruçeşme, 0212/259-5919, www.reina.com.tr), with its multilevel restaurants featuring nouvelle cuisine and pizza, a bar set over the Bosphorus, and a nightclub.

alley in Beyoğlu

Frequented by Sting, Selma Hayek, and Uma Thurman, Reina is the place to rub elbows with Hollywood's A-list come summer (if you can get in).

The best nightclub for die-hard dancers is **Sortie** (Muallim Nacı Cd. 54, Kuruçeşme, 0212/327-8585, www.sortie.com.tr). This is the place to strut your stuff, with more than 900 square meters of throbbing fun along the Bosphorus's European shore.

Another high-class foray into Istanbul's highly competitive nightlife scene, **Anjélique** (Muallim Nacı Cd., Salhane Sk. 5, Ortaköy, 0212/327-2844, www.istanbuldoors.com) at first seems simplistic in design. But architect Mahmut Anlar's strategically placed angled mirrors create a magical environment that reflects the Bosphorus's shimmering waters throughout the space come nighttime. The Wolfgang Puck-like pizzeria on the first floor gets busy, but Anjélique's nightclub is what really draws the crowds.

Vogue (Spor Caddesi, Beşiktaş Plaza Blok A, 13th Fl., 0212/227-4404, www.

istanbuldoors.com) still features some of the best entertainment in town. Its three terraces house a bar and two restaurants that are set high enough to offer some mind-boggling views of the straits. Its Book of Wines is another plus, with more than 200 vintages accompanied by food pairing suggestions.

Indigo (Istiklal Cd., Akarsu Sk., Mısı Apt. 1-5, Galatasaray, 0212/244-8567, www.indigo-istanbul.com, 10pm-5am Fri.-Sat.) is set high atop a historical building in Beyoğlu. It's where Europe's best DJs flock to spin their LPs for a 20-something crowd and a hypnotic light show.

For R&B and hip-hop, try the white Hellenic pillars and white lounges of **Riddim** (Sıraselviler Cd. 35/1, Taksim 0212/251-2723, www.riddim.com.tr, Tues.-Sun.).

Getting more international press than other venues, **360°** (Istiklal Cd. 163, Mısır Apt. 8th Fl., 0212/251-1042, www.360istanbul.com) is where the party's at almost every night, particularly on summer evenings when the club's glass wall opens onto a terrace. The spacious restaurant provides spectacular 360-degree views of the city—perfect at sunset—and has an unexpected mix of Thai and Turkish dishes on the menu. After 11pm the place vibrates to the latest tunes spun by guest DJs. The space itself may be difficult to find, as it is set atop an apartment building that blends seamlessly with its surroundings. Its sister club on the Asian shore, **360° East** (above Hilton Doubletree Hotel, Albay Faik Sozdener Cd. 31, Kadıköy, 0216/542-4350) duplicates the classy style, quality cuisine, and party anthems until late. The views from the eastern venue are more spectacular, especially at sunset as the sun seemingly dips into the Marmara Sea behind the minarets of Istanbul's European side.

Closer to the hotels of Sultanahmet, the hidden **Şah Bar** (Incili Cavus Cikmazi, 9, cell tel. 0533/557-7578, www.sahbar.com) is the only late-night venue in the tourist district. It gets busy around 11pm when the restaurants start to close. The latest Western hits are spun alongside a bar brimming with beverages. It has a mix of young and mature patrons, with several spaces to dance with other travelers or chill out away from the thumping party tunes.

Live Music

The arrival of the Istanbul Modern Museum in 2004 revitalized the lower part of Beyoğlu, a part of town all but forgotten for decades. The exhibition space of the museum, along with its spiffy rooftop café, brought back the crowds, including live music aficionados. This growing interest in live music has driven up ticket prices and has introduced a whole new spectrum of sound to the city. There are now plenty of performance venues. Reserving tickets in advance is recommended, as the following venues tend to be little more than holes-in-the-wall.

Babylon Istanbul (Seyhbender Sk. 3, Asmalı Mescit, 0212/292-7368, www.babylon.com.tr) is considered one of the world's top 100 bars, and for good reason. This intimate space features local and international performers belting out tunes in genres like Latin jazz, indie pop, reggae, funk, and hip-hop. The Byzantine backdrop combines with state-of-the-art lighting and sound to create a special ambiance that's uniquely Istanbul.

Just down from the Galata Tower, **Nardis** (Kuledibi Sk., Galata, 0212/244-6327, http://nardisjazz.com) features mainstream jazz at its best. Set in the bowels of a brick enclave, which only enhances sound quality, Nardis gets packed quickly, so get here close to opening time: 9:30pm Monday-Friday, 10:30pm Saturday-Sunday.

Tucked away in the 19th-century Suriye Pasaji, just off Istiklal, **Quit Bar** (Balyoz Sk. 7/1, Asmalı Mescit, 0212/245-3176, www.quitistanbul.com) epitomizes Istanbul's "hidden gem" market for evening entertainment. The owner and guest performers flaunt their brand of music, from soul and funk to garage, disco psychedelic, folk, and more. The owner's reputable history in the Istanbul music scene makes this a popular place for local musicians, artists, and their muses.

Get your hips ready for Balkan beats, salsa, reggae, and world music at **Araf** (Balo Sk. 32, 0212/244-8301, hwww.araf.com.tr). Perched on the top two floors of an old Taksim building, the bar has performances and DJs every night of the week, plus great night views of Istanbul.

Turkish Nights

Extremely trendy with visitors, Istanbul's dinner cabaret Turkish Nights are relegated to the European side of town. Expect an evening of traditional Turkish music, folk dancing, belly dancing, and singing combined with several courses of mediocre cuisine. It's wise to reserve a space in advance through your hotel, as these venues can get packed. Dinner service typically begins at 8pm daily, and the prix fixe menu includes all entertainment and drinks but not gratuities. Shows are usually over by 11pm and include free transfers to and from your hotel.

For more than 50 years **Kervansaray Restaurant & Night Club** (Cumhurriyet Cd. 52A, Harbiye, 0212/247-1630, www.kervansarayistanbul.com, €95, includes 2 drinks) has been thrilling guests nightly with sumptuous platters, drinks, and rambunctious music and dancing. An arabesque venue replete with tables dressed in white linen, this traditional nightclub entertains more than 150 diners with live music, belly dancers, and folk-dance groups. Along the same lines and close to Sultanahmet, the **Gar Gazino** (Mustafa Kemal Paşa Cd. 3, Yenikapı, 0212/588-4045, www.garmuzikhol.com, €60), an all-inclusive destination, has the added bonus of Kafkas dancers that spin on their knees and leap up, with a few extra surprises thrown in. For ambiance, the dance shows at **Hodjapasha Cultural Center** (Hocapaşa Hamam Sk., 3B, 0212/511-4626, www.hodjapasha.com, 70TL) are unique in that the performances by folkloric troupes and male and female belly dancers are within the walls of a 550-year-old hamam. Tickets for Hodjapasha are for the show and light refreshments only.

The neo-Lebanese cabaret restaurant **Arabesque** (Taşkışla Cd. 19, Maçka, 0212/231-0356, 160-220TL) offers belly dancing and singers belting Western pop hits in an atmosphere of *1001 Arabian Nights* meets neon lights and graffiti by Beirut artist Yahya Muhakkin. What sets this restaurant above the rest is the decor and the breathtaking views of the Bosphorus. The fixed menu is cheaper Monday-Thursday, with prices increasing for the weekend.

Gay and Lesbian

Istanbul's lesbian, gay, bisexual, and transgender community has steadily grown thanks to an influx of gay and lesbian expatriates along with a few Turkish pop icons who have come out. As a result, the LGBT nightlife scene, primarily concentrated around Beyoğlu, is vibrant. For comprehensive listings and advice about the LGBT scene, visit **IstanbulGay.com** (www.istanbulgay.com), or contact travel specialists **Pride Travel** (Incili Çavuş Sk. 33/11, 0212/527-0671, www.travelagency-turkey.com).

Renowned as a meeting place and much tamer than the surrounding clubs, **Sugar & Spice** (Saka Salim Cikmazi 3/A, Galatasaray, 0212/245-0096) is a café in a narrow alley opposite the St. Antoine Church and is mostly patronized by the city's trendy men. For women, **Bigudi Club** (Mis Sk. 5/5, Taksim, cell tel. 0535/509-0922) is the weekend mecca for Istanbul's lesbian community on Saturday evening.

Hidden in the streets of Beyoğlu, **Tek Yön** (Sıraselviler Cd. 63/1, 0212/245-1653, www.clubtekyon.com, 10:30pm-5am daily) moved to a bigger venue in 2009 and is Istanbul's most popular gay venue. Once frequented mainly by bears, it's now an all-round venue for gay men of all shapes and sizes. Go-go dancing and drags show are often on the stage, but beware of escorts and rent boys lurking in the crowd. Another option is **X Large** (AOS Sitesi, G:52. Sk. 12/1, Maslak, 0212/243-3533, 11pm-5am Fri.-Sat.). The cover charge and drinks cost more, but the floor shows are more professional, and the venue is away from Taksim in more upmarket digs in Maslak. Unlike Tek Yön, known to be somewhat misogynist, XLarge is a mixed crowd of LGBT and straight people with open minds.

PERFORMING ARTS

Aside from its nocturnal drinking and dancing destinations, Istanbul also has a variety of traditional shows, including ballet, folk dance, and classical music. The **Akbank Arts Foundation** (www.akbanksanat.com) runs a yearlong program of theater, classical music, and jazz at venues throughout the city; visit the website for more information. Since 2007, **Garajistanbul** (Kaymakan Reşat Bey Sk. 11a, Galatasaray, 0212/244-4459, www.garajistanbul.org) has featured the most cutting-edge performing arts most nights of the week. Tickets for festival and events can be purchased through www.biletix.com.

FESTIVALS

While festivals take place year-round, Istanbul's festival season typically runs April-July and kicks off with the showy **Tulip Festival-Istanbul** in April. For a month, virtually every roadside, roundabout, and freeway median is dressed in every variety of the indigenous bloom. A little-known fact is that the tulip is not native to Holland; rather, the tulip was brought to Western Europe by the Ottomans under Süleyman the Magnificent. April is also the time when the **Istanbul International Film Festival** (various locations, 0212/334-0700, www.iksv.org) begins. The festival showcases the best of contemporary and classic films from local and foreign filmmakers through screenings, classes, and speeches on movie-related topics. Movie stars are known to make cameo appearances throughout the three-week event.

The Istanbul Foundation for Culture and Arts (www.iksv.org) backs the film festival with the **International Istanbul Theater Festival** in May-June, and the **Istanbul Music Festival** is also in June, featuring an acclaimed classical music concert series in the most unforgettable venues the city has to offer. Also in May-June is the foundation's **Istanbul International Art and Culture Festival,** which includes workshops and conferences on the advancement of theater and dance in Turkey. But by far the most anticipated festival run by the foundation is **Istanbul's International Jazz Festival** in July. A bevy of top musicians and lyricists perform to sold-out crowds in a variety of venues citywide. The highly acclaimed **Istanbul Biennial,** typically held every other September, is a forum for international and local artists to come together to celebrate and discuss the world of visual artistry.

Highly anticipated each year and attended by some 50,000 youthful folk, the multiple-day outdoor **Rock 'n Coke** (www.rockncoke.com) concert highlights *Billboard* magazine's chart-toppers in September.

Shopping

Shopaholics beware! Istanbul has tons of antiques as well as trendy brands at modern multiplexes that are sprouting like wildflowers all over the city. Knowing where to go for what is key. There's the tried-and-true **Grand Bazaar** to hone bargaining skills while taking in one of the oldest structures of its kind. The dirt-cheap catch-all of **Tahtakale,** lining the hill between the Grand Bazaar and Eminönü, near the exotic foodstuff of the **Spice Bazaar,** is also worth a look, as are the nifty Ottoman antiques located in Beyoğlu's **Çukurcuma** neighborhood, adjacent to the rear of Galatasaray High School. At the start of Galip Dede Caddesi, just off Istiklal, are **Tünel's** old music shops, where timeworn sheet music and new instruments can be browsed. When you've had enough antiquing and memento hunting, do like Istanbul's élite and head for the designer label-filled **Istiniye Park** in its namesake neighborhood, or Nişantaşı's posh **City's** shopping complex, or better still **Istanbul Forum,** with shops and plenty of attractions the kids will love. Better shops offer shipping services. With the exception of the Grand Bazaar and Spice Bazaar (Mon.-Sat.), retail shops are generally open 10am-10pm daily.

BOOKS, MAPS, AND MUSIC

To browse books and CDs new and old, nothing compares to Istiklal Caddesi. Chain stores like **D&R** (www.dr.com.tr), **Istanbul Bookstore** (www.istanbulkitapcisi.com), and **Remzi** (www.remzi.com.tr) are peppered throughout Istanbul, but Beyoğlu's central location enables sightseers to pop in for a quick purchase without going out of the way.

For English books, **Robinson Crusoe 389** (Istiklal Cd. 195A, 0212/293-6968) has been the go-to shop for expatriates for decades. Its tall shelves have a good assortment of fiction and nonfiction, including travel guides focusing on Istanbul and Turkey. Flanking Galatasaray High School is **Homer Kitabevi** (Yeni Çarşı Cd. 12/A, 0212/249-5902, www.homerbooks.com), where academics flock for Ottoman- and Turkish-interest titles, such as religion-centric literature, women's issues, photography, and architecture. On Istiklal, just 20 meters from Galatasaray gates toward Tünel, **Insan Kitap** (İstiklal Cd. 96, 0212/249-5555, www.insankitap.com) is modern bookstore with a comprehensive selection of travel guides for your next destination. **Mephisto** (Istiklal Cd. 125, Beyoğlu, 0212/249-0696, www.mephisto.com.tr) is a great for books and CDs of all genres.

Around Sultanahmet, two bookshops share the same owner: **Galeri Kayseri** (Divan Yolu Cd. 58, 0212/512-0456, www.galerikayseri.com) offers the expected array of tomes on everything spectacular about Turkey and Istanbul, such as the cuisine, culture, history, and architecture; the newer store, **Bookshop Istanbul** (Divanyolu Cd. 11, 0212/516-3366), offers about the same just up the street on the opposite side. The prices for travel books in Sultahamet are inflated because of the tourism trade; head to Istiklal Street for more reasonable prices.

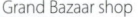
Grand Bazaar shop

CERAMICS

Sultanahmet has myriad stores selling typical Turkish artisanal crafts, but **Caferağa Medresesi** (Caferiye Sk., Sultanahmet, 0212/513-3601, www.tkhv.org, Tues.-Sun.) has a selection of perfect gifts and souvenirs. This 15th-century theological complex, one of Mimar Sinan's architectural gifts, was all but forgotten until artisans united and refurbished the structure's string of cubicles and classrooms into workshops and retail space. Here you can make your own gifts in hands-on art classes promoting local artistry such as *ebru* (marbling), porcelain painting, glass painting, pottery, and calligraphy (80TL, 60 minutes).

When then-Pope Benedict XVI came to town in 2006, he received a departing gift commissioned by Tahir Eğinci, owner of **Iznik Classics** (Arasta Bazaar, 119, Sultanahmet, 0212/517-3608, www.iznikclassics.com). His creations, along with piles of more affordable yet beautifully mass-produced items, are superb. There's bound to be something for every taste and budget, or visit the other locations (Iç Bedesten, Serifağa Sk. 188, Grand Bazaar, 0212/520-2568; main gallery at Utangaç Sk. 17, Sultanahmet, 0212/516-8874).

If you're looking for standard ceramics without hefty price tags or the assault on your senses of the bazaar, head to **Tribal Art Hand Craft House** (8-10 Çatalçeşme Sk., Sultanahmet, www.tribalarthome.com). The store, one street north of the T1 tramline, has a massive selection of textiles, lanterns, glassware, jewelry, and other trinkets for friends back home.

JEWELRY

Goldsmiths at the Grand Bazaar and Sultanahmet as well as at chain stores peddle unique pieces, including new designs and *nazar boncuk* (Turkish evil eyes), set among diamonds or strung on simple 22-karat gold chains. Turkey has a long tradition of jewelry artistry, particularly in Istanbul. If you can't find what you're looking for, Murat Ismailli, better known as the Jewelry Magician, follows his family tradition and custom-crafts pieces to order. Ismailli's shop **Dilara Kuyumculuk** (Iç Bedesten 28, Grand Bazaar, 0212/512-8364) offers a wide variety of gilded opulence and irresistible trinkets. A good way to compare is to request prices for items along Bazaar's Nuruosmaniye Caddesi, where some of the more flamboyant and generally more expensive gemologists are. For custom-made yet strictly Turkish baubles, head east of the Grand Bazaar's Kilitçiler Gate to **DesignZone** (Ali Baba Türbe Sk. 21/4, Nuruosmaniye, 0212/527-9285), where artist-entrepreneur Özlem Tuna displays her tulip-inspired collection along with busts, earthly ceramics, and her alaTurka candle series.

In upmarket Nişantaşı, diamonds may be king, but novel **Rumî** (Şakayık Sk., Ihlamur Palas Apt. 42/4, 0212/240-4360, www.rumi-jewelry.com), headed by designer Erdal Tekisalp, embraces simple styles reflecting authentic Turkic and Anatolian epochs. Some pieces are inspired by Neolithic artifacts, while others evoke more recent examples of Hittite embellishments. There's also the Turkish gone-global manufacturer **Altınbaş** (Divanyolu Cd. 80, Sultanahmet, 0212/513-9288, www.altinbas.com), respected nationally for some of the finest rocks, particularly in solitary settings, as well as earrings and necklace sets. Finally, for a treasure trove of more affordable costume and dress jewelry, immerse yourself in the central **Iç Bedesten** of the Grand Bazaar. There's a warren of silver, antiques, and jewelry stalls here where haggling is a must.

MALLS

Istanbul is a mecca of megaplexes. Not just a compilation of stores, these shopping centers are floors upon floors of mammoth brands, swanky couture, cafés, and eateries, all appealing to the fickle upper-middle-class Türk. Malls sit at virtually every cardinal point, but do check out the gargantuan **Istiniye Park** (Istiniye Bayiri Cd., 0212/345-5555, www.istinyepark.com), towering over its namesake neighborhood over the Bosphorus's northern flank.

Nişantaşı's **City's** (Teşvikiye Cd. 162, 0212/373-3300, www.citysnisantasi.com) is the *crème de la crème*. No plastic cutlery or trays here; forgo the burger and opt for a steak au poivre at L'Entrecôte de Paris, a bistro that has won the hearts of well-heeled foodies. Fashion rules this neighborhood, but little did the developers know that the big-name restaurateurs they brought would overshadow City's world-class boutiques, such as Jean Paul Gaultier's first ever shop.

West of Sultanahmet, accessible by the M1A metro from Aksaray and Yenikapı, is the mega **Forum Istanbul** (Şehir Parkı Cd., Kocatepe, 0850/222-0724, www.forumistanbul.com.tr), complete with 265 brand-name shops, restaurants, cinemas, the **Turkuazoo Aquarium** (www.turkuazoo.com, 32TL adults, 24TL ages 3-16), and **Jurassic Land** (www.jurassicland.com.tr, 28TL adults, 22TL ages 2-16 years). This is a must for any modern-day shopping enthusiast and makes a great day out for the kids.

SWEETS

"Eat sweet, talk sweet" goes the popular Turkish saying. Indeed, after trying some sugary, nutty concoctions such as flaky baklava, hard candy, or the famed *rahat lokum* (Turkish delight), it's easy to understand why. Historic candy maker **Ali Muhiddin Hacı Bekir** (Hamidiye Cd. 83, Eminönü, 0212/522-0666, www.hacibekir.com.tr, 9am-8pm daily) set up shop upon arrival in Istanbul from his Black Sea hometown of Kastamonu in 1777. Hacı Bekir—a title afforded to those who've completed the *hac* (pilgrimage) to Mecca—created a softer chew that bowled over the harem, and started a tradition that has been practiced under the same roof for longer than any other business in town. These sumptuous morsels can also be purchased in Beyoğlu (Istiklal Cd. 83, 0212/245-1375) or in Kadıköy (Muvakıthane Cd. 14 & 16, 0216/336-1519).

For a heavenly bit of a different texture, **Güllüoğlu Baklava & Café** (Kemankeş Cd., Karaköy, 0212/249-9680) offers baklava in no less than 12 varieties, sold by the gram. Stumped? Try the *sütlü nuriye* baklava made from hazelnuts imported from Ordu. For a smorgasbord of purely Turkish desserts, **Saray Muhallebicisi** (Istiklal Cd. 173, Beyoğlu, 0212/292-3434, www.saraymuhallebicisi.com, 6am-11pm daily) has been offering flaky pastry and creamy dairy desserts for more than seven decades. Sample the *tavuk göğsü* (chicken breast)—a rice pudding made with finely chopped chicken breast. Saray is also known for its *ekmek kadayıfı* (bread morsels baked in syrup), served with a heaping dollop of thick clotted cream.

TEXTILES, LEATHER, AND CARPETS

For Istanbul's in crowd, it doesn't get any better than **Sivaslı İstanbul Yazmacısı** (Yağlıkçılar Cd. 57, Grand Bazaar, 0212/526-7748). This is one of the oldest drapery stores in town, where fashion icons like Rifat Özbek, Hussein Chalayan, and Dolce & Gabbana have come to purchase fabrics. Intricate needlework, hand-printed fabrics, pricey antique lacework, and newer lace tatted by women deep in the Anatolian hinterland hang side by side in this small atelier. **Doğan & Özgür Bilgili** (Takkeciler Sk. 93-95, Grand Bazaar, 0212/527-6359, www.bilgili.info) is where Bill and Hillary Clinton dropped by for well-tailored fine leather jackets and full-length coats. For organic Turkish bathrobes, towels, and hamam products, you can't go wrong with **Jennifer's Hamam** (Arasta Bazaar, No. 135, 0212/518-0648, www.jennifershamam.com). For a versatile pashmina, **Igüs Eşarp** (Yağlıkçılar Cd. 80, Grand Bazaar, 0212/512-2538, www.igustekstil.com) has every possible shawl imaginable, from premium silk, wool, and velvet to viscose. Rugs are the mainstay at **Noah's Ark** (Ticarethane Sk. 5A, 0212/511-8050, www.noahsarkcarpetskilims.com), a well-respected shop away from the pricier Grand Bazaar run by brothers Hamza and Yusuf Yildiz. Looking for silk? Head to **Ipek** (Istiklal Cd. 120, Beyoğlu, 0212/249-8207) for scarves so luxurious they should be framed, not worn. Men will also find silk ties and cravats.

Buying an Authentic Rug

Exactly when Turkish nomads began weaving animal hair to create yurts is unknown, but it's safe to assume that the practice dates well before the 5th century BC. That's according to the carbon dating of the oldest knotted-pile carpet ever found, an impressive 3.5-square-meter rug that belonged to a Scythian prince and features the famed Turkish double knots—some 347,000 of them per square meter. By then, the practice of weaving had evolved from a need basis to an artful pursuit. Rug-making was introduced to Anatolia by the Selçuk Turks sometime in the 11th century, and nomadic Yörük tribes advanced their craft by introducing fine silks, new colors made from vegetable dyes, and innumerable weaving forms. Eventually, palatial-size rugs—mostly made of silk—were used in imperial residences. For these, sultans conferred with the master artisans of Hereke, an area that has continued to produce some of the world's finest (and priciest) woven floor coverings.

Finding an original, one-of-a-kind rug—knotted-pile carpet or woven, flat kilim—depends on taste, budget, and the right seller. Taste is easy: you like it, you buy it. From the heavy floral patterns and deep hues used in Bergama to the fine silks and wools used to create the tiniest of blooms on a Hereke, more than a dozen styles and a variety of sizes are available. Budget, however, is a little more difficult: Original pieces run the gamut from US$80 to US$80,000 or more, depending on size, age, condition, and quality of materials. Prices also increase according to sheen, depth of hues, and complexity of design.

Here are a few things to know before selecting that perfect piece:

- Colors and symbols have meanings that date back to paganism. Red, the dominant hue, symbolizes wealth, joy, and happiness. Green represents heaven; blue stands for nobility and grandeur; yellow keeps evil away; black keeps worries at bay. The scorpion symbolizes pride and liberty. Weavers use images of the ram's horn (fertility, heroism, and power) and the evil eye to convey their happiness and piety.

- Shops sell antique and new rugs as well as replicas of historical rugs. If a seller tries to pass off an antique that shows no signs of wear and tear or repair, it may be a new rug that has been artificially aged.

- Machine-made rugs are less expensive than handwoven rugs, but they're typically created with synthetic or inferior fabrics, have poor stain resistance and low structural integrity, require more maintenance, and have virtually no resale value. Superior quality, hand-knotted carpets retain their market price well.

- The rules of the buying process are simple. Expect glasses of tea while the owner's staff unfurls his wares. Keep the ones that appeal to you and send the rest back. If you're in the mood to buy, start haggling. The owner's starting price may be anywhere from 30 to 50 percent above the intended selling price. If you're not buying, tell him you'll return and thank him for his time and effort. It pays to shop around. Stick to a predetermined budget, and whatever you do, do not follow a guy from the street to a carpet shop; you'll be paying more to cover his commission.

For more on Turkish carpets, peruse Jon Thompson's *Oriental Carpets: From the Tents, Cottages and Workshops of Asia*. For an on-site lesson on the art of handwoven carpets or to purchase from a reputable dealer, head to **Noah's Ark Carpets And Kilims** in Sultanahmet or **Kemal Erol** in the Grand Bazaar. Both can organize international door-to-door delivery.

Sports and Recreation

For a long time, athletics—and exercise in general—were relegated to professionals or youths, but now a visiting jogger or swimmer will find that he or she doesn't have to go it alone in Turkey. Jogging, tennis, sailing, and trendy body workouts like yoga are increasingly popular. Istanbul is peppered with arenas devoted to well-being, in addition to gyms and spas provided by the better hotels in town. On weekends, head out early to beat the crowds and traffic.

HIKING AND BIKING TRAILS

Riding a bike in old Istanbul is not advised due to the rough cobbled roads, narrow lanes, pedestrian traffic, and the inability of drivers to share the road. Forget Beyoğlu too with its hilly terrain. The Asian side, however, is a different story. A marked two-kilometer stretch along the Sea of Marmara, the **Dalyan-Bostancı** is a paved route along Istanbul's Anatolian shore that beckons crowds on the weekend. Lapped by sea below, the elevated path features outdoor training areas with rudimentary exercise machinery, parks for children, tiny cafés, and extensive landscaped lawns. To get here, ride the Eminönü ferry to Kadıköy and hop on a *dolmuş* headed for Bostancı.

Büyükada is unrivaled for serious joggers, hikers, or bikers. The 15-kilometer trail circles the island and offers serious sports enthusiasts a run for their money, while a shorter 8-kilometer path crisscrosses the isle.

On the European side, the closest jog-worthy track to the tourist area is through **Gülhane Park** and out to the coastal footpath lining the Sea of Marmara. Some 21 kilometers from Taksim is **Belgrade Forest** (Sarıyer, 0212/559-2549), a former imperial hunting venue that now welcomes hikers and cyclists along its six-kilometer walking path. Taking a taxi or a rental car is recommended. Alternatively, bus 42T from Taksim Square stops at Bahçeköy, which is just a short walk from the park's entrance.

Unison Travel (0212/256-4192, www.unisonturkey.com) offers a range of green-thumb tours for those interested in exploring Istanbul's gardens and parks.

SAILING

The city's largest leisure marina sprawls along the Sea of Marmara at Kalamış/Fenerbahçe, on Istanbul's Asian shore. The first port of call for any sailor is to contact the city's first professional sailing school, **Istanbul Sailing Academy** (0216/449-9560, www.istsailing.com), located at Kalamış Marina (Münir Nurettin Selçuk Cd., 0216/346-2346, www.seturmarinas.com). The Academy offers a range of social events, sailing programs, and training for beginners to advanced seafarers. Also for beginners, the nearby **Istanbul Sailing Club** (İstanbul Yelken Kulubu, Tur Yolu Sk., Fenerbahçe, 0216/330-0633, www.istanbulyelken.org.tr) will help you set sail on a new hobby. Along the European shore, the **Ataköy Marina** (Sahilyolu, Ataköy, 0212/560-4270, www.atakoymarina.com.tr), out by the Sheraton Hotel, provides mooring space, sailing lessons, and a great meal in the club-like eatery, where the dining room overlooks the Sea of Marmara.

BEACHES

If your itinerary doesn't call for a stopover on Turkey's Aegean or Mediterranean coasts, beaches are accessible in Istanbul as a day trip, either on the Sea of Marmara or the Black Sea, at opposite ends of town. Starting with the warmer and calmer waters of the Sea of Marmara, the Princes' Islands offer some great seaside lounging options and an idyllic escape from sightseeing. According to locals, the quality of the water is questionable, but the recent return of indigenous dolphins proves that the municipality cleaned the shore to some extent. Unlike on U.S. beaches, those on patrol are not necessarily lifeguards but rather hired hands who collect user fees for parasols and chaise longues. Swim with care, particularly around the shore of the Black Sea.

In the Marmara Sea, the Princes' Islands' Büyükada has a nice array of beach clubs, including **Nakibey** (0216/382-4501) and **Yoruk Ali Beach** (0216/382-7341). You can bask in the serenity of the archipelago away from the concrete jungle across the Marmara. Heybeliada's cove is open to the public, and its **Green Beach Club** (0216/351-1600, www.clubgreenbeach.com) is the Turks' fun retreat, filled with banana floaties, tons of swimming, and other activities. Entry to beach clubs on the island vary from 30TL upward. The cost includes your sun bed and umbrella as well as the boat service that departs from the ports to reach the clubs. Restaurants with roaming waiters are on standby at all beach clubs to take your food and drink orders.

Along the Asian shore, the small beaches of **Caddebostan, Suadiye,** and **True Blue Beach Club** (Fenerbahçe, 0216/550-5470) hug the coast along the Sea of Marmara, and they get crowded once school is out. Their proximity to the shopping mecca of Bağdat Caddesi offers the exhausted shopper a respite.

The Black Sea resort city of Kilyos, however, is the pick of the bunch and well worth the 38-kilometer trip from Taksim. Always refreshing, the Black Sea's cooler waters have an occasional undertow that swimmers should be wary of. This shore's hottest beach club is **Suma Beach** (Boğaziçi Kampus Yolu, 1/A, Kilyos, 0212/203-0863, from 40TL). Thanks to Suma's shuttle service from Darüşşafaka metro station, if you time it right, you can whiz from Taksim to the beach in an hour by combining the M2 metro with the shuttle service. Entry fees to the beach increase if you want to stay for the evening entertainment. In 2013, it was the hottest summer destination. Follow the Suma Beach Facebook page to know when the shuttle leaves and what events are planned. Along the same stretch of beach is **Solar Beach** (Turban Cd. 4, Kumköy, İstanbul, 0212/201-2086, www.solarbeach.com.tr, from 25TL). The website details the range of shuttle services.

POOLS

Even if your hotel doesn't have a pool, there is still the possibility of lounging poolside. Most

Istanbul marina

five-star hotels allow outsiders to drop in for a fee that allows access to the pool, sauna, gym, and other facilities. It's not cheap: The facilities at **Çırağan Kempinski Hotel** (Çırağan Cd. 32, Beşiktaş, 0212/326-4646, www.kempinski-istanbul.com, 7am-8pm daily, Mon.-Fri. €100, Fri.-Sun. €160) are just steps from the Bosphorus. The daily fee includes access to the heated indoor and outdoor pools, a jetted tub, and a sauna. In addition to the sublimely thick towels of fine Turkish cotton, the cuisine at the poolside gazebo is on par with the Kempinski's renowned luxury.

Just off Taksim Square is a hotel district called Talimhane. The three- and four-star hotels with pools here offer the cheapest drop-in rates for nonguests to cool off. They are by no means five-star quality, but if you want a dip on a rooftop terrace, this option is easier on the wallet. The **Taksim Gonen Hotel** (Aydede Cd. 15, Talimhane, 0212/297-2200, www.taksimgonen.com, 40TL) is one such hotel where you can relax at the small rooftop pool, just five minutes' walk from Taksim Square.

A personal favorite, because it feels like Saint-Tropez meets the Bosphorus, is poolside at Suada, also known as **Galatasaray Island** (Kuruçeşme, 0212/263-7300, www.suadaclub.com.tr, pool 10am-7pm daily, 100TL). This is where fashionable *Istanbullus* sunbathe in summer, and compared to five-star hotel fees, it's excellent value for money due to its classy ambiance, location in the Bosphorus, and dining options in three reputable restaurants on-site. Travel 1.5 kilometers past the Bosphorus Bridge to Kuruçeşme Park; a boat here shuttle guests to the island throughout the day and night. Get here early to secure your poolside chaise longue. The restaurants are open until late, long after the pool closes.

SPECTATOR SPORTS

Istanbul has hosted some big-name events such as the Istanbul Grand Prix and the Red Bull Air Race. The city was even a contender for the 2020 Olympics, coming in second to Tokyo. These days the annual events list has dwindled somewhat, but there are a few beloved events that continue to lure athletes to the city.

The **Istanbul Marathon** (www.istanbul-marathon.org) takes place every November and has attracted international runners for over three decades. The event features the 42-kilometer marathon as well as 8-, 10-, and 15-kilometer fun runs. It's the only marathon in the world to span two continents, with thousands of runners crossing the Bosphorus Bridge and passing significant historical sights before finishing in old Istanbul.

Over 1,500 local and international competitors visit Istanbul to partake in the 6.5-kilometer swim in the **Bosphorus Cross-Continental Race** (http://bogazici.olimpiyat.org.tr) from Asia to Europe every July. Also among the big spectator events held mid-year is the **World Tennis Association's Istanbul Tennis Cup** (www.wtatennis.com).

During the last week of July, the **Burn Kiteboard World Cup** (www.prokitetour.com) brings young talent to the popular kitesurfing location of Burç Beach in Kilyos, on the Black Sea. Finally, the **International Sailing Week of Istanbul** (www.istanbulyelken.org.tr) commences the third week of every August from the Istanbul Sailing Club's Fenerbahçe marina, with a lavish opening ceremony. For spectators, the regatta is a dazzling sight, with ballooning sails against the blue waters of the Sea of Marmara.

Hamam: The Great Scrub-Down

Humid hamams were the center of community life during the Ottoman era. Among the echoing sounds of running and splashing water, men emerged from the aromatic *köpük* (lathering of soap) having forged new business deals; women, in the separate female section, lay on the *göbektaşı* (heated marble dais) with one eye open, checking out potential wives for their sons. These days, foreigners can partake in the ritual with a scrub, wash, and massage within the marble walls of historic bathhouses.

While every town listed in this guidebook has hamams, the more touristed the town is, the more the temperature drops and the less authentic it gets—and no one likes a cold bath. The following hamams in Istanbul will get your temperature up, slough off dead skin, and reinvigorate you. Hamams are generally open 8am-10pm daily, sometimes later; time your visit to hear the call to prayer echo from mosques outside as your attendant washes you down—it's simply magical.

Traditional *peştemal* (towel), *kese* (exfoliating glove) and *takunya* (slippers) are provided as part of the packages listed. Generally, you strip down to your bathing suit or underwear, though most baths have clients who get fully naked. Do what you're comfortable with, but do wear coverage if it's provided. Expect bath attendants to wear very little as well.

The grandest bath of all is the impressive **Ayasofya Hürrem Sultan Hamamı** (0212/517-3535, www.ayasofyahamami.com, from €80), between the Blue Mosque and Ayasofya. Built in 1557 by Sinan for the infamous Lady Roxelana, the structure was recently renovated to become the bath for today's elite. Bath packages are expensive, but the service will leave you feeling like a royal. Men and women are in separate sections.

Cemberlitaş Hamamı (Vezirhan Cd. 8, Cemberlitaş, 0212/522-7974, www.cemberlitashamami.com.tr, from 90TL) is steps west of Sultanahmet on the way to the Grand Bazaar. One of Istanbul's most historic hamams, Cemberlitaş was designed by imperial architect Mimar Sinan in the mid-16th century and offers Thai, aromatherapy, and Indian head massages as well as mud masks and beauty therapies. There are separate sections for men and women.

Featured in Patricia Schultz's *1,000 Places to See Before You Die*, **Cağaloğlu Hamamı** (Yerebatan Cd., Sultanahmet, 0212/522-2424, www.cagaloglunamami.com.tr, from €50 for complete bath service) may only date back to the mid-18th century, but it has remained the bath of choice for visiting glitterati, including Britain's Edward VIII and Florence Nightingale. The ambiance is delightful, but it does lack the massage packages that other hamams offer.

Mixed-gender couples can bathe together at **Süleymaniye Hamamı** (Mimar Sinan Cd. 20, Süleymaniye, 0212/519-5569, www.suleymaniyehamami.com.tr, from €35), built for Süleyman the Magnificent in the mid-16th century by imperial architect and friend Mimar Sinan. You'll need to reserve a spot, and you may be sharing the hamam with other couples, but the bath's steamy temperature is one of the most authentic available. Men are given a towel and women are given a disposable bra and shorts.

In Beyoğlu, **Tarihi Galatasaray Hamamı** (Turnacıbaşı Sk. 24, Beyoğlu, 0212/249-9456, www.galatasarayhamami.com, 135TL full service) was commissioned by Sultan Beyazit II in the early 16th century, as an extension to the famed Galatasaray Lisesi (school). Both its women's and men's sections are favorites of Beyoğlu's upper crust, and the staff's no-nonsense cordiality has lured Hollywood's elite, including John Travolta, who went all out on the Pasha Package (full service with oil massage, 170TL).

Those arriving by cruise ship will appreciate the convenience of Mimar Sinan's **Kılıç Ali Paşa Hamamı** (Hamam Sk. 1, Tophane, 0212/393-8010). Built in 1580 as part of the Tophane mosque complex, this newly renovated hamam offers a traditional hamam ritual package (130TL) and full-body massage (140TL) and a unique "hamam ritual with children" (100TL) for mothers and young daughters and father and sons to bath together in the tradition of Ottoman times.

Üsküdar Çinili Hamamı (Cavusdere Cd., Murat Reis Mahallesi 0216/553-1593, www.cinili-hamam.com, from 42TL) on the Asian side is a gorgeous set of authentic Turkish baths, commissioned by Sultan Ahmet I in 1648 for his Bosnian wife, Köşem Sultan. It's one of the few that has withstood the test of time and remains much as it did when it opened. Çinili features separate sections for women and men.

Accommodations

Picking the ideal place to stay in Istanbul can be daunting. First-timers should stay in the "old town" neighborhoods of Sultanahmet, Gülhane, or Sirkeci with proximity to the sights and where public transportation is plentiful. Accommodations in more modern Beyoğlu are also an option; it's just 20 minutes by tram to the old town and gives a different, more realistic perspective on the city due to the male-to-female ratio of locals being more balanced (in Sultanahmet, visitors often ask, "Where are the women?"). Asian side digs are great for shopping enthusiasts and sailors who want to make the most of the Kalamış marina. Nothing beats splurging on a room by the Bosphorus at one of the newer five-star or boutique hotels nestled in an old Ottoman mansion or palace, if you have the resources. If you're traveling solo or as a family, avoid Aksaray near Sultanahmet. This seedy area is known for cheap lodging and lacks the friendly feel found elsewhere. For all locations, reserve well ahead of time to secure a room and get better rates.

The quality and rates of Istanbul's hotel rooms run the gamut from the most expensive suite at the Cırağan Kempinski (€30,000) to a dorm bed at a youth hostel (€14). A large selection of smaller boutique inns caters to all budgets and tastes. Best of all, hotels and B&Bs add custom touches to ensure that guests are pleased, thus guaranteeing that sought-after word-of-mouth recommendation. Türks are generally sticklers for cleanliness, so expect lodgings to be pristine.

Hostels, guesthouses, and inns are the least expensive accommodations. Some feature a variety of options, from family rooms with en suite baths to multiple-bed dormitories with shared facilities. A few businesses make extra money with a travel agency on site, offering economical tour packages and other related services, or by taking commissions on bookings. If they recommend one tour or event booking over another, it's usually because they have a commission deal with a specific company. That's not to say you shouldn't book through them, but shop around for the price and program you want.

It pays to research room rates online with sites such as www.booking.com and www.hostelbookers.com and by calling the hotel directly to compare which source has a better deal. Discounts for longer stays and for cash payment are common if you ask. Confirm if there are any additional hotel charges, which generally include the value added tax (VAT); if the information doesn't guarantee that it does, do inquire, as the extra fee can add up quickly.

Lodgings throughout Turkey typically include Wi-Fi access and breakfast in the room rates, even for a dorm bed. If the establishment does not include a morning meal, which is rare, ask for directions to the neighborhood *fırın* (bakery). Summer can be torrid, so ask about air-conditioning, which older, smaller B&B's may not provide. Noise can also be a factor, particularly in neighborhoods like Taksim and Sultanahmet. Assure a restful night by booking a room away from the main drag. It may be exotic, but the crack-of-dawn call of the *müezzin* is sure to wake anyone not used to it. Securing lodgings away from this noise is difficult given the more than 2,600 mosques in the city.

Peak season rates are listed throughout this guidebook; during the off-season (Nov.-Mar.), rates are at least 10 percent lower.

SULTANAHMET AND VICINITY
Under €100

The best value for the money is ★ **Antique Hostel** (Kutlugün Sk. 51, Sultanahmet, 0212/638-1637, www.antiquehostel.com, from €12). Known for its lavish complimentary breakfasts and rooftop terrace, Antique has redefined the hostel experience to include satellite TV and air-conditioning in all its sparkling clean dormitory-style rooms, singles, doubles, quads, and family rooms. Preferred by young adults, rooms here are also available facing the Marmara Sea at a fraction of the cost of neighboring lodgings. Another good option for the budget traveler is ★ **Hotel Yunus Emre** (Şıfa Hamamı Sk. 30, 0212/638-4562, www.yunusemrehotel.com, from €50), with satellite TV, air-conditioning, blow-dryers, and breakfast. Pleasant pastel decor adorns pristine rooms with ample baths, and the rooftop terrace facing the grand Blue Mosque will delight. Check the website for special deals.

For backpackers, the **Orient Hostel International** (Akbiyik Cd. 13, 0212/517-9493, www.orienthostel.com, from €9) is a good base for an inexpensive Istanbul stay. Thanks to its on-site travel agency, guests can easily book the Orient's popular tours, such as those to Cappadocia or to the battlefields of Çanakkale. The place is best-known for its Terrace Café & Restaurant, great views, boisterous bar, and large collection of narghile flavors. Rooms range from a 30-bed dorm through four- and six-bed dorms, doubles, and suites.

For self-catering travelers, there is no sweeter home away from home than **Topkapı Apartments** (Demirci Resit Sk. 11, Sultanahmet, 0212/511-8050, www.topkapiapartments.com, from €65). Each of the four rooms offers short-term studio living with a double bed, a sofa, a kitchen, and a bath. For fresh air, retreat to the rooftop with views to the Marmara Sea. A supermarket and Wednesday market is close by to make your own meals in your vacation abode.

€100-200

The **White House Hotel** (Çatalçeşme Sk. 21, Sultanahmet, 0212/526-0019, www.istanbulwhitehouse.com, from €169) was voted by Tripadvisor travelers as one of the best hotels of the city in 2010, 2011, and 2012. From its opulent gold-on-white Ottoman interior to a rooftop restaurant with a view of the Bosphorus Bridge, Ayasofya, and Topkapı Palace, this hotel offers all the special touches mid-range travelers seek. The proximity to the Basilica Cistern, tramway, and some of the best restaurants in Sultanahmet will certainly please.

★ **Hotel Empress Zoe** (Akbıyık Sk. 10, Sultanahmet, 0212/518-2504, www.emzoe.com, from €140), next to a mid-15th-century hamam, has a lobby that exudes historical charm, with ancient walls and barrel Byzantine vaulted passages. If the lush patio reminds you of California's landscaped gardens, that's because Zoe's owners, Christina and Ann Nevens, are from San Francisco. Filled top to bottom with frescoes, the rooms are adorned in traditional Anatolian furnishings, some even boasting hamam-like marbled baths. The best rooms are the suites, some with adjoining terraces that feature scenery of the gardens or Marmara Sea. Browse the website to pick a room and get rates.

For a room possibly more exotic than the surrounding neighborhood, **Kybele Hotel** (Yerebatan Cd. 35, Sultanahmet, 0212/511-7766, www.kybelehotel.com, €150) fits the bill with glass lamps hanging from every ceiling, including more than 1,000 lamps in Kybele's lobby. A bit quirky at best, the veritable treasure trove inside is the accumulation of a trio of antiquing brothers whose Ottoman doors, calligraphic works, and other objets d'art are just a few items in this compact lodging less than 100 meters from the entrance to Basilica Cistern and Ayasofya.

Located a short walk from the Sirkeci tram and Marmaray stations and near the Spice Bazaar is the environmentally friendly **Neorion Hotel** (Orhaniye Cd. 14, Sirkeci, 0212/527-9090, www.neorionhotel.com, from €154). This modern 58-room hotel opened in 2011 and has fast become one of Istanbul's most popular. Services include complimentary afternoon tea, a rooftop terrace, and a luxury spa center with an indoor pool and a jetted tub.

For Old World accommodations, nothing beats ★ **Yeşil Ev** (Kabasakal Cd. 5,

Sultanahmet, 0212/517-6785, www.yesilev.com.tr, from €170). Set along picturesque Kabasakal, abutting the Topkapı Palace's perimeter, the "Green House" has late-18th-century furnishings that transplant guests to the decadence of the Ottoman Empire. It was once an aristocratic abode, and its 19 rooms, layout, and facade have been flawlessly recreated with 21st-century comforts.

Over €200

Rated Europe's best hotel by *Travel + Leisure* magazine in 2007 and second in the glossy's best overall value rating, the **Four Seasons at Sultanahmet** (Tevkifhane Sk. 1, Sultanahmet, 0212/402-3000, www.fourseasons.com/istanbul, from €560) was refurbished from the rubble of a prison and galvanized in celluloid by the hit movie *Midnight Express*. This 65-room neoclassical hotel offers the most luxurious accommodations near the tourist magnets of Ayasofya and the Grand Bazaar, just a 15-minute dash away. True to form, the service at this location is immaculate.

BEYOĞLU AND TAKSIM

The district of Beyoğlu consists of about a dozen neighborhoods all sharing mid-19th-century architecture in a modern hub of foot and vehicular traffic. At the storied hotels of Galata and Tepebaşı, a neighborhood undergoing a culinary renaissance, the chain lodgings over the bustle of Taksim Square, or the posh digs of Nişantaşı, you'll be pleased if you like action and being close to the shopping strip of Istiklal Caddesi.

Under €150

The pleasant surprise in Beyoğlu is **Galata Residence** (Felek Sk. 2, Galata, 0212/292-4841, www.galataresidence.com, from €100). Built in 1881, this is Istanbul's first apartment building and today has large and small apartments to accommodate self-catering travelers wishing to escape the tourist precinct across the Golden Horn. Some of the top-floor two-bedroom apartments have views to the Bosphorus that share real estate with the Ege & Rum Restaurant. The quaint decor reflects the belle epoque period in which the building was constructed atop a 19th-century Genoese storeroom. The vaulted Café Mahzen is now nestled in this catacomb-like structure, providing a cozy ambiance for afternoon tea.

For the swankiest of boutique hotels tucked in a Taksim side street, ★ **Lush Hip Hotel** (Siraselviler Cd. 12, Cihangir, 0212/243-9595, www.lushhiphotel.com, from €99) is all about the trends. Its mundane facade belies the all-encompassing richness of its interior decor, with each room offering a different vibe, from classic Ottoman to Warhol-esque pop art. With 42 rooms, this award-winning hotel offers special package deals for honeymooners, historians, and even those who want to take in the serenity of the Lush Day Spa on-site.

Le Grand Hôtel de Londres (Meşrutiyet Cd. 117, Tepebaşı, 0212/245-0670, www.londrahotel.net, from €40) oozes with *Orient Express* charm throughout its lobby and dining room, which retains the grace of 1892, when the hotel was built. The expected 19th-century touches, bold velvet curtains, gilded design, and grand piano bar delight guests seeking the charisma of old "Stamboul." The hotel has undergone a number of lengthy renovations to provide a slice of history that will appeal to budget and mid-range travelers.

Situated less than five minutes' walk from Taksim Square is the **Marions Suites** (Purtelas Sk. 12, Taksim, 0212/243-2424, www.themarionssuite.com, from €129). With its secret garden and large, bright suite rooms, Marions is one of the newest darlings in the Taksim hotel district to offer modernity so close to the action on Istiklal Street. For less than €200, the enormous penthouse suite with kitchenette, lounge, and private outdoor terrace is a chic home-away-from-home with touches of luxury, ideal for couples and honeymooners.

Backpackers will also find a place to call home in Beyoğlu. The hostel with a solid reputation for style, location, and cleanliness is **Bella Vista** (Turan Cd. 50, Taksim, 0212/361-9255, from €11). Nine small yet cozy dorm and private rooms are located 300 meters from Taksim Square, Istiklal Street, and the metro station. A café that caters to vegetarian travelers is the heart of the hostel, while six floors up is the place to take in the views of Beyoğlu. The staff work hard to welcome guests with movie nights, musical jam sessions, and other social events, creating a friendly electric vibe.

Over €150

Close to Taksim Square, the **Divan Istanbul** (Asker Ocağı Cd. 1, Şişli, 0212/315-5500, www.divan.com.tr, from €287) is the Divan brand's flagship hotel, completely refurbished in 2011 and designed by acclaimed architect Thierry Despont, who placed his signature style on the Getty Center in Los Angeles and the home of Bill Gates. Modern elegance combines with the oriental allure of contrasting colors that flow throughout the hotel's 191 guest rooms, restaurants, bars, pool, and spa center. For the best Japanese food in the city, take a seat in the Maromi Restaurant for lunch or dinner. With the mission "to be legendary," expect only first-class service and high-quality style at the Divan Istanbul.

The historical ★ **Pera Palace Hotel Jumeirah** (Meşrutiyet Cd. 52, Tepebaşı, 0212/377-4000, www.jumeirah.com, from €196) is one of the grand old abodes from the days when the *Orient Express* steamed into Istanbul Gar. Built in 1894 as the first European hotel in Turkey, it once served as a chic terminus for distinguished *Orient Express* guests like Greta Garbo and Alfred Hitchcock. Agatha Christie partly penned *Murder on the Orient Express* here, and Atatürk would sojourn in room 101 on occasion,; it now houses a museum dedicated to his life. The Grand Hall and regal touches like the red-carpeted floor, crystal chandeliers, and thick marble columns throughout still greet guests. The rickety gilded cage elevator remains for display purposes only, alongside newer versions. Opt for accommodations on the 2nd floor or higher, which have views of the Golden Horn and beyond. The hotel is managed by the same chain responsible for Dubai's seven-star Burj Al Arab.

BOSPHORUS

Refurbishing Istanbul's *yalılar* has been a hobby for the rich for more than 150 years. Some have done this elegantly; others have gaudily splattered their wealth to impress the neighbors. But less than a handful were able to recreate the atmosphere that led to 19th-century French scribe Lamartine's eloquent statement: "The Bosphorus can be described as an avenue of water surrounded by mansions one more beautiful than the other. Believe me, if fate had granted you one of these, you would never think of leaving to your last day." Spending the night in one of these mansions is an Istanbul experience that can be easier on the wallet than you might expect. An online search could reveal some advantageous packages to stay in a piece of Bosphorus real estate for a night or a weekend. Most waterside hotels offer guests boat or car transfers to facilitate travel across the straits.

European Shore

For secluded luxury, nothing beats ★ **Hôtel Les Ottomans** (Muallim Naci Cd. 68, Kuruçeşme, 0212/359-1500, www.lesottomans.com, from €800). Socialite Ahu Aysal dished out some €65 million of her family's fortune to turn the eyesore that was once the 19th-century Muhsinzade Paşa Waterside Mansion into the most exclusive and unique property. Epitomizing traditional Ottoman decor with handpicked antiques and luscious fabrics, 10 rooms, each a haven of serenity in itself, are packed with luxurious touches like the latest in technology. Astounding to the say the least, the Ottomans experience is heightened with the award-winning Claudalie Vinotherapie Spa, a 1,950-square-meter facility earmarked to allay the stresses of hours of sightseeing through individualized treatments. From butler to yacht services, and the masterful tweaking of local gastronomy with international accents, Les Ottomans is an unforgettable experience.

Not exactly on the water, but a location that hovers sublimely close to it, is the **W Istanbul** (Süleyman Seba Cd. 22, Beşiktaş, 0212/381-2121, www.whotels.com, from €185). It is the Starwood Hotels & Resorts' first foray into the fickle European market with their heavily branded hotel replication concept. That means that guest services (like the FIT Centers, pillow menu, and Whatever/Whenever concierge service) and accommodations have been streamlined worldwide to produce an identical experience from, say, New York to Doha. Totally neo-Zen, with a slate of lip-smacking colors, serenity rules supreme on the upper floors, while grooviness governs the ground floor with W's selection of eateries and lounge bar. The hotel is located in the historic Akaretler Row Houses, one of Istanbul's chicest rejuvenated neighborhoods, and former staff quarters of the Dolmabahçe Palace.

If Dolmabahçe is the *valide sultan* (imperial mother) of the shore, then **Çırağan Kempinski Hotel** (Çırağan Cd. 32, Beşiktaş, 0212/326-4646, www.kempinski-istanbul.com, from €384) is the lady-in-waiting. Renovated in 2008 to enhance the palace's original oriental decor and peppered with the eclecticism so fashionable in the late 18th century, this is the real deal for those seeking imperial digs while in town. For the very wealthy, there is the ridiculously lavish 510-square-meter Sultan Suite (€30,000 per night), where the 24-hour butler and chef service cater to your every whim. But don't let that be a deterrent to enjoying one of the smaller rooms, all offering video and music on demand as well as luxurious baths. With the exception of the Park View rooms, all accommodations come with a view of the Bosphorus. Private cabanas on the lawn surrounding the hotel's pool, one of the largest in town, which is heated in winter, come with complimentary fresh fruit, bottled water, and even a cabana boy to take your order.

Inaugurated in mid-2008, the decade-in-the-making **Four Seasons Istanbul at the Bosphorus** (Çırağan Cd. 28, Beşiktaş, 0212/381-4000, www.fourseasons.com/bosphorus, from €560) is nestled in a refurbished colossal 19th-century waterside palace on the Bosphorus. Boasting a 10-room spa facility and quayside pools on Europe's western edge, Istanbul's second Four Seasons location offers the spotless service that garnered its sister location in Sultanahmet the best European hotel award from *Travel + Leisure*. The hotel's least expensive offering, the 45-square-meter Superior Room, may house a widescreen LCD TV, but what makes it unique is its luxurious floor-to-ceiling marble and en suite bath with a soaking tub and separate glass-enclosed shower space.

Asian Shore

With a modern minimalist interior decor that belies its historical facade, the lobby of ★ **A'jia Hotel** (Ahmet Rasim Pasa Yalisi Halide Edip Adıvar Cd. 27, Kanlıca, 0216/413-9300, www.ajiahotel.com, from €300) welcomes guests with a cool white and beige palette. This is Istanbul's truly first high-class boutique hotel. The water views from 16 of A'jia's rooms are particularly superb due to the slight elevation the building enjoys. Guests are pampered with bathrobes, towels, and slippers of chunky Turkish cotton and goose-feather down comforters covering king beds. Internet access and LCD TVs are some of the location's amenities, along with the property's small commuter boat.

The award-winning ★ **Sumahan On The Water** (Kuleli Cd. 51, Çengelköy, 0216/422-8000, www.sumahan.com, from €410) is the only hotel of its kind refurbished from the rubble of a *rakı* refinery. Darker tones with contemporary architecture—think of a loft by the water—and dazzling views from every room were conceived by the architects, the Turkish-American couple Nedret and Mark Butler, who also own the spectacular property. The reflection of the sun's rays bouncing from the water creates an ever-changing atmosphere within the Sumahan. Staying the night near the historic village of Çengelköy is an added bonus. The Sumahan's incredibly popular Tapasuma restaurant is one of Istanbul's newest elite haunts to savor delectable fish and tapas.

Situated in a refurbished aristocratic residence is the **Bosphorus Palace Hotel** (Yalıboyu Cd. 64, Beylerbeyi, 0216/422-0003, www.bosphoruspalace.com, from €175). Seemingly stuck in time, the neo-Ottoman residence offers 14 opulent guest rooms, dressed in the rich fabrics and antique furnishings reminiscent of the residence's heyday. Near Beylerbeyi Palace, this boutique hotel may be a continent away, but it's close to the Bosphorus Bridge and IDO ferry terminal. One of the most affordable hotels along the straits., the Bosphorus Palace also has complimentary Internet access, satellite TV, secretarial services, baths equipped with robes of the thickest Turkish cotton, separate showers, and blow-dryers.

ASIAN SIDE

Preferred for its more suburban feel and its proximity to Istanbul's Sabiha Gökcen Airport, the Asian side offers a variety of accommodations, from five-star luxury to boutique hotels and inns (although choices are limited compared to those on the European side). Aside from bragging rights for having stayed on an entirely different continent, consider the greener, slower-paced Asian side, where culinary and shopping expeditions are on par with those on the opposite shore. Getting to the sights of Sultanahmet and Beyoğlu is an enjoyable half-hour ferry ride or a four-minute Marmaray train trip between Üsküdar on the Asian side and Sirkeci on the European side.

Under €125

Since its 2006 renovation, **Hotel My Dora** (Recaizade Sk. 6, Kadıköy, 0216/414-8350, www.hotelmydora.com, from €60) has been a breath of fresh air in the transportation hub of Kadıköy. It is relatively small, with about three dozen rooms. Epitomizing quirkiness, each room boasts a different style of decor—from quirky industrialism with red splashes to classic furnishings replete with wooden accents throughout. Featuring spotless baths, My Dora is a smart choice for discriminating travelers and those abiding to a strict budget. Choose a front-facing room on one of the top floors for stunning views of Sultanahmet and Haydarpaşa.

Steps away from Kadıköy's hectic open-air market, **Zumrut Hotel** (Reşitefendi Sk. 5, Kadıköy, 0216/450-0454, www.kadikoyzumrutotel.com, from €50) is an economical solution for the travel-savvy. With just two stars, it packs barebones accommodations with the necessities, like air-conditioning, satellite TV, and Wi-Fi access. Expect clean accommodations and a copious complimentary breakfast buffet.

Nestled along what was once one of Istanbul's prized holiday resorts, **Hotel Suadiye** (Plaj Yolu 25, Suadiye, 0216/445-8424, www.hotelsuadiye.com, from €99) is a hybrid of boutique charm with all the expected comforts of a chain hotel. Overlooking the Sea of Marmara and the picturesque Princes' Islands, the Suadiye offers quiet accommodations just steps from the shopping and dining haven of Bağdat Caddesi. Spacious bedrooms have large tiled baths, and along with Wi-Fi, a myriad of business services and facilities are offered.

Over €125

Rich textures and ornate decor abound at **Wyndham Istanbul Kalamış Marina** (Kalamış Fener Cd. 38, Kalamış, 0216/400-0000, www.wyndham.com, from €140). This five-star designer hotel lies adjacent to the exclusive Kalamış marina and shopping district of Bağdat Caddesi. Bulging with amenities, the location is renowned for its wellness facilities, seven restaurants and bars, and 210 rooms and suites that look out either to the city or Marmara Sea and the Princes' Islands. Families can laze by the outdoor infinity pool that stretches toward the marina, or enjoy the children's play area connected with the Blue Harmony Spa.

ADALAR (PRINCES' ISLANDS)

The Princes' Islands are an ideal locale to stay the night, particularly in Büyükada's uptown or nostalgic digs. ★ **Splendid Hotel** (23 Nisan Cd. 53, 0216/382-6950, www.splendid-hotel.net, from €150) is the best on the island. The accommodations are a bit overpriced, but the sunset, particularly from a top-floor room, makes staying here worth the cost. Set in an art nouveau building that hosted Edward VIII and other dignitaries, the lobby and grounds are a pleasing mix of Greek and Ottoman touches with 70 rooms, four suites, and a pool. The ★ **Büyükada Princess** (Iskele Cd. 2, south of the port, 0216/382-1628, www.buyukadaprincesshotel.com.tr, 220TL) is the island's most famous and oldest hotel at over a century. An upscale bar was added during the latest round of renovations. Its sea-facing facade features a scenic pool, a wet bar, and geranium-lined balconies. Expect the best in accommodations. **Naya Retreat** (Yılmaz Türk Cd. 96, 0216/382-4598, http://nayaretreats.com, from €80) is an inn that doubles as Istanbul's best yoga and meditation retreat. Naya is set in a refurbished white wooden mansion and is the entrepreneurial venture of free-spirited expatriate Ludwig Lehner. Don't confuse this for a conventional boutique hotel: Read the house rules on the website before booking to understand what's on offer.

On Heybeliada, the **Halki Palas** (Refah Sehitleri Cd. 94, Heybeliada, 0216/351-0025, www.halkipalacehotel.com, from €100) is a little gaudy, but still is the best option to bask in the ultimate comfort and supreme serenity of the smaller isle.

AIRPORT HOTELS

Attracting largely business clientele, airport accommodations are typically large international chains that provide streamlined and replicated rooms and facilities. Check for conventions occurring during your stay, which may raise the room rates and the noise level of the hotel's public facilities. On the plus side, the commute to and from the airport is a snap.

For a no-brainer, stay at **TAV Airport Hotel** (International Terminal, Atatürk International Airport, 0212/465-4030, www.tavairporthotel.com) without even leaving the terminal. Awesome for transit passengers requiring a few hours of rest, its 46 "air side" standard rooms are within the airport's security zone, meaning there are no traffic hassles and it's for international travelers only. Rented in three-hour increments (from €102 for the first 3 hours), these rooms are ideal to complete some work, get a horizontal nap, or shower away the stresses of a long transcontinental flight. The remaining 82 "land side" standard, superior, executive, and suite rooms (from €118) serve the nontraveling public with the same three-hour deal as well as overnight and extended stays. The hotel's fitness center also offers a chance to get the muscles moving between flights. Overlooking the tarmac, the Sky Restaurant's Turkish specialties are great for hotel guests, or travelers seeking a more serene dining environment than the airport's food court.

The ★ **Renaissance Polat** (Sahilyolu Cd. 2, Yeşilyurt, 0212/414-1800, www.marriott.com, from €103) is a block of mirrored concrete towering over the Sea of Marmara. All rooms and public spaces offer wireless high-speed Internet and entertainment options. Although a bit stark, rooms are spacious, and most offer large windows that provide uninterrupted sea views. Pick from seven international dining and bar options, including the Champions American Sport Bar & Restaurant, which serves an American and Mexican menu with the requisite widescreen TV to watch sports. The Bier Stube Restaurant boasts strictly German fare, the Daphne specializes in Mediterranean dishes, and the Royal China Chinese Restaurant caters to guests desiring Szechuan cuisine.

Istanbul's mainstay by the sea and airport,

the **Çınar Hotel** (Fener Mevkii, Yeşilköy, 0212/663-2900, www.cinarhotel.com.tr, from €173) was one of the first local hotels to combine luxury accommodations and superior catering, in 1958. The hotel's modern rooms with balconies facing either the sea or a garden offer a pleasant respite between flights, and unlike most hotels, Çınar does border a sandy beach that leads into the Marmara Sea. If the beach looks unappealing, a workout in the health club or a lazy hour or two by the outdoor pool is not a bad way to pass the time.

Food

Eating is half the fun of traveling in Turkey. In cosmopolitan Istanbul, the national Anatolian cuisine, influenced by Arabic, Armenian, Georgian, Russian, Greek, and Mediterranean flavors, is enhanced by the regional seafood. Don't pass up Istanbul's renowned Ottoman cuisine or you will be denying yourself the rich and complex compilation of tastes and textures that emerged from the imperial kitchens of the Ottoman palaces lining the Bosphorus. Istanbul's street fare is also peppered with interesting finds, like the *balık ekmeği* (fish sandwich), found near the docks at Eminönü. The ubiquitous grilled-cheese toast, best with a steaming cup of fresh tea or a cold glass of *ayran* (yogurt drink), is a popular alternative. Ditto for the simple *simit* (circular sesame seed baked bread). The *dürüm* (lavash bread filled with thin slices of meat roasted on a spit) remains the crowd favorite for a quick and filling snack. A midday stop at any busy diner reveals a menu chockfull of interesting dishes.

Primarily due to its location, Istanbul offers eclectic fusions of various cuisines as well as a myriad of fine restaurants specializing in classical European gastronomy or cutting-edge cuisine. Nowadays it's also possible to find international chains, such as Jamie Oliver's signature **Jamie's Italian** (Zorlu Center, Zincirlikuyu Cd., Beşiktaş, 0212/353-6808, www.jamieoliver.com, 30TL) and even a **Hard Rock Café** (Meşrutiyet Cd. 3, Asmali Mescit, 0212/251-7444, www.hardrock.com) among the traditional *lokantalar* (canteen-style restaurants).

Sultanahmet has rather few gastronomical restaurants. Eateries here tend to focus on international dishes mixed with regional kebabs and Ottoman classics. Locals head to Beyoğlu and beyond for unique culinary fare. For the latest in cutting-edge gastronomy, head to Şişli's Nişantaşı or the Bosphorus shore in Ortaköy and Kuruçeşme. You'll find some of the city's best elite culinary destinations, with prices to match. Another good option is Bağdat Caddesi on the city's Anatolian side, where most bistros cluster on the street's eastern end, toward the neighborhoods of Suadiye and Bostancı.

Retailers and restaurateurs are required by law to post prices at the front door, but some eateries list the dishes and not much else. If this is the case, confirm prices before ordering and ensure that the bill matches those previously quoted. This is advised at seafood restaurants, particularly those lining the underbelly of the Galata Bridge. Mid-range and fine-dining restaurants may impose a per-person fee called a *kuver* (cover) of 3-10TL per head, which basically covers water and bread. Other establishments add a 10 percent service fee automatically covering a tip for the waiters. These fees are typically not listed on the menu, just on the final bill. Check with your host on arrival so there are no surprises. If the service fee is not included, a tip of around 10 percent of the total price is advised, particularly if the service was attentive.

English and other languages may be spoken at upscale establishments, where reservations are helpful. Hotel concierges can be helpful too in making reservations and suggesting where to dine.

Unless otherwise stated, upscale restaurants, which are generally located in hotels, serve food from noon to 3pm and from 5pm until at least 11pm. Most eateries outside hotels continue service through the day from 8am or 10am to midnight.

Lastly, avoid feeding the multitude of cats begging for scraps along terraces. Throwing one piece of fish or even bread will summon felines and irk managers who try to keep them away. Why are there so many? Legend has it that the Prophet Muhammad, who promoted love of all creatures in return for a blessed life, discovered his favorite cat, Muezza, sleeping on the sleeve of his robe while dressing for prayer. Rather than disturb her, he cut the robe and left her to sleep peacefully. Muhammad's fondness for felines is now reflected throughout the Muslim world.

SULTANAHMET AND VICINITY
Turkish and International

Accessible while inside the Topkapı Palace walls, **Konyalı Topkapı Sarayı Lokantası** (Sultanahmet, 0212/513-9696, www.konyalilokantasi.com, 30TL) has remained the gathering place for international heads of state since the early 1970s when Richard Nixon, Queen Elizabeth II, and Benazir Bhutto ate here. Its authentic Ottoman cuisine, which includes lots of pricey kebabs, is prepared just steps away from the imperial kitchens from which it originated. The main dining room is elegantly decorated. The adjoining bistro, however, offers similar fare at a fraction of the price as well as great sea views. Try the Ottoman sherbet drinks on offer, which have been created with in-season fruit based on recipes found in the palace archives.

One of the top picks for Turkish cuisine in Sultanahmet is actually the food you cook yourself at ★ **Cooking Alaturka** (Akbıyık Cd. 72a, Sultanahmet, www.cookingalaturka.com, 0212/458-5919, €60). This cooking school offers foreigners a hands-on overview of Turkish and Ottoman cuisine guided by the skills of a Turkish chef. The chef helps prepare a five-course meal with fellow classmates before they savor the results at the end of class. Grand chef and expatriate owner Eveline Zoutendijk has created the airy pint-size restaurant that features six set menus. There's also a collection of Turkish foods available for purchase, including red pepper flakes and pomegranate extract. You don't need to be a student here to enjoy the food; drop-ins and dinner reservations are both welcome.

Sarnıç Restaurant (Soğukçeşme Sk., Sultanahmet, 0212/512-4291, www.sarnicrestaurant.com, 45TL) is set in a 1,500-year-old Roman cistern that flanks Topkapı Palace. It is striking, with a roaring fire in a large rock chimney, backed by soaring colonnades with humongous domes aloft and hundreds of candlelit tables that raise expectations for great things to come. The large space can get noisy, but the menu is above average, and although it's much pricier than its neighbors, where else can you dine in a such historical setting? The fare is a meaty fusion of French, Turkish, and seafood.

Looking to impress that special someone or see Istanbul's finest landmarks from great heights? Take to the rooftop of **Seven Hills Hotel** (Tevkifhane Sk 8, 0212/516-9497, www.sevenhillshotel.com, 25TL), to dine on seafood and Turkish fare in an open-air restaurant with the majestic Blue Mosque and Ayasofya on one side and the Marmara Sea and Asia coastline on the other. Meals cost a little extra because it's all about the views. If you're watching your pennies, it's just as nice to recline here for mid-afternoon tea or a drink at sunset. Go before sunset and stay until the call to prayer for a truly memorable experience.

For genuine Turkish and Kurdish hospitality, visit the owner-operators at the cozy ★ **Fuego Café and Restaurant** (Incili Cavus Sk. 15A, Sultanahmet, 0212/531-3697 www.fuegocaferestaurant.com, 25TL). Located a short walk uphill from the Basilica Cistern in a lively pedestrian side street, you can people-watch as you enjoy high-quality international, Turkish, and Ottoman cuisine.

The moussaka and *Hûnkar beğendi* (tender chunks of lamb served over eggplant purée) are personal favorites, and the succulent *şiş* kebabs are some of the best in town. The bar staff mix up a pretty good cocktail, too, which is hard to find in Istanbul. Dine alfresco on the street, inside, or in the upstairs salon.

Pull up a chair overlooking one of the busiest cobblestone streets of old Istanbul at the much loved ★ **Albura Kathisma Café and Restaurant** (Akbıyık Cd. 36-38, 0212/517-9031, www.alburakathisma.com, 25TL). This restaurant offers a meal for every taste and budget from international favorites, such as pasta and salads, to sumptuous Turkish cuisine. Enhance your dining experience by matching your dish with a Turkish wine from the lengthy wine list. After dining, wander to the back of the restaurant, turn right, and step back in time to the Byzantine-style chambers of the former Magnaura Palace. It's one of Sultanahmet's best-kept secrets.

Seafood

Compared with Istanbul's waterside neighborhoods, Sultanahmet has few seafood options. You'll find fish on the menu of most establishments, but the top pick for seafood specialists is ★ **Giritli Restaurant** (Keresteci Hakkı Sk. 8, 0212/458-2270, www.giritlirestoran.com, 125TL). This isn't a tourist restaurant but rather a local haunt loved for its Cretan offerings, and there's no need to bargain for the catch of the day or check the bill for tricky accounting because the generous prix fixe menu comes with plenty of *mezeler,* grilled seafood, dessert, unlimited water, *rakı,* wine, and beer. Come with an appetite and devour the cuisine within the walls or the courtyard of a historic Ottoman home. Dishes other than seafood can be made on request. In summer, make a reservation to secure a table in the courtyard.

Quick and Inexpensive

Come *Ramazan* (Ramadan), there's one eatery in town that has lines of locals hankering for a meal to break their fast. What they're waiting for is the *köfte* (meatballs) at **Tarihi Sultanahmet Köfteci** (Divanyolu Cd. 12, Sultanahmet, 0212/520-0566, www.sultanahmetkoftesi.com, 20TL). Packed every day and night, the restaurant has a slim menu with a choice of *köfte* or lamb *şiş* (skewered)—but who needs an enormous selection when the meatballs are so sumptuous? Who knew ground lamb with breadcrumbs could be grilled to such perfection? Obviously Mehmet

There's always time for afternoon tea.

Seracettin did when he began serving those walnut-size patties in 1920. Try them with rice and a fresh white bean salad, best enjoyed with *limon* (lemon) rather than vinegar, and the watered-down yogurt drink *ayran*. Top it all off with a hefty slice of delicious *irmik helvası* (sweetened semolina with pine nuts). The food is definitely worth the wait, but go easy on the chili flakes, they've got kick!

On route to the Grand Bazaar from Sultanahmet, turn right at the Çemberlitaş tram stop to find **Makarna Sarayı** (Vezirhan Cd. 18, 0212/528-2938, www.makarnasarayi.com.tr, 15TL) is a modest casual *lokanta* where you can choose between the unique lamb kebab roasted with infused vegetables, or grab a tray and start pointing and selecting from the choices of pastas, *dolmalar* (vegetables stuffed with savory rice), casseroles, and soups. The price will vary depending on how many dishes you select. Wash the meal down with a freshly squeezed juice from the front of the store. If pomegranates are in season, try some squeezed with orange for a zesty taste. This place is ideal for a homey lunch break before hitting the labyrinth of bazaar streets.

A morning at the Grand Bazaar can leave one feeling overwhelmed and hungry; fortunately there are plenty of cafés where you can rest and revive. The best of the bunch though is located outside gate 16: **Keyf-i Mekan Cafe and Restaurant** (Tığcılar Sk. 48, Grand Bazaar, 0212/522-5861, 15TL). This cozy rustic café with exposed dark brick walls and wooden fixtures churns out homemade classics brimming with terrific taste. Incidentally, *keyfi* (living a life that's full of pleasure) is a way of a life in Turkey. Choosing to dine here with the *mezeler* of the day or grills from the menu will surely bring some *keyfi* to your lunch break.

AROUND BEYOĞLU
Turkish

Wine lovers will appreciate a before-dinner wine tasting session at **Sensus** (Büyükhendek Cd. 5, Galata, 0212/245-5657), a few steps from the Galata tower. Known as a wine and cheese boutique, rows and rows of Turkey's best wines are available for purchase or to sample for a fee. Doubling as a wine cellar, you're free to take a seat and match your samples of reds or whites (35TL, 5 types) with the selection of *mezeler* from the menu. Indigenous white grapes include the light and fruity *Sultaniye* and the drier *Narince*. For reds, the full body *Boğazkere* or the softer *Öküzgözü* may impress. Blends of these are worth tasting if available.

A fixture in Taksim since 1888 for some of the most sumptuous Ottoman and Turkish fare in town, **Hacı Abdüllah** (Eski Sakızağacı Sk. 9A, 0212/293-8561, www.haciabdullah.com.tr, 25TL) is filled with shelves of homemade fruit compotes that make their way into the house's desserts. The *Hûnkar beğendi* (Sultan's delight) is popular, and so is the traditional *türlü* (mixed vegetables). Usually hard to find, the sun-dried eggplant *dolma* has diners begging for seconds.

With more traditional entrées than any other restaurant on the strip, ★ **Otantık** (Istiklal Cd. 80A, Galatasaray, 0212/293-8451, 15TL) is renowned for its homemade *yufka* (paper-thin dough) rolled and cooked by local women right at the entrance. Filled with kilims and pillow-backed banquettes, Otantık's window tables on the upper floors are ideal for watching hectic Istiklal below. The thick lentil soup is a mainstay and warming during Istanbul's chilly season. Follow it up with a *gözleme* (Turkish pancake) filled with lamb, feta, or spinach and a crispy shepherd's salad with diced tomato, cucumbers, onions, and parsley.

The **Istanbul Culinary Institute** (Meşrutiyet Cd. 59, Tepebaşı, 0212/251-2214, www.istanbulculinary.com, 20TL) is part school, part Turkish gastronomical diplomat, and part restaurant. What owner Hande Bozdoğan has done superbly, though, is reawaken local taste buds to the incredible richness of Anatolian cuisine, with seasonable farm-to-table ingredients. The atmosphere is of a simple bistro with a clean and minimalist Nordic decor. The best option at this charming eatery is the table d'hôte (100TL), the day's prix fixe menu. Visit the website for the daily offerings, or simply show up and be surprised.

International

For a smart, mid-priced restaurant, try ★ **Kitchenette** (The Marmara Istanbul, Taksim Meydanı, 0212/292-6862, 25TL) by Taksim Square. Try their avant-garde hamburger, a grilled patty of ground lamb and beef served on buttered homemade bread and packed high with sautéed spinach, cinnamon onions, and cheddar cheese. For those watching their diet, the "Fit for You" menu has 15 low-calorie meals that will go easy on the waistline. Kitchenette outdoes its counterparts by consistently providing attentive service and a fresh menu. This is a great breakfast, lunch, or dinner alternative as well as a great spot to experience Taksim Square's buzz. Give your taste buds a treat with any one of their contemporary desserts. A macaroon platter, perhaps?

The Cihangir neighborhood, between Istiklal Street and the Bosphorus, is a Bohemian warren of gourmet pleasures. Restaurants and cafés have emerged here to cater for expatriates and local socialites who pay big prices to secure a piece of Old World real estate in downtown Beyoğlu. You can enjoy the same sweeping Bosphorus views at **Kat 5** (Soğancı Sk. 7, 0212/293-3774, www.5kat.com, 35TL), an elegant setting worthy of the cover of *Vogue Living*. The rooftop restaurant is famous for its generous buffet lunch menu (55TL pp, 11am-2:30pm daily) and the evening three-course prix fixe menu (from 95TL pp), consumed either downstairs in a French provincial style dining space or upstairs on an open-air terrace. À la carte menus are also available for breakfast, lunch, and dinner.

Tired of Turkish food? Try the Thai and Southeast Asian dishes created by the Thai Royal family's former chef, Miss Nuch, at ★ **ÇokÇok Thai** (Meşrutiyet Cd. 51A, Tepebaşı, 0212/292-6496, www.cokcok.com. tr, 25TL). The food is just marvelous, and so is the Asian decor over two floors and a summertime outdoor patio. ÇokÇok ("chock chock," meaning "plentiful") flies in the freshest ingredients from Asia to produce dishes that have garnered the Best Ethnic Restaurant in Turkey label from gourmet critics. The food menu features contemporary Thai fare with a European twist, while the cocktails have a unique Southeast Asian flavor, unlike anywhere else in Istanbul.

Quite possibly the best café for rooftop views of old Istanbul, the Bosphorus, and the 19th-century homes of Galata can be found at **Galata Konak Cafe** (Haci Ali Sk. 2, Galata, 0212/252-5346, www.galatakonakcafe.com, 25TL). The menu here offers enough variety, with nothing too mind blowing, but what sells this place is certainly the view and the desserts. Find out when the sunset evening call to pray will be, take a seat here with a tea or coffee (don't forget the cake), and hear the echo of a thousand *müezzinler* singing the Islamic call to prayer. The moment really is stunning.

Seafood

If you've climbed the Galata Tower and are searching for a friendly low-fuss meal, grab a table at the tiny **Fürreyya Galata Balikcisi** (Serdari Ekrem Sk. 2, Galata, 0212/252-4853, www.furreyyagalata.com, 20TL). This modest restaurant, with a basic menu, lures diners looking for fresh seafood cooked to perfection. The *balık dürüm* (fish wrap) is popular, as are the restaurant's seafood take on the Turkish culinary traditions of *köfte* and mantı (Turkish ravioli) made with fish instead of meat. A recommendation from Ismail, the owner, also ensures a pleasant meal.

For a traditional *meyhane* (Turkish tavern) experience, ★ **Asmali Cavit** (Asmalımescit Cd. 16/D, 0212/292-4950, 25TL) is a lively option off Istiklal Street that attracts a solid local following on the weekend. You do need to reserve ahead to secure a table as the place is tiny and popular. This is a place to experience a typical Saturday night out with the locals. Expect an abundance of *mezeler,* seafood, and *rakı*, sometimes burned off with rounds of spontaneous dancing. Musicians who play *fasıl* traditional music with a violin, clarinet, and *darbuka* will often work the dinner crowd into a party mood. Other popular *meyhane* locations are Nevizade Street and Çiçek Passage, off Istiklal Caddesi.

Quick and Inexpensive

For home-cooked food just like a Turkish mama would make, head to **Helvetia** (Gen. Yazgan Sk. 12, Asmalı Mescit, 0212/245-8780, 15TL), a modest little diner filled with young and groovy locals. Don't expect white tablecloths or table service; this is a no-frills treasure with generous servings of *mezeler*. Simply point to the vegetarian and meat options on the counter and take a seat in the communal dining space. The food is so good and affordable you may come back for more.

Dirt cheap and always good, **Köfteci Hüseyin** (Kurabiye Sk. 14, Taksim, 0212/243-7637, 15TL) is a hole-in-the-wall that caters to blue-collar workers in a backstreet of Istiklal Caddesi. English is minimal, as is the menu. It's *köfte* (meatballs) cooked to perfection, with *piyaz* white bean salad. Locals line up for this every day, so avoid the lunch line.

With counters and meals overflowing with chocolate, **J'adore Chocolatier & Café** (Emir Nevruz Sk. 22, Galatasaray, 0212/249-0333, 10TL), is a hidden gem where many shoppers retreat for a coffee break after pounding the pavement of Istiklal Caddesi. It's so popular with the locals that you may need to wait for a seat in the tiny café. The wait will be worth it, though, with choices of desserts like chocolate pie, chocolate fondue, various flavors of hot chocolate, and the Beatrice chocolate cake. You can purchase gifts from the counter on the way out.

ALONG THE BOSPHORUS
Turkish

Armed with a credit card, head for **Tuğra** (Çırağan Palace Kempinski, Çırağan Cd. 32, Beşiktaş, 0212/236-7333, www.kempinski.com, 60TL) for what is arguably the best

dinner on the Bosphorus

fine dining Ottoman cuisine—and views—in town. The menus are seasonal and available on the website, with prices listed. Taste the dishes that made sultans in this very palace swoon, like *Külbastı*, a 18th-century dish of lamb or fish atop smoked eggplant puree, with a wild herb patty, and pomegranate and red onion relish. To complete the experience, savor a candy stick rolled at the table from the *macun,* an authentic sweets trolley that winds through the tables of this gastronome's opulent paradise.

Istanbul's latest culinary sensation, **Tapasuma** (Kuleli Cd. 43, 0216/401-1333, www.tapasuma.com, 60TL) is set in an old Ottoman distillery on the banks of the Asian shore as part of the Sumahan on the Water Hotel. An enormous selection of *mezeler* and contemporary Turkish fare await guests who have the option of arriving from Europe via the private *Sumahan I* from Kuruçeşme, north of the Bosphorus Bridge. It's a popular place for business meetings, and for travelers it's ideal to get away from the hustle of the European shore to celebrate a special occasion.

International

Degustation menus are catching on in the elite restaurants that cater to business meetings and romantic occasions. Overlooking the Bosphorus, just down from Taksim Square, ★ **Topaz** (İnönü Cd. 50, 0212/249-1001, www.topazistanbul.com, 60TL) is one, impressing high-end diners looking for something different. Topaz claims to be "continually pushing the boundaries, developing a reputation for gastronomic boldness," which they achieve with seven-course Ottoman and Mediterranean degustation menus (245TL with wine, 145TL without). Included are decadent samples of Ottoman palace classics and traditional recipes reinvigorated for the contemporary palate. The à la carte menu is available for more affordable options.

If *Sex and the City* were filmed in Istanbul, the internationally renowned **Zuma** (Salhane Sk. 7, Ortaköy, 0212/236-2296, www.zumarestaurant.com, 100TL) would be the perfect hangout for the gal pals. A neo-Zen lounge and bar grace the upper floor, while the restaurant boasts a stylish neon-bathed sushi bar and the Robata Grill. Zuma's forte is their presentation of the informal Japanese culinary experience of the *izakaya*, in which a series of small plates are served for all to try. The Istanbul location, according to local clientele, surpasses the original locations worldwide, thanks to the wonderful scenery afforded by the straits and the Bosphorus Bridge on its doorstep. Try the signature spicy beef tenderloin with Sakura (a raspberry infused sake mixed with cucumber, vodka, and lime) or go all out with the multicourse tasting menu (200TL, excludes drinks).

Seafood

Istanbullus know where to eat fish, and those with enough time head to the adjoining Asian outposts of Beylerbeyi and Çengelköy, both noted for their superior catches, particularly *palamut* (a tender tuna), and the meaty mussels that line their banks. Aside from a plethora of popular fish stands, **Çengelköy Iskele Restaurant** (Çengelgöy Iskelesi Meydanı 10A, 0216/321-5505, www.cengel-koyiskelerestaurant.com, 40TL) is a fish eatery with a rooftop balcony that's literally over the straits facing the Bosphorus Bridge. You may find yourself seated next to one of Turkey's wealthiest elite. Come for lunch if time allows; weekend evenings tend to be packed and rather loud.

ASIAN SIDE
Turkish

While there is not much to see in Üsküdar, many *Istanbullus* recommend taking a ferry to the Asian port just to try **Kanaat Lokantası** (Selmanipak Cd. 9, 0216/341-5444, www.kanaatlokantasi.com, 25TL, cash only). As one of the oldest eating establishments in Istanbul, this iconic business has dedicated itself to *ev yemekleri* (heartwarming home food) since 1933. This place gets crowded during lunch hour, so plan to dine later on. If you're looking for inspiration, Turkey's national dish, *etli kuru fasulye*, is white beans stewed in tomato sauce with lamb chunks; or stuffed onions are nicely paired with dozens of the chef's daily specialties. Don't expect much aside from fast friendly service and hearty food.

Specializing in slices of tender kebabs and grilled meats, **Niyazibey** (Ahmediye Meydanı 1, Üsküdar, 0216/310-4821, www.niyazibey.com, 20TL) never disappoints. Also great here is *perde pilavı*, a complex dish traditionally served at weddings throughout Anatolia. The dish is decorated with a crust that symbolizes a new couple's house: Nuts represent the couple and currants are all their future progeny. And a kebab house would be remiss without a *künefe*, a baked dessert consisting of *kashkaval* cheese wrapped in hair-thin pastry dough and sweetened with sugar.

Cooks of Antep cuisine, from Turkey's southeastern city of Gaziantep, are famous for their creative touches on traditional Turkish fare such as the *ciğer kebap* (liver kebab), *lahmacun* (Turkish pizza with ground lamb), and baklava. ★ **Develi** (Münir Nurettin Selçuk Cd., Kadıköy, 0216/418-9400, www.develikebap.com, 25TL) is a great choice to sample the fare from an Antepian kitchen. Set along the docks of Istanbul's most luxurious marina, its location is stunning.

International

The mirrored walls and ornate ceilings of the 19th-century white wooden *köşk* (mansion) that houses **Café Zanzibar** (Cemil Topuzlu Cd. Köşk Sk. 102A, Caddebostan, 0216/385-6430, www.cafezanzibar.com.tr, 40TL) is elegance defined, with a garden of creeping vines and lush potted ferns right on the Sea of Marmara—a little oasis far from the noise of downtown Istanbul. The menu is a mix of gourmet Italian, French, and Turkish cuisine, a little pricier than most, but certainly unique. To get here, cross over to Asia via ferry or Marmaray train and take a taxi.

Seafood

A great place for *mezeler* and fish, ★ **Foça** (Turgut Özal Blv. 110, Küçükyalı, 0216/519-8686, www.focarestaurant.com, 50TL) is reminiscent of the battery of boats just across the way from the restaurant. A walk inside the main cabin of this pseudo-ship reveals both interior seating and a large terrace. No one does *lakerda* (fried calamari) like Foça. A large colorful room full of activities for the little ones will also be appreciated by families.

For the feel and spread of an old-meets-new *meyhane*, head to Tarihi Moda Port to ★ **Cibalikapı Balıkçısı** (Yolu Moda Cd. 163A, Moda, 0216/348-9363, www.cibalikapibalikcisi.com, 30TL). While there is a tasting menu (100TL) featuring the freshest daily catch, it's only available for groups of 10 or more. The degustation menu (160TL) is perhaps more viable for two people and a great way to have the best dishes in the house, but à la carte is also possible. The atmosphere is traditional, with splashes of contemporary touches throughout the indoor and outdoor dining areas. The courtyard is the place to be in summer, and like all *meyhaneler*, best enjoyed in the company of friends.

Quick and Inexpensive

A favorite of the international media, ★ **Çiya Sofrası** (Güneşlibahçe Sk. 43, Kadıköy, 0216/330-3190, www.ciya.com.tr, 20TL) boasts hundreds of Turkish, Ottoman, Seljukian, Jewish, and Middle Eastern specialties. More of a food anthropologist than a chef, Gaziantep-born owner Musa Dağdeviren continues to add to Çiya's culinary anthology. It translates into good home-cooked fare in a chic bistro atmosphere as well as a tantalizing taste-bud trip into Turkey's outer regions and beyond. The menu changes daily. *Mezeler* are weighed to create an affordable entrée. Select two to three dishes to share from the chef at the counter, leaving room for the *kabak tatlısı* (pumpkin dessert) or *domates tatlısı* (tomato dessert) if you can.

ADALAR (PRINCES' ISLANDS)

The archipelago's proximity to the cooler waters of the Bosphorus ensures that the straits' best fish are brought in daily and served alongside the Sea of Marmara's catch of the day. As such, most restaurants on the islands offer seafood as main courses, along with some of the requisite *mezeler*. ★ **Ali Baba** (Gülistan Cd. 20, 0216/382-3733, www.alibababuyukada.com, 25TL) is renowned for its consistent quality and for not gouging its foreign clientele. *Mezeler* like octopus salad and stuffed mussels, followed by a main course of the islands' renowned red mullet, have been Ali Baba's forte for decades. For those not keen on fish, on Büyükada you can also find vegetarian, chicken, and beef dishes. **Akasya** (next to Splendid Palace Hotel, 0216/382-1050, 20TL) offers simple and inexpensive meals of pizzas, pastas, steaks, and grills in a pleasant contemporary courtyard away from the busy streets near the port. The master bakers have been luring mainlanders to **Büyükada Pastanesi** (Recep Koç Cd.

42, 0216/382-4303) since the turn of the century with its famous local bread and sweet pastries. The freshly baked goodies like the *lokum* (Turkish delight) cookies are great to take along on an island picnic.

Heybeliada is known for its lively Greek fish restaurants, among them ★ **Halki** (Ayyıldız Cd. 24, 0216/351-8595, 25TL). Halki's appetizer trays are as varied as their ramekin dishes are sumptuous.

Before leaving any of the islands, it's a tradition to eat a creamy Turkish *dondurma* (ice cream) piled high atop a waffle cone. The recipe includes salep (from a species of orchid) and mastic, making it smooth, slightly sticky, and oh-so-good.

Information and Services

VISITOR INFORMATION

While there are many tourism offices throughout town, the most helpful ones, aside from the locations at Atatürk International and Sabiha Gökçen Airports, are in the heart of Sultanahmet (Divanyolu Cd., 0212/518-1802), down from the tram stop on the right, and the Taksim branch (Taksim Meydanı, 0212/245-6876). There are also smaller offices in Beyazit Meydanı (near the Grand Bazaar, 0212/522-4902); Istanbul Gar (0212/511-5858) in Sirkeci; Karaköy Seaport (0212/249-5776); and one run out of the Hilton Hotel Arcade (0212/233-0592) in Harbiye, north of Taksim Square. Most offices are open 9am-5pm daily, but the hours are often extended to 6pm in summer and depending on foot traffic. With true Turkish hospitality, staff assist with most requests; maps and general information are also available.

Due to the intricate web of roads, printed maps from tourism offices are never quite sufficient or accurate to use to navigate. To get a grasp of the lay of the land, check out Google's interactive maps online for arguably the most thorough layout. Using your smartphone, take screen shots of the locations you want to visit, such as the Grand Bazaar map (www.grandbazaaristanbul.org). This will give a quick reference out on the streets if you don't have data connectivity. Accurate paper maps can be purchased at information kiosks and bookstores.

Luggage Storage

Most lodgings allow secure luggage storage, even if you decide to travel out of the city and don't want to take all your bags. Most transportation hubs also provide lockers or storage offices. Located in the international arrival terminal of **Atatürk International Airport,** the check-in **Emanet Bagaj** facility can hold luggage—ensure that it's locked—for a daily fee ranging 12-25TL. Its smaller counterpart on the Asian side, **Sabiha Gökçen International Airport,** also provides the same service.

MONEY

Both Atatürk International and Sabiha Gökçen airports have several Automated Teller Machines (ATMs) and currency exchange bureaus, where most currencies can be converted into Turkish liras (TL). Banks and ATMs are not hard to find all around the city. During banking hours (9am-noon and 1pm-5pm Mon.-Fri.), ensure your safety by using ATMs attached to banks during working hours, so if something goes wrong—like your card being swallowed by the machine—personnel are close by to remedy the situation. As in any big city, ATM scams do occur and are more prevalent after hours and on weekends. Be wary of people loitering near ATMs, and if anyone randomly tries to help you, stop what you are doing immediately—don't touch any keys that might give away your PIN.

COMMUNICATIONS
Mail
To purchase stamps, send letters (under 2 kilograms), or receive telegrams, the main post office close to Sultanahmet is **PTT** (Büyük Postane Cd. 1/25, 0212/511-3818, www.ptt.gov.tr, 8:30am-5pm Mon.-Fri., 10am-3:30pm Sat.), located in Sirkeci between Istanbul Gar (the train station) and the Egyptian Spice Bazaar. Other branches are open shorter hours; check with your hotel for the nearest one.

Internet Access
Aside from providing telephone and fax services, most hotels provide free Wi-Fi for guests either in public areas or throughout the hotel, as do cafés. If you're traveling with a laptop or smartphone, surfing the Internet is as easy as requesting the password *(şifre)* from your host. It's not difficult to browse the Web or video chat once connected. Internet cafés still exist; ask your hotel where the nearest one is located.

EMERGENCY SERVICES
For urgent medical services, dial 112; police, 115; and the fire department, 110. All emergency numbers provide English-speaking staff. If a crime has been committed against your person, such as theft, make a report at the local *karakol* (police station) closest to the incident. The **Turizm Polisi** (Yerebatan Cd. 6, Sultanahmet, 0212/527-4503), located in the yellow Ottoman mansion opposite the Basilica Cistern, is the law enforcement branch for foreigners in Istanbul. Be aware that you might get the runaround when reporting the crime to the correct police station; such are the bureaucracy pains of a large city.

The following private hospitals have English-speaking emergency, inpatient, and outpatient services: **American Hospital** (Güzelbahçe Sokak, Nişantaşı, 0212/311-2000, www.americanhospitalistanbul.org); closer to Taksim and Sultanahmet, the **Universal German Hospital** (Sıraselviler Cd. 119, Taksim, 0212/293-2150, www.universalinternational.org) and the state-run **Taksim First Aid Hospital** (Sıraselviler Cd. 112, Taksim, 0212/252-4300). For the Asian side visit the private **Acıbadem Hospital** (Tekin Sk. 18, Kadıköy, 0216/544-4664, www.acibademinternational.com). All of these facilities are open 24 hours daily, and you can expect first-rate care, equipment, and facilities. Ask about costs and the process of claiming travel insurance upfront.

Getting There

AIR
Atatürk International Airport
Istanbul's **Atatürk International Airport** (IST, 0212/463-3000, www.ataturkairport.com) is in Yeşilköy, about 20 kilometers west of Sultanahmet and 23 kilometers west of Taksim. Turkey's largest air hub and Europe's fifth busiest has two efficient modern terminals: one for international flights, with a level for arrivals and another for departures, and the other for domestic flights. To cope with increasing air traffic, a third airport is planned for near the Black Sea coast, expected to open in 2019.

Visas were once issued at the airport, but now visa applications must be completed online prior to arrival at www.evisa.gov.tr. Luggage carts can be unlocked with a one-lira coin in the baggage claim hall. Currency exchange kiosks are available just past passport control to get some coins before retrieving your luggage. Along with restaurants, cafés, and executive lounges, services like car rentals, a florist, currency exchange kiosks, banks, ATMs, and even a hotel are within the airport's security zone and available to passengers.

There are various options to get into the city. Some hotels provide convenient free transfers for guests who book three or more nights. By far the most convenient solutions to reach any destination in Istanbul are to hail one of the myriad yellow **taxis** (40TL to Sultanahmet, 30 minutes; 50TL to Taksim, 40 minutes) waiting by the passenger loading zone outside the airport terminals, or to board an airport shuttle, such as the Havataş coaches. If your baggage is not excessive, board the **Hafif Metro** (M1A light rail system) in the basement of the international terminal and whiz into town in less than an hour. Transfer to Sultanahmet by changing to the T1 tram bound for Kabataş in Zeytinburnu, or stay on the train until Yenikapı to transfer to the M2 metro for stations along this line to Taksim. For the Asian side, transfer at Yenikapı to the Marmaray line to Üsküdar.

Sabiha Gökçen International Airport

Sabiha Gökçen International Airport (SAW, 0216/588-8000, www.sabihagokcen. aero) is located in the Asian town of Pendik, 43 kilometers southeast of Taksim Square, at least an hour's journey. The airport hosts mostly charter flights by low-cost European and domestic airlines as well as some domestic routes by Turkish Airlines and Pegasus Airlines. Jam-packed around the clock, Istanbul's second airport is a popular departure spot for *Istanbullus* heading out on vacation or business. If you're taking a domestic flight, double-check your departure airport; many travelers have arrived at Atatürk Airport to find that their flight departs from Sabiha Gökçen Airport, 70 kilometers away.

Aside from taxis, there are also Havataş airport shuttles available to Taksim and Kadıköy, and to Sultanahmet with private providers.

Airport Shuttles

The comfortable coaches of **Havataş** (444-2656, www.havatas.com, every 30 minutes 4am-1am daily) airport shuttle services depart from the front of the terminals at Atatürk Airport (10TL, 40 minutes) and Sabiha Gökçen Airport (13TL, 90 minutes) for the ride to Taksim, terminating adjacent to the Divan Hotel on Abdülhak Hamıt Caddesi. Another service departs from Sabiha Gökçen Airport bound for Kadıköy (8TL, 30 minutes). These services do not drop passengers in Sultanahmet; a taxi or public transportation via the F1 Taksim-Kabataş funicular and T1 tram from Kabataş to old Istanbul is required.

Door-to-door airport shuttles are available and can be booked through your hotel or **Istanbul Airport Shuttle** (0212/518-0354, www.istanbulairportshuttle.com, from €20). Double-check its itinerary, though, as you may be the last to be dropped off, and Istanbul traffic can make this a long journey. Also, check with your airline, as some companies provide a shuttle service to tourist districts.

TRAIN

The international ***Bosphorus Express*** departs every night from Istanbul's European side, traveling to Sofia, Bulgaria (€19-28, 12.5 hours) and Bucharest, Romania (€38-56, 20 hours). The return express service to Istanbul from these destinations arrives around 7am every morning. As rail upgrading work continues, check the departure and arrival terminal in Istanbul with the international ticket office (0212/527-0050) inside Istanbul Gar in Sirkeci. Couchette and sleeper supplements are available, and passengers with European InterRail passes (www.interrail.eu) can use this service.

The financial crisis in Greece has led to the cessation of international rail service to Thessaloniki or Athens for the time being. If you're planning a trip across the Greek border, contact the **Turkish State Railways** (444-8233, www.tcdd.gov.tr) to see if service has been restored.

The 533-kilometer high-speed train service to the Turkish capital, Ankara, opened in 2014, reducing the travel time to Ankara (80TL) to three hours, and challenging the airlines and coach companies for convenient travel between the two cities. The service from Ankara terminates at Pendik on the Asia side.

BUS

Bus travel is the easiest, cheapest, and most popular method of travel in Turkey—that is, if a high-speed train is unavailable. Although once outrageously expensive, domestic routes are usually cheaper than airfares, though an airfare sale may make it worthwhile to spend a little extra to save time. There are two major bus stations: **Büyük Istanbul Otogar** (M1A metro stop Otogar in Bayrampaşa) is the enormous main terminal, also referred to as Bayrampaşa or Esenler *otogar* (bus station) 12 kilometers northwest of Sultanahmet; **Harem Otogar** is on the city's Asian side, just south of Üsküdar port. There are also other stations located around the city.

Büyük Istanbul Otogar serves hundreds of small and large companies with thousands of lines, connecting points throughout Turkey, Greece, Bulgaria, and Central and Eastern Europe. Travel with **Ulusoy** (444-1888, www.ulusoy.com.tr), **Varan** (0212/692-9595, www.varan.com.tr), or **Metro Turizm** (444-3455, www.metroturizm.com.tr), some of the largest and most dependable coach companies in Turkey. Bus tickets can be bought via travel agents in touristed areas or from bus company ticket offices scattered around the city. Tickets may include shuttle service to the relevant *otogar* of departure. It may pay to shop around for the best deal. Purchasing coach tickets online is possible but is often problem-prone.

CAR

If you are arriving by car from Ankara, any other Turkish city, or neighboring European countries, you'll find ample road signs, but they are posted very close to the exits or places they indicate. For this reason, it is advisable to stay in the outside lane.

Getting to Istanbul from Europe is simple by following the O-3/E80 Trans-European Motorway (TEM). To reach Istanbul's Asian territories, turn left onto highway O-2 to travel over Fatih Sultan Mehmet Bridge, or continue the TEM to highway O-1 to travel over the Bosphorus Bridge, closest to Üsküdar and Kadıköy. Once in Istanbul, leaving the car in the hotel's parking lot is recommended.

If you plan to drive cross-country, rent a vehicle at the end of your Istanbul stay so you won't have to worry about it while in town. Recommended car rental agencies at Atatürk International Airport include **Avis** (0212/465-3454, www.avis.com.tr); **Hertz** (0212/465-5999, www.hertz.com.tr); **Budget** (0212/465-0240, www.budget.com); and **National** (0212/465-3546, www.nationalcar.com). The main TEM is about seven kilometers north of the airport, meaning you won't need to contend with narrow alleys and traffic downtown.

BOAT

Arriving cruise ships dock at Karaköy's **International Maritime Passenger Terminal** just northeast of where the Bosphorus meets the Golden Horn. The T1 tram's Karaköy stop is a five-minute walk from the port following the shoreline southwest.

The **IDO** (Istanbul Deniz Otobüsleri, 0212/444-4436, www.ido.com.tr) car ferries and fast passenger boats crossing the Sea of Marmara from Bandırma (2 hours), Yalova (75 minutes), and Bursa (95 minutes) arrive at Yenikapı on the European shore near Sultanahmet. From there, take the Marmaray train into Sirkeci and the Asian side; the M1A Hafif metro to Atatürk Airport; the M2 metro via Taksim Square; or a taxi. IDO fast ferry services from Yalova to Pendik (45 minutes) and Bostancı (65 minutes) are also available.

Getting Around

If it weren't for its manic traffic, Istanbul would be idyllic. But what has become one of the largest cities in the world, with an estimated 17 million residents, is also one of the worst when it comes to commuting in a private vehicle. In the future, a third bridge will hopefully relieve some of the stress caused by vehicular traffic, but recent projects like the sinking of Taksim Square and the Marmaray have done little to curb congestion. Do as most locals do and opt for walking and public transportation.

Every time you access a tram, funicular, metro train, or Bosphorus ferry, you need to buy a *jeton* (token) for 4TL pp per journey from the ticket machines near your point of departure. Fares to and from the Princes' Islands are higher, and cash fares and *jetons* are not accepted on municipal buses—only an **IstanbulKart** will buy you a seat. Significant discounts are in reach when you purchase an IstanbulKart from confectionary kiosks near tram and metro stations and selected bus stops. Pay a nonrefundable 10TL for the card and then add value at the kiosks when needed. With an IstanbulKart the fare per person is reduced to 2.15TL. One card is good for up to five people. If you plan to use public transit a lot, it is a solid investment. Simply swipe the card, once per person, at the turnstiles. For more information about public transportation in Istanbul, visit **Istanbul Ulasim** (www.istanbul-ulasim.com.tr) for metro, light rail, trams and funicular information, and **IETT** (www.iett.gov.tr) for municipal buses.

TRAMWAY

Istanbul's tramways are an asset for visitors: the main T1 tram zips from Kabataş along the Bosphorus through Karaköy, crossing the Galata Bridge to Eminönü and Sirkeci, where connections to the Marmaray are possible. Once in Sirkeci it climbs the hill into Sultanahmet, following Divan Yolu into Beyazıt—the stop for the Grand Bazaar—then through Aksaray, followed by the city walls to Topkapı (for transfer to the T4 tram that passes Edirnekapı for Chora Museum and on to Mescid-I Selam). The T1 tram snakes along to Zeytinburnu—the interchange for the M1A Hafif metro to Atatürk Airport—to finally reach its last stop of Bağcılar. The service is supposed to run every two minutes, 6am-midnight daily, but the arrival times are haphazard. Sometimes they're more frequent, sometimes less.

The Taksim-Tünel **Nostalgic Tramway** noisily clatters the length of Istiklal Caddesi every 10 minutes, from Taksim Square to the entrance of the funicular station at Tünel. The T3 tram (7am-9pm daily) loops through the shopping strip of Bahariye and the enclave of Moda, from the port of Kadıköy on the Asian side every 10 minutes, taking about 20 minutes to do the full loop.

FUNICULAR

Two funiculars climb the steep hill either end of Istiklal Caddesi. Tünel, the second-oldest of its kind in Europe, saves passengers the steep climb from Karaköy through the backstreets of Galata en route to Tünel. It runs about every five minutes 6am-10pm daily. The second and newer funicular (F1, 6am-midnight), built in 2005, bypasses the hectic traffic from Kabataş to Taksim Square every three minutes with an underground ride that takes less than three minutes.

METRO AND LIGHT RAIL

Istanbul's main metro, **M2,** runs every four minutes 6:15am-midnight daily from Yenikapı, on the Marmara coast, through to Taksim Square, Şişli, and Levent (a haven for shopping malls) before terminating at Seyrantepe near the Black Sea in 35 minutes.

The light-rail system, called **Hafif Metro**

(M1A), links Yenikapı with the Büyük Istanbul Otogar, before later terminating at Atatürk International Airport every five minutes 6am-midnight daily.

MARMARAY

The full 76.3 kilometer, 104-minute Marmaray rail line from Halkalı on the European side to Asia's Gebze train station is due to be completed in 2015. The first stage of the project, between Yenikapı and Ayrılık Çeşmesi, which included a 1.4-kilometer tunnel 55 meters below the Bosphorus, was delayed significantly due to the discovery of marine artifacts, shipwrecks, and jewelry, now displayed in the Istanbul Archaeology Museums. The section that was due to open in 2009 finally opened to much fanfare in 2013 to coincide with the 90th anniversary of Republic Day. The **Marmaray** (www.tcdd.gov.tr) cuts the 25-minute ferry journey between Asia and Europe down to just four minutes between Sirkeci and Üsküdar (though nothing can beat the Bosphorus breeze and the view of Istanbul's peninsula, which is why many *Istanbullus* continue to use the ferries). The fare on the Marmaray is the same as for the trams, trains, and ferries (4TL pp, 2.15TL with an IstanbulKart).

BOAT

The ferries that zigzag the Bosphorus and travel to the Princes' Islands are operated by **IDO** (0212/444-4436, www.ido.com) and **Şehir Hatları** (0212/444-1851, www.sehirhatlari.com.tr), with the latter serving ports along the Golden Horn. This mode of transportation is pleasant, particularly sitting atop the deck sipping *çay* and feeding seagulls pieces of *simit* purchased onboard. The main docks are situated in Eminönü, Karaköy, Kabataş, and Beşiktaş on the European side, and Üsküdar and Kadıköy on the Asian side. For an updated list of routes and schedules, check the websites or pick up a timetable at any of the ports listed. Take note of the last ferry back from Asia; otherwise it's a *dolmuş* or a pricey taxi ride back to Europe.

Fast boats by IDO, known as *hızlı feribot*, are catamarans that traverse the longer routes among Kadıköy and Bakırköy, Bostancı, Princes' Island, and Kabataş, in addition to a few others, for extra cost.

MUNICIPAL BUS

Istanbul's public bus system is extremely reliable and inexpensive, but most visitors don't use them simply because the tram, funicular, ferries, and metro services take

Haydarpaşa Train Station and ferry

you where you need to go. Bus routes and schedules are available online at www.iett.gov.tr; busy routes run on average every 15 minutes. The main stations used by visitors are Eminönü, adjacent to the Galata Bridge; below Taksim Square; and by the ports of Kabataş, Üsküdar, and Kadıköy.

Istanbul also has a **Metrobus** (www.iett.gov.tr) system that shuttles 700,000 locals daily via an express lane highway, but this crowded, often unpleasant mode of transportation is away from tourist attractions and unlikely to be used by travelers.

DOLMUŞ

Like the municipal buses, *dolmuşlar* are rarely used by visitors, but on occasion those who like to get off the beaten track will find these a good way to get around. The hubs of Taksim, Aksaray, Üsküdar, and Kadıköy have several *dolmuş* services that crisscross the city through a defined route at a set price (generally 2-5.50TL one-way). The *dolmuş* (literally meaning "stuffed") used to be a classic ride in a vintage car, but nowadays they are lackluster yellow minibuses with the destinations posted on the side windows. These minibuses become convenient after at 11pm when the IDO ferries between Europe and Asia stop running.

TAXI

Taxi services are popular and inexpensive in Istanbul compared to other world cities. These yellow vehicles, which have a 24-hour base fare of 2.95TL, with 1.70-1.90TL added for every kilometer thereafter, are everywhere. Delays in traffic and toll roads will add to the fare.

Most cabbies are decent individuals, but quite a few will cheat visitors. If asking for a taxi to Topkapı Palace, make sure it's the palace and not the neighborhood, a costly detour and a successful stunt pulled by a few cunning drivers. Others will claim *çok* (lots of) traffic to give you the classic scenic route through the city that adds to your fare. Avoid taxis waiting along the tramlines of Sultanahmet or near five-star hotels; they're dying to take you the long way. Ask your hotel what the likely fare would be so you can politely challenge a driver if you're overcharged. Hotels and restaurant will gladly call taxis for you, using reliable companies. That said, some budding entrepreneurs will suggest a private transfer to get you back to your hotel to get a commission. One taxi for four people should set you back about 20TL between Taksim and Sultanahmet. If the cost of the minibus is more than this, don't be afraid to decline the offer. Finally, a friendly *merhaba* or *selam* (hello) when you get in the taxi may help with international relations and customer service. Cabbies do not expect gratuities, but locals typically round off the fare to the next lira.

CAR

Driving through Istanbul is a nightmare; parking is even worse. If you must, take a deep breath and prepare for hectic traffic, double- or triple-parking, constant honking that mean anything from "hello" to "get out of my way," angry drivers, and gas prices three times higher than back home.

Avoid rush hour traffic in and around Istanbul, 7am-9am and 3pm-8pm Monday-Friday, and Sunday afternoons, unless sitting in the car for hours is on your itinerary. Street signs and road rules exist but are taken as mere suggestions that often go unheeded. Some streets are one-way, with alternates going in the opposite direction. But even those are fair game. If you get caught bumper-to-bumper with an oncoming vehicle, be the wise one and back up. Bus drivers pull out into lanes without checking their rearview mirrors. Expect the unexpected and leave more than ample distance between vehicles. Crosswalks are never places to stop unless you want to bear the wrath of car horns.

If you do arrive to the city with a vehicle, consider parking it in the hotel's underground lot or a municipal parking facility for a small fee. Generally staffed by an attendant hired by the municipality, street parking is inexpensive, as little as 3TL per hour up to 20TL for a 24-hour period.

Thrace and the Sea of Marmara

Marmara Denizi
  (Sea of Marmara) 120
Edirne 140

Gelibolu Yarımadası
  (Gallipoli Peninsula) 147

After an eyeful of Istanbul, many visitors head for the irresistible golden sands of southwestern Anatolia, but few visit the farther reaches of the Marmara Denizi (Sea of Marmara) or north into Trakya (Thrace). What they miss is the area's unique mix of Balkan and Greek origins, a trove of stunning early Ottoman architecture, and a string of fishing villages that have barely changed over the centuries.

The Sea of Marmara is bounded on the north by Thrace and on the south by northwestern Anatolia. Its western reaches bottleneck into the strategic Dardanelles Strait, the maritime channel where Alexander the Great conquered the Persians in the 4th century BC. On Thrace's craggy southwestern tip, Gelibolu Yarımadası (Gallipoli Peninsula), a lush national park, commemorates the thousands of Australian, New Zealand, and other Allied troops and Ottoman troops who lost their lives in the bloody conflict here during World War I. To the east, the Sea of Marmara flows between low coastal crags into the Bosphorus Straits.

Thrace is bordered by Greece and Bulgaria and by the Black, Aegean, and Marmara Seas. Fields of sunflowers—cultivated mostly for their oil—bloom into an endless yellow blanket in summer. The pine forests that once cloaked Thrace's southern flank have given way to the more lucrative real-estate industry. The Ottoman capital of Edirne is the main highlight of Thrace. It's also its largest city, a living museum of sorts, with pristinely preserved Ottoman bridges, mosques, and caravanserais. Aside from Selimiye Camii (Selimiye Mosque)—considered to be Ottoman master architect Mimar Sinan's greatest feat—Kırkpınar Yağı Güreşleri (Kırkpınar Oil Wrestling Festival) remains Edirne's tourism draw, attracting thousands of visitors annually. Edirne also makes for a quick getaway into neighboring Greece, Bulgaria, or Eastern Europe.

The southern edge of this area is noted for its thermal activity and some less-than-stellar beaches packed in summer with Istanbul's middle class. The bucolic countryside unfurls along a series of hills that

Previous: Bursa's coastline; Yeşil Türbe, tomb of Sultan Mehmet I. **Above:** the Green Mosque in Iznik.

Highlights

★ **Yeşil Cami (Green Mosque):** Take a day trip to Bursa to bask in the beauty of the Green Mosque, an early-Ottoman architectural gem. The best time to visit is June, when silk merchants flock en masse to the former Ottoman capital's impressive bazaar (page 121).

★ **Çekirge:** Reduce stress sultan-style in the tepid effervescence of these thermal baths, made famous by the Romans (page 128).

★ **Iznik Şehir Surları (City Walls):** Climb Iznik's 1,900-year-old city ramparts, near the town's majestic Istanbul Gate, and view the sleepy lake just to the west of the walls (page 135).

★ **Selimiye Camii (Selimiye Mosque):** Architecture devotees will fall in love with Selim's Mosque, considered Mimar Sinan's pious masterpiece (page 140).

★ **Kırkpınar Yağı Güreşleri (Kırkpınar Oil Wrestling Festival):** In this centuries-old annual Oil Wrestling Festival, men wrestle to win the golden belt (page 143).

★ **Gelibolu Yarımadası Tarihi Milli Parkı (Gallipoli National Park):** Pay homage to the tens of thousands of fallen heroes who gave their lives over the strategic Dardanelles during World War II (page 147).

Look for ★ to find recommended sights, activities, dining, and lodging.

give way to Bursa. Another of the Ottomans' erstwhile capitals, Bursa is now a progressive city teeming with industry and artists. Iznik is a sleepy lake town where organized Christianity essentially got under way and the art of intricate faience was mastered. To the west, Kuş Gölü is a popular rest stop for graceful flamingos and hundreds of other migratory bird species. The southern region's back roads, with their prolific agriculture and abundant heritage, offer a glimpse of the Anatolian richness that awaits the traveler deeper into the countryside.

This region is a delight for foodies. A trip to Bursa isn't be complete without lunching on its famed Iskender Kebab—slices of tender lamb drenched in tomato sauce and melted butter—or a juicy peach come July. Fried liver is also popular in Edirne and northwest of Istanbul. Bounded by the warmer waters of the Sea of Marmara, fishing villages like Eceabat boast delicate fish like gilthead bream and red mullet.

Thrace and the Sea of Marmara regions provide a stunning array of destinations close to Istanbul, and unique history for travelers to discover.

PLANNING YOUR TIME

Visiting each of the destinations along the Sea of Marmara and Thrace can be easily completed in one- or two-day trips from Istanbul, with late spring and early fall the best time to visit.

The climate of the Sea of Marmara and Thrace is quite seasonal. Winters can be bitterly cold, with storms thrashing the western coast of the Gallipoli Peninsula, often making boat transportation impossible. On Uludağ, near Bursa, snow on the mountain lures domestic travelers for skiing holidays from December to April. Summers can be torrid, but not as unpleasant as the broiling heat of the southern Aegean or Mediterranean coasts. Making the trip more worthwhile in summer are the massive sunflower meadows, providing a splash of yellow in the agricultural landscape where, come winter, goatherds steer their charges over a land left bare by the tobacco and wheat harvests.

Other than Edirne's Kırkpınar Oil Wrestling Festival (July) and Anzac Day (April 25) at Gallipoli, this territory remains somewhat undisturbed by tourism, making these side trips a great way to get to know Turkish culture.

Marmara Denizi (Sea of Marmara)

Extending west from its easternmost Bay of Izmit, the Sea of Marmara is sprinkled with hidden natural delights and relics spanning several millennia. Known as Propontis in antiquity, the Sea of Marmara separates the Aegean Sea and the Bosphorus that leads to the Black Sea. The once fertile plains just beyond the low verdant crags that separate Marmara's southern coast have given way to the nation's industrial backbone, thanks to the area's proximity to Istanbul. It has become one of Eastern Europe's manufacturing powerhouses, primarily in the automotive sector. But agriculture remains the focus of this area, with both independent farmers and food processing giants. Olives are still the region's most prominent product. Also of note are the natural Thelasso therapies at Termal or Çekirge and the region's attractive tributes to the empires of bygone eras that once that ruled these lush mountainous lands. This western tip of Anatolia mirrors the boundless pleasures to be found inland.

BURSA

Bursa is synonymous with affluence. Its modern periphery sprawls from the fertile slopes of Uludağ (Great Mountain) to incorporate an industrial center. It was once nicknamed *yeşil* (green) Bursa, but more than three decades of industrialization and growth have replaced a good portion of the fields and woods that inspired that moniker. Its insatiable appetite for labor continues to beckon migrant workers from rural and eastern Anatolia by the busload. With a growing population of 1.7 million, Bursa is one of the country's largest cities. However, unlike Istanbul and Ankara, it is not frenzied and disorderly. In fact, the noted spa hamlet of Çekirge and the ski resort of Uludağ inspire relaxation. Home to a bevy of artists, from silk weavers to painters and singers, Bursa is known for its progressive liberalism, which stands out in Turkey's increasingly conservative climate.

Bursa was once an important stop on the Silk Road. But it really wasn't until the arrival of the Romans that the therapeutic powers of its indigenous hot springs in Çekirge were exploited. Roman emperors constructed edifices and attractive marble bathhouses around the springs. Later, the Byzantines introduced silk production. In 1326, Osman Bey—after whom the Osmanlı (Ottoman) Empire was founded—conquered the city. This crucial event transformed the semi-itinerant Osman tribe into what would become the imperial Ottoman dynasty. Unquenched, Osman Bey's son, Orhan Gazı, set his sights on the west while lavishing his capital, Bursa, with the spoils of war. The city's trade flourished; the budding empire minted its first coins; and imperial silk production rose to an all-time high. During the 17th century, Bursa became renowned for carriage-making; the industry continues today with more modern vehicle production by Oyak-Renault. Both Coca-Cola and PepsiCo headline Bursa's food and beverage producers.

Despite its modern factories, Bursa has many historic architectural relics, from mosques to the Byzantine baths. Other notable delights include *kestane şekeri* (candied chestnut sweets) and perhaps the world's best peaches, available in summer.

While most tours breeze through in one long afternoon, Bursa deserves a couple of days. Earmark a full day to leisurely sightsee, haggle for silk in the old bazaar, attend a local Karagöz-Hacivat puppet show, and relax in Çekirge's hot springs. Top it off with a ride in the cable car that zips up to Uludağ for a bird's-eye view of Bursa's magnificent landscape. Avoid day trips to Bursa on Monday, when most museums are closed. More information about Bursa can be found in English at www.bursa.com.tr.

Sights

As is the case throughout Turkey, all mosques are open daily except at prayer times. Entry is free, but donations are advised. Most museums are open 8:30am-12:30 and 1:30pm-5:30pm Tuesday-Sunday.

★ YEŞİL CAMİ (GREEN MOSQUE)

Yeşil Cami (Yeşil Cd., off Atatürk Cd., Yıldırım, free) is one of the country's more ornate mosques, set in the Ottoman dynasty's early Çelebi Mehmed Social Complex. Commissioned in 1412 by Mehmet I (also known as Çelebi Mehmed), the emerald building was the foundation of Ottoman architecture. Its showy white carved marble entrance and the vibrant color throughout proved that a mosque could be both architecturally daring and a bona fide religious sanctuary—a far cry from the atonal and austere Persian and Selçuk styles of architecture that previously seen throughout Anatolia. Aside from its architectural significance, Yeşil Cami also glorifies Mehmet I's triumph in a decade-long power struggle with his brothers after the death of their father, Beyazıt I.

Moving beyond the elaborate archway, a mammoth 14-meter-high niche in the wall, called a *mihrab*, points to Mecca. Just past and above the entrance is the ornately tiled sultan's **Imperial Loge,** a private suite that's closed to the public. The building is named after the green faience located throughout the space. The free use of ceramics was a new trend, which became all the rage in later religious monuments and propelled Iznik tile mastery to the cultural forefront.

Opposite, the **Yeşil Türbe** (Green Tomb) holds the remains of Mehmet I, completed just 40 days before he died. Most visitors to Bursa

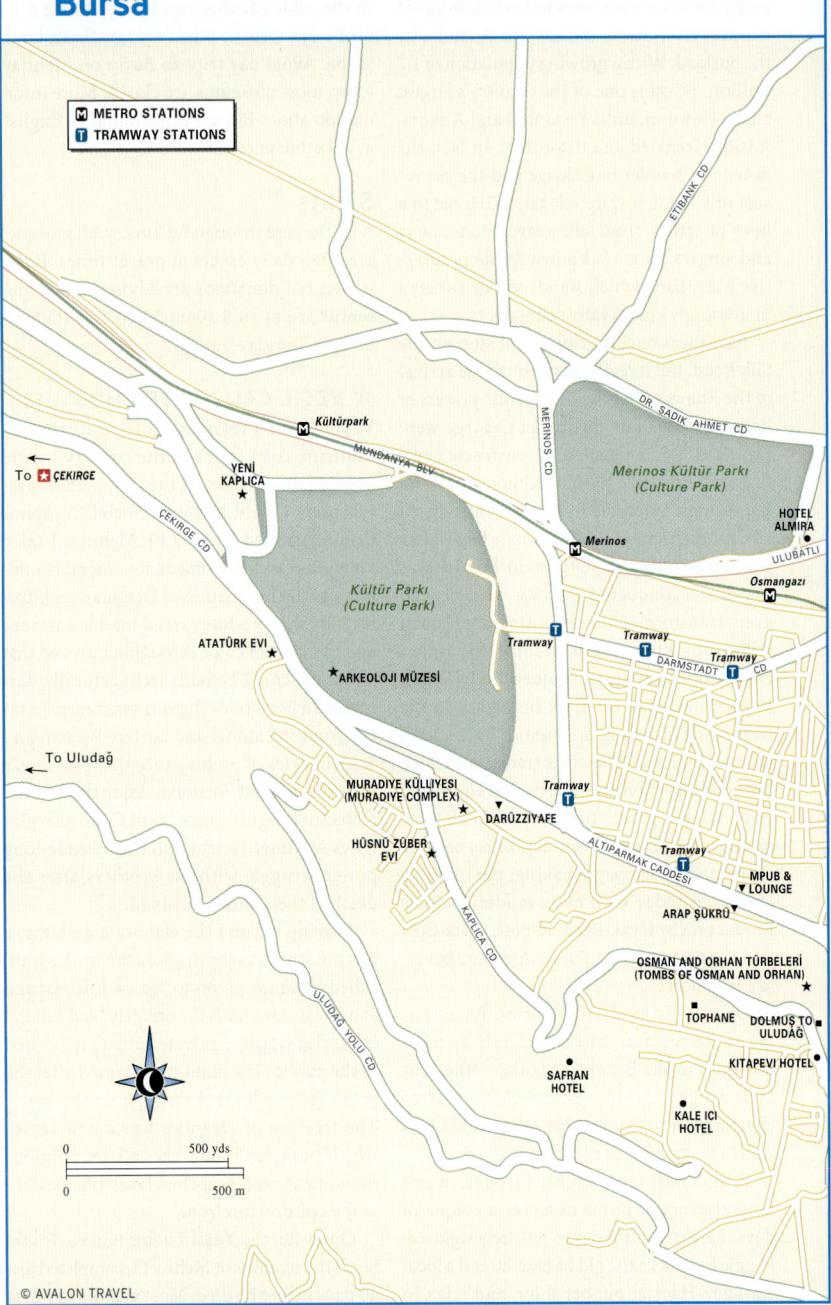

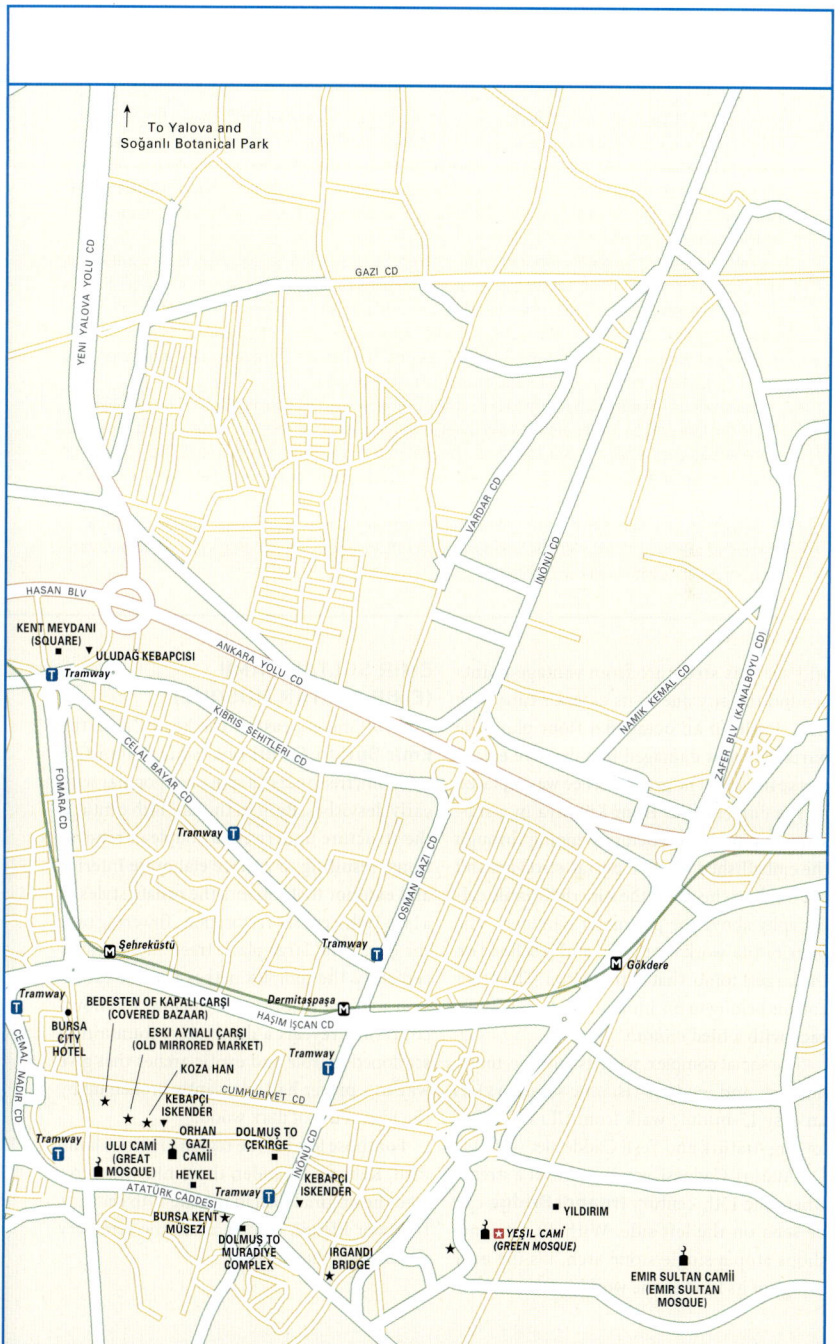

Birds of Paradise

Küş Gölü (Bird Lake, also called Manyas Lake), just 16 kilometers south of Bandırma on the Bandırma-Balikesir Highway, is the richest habitat for local and migratory birds in Turkey. Some 239 species feed, rest, and breed here in May-June on their way to Europe and in September-October on their return to warmer climes in Africa. Declared a conservation area in 1959, the 64-hectare **Kuşcenneti Milli Parkı** (Bird Paradise National Park, 7am-5:30pm, 4TL), adjoining Bird Lake, is a veritable ornithological heaven come spring and fall.

Hundreds of graceful posers, including tufted herons, large spoonbills, glossy ibis, black cormorants, and leggy storks nest in the willow copses along the banks of the lake. Observation towers allow a close look at some rare species. Endangered yellow-beaked Dalmatian pelicans gather by the dozen on specially built platforms in May-June. The lake provides the birds with plenty of fish, particularly in spring when the placid waters teem with 23 species. The habitat, comprising rich vegetation that grows on bird droppings, is ideal for the growth of insect larvae.

Most species of large birds return to the same nesting sites, often conveniently utilizing last year's. While the lake and its levees are typically quiet, arguments over territory do arise among the birds. Once settled, they repair any damage caused by winter storms and move in to lay and hatch their eggs in tandem. Moorhens, ducks, coots, and geese nest in reeds and rushes, while egrets, night and purple herons, glossy ibis, and pelicans arrive in early March to nest on higher platforms.

Despite its small size, Kuşcenneti's unique natural features, observation towers, lakeside restaurants, and picnic areas are an excellent destination for bird aficionados visiting Bursa and the northwestern coast of Anatolia with their own vehicles.

---

will see this structure from vantage points around the city due to its exterior turquoise tiles. Built on an octagonal floor plan, the burial site was damaged in a massive earthquake in 1855. The green faience was replaced by the current tiles from Kütahya in a subsequent renovation. Before stepping through the embellished wooden portal, stroll around the tomb to check out the superb Koranic calligraphy above the perimeter windows. The interior tile-work is original and is echoed on the largest tomb, that of the sultan. The other coffins belong to his immediate descendants, each with a tiled *mihrab*.

The social complex, with its mosque, tomb, hamam, and *medrese* (Islamic seminary), is an easy 15-minute walk from Ulu Cami following Atatürk and Yeşil Caddesiler (streets). On Atatürk Caddesi, you'll pass over a stream where the 15th-century **Irgandi Bridge** can be seen on the left side. With 30 artisanal shops atop a single stone arch, it's the only bridge of its kind in the world.

EMIR SULTAN CAMII (EMIR SULTAN MOSQUE)

Just 700 meters east of the Yeşil Cami, the **Emir Sultan Camii** (via Emir Sultan Cd. Yıldırım, free) marks a spot once popular with early dervishes. Built in the late 14th century, the structure underwent a couple of renovations, resulting in a more elaborate interior and exterior that mirrors the ornate styles of a late-19th-century restoration. Towering over the city, amid large plane trees and a nearby cemetery, the complex makes a serene excursion with views of the city below. Its showy courtyard reveals a diminutive fountain of scalloped marble and exotic arches that give way to a prayer hall, pleasantly broken up by the liberal use of dark wood.

For those fond of the region's famous lamb dish, Kebapçı Iskender, the genius who created the original dish in the late 19th century, Iskender Efendi, is interred in the cemetery just outside the mosque.

MUSEUMS

The **Türk Islam Eserleri Müzesi** (Turkish and Islamic Arts Museum, Yeşil Cd., Yıldırım, 0224/327-7679, 8:30am-12:30 and 1:30pm-5:30pm Tues.-Sun., free), housed in the 15th-century *medrese* of the Çelebi Mehmed Social Complex, is in need of a little upkeep but contains a small collection of Iznik ceramics, manuscripts, Karagöz puppets, and dervish artifacts.

The ultramodern **Bursa Kent Müzesi** (Bursa City Museum, Kent Square, 0224/220-2626, 9:30am-5:30pm Tues.-Sun., 1.50TL with BuKart, purchased on-site) is housed in Bursa's old courthouse. Three floors depict the city's 7,000-year history, along with that of its conquering warlords on the ground floor; the upper floor details Bursa's recent history and its artists. The reconstruction of more than a dozen handicraft workshops and a short history of the area's silk production industry can be found in the basement. The information panels are entirely in Turkish, and an English guidebook provided at the front door does little to fill the gap, so visit with a Turkish speaker or just take in the interesting exhibits.

ULU CAMI (GREAT MOSQUE)

The **Ulu Cami** (Atatürk Cd., free), commissioned by Beyazıt I in 1396, serves as a beacon to the faithful. It rises as an immense rectangular brick heap, crafted from stone quarried from nearby Uludağ. It is topped by 20 domes and a massive solitary minaret. An example of Selçuk architecture, square columns support the mosque's domed roof and break the vastness of the interior hall. The interesting burbling **şardivan** (a fountain for ritual cleansing), smack in the hall's center, adds a little serenity to the ambiance. Recently added, the domed glass above allows much needed light to penetrate the otherwise dark sanctuary. The *minbar* (pulpit) is elegantly carved out of walnut and exemplifies the artistry of early Ottoman woodcrafters.

BURSA BAZAAR

Just north of Atatürk Caddesi in Osmangazi, central Bursa is a beguiling centuries-old beehive of trade. Unlike Istanbul's version, **Bursa Bazaar** (9am-7pm daily) is airy, with plenty of *hans* (inns) doubling as open tea gardens that offer ample opportunities to relax. The bazaar is on the doorstep of Ulu Cami and is bounded by Cemal Nadir Caddesi to the west; the pedestrianized Cumhuriyet Caddesi to the north; and İnönü Caddesi to the east.

Emir Han, established in 1336, is the first structure you come to, just north of Ulu Cami.

the roofs of Bursa's historic bazaar

Today, it offers an arena to discuss politics over tea by a burbling fountain surrounded by palm trees, firs, Islamic bookshops, and gold jewelers. Centuries ago, caravans traveling the Silk Road stopped here. The camels brayed in the courtyard as trade was conducted with the locals. First, the *han* peddled **kepenek** (felt coats for shepherds), but later spices and food were the mainstays; in the 20th century, textiles and weaving took over before the merchants of today moved in. Just east is **Eski Aynalı Çarşı** (Old Mirrored Market). Prior to welcoming trade, it served as the first Turkish bath built by the Ottomans, called the Orhan Gazı Hamamı. Constructed in 1339, today it's a covered passage where you'll find the master puppeteer Şinasi Çelikkol's **Karagöz Antiques** (www.karagozshop.com). His store is overflowing with Bursa's famed colorful translucent Karagöz and Hacıvat shadow puppets, generally made from leather or camel hide. If Şinasi is in the shop, he'll gladly put on a mini show so you can see the material of this 700-year-old art form come to life. **Koza Han** (Cocoon Market) is a five-centuries-old two-story brick building crested with a series of chimneys. Built by Beyazıt II, this trading structure was beautifully revamped thanks to the Aga Khan Foundation in 1985. Encompassing a large courtyard shaded by plane trees is the octagonal **Beyazıt II Mosque.** Farmers of old gathered annually to peddle the silk cocoons that brought Bursa its textile fame. Today's world-famous Bursa *ipek* (silk) is sold in the finished form, mostly on this *han*'s second floor. Farther east, the **Çiçek Pazarı** (Flower Market) is a fragrant spectral spray of blooms whose final scent leads through to the **Tuz Pazarı** (Salt Market), on the right side. Across İnönü Caddesi is the **Demirciler Çarşısı** (blacksmiths bazaar), where welders still practice their trade.

Wander back toward Ulu Cami to explore the **Kapalı Çarşı** (Covered Market), a labyrinthine vaulted market geared toward local needs rather than visitors. This translates to lower prices and a good opportunity to try haggling. If you're interested in purchasing anything, ask if shipping can be arranged rather than schlepping it home in a suitcase.

At the center of the covered bazaar is the market's oldest structure—the 14th-century ***bedesten*** (marketplace). Built by Beyazıt I, it was partly leveled during the 1885 earthquake and by fire seven decades later. Rebuilt each time, it's known today as the **Kuyumcular Çarşısı** (Jewelers Market), where lines of modern shops sell gold.

ORHAN GAZI CAMII (ORHAN GAZI MOSQUE)

Abutting the Koza Han to the south, **Orhan Gazı Camii** (Atatürk Cd., free) was commissioned in 1339 by the warlord of the same name. Instead of the traditional square floor plan, this sanctuary retained the T-shaped structure of the *zaviye* (dervish hall) it replaced. Despite the natural calamities that befell this mosque, various restructuring efforts have maintained the original layout, with cubicles lining the main prayer hall.

OSMAN AND ORHAN TÜRBELERI (TOMBS OF OSMAN AND ORHAN)

The remains of a *hısar* (fortress)—also referred to as Tophane—mark Bursa's oldest relic, overlooking Cemal Nadir Caddesi. Dating back to Roman Prusa, the last vestige of a thick city wall, surrounding what was once an acropolis, is still visible. The arrival of the Ottomans signaled Bursa's expansion into the valley, with the hillside of more upscale architecture including the few remaining *konaklar* (residences) that grace this lofty part of town.

Climbing Osman Gazı Caddesi, turn right into the Timurtaş Paşa Park to access the side-by-side **Osman and Orhan Türbeleri,** the tombs of father and son Osman Bey and Orhan Gazı Osman, who took most of Anatolia and Thrace from the Byzantines and founded the Ottoman Empire. The beautiful baroque structures that house the tombs were Sultan Abdülaziz's contribution to his forebears, after the earthquake of 1855 leveled the original building. The path dividing the two tombs leads to one of three 19th-century **clock towers** that once doubled as fire watch towers. The peaceful park is filled with tea gardens with outstanding views of the bazaar rooftops set against a backdrop of the Yeşil Türbesi and Uladağ in the distance.

MURADIYE KÜLLIYESI (MURADIYE COMPLEX)

At the western end of central Bursa, **Muradiye Külliyesi** (II Murat Cd., off Kaplıca Cd., Muradiye), a theological complex, marks the last imperial structure to grace Bursa. Built in 1426 for Sultan Murat II, the mosque, with its burst of color and intricate *mihrab,* is reminiscent of Yeşil Cami on the city's opposite hill. The old seminary on the grounds doubles as a cancer research center today, and the original poorhouse and kitchens are now the Darüzziyafe restaurant, which serves exceptional Ottoman cuisine. Murat II was the son of Yeşil Cami's Mehmet I and father of Mehmet II, the conqueror of Istanbul.

Situated behind the mosque in a fragrant rose garden is a burial ground with 12 tombs, the largest that of **Sultan Murat II.** Interestingly, he requested that his mausoleum remain open so that the rain, prevalent in the region, would fall on his tomb—perhaps as regular ablutions in an eternal state of piety. His sons, slain by their stronger brother in a struggle for the throne, are also buried here. Alongside them are tombs of imperial descendants who suffered similar fates decades later. Unlike other Islamic chieftains, the heir to the Ottoman dynasty was not designated before a sultan's death, making the position fair game for any of the many able-bodied male progeny who from the crowded harem. Son of Beyazıt II, Sultan Selim, a.k.a. "The Grim," is a prime example of the brutality among the heirs. The remains of his older brother are interred in the **Şehzade Ahmet Türbesi.** The bloody sultan insured his supremacy by killing three of his own sons, another brother, and a half a dozen nephews.

Back out on Murat Caddesi, west of the mosque is **Ulumay Museum** (0224/221-3542, 8:30am-12:30 and 1:30pm-5:30pm Tues.-Sun., 5TL), which displays various costumes and jewelry from the Ottoman period inside the Ahmet Paşa Medrese. The information is in Turkish, but essentially the first word in the display is the city of origin for the costume. Just up from the costume museum toward the main drag, the **Osmanlı Evi Müzesi** (Ottoman House Museum, entrance off the

Silk cocoons were once traded at Koza Han (Cocoon Market).

side street, 0224/222-0868, 8am-noon and 1pm-5pm Tues.-Sun., free) is believed to be the former mansion of Sultan Murat II and allows visitors to see the interior of a humble 17th-century Ottoman mansion. All the museums in the complex are closed Monday.

Along Kaplıca Caddesi is the Murat II hamam, and one street back from the main road is the living museum of **Hüsnü Züber Evi** (Hüsnü Züber House, 0224/221-3542, 10am-noon and 1pm-5pm Tues.-Sun., free). This authentic 1836 *konak* (residence) was painstakingly restored by local woodwork and sketch artist Hüsnü Züber in 1988 to display his works. Turkish-speaking staff will escort you around the house to show you the humble living areas upstairs and Hüsnü's woodwork and sketches downstairs, which include a large collection of ornate wooden spoons amassed from various regions in Anatolia.

AROUND KÜLTÜR PARKI (CULTURE PARK)

Northwest of the Muradiye Complex and set amid the tea gardens and playgrounds of the expansive **Kültür Parkı** (Çekirge Cd.), the **Arkeoloji Müzesi** (Archaeological Museum, 0224/334-4918, 8:30am-12:30 and 1:30pm-5:30pm Tues.-Sun., 5TL) boasts a fine collection of Byzantine and Roman stone relics, such as sarcophagi and statues found locally, as well as glassware and jewelry collected throughout Anatolia.

Amid immaculately landscaped gardens, the **Atatürk Evi** (Atatürk House, Çekirge Cd., 0224/334-7716, 8:30am-12:30 and 1:30pm-5:30pm Tues.-Sun., free) was the home of the father of modern Turkey during his 13 visits to Bursa. Built in 1895, the residence offers a glimpse of the statesman's inner sanctum, replete with personal effects on two of the three floors open to the public.

Bursa has abundant natural hot springs, making it an ideal place to partake in the bathing ritual of a hamam. One of the most popular local baths is **Yeni Kaplıca** (New Thermal Spring, Eski Mudanya Cd., 0224/236-6955, 6am-10pm daily, 60TL for full scrub and massage), with a series of three bathhouses. They're not touristy at all—in fact, staff do not speak English, and most clients are Turkish, so expect an awkward moment or two being the only *yabancı* (foreigner) in the bath. The men's and family hamams, with their ornate domes, date back to Byzantine emperor Justinian I, but the lackluster women's bath, essentially an uninspiring four-wall structure out back, is more recent. The hot spring temperature in all baths is 45°C, said to help with ailments like rheumatism. Despite their purported natural healing qualities, only go if you can use the male baths, and get the full package; for women, head to Cekirge's Eski Kaplıca for a nicer experience. You could also save yourself 15TL by bringing soap and a *kese* (scrubbing glove) from the market; otherwise you'll need to buy these here at higher prices. Disposable underpants are also provided, but bring your own if crumpled medical wear is not your thing. You'll see the domes of Yeni Kaplıca from the platform of the Kültürpark BursaRay metro stop. From there, it's a five-minute walk across a park.

★ ÇEKIRGE

About five kilometers west of Bursa's center, **Çekirge** sprawls along a foothill of lush Uludağ with upscale old residences and hotels that feature in-house thermal baths that date back to Roman times.

Built by Byzantine Emperor Justinian I and his wife, Theodora, in the mid-6th century, **Eski Kaplıca** (Old Baths, Eski Kaplıca Sk., 0224/233-9300, 7:30am-10pm daily, 30TL women, 35TL men) is a grand marble structure where people seeking the thermal baths' therapeutic benefits while away the hours. It was renovated by the adjacent Kervansaray Termal Otel, conveniently connected by a modern walkway. The Old Baths feature separate opalescent marble pools for men and women, hamams, and adjacent cool pools. The hamam treatment with scrub, soap lather, and wash is 15TL extra.

Located just up the hill from the Old

Karagöz-Hacıvat: Turkey's Beloved Shadow Puppets

Popularized by the Ottomans, Karagöz (Black-Eye) and Hacıvat represent the class struggle still present in modern Turkey. Often deceitful and lewd, Karagöz personifies the uneducated public, while Hacıvat epitomizes the cultivated few through his refined Ottoman-Turkish speech. The fun is that Karagöz's street smarts always trumps Hacıvat's learning, although the former's harebrained schemes always backfire.

The origin of this famed duo is unclear. The 17th-century travel and cultural essayist Evliya Çelebi believed that the puppets memorialize ironworker Kambur Bâli Çelebi (Karagöz) and the master mason Halil Hacı İvaz (Hacıvat). The two worked side-by-side during the construction of Ulu Cami during the reign of Sultan Orhan (1324-1362), often bantering so humorously that hundreds of employees stopped work to listen. Construction slowed to a halt, so angering the sultan that he ordered the duo executed. The sultan was plagued by remorse, and his commissioner tried to cheer him up by improvising the first shadow puppet performance of Karagöz and Hacıvat, using his white turban as a background and his camel-hide sandals in lieu of the deceased comedians.

Karagöz plays are structured in four distinct sections. The *mukaddime* (introduction) starts with Hacıvat reciting a *semai* (poem), followed by a prayer. He then tells the audience that he's looking for his friend Karagöz, calling his sidekick to the stage. A *muhavere* (dialogue) ensues between the duo, followed by the third part, the *fasıl* (main plot). The *bitiş* (conclusion) features an argument between Karagöz and Hacıvat, in which the latter berates his sidekick for ruining the topic at hand, and the former replies, "May my transgressions be forgiven."

Karagöz puppeteers are called *hayalî* (illusionist). One *hayalî* impersonates each of the shadow play's characters by performing songs and adopting dialects. An apprentice sets up and takes down stages and hands the puppet master the puppets as required. The puppets themselves are still crafted of camel hide, just as they were for the first performance 700 years ago.

Baths, **Hüdavendigâr I Murat Camii** (I Murat Cd., free) mosque took more than two decades to build, perhaps because its commissioner, Sultan Murat, was constantly waging war against enemies in the Balkans. The name *Hüdavendigâr* (Creator of the Universe) was humbly affixed by Murat himself. The mosque has a unique inverse-T shape and features a *medrese*, once used by traveling dervishes, on the ground level. Inaugurated in 1385, the complex features a rather bland prayer hall, highlighted only by an ornate *mihrab*. Just across the street, the huge tomb of Murat I was built after he was slain in Kosovo in 1389 during a Serbian-led rebellion to free Balkan territories from Ottoman rule.

While in the neighborhood, families might like to drop in to the **Karagöz Museum** (Çekirge Cd. 159, 0224/232-2590, 8:30am-12:30 and 1:30pm-5:30pm Tues.-Sun., 5TL) to see a tribute to Bursa's famous Karagöz-Hacivat puppets. Collections of original puppets with semitransparent camel hide are on display with a complimentary show every Wednesday (11am and 2pm) and Saturday (11am).

Festivals

For three weeks starting in mid-June, Bursa's **Uluslararası Festival** (0224/234-4912, www.bursafestivali.org) is the annual tribute to the city's performing arts. Organized by master puppeteer Şinasi Çelikkol, the five-day **International Golden Karagöz Dance Competition** (0224/234-4912, altinkaragoz.org) is staged annually in Bursa's open-air culture park during the first half of July.

Nightlife

At twilight, hoards of residents emerge from workplaces and houses to stroll in the parks of green Bursa. Particularly on weekends, the parks are where you'll find most people socializing with friends and family in tea gardens and cafés. When the sun sets, Bursa's throbbing nightlife explodes, rivaling Istanbul's evening entertainment options thanks in part to the legions of youths attending nearby Uludağ University.

For anyone over age 30, there's no better place to stroll cobbled lanes or take in the nightlife than **Arap Şükrü** (Sakarya Cd.), below the citadel's towering stone walls of Tophane. You'll find fish restaurants serving *rakı* (an aniseed-flavored aperitif) lined up in this famous former Jewish quarter. Like Istanbul's Nevizade Street, ensembles of dueling *darbuka* (drum) and violin-playing musicians roam the area from 9pm to entertain the dining and drinking masses.

Calling all revelers: **Kat3 Bar** (Emek Cd., 19, 2nd Fl., Nilüfer, 0224/443-2272) is a pub, disco, and restaurant all in one away from central Bursa. There's a different theme every night, including karaoke every Thursday. For another all-inclusive location, **Club Vici** (Mudanya Yolu, Çağrışan Mevkii 7, 0224/244-7373, www.vici.com.tr), also in Nilüfer, boasts both sizzling outdoor and indoor dance floors for 2,000 people as well as a bar and restaurant. The unassuming but always fun **MPub & Lounge** (Altıparmak Cd. 9D, 0224/220-9428) is closer to central Bursa and Arap Şükrü, where locals hang out over beer during the week. Live DJs work their magic on Friday and Saturday.

Accommodations

Typically, accommodations in Bursa's chaotic Merkez (center) are geared toward businesspeople, while the neighborhoods of Tophane and Çekirge are more relaxed, with thermal spa amenities overflowing on the main drag of the latter.

For a mid-range option in the center of the action, the ★ **Kitapevi Hotel** (Burcustu Sk. 2, Tophane, 0224/225-4160, www.kitapevi.com.tr, €95-175), meaning "book house," does cater to bookworms with a collection of novels in most rooms, but its fine Ottoman architecture set among a serene verdant garden will appeal to any traveler. Each room is uniquely decorated; choose one shaded by a magnolia tree, one with a Turkish bath, and in winter, request a room with a fireplace. Finishing touches like complimentary afternoon tea and a restaurant offering international cuisine make this hotel a top pick in Bursa.

The owners of **Kale Ici Hotel** (Dolaplı Sk. 3, Tophane, 0224/223-1707, www.kaleiciotel.com.tr, 250TL) have retained the charm and authenticity of this 250-year-old Ottoman mansion. Large living spaces connect seven rooms that are fashioned with colorful velvet furnishings atop wooden floorboards decorated with Anatolian wool carpets. Resting here is divine, with home comforts such as bay windows in some rooms and a garden sporting a magnolia tree as old as the mansion it shades.

As a restored Ottoman abode, the **Safran Hotel** (9. Ara Sk. 3, Tophane, 0224/224-7216, www.safranotel.com, from 70TL) cheers up its guests with a saffron-hued facade and comfortable amenities in nine standard rooms and suites. The rooms are less opulent than neighboring venues, but the location in the old city means you're still close to all attractions of the citadel and bazaar quarter.

Bursa City Hotel (Durak Cd. 15, 0224/221-1875, €60) is an excellent central option for those on a budget. It's possible to get a single room here for as low as €35, and the room is fully renovated with brand-new baths and clean rooms with white tufted headboards. The hotel also has a rooftop terrace with a view of the busy pedestrian street below.

For five-star accommodations in downtown Bursa, the five-star ★ **Hotel Almira** (Ulubatlı Hasan Blv. 5, Merkez, 0224/250-2020, www.almira.com.tr, from €170) has perhaps the most elegant and modern rooms. While the Almira excels at taking care of Bursa's business guests, those here for pleasure will not be shortchanged. On-site facilities include a full-service spa, a salon, a hamam, an oxygen bar, and restaurants that feature top-notch food and entertainment to match.

The 29 pricey rooms at the special-class **Otantik Club Hotel** (Botanik Parkı, Soğanlı, 0224/211-3280, www.otantikclubhotel.com, €60-90) boast classic Ottoman decor that makes guests feel like sultans. Expect modern amenities, including Internet access, satellite TV, air-conditioning, and a large pool. Its top-notch restaurants serve superb fish fare as well as Italian, French, and Turkish cuisine. The nearby botanical gardens make for a great after-dinner stroll. The hotel is located on the outskirts of the city west of Yeni Yolova Yolu.

In Çekirge, ★ **Hotel Gönlüferah 1890** (I Murat Cd. 20, Çekirge, 0224/232-1890, www.gonluferah.com, €75-105) achieves utter luxury with a captivating mix of Ottoman classic furnishings and modern design, including canopy beds and plush carpets, in a spectrum of dazzling color. Valley views abound. The Zoe Spa offers 12 custom massage options. Plasma-screen TVs and divine haute cuisine at the upscale À La Carte restaurant round out the exquisite experience.

The **Demirci Otel** (Hammamlar Cd. 33, Çekirge, 0224/236-5104, €30) may be humble, but it's always a good bet for the cleanest, most inexpensive lodgings in pricey Çekirge.

Food

Bursa is renowned for its kebabs, in particular the authentic and ubiquitous spit-roasted, tomato sauce-slathered Iskender Kebab. You'll find these modest Iskender eateries and *izgara* (grill) restaurants on every street with little variety in the offerings. However, a burgeoning haute cuisine movement, typically in upscale hotels, is getting nods from the gastronomes of Istanbul. You'll also find well-respected chain restaurants such as the upmarket and highly recommended **Meshur Tavaci Recep Usta** (Erdoğan Binyücel Cd. 5/1, Nilüfer, 0224/452-4004, www.tavacirecepusta.com, from 25TL). Also found in İzmir and other cities, this Turkish restaurant combines a showering of complimentary dishes in an elegant dining setting with a menu starring Recep Usta's famous *kaburga dolması* (lamb ribs stuffed with flavored rice) so succulent that the meat falls off the bone. The restaurant is located out of town off the D200 highway (metro stop: Altınşehir); reserve a table to avoid disappointment.

★ **Kebapçı Iskender** (Ünlü Cd. 7, 0224/221-4615, kebapciiskender.com.tr, 20TL) has been in business and serving its patented recipe of sliced pit-roasted lamb since 1867. What started as Iskender Efendi's restaurant, serving food to tradespeople in the local bazaar in 1850, grew into a brand that extends throughout the city and farther—check their website for locations, which include one conveniently adjacent to Koza Han. Even the popular vertical revolving spit was invented here as a way to provide a more hygienic cooking method, rather than rotating the circular slab of meat over a fire in the ground.

The Iskender Kebab at **Uludağ Kebapçısı** (Kent Meydanı AVM shopping center, 0224/255-5556, 15TL) challenges Iskender's version for the best kebab in town. Cemal and Cemil Usta, the managing owners of the business for over four decades, added this location in the heart of Bursa to their original diner (Uluyol Şirin Sk. 12, 0224/251-4551) in a blue-collar suburb. The meat and creamy yogurt is farm-fresh. Top it all off with a dessert of *sütlü irmik helva* (sweetened milk and semolina) for a full belly.

For Ottoman fare in a historical location, head to rustic ★ **Darüzziyafe** (II Murat Cd. 36, Muradiye, 0224/224-6439, www.daruzziyafe.com, 25TL) in the restored poorhouse of the 15th-century Muradiye Complex. Choose among 400 different dishes and dine at one of the rows of tables that pack the hall. In summertime, outside seating provides the perfect setting to savor *Ali Nazık Kebabı* (stewed lamb in sautéed eggplant).

The first fish restaurant to open in Bursa, ★ **Arap Şükrü** (Sakarya Cd. 4, 0224/220-6716, 25TL) is so famous with locals that its name is used as a location marker in the city's former Jewish enclave, where families escaping Spain settled during the reign of Beyazıt II in 1492. While there's a host of similar diners crowding Sakarya Street, Arap Şükrü is the original, and its long-standing consistent popularity speaks volumes for its quality. The sidewalks in summer and winter offer added seating and people-watching options. Not into fish? There are plenty of meat specialties as well. A *kuver* (service charge) of 3TL pp is added for bread and water.

Information and Services

The **Tourist information Office** (Atatürk Cd., just east of Ulu Cami, 8am-noon and 1pm-5pm Mon.-Fri.) provides information regarding *dolmuş* (communal taxi) stops, hotels, spas, restaurants, and other local destinations.

Like Istanbul, Bursa is a large city filled with modern conveniences. Banks and ATMs are mainly located along Atatürk Caddesi and Namazgah Caddesi. Most businesses accept credit cards; but for bargaining, cash still rules. Currency exchange booths are located in the bazaar and at the bus and airline terminals.

Getting There

The best way to get to Bursa from Istanbul is with **IDO fast ferry** (0212/444-4436, www.ido.com.tr) from Yenikapı (from 39TL, 1.5 hours, 2 trips per day) or Kadiköy (from 21TL, 2 hours, once per day) straight into Bursa's Güzelyalı port. **BUDO fast ferry** (Bursa Deniz Otobüsleri, 444-9916, https://budo.burulas.com.tr, 20TL) runs more services daily between Istanbul's Kabataş port near Taksim Square and Mundanya port. At the front of the both Bursa ports, board the yellow bus to the Emek BursaRay metro station (2.50TL with BuKart, 30 minutes) to take the BursaRay to Şehreküstü station downtown (2.50TL with BuKart, 35 minutes). The ferry from Yenikapı also accommodates vehicles (from 150TL). Take the D575 highway from the ports to central Bursa.

Even faster is the new seaplane by **Seabird Airlines** (0850/811-0732, www.flyseabird.com) that touches down in Bursa's Gemlik port 18 minutes from the Golden Horn. Tickets are purchased from Burulaş (444-9916, www.burulas.com, 100TL, 3 trips per day).

Intercity **coach** services to Bursa terminate at the *otogar* (Yeni Yalova Yolu), 10 kilometers north of the city center. To reach Atatürk Caddesi, board yellow bus 38 outside the terminal (2.50TL, 30 minutes), or for Çekirge, take bus 93.

Bursa Yenişehir Airport (YEI, 0224/781-8181, www.yenisehir.dhmi.gov.tr) has domestic and international flights, with yellow bus 80 (6TL with BuKart) transporting travelers the 50 kilometers to Kent Square.

Getting Around

Walking central Bursa is the best way to explore the city, but to reach Çekirge (2TL) or Muradiye (1.75TL), take a four-seat white sedan *dolmuş* from their designated stations. Cash fares are paid directly to the driver.

Burulaş (www.burulas.com.tr) manage all public transportation, including the **BursaRay Metro** lines 1 (to Emek) and 2 (to Üniversite) and the **yellow buses,** including the bus to and from the *otogar*, and the *teleferik*, the cable car to Uludağ. The **red tram** does a small loop of central Bursa. A **BuKart** is required for all public transport (2.50TL per trip) and can be bought from metro stations or from confectionary kiosks near stops; look for the word "BuKart" or *dolum* on kiosks. Bus drivers will not accept cash fares. Buy a BuKart before boarding, and validate it on the bus. **Taxis** are also an option; a ride across town from Kent Square to Çekirge is no more than 15TL. Fares to Yeşil Cami are under 10TL. With a number of one-way roads, driving in Bursa can be complicated. Park the car and rely on public transportation for this city.

ULUDAĞ

Uludağ (Great Mountain), 36 kilometers south of Bursa, is Turkey's favorite ski resort. It is also regarded as the mythological Mysian Olympus, where the gods supposedly watched the battle of Troy. The massif's flanks make up the **Uludağ Milli Parkı** (entrance gates in Karabelen, 5TL per vehicle) a national park of towering conifers and wildlife bisected by trails that wind up to the 2,543-meter summit. Come summer, legions of cars packed with picnickers sputter up Uludağ to claim their piece of meadow for half-day trips. The mountain also provides spectacular scenery, diverse flora, and newly marked trails for trekkers. Pack a picnic lunch, or dine at the restaurants atop the mountain. But don't dismiss the unpredictable weather—summer wind storms are not unheard of—and bring the necessary gear, including a cell phone, even if you're only setting out for a couple of hours.

Come winter, the area of Oteller, 18 kilometers up the mountain from the park gate, is a winter wonderland, with numerous lifts operated by various resorts (from 70TL per day). Lift tickets are sold at hotels, which also have ski clothing and equipment rentals (from 100TL per day). The slopes are ideal for beginner and intermediate skiers, with expansive fields appealing to cross-country skiers as well. Come in late January or early February to avoid the packed winter break season.

Accommodations

Towering amid an expansive meadow is the ★ **Monte Baia Hotel** (2.Oteller Bölgesi, 0224/285-2383, www.baiahotels.com, 560TL full board in winter). It offers a ton of amenities, including babysitting services, a day spa, a chill-out lounge with a fireplace, a disco, and so much more. With over 180 rooms, the Monte is part of the Baia chain, renowned for its attentive service and cleanliness in ultra-modern luxury. Lower down the slopes, **Hotel Genç Yazıcı** (1.Oteller Bölgesi, 0224/285-2340, www.grandyazicihotels.com, 550TL full board in winter) has a ski school, equipment rentals, and a cozy chalet ambiance. The spacious, comfortable rooms are decked out with dark wood finish, some offering views of the mountain. The terrace is the best place to people-watch the skiers of all skill levels take on the snow.

Getting There

There are two ways to reach Uludağ from Bursa. The first is a must, weather permitting: the *teleferik* (cable car). If it's operating, hop on a *dolmuş* marked "Teleferik" on Osman Gazi Caddesi in Tophane (9TL). A wait is possible as the vehicle only starts its journey when the car is full. Departing approximately every half hour, the 30-person **Teleferik** (Teleferik Caddesi, 8am-10pm daily summer, 10am-5pm daily winter, 10-15TL pp) takes about 30 minutes to reach the top. A lift change is necessary at Kadıyayla for the final climb to Sarıalan, ten kilometers down from Oteller. A *dolmuş* from Sarıalan travels to the hotels. There is also a two-person gondola (10TL pp) that continues three kilometers up the mountain to Çobanakaya. Ski equipment cannot be taken on the *teleferik*, so rent your equipment on the mountain.

The *dolmuş* from Tophane (Osman Gazi Cd.) in Bursa is more frequent in winter and departs from when full (9TL), winding its way up the 50-minute route to Sarıalan. **Taxis** from Bursa travel to Uludağ (120TL for Oteller), but a return may be negotiated if you're doing a day trip, as drivers are reluctant to go back empty. With all transportation, return to Bursa before dark unless you have accommodations booked.

If you're **driving,** you'll need tire chains in winter (Dec.-Apr.) to get through the park's gate eight kilometers before Sarıalan. These may be purchased at inflated prices from sly entrepreneurs along the roadside.

IZNIK

A farming city sprawling through an abundant valley formed by the Bithynian peaks, Iznik is set amid olive and peach orchards, punctuated by soaring cypress and an enormous lake. Its agricultural trove is not unlike many of its sister cities throughout the Aegean. However, its past is a long history of faith and capitulation to countless tribes, kingdoms, and empires.

Iznik's lake is a bird-lover's paradise, but in 2014 it grabbed national media attention

Iznik

when divers discovered a 1,600-year-old Byzantine basilica just 20 meters from the shore. Also in the headlines were the 2,000-year-old Hellenic-style tumuli, unearthed near the town's necropolis. Needless to say, ongoing excavations continue to reveal this town's diverse past, so check in with the tourism office for new sites to explore. After viewing many of Istanbul's or Bursa's historical monuments, many visitors head to Iznik primarily to browse and buy locally made faience, but many discover the town's momentous significance in the birth of organized Christianity. In fact, many Christians considered Nicaea (Iznik's Roman name) the third among holy cities after Jerusalem and the Vatican. Little remains of its early history except for a scattering of city walls and a few lackluster monuments. Overall, unless you're into ceramics or faith-based tourism, you can bypass Iznik altogether in favor of Bursa.

Following an original Hellenic city plan, Iznik is basically a flat city surrounded by high fortifications. Most sights are within the city walls, which have four cardinal gates: Istanbul, Lefke, Yenişehir, and Göl (Lake). Atatürk Caddesi connects the gates from north to south, 1.5 kilometers apart, and Kılıçaşlan Caddesi runs 1.3 kilometers from east to west, with Ayasofya right in the middle. Earmark half a day to visit the sights with lunch near the Ayasofya or by the lake.

History

Iznik was controlled by many ancient Greek kingdoms. It was rebuilt in 316 BC as Antigoneia in honor of the one-eyed Macedonian King Antigonus, who claimed the city several years after the death of his commander, Alexander the Great. But conspiracy among the ranks led to his demise, and one of the scheming generals, Lysimachus, became Iznik's new ruler. The former general renamed the city Nicaea after his wife. For the next two centuries, the city served as the center of the Bithynian realm and a bastion of trade. In 74 BC, its title, along with control of neighboring cities throughout the region, was transferred to the Romans. The rise of nearby Nicomedia—today's Izmit—produced a vehement battle for supremacy between the two cities. It was eventually settled by the reading of an official decree entitling the latter the status of metropolis. After temporary invasions by the Goths of the west and the Persians from the east, Nicaea surpassed its previous grandeur under the Byzantines.

The 4th and 8th centuries AD proved fortuitous for the city and budding Christianity, as two church meetings would cement the religion's foundation and its principles. The first, convened by Constantine the Great in 325, saw the creation of the Nicene Creed, a document establishing the divinity of Christ. The second, held in Nicaea's Hagia Sophia (Ayasofya) Church in 787, settled the Iconoclastic Controversy. This raging dispute over the depiction and veneration of holy figures ended in the rift between the Orthodox and Roman Catholic churches.

After serving as a Byzantine buttress against the advancing Turks in the early first millennium, Nicaea reclaimed its prosperity and was lavished with majestic edifications and fortifications by Justinian I during the 6th century. In 1078 it took the Selçuk Turks an entire year to break through the thick walls and conquer the city within. Crusaders would come knocking at the behest of Byzantium less than 20 years later. But during an overnight strategic sleight, the Byzantines, who had arrived moments before Europe's army, raided the city and reaped its riches. When the Venetians took Byzantium in 1204, Emperor Theodore I retreated to Nicaea and named it the capital of the Byzantine Empire.

The advancing Ottomans conquered Nicaea in 1331. Sultan Orhan I ordered the destruction of its buildings, with the remaining rubble to be used in the construction of mosques and the first Islamic theological school. After the conquest of Constantinople in 1453, Iznik lost its importance. It would soon regain some of it—at least artistically—when Sultan Selim I ordered all the ceramics artisans from the newly conquered Persian city of Tabriz to move west to Iznik. Inspired by ornate Chinese porcelain and Islamic motifs, the tile makers created impressive faience—tin-glazed pottery. By the 1700s, the city's artistic renown and the art form declined, leaving behind agriculture as its main industry. Thanks to demand from the tourism sector, Iznik's ceramics industry has rebounded.

Sights
★ IZNIK ŞEHIR SURLARI (CITY WALLS)

Some five kilometers in length, the **Iznik Şehir Surları** didn't fare well. The majority of the more than 100 watchtowers that soared from the fortifications lay mostly in rubble. What remains intact now are three of the original four monumental gates, plus a few smaller gates and sections of the wall some 10 meters high. The **Istanbul Gate,** in the north, boasts a triumphant arch honoring Hadrian between its inner and outer gateways, while the **Göl**

Kapıları (Lake Gate) is little more than an opening through the walls. **Lefke Gate,** to the east, is well maintained and comprises a central gateway with two side portals. Built by Proconsul Plancius Varus to honor Hadrian's visit in AD 123, the main gate's outside facade is replete with ornate scenes of warfare etched into its stonework. Climb through the gate for spectacular city views. Finally, the Selçuks, Ottomans, and Byzantines repeatedly breached the fortifications through the **Yenişehir Gate** to the south.

AYASOFYA CAMII (MOSQUE OF AYASOFYA)

Not much more than a roofless shell for many years, the **Ayasofya Camii** (Atatürk Cd., 0224/757-6297, 9am-5pm Tues.-Sun., free) became a functioning mosque again in 2011. Set amid a fragrant sunken rose garden, the seemingly freestanding structure offers little for the visitor except a discolored fresco of the Virgin Mary, Jesus, and John the Baptist in an area once used as the nave. There are also portions of an 11th-century mosaic floor protected by barricades to prevent pedestrian damage. Constantine commissioned the original building. It succumbed to a massive earthquake and was then rebuilt entirely by the culturally inclined Justinian I before being converted into the Ulu Mosque in 1331. The Mongol invasion in the early 14th century brutally damaged the structure, and a fire some 200 years later caused further decline. The ill-fated place of worship fell into the able hands of Mimar Sinan, who lavished the building with Iznik tiles in a complete renovation in the 16th century. Fierce fighting between Greek and Turkish troops in 1922 again damaged the sanctuary. As with most mosques, avoid visiting during local prayer times, and dress modestly by covering exposed shoulders, legs, and, for women, the hair.

IZNIK ARKEOLOJI MÜZESI (IZNIK ARCHAEOLOGICAL MUSEUM)

Across the street from Yeşil Cami, **Iznik Arkeoloji Müzesi** (Müze Sk. 11, 0224/757-1027, 9am-1pm and 2pm-5pm Tues.-Sun., 3TL) is housed in the Nilüfer Hatun Imareti, the shelter built by Murat I in 1388 in tribute to his mother. She was a smart and artistically gifted Byzantine blue blood, who, through a twist of fate, was snatched by Sultan Osman the day she was to marry the Greek Prince of Bilecik. Her father, the Prince of Yarhısar, had

city walls and Istanbul Gate of Iznik

lured Osman to the wedding ceremony to assassinate him. Aware of the scheme, Osman stole the soon-to-be princess. She went on to marry Osman's son, Orhan, and subsequently controlled the Ottoman State during her husband's many conquests. The building was used as a hospice for the Ahi Brotherhood of skilled artisans long before it was rededicated to Nilüfer.

The grounds are a catchall for tombs and statues dating back to the Romans, the town's stint as a Byzantine capital, and the early Ottoman era. On display are samples of original Iznik tile work, such as the complex red faience; ceramic artifacts from the mid-1500s; an intact Roman sarcophagus; and samples of Ottoman craftsmanship such as weaponry, weaving, and kitchenware.

OTHER MOSQUES

Crouching amid lawns and sporadic firs, the **Yeşil Cami** (Green Mosque, Müze Sk.) near Lefke Gate provides a splash of color in Iznik's prevailing dowdiness. Its petite single minaret, tiled in red, white, and turquoise, replaced the emerald hue the monument was named after. Its colorful spire tips off visitors to the wealth of faience within the thick brick walls it towers over. The ornate etchings on the marble portico lead into a sanctuary that was custom-built in 1378 for Çandarlı Kara Halil Hayrettin Paşa, a commander who led sultan Orhan I's army and later served as grand vizier under the subsequent sultan, Murat I. Like the minaret, the inner sanctum's red, blue, and white faience challenge the mosque's green moniker.

Farther west, the **Hacı Özbek Camii** (just north of Kılıçarslan Cd., between Mevlânâ and Eşrefoğlu Sk.) is the town's oldest mosque, one that has been the target of inept beautification schemes. And just to its north, the green outdoor **Eşrefzade Abdullah Rûmî Tomb** encases the remains of a noted Sufi mystic. Adjacent is a solitary minaret with Iznik tiles as a memorial for a mosque that destroyed during the War of Independence in 1922.

OTHER HISTORICAL BUILDINGS

The **Süleyman Paşa Medresesi** is located on the street of that name. This chimneyed structure was built by Sultan Orhan as the first theological school in the empire, right after he conquered Nicaea in 1313. While it's still functioning after 700 years, the *medrese* also houses a few tile ateliers and shops at affordable prices.

Near the Ayasofya is the 15th-century **II Murat Hamamı** (1 block south of Ayasofya, 0224/757-1459, 7am-11pm daily, men only). What was once the women's section now serves as a showroom for dazzling ceramics. Across the road are the excavations of former tile-making workshops.

Just east of the *otogar*, a fenced-off scattering of stones below ground level are the vestiges of the imperial **Church of Koimesis.** It was built for Byzantine emperor Theodore I, who fled Constantinople after the Venetian Crusaders overtook the city in 1204. West of Atatürk Caddesi toward the south gate is the ruined 15,000-seat **Roman Theater** and the smaller **Saray Gate,** which led to Sultan Orhan's palace. The theater grounds are also closed to visitors.

IZNIK FOUNDATION

The **Iznik Foundation** (Sahil Yolu, 0224/757-6025, www.iznik.com) was established in 1993 to research the method for creating Iznik's semiprecious decorative tiles and train modern-day artists to promote this Ottoman art form to the world. You can visit the foundation in Iznik or Istanbul and see their work in action and even buy a souvenir or two. Little information existed as to how the quartz tiles were created in the 15th century, hence the mission of the foundation. This stunning faience is celebrated for its unique composition of quartz, quartzite, and clay and for its underglaze of diverse decorations using regional flora and symbolism on a white base. Stunning bold blues were initially used, while turquoises, reds, and yellows are synonymous with the art form's heyday in the 16th century. It was in such demand a century later that 300 workshops existed in Iznik, before the eventual demise of the Ottoman empire.

Accommodations

Iznik has few upscale hotels, and the few that exist are jam-packed during the holidays and summer. Book far ahead or opt to stay in Bursa's myriad of no-frills lodgings and boutique hotels. The ★ **Çamlık Motel** (Göl Sahıl Yolu, 0224/757-1362, www.iznik-camlikmotel.com, 120-150TL) remains the best and most reliable place to spend the night. Right on the lake, the hotel has a garden and bright minimalist rooms with full amenities. The facility's rustic restaurant surpasses any other in town. Samples of Iznik Lake fish and seafood are served under plane trees by the placid lake.

For an economical solution, **Cem Hotel** (Sahıl Yolu 34, 0224/757-1687, www.cemotel.com, 150TL) has a variety of accommodations, from spacious standard rooms to even larger suites with balconies and views of the lake. Enjoy the complimentary farm-fresh breakfast and go back for more locally grown produce at the hotel's restaurant, open for lunch and dinner.

Also a good bet, **Kaynarca Pansiyon** (Gündem Sok 1, 0224/757-1753, www.kaynarca.net, from 25TL) is a favorite with backpackers because of the dorm and budget private rooms. Here you'll Ali, a friendly host who dishes out lots advice and information about the things to see and do in Iznik. Don't expect air-conditioning or anything flashy, but Kaynarca has an excellent location close to the sights and the bus station. The hotel doesn't take reservations.

Food

Iznik's best restaurants are located at the Çamlık or Cem Hotels, whose lakeside eateries provide a mesmerizing location to break bread. Most visitors to Iznik will simply need a quick and easy pit stop for lunch between site visits. **Kenan Çorba and Izgara** (Atatürk Cd., across from Ayasofya, 0224/757-0235, 15TL) is a delicious restaurant with five soups and at least 10 homemade Turkish dishes on offer. Point and select the dishes you want once the chef explains the daily menu. Another hole-in-the-wall popular with the locals is **Kofteci Yusuf-Iznik Imren** (Atatürk Cd. 73, 0224/757-3597, 15TL); although part of a chain, this large eatery is conveniently close to the attractions and packed for lunch daily. The menu has a mix of grills, *köfte* (meatballs), and salads.

Information and Services

Near the town's center, you'll find plenty of ATMs on Kılınçaslan Caddesi. A small cabin for the **Tourism Office** (Atatürk Cd., 0224/757-1933) shares the courtyard of the Ayasofya.

Getting There

The fastest way to reach Iznik from Istanbul is to board the **IDO fast ferry** (0212/444-4436, www.ido.com.tr) to Yalova (8:30am-8pm daily, 75 minutes, from 18TL pp, from 110TL with a car and 4 passengers) that departs at least five times daily from Yenikapı. The M1 and M2 metro and Marmaray train lines all connect to Yenikapı from locations throughout Istanbul. Another IDO ferry departs from Pendik on Istanbul's Asian side (7am-9:30pm daily, 45 minutes, from 9TL pp, from 82TL with a car and 4 passengers) at least 11 times daily. In Yalova, transfer to the **Nolu Koop dolmuş** (departs hourly, 10TL) to Iznik at the bus station west of the ferry terminal; otherwise, if you have your own vehicle, follow the D575/E881 highway from Yalova and turn left onto the D150 before arriving in Iznik via the D595 (60 kilometers, 60 minutes).

A *dolmuş* linking Iznik *otogar* to Bursa *otogar* (5:30am-7:30pm daily, 85 kilometers, 75 minutes, 10TL) departs every 15-45 minutes.

TERMAL

Termal is an ideal stop for rejuvenation on any leg of an itinerary around Bursa and Iznik. Just 12 kilometers southwest of the Yalova port, **Termal** (Yalova Thermal Hot Springs Resort, 0226/675-7400, www.

yalovatermal.com, bath and spa facilities 8am-10pm daily) is a massive complex of geothermal activity. Roman emperors were the first to claim the warm waters rising from underground some 17 centuries ago. Justinian I commissioned large marble baths for his personal use, but years of fierce battles and major earthquakes ravaged the structures. Rediscovered under a pile of earth in 1900, Sultan Abdülmecid commissioned a major renovation of additions to the imperial facilities. Turkish Republic founder and leader Mustafa Kemal Atatürk so enjoyed Termal's restorative powers that he had an elegant series of pavilions, surrounded by exotic landscaping, built in 1929. This estate overlooks the complex. While the area's population swells during the summer from 45 to 500, the resort, with its surrounding web of trails and streams, beckons anglers, hikers, and bathers year-round.

Across the parking lot at the entrance of Termal, the **Atatürk Evi** (Atatürk House) is at the end of a wooded path on the left. Beyond the exotic landscaping, the quaint house provides an intimate look at this very public figure's inner sanctum. The first and most popular bath is **Kurşunlu Banyo,** named after its lead-covered dome. Head to its outdoor facilities (20TL for 90 minutes), which are perfect for families. Or follow in Emperor Justinian's steps and opt for the indoor pool and sauna (25TL for 90 minutes). The superior 1,600-year-old **Valide Banyo** (13TL for 90 minutes) offers separate bathing sections for women and men. The 26 private bathing rooms at the **Sultan Banyo** (22TL for 60 minutes) are the more comfortable options and are typically frequented by more conservative users. Massage services are also available throughout the complex.

Awakening to the potential of health-oriented tourism, the entire complex has been revamped by the on-site office of the Ministry of Health. They also manage Termal's five hotels. Once drab and threadbare, these lodgings have been whipped into appealing facilities.

★ **Çınar** and **Çamlık** hotels (from 210TL) together offer 100 alluring rooms. Inspired by two 100-year-old sycamore trees in the yard, the Çınar surrounds a large welcoming courtyard with a bustling café. Çamlık's bar and restaurant may be a better bet for grown-ups. A third property, the **Apart Hotel,** is specifically intended for large groups with six rustic air-conditioned apartments. Booking all accommodations can be done at 0226/675-7400 or www.yalovatermal.com. Rooms rates include bed, breakfast, and unlimited access to the baths. Full-board rates, which include lunch and dinner, are also available. The prices quoted above are midweek; weekends have a minor surcharge for baths and accommodations.

Getting There

From Bursa, take an hourly *dolmuş* from Bursa *otogar* (1 hour, 13TL) to Yalova and transfer to the *dolmuş* to Termal (every 10 minutes, 3TL) at the bus station west of Yalova port. From Yalova Port, travel along Çınarcık Yolu to the Termal parking lot with private vehicle or *dolmuş* (3TL) that shuttles passengers every 10 minutes from the bus station west of Yalova Port. **IDO fast ferries** (0212/444-4436, www.ido.com.tr) to Yalova depart from Istanbul's Yenikapı (European side) and Pendik (Asian side) ports.

Edirne

The largest city on the Thracian Peninsula, Edirne spreads along a hill above the valley where the Tunca and Meriç Rivers meet. A trading post for ancient Romans making their way to Asia Minor, its status rose steadily with the Byzantines and was punctuated by a stint as the second capital of the Ottoman Empire (1365-1453) until Constantinople was conquered. After this time, Edirne remained a favored summer retreat for the Ottoman dynasty, as well as the preferred launching site for assaults on Europe. Travelers visit in early July for the city's annual Kırkpınar Oil Wrestling Festival and to get an eyeful of its exquisite Ottoman and Roman architectural relics. April also sees larger crowds that gather to see the city's symbol, the tulip, come to life with spectacular displays of color.

Historians have pinpointed Edirne's beginnings in the 7th century BC, when it served as a settlement for the warmongering Thracian tribes known as Uskadama. Nine centuries later, Edirne became a bastion and a stop on the Via Egnetia, an early road linking Byzantium to the rest of the Roman Empire. This major passage to and from Asia Minor expanded and was renamed by Roman emperor Hadrian as Hadrianopolis. Abbreviated some time later to Adrianople, the city witnessed Licinius's vicious loss to Constantine in AD 323, and Valens's slaughter at the hands of the bloody Visigoths some four decades later. Countless battles and sieges continued in the next millennium, and Edirne grew into a fitting center for weaponry.

Aiming to encircle and starve Constantinople, Murat I's Ottoman troops finally conquered Adrianople in 1363. The city was soon made a capital and renamed Edirne.

After the Turks and Allies ratified the Treaty of Sèvres in 1920—an agreement that shattered the former Ottoman Empire into regions shared between the victors of World War I—Edirne fell under Greek military rule. But even that was short-lived, as Mustafa Kemal Atatürk bloodily reclaimed it just months later.

Edirne is an ideal day trip from Istanbul. Leave early for the 2.5-hour coach ride and spend the rest of the morning checking out the mosques and the Edirnekâri—the city's unique Ottoman homes—before foraging for treasures in the covered bazaar's *bedesten* (marketplace). In the afternoon, stroll down to the banks of the Meriç River to view Ottoman bridges and settle at a waterside tea garden for *çay* (tea).

SIGHTS
★ Selimiye Camii (Selimiye Mosque)

The great Mimar Sinan considered the 16th-century **Selimiye Camii** (Taş Odalar Sokak, free) to be his finest work, and critics agreed. The mosque was commissioned by Sultan Selim II, Sultan Süleyman and Hürrem Sultan's son, but it never welcomed its benefactor. Selim the Sot, as he was commonly known, died of a fever a year before the building's completion. Much smaller than Süleymaniye in Istanbul, the ornate interior of Selimiye is what propels it to greatness. At 60 meters in height, the four soaring minarets also add to its majesty.

As you enter through the west gate, you encounter a spectacular dome held up by eight conspicuous columns towering over a circular prayer hall. The *mihrab* is tucked in an alcove in true Abazid style; it's pushed back far enough to allow just enough depth for sunlight to filter through three sides, bathing the space and its extensive glittering tiles in natural light. Almost 30 meters in diameter, the interior of the dome boasts sumptuous calligraphy highlighted by the daylight shining through 45 windows at its base. The Iznik faience, including the tiles that beautify the

Edirne

mihrab, explodes in color and floral inspiration. The *minbar* is carved of fine marble.

The surrounding complex features a busy *arasta* (row of shops) that dedicated to indigenous artwork, along with several seminaries. With an assortment of early Ottoman relics and a nod to the popular sport of oil wrestling, the **Turkish and Islamic Arts Museum** occupies the main *medrese*. There's also the tomb of Selim II and those of his three daughters tucked into a mausoleum embellished with etched mother-of-pearl.

Other Mosques

Named after the three balconies on its loftiest minaret, **Üç Şerefeli Cami** (Mosque with Three Galleries, Hükkümet Cd., free) beautifully depicts the mid-15th-century transition from Selçuk architecture found in western Anatolia to the budding complexity of Ottoman-style buildings. This is the first mosque to boast a central dome over its prayer hall and to include four subsidiary domes. Earlier structures feature a series of small domes that crown abutting double-walled structures. This mosque's fountain appears outside, also a first of its kind. The fountain started a trend adopted by later imperial architects.

Eski Cami (Old Mosque, rotary at Talat Paşa and Mimar Sinan Cd., free) was built in 1413 for Sultan Mehmet I. Similar to Ulu Cami in Bursa, Eski Cami is a nine-domed building of cut stone with a portico of five bays on its northern flank and a minaret gracing its northwest corner. Massive square columns embellished with Koranic calligraphy, added in the late 19th century, break up the extensive red carpeting inside. Just across the street, the *bedesten* (Mon.-Sat.) is Edirne's first enclosed market. It was built by Mehmet I to generate revenue for the upkeep of the mosque. It consists of 14 vaulted chambers, fashioned after its predecessor in Bursa, that are quite ordinary and disorganized.

On a hill northeast of the city overlooking Sarayiçi, just a brisk 10-minute walk northeast of Selimiye Mosque, is the diminutive **Muradiye Camii** (Mimar Sinan Cd., free). It was built in 1435 as a *tekke* (convent for the Mevlevi order) but was inaugurated as a mosque. Its construction is based on the reverse T-floor plan prevalent in that era. The Muradiye is known for its variety of hexagonal—not square—tiles that interlock with triangular turquoise faience to create a unique backdrop. The tomb of Musa Kasîm Efendi, the Ottoman Empire's last Islamic judge, is in the adjoining cemetery.

On the northwestern end of Edirne, across the Tunca River, the immense **Ikinci Beyazit Külliyesi** (II Beyazit Cd.) is a feast for the eyes and a haven for the harried. Completed in 1488, this complex remained the largest of its kind in the Islamic world for more than a century. Along with a mosque, there are several buildings that make up the complex: a *darüşşifa* (hospital), soup kitchens, *medreseler*, hamams, a mill, depots, and even a bridge. For 200 years, the *darüşşifa* was a world-renowned hospital for treating eye diseases and mental ailments. At a time when Europeans burned the mentally ill at the stake for being cohorts of the devil, at this complex, treatment for the mentally ill included fragrance therapy. Meals prepared with exotic fowl, such as partridge and pheasant, supposedly treated certain afflictions. Sound therapy with live music and natural running water were also popular healing methods. Today, this building serves as the not-to-be-missed **Sağlık Müzesi** (Health Museum, 0284/224-0922, www.saglikmuzesi.trakya.edu.tr, 9am-6pm daily, 5TL), which displays original patient quarters as well as the Ottomans' innovative healing methods.

Edirne Müzesi (Edirne Museum)

Built around a large courtyard across the street from the Selimiye Camii, the **Edirne Müzesi** (Kadirpaşa Mektep Sk. 7, 0284/225-1120, 8am-noon and 1pm-5pm Tues.-Sun., 3TL) offers a broad slice of Edirne's history, with displays of early Ottoman relics that include brass- and copper-weighing instruments and nacre-inlaid furniture as well as reconstructed suites of Ottoman houses that include a circumcision room. The museum's collection spans prehistory to the Republican Era. Ancient Roman fluted-glass perfume bottles are on display in the archaeological section. The ethnography section boasts interesting early Ottoman knickknacks.

Makedonya Kulesi (Macedonian Clock Tower)

After getting word that the Russian army was en route to capture Edirne, its governor, Cemil Paşa, blew up the city's large ammunition armory, eradicating in a moment Roman emperor Hadrian's magnificent 1,700-year-old Clock Tower castle (Mumcular Sk.). Only one of the four original corner towers remained standing after four days of explosions. It was restored in 1875 and renamed the **Makedonya Kulesi.** Ongoing archaeological digs have unearthed parts of the city walls and a Byzantine church in the vicinity.

Kaleiçi

The **Kaleiçi** is Edirne's Sultanahmet, with a plaza-like network of cobbled streets in true Roman fashion. Edirne's **Great Synagogue,** which was Europe's third largest in 1906, is at the end of Maarif Caddesi, just north of Darül Hadis Caddesi. Kaleiçi also has spectacular specimens of Edirne's unique wooden architecture.

Ali Paşa Çarşısı

Just east of Hürriyet Meydanı (square) is **Ali Paşa Çarşısı,** one of Edirne's covered markets. It was built in 1568 by Mimar Sinan at the request of grand vizier Semiz Ali Paşa. The structure was ravaged by fire in 1992. Some of the 130 shops were reconstructed with great care, as was the structure's remarkable central dome.

★ Kırkpınar Yağı Güreşleri (Kırkpınar Oil Wrestling Festival)

During the first week of July, masses descend on a stadium in Sarayiçi, two kilometers northwest of the city center, to take part in the six-centuries-old **Kırkpınar Yağı Güreşleri.** The fun is watching the action of muscular grown men oiled and clad in tightly fastened mid-calf pants. While there are many similar competitions throughout Anatolia, none compare to the seven-day Kırkpınar festival, which welcomes domestic and foreign

interior decoration of Selimiye Camii

luminaries, janissary bands, folk dance troupes, and merchants. The festival has various activities for the entire family.

The Kırkpınar Oil Wrestling Festival may be the world's oldest wrestling contest, held continuously every year since 1357 in Rumelia (modern Thrace). Believed to have originated from deep in central Asia, this ancient battle of might was brought to the Anatolian plains by Turkic nomads. As the Ottomans conquered their way to Edirne during the mid-14th century under the command of Süleyman Paşa, troops wrestled each other during their down time. The myth behind Kırkpınar is that on one occasion, 40 able men began wrestling through eliminatory bouts that finally pitted the top two. They battled beyond exhaustion and eventually died. The duo was buried by a fig tree near Edirne. Once the town was under Ottoman control in 1363, the remaining members of the band of 40 arrived at Ahırköy Meadow, where a clear spring gushed forth near that fig tree. The location was named Kırkpınar (Forty Sources) for the wrestlers who took part in the apocryphal wrestling match.

At over 650 years old, the festival is steeped in tradition, which includes a series of rules and practices. During the Ottoman era, wrestling matches outside palace walls were organized solely at fairgrounds, during weddings, and in the homes of the wealthy. As master of ceremonies, the Kırkpınar Yağlı Güreş Ağası (Ceremonial Lord) provided guests with continuous entertainment, lodging, and food, and was also responsible for calling the wrestlers and ensuring that the games followed traditional rules. Today, the municipality has assumed this task due to the event's popularity and rising costs.

The çazgır (emcee) introduces each wrestler by name, title, and competency to the jury and spectators. Then the wrestlers are matched through a draw, after which prayers and verses are recited. The clothing abides by tradition, as does the oiling. A competitor collects dripping oil with his right hand and spreads it to his left shoulder, repeating the process with the left hand. Opponents are expected to oil each other's backs.

The longest-reigning champion, Ahmet Taşcı, won the golden belt—the award given to the başpehlivan (top wrestler)—no less than nine times during the 1990s.

Sarayiçi

The leafy area of **Sarayiçi** that hosts the festival for oil-clad wrestlers was once the

Young boys from the Roma community leap giant fires to purify their soul for Hidrellez.

Ottoman dynasty's hunting grounds and Saray-I Cedid (New Palace) where Sultan Mehmet II planned his successful attack on Constantinople. Since 2009, archaeologists have been working to restore this grand structure, commissioned by Murat II in 1450 and completed by his son Mehmet (The Conqueror). It later served as an artillery armory in the 19th century before the Governor of Edirne ordered its destruction in 1878. The ruins, which include the palace kitchen and baths where Hürrem once bathed, can be seen by walking over the small Fatih Bridge outside the stadium.

Sarayiçi also comes alive with the Romany 9/8 rhythm on May 5-6, when the Roma community celebrate the **Hidrellez** (Coming of Spring Festival) with music and dancing, along with folkloric activities such as purifying one's soul by jumping over a fire or plunging into the freezing Tunca River, done at sunrise on May 6. Locals will also come to support the bathers and throw wishes, written on paper, into the water, believing Saint Hızır will grant them good luck. Bring plenty of spare change to tip the musicians who play throughout the crowd.

Bridges

Just outside the city center, Edirne's imposing bridges inspired many folk songs. Linking the thickly wooded shores of the Tunca River, the most elaborate bridges are masterpieces of Mimar Sinan. The oldest example, which links both levees with 27 arches, was commissioned in the second part of the 13th century by Byzantine emperor Michael Palaelogus. It became known, however, for its restorer Gazı Mihal Bey more than 100 years later. The 12-arch **Şahabettin Paşa Köprüsü,** also known as the Saraçhane Köprüsü, was erected in 1451. Mehmet I's **Fatih Köprüsü** followed a year later. Mimar Sinan's **Saray Köprüsu,** also known as Kanunı, was built in 1560 to honor Süleyman the Magnificent. The commission of **Ekmekçizade Ahmet Paşa Köprüsü** in 1608 and the mid-19th-century **Yeni Köprü,** at the confluence of the Meriç and Arda Rivers, are the most contemporary additions.

ACCOMMODATIONS

Don't expect much from Edirne's accommodations, but there are a couple of gems worth looking at. You may have to communicate via email to book hotels as English speakers are rare.

Rüstem Paşa Kervansaray Hotel (Iki Kapili Han 57, 0284/212-6119, www.edirnekervansarayhotel.com, from €60) is a centrally located 76-room historical hotel. Mimar Sinan was involved in this construction, and the rooms overlook a quiet, romantic courtyard flanked by a bar and terrace restaurant. The bare rooms don't justify the rates, and there are better options in town, but if you're a lover of nostalgia, this could be for you.

There's no better place to stay than ★ **Hotel Edirne Palace** (Vavlı Camii Sk. 4, 0284/214-7474, www.hoteledirnepalace.com, €60). The hotel has 35 pristine, inviting rooms with embossed cream wallpaper and contemporary white furniture, giving the ambiance a fresh and modern feel in the historic center of town. The quality of the rooms, large complimentary breakfast, and convenient location make it comfortable without the hefty rates.

Taşodalar Otel (Taşodalar Sk. 3, behind Selimiye Mosque, 0284/212-3529, www.tasodalar.com, €80-215) is a 600-year-old mansion of the Saray-I Atık (Old Palace) that was built by Murat I in 1365. The palace witnessed the birth of Fatih Sultan Mehmet in 1432 (he was just age 21 when he conquered Istanbul), but it was largely destroyed by Selim the Sot to make way for his grand mosque, now across the lane. Today this historical mansion boast an on-site restaurant, a terrace, and 12 rooms decked out in an Ottoman style that suggests time has stood still. If only those walls could talk!

Solo travelers looking for budget digs won't find a hostel in Edirne, but you can snare a single room in a hotel for around €20 with some online searching. Start your search with **Saray Hotel** (Eski Istanbul Cd.

28, 0284/212-1457, www.edirnesarayhotel.com, €20-60), with its checkerboard-inspired rooms, a great deal for the buck. If the decor seems an assault on your senses, retreat to the rooftop to take in great views of the town.

The nicest hotel in Edirne is the upscale **Rhys Hotel** (Talatpaşa Cd. 82/A, 0284/213-0797, www.ryshotel.com, €85-120). Located two kilometers east of the Selimiye Mosque, this new lodging is packed with amenities: A day spa complete with a sauna, jetted tub, and massage options complement high-quality restaurants, a bakery, complimentary newspaper service, and 70 elegant and spacious rooms and suites. The rooftop **Vargo Restaurant & Bar** is the place for guests and nonguests alike to enjoy international and Turkish fare while taking in panoramic views of the city.

FOOD

For meat-loving Turks, visiting Edirne without tasting its homegrown delicacy of fried *ciğer* (liver) is akin to lunacy. The restaurant that's hot on everyone's lips (partly because of their fiery peppers) is **Aydın Tava Ciğer** (Tahmıs Çarşışı 12, 0284/214-1046, www.aydintava.ciger.com, 15TL). Expect to wait for a seat in this tiny, modest restaurant—it's always packed, but the wait is worth it.

If the thought of eating peppers and giblets isn't appealing, there are plenty of other vegetarian and meaty options, particularly the Edirne *köfte*—a plump, silver dollar-size patty. One place to try these is on the Meriç River at **Lalezar** (Lozan Cd. 6, 0284/223-0600, www.lalezaredirne.com, 25TL). It's a traveler favorite, with a large menu featuring grilled meats, *pides*, and salads. Adults will love the view of the river, but kids will find the playground more appealing.

Famed food critics, TV personalities, and politicians plan daily trips around lunch at ★ **Meşhur Çiğerci Kazım Usta** (Osmaniye Cd. 43, 0284/212-1280, www.cigercikazimusta.com, 15TL). Established in the covered bazaar in 1967, Kazım Usta relocated to a much larger building near the fish market to accommodate the growing lines at the door. To avoid the intense fumes generated by the overworked fryer, upper-level seating is recommended. Savor the fried spicy red pepper and lentil soup along with mounds of crusty bread.

Vegetarians will appreciate meals served up at **Melek Anne Homemade Food** (Maarif Cd. 18, 0284/213-3263, www.melekanne.com, 20TL). Melek Anne, meaning "angel mother," is a quirky café open for breakfast, lunch, and dinner. From the front door of this Ottoman abode you're greeted with the vibrant reds and greens that meet the splashes of purple and yellow inside and through to the quaint leafy courtyard. The prices are not listed, so check prior to ordering. If you need recommendations, you can't go wrong with *patlıcan musakka* (eggplant moussaka), *kabak* (zucchini), *biber* (peppers), or *dolması* (vegetables stuffed with savory rice).

INFORMATION AND SERVICES

The majority of ATMs are located around Hürriyet Meydanı (look for the big red tulips off the main drag) and along Saraçlar Caddesi, where the post office—**PPT** (0284/212-6201, 8:30am-5pm Mon.-Fri., 10am-4pm Sat.)—can also be found. Mostly geared for Turks, the **Tourism Office** (Hürriyet Meydanı, 0284/213-9208) provides limited information in most Western languages.

GETTING THERE AND AROUND

For an enjoyable ride to Edirne, hop on a **coach** (25TL one-way) for a day trip from Istanbul's Bayrampaşa Otogar to Edirne's *otogar*, which is eight kilometers east of the city square. **Metro Turizm** (444-3455, www.metroturizm.com.tr) and **Ulusoy** (444-1888, www.ulusoy.com.tr) coaches depart every hour for the 230-kilometer, 2.5-hour journey northwest along the Trans-European Motorway (E80). Once in Edirne, a *servis* (free shuttle bus) from the coach company or *dolmuş* (2TL) takes passengers to Hürriyet Meydanı; taxis are also available.

Construction on the rail line between Edirne and Istanbul has reduced the number of trains to once per day Friday through Sunday. Until work is complete, travel by rail is a much slower option (5.5 hours) between the cities. More information on rail services can be found at www.seat61.com.

By **car,** the route via the E80/O-3 toll road tends to take two hours (7.25TL standard vehicle toll from European Istanbul). Alternatively, the D110-E84 highway, with no tolls, hugs the northern coast of the Marmara and is a circuitous scenic option that almost doubles the transit time with traffic congestion. Traveling into Turkey from Bulgaria involves taking the E80 through Kapitan–Andreevo and Kapıkule, about 20 kilometers northeast of Edirne. From Greece, the border town of Pazarkule is the first Turkish town, less than eight kilometers from Edirne.

Gelibolu Yarımadası (Gallipoli Peninsula)

Every year on April 25, Australians and New Zealanders flock to the cemeteries and the memorialized combat zone of the national park on the peninsula for a dawn ceremony marking the anniversary of the Allied landings during World War I. Other than this day, only weekending Turkish families visit the rolling plains and undeveloped beaches of the pristine peninsula, north of the strategic Dardanelles. Perhaps left unspoiled as a reminder of the tens of thousands who perished trying to breach or defend the straits, Gallipoli Peninsula inspires serene contemplation of the region.

★ GELIBOLU YARIMADASI TARIHI MILLI PARKI (GALLIPOLI NATIONAL PARK)
Before You Go

Gelibolu Yarımadası Tarihi Milli Parkı is quiet year-round except on Anzac Day (Apr. 25). The event has ballooned in popularity during the last decade in the lead up to the centenary of the landings in 2015. To avoid inflated rates for everything from flights to hotel rooms as well as dense crowds, avoid the second half of April altogether. Otherwise, you'll join the patriotic green and gold-clad Aussies and the black-garbed Kiwis during this busy time.

One could spend days visiting the 20 or so main sites in the park. If you are exploring on your own, the best plan is to divide the park into two: the northern Gallipoli cemeteries and trenches, where the Anzac forces landed in 1915; and the southern section, Cape Helles, where the French and British troops were positioned.

Touring the park, which spans 37 kilometers of rough backcountry from top to bottom, is nearly impossible without a vehicle. Using a local *dolmuş* is not advised as the significant landmarks are far apart and the service infrequent. Driving or joining a tour are the best options. Visitors in search of a tour guide on-site can look around Eceabat, Çanakkale, or Kilitbahir; but for better rates, book ahead with one of the agencies listed below.

If you are attending the Anzac Day ceremonies, allocate at least two days for this moving experience. Most operators transport guests from Istanbul to the Anzac Commemorative Site in the late afternoon of April 24. On arrival the guide will direct you to your patch of grass or grandstand to camp under the stars until the end of the Dawn Service (6:30am Apr. 25). While there is no shelter, food stalls and portable toilets are provided for the 10,000 guests. Films about the Gallipoli campaign play through the night as temperatures dip 0°C. Pack warm gear and sleeping bags, but make sure they're lightweight, as daytime temperatures can reach 20°C, and you'll get hot hiking the 1.5 kilometers uphill to the Australian service (10am) at Lone Pine, and then 3.2 kilometers on to Chunuk Bair for the New Zealand service (11:30am). Guests can be picked up at Lone Pine or Chunuk Bair for transfer back to Istanbul. Private vehicles cannot access the site on Anzac Day, which is why joining a tour is advised. The Australian government has more information about the commemorations at www.dva.gov.au.

Tours

Since the park is such a big draw, buses depart almost hourly for Çanakkale from Istanbul. Myriad packages, even private tours of the memorial, are available through a variety of tour operators. The best all-around package if you are short on time is a day tour from Istanbul run by **Crowded House Hotel & Tours** (Huseyin Avni Sk. 4, Eceabat, 0286/814-1565, www.crowdedhousegallipoli.com, €78). The tour includes an early pickup from your Istanbul hotel, a five-hour commute to Eceabat, lunch in Crowded House Hotel's secret garden, followed by a five-hour tour of the northern sites, arriving back to your Istanbul hotel late in the evening. Crowded House can also book half-day tours (€30) for the northern and southern Helles sites as well as boat cruises and snorkeling tours over the wrecks off the peninsula if you want to spend more time exploring the area. Another local choice for tours is the dependable **Hassle Free Tours** (Cumhuriyet Meydani 59, Çanakkale, 0286/213-5969, www.anzachouse.com). Most tours focus on the northern section of the site, so if you'd like to see more, base yourself in Eceabat or Çanakkale for a day or two to make the most of the tours on offer. For trekkers, walking is feasible with the right gear: hiking boots, long pants, a sun hat, a good map, and plenty of bottled water. For more detailed historical information and a downloadable hiking audio guide to 14 of the northern sites, log onto www.anzacsite.gov.au. The 2005 documentary *Gelibolou*, directed by Tolga Örnek, available in English with narration by Sam Neill and Jeremy Irons, is also essential viewing.

History

In August 1914, Enver Paşa, the Supreme Commander of Turkish Forces, signed a secret alliance with German ally Kaiser Wilhelm II with the aim of regaining the eastern province of Kars, which was ceded to Russia during the Russo-Turkish Wars of 1877. Or so he thought; the deal provided the Ottomans much-needed weaponry from Germany, and in return allowed the Germans to maneuver two warships through the Dardanelles to escape British pursuit. A few months later, all hell broke loose when this newfound military alliance used the same two ships, backed by the Ottoman Navy, to raid a handful of Russian ports. Russia was forced to declare war on the Ottoman Empire, and the British saw an opportunity to take Ottomans out of the conflict by launching a strategic attack on the capital, Istanbul.

The plan, organized and coordinated by then-First Lord of the Admiralty Winston Churchill, was two-pronged: to destabilize the Ottoman batteries guarding the Aegean coast, followed by an allied French and British naval push through the Dardanelles. On March 18, 1915, under the command of Admiral de Roebeck, a seven-hour sea offensive saw Allied warships penetrate 11 kilometers through the straits before being forced to retreat. This single event cost the lives of more than 20,000 combatants. The Allies later realized that their Turkish opponents had been on the verge of capitalizing on that fateful day, for they had all but exhausted their ammunition. Retreating to the Greek island of Limnos in the Aegean Sea, the Allies took roughly a month to prepare a ground offensive to secure the Gallipoli Peninsula, Dardanelles, and the Asian coastal region to the south. The strategy was implemented on April 14. British and French troops were to land near Cape Helles on the peninsula's southern tip, while Anzac forces aimed for the western flank. The plan was for the two flanks to rejoin somewhere in between.

Little did they know that the Turks had also regrouped. With the Ottoman army's 9th infantry division showing impossible resolve, the Anglo-French offensive only succeeded in gaining a single beach and little scrubland after months of warfare. The Anzacs were not so lucky when they botched their landing: The troops reached Arıburnu's massive cliffs far north of their intended target of Kabatepe's wide-open beach. The precipitous terrain impeded their inland progress, as did the resilient counteroffensive commanded by Ottoman Lieutenant Colonel Mustafa Kemal Atatürk, who went on to establish the Turkish Republic less than a decade later. The Turks pushed the Anzacs back over the crags and strengthened their lines over the next few months. Some of World War I's goriest trench warfare ensued between the Johnnies (Anzacs) and Mehmets (Turks). Both sides cleared away the other's dead despite frostbite in the winter and widespread epidemics of enteric fever and dysentery. Turkish and Anzac troops, some entrenched just eight meters apart, engaged each other in conversation once the bell signifying the end of combat for the day would ring. So close was their proximity that a despondent Atatürk led his men into battle with these words: "I am not asking you to attack; I am ordering you to die. For in the time it takes for us to die, other soldiers and commanders will arrive to take our place."

It wasn't until December 1915, after a handful of ineffective campaigns, that the Allies issued the first order to withdraw. In nine months and one of the war's goriest conflicts, 130,784 combatants died, more than 70 percent of them Turks, and 392,338 were wounded. The blame for the botched offensive was laid squarely on British command, with repercussions including Churchill's demotion to Minister of Munitions and a loss of faith in British prime minister Herbert Asquith's single-party Liberal government. For the Aussies, Gallipoli was their first military conflict after gaining independence from Britain, a galvanizing turning point for the then fledgling state. For the Turks, little was said, except that they maintained their centuries-old reputation for ferocity and bravery in battle. And, for Atatürk, his military success at Gallipoli cost him dearly five years later when he rallied just a handful of Turks for the War of Independence. Following the 1918 Armistice, the French and British returned to Gallipoli to officially bury their dead.

Northern Sights

Opened in 2012, the US$80 million **Çanakkale Destanı Tantıtım Merkezi** (Kabatepe Simulation Center, Kabatepe, 0286/810-0050, 9am-5pm daily, 13TL) is a good place to start a tour of Gallipoli—just follow the signs from Eceabat. Guests are given a headset at the ticket booth to watch and listen to 3-D re-creations of the Gallipoli campaign in 11 galleries that also display uniforms and personal effects from the war. Poignant displays show the weaponry used and the bullets fired, including the bullet-pierced skull of a Turkish soldier.

Heading westward, a 600-meter uphill climb leads to the camping grounds and ferry docks of **Kabatepe.** Following the coastal road for a couple of kilometers north leads through the cemeteries of **Shell Green, Beach,** and **Shrapnel Valley.** At Beach Cemetery you'll see one grave with more red poppies, a symbol of remembrance in Commonwealth countries, than most; this is the burial site of Private John Simpson Kirkpatrick, a British-born Anzac immortalized in the legend "Simpson and His Donkey." As a stretcher bearer, Simpson evacuated the wounded from the front lines with donkeys found near the battlefields. His extraordinary feat of courage occurred under constant gunfire until he was mortally wounded three weeks after the landing.

Farther north is **Anzac Cove,** the Aussie and Kiwi ill-fated landing site. This is where Anzac forces were ordered to climb over the crag with lines of Turkish infantry guns pointed at them from the ledge above. Atatürk commanded the Ottoman troops to that spot, ignoring his orders to station his men at Cape Helles. Failing miserably to gain the cliffs, the remains of thousands of doomed Anzacs are buried in rows of marked graves along this Gallipoli coastline. Atatürk's stirring 1934 tribute to the enemy is memorialized in marble nearby:

> Those heroes that shed their blood
>
> And lost their lives …
>
> You are now lying in the soil
> of a friendly country.
>
> Therefore, rest in peace
>
> There is no difference between the Johnnies
>
> And the Mehmets to us where
> they lie side by side,
>
> Here in this country of ours.
>
> You, the mothers, who sent their
> sons from faraway countries …
>
> Wipe away your tears.
>
> Your sons are now lying in our bosom
>
> And are in peace.
>
> After having lost their lives
> on this land, they have
>
> Become our sons as well.

Anzac Cove meets the cemetery of **Arıburnu** just south of the **Anzac Commemorative Site** at North Beach, where the annual memorial ceremonies are held on April 25. Farther north you'll come to the graveyards of **Canterbury,** New Zealand's **No. 2 Outpost** and **Embarkation Pier.**

Head back toward the Kabatepe Simulation Center, but before reaching the museum, take the inland loop road that passes the remaining sites of interest. The first stop is the **Unknown Soldier Monument,** depicting a Turkish soldier carrying a wounded Brit back across enemy lines. This poignant memorial was inspired by Australian governor general Lord Casey during a visit to the peninsula in

Anzac troops landed at Anzac Cove on April 25, 1915 under heavy artillery fire from Ottoman soldiers.

1967. While serving as a lieutenant during the campaign, Casey witnessed a Mehmet carry a wounded British soldier from a Turkish position, back to his comrades in Allied trenches, just meters away.

A few hundred meters ahead is **Lone Pine** (Kanlı Sırt), where Aussies mounted a large offensive the evening of August 6 to divert the Turks away from Suvla Bay, where the Brits were landing. The battle here alone, often with one-on-one combat, saw more than 9,000 casualties for both sides in four days and was regarded as a small victory for the Anzacs, though they gained little ground. The cemetery is named after the sole Aleppo pine that existed here during the battle; the Turks had chopped down the rest of the trees to construct their trenches, leaving just one. The tree now in the center of the cemetery is seeded from the original.

Continuing on, the road past **Johnston's Jolly** and **Quinn's Post** cemeteries follows the previous no-man's-land between the narrow line of trenches, literally meters apart.

Beneath, a large system of tunnels was dug to provide supply lines.

About one kilometer farther on from Lone Pine is the **Turkish 57th Regiment Memorial,** the first Ottoman regiment to attack after the landings, led by Atatürk. The statue at the front of the memorial is that of Hüseyin Kaçmaz and his granddaughter. Hüseyin was the last surviving Turkish Gallipoli veteran, who died in 1994 at age 110. Incidentally, his children can recount his war stories and how he first tasted chocolate after the Johnnys hurled bars into the Ottoman trenches in a sign of Aussie mateship.

Farther uphill, the road forks; bear left to pass the **Mehmet Çavuş Monument,** which commemorates the Mehmetçikler (Turkish soldiers) who died defending their native soil from these high ridges. The path then leads to **The Nek,** the site of one of the most tragic and senseless losses of life for the Anzacs during the campaign. On August 7, a mishap of ill-timed military actions and commands saw four waves of 150 men from the 3rd Light Horse Brigade gun downed in a 30-meter charge to the impenetrable Ottoman line of defense. The event killed 314 men in 15 minutes—almost half the troops of Victoria and Western Australia's 8th and 10th Lighthorse Regiments—and was described at the time by one commander as "bloody murder." The series of ill-fated events at The Nek are featured in the 1981 movie *Gallipoli*.

The last and highest site to visit is **Chunuk Bair,** the southern summit of Sari Bair, which saw a successful charge by New Zealand and British soldiers on August 8, momentarily gaining control of this strategic position. A counterattack by Atatürk's troops two days later had them retreating back down the slopes. Today, you can take in the view here as well as photograph the trenches and numerous memorials.

Cape Helles

Largely skipped by visitors but not forgotten, the region southwest of Kilitbahir is known as **Cape Helles,** where the Anglo-French offensive was launched. Near the main intersection in Alcıtepe village, 16 kilometers from Kilitbahir, is a privately owned **War Museum** (9am-5pm daily, donation). Proprietor Salim Mutlu has amassed a small but interesting collection of war memorabilia, such as artillery, medals, and letters laboriously handwritten by the soldiers to their families waiting for their return. Past the village, the road continues to several cemeteries and monuments along the tip of the peninsula.

The southernmost farming village of **Seddülbahir** contains a beach, a port, and the remains of an Ottoman fortress. Just over one kilometer to the west is the stark **Cape Helles Memorial Center,** a tall obelisk honoring the 20,000 British who fought during the arduous nine-month campaign. This monument provides an ideal place from which to watch cargo ships lazily pass through the straits. On August 15, 1915, just after 6am, the Brits landed at the mouth of the straits, barely 300 meters to the west, producing a hailstorm of bullets at **V Beach.** Thousands of lives were lost as the Brits tried to press their ships through the channel and force the greatly outnumbered Turkish line into retreat. Between Helles and V Beach is a memorial displaying models of trenches dedicated to Yahya Çavuş, the sergeant who commanded the initial defense of the peninsula; there are also British cemeteries here.

Eight kilometers northeast of Seddülbahir is the **French War Memorial and Cemetery.** The moving monument contains a handful of ossuaries and endless rows of metal crosses. In March 1915 the 10,000 French troops, including those from the country's colonies, mainly North Africans, descended on the Asian shore at Kumkale and had no problem claiming the outpost. They then joined the British front, where they suffered near annihilation. Just east, the 44-meter-tall **Abide Memorial** honors the martyrs of Çanakkale, all the Turks who lost their lives during the Gallipoli campaign.

Accommodations

If you plan to stay overnight in the region, there are several options. Modern hotels are available in Çanakkale, just across the straits. If you need a simple clean space that's inexpensive, Eceabat is worth a look. The outposts of Seddülbahir and Kum Limanı also have a number of small motels, but their isolation makes them almost inaccessible in the evening, unless you have your own transportation.

In Eceabat, the **Hotel Cassa Villa** (Camburnu Sk. 75, Eceabat, 0286/814-1320, www.otelcasavilla.com, from 75TL), is ideal for those with their own wheels and offers nine rooms with balconies, one kilometer from the Çanakkale-Eceabat ferry port. The big bonus here is the expansive garden where breakfast is served in view of the Dardanelles. Each room is decorated with its own unique style and color by the owner, Birgül Ejder, so it may pay to visit the website and request the room suited to your tastes.

For the best in inexpensive and pristine lodgings just opposite the port, ★ **Crowded House** (Huseyin Avni Sk. 4, 0286/814-1565, www.crowdedhousegallipoli.com, €25-40) offers 27 basic rooms with en suite baths, air-conditioning, and complimentary breakfast. Both family- and backpacker-oriented, the hotel is owned by amicable duo Ziya Artman and Polat Cenboz, who are always happy to share their extensive knowledge of the peninsula, assist with tours, and offer a host of fun activities. The tours also hire highly qualified guides such as the legendary Bülent Yilmaz Korkmaz, affectionately known as Bill. After your tour, sojourn to the hotel's secret garden for a refreshing drink with fellow travelers.

Hotel Ejder (Ataturk Cd. 5, 0286/814-2697, 100TL) is earning good reviews for its friendly service, simple clean rooms, and location just 500 meters from the port. Request a room with a balcony for extra space or take to the rooftop terrace for a breezy view of the Dardanelles.

For out-of-the-way rustic accommodations, ★ **The Gallipoli Houses** (Kocadere Village 29, 0286/814-2650, www.thegallipolihouses.com, €55-105) offer renowned complimentary breakfasts and dinners, home-cooked by owner and tourism specialist Özlem Gündüz. With her significant other, Belgian historian Eric Goosens, the duo have provided an unequaled experience, merging European elegance and Turkish hospitality in this idyllic traditional stone B&B with 10 simply furnished rooms. Book the largest Kocadere room, with a balcony and views of the village and the Aegean Sea.

In Seddülbahir, **Pansiyon Helles Panorama** (atop Seddülbahir Hill, 0286/862-0035, www.hellespanorama.com.tr, 35TL) is a gem that stares straight at the colossal Abide monument and the Aegean Sea. Superior in service and lodgings, the only downside here is that the baths are shared, but the local knowledge and hospitality of Erol and Naile Baycan are worth the stay in this unique setting.

Food

Outside Çanakkale and the excellent restaurants in some of the hotels of this area, fish lovers will revel in Eceabat. Along the harbor are a variety of fish restaurants, but none equal ★ **Liman Balık Restoran** (Istiklal Cd. 67, 0286/814-2755, www.limanrestaurant.net, 20TL), with great views of the straits. Eight prix fixe specials (20-38TL) please carnivores and vegetarians alike. The set menus include five dishes, though you can also order off an à la carte menu.

Information and Services

Everything you need, such as ATMs, is located around the port where the car ferry to Çanakkale departs. The nearest tourism office is in Çanakkale, and your hotel front desk will have local tourism information. The post office, **PTT** (Cumhurıyet Cd. 38, 8:30am-5pm daily), is available for currency exchange, adding value to HGS (toll road) cards, and postal services.

Getting There and Around

You can reach Eceabat by air, coach, and ferry via Çanakkale, the nearest transportation hub for Eceabat on the other side of the Dardanelles. Once in Çanakkale, head to the port to board the hourly **ferry** (0286/444-0752, www.gestasdenizulasim.com.tr, 2.50TL pp, car and passengers 29TL) that transports you to Eceabat in 25 minutes, every hour on the hour. Otherwise, the quickest and most common way independent travelers reach Eceabat is via **coach** from Istanbul (45TL, 5.5 hours) with **Kamil Koç** (444-0562, www.kamilkoc.com.tr), **Metro Turizm** (444-3455, www.metroturizm.com.tr), or **Truva Turizm** (444-0017, www.truvaturizm.com); get tickets either online or via their sales offices in bus stations and touristed areas.

Drivers should take the E80/O-3 (Trans-European Motorway) in Istanbul, a toll road, and exit at Kınalı (standard vehicle toll from European Istanbul 3TL). Continue on the E84 until Kesan, then turn left onto the E87 and follow this highway to Eceabat.

The Northern Aegean Coast

Çanakkale and Truva (Troy) 159
Bergama (Pergamum).......... 184
İzmir............................ 191

The northern Aegean has thrived for thousands of years on the fertility of its soil and the beauty of its shores. The Bay of Edremit is known as the Olive Riviera due to the orchards and hundreds of olive processing factories that dot the region, and verdant plateaus are home to the Yörüks (nomadic herders), who've prospered for centuries from farming and artisanship high in the hills.

The Aegean provides an array of activities for sun and sea worshippers. With a slew of boutique hotels, the seaside resorts of Assos, Ayvalık, Foça, and Çeşme are the jewels of the region. Divers revel in the offshore scenery, and there are the very rare Mediterranean monk seal near Foça, spectral undersea rock formations, secluded coves, and varied fauna all along the coast. Near Çanakkale is the increasingly popular island of Bozcaada, the smallest of Turkey's two remaining isles in the Aegean Sea. Bozcaada has been feted since antiquity for its wine. Today, its cobblestone backstreets and picturesque beaches are hosting Turks who want to vacation away from the crowded resorts to the south.

The area's natural beauty and abundance has lured civilizations from near and far for eons. Virtually every empire of the Mediterranean region called this region home at one time, including the Persians, Lydians, Visigoths, and Romans. The sheer wealth of historical sites is amazing. From the heavily visited legendary ancient cities of Truva (Troy) and Bergama (Pergamum) to the remnants of the centuries-old synagogues and Orthodox churches of İzmir, the northern Aegean coast offers historical wonders alongside its calm, cool waters.

At virtually every stop, you'll find dishes crafted of delectable ingredients sprouted from land so rich that the amicable locals often joke that no sowing is required. The archipelago around Ayvalık is filled with *papalina* (baby sardines), fried and served in mounds in the summer, which Turks and their Hellenic neighbors travel long distances for. The region is also famed for its fabulous herbs. For an inside view of this bounty, check out a *pazar* (farmers market), where Yörük

Previous: harbor of Assos; Sanctuary of Trajan, Pergamum. **Above:** replica of the Trojan Horse, Troy.

Look for ★ to find recommended sights, activities, dining, and lodging.

Highlights

★ **Truva (Troy):** Try to keep track of the many incarnations of Troy at this ancient spot, located at the western tip of the Biga Peninsula (page 165).

★ **Bozcaada:** With its scenic green landscape, Bozcaada is an ideal island to frolic in the waves, catch some rays, and sip a local vintage (page 170).

★ **Assos:** Check out what is arguably the most picturesque village on the Aegean. From its heights, the Doric Temple of Athena affords breathtaking sunset views (page 176).

★ **Bergama's Acropolis:** Explore the magnificent ruins and stand at the foundation of the former Altar of Zeus. The steep terraces look out onto the fields of ancient Pergamum (page 187).

★ **Foça:** Laze through this nostalgic Greek enclave and find the perfect terrace along the city's old fishing wharf to enjoy the day's luscious catch (page 189).

★ **Sart (Sardis):** Check out one of the richest cities of antiquity—the first to mint coins—and its ruins, spanning 5,000 years (page 202).

★ **Alaçatı:** Rub elbows with the country's wealthy and fashionable in this party outpost, popular for its water sports, boutique hotels, and flamboyant nightlife (page 206).

women clad in traditional and colorful garb peddle seaweed, homespun carpets, olives, and honey.

What makes this region memorable is its laid-back atmosphere and welcoming spirit. Northern Aegeans are known for their brand of celebrated Turkish hospitality, exemplified when, for example, non-English-speaking Turks run off to find an English-speaking local to help travelers.

PLANNING YOUR TIME

Most coach tours swoop through this area in a day or two from Çanakkale to the relics of Troy and Bergama and end in either İzmir or the southern Aegean. Instead, take your time and discover the serene points in between. Devote the first day to touring the busy port city of Çanakkale, followed by ancient Troy or Gallipoli. From there, insert a day or two on the sleepy isle of Bozcaada or head south to the ancient port city of Assos. Spend the evening around Assos's wharf and bed down in one of its luxurious B&Bs. After a day in Ayvalık and Cunda island, visit ancient Pergamum's abundant Greco-Roman ruins in Bergama. Early in the afternoon, head to quaint Foça, 105 kilometers to the south. When sated, set the compass due south for the religious treasures of biblical İzmir—Turkey's third-largest city and port. Earmark the next day for Sardis's gorgeously intact Byzantine shops and baths complex.

For a longer itinerary, in summer, insert a couple of days on the Çeşme Peninsula or opt for a boat trip to lush, green Lesbos—a Greek island whose ancient fortifications hold monuments that retrace some 3,000 years of history.

Spring and fall are known for showy bougainvillea in the villages. Most festivals in this culturally rich area occur between June and September, including the annual Bergama celebration of its ancient history and various annual odes to the harvest of local fruits. Gusty winds batter the Aegean coast and reduce tourism to a trickle in winter. Buses and ferries between smaller towns such as Assos, Çeşme, and the island of Bozcaada becomes infrequent—an inconvenience for travelers without a car.

HISTORY

The northern Aegean coast is the top of a circle that encompasses the ancient Greek realm of Asia Minor. Major cities were populated by the prominent kingdoms of the day—early Romans, Greeks, Persians, and finally the Ottomans. This large chunk of land traces some of its known history to the ancient Greek site of Troy, immortalized in Homer's *Iliad* and *Odyssey.* Troy dates to the late Bronze Age, 5,000 years ago. No less than 12 different communities were built on the original ruins, nine of which are clearly detailed on-site. The most recent layer is dated to the first century BC. The region's interior may date back even earlier. Ruins like those found in Sart (Sardis), 105 kilometers east of İzmir, hold remnants attesting to the city's continuous role as a major metropolis for more than 5,000 years. Exceptionally fertile lands and a temperate climate provided endless and varied sustenance. Polytheistic kingdoms gave way to Judaism, Christianity, and Islam, which lived peacefully side-by-side for centuries.

Çanakkale and Truva (Troy)

The top of the northern Aegean territory is Anatolia's westernmost point, where its low coastal crags taper off into the Dardanelles. Çanakkale sits at the strategic narrowest point between the Thracian shore and Anatolia. The landscape is steeped in mythology, including the myth in Homer's story about Zeus's son, Dardanus, who built a city on the Asian shore of the passage and named it after himself; the name of the straits today, the Dardanelles, is a corruption of that moniker. Another myth tells of young Leander, a resident of Abydus, an ancient Asian outpost along the southern shores of the straits, who swam across the treacherous straits to the town of Sestus to embrace his love, Hero. But the torch Hero lit to guide her lover blew out, and Leander lost his way and drowned. The story piqued poet Lord Byron's interest and he, too, was inspired to cross the channel in 1810.

The epic ruins at Troy, about 30 minutes' drive west of Çanakkale, reflect more than just Homer's romanticized accounts of the decade-long Trojan Wars; they impart 5,000 years of continuous history through the layers of relics.

Just off the Aegean coast, the island of Bozcaada offers wine and sandy beaches. Back on the mainland, a few other Roman, Greek, and Ottoman historical sites near Çanakkale and Troy are interspersed with sleepy villages. Along the route you'll see fields of wheat, sunflowers, wildflowers, olive trees, and the occasional turtle.

ÇANAKKALE

A busy port town along the Dardanelles, Çanakkale serves as a base for travelers headed to Troy and Gallipoli National Park. Unexpected perhaps is the busy nightlife the city offers, thanks to a booming student population attending the local Onsekiz Mart Universitesi and the masses of Australians who descend on the scenic harbor and the bars on Fetvane Sokak in late April for Anzac Day. Aside from being Turkey's second-busiest transcontinental transportation hub, after Istanbul, Çanakkale's blue-collar interior

the port town of Çanakkale

Çanakkale

abounds with food processing and manufacturing plants.

Thanks to its position at the narrowest point—1,200 meters—along the 60-kilometer Dardanelles, the area known as Çanakkale boasts a 5,000-year history. This geopolitically important location has been continually inhabited and has weathered conquests and bloodshed since antiquity. In 480 BC, the Persian army, led by Xerxes I, crossed the channel to conquer Macedonian lands. Alexander the Great's Macedonian troops successfully reversed the gory takeover in the opposite direction 150 years later. Alexander sacrificed a bull here to appease the sea god Poseidon to ensure a peaceful crossing.

The channel was historically known as Hellespont, a name from the myth of Helle and Phrixus, the children of the cloud goddess Nephele and King Athamas. The king fell in love and later married Ino, abandoning his previous wife, Nephele. Her retreat caused a great drought. Ino, jealous of the children, was persuaded the drought would end if Athamas would pacify the gods by sacrificing Helle and Phrixus. Getting wind of this, Nephele sent her twins away astride a flying ram with a golden fleece. While in flight over the Dardanelles, Princess Helle fell into the water and drowned.

The Dardanelles were crucial to the defense of Constantinople during Byzantine times. Knowing this, the Ottomans conquered the passage in the 14th century in order to control its maritime traffic, and consequently gained control of the Byzantine capital. In 1462, Mehmet the Conqueror planned the construction of two bastions on either side of the channel—Kilitbahir Hısarı on the European shore and Kale-I Sultaniye on the other—to deter the eastbound passage of Christian boats and to further secure Istanbul.

At the start of the 19th century, the Russian Empire sought control of the Dardanelles, launching a century-long struggle among the flailing Ottoman Empire, the Allies, and the Russians for supremacy over the straits. During World War I, the nine-month Gallipoli campaign for control of the Dardanelles left 130,784 combatants dead.

If time allows, spend half a day in Çanakkale along the pier and take in the significance of its geography and the succulent seafood at one of the waterside restaurants. Allow a day to explore the artifacts from the Gallipoli Campaign and the ancient relics of Troy.

Sights

One street back from the port in the square between Yalı Caddesi and Fetvane Sokak is the five-tiered, four-sided **Saat Kulesi** (Clock Tower). The tower was built in 1897 from local Ayvalık stone with 10,000 gold coins bequeathed by Emilio Vitalis, a wealthy Italian merchant and consul who lived adjacent to the square.

Walking down Yalı Caddesi leads to the gates of the **Military Museum and Çimenlik Fortress** (0286/213-1730, www.denizmuzeleri.tsk.tr, 9am-noon and 1:30pm-5pm Tues.-Wed. and Fri.-Sun., 5TL). Also known as the Deniz Müzesi (Naval Museum), this complex overlooking the Dardanelles consists of several exhibition spaces depicting the 1915 Çanakkale Naval Battle and Campaign. Between the entrance and the fortress is a large park displaying the weaponry and anchors of World War I. The remnants of *UB-46*, a 37-meter German submarine, lies in the middle of the park. The wreckage was recovered in Istanbul in 1993, years after the submarine was destroyed by a mine in the Black Sea in 1916.

Beyond the park is the entrance to the 15th-century **Çimenlik Fortress** (Kale-I Sultaniye), comprising an entrance hall, a forecourt, and a main fortress. Images of the fortress's military history adorn the entrance hall, with the forecourt housing the Fatih and Abdulaziz mosques—the later showing copies of some of the world's oldest maps drafted by Ottoman admiral and cartographer Piri Reis in the 16th century. In the forecourt you can also view a 38-centimeter unexploded shell from the British battleship HMS *Queen Elizabeth*. It left quite an impression on the fortress—a large hole in its northern wall. Upstairs in the main fortress are three levels devoted to the 1915 Gallipoli Campaign.

Before leaving the museum, visit the replica of the *Nusrat* minelayer. The original ship played a crucial role in hampering the Allied attacks of March 18, 1915, by replacing mines at night on seabeds that had been previously cleared by French and British minesweepers.

Located near the Naval Museum is the busy shopping strip of **Çarşı Caddesi.** A leisurely stroll up the street leads to the touristy **Aynalı Çarşı** (Mirrored Bazaar), a covered walkway selling the typical wares of a traditional bazaar. Originally built in 1889 but damaged in World War I, the bazaar reopened in 2007 after a restoration.

Take in the mementos and legendary stories of the city at the **Çanakkale Kent Müzesi** (Fetvane Sk. 31, 0286/214-3417, www.

canakkalekentmuzesi.com, 10am-7pm daily Apr.-Aug., 9am-5pm daily Sept.-May, free). The who's who of Çanakkale's past is shown in a timeline of events, giving perspective to the region's history and attractions. Guidebooks are available in English.

Rest and reenergize down the street in the pleasant cobblestoned sanctuary of **Yalı Han** (Fetvane Sk. 28, 10am-midnight daily). Sip *çay* (tea) or savor the aroma of Turkish coffee alongside übercool city folk in this 19th-century meeting place for travelers.

Returning to the port, walk along the pier adjacent to Kayserili Ahmet Paşa Caddesi to meet a real movie star—the towering **Trojan Horse** from the 2004 film *Troy*. An educational 3-D model of the ancient city of Troy can be found close by its hooves.

The dominating German **Krupp Fortress Gun** on Cumhuriyet Caddesi was used by the *Mehmetçik* (Turkish soldiers) on March 18, 1915, to defend the city from the Franco-British naval fleet.

ARKEOLOJI MÜZESI (ARCHAEOLOGICAL MUSEUM)

Çanakkale's **Arkeoloji Müzesi** (100. Yıl Cd., 0286/217-6740, 9am-5pm daily, 5TL) contains astoundingly detailed terra-cotta statues, coinage, gold jewelry, bronze, and glass perfume bottles recovered from digs around the region, including those salvaged from the nearby Dardanos tombs in 1974. There's also a small array of relics unearthed at Troy in the 19th century by Heinrich Schliemann and artifacts collected from the necropolis on Bozcaada.

To reach the museum, take a municipal bus going to Kepez from the bus stop on Kayserili Ahmet Paşa Caddesi, in front of the port. The bus will travel through the town, crossing a small bridge on Atatürk Caddesi, where the *dolmuş* (communal taxi) for Troy departs. A few stops after the bridge is the Pazar Pazarı bus stop. Get off here, and the museum is ahead on the left by the traffic lights. Active types may enjoy the easy 25-minute walk between the port and museum.

The star of the blockbuster *Troy* is now a star attraction in Çanakkale.

Events

War commemorations are held each year at two different times. The Turks celebrate **Çanakkale Deniz Zaferi** (Çanakkale Naval Victory) on March 18, the day Ottoman armed forces foiled the Allied naval push through the strait. Kiwis and Aussies honor their tens of thousands of war dead on **Anzac Day** (Apr. 25) at dawn, the time and date of the ill-fated Allied landings in 1915. An internationally televised ceremony is followed by various commemorative services throughout the historic peninsula.

Celebrated in mid-August since 1963, the **International Troy Festival** (Çanakkale Municipality, 0286/217-1079, www.canakkale.bel.tr) resuscitates ancient Troy with guided tours, reenactments, and folkloric performances in addition to a variety of art and film exhibitions.

Nightlife

With 37,500 university students residing in the town and a steady stream of travelers,

Çanakkale has a good vibe after the sun sets over the Gallipoli Peninsula, particularly in summer. Bars are found along Fetvane Sokak, Matbaa Sokak, and all along the pier. For a local favorite head to Eskibalıkhane Sokak near the ferry and look for the 1960s Chevy protruding from the roof of **Benzin Café & Bar** (0286/212-2237, until 2am daily). This American diner-inspired café caters to budget-conscious local students with a comprehensive menu of affordable snacks, entrées, and cocktails. Pucker up for the rum and mint-laced Cocos Kiss—a refreshing drink to end a day's touring. For live music and DJs, **TNT Bar** (Saat Kulesi Meydanı 6, 0286/217-0470) attracts locals and travelers looking to rock out in a casual setting. The crème de la crème of Çanakkale nightspots is **Lodos** (Nara Sk. 1, 0286/217-2079), where groovers can dance on the waterfront overlooking the Dardanelles or recline on lounges encircling the dance floor.

Accommodations

As a waypoint between continents, Çanakkale is filled with assorted lodging options. Be forewarned: Around Anzac Day (Apr. 25) there can be no vacancies for a week. Unless you're here to honor the fallen, avoid the second half of April.

European provincial style on the Dardanelles is at ★ **Hotel Limani** (Yalı Cd. 12, 0286/217-2908, www.hotellimani.com, from €82). Owner Hüseyin Yalman and his wife, Hulya, lived in each of the 32 rooms for 1.5 years to perfect the hotel experience; the results are seen in the European decor and modern comforts throughout. The terrace suite, with a private balcony, will impress, as will breakfast served just meters from the shore.

Anzac Hotels owns four hotels in the city, each with similar attractive decor, knowledgeable staff, and complimentary tea coffee with Turkish delight. The **Grand Anzac Hotel** (Kemal Yeri Sk. 11, 0286/216-0016, www.anzachotels.com, from €40) is one of the newest, with 37 rooms on four floors, located close to the clock tower. After exploring Troy and Gallipoli, appreciate relaxing in the comforts of the hotel watching complimentary screenings of the film *Troy* and the 1981 Australian war movie *Gallipoli*. Discounts for accommodations are available; check the website.

Another Anzac Hotels lodging is the newly renovated historical **Kervansaray Hotel** (Fetvane Sk. 13, 0286/217-7777, www.otelkervansaray.com, from €45). This century-old redbrick judge's mansion has maintained the simple grandeur of Ottoman times with high ceilings, polished floorboards, and regal style. Rooms facing the tranquil garden for the guests have afternoon sun. A new annex with eight rooms complements the classical design of the main building with the modern amenities of its sister hotels.

Next door to Kervansaray is the incredibly inexpensive **Efes Hotel** (Talat Orhan Salcioglu Sk. 13, 0286/217-3256, from 60TL). Mrs. Yetimoğlu has proudly owned the hotel for 35 years and offers friendly hospitality, complimentary breakfast, and basic lodgings. The rooms, while showing their age, are clean and large, with the better rooms overlooking the garden or facing Fetvane Sokak.

Backpackers searching for a shared dorm room or basic private rooms will find **Hotel Anzac House** (Cumhuriyet Meydanı 59, 0286/213-2550, www.anzachouse.com, dorm 30TL, private room from 70TL) just a short walk from the port. Comforts are limited, with shared baths, and a few rooms have air-conditioning, but on the upside, Hassle Free Travel Agency is on-site for travel planning.

The only five-star hotel in Çanakkale, the 274-room **Hotel Kolin—The Hellespont** (Kepez, 0286/218-0808, www.kolinhotel.com, from €130) was built for the demands of visiting dignitaries. Glitterati such as Prince Charles enjoy sumptuous spa options, an indoor-outdoor pool, and a myriad of restaurants, bars, and sporting facilities. The hotel is located in Kepez, away from the main sights of the city but with panoramic views of the strait.

Food

Çanakkale is a place to revel in seafood, especially the ubiquitous sardines. The best dining options are at the waterside restaurants lining the pier, where you'll find typical Turkish "fast-food" fare in addition to local specialties like *peynirli helva* (sheep cheese and semolina), *şakşuka* (Mediterranean veggies cooked in olive oil), just-harvested mussels, and everything else from the water. Expect most dishes to be generously drizzled with local olive oil with lemon zest. For wine pairings, try one of the Eceabat wines by Suvla or any of the recommended wines from Bozcaada.

To savor Çanakkale's bounty, try the six-decade-old **Yalova Restaurant** (Gümrük Sk. 7, 0286/217-1045, www.yalovarestaurant.com, 22TL). Known for its mezes, this place also serves a vast range of local seafood, including oysters and melt-in-your-mouth anglerfish. Reserve a table by the window or on the rooftop terrace and dine as the sun sets over the Gelibolu Peninsula.

The smaller **Sea Side** (Balıkhane Sk. 3, 0286/214-2726, 18TL) is a cheaper and equally satisfying option for fish restaurants by the port with homegrown musicians playing for diners every night of the year.

Dine meters from the water at **Café du Port** (Yalı Cd. 12, 0286/213-5970, www.cafeduport.com.tr, 18TL), owned by the Limani Hotel and with a comprehensive menu showcasing local favorites as well as Italian pastas, risotto, and Asian noodles.

For cheap an and cheerful meals, **Gülen Pide** (Cumhuriyet Meydanı 27A, 0286/212-8800, 10TL) and **Doyum Pide Kebap Restaurant** (Cumhuriyet Cd. 13, 0286/217-1866, 15TL) both offer a selection of regional cuisine, kebabs, *pide*, and pizzas. Yalı Caddesi is also lined with *döner* kebab shops that will fill the belly for under 10TL.

Along the trendy waterfront, the always hip and dependable **Café Notte** (Kayserili Ahmet Paşa Cd. 40, 0286/214-9111) is not only an evening spot infused with a chic continental feel, it's also a modern café that features a gourmet shop of regional produce, including a great selection of Turkish wines.

Minimarts selling drinks and snacks are found throughout the city, with the major Carrefour supermarket next to well-known fast-food chains on Atatürk Caddesi, near the *eski* (old) *otogar* (bus station).

Information and Services

As the district's main city, Çanakkale's **Turizm Danışma** (Tourism Office, 0286/217-1187) is on the right just after you leave the port; it has detailed maps and brochures pertaining to the region. Postal services can be found at the **PTT** outpost by the port or at the main office on Inonu Caddesi (8:30am-5:30pm Mon.-Sat.), which opposite the **Çanakkale State Hospital** (0286/217-1098). ATMs are located throughout town; branches of national banks are located along Çarşı Caddesi, with a currency exchange office located just up from the Tourism Office on Cumhuriyet Meydanı.

Getting There

AIR

Regular one-hour direct flights from Istanbul to Çanakkale are provided by **Bora Jet** (0212/465-2878, www.borajet.com.tr). Taxis (25TL) and local buses are available for transportation between the airport and the city center and port, about three kilometers apart. The bus costs 2.50TL but requires the purchase of either a KentKart (4.50TL) or a Kullanat Kart (0.80TL).

BUS

A new Çanakkale *otogar* is served every day by coaches from major cities. Purchase tickets from **Kamil Koç** (www.kamilkoc.com.tr), **Metro Turiszm** (www.metroturizm.com.tr), or **Truva Turiszm** (www.truvaturizm.com) either online or at their sales offices in bus stations and touristed areas. Tickets can also be purchased from selected travel agencies, but shop around for the best fares. Approximate prices and travel times to Çanakkale, with breaks: Bayrampaşa Otogarı in Istanbul

(60TL, 6 hours); Ankara (65TL, 12 hours); Bursa (35TL, 5 hours); Edirne (45TL, 3 hours); and İzmir (45TL, 6 hours).

Coaches from Istanbul include a 25-minute ferry from Eceabat to the port of Çanakkale. You can take the coach at either *iskele meydani* (port) before it terminates at the Çanakkale *otogar,* six kilometers away. Coaches from cities on the Anatolian side terminate at the *otogar.* Transfer there for the bus company's free *servis* (free shuttle bus) which drops passengers near the sales offices next to the Çanakkale port.

FERRY

From Istanbul, take the smooth **IDO fast ferry** (www.ido.com.tr, 2 hours, from 39TL pp) from Yenikapı (near Sultanahmet) to Bandırma, a seaside port on the Anatolian side. At Bandırma, board a local bus (1.75TL) from the bus station as you exit the port and travel through the town and industrial area for 20 minutes to the *otogar.* Truva and Kamil Koç (25TL, 2.5 hours) have direct coaches from here to Çanakkale. Ferry tickets can be bought from the IDO website or at Yenikapı port. Buy in advance for the best fares. Using the ferry can be a faster option than the direct coaches from Istanbul, but coach connections in Bandırma can delay arrival to Çanakkale.

CAR

From Istanbul, take the E80-TEM (Trans-European Motorway), a toll road, and exit at Kınalı. Continue on the E84 highway until Kesan, then turn left onto the E87 and follow it to Eceabat. Once there, watch for the road signs directing you to the Çanakkale *feribot* (ferry), which crosses to Çanakkale every hour on the hour 24 hours daily in 25 minutes. There's another crossing at Kilitbahir, three kilometers farther west, where smaller ferries take 15 minutes to cross the strait. Both services are run by **Gestaş** (0286/444-0752, www.gestasdenizulasim.com.tr, 2.50TL pp, car and 7 passengers 29TL). Schedules and fares are online and posted at Çanakkale's docks. Tickets are purchased at the port of departure. The whole journey between Istanbul and Çanakkale takes five to six hours.

Alternatively, take the **IDO fast ferry** (www.ido.com.tr, 2 hours, from 131TL per vehicle, 33TL pp) at Istanbul's Yenikapı seaport to Bandırma. This itinerary cuts 45 minutes from the older route. The remaining 160 kilometers west from Bandırma to Çanakkale takes about two hours.

Getting Around

Taxis are widely available, but if you stay near the port, restaurants and most attractions are within walking distance. If you intend to use the municipal **bus** to reach the *otogar* or Archaeology Museum, a **KentKart** (4.50TL) or a **Kullanat Kart** (0.80TL)—prepaid swipe cards similar to the IstanbulKart—is required. Both cards require you to add credit for fares, with the latter allowing top up for two journeys only. Cash fares are not accepted on municipal buses. Kiosks displaying the KentKart logo sell the cards, which you swipe when boarding the bus (1.50TL-2.50TL per journey). Municipal buses for the Çanakkale *otogar* can be hailed from Cumhuriyet Caddesi opposite Hotel Anzac House, or if you have a ticket with an intercity coach company, a *servis* bus to the *otogar* will depart near sales offices by the port.

★ TRUVA (TROY)

The sweeping tales of demigods, epic voyages, and a wooden horse were once assumed to be only legends in the Homeric texts, until the ruins of Troy were discovered in the late 19th century.

The possibility of finding the riches known as Priam's Treasure led German-born Heinrich Schliemann on a three-year dig culminating in 1873 when he discovered a collection of copper instruments and weapons, a chest of gold and silver jewelry, and a myriad of goblets made of precious metals. While a fraction of the hoard remains in Turkey, thanks to a trade Schliemann made with the Ottomans to extend his permission

The Truth About Homer's Trojan Wars

Remember beautiful Helen, whom Homer wrote about in the *Iliad* 3,000 years ago? She's said to have launched a decade-long conflict between two nations. Was it myth or actual history? Archaeologists have spent lifetimes digging for facts that would corroborate the Greek bard's lofty epic.

Homer's tale hinges on Helen, a Greek king's wife who is seduced by the Trojan prince Paris, who carries her off to the glorious city of Troy. The Greeks' fiercest king, Agamemnon, marshals an army, and with 1,000 ships lays siege to Troy to bring back Helen. The battle wears on for a decade, but Troy's fortifications remain impregnable, so the Greeks resort to trickery and hide Greek soldiers inside a wooden horse just outside the city. The Trojans pull the supposed peace offering inside, and the soldiers leap out and open the city gates.

While most academics agree that Homer composed the story in the 8th century BC, they also concur that the events at Troy might have occurred centuries before his lifetime in the late Bronze Age, when the Greeks first used writing. The invention of bronze revolutionized weaponry and warfare, hence the Trojan war is thought to have happened around 1200 BC. Evidence of the existence of Troy was found by the site's first amateur excavator, Heinrich Schliemann, in 1870.

Based on geographical clues gathered from Homer's texts, Schliemann accurately guessed Troy was located on a hill on the northwestern tip of the Biga Peninsula. Fifteen meters below the surface, Schliemann and his team of 200 discovered a walled palace, with a paved ramp wide enough to accommodate two chariots leading to the gate of a city—exactly as Homer described.

Schliemann was sure he'd found Troy, but the world was skeptical. The subsequent discovery of a hoard of precious jewels proved it had been home to prosperous and advanced people. As an amateur, however, Schliemann was unable to date the layers of the site. The team did not account for one well-known archaeological fact: Ancient civilizations erected cities on top of previous settlements, creating sequential layers. Troy is composed of nine distinct strata, each representing a different era and totaling 4,000 years of continuous inhabitation. The bottom layer dates to 2500 BC, the time when the Egyptians erected the pyramids. The top layer dates to the era of Christ.

As the science of archaeology evolved, more sophisticated tools were used to date Schliemann's findings, which turned out to be more than 1,000 years too old. Schliemann had dug too deep, to the late Bronze Age, the ninth layer. Homer's Troy was higher up, around the sixth layer's fortification walls. Here, excavations revealed physical structures, including towers, wide streets, tall gates, and a regal citadel that matched the story precisely. But while the city may have been wealthy and powerful, with walls that could have withstood a decade of siege, the site of Troy was much smaller than Homer's portrayal.

In 1988, German scientist Manfred Korfmann, along with a team of international archaeologists, turned their focus on the eight-meter-high fortification walls of the site and discovered that while these were indeed thick defenses, the ancients had made one basic error in their construction: The gates in the walls had no closing mechanism. The fact that fortifications of this size could have been built without any defenses perplexed Korfmann. Could it be that the city extended beyond what had already been discovered?

Almost a century after Schliemann's workers first dug, excavation resumed. Korfmann's team used magnetic imaging to explore underground, which led to the amazing discovery of a Roman city based on a grid plan hidden beneath the fields. Korfmann spotted one feature so faint that it could easily have been overlooked: A line between the walls that vacillated inward and outward. Excavation at

to dig, the bulk of the precious artifacts were smuggled out of the country. Most ended up at the Imperial Museum of Berlin, where it stayed until the Red Army shipped it to the former Soviet Union in 1945. After decades of the Russian government denying its existence, the treasure mysteriously appeared at Moscow's Pushkin Museum in 1993.

For some, Troy seems like just a collection of rocks; for others, it is a testament to the reality of Homer's tales. For scientists, the ruins provide a unique opportunity to detail the

this spot revealed a deep ditch that extended 700 meters around the mound. Korfmann believed that this was the massive defense Homer spoke of, one that was designed to stop chariots. This marked the actual outer limit of the lower city, and carbon dating of remains found in the ditch confirmed the late Bronze Age time frame. This sizable city, with 4,000-8,000 inhabitants, more closely matched the size described in Homer's tale.

Korfmann's team found evidence of violence in the lower city in the form of arrowheads, evidence of a catastrophic fire, and skeletons, providing undeniable evidence of a city that defended itself against a considerable enemy.

With the identity and size of Troy clearly defined, only a couple of questions remained: Were Troy's attackers really from Greece, as Homer said? And had they really been able to put together an armada of 1,000 warships? According to historians, this bit of Greek history occurred during the Mycenaean era. Greek archaeology professor Spyros Iakovidis, who has spent his career excavating ancient Mycenae, the capital of ancient Greece at that time, says that Mycenae was commanded from a palatial citadel from which a web of roads unfurled to each part of its dominion. And a military attack against any enemy state of Bronze Age Greece such as Troy may well have been launched from here.

The legendary might of these ancient Greek warriors as related by Homer was proved when a mass of graves was unearthed inside a walled cemetery within the fortifications of the Mycenaean citadel. Skeletons of men wearing colossal gold death masks and ornate ceremonial armor were found. These Mycenaean warrior chiefs, each buried with weapons of war, were dated to the late Bronze Age. Some were buried with as many as 40 or 50 swords, a collection of weapons gathered during a lifetime, each attesting to the warrior culture described by Homer.

But no shred of evidence linked these fabled combatants to Troy, nor to the myth that they had sailed en masse to recover Helen. Further excavation revealed that the Mycenaeans were in the midst of a massive rebuilding program that required great natural resources, so they looked east to fulfill what they lacked in their realm: tin to make bronze weapons and tools, and gold. Greed, not love, drove the Mycenaeans to lay siege to Troy.

A shipwreck on the seabed south of Troy hints that the Trojans had enough riches to incite the Mycenaeans to launch a massive attack. Turkish archaeologist Cemal Pulak found 11 tons of bronze as part of this Bronze Age shipwreck. Ornate gold ostrich eggs from Africa or Asia were found alongside goods from all over the known world. If this large ship had docked at Troy, the city may have been one of the major ports along the Aegean, a highly strategic trading position along the narrow Dardanelles.

Korfmann believed that Troy capitalized on this geographic advantage. It was the largest city along the Aegean coast and one of the wealthiest of its era. Besides the Mycenaeans, its location was envied by another landlocked civilization: the Hittites to the east.

According to renowned Hittite researcher Trevor Bryce, who has studied the Bronze Age tablets left behind by Hittites, references to battles over a region named Wilusha appear in the texts. Wilusha was similar to the name Wileos, the name the ancient Greeks used for Troy. The tablets chronicled protracted conflicts involving the Mycenaeans and showed that Mycenaean warriors had fought at Wilusha's gates.

As for the Trojan Horse, however, archaeological research shows no evidence of its existence outside the Greek bard's imagination.

evolution of urbanization and development at a single site over a long stretch of time.

It takes about 90 minutes to walk through Troy on a comfortable timber platform that runs through the site. Shade is minimal, and the summer heat warrants bottled water, a hat, and sunscreen. While the path is dotted with informative signs about significant locations, most visitors are bused in with guides. The new US$10 million Troy museum is set to open in 2015 near the current archaeological site and will feature galleries of relics found here above and below ground.

History

The self-taught archaeologist Schliemann began excavating a hill then known as Hısarlık in 1870 after securing the permission of an American consular attaché who had just purchased the plot from the Ottomans. Schliemann unearthed a knoll that in time extended to almost 15 meters in depth and unveiled layers of civilization.

Schliemann's findings and later archaeological digs revealed that the deepest tier, called **Troy I** (3000-2600 BC), was a flourishing mercantile outpost with a collection of clay houses. Their carbonized remains indicate a sweeping fiery end. The second layer, **Troy II** (2600-2250 BC), includes broad terraces and a much larger and more complex settlement. The metal coins with distinctive Mesopotamian characters found at this level indicate that trade may have been an integral part of the economy. **Priam's Treasure,** which Schliemann so desperately sought, was found in this stratum. The common villages of **Troy III-V** (2250-1800 BC) mark a lull in the evolution of this ancient Hellenic settlement. **Troy VI** (1800-1300 BC), just above, was colonized by the Mycenaeans—Greeks of the Bronze Age. These settlers built 10-meter-high fortifications and a prominent acropolis, all of which were destroyed by a massive earthquake. Late-19th-century archaeologist Wilhelm Dörpfeld argued that this level—the sixth stratum—constituted the city of King Priam, but modern academia has found that **Troy VIa** (1300-1260 BC) was the actual bastion of King Priam that fended off repeated Greek attacks during the decade-long Trojan Wars, the period that Homer immortalized in verse. A large cache of emergency supplies was found buried in beneath this layer. Two subsequent incarnations, **Troy VIIb1** and **VIIb2** (1260-700 BC) were humble trading posts, while **Troy VIII** (700-350 BC) was repopulated by Greeks from the nearby islands Lesbos and Tenedos. Lastly, **Troy IX,** or Ilium Novum (1st century AD), was visited by Alexander the Great after he conquered the Persians at Hellespont in 334 BC. Since Alexander considered himself a direct descendant of Achilles, the Greek hero of the Trojan Wars, he beautified the city of his presumed heroic ancestor and swore to erect a Temple of Athena within its walls.

Troy was entirely renovated at the behest of the first Roman emperor, Augustus. Under the Byzantines, Constantine thought about endowing it with the status of capital for his fledgling Eastern Roman Empire (3rd century AD), but the more strategic coastal outpost of Byzantium, today's Istanbul, was founded after a push eastward. Much like Efes, its larger sister to the south, retreating seas reduced trading potential and caused Troy's decline.

Sights

Beyond Troy's **entrance** (0286/283-0536, 8:30am-7pm daily summer, 8:30am-4:30pm daily winter, 20TL, 10TL audio guide, 90-minute guided tour 120TL) is the large **Trojan Horse** that has come to symbolize this UNESCO World Heritage Site. It was carefully constructed by the Turkish Ministry of Tourism, following details found on ancient local coins. Today, visitors can climb into the horse and peer out the windows for a souvenir photo. Near the wooden horse a café and **visitors center** sell maps and color-coded guidebooks that highlight the site's history and ongoing research.

Beyond the equine plaza is a path that eventually loops through the entirety of the site. At the beginning of the path, the small structure on the right, behind the wooden horse, is the excavations building for researchers. In front are storage vases used for olive oil and copper conduits used by the Romans to pipe water from nearby Mount Ida. On the left are the displaced marble columns of the Temple of Athena. The trail leads up some steps to a wooden platform with a panoramic view the site. The white canopy in the distance signifies the highest point of Troy. A sign on the right bears the names Ilios (Troy's ancient Greek name) and Wilusa (the city's name in 13th century BC Hittite sources). Follow the timber path beyond the sign, down the stairs to a junction of two walls on the left. Face the sloping limestone wall of irregular stones for an orientation to Troy's iconic walls. The sloping wall, built to withstand earthquakes, is the remnants of Troy VI. The more organized cut-limestone wall to the left is from Troy VII. To the right, the wall lining the path belongs to Troy VIII, and opposite the slopping wall are the remnants of the Romans' Troy IX. These different textures and configurations allow you to recognize the various eras throughout the site. Continue along the path, and as it turns left, look for the two facing defensive walls that ensconced the **East Gate.** Go up more steps to the Greco-Roman remains of the **Temple of Athena,** which dates to Ilium Novum (1st century AD). Unfortunately, much of this monument was destroyed when Schliemann's crew dug a trench beneath in search of Priam's Treasure. The highest terrace above, once the forecourt of the temple, is where visiting dignitaries—such as Persian king Xerxes and Alexander the Great—paid homage to the deity. Linger a minute to gaze at the Dardanelles and the cultivated plains of Scamander, over which the Aegean once extended. At the bottom of the path is a mishmash of temple remnants that reveal part of the temple's ceiling. Look closely for the small flowers, each one unique. Some say the temple's architect used flowers as a signature.

Farther along the path are the foundations of the houses of **Troy I.** These were constructed according to the traditional Bronze Age Greek Megaron Plan—a rectangular hall, entered through an open two-columned portico, with a central hearth. Farther on is **Schliemann's First Trench,** the heart of the site, depicting more than three millennia of ancient civilizations, from the top Ilium Novum stratum to Troy I at the bedrock. Continue down the stairs to see the remarkable **stone ramp** used during ceremonies that led up to **Troy II.** Just to the left, inside the walls, is where Schliemann unearthed Priam's Treasure. The next stop is a complex believed to have held Troy IV's **Palace of Priam,** then farther along is a Hellenic **sanctuary** where ritualistic sacrifices to the deities of the era were conducted. For fans of the 2004 movie *Troy*, the **Skaian Gate** (South Gate) is where Hector and Achilles fought their duel. The area beyond is littered with Roman monuments, including the **Odion** (Theater) and the **Bouleuterion** (Senate). Just beyond the theater, near signpost 11, look for the long marble entablature with

the ruins of the legendary ancient city of Troy

the Greek inscription facing the path. Could it say, "Tonight's show, starring . . . ?" From here, return to the Trojan Horse.

Getting There

Troy is about 25 kilometers southwest of Çanakkale. If you're **driving,** take the Çanakkale-İzmir Highway (E87) and turn right when you see the brown tourism sign for Truva (Troy). The entrance is six kilometers from this turnoff.

Transportation from Çanakkale to Troy is available via an hourly ***dolmuş*** (5TL) that leaves every hour on the half-hour from the station below the Sarıçay River Bridge, off Atatürk Caddesi. Return service departs every hour on the hour from the parking lot near the wooden horse. Both services run at minimum 9am-5pm daily. Schedules can be provided by the Tourism Office in Çanakkale. Transportation tariffs and schedules to and from Çanakkale—as many other services in Turkey—may change at a moment's notice. For this reason it's wise to schedule a tour with an independent travel agency. **Crowded House** (0286/814-1565, www.crowdedhousegallipoli.com) provides morning and afternoon tours of Troy (€30) with excellent guides and transfers to the site. Day tours from Istanbul with lunch, transfers, and a guide (€78) can also be arranged.

★ BOZCAADA

The Greek historian Herodotus declared that God created Bozcaada so that people could live longer. This thimble of an island is inherently Turkish yet also fundamentally Greek, combining both cultures in sites and activities that are a treat for the senses. Vines bearing succulent clusters of grapes grow ubiquitously over colorful and rustic abodes, tractors and horse carts share the cobbled roads with the latest cars from Istanbul, fresh-picked local produce is served to guests seated on rickety tables and chairs, and out of town, rugged cliffs give way to sandy turquoise beaches.

This isle is a gem, renowned for ages for its grapes, wines, red poppies, and stories. Homer's demigods may have battled in Troy, but they amused themselves on Bozcaada (or Tenedos, as the Greeks call it). The Achaean fleet hid behind Tenedos as the Trojans succumbed to the tactics of the wooden horse in Troy, and the British used the island as a supply base during World War I. If exploring the northern Aegean in summer, consider spending a few days on Bozcaada to appreciate the island's role in the creation of modern Turkey.

The lofty stone walls of a fortress greet visitors on arrival, but the sleepy Greek architecture of the backstreets quickly lightens the mood. The island was home to a majority of Greeks until the signing of the Treaty of Lausanne in 1923, when Tenedos was handed over to the new Turkish Republic. While the island was excluded from the wider population exchanges between Turkey and Greece, political maneuvering and discrimination from the 1950s onward slowly persuaded Greek families to emigrate to Greece, the United States, and Australia. Today, a small number of Greek families remain, and there are distinct Greek and Turkish neighborhoods in the island's only village. These pretty neighborhoods, combined with the abundance of local produce and attractions, lures artisans, gastronomists, oenophiles, and adventure seekers alike, and a number of events and festivals celebrating these interests ensure a steady flow of international and domestic visitors from May to September.

Traveling to Bozcaada from October to May is dependent on the weather, as *poyraz* and *lodos* (northerly and southwesterly winds, respectively) begin to disrupt ferry services. Most business owners shut up shop as tourism wanes in October. Confirm the weather conditions before departure or you could be stranded for days during fierce windstorms. For ferry details, visit **Gestaş** (www.gestasdenizulasim.com.tr/en) or **Bozcaada Rehberi** (http://en.bozcaadarehberi.com).

Sights

Bozcaada is rich in history. From the Persians and Greeks to the Romans and Ottomans, civilizations were quick to claim this outpost at the mouth of the strategic Dardanelles. Not much remains of these empires except for the well-preserved **Fortress of Bozcaada** (10am-1pm and 2pm-6pm daily summer, 5TL) located on the island's northeastern cape. The founder of the fortress remains unknown, but the Venetians, Genoese, and Byzantines all occupied the stronghold at various times. When the Ottomans arrived in 1455, Fatih Sultan Mehmet ordered its complete renovation, adding the 10-meter-wide moat and drawbridge to separate the structure from the island. The Venetians attacked, and again the fortress underwent a number of renovations. Today, you can visit its stark interior, climb its highest tower, and photograph views of the northern Aegean and town below.

For over 15 years Hakan Gürüney has passionately researched and collected 7,000 items of memorabilia about Bozcaada and placed them on display on two floors of an iconic 19th-century Greek home. The **Tenodos Museum** (Lale Sk. 7, www.bozcaadamuzesi.net, 10am-8pm daily summer, 5TL) showcases his efforts with a captivating collection of nostalgic photos, Ottoman documents, private letters from World War I, personal possessions of Greek families, and tributes to the local fishing and wine industries. Explore Hakan's finds to gain an appreciation for the island's poignant past.

Located next to the museum is the **Bozcaada Sanat Galerisi** (Bozcaada Art Gallery, Lale Sk. 9, cell tel. 0542/811-6416, 10:30am-10pm daily, free). Internationally known Turkish artist Belgin Şahin hosts exhibitions of local and domestic artists in various media and creates a cultural center for the island with poetry nights, workshops, and symposia in the gallery's Itırlı Bahçe (Fragrance Garden). This serene courtyard is a place to relax and sip homemade lemonade with ginger while admiring the many herbs and flowers that adorn the garden.

The second gallery on the island, **Rengigül Art Gallery** (Emniyet Sk., cell tel. 0532/481-7999, 9am-1pm and 5pm-11pm daily, free)

also has regular exhibitions by Turkish artists and is managed by Istanbul stained-glass artist Nurten Erdinç.

Meryem Ana Kilisesi (Church of Mary, 8am Sun. mass) is situated in the heart of the Greek Cumhuriyet *mahallesi* (neighborhood). While the inscription above the church's front door indicates that it was built in 1869, the local Orthodox population maintains that the Venetians were the first to construct a church on this site some four centuries earlier.

In the Turkish Alabey *mahallesi* the minarets of two mosques can be seen: the red 17th-century hewn-stone **Alabey Mosque** (Alabey Cami Sk.) and the **Yalı Mosque** (Cami Sk.), restored by Ottoman admiral Köprülü Mehmed Pasha in 1655 after the Venetians destroyed the original structure.

After indulging in the island attractions, view the sunset over the Aegean Sea near the wind turbines and privately owned **Polente Feneri** (lighthouse) on the westernmost point of Bozcaada. A popular **Ada Turu** (Island Tour, departs 6:30pm, 2.5 hours, 15TL) takes visitors to watch the sunset, with photo opportunities along the way. Pack something to sit on as well as drinks, as there are no amenities in this remote area. The tour departs between the police station and the port; buy tickets on the bus.

Wineries

According to legend, the Greek mythological hero Tenes, for whom the island was originally named, found a wild kuntra grape leaf along Poyraz Harbor and replanted it. The Greeks were avid viticulturists, as seen in Homer's *Iliad* and on ancient Tenedosian coins. With the arrival of the Turks in the early 20th century, the practice was largely abandoned except for edible varieties, but in 1925 Yunatçılar Şarapılık revived the industry. The industry struggled in subsequent decades as wine trailed *rakı* (Turkish aperitif) as Turks' drink of choice. But thanks to an injection of cash from the then Turkish government in the late 1990s to modernize wine-producing facilities, combined with the fact that wine was in vogue, the area's vintners grew. Today, more than five million vines produce 1,600 tons of edible grapes and 3,780 tons earmarked for viniculture. While indigenous grapes like kuntra, vasilaki, and karalahna still produce a spectrum of strictly Turkish wines, finer and more profitable French wine grape varieties, including chardonnay, merlot, and cabernet sauvignon, were introduced in the late 1990s.

Conservative alcohol laws passed in 2013 forbid advertising and marketing activities that promote consumption of alcohol, so tastings and tours of the wineries are now restricted. Websites promoting wineries are also illegal, but learning about the wineries at their shops in the village and purchasing bottles is warmly welcomed.

The island's 3,000-year-old winemaking legacy is evident in almost every household but there are just six vineyards. **Talay Şarapçılık** (Talay Winery, Lale Sk. 5, 0286/697-8080) peddles vintages from dry whites to dessert clarets. **Ataol Şarapçılık** (Çınar Çeşme Sk. 3, 0286/697-8404) has been producing wines since 1927. **Corvus Vineyards** (Çınar Çeşme Sk., 0286/697-8181) offers robust wines using all four of the island's indigenous grapes. The first Muslim winemakers on the island and the island's oldest institution, **Yunatçılar Şarapçılık** (Emniyet Sk. 24, 0286/697-8055), also known as Çamlıbağ, produces 10 distinctive whites and reds. The newest wineries on the island, **Amadeus** (Ayazma Yolu, cell tel. 0533/371-0470), owned by Oliver Gareis, and **Gülerada Şarapçılık** (Tuzburnu Yolu, 0286/697-0177) yield reputable collections from the island's indigenous and imported grapes.

Events

Community events and festivals are held throughout the peak season, with the **New Balance Half Marathon and 10K Run** kicking events off the second week of May. The third week of May, Bozcaada residents and visitors launch kites from the fortress for the **Bozcaada Uçurtma Festivali** (Kite Festival). Make your own kite or fly one provided by the municipality. July 26 is the Greek Orthodox **Ayazma Festival,** with a feast and dancing under the plane trees of Ayazma Monastery to honor Saint Paraskevi. In early August, prominent Turkish journalist and media scholar Huluk Şahın hosts the two-day **Day of the Poets and Homer Readings.** At sunrise on the second day, join international guests and literature lovers on Arkdeniz Beach, behind the fortress, and enjoy the words of Homer's *Iliad* and *Odyssey* read in several languages.

The first weekend of September sees the wine of the island celebrated with the two-day **Bozcaada Vintage Festival,** also called the Harvest Festival, where the newly harvested grapes are paraded through the streets before a concert, grape contest, and beauty pageant in the fortress. The second weekend of September is the **Bozcaada Lezzet Festivali** (Local Tastes Festival), where international chefs cook delicious dishes with the island's produce. Check with the Bozcaada Turizm Işletmecileri Derneği (BOZTID, www.boztid.org.tr) for up-to-date information on dates and venues for both festivals.

Nightlife

Bozcaada's nightlife revolves around the foot of the castle. **Polente Café** (Iskele Cd., 0286/697-8605, 8am-2am daily) is Bozcaada's busiest night haunt, serving a wide selection of coffees and wines, and the perfect hangout any time of day. Along the waterfront is the secluded **Fuska Café and Bar** (Kazanlar Sk. 20, 0286/697-0429), with soft table lighting, gentle waves lapping the shore, and the illuminated fortress in the near distance making it a magical setting for savoring an evening nightcap.

Sports and Recreation

Bozcaada's geography is perfect for sport enthusiasts. Whether it's diving, cycling, or even riding a scooter, there are plenty of novel ways to experience the island. Cycling around the island, however, isn't for everyone. Limited shade, regular inclines, and the lack of facilities such as places to buy water can make it

Bozcaada's popular Ayazma Beach

exhausting. Pack plenty of water and take the inland road (Ayazma Yolu) to reach Ayazma Beach rather than the more mountainous coastal route.

WATER SPORTS

The southwest coast offers snorkeling and scuba diving options. **Sulu Bahçe** (Water Garden) lives up to its name: It's an underwater cliff that extends down 20 meters, filled with colorful corals and finned creatures. **Mermer Burnu** (Marble Cape), near the Akvaryum beach, is home to seal caves, frisky octopi, colorful sea sponges, and a seabed littered with ancient artifacts, from amphorae to large ceramic slabs. The most amazing and deepest dive remains **Kalın Burun,** accessible only by boat, where antique clay oil and wine amphorae as well as a shipwreck pepper the seafloor at a depth of 30 meters. Scuba diving and night dives require permission from authorities. Artifacts must be left in place to preserve the seabed. **Seahorse Dive School** (Yat Limanı, cell tel. 0536/979-7122,

dives from 100TL) offer courses and discovery dives.

Boat tours (11am-6pm daily, 60TL) include lunch and are a great way to discover coves that are inaccessible by vehicle and make new friends. The boat departs in front of the fortress near the port.

The extreme sport of kitesurfing has gained popularity on the island Çayir Plajı; enthusiasts need to bring their own equipment. For other extreme options, **Deniz Yidliz** (Ayazma Beach, cell tel. 0532/662-1368, www.denizyildiziada.com) has sailboards, paddleboats, and canoes for rent as well as a speedboat for wakeboarding, banana boating, and sea biscuit (inner tube) rides.

BEACHES

Bozcaada's southwestern coast is filled with picturesque sandy shores. The Aegean's waters are clean thanks to the area's prevailing winds. The waters are also free of seaweed but are cold. The most popular shore to throw down a towel is **Ayazma,** with its indigo waters ringed by low shrubby crags. Accessible by public transportation, this beach is the only one to provide facilities such as restaurants and restrooms. Rent beach chairs (5TL) and umbrellas (5TL) for the day or bring your own. Other less crowded beaches are accessible with a car and combine privacy and convenience. The sandy coastline **Ayana** and **Akvaryum Koyu** to the south and the often windy **Tuzburnu** to the east are also good choices, but bring your own water and shade. **Habbele** has a private beach, but you can sunbathe in the public section.

Accommodations

Bozcaada offers a range of lodging options, all with adjacent dining facilities for breakfasts that showcase local produce. There is no shortage of picturesque whitewashed B&B and small hotels in the town. If you have a car, staying one of the vineyard guesthouses may appeal, but English-speaking hosts are hard to find. As with most places covered in this book, in summer you must have a room reservation arranged before you arrive. The high season runs mid-June to mid-September; most facilities shut down November to April.

Leave your shoes at the door and instantly feel at home year-round at ★ **Aliki Konukevi** (Eylül Cd. 58, 0286/697-0554, www.alikikonukevi.com, from 180TL). British owner Liz Bilen and husband Ersin live in this beautifully renovated Greek home that offers two English-style B&B rooms with a shared bath. Whether it's enjoying Bozcaadan wine at sunset on the rooftop terrace or relishing in the generous breakfast of island produce, Liz and Ersin's warm hospitality and local knowledge makes Aliki a sought-after lodging on Bozcaada.

Located closer to the fortress, the refurbished Greek townhouse of **Kaikias** (Duvarlıkuyu Sk. 1, 0286/697-0250, www.kaikias.com, from 280TL) offers a refined, sensual ease. Designed by architects and owners Handan and Ismail Beydili, this opulent, romantic hotel has ornate Greek furnishings and four-poster beds draped in white curtains to make you feel like a VIP. Aside from a delectable complimentary breakfast, Kaikias guests have access to a private pebble beach meters from the hotel with timber sunbeds and umbrellas overlooking the fortress.

On the budget side, **Kale Pansiyon** (Inönü Cad 69, 0286/697-8617, www.kalepansiyon.net, 40-60TL) feels like overnighting in someone's meticulously clean spare bedroom. Enjoy a copious breakfast of farm-fresh produce on a vine-covered terrace that affords views over the castle. Kale has some of the cleanest baths on the island, with the more attractive rooms located in the building down on the right.

Over in the Alabey neighborhood, wine connoisseurs may appreciate lingering in the secret garden or perusing the art gallery of **Hotel Armagrandi** (Dolaplı Sk. 4-6, 0286/697-8424, www.armagrandi.com, from 150TL), a historic wine factory converted to a rustic hotel with 25 modern rooms, most with exposed rock that create a cozy setting. The standard rooms and suites offer fine comforts and ambience.

Food

Expect Greek dishes combined with classic Turkish fare, and indigenous grapes in the most unexpected places, like Aegean sardines in grape leaves. Coal-grilled octopus and stuffed squid are island specialties that accompany the local white wines beautifully. Herbs sprout from every crack on Bozcaada and often find their way into tasty omelets, *gözleme* (Turkish pastry), and mezes. Bozcaada's unique delicacies include red poppy liquor, olive jam, and tomato marmalade. Mostly closed during the off-season, the majority of restaurants are located around the harbor, at hotels, and along Ayazma Beach. Service can be a little slow at times, but that's island life; enjoy it while you can.

Bozcaadan cafés are an island institution. One of the most popular is **Ada Café** (Çınar Çeşme Sk. 4, 0286/697-8795, 8am-1pm daily, 15TL). The small menu offers breakfast and café-style snacks, but the attraction is the drinks and dishes infused with poppy syrup. Try the juice, in which poppy petals are soaked in water and flavored with sugar.

After fish and mezes along the Aegean coast, travelers will revel in the broader selection of international flavors served all day long at Lisa Lay's **Café at Lisa's** (Kurtuluş Cd., 0286/697-0182, 9am-1am daily, 15TL). Delight in truly delicious gourmet pizzas, pastas, Asian dishes, and crepes, finished off with a slice of chocolate cake and a real cappuccino underneath a plane tree. The café also has a generous list of Bozcaadan and Eceabat wines. Lisa is an Aussie with her finger on the pulse of the island. She produces the Adapost-Bozcaada's first online gazette in Turkish and is a wealth of island knowledge for visitors.

Seafood and meze restaurants are in abundance along the harbor, but for a more secluded seaside location, dine at **Martı** (Kale Arkası 20, 0286/697-8215, www.martirestaurant.com.tr, 20TL). Couples will adore the romantic ambiance and soothing world music, while families will giggle getting to know the restaurant's friendly goose. Dishes here are famed for Aegean herbs and seafood cooked to perfection. Try the succulent swordfish casserole paired with a glass of *çavuş* wine from one of Bozcaada's indigenous grapes.

Choosing a dining location in the backstreets of the Cumhuriyet neighborhood can be an overwhelming experience, with so many colored chairs and tables on offer, but ask the *Bozacaadali* (residents) for recommendations and you'll be sent to **Sandal** (Alsancak Sk., 0286/697-0278, www.bozcaadasandal.com, 20TL). Look for the rowboat protruding from the wall and the cobalt-blue chairs to locate this restaurant, owned by Ahmet Bölük. Meals are best shared, with several mezes followed by today's catch. The stuffed octopus is highly recommended.

Sun-lovers lazing on Ayazma Beach are likely to feel famished by mid-afternoon, so thankfully third-generation Bozcaadan restaurant **Koreli** (Ayazma Mevkii, 0286/697-8098, www.korelibozcaada.com, 8TL) is open in summer, serving up *gözleme* (Turkish pastry), *mantı* (Turkish ravioli), and *köfte* (meatballs) in a casual beachside setting. Farther up the road, similar fare can be found at the well-known **Vahit'in Yeri** (Ayazma Mevkii, 0286/697-0130, 10am-midnight daily, 8TL). Vahit peddled *köfte* in a mobile stand before opening the first restaurant at Ayazma and now owns his share of shore beneath the shady trees, where he still offers some of the juiciest meatballs by the beach.

The brown paper bags of **Çiçek Pastanesi** (Alabey Meydanı, 0286/697-8226, 8am-midnight daily, www.bozcaadacicekekmek.com) are the most fashionable on the island. Drool over cabinets filled with decorated cakes, almond cookies with gum, *açma* and *poğaça* (baked rolls), savories, and ice cream. Devouring a Çiçek dessert in the main square of the Alabey neighborhood is an island ritual.

Information and Services

The **Bozcaada Turizm Işletmecileri Derneği** (BOZTID, cell tel. 0531/784-3173, www.boztid.org.tr, 9:30am-6pm daily summer) has a cabin on the right as you leave port for information. Other helpful services include the **Police** (İskele Cd., 0286/697-8010), **Hospital** (20 Eylül Cd., 0286/697-8051), and **PTT** (post office, Çınar Çeşme Cd. 4, 0286/697-8170). ATMs and taxis are located just off Çınar Çeşme Sokak near the PTT.

Getting There

A *dolmuş* (10TL, 1.5 hours) service operates between Geyikli port and the Çanakkale *otogar;* another *dolmuş* travels between the port and Ezine *otogar* (4.50TL, 25 minutes) year-round. In peak season, coach companies will also drop passengers off at the port, but in winter they divert to Ezine *otogar* for the *dolmuş*, where passengers transfer to the Geyrikli *dolmuş*. **Taxis** are also available to transport people to the port year-round.

By **car,** follow Geyikli or Bozcaada signage on the Çanakkale-İzmir highway (E87).

All Bozcaada visitors board the **Geyikli-Bozcaada ferry** (Gestaş, 0286/444-0752, www.gestasdenizulasim.com.tr, 6TL pp, 58TL per car round-trip) from Geyikli, south of Troy, and arrive at the Yükyeri Ferry Dock on Bozcaada within 30 minutes. Purchase round-trip tickets at the ticket booth at Geyikli dock. In peak season, boats generally depart Geyikli every two hours 8am-10pm daily. From Bozcaada, the ferry departs at 7:30am and runs every two hours 9am-9pm daily. Hourly service is available Friday to Sunday. Those with cars should arrive at least an hour prior to departure as boats get crowded during summer. In winter (Oct.-May), ferries depart four times a day, subject to weather conditions. Check schedules in winter by calling **Gestaş** (0286/444-0752).

For something unique, take off over the minaret-dotted skyline of the Golden Horn in Istanbul and land by the beaches of Bozcaada with **Seabird Airlines** (0212/310-2330, www.flyseabird.com, from 177TL, 80 minutes). Seabird flies four times a week to the island; tickets can be purchased online.

Getting Around

Transportation on the island is by private vehicle or by renting a bike or a scooter from Deniz at **Rent a Car** (Çınar Çeşme Cd., cell tel. 0545/541-9515, bikes 25TL, scooters 70TL, SUVs 100TL for 24 hours). The best way to get to the beaches is by ***dolmuş.*** June to September, **minibuses** to Ayazma and Habelle beaches (3TL) await passengers between the police station and the port and depart every 15 minutes from morning to sunset daily. Evening schedules vary, so check timetables with BOZTID at the cabin near the port and make note of the one of the taxis' phone numbers, just in case.

BIGA YARIMADASI

Looping westward from Çanakkale, the ruins and barren coastline of the desolate Biga Yarımadası, history's Troad, rarely attracts visitors but can provide a scenic route between Çanakkale and Assos, if time permits, for those with a private vehicle.

One kilometer from Dalyanis is a collection of what is estimated to be more than 400 hectares of decrepit Hellenic ruins, originally called **Alexandria Troas.** Established in 310 BC, this city was the main port of northwestern Asia Minor and gradually expanded both in size and wealth to become the Troad's richest settlement. Today, the remains of its grandeur include baths and a gymnasium dating back to AD 135, a two-basin harbor now almost entirely covered, vestiges of a 10-kilometer-long strip of fortifications, and the aqueduct built by Trajan almost 2,000 years ago. Much like Troy, the city began a long decline in the 3rd century AD, mostly attributed to the diversion of trade to the newly established imperial seat of Constantinople.

Farther south, the expanding town of **Gülpınar** reaps the benefits of tourism thanks to the **Apollo Smintheus Temple** (8:30am-5pm daily, 5TL), along with its small adjoining museum (9am-7:30pm daily Jun. 15-Aug.). The altar was a gift to Apollo from the people of the Troad in appreciation of his staunch commitment to the Trojans in the decade-long war against the Achaeans in the 2nd century BC. Apollo was the king of Tenedos and the patron of ancient Chryse—today's Bozcaada and Gülpınar.

Farther south, the fishing village of **Babakale** surrounds a large Ottoman fortress, which was entirely renovated in 2000. Sultan Ahmet III was forced to dock his armada at Babakale during a fierce storm. In gratitude to the Turcoman population who had assisted his troops during their layover, the sultan commissioned this massive citadel in 1725 to deter pirates from raiding the village.

Getting There

Dolmuşlar are available via Ezine but are infrequent and time-consuming; a **private vehicle** is advised. South of Troy, turn off the E87 for Pinarbasi, and follow the narrow road through villages to Geyikli, then onto Dalyan. From here it is possible to drive through the peninsula via rural roads to access Gülpinar and Babakale. The road from Gülpinar continues on to Assos.

★ ASSOS

About 20 kilometers south of Ayvacık is the tiny scenic town of ancient Assos. Also called Behramkale, the town has three unique settlements connected by steep narrow roads that wind through farming areas and ancient Greek and Roman ruins. The cobbled paths and stone buildings of the panoramic Behramkale village sit atop jagged red cliffs that overlook the beaches and boutique hotels of a charming *iskele* (harbor). Four kilometers away is Kadırga pebble beach—made popular by eager Turkish tourists seeking the sun and temperate waters of the Aegean.

The main draw at Assos is the famed **Temple of Athena** at the crest of Behramkale village. As the acropolis for the ancient Assos, the temple offers uninterrupted views of the Greek island of Lesbos, the long arch of the Bay of Edremit, and the Biga Peninsula.

Assos is steeped in history from the time it was founded in the 10th century BC by

Aeolian colonists from the city of Methymna on nearby Lesbos. The city prospered under the rule of Blythinian banker Eubulus during the 4th century BC. Eubulus's former eunuch, Hermeias, who had studied under Plato and Aristotle in Athens, gained his freedom and rose to prominence to become Assos's next ruler. During Hermeias's reign, his former teacher Aristotle founded his—and Assos's—first school of philosophy, in 348 BC. The philosopher went on to marry Hermeias's niece, Pythia, before returning to Lesbos. Some years later, the Persians invaded Assos and tortured Hermeias to death. Alexander the Great reconquered the city in 334 BC. Saint Paul visited Assos on his way to Lesbos during his third missionary trek through Asia Minor between AD 53 and 57. Soon after, the once prosperous city dwindled into a sleepy fishing village, until its ruins attracted the young American archaeologist Francis Bacon, an Assos expedition leader, in 1880.

Once an isolated summer hangout for a few sophisticated *Istanbullus,* Assos's upmarket popularity has hit a crescendo for those wanting to escape the crowded resorts dotting the south. Sun-lovers may like to stay two or more nights to relax by the sea; otherwise, a detour en route to Ayvalık to visit the temple, ruins, and harbor over a few hours offers a pleasant break on a long journey.

International tourism is on the rise, but local services and infrastructure haven't caught up. There are ATMs in the village but no postal services or visitor information offices. Most hotels can exchange currency, accept credit cards, and provide regional information to visitors. More information on Assos can be found at www.en.assosrehberim.com.

Sights

On reaching the narrow cobblestone streets of the hilltop Behramkale village, follow the road lined with market stalls up to the ticket booth for the Temple of Athena and the **Hüdavendigar Camii.** Sultan Murat I, a diplomat who unabashedly nicknamed himself Hüdavendigar, meaning "master" in Persian, commissioned this mosque. A marble slab depicting a Greek inscription above the building's entrance confirms that the mosque was constructed from building blocks pilfered from the church it replaced.

Atop the hill is the 6th-century-BC **Temple of Athena** (0286/721-7218, www.muze.gov.tr/assos-en, 8am-7pm daily summer, 8am-5pm daily winter, 10TL). Only a few of the original altar's original 44 Doric columns remain; the

The tiny harbor of Assos is ideal for a swim and seafood lunch.

rest of the structure was reconstructed with blocks of unsightly concrete.

Artifacts from ancient Assos litter the hillside within the crumbling four-kilometer-long fortification system. Accessible from the road leading to the harbor, the **necropolis** and **sarcophagi** are fashioned of locally quarried stone known for its caustic qualities. Interestingly enough, the term *sarcophagus*, originally meaning "flesh-eating," was coined in Assos. According to Pliny the Elder's accounts (AD 23-79), bodies buried in the corrosive material were consumed within 40 days. Scientists later attributed the stone's properties to its high alum content. Ironically, Assos's indigenous stone is impossibly difficult to work. The towers and gates within the **city walls**—one of the best-preserved fortification systems in Turkey—are impressive. Lower still are a 2nd-century-BC **agora,** a **theater,** and a **gymnasium** constructed on an area that was once two terraces.

Just out of Behramkale on the old road to Ayvacık are the pointed arches of the mid-14th-century Ottoman bridge, **Hüdavendigar Köprüsü,** built for Murat I (The Master).

Accommodations

Assos, reputed for its excellent but pricey boutique hotels, also offers an entire range of lodging options in Behramkale and the harbor, where the majority of visitors stay. Accommodations rates can vary greatly among phone quotes, internet sales, and in person, so it pays to shop around and negotiate half-board deals, which include dinner. Most lodgings are beautifully refurbished warehouses or abodes built of antique stone. All rooms in the harbor include free access to the wooden piers that extend from the pebble beach over the glistening blue waters of the Aegean. Yes, it's as gorgeous as it sounds.

Lovers of the outdoors can find campsites and air-conditioned bungalows just past the harbor on the road that bends around the hotels and restaurants. The pick of the bunch is **Yelken Camp** (Iskele Mevkii, 0286/721-7433, www.yelkencamp.com, tents 25TL, bungalows from 120TL half-board, summer only). Bungalows have en suite baths, and a barbecue dinner is cooked and served overlooking the beach.

Set in a refurbished gray-stone *keravasaray* (caravanserai), the four-star **Assos Kervansaray** (Iskele Mevkii, 0286/721-7093, www.assoskervansaray.com, from €130 half-board) is packed with features like an indoor and an outdoor pool, two restaurants, and a private pier leading to the Aegean. The better rooms boast antique decor and balconies with stunning sea views.

Opened in 2012, the family-run ★ **Hotel Behram** (Iskele Mevkii, 0286/721-7016, www.assosbehramhotel.com, from 150TL) is an excellent value, located right on the harbor with 17 well-appointed modern rooms within a renovated harbor warehouse. Breakfast, served by the water overlooking Lesbos, is possibly the best on the Aegean coast.

Up the hill in Behramkale are the charming stone boutique hotels and *pansiyons* of the village. The überchic ★ **Assosyal** (Behramkale Köyü 8, 0286/721-7046, www.assosyalbutikotel.com, 200TL) is a design hotel adorned with contemporary divans and industrial sculptures by Sedat Abayoğlu, set against uninterrupted views of Mount Ida. The hosts know guests won't venture too far from this homey luxury, so meals are served in a choice of attractive dining areas.

On the low-budget end but packing tons of charm, right in Behramkale, the **Eris Pansiyon** (Behramkale Köyü 2, 0286/721-7080, http://erispansiyon.com, 120TL) is owned by a retired American couple from New York. No pretense here, just three simple rooms, a terrace with views of the valley, Mediterranean gardens, and delicious complimentary afternoon tea.

Food

As in other Aegean towns, fresh seafood and a selection of hot and cold mezes and kebabs rule menus here. While most hotel

Yörüks

The colorful artisanal works of the Yörüks (nomadic herders), one of the oldest tribes of modern Anatolia, pepper the Aegean and Mediterranean coasts. From beautiful carpets to simple fine cookery, their mastery of homemaking on the range has evolved through 1,000 years of nomadic life.

Just a few Yörüks remain nomadic, but more than 1,000 years ago, these nomads moved south from their home in today's southwestern Kazakhstan. Yörüks inundated western Anatolia after the Selçuks conquered the Byzantines in in 1071. Although they're kin to the Turkmen and other Anatolian ethnicities, the Yörüks have predominantly Caucasian traits. As the Ottoman Empire expanded, some settled farther west, in the Balkans, Macedonia, Thrace, and Cyprus.

Today, Yörüks assimilation into the Turkish fabric is almost seamless. Proud of their heritage, they take every opportunity to differentiate themselves from the other ethnic groups in Turkey, including the Alevis, Turkmen, Roma, Kurds, Circassians, and Arabs. The "real" Yörüks, those deeper in Anatolia, still continue transhumance, the seasonal movement of livestock from one grazing ground to another.

Their name, a phonetic take on the word *yürü* (meaning "to walk"), honors their nomadic existence. Their songs and crafts represent one of the last remnants of the true Turk, one whose nomadic culture has stood fiercely against Ottoman dominance. Apt at weaving kilims and other crafts, Yörük women relate their heritage through design, making each item as unique as the person who created it.

---

deals include an evening meal, for a uniquely Assosian dish, try the Sea Bass à la Aristotle at **Uzun Ev** (Iskele Mevkii, 0286/721-7007, 22TL), said to be from *Deipnosophistae*, an ancient cookbook by Athenaeus.

A trip to Assos is not complete without trying the award-winning dishes of thespian-turned-chef extraordinaire Lütfi Oğuzcan at **Biber Evi Restaurant** (0286/721-7410, www.biberevi.com, 20TL). Foodies are drawn to Biber Evi (Chili House) for Lütfi's personalized culinary offerings, with ingredients plucked fresh from his kitchen garden. Reservations are essential.

For a cheap bite in a peaceful garden setting in the village, the **Panorama Restaurant** (Behramkale Köyü 71, 0286/721-7037, 10TL), on the hillside halfway to the temple, is an ideal retreat from the sun and offers magnificent views to Lesbos. The *gözleme* (Turkish pancake) is a good lunch time snack, but dining among the flowers means trying the Aegean specialty *kabak çiçeği dolması* (zucchini flowers stuffed with spiced rice).

Getting There and Around
BY BUS AND *DOLMUŞ*
Assos can be reached via *dolmuş* from Ayvacık and Küçükkuyu *otogarlar* (bus stations). Minibuses departing from Çanakkale (10TL, 1.5 hours) and coaches from Istanbul (40TL, 7 hours) connect to Ayvacık *otogar*, and from here, board the hourly *dolmuş* to Assos (6TL, 40 minutes). Travelers from Bozcaada also arrive at Ayvacık *otogar*. From the Bozcaada ferry harbor in Geyrikli, take the *dolmuş* to Ezine *otogar* (4.50TL, 25 minutes). At the *otogar* exit, turn left to see the E87 highway 50 meters ahead, where you can hail the Çanakkale-Ayvacık minibus (5TL, 45 minutes) as it nears the traffic lights. Küçükkuyu *otogar* is the transit point for Assos if traveling from Ayvalık (20TL, 2.5 hours), İzmir (30TL, 4 hours), Bursa (33TL, 5 hours), or Ankara (65TL, 10 hours). Adjacent to the Küçükkuyu *otogar*, on the E87/D550 highway, hail a *dolmuş* going to Assos/Behramkale (5TL, 1 hour). The *dolmuşlar* from Ayvacık and Küçükkuyu go to Kadırga beach before dropping passengers in Behramkale village and then Assos harbor.

The same *dolmuş* services run every 30 minutes in summer between the harbor and village (3TL one-way). The *dolmuş* station at the harbor is 50 meters uphill from the water's edge. In winter, the *dolmuşlar* operate less frequently.

BY CAR

The fastest route to Ayvacık or Küçükkuyu from Çanakkale or İzmir is highway E87/D550. Interior roads from Ayvaçık and Küçükkuyu meet at a crossroads on the doorstep of Behramkale and have clear directional signposts. Take the road to the *iskele* and turn left where the statue of Aristos stands to reach the village, or ignore the statue and continue down the road to reach the harbor. There are literally two streets in the village and one street for the harbor, making navigation easy.

AYVALIK

Arriving in Ayvalık is misleading: With its slew of prosaic two-story compounds, it's not exactly the resort town that guidebooks praise. Reaching the heart of Ayvalık, however, reveals a pleasant blend of historic and modern features based on fishing, tourism, and olive oil production. This seaside city of 35,000 year-round residents is sprinkled with decaying Ottoman Greek homes along a mishmash of cobblestone alleys that lead trucks, scooters, and horses to shores filled with restaurants, shops, and boat cruises.

Offshore of Ayvalık is an archipelago of 24 islands. The largest, Alibey, also called Cunda, features stone town houses revitalized as B&Bs, lively cafés, fish restaurants, and the Greek Orthodox Taksiarchis Church—a major landmark for the island. The island was renamed Alibey for a hero of the Turkish resistance. Most Turks call it Cunda, but true locals of Cretan origin call it Moschonisi, Greek for "scented island."

Staying a night or two to explore the cobbled lanes, local cuisine, and Cunda is recommended for travelers en route to İzmir, Bergama, or Selçuk. The town is most active on Thursday, when a busy farmers market, stretching out from Barbaros Caddesi and beyond, provides locals with bargains galore.

Sights

Roaming the maze of backstreets en route to the major landmarks is a pleasant way to absorb the personality of the town, with its

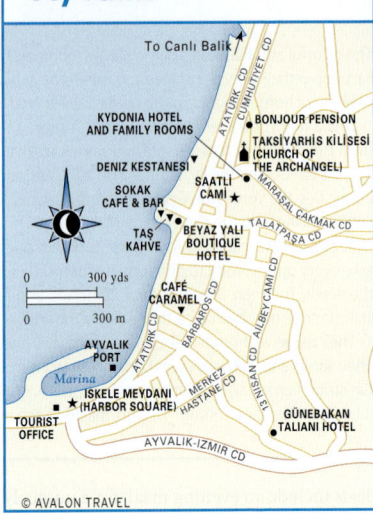

Greek homes in various colors and conditions. Starting at Iskele Meydanı (harbor square), head up one of the lanes linking the shore to the hill to **Saatli Cami** (Mosque with a Clock). Today's mosque was actually the Agios Ioannis Church, which converted to a mosque in the early 19th century. The belfry and clock attest to its original Greek Orthodox status. Agios Ioannis's frescoes were whitewashed over in the conversion.

Just streets away, the **Taksiyarhis Kilisesi** (Church of the Archangel, Mareşal Çakmale Cd., 9 Sk. Ara, 10am-7pm daily, 5TL) avoided conversion to Islam. Its famed architecture and marble work has survived since the church's inauguration in 1873, and a refurbishment completed in 2013 revived the building's heavenly ambiance with newly painted frescoes depicting the life of Jesus.

Nearby at **Tarlakusu Gurmeko Kafe** (Cumhuriyet Cd. 53, 0266/312-3312, www.tarlakusu.com), owners Ayfer Özcan and Ali Eroğuz celebrate the wealth of talented artists and Aegean produce in Ayvalık. The duo offer cooking classes (80TL pp) as well as art and drama classes in a renovated dairy factory. Visitors can relax and revive in the

Taksiyarhis Kilisesi (Church of the Archangel)

koruk suyu (green grape juice). Indulge in a glass before moving onto the next site.

South of Ayvalık's downtown, along the coastal road, is a steep climb through the scented pine groves to a hilltop known as **Şeytan Sofrası** (Satan's Table). This lofty scenic spot is said to possess a rock with the devil's footprint, left when he jumped over to Lesbos. The lookout boasts open-air cafés and views of the archipelago. Farther south, travelers can find the seven-kilometer sandy beach of Sarımsaklı, and the quieter Badavut beach where umbrellas and sun lounges can be rented for 10TL.

Across a long jetty, about 1.5 kilometers north of Ayvalık's main square or via a 20-minute boat ride, lies **Cunda**—a.k.a. Alibey Adası. Great for a lunchtime or evening stroll, the island has plenty of souvenir shops, ice cream, and cafés to pass some lazy hours. Worthy of a visit is Cunda's own **Taksiyarhis Kilisesi** (Church of the Archangel) and the panoramic **Sevim & Necdet Kent Library and Nostalji Café** (Garip Sk. Aralığı 5, 0266/327-3300, www.rmk-museum.org.tr, 9am-5:30pm daily) with its hilltop windmill; both can be seen on arriving in the harbor. Street signs are pretty much nonexistent here, but the main village of the island is small enough to get your bearings. For those with vehicles, the undulating road that leads to the northern **Patriça Doğa Parkı** (Patrica Natural Reserve) features curbside fountains and an ever-changing scenery of olive groves and thyme bushes. At the end of the road is the privately owned **Ayışığı Manastırı** (Moonlight Monastery), which was built in 1751 for an Orthodox brotherhood. Of the eight friaries founded on Cunda, Agios Dimitrios Ta Selina—Moonlight Monastery's Greek name—was by far the most famous. There are plans to open it once a week to visitors. Ask at your hotel for updates.

contemporary setting with a selection of coffees and café-style treats. Browse the olive oil, organic products, and herbal teas for sale.

Close to Ayvalık's neoclassical Greek church-turned-mosque, **Çınarlı Cami** (formerly Ayos Yorgis) is the headquarters of a socioenvironmental empowerment project, **Çöp(M)adam** (13 Nisan Cd. 14 Sk. 1, cell tel. 0533/233-7794, www.copmadam.org). This corner store is a workshop and salesroom for chic bags, aprons, jewelry, and other stylish items made from unwanted cloth, plastics, and metal, given new life by American Tara Hopkins and her team of local women who sell their designs on-site. The project benefits the environment through recycling and provides an income for women who have never earned a salary. The product tags read *Güle güle kullanın,* meaning "Use this with a smile." Those interested in the artisans of Ayvalık can ask Tara for an excellent arts-and-crafts map of the town. Right next door to Çöp(M)adam is **Şeytanın Kahvesi,** famous for their bitter powdery yet refreshing

Diving and Cruises

The waters off Ayvalık are rumored to hold the lost city of Atlantis. Try your luck at discovering its ruins, or just enjoy the water with one of the few certified dive operators that have sales booths along the harbor front. **Körfez Diving Center** (Atatürk Blv. Özaral Pasajı 617a-30, 0266/312-4996, www.korfez-diving.com, 135-650TL) has packages from a one-day, two-dive tour to a full two-day course five beginner dives.

For an excellent value-for-money day out, board one of the daily island-hopping boat cruises from the harbor. Swim and explore the archipelago aboard the *Bambi* (Turan Tuncer Cd. 11, 0266/312-5760), or for games and dancing, join the Turkish party people on the *Ege Tur-1* (Atatürk Blv., cell tel. 0533/327-9159). Both cruises (25TL, lunch included) depart at 10:30am daily and return to Ayvalık at 5pm. Tickets can be bought directly from the cruise company at the harbor.

Thea Saling (Cumhuriyet Cd. 167, 0266/312-7458, www.theasailing.com) departs from Cunda with a fleet of yachts available for daily or weekly rental. Ask for a crew and a captain, or sail yourself.

For a day tour of Lesbos (also known as Lesvos and Mitilini), just off Ayvalık's coast, contact **Meis Turizm** (0266/312-4152, www.meisturizm.com, 9:30am-6pm daily, €55 pp), offering a guided tour in English; Meis can also arrange ferry tickets with Jale Lines or **Turyol** (Atatürk Blv. Güzide Apt. 296/2, 0212/293-2326, www.turyolonline.com) ferries to travel independently to Lesbos (from €30 pp, €60 per car). From May to October, departures to Lesbos are scheduled for either 9am or 9:30am and 6pm Wednesday and Friday-Sunday and 6pm Monday-Tuesday and Thursday.

Accommodations

Lodging in Ayvalık runs the gamut from antique B&Bs to unpretentious boutique hotels. It can get noisy in the heart of the town with the narrow cobbled lanes echoing every sound during the day, but things quiet down at night. Travelers are advised to make reservations via the internet, as fluent English is not common in some hotels.

Oozing charm, the architecturally significant ★ **Bonjour Pansiyon** (Fevzi Çakmak Cd., Çeşme Sk. 5, 0266/312-8085, www.bonjourpansiyon.com, 100TL) exemplifies Ayvalık's past. Once the French consulate, the entrance is filled with ornate antiques and century-old painted ceilings, while the quiet rear gardens and divan are for a breakfast feast. Bonjour has 12 rooms in two buildings with shared baths.

Families will appreciate the location and immaculately kept rooms of **Kydonia Hotel and Family Rooms** (Fethiye Cd. 125, 0266/312-3672, www.kydoniahotel.com, from €80). Opened in 2013 by Ünal Çakmak and Kurtuluş Gülmez, the renovated century-old Greek home has large rooms with private baths, some with balconies. An on-site travel agency with English speakers and a large rooftop terrace is a welcomed treat for independent travelers.

Also offering quaint family and standard rooms is the **Günebakan Taliani Hotel** (13 Nisan Cd. 163, 0266/312-8484, www.talianihotel.com, from 140TL). The hotel, set in a lush garden away from the bustling town, has magnificent views of the bay and is ideal for those with vehicles who want to avoid the traffic downtown. Famed for its breakfast of regional produce, this family-owned hotel offers quintessential Turkish hospitality.

Rustic elegance and luxury meld beautifully at **Beyaz Yalı Boutique Hotel** (Gümrük Cd. 51, 0266/312-3200, www.beyazyali.com, from 350TL). Walk into this waterfront mansion and feel at home with its welcoming foyer and large lounge area with a fireplace under a lofty ceiling. The courtyard on the Aegean shore with a private pier has the look that chic design magazines drool over.

While a half-day visit is recommended for Cunda, lavishly appointed boutique hotels are abundant in the quiet picturesque streets of the island. Canan and Oktay Fergan, owners of ★ **YundAntik Konukları** (Hayat Cd. 25-27, 0266/327-3060, www.yundantik.com, from 250TL) are renowned for providing impeccable services and 14 luxurious rooms equipped with all modern amenities. Breakfast and complimentary afternoon tea will make visitors feel right at home in the guesthouse's elegant courtyard.

Food

Warmer waters bring *papalina* (baby sardines) to Ayvalık, which Turks drive across the country for. As is the case throughout the Aegean, tons of seafood and fresh herbs, including *istifno* (a kind of greens) and *radika* (chicory), show up in a myriad of appetizers that are best enjoyed along Cunda's pier or Ayvalık's seaside promenade. One of Ayvalık's most uninspiring culinary claims to fame is the *Ayvalık tost*, which is, yes, toast. Bread is piled with cheese, tomatoes, sausage, mayonnaise, and tomato sauce and toasted—not exactly memorable but still a satisfying on-the-go snack.

For fish restaurants in Ayvalık, families will enjoy watching the schools of fish swim under the busy pier at **Canlı Balik Restaurant** (Sahil Boyu 3, 0266/312-4555, 25TL), while couples will value the serene and more private **Deniz Kestanesi** (Karantina Sk. 9A, 0266/312-3262, www.denizkestanesi.com, 20TL). Both are located on the water's edge and have attentive staff serving up fresh seafood and a generous variety of hot and cold mezes.

Two streets back from the Finnisbank, near the seaside bus stop and Tansaş supermarket, is Yasemin Arbak's hidden French provincial **Café Caramel** (Barbaros Cad 9. Sok 18A, 0266/312-8520, 9am-8pm Mon.-Sat., 15TL). The high ceilings are reminiscent of the building's former life as a holding yard and lodging for camels and their owners. Yasemin has transformed the space into "little France" serving up a small menu of delicious pastas and homemade desserts from the cottage-style kitchen on-site. Adding to the allure of the café are the antiques and trinkets for sale. Reservations are essential for evening meals.

Rub shoulders with the locals in a genuine lively *meyhane* (pub) at the **Tik Mustafa'nin Yeri** (Tenekeciler Sokağı, 0266/312-3830, 20TL). In the back alleyways dedicated to the crafts of local metal workers, expect mezes, seafood, regional kebabs, music, and possibly singing as the *rakı* settles in.

For an after-dinner drink, wander over to Matbaah Sokak, between the PTT and the harbor. The street is lined with bars and clubs playing a variety of music genres until late, or head closer to the harbor to **Sokak Café & Bar** (Gazinolar Cd. 7, 0266/312-1255) to relax in a beanbag on the water and smoke a fruity water pipe while listening to Turkish musicians play acoustic sets.

On Cunda, for a welcome break from fish restaurants and mezes, see the cosmopolitan café menu at **Uno** (Çarşı Cd. 1, 0266/327-1828, www.cundauno.com, 15TL), to the right and a street back from the harbor. Uno's menu of burgers, pastas, and pizzas served in the shade on a comfortable patio is a good stop when sightseeing on Cunda. Up the road, **Ayna** (Çarşı Cd. 22, 0266/327-02725, www.ayna-cunda.com, 20TL) has a more pricey gourmet menu of local produce in an attractive indoor-outdoor dining space. Before leaving the island, visit the 150-year-old **Taş Kahve** (Stone Coffee, along the esplanade). It's a regional landmark, with its tall stained glass windows and high ceilings. All the seats face the water—perfect for people-watching along the harbor.

Information and Services

The Ministry of Tourism's main **Tourism Office** (İnönü Cd. 11, 0266/312-2122, 9am-7pm daily) is located one kilometer from the main harbor, just past the marina. A smaller municipal tourism booth is located near the bus station on the seaside, but it's rarely open. Next to this booth is a useful map and information concerning the sites and history of the town. The **PTT** (Atatürk Blv. 49, 0266/312-1003, 8:30am-5pm Mon-Sat.) post office, banks, and ATMs are on Atatürk Bulvarı, the town center's main thoroughfare. The **Ayvalık State Hospital** (0266/312-1035) is located opposite the marina.

Getting There and Around

Coach connections to Ayvalık can be arranged with many of the national companies, such as **Truva** (www.truvaturizm.com) or **Varan** (www.varan.com.tr). Coaches will drop passengers at a gas station two kilometers from Ayvalık, where a *servis* transfers you to the town *otogar*. A taxi maybe required to get from the *otogar* to your hotel; otherwise it's a 10-minute walk to the harbor. Coach sales offices are located by the harbor.

If **driving,** turn right onto Edremit Caddesi off the E87/D550 highway to reach the town center. Alternatively, drive to the next turnoff—the Ayvalık-İzmir Caddesi. Both roads lead to the main Atatürk Bulvarı.

The municipality's public transportation is very convenient. Most **buses** run the length of Atatürk Bulvarı to the beaches of Sarımsaklı and Badavut to the south (2.50TL) and to the *otogar* and Cunda (Alibey) Island (2.50TL) in the north. The buses all pass the bus station in the middle of town on Atatürk Bulvarı—the ideal place to board. Ayvalık's four-seater *dolmuşlar* (2TL central area, 2.50TL to Cunda), with white and red stripes, run the same route from their main stop in Armutçuk in the north to Sefa, near the marina to Cunda. A **boat shuttle** (3TL) connects Ayvalık's harbor to Cunda in just 20 minutes, generally every hour on the hour 10am-midnight daily. Tickets for all local transportation services are bought once you board the vehicle or vessel. **Avis Car Rental** (Talatpaşa Cd. 61, 0266/312-2456) has a range of vehicles for those who want to explore the greater area by car.

Bergama (Pergamum)

Ideal as a full-day trip from Ayvalık or İzmir, Pergamum's succinct historical layers make it a living testament to Asia Minor's tumultuous past. Two of the Mediterranean's best archaeological sites are located here—the Acropolis and the Asclepeion of ancient Pergamum. The city, called Bergama in Turkish, is also home to the Red Basilica—today's Kızıl Avlu (Red Court)—which appeared in the Christian Bible's Book of Revelation. But aside from its tourist trappings, Bergama's cobblestone lanes, home to rickety Ottoman and Greek abodes, and its industrious downtown are uniquely entwined with ancient artifacts; it's worth an overnight stay.

Ancient Pergamum is noted for its stunning ruins, most of which date to Eumenes II's illustrious reign (197-156 BC). Found in the elevated Acropolis—the old city's cultural, religious, and legislative hub—the ruins include a bluff-hugging amphitheater, the ornately chiseled gate of the Temple of Athena, and remnants of colossal palaces. Pergamum's ordinary citizens thrived in the city below. Also here are the remains of the Asclepeion, one of the earliest and most prominent medical centers of antiquity.

HISTORY

While Pergamum traces its beginnings to the 10th century BC, Lydian king Croesus brought it to prominence around 560 BC. About a decade later, the Persians conquered Pergamum as part of the Lydian realm and ruled the city until Alexander the Great's powerful army reclaimed all Asia Minor in 334 BC. On Alexander's untimely death 11 years later, his top general and administrator of Asia Minor, Lysimachus, turned the city into a military base and treasury for a reported 9,000 talents—as much as 245 tons—of gold. But while Lysimachus was away campaigning, he entrusted his favored lieutenant, Philetaerus the Eunuch, with guarding the city and its wealth. When Lysimachus died in 281 BC, Philetaerus adeptly managed to stay in control and used this trove to found the dynasty of the Attalid Kings. In the following 15 decades, Pergamum flourished into the capital of what in time would become Anatolia's most important kingdom

the vaults of Pergamum, high above today's Bergama

and one of the most revered cultural centers of ancient Greek civilization. Additions like the Altar of Zeus and the grand library under the reign of Pergamum's most illustrious king, Eumenes II, propelled Pergamum's grandeur to rival Alexandria and Antioch during the first half of the 2nd century BC. But Attalus III, lacking a direct heir, bequeathed the city in 133 BC to Rome. Four years later, the kingdom of Pergamum became the Roman province of Asia, losing some of its economic and political power but continuing its growth as a cultural and intellectual center. During Byzantine rule, Pergamum was a considerable Christian center, its church mentioned as one of the Seven Churches of the Revelation. In AD 262, the marauding Goths arrived, signaling the beginning of a lengthy demise.

In 1871 Karl Humann, a young German engineer managing the construction of a road through Pergamum, "discovered" the ruins of Pergamum, while scavenging the area for building material. Instantly switching professions, the new archaeologist uncovered an impressive cache, including the Altar of Zeus and the Temple of Athena's ornate propylaeum. Both were sent to the Pergamum Museum in Berlin.

SIGHTS

Start at the old town center, where an archaeology museum puts the ancient city's achievements and timeline into perspective. Just over one kilometer west lies Pergamum's famed medical center, the Asclepeion, which can be followed by a visit to the Acropolis, five kilometers north. The town synchronizes the opening hours of all sites, 8:30am-6:30pm daily in summer and 8:30am-5:30pm daily the rest of the year. Alongside the parking lots of the Acropolis and Asclepeion are merchants peddling handsome souvenirs, such as onyx statues and vases, at half the prices seen in Istanbul. Stock up with a couple of water bottles sold here, particularly during the heat of summer, which can top 40°C.

Arkeoloji Müzesi (Archaeology Museum)
Pergamum's small but informative **Arkeoloji Müzesi** (Cumhurriyet Cd. 10, 0232/631-2883, 5TL) displays discarded objects the Germans didn't think worthy of carting off to Berlin, mainly statues and gravestones found among Pergamum's extensive ruins. Aside from a mock Altar of Zeus painstakingly reproduced by museum staff, see the museum's ethnographical displays of indigenous life and crafts as well as clothing and kilims (Turkish carpets).

Kızıl Avlu (Red Basilica)
Known as the Red Basilica for the color of its stone, the 2nd-century-AD **Kızıl Avlu** (Kinik Cd., 5TL) was built during the reign of Hadrian as a temple to honor Egyptian gods Isis, Serapis, and Harpocrates. This massive pile of red bricks 900 meters from the Archaeology Museum straddles the Bergama River, which flows into two tunnels below the structure. Just before entering the site,

the **Kurtuluş Camii** (Liberation Mosque) is tucked inside one of this great church's towers.

Mentioned as one of the Seven Churches of Revelation in the Christian Bible, Saint John the Apostle sent one of his ominous letters to this church, noting that the city held the throne of Satan, perhaps in reference to the Altar of Zeus. The Byzantines converted this huge edifice into a basilica in the 5th century AD.

Asclepeion (Temple of Healing Arts)

One of the foremost medical centers of its time, the **Asclepeion** (www.muze.gov.tr, 20TL) was both a sanctuary and a healing center built to honor the god of healing, Asclepius. It was founded in the 4th century BC by Greek poet Archias, an Antiochian who had been cured at a similar center in Epidauros in Greece. Pergamum's Asclepeion was the world's first psychiatric hospital and the first natural therapy center using music, theater, massage, mud, diet, bathing, and therapy derived from dream analysis. The likes of Marcus Aurelius and Hadrian were treated here.

But it wasn't until Galen, the foremost Roman physician after Hippocrates, that the center became significant. Born in Pergamum, Galen used anatomical studies of animals and observations of human bodily functions made during his medical studies in Smyrna, Alexandria, and Corinth to cure severely traumatized patients at Pergamum's gladiator school. His insights into the circulatory and neural system remained in use until the late 1500s.

A stroll through the Asclepeion begins along the stone path, Via Tecta, Pergamum's Sacred Way. Once flanked with bustling shops, the path leads to the remains of a column carved with snakes, the symbol of Asclepius. Just as a snake sheds its skin, patients sought to shed their illnesses here. Note the signs at the entrance leading to the Pergamum's famed library to the right, and the 3,500-seat Roman theater, both used to entertain patients. Nearby is the **Sacred Fountain,** where modern visitors may still benefit from its alleged curative powers. Finally, listen to the trickling of water from the holy springs and follow the sound to the 70-meter tranquil underground passage to the **Temple of Telesphorus,** also known as the circular treatment building, honoring a god who symbolized recovery from illness. The **Temple of Zeus Asclepius,** built during the

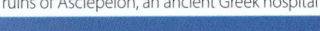

ruins of Asclepeion, an ancient Greek hospital

reign of emperor Hadrian, is adjacent to the treatment building.

To reach the Asclepeion, head west, uphill, for approximately one kilometer by following signs along Galinos Caddesi. It's possible to walk, but in the heat of summer, taking a taxi to both the Asclepeion and the Acropolis is advisable. Also, bear in mind that the Asclepeion borders a large military installation; all nearby streets are closed to traffic at sunset. Refrain from taking photos of the military base to avoid a run-in with the local authorities.

★ Acropolis

Some 365 meters in elevation along steep terraces that reveal stunning views of the modern city below, the **Acropolis** (www.muze.gov.tr, 25TL, audio guide 10TL) was the center of the Attalid Kingdom. Blue dots now show a suggested route around the site, but these can be difficult to see. Roaming the Acropolis freely is easy as significant sites have information posts, and there are timber walkways over hazards in some areas.

Uphill from the entrance, the partly reconstructed **Temple of Athena** is missing its propylaeum, which was carted off to Berlin's Pergamum Museum in 1871. The Temple is adjacent to Pergamum's noted **Library.** Some 200,000 texts were housed in this structure, which was greatly expanded by cultural aesthete Eumenes II. He's said to have borrowed tomes from some of antiquity's largest libraries without returning them, and even exchanged gold for the works of Aristotle. Eumenes's unrelenting drive to build the library so concerned Egyptian kings—the sole producers of papyrus during the era—that they stopped exporting it to Pergamum, fearing that its book repository would surpass theirs. Eumenes, ever the problem solver, launched a race to find an alternative printing medium, offering a large reward. And that is how *pergamenum* (parchment), the ancient Egyptian method of specially treating and extending animal skin, was revived. In the end, Mark Anthony ransacked the library,

lavishing his beloved Cleopatra with the repository's greatest titles.

Just over the edge, ancient Rome's steepest **amphitheater** once seated 10,000 comfortably. Some 80 rows extend in three tiers over 30 meters on the flank of a vertiginous cliff. Its innovatively portable stage was carted off between performances to allow free access to the **Temple of Dionysus,** located stage left.

Doubling back up to the top of the hill via an **arched corridor and vaults** leads up to the **Sanctuary of Trajan,** which was built in AD 125 by Roman emperor Trajan's successor, Hadrian, in his and Zeus's honor. This shrine was also partly reconstructed by German archaeologists; its splendid Corinthian columns are a mix of original material and aptly etched modern marble blocks. For dizzying scenery of the valley and aquifer beyond, cross the ruins of the ancient city's walls toward the remains of the **arsenal** and the **pillared cistern.**

On the return to the entrance, the road leads through the remains of six royal residences, including the **Palaces of Attalid I** and **Eumenes II.** Below the Temple of Athena is where the **Altar of Zeus** once stood. Just the foundations of the altar beneath two large evergreen trees can be seen, but this is enough to imagine the grandeur of this shrine. The shrine was commissioned by Eumenes II to honor his father's victory against the Gauls in the late 2nd century BC. If you don't want to miss anything, walk past the Altar of Zeus down to the **Roman baths,** the **Middle City** with its **gymnasium,** the **Temple of Demetre,** and Pergamum's **Lower Agora.** Holes in the fence may lead walkers back to town, but profiteers of the Acropolis Teliferik (cable car) try to prevent this exit. The fastest way to the Acropolis is by taxi or via the swaying Teliferik (10TL pp one-way) that transports visitors in eight-seat capsules above the ruins. Passengers of tour coaches and buses will also access the ruins via the Teliferik, as turning around was not part of the lift's design. Walking the long road up to the Acropolis is possible, or ask a local for the latest shortcut in the fence.

ACCOMMODATIONS

Make a beeline for ★ **Athena Mansion** (Imam Çıkmazı 17, 0232/633-3420, www.athenapension.com, dorm €12, rooms from €40), an 18th-century Arapoğulları mansion in the heart of the old town that owner Aydın Sengul has lovingly renovated into an affordable oasis with views of Pergamum. The *pansiyon* has a five-bed dorm with a shared bath, double rooms and family rooms with private en-suite baths, and a cozy lounge area overlooking an enormous garden with a sought-after hammock. Kicking back and taking in the cool breeze here may mean postponing other travel plans.

Sleep with the mythological gods or goddesses of ancient Pergamum in a renovated 19th-century Greek home, **Hera Hotel** (Tabak Köprü Cd. 13, 0232/631-0634, www.hotelhera.com, from €80). The hotel has 10 ornately decorated rooms, each named after a god or goddess. Kilims, antiques, and wooden floorboards embellish three floors, including a wine cellar. Proud owners the Oflaz family exude Turkish hospitality with personal service, such as dinner and tour bookings. A generous breakfast is also served on the terrace with views of the town and Pergamum's ruins above.

FOOD

Gourmet restaurants have yet to hit Bergama, but oodles of local eateries have tasty, homey dishes. Don't be put off by restaurants with bains-marie (stainless-steel double boilers): These bowls produce the tastiest dishes throughout Turkey. Between visiting sites, the hungry can refuel at ★ **Bergama Sofrası** (Bankalar Cd. 44, 0232/631-5131, 8TL), next to the Hacı Hekim Hamamı. This clean establishment looks like a modern-day fast-food eatery from the street, but inside is a counter full of authentic specialty dishes like *etli lahana dolma* (cabbage leaves stuffed with meat and flavored rice), *terbiyeli köfte* (rice and ground beef meatballs in broth), soups, grilled meats, and more. Order your meal by pointing to the dishes on the counter or select your meats from the cabinet. Along Bankalar Caddesi is **Paksoy Pide** (Istiklal Meydanı 39, 0232/633-1722, 4TL) serving up *pide* (flatbread topped with cheese or lamb) and soups. Another good choice for lunch and dinner is **Akropolis Restaurant** (Ittihat at Terakki Cd., 0232/632-7722, 15TL) on the hill between the Acropolis and the town site. Choose between indoor or outdoor seating with a selection of mezes, vegetarian or meat dishes such as lamb chops, or spicy kebabs. The restaurant is one of the few places to get wine, beer, and spirits with your meal. Another location to enjoy a coffee or wine with a snack is the **Red Basilica Hotel & Cafe** (Kınık Cd. 77B, 0232/632-7601, www.redbasilica.com, 8TL). The menu is small, but the location overlooking the Red Basilica is perfect at sunset.

INFORMATION AND SERVICES

The Turkish Ministry of Tourism, Pergamum's **tourist office** (Cumhuriyet Cd., 0232/631-2851, 8:30am-5:30pm Mon.-Sat.) is located next to the archaeological museum. All bank and mail services are located along the stretch of Cumhuriyet Caddesi that becomes Bankalar Caddesi.

GETTING THERE AND AROUND

Pergamum's *otogar* is on the Bergama-İzmir Yolu, seven kilometers from town. There are hourly **buses** to and from Ayvalık's *otogar* and seaside bus station (Dikili-Bergama *dolmuş*, 10TL, 1.5 hours) and İzmir's main *otogar* (12TL, 2 hours), while connections to Istanbul and Ankara are offered once daily. Catch a taxi (20TL) or the regular *dolmuş* (2TL) service for the seven-kilometer commute into town from the *otogar*. The *dolmuş* from Ayvalık and İzmir and coach companies will also drop off and pick up at their sales office in town on the corner of Böblingen Caddesi and Kayhan Caddesi, and close to the Red Basilica on Eski Elektrik Fabrikası Caddesi.

If arriving by **car,** follow the İzmir-Çanakkale Yolu (E87) five kilometers past

Eski Foça's small sea is lined with dining options.

Ovacık, and turn onto the D240 highway, where road signs lead drivers the rest of the way.

Navigating around Pergamum's somewhat remote sites on foot is feasible during winter. Otherwise, and particularly for the sake of time, negotiate transportation to and from and between the two main sites—the Asclepeion and the Acropolis—with a **taxi.** Taxis only allow for a short hop through the various sites and should cost no more than 40TL for the round-trip from town. Add another 20TL if traveling from the otogar. The archaeology museum and Red Basilica are within walking distance within the town center.

★ FOÇA

If the northern Aegean is the oyster of Turkey's western coast, Foça is its pearl. Its Greek townhouses and Ottoman mansions are side by side and fill with cultivated Istanbullus come June. The harbor town's population then soars well beyond its 15,000 year-round residents. The cool coastal waters are also reputed as a resting site for the Mediterranean monk seal, one of the world's most endangered mammals, estimated to be have a population of just 400.

Essentially divided into two parts, Yeni and Eski Foça—New and Old Foça, respectively—the old part of town sprawls along two bays: Büyük Deniz (Large Sea) to the south is home to a commercial port; Küçük Deniz (Small Sea) to the north is the touristed area. Nineteen kilometers from its sister city, much smaller Yeni Foça seems forlorn in its remoteness. Located 70 kilometers north of İzmir, Eski Foça is a delightful afternoon jaunt from the city or a picturesque lunch stop, breaking up a long journey to Selçuk.

Historically, Foça was known as Phocaea, an Ionian city dating to the 9th century BC. In 547 BC when Cyrus the Great of Persia conquered Lydia and all of its previously annexed Ionian territories, Phocaeans abandoned the city rather than succumb to Persian rule. As for Yeni Foça, it may be called new, but it was actually settled by the Genoese in 1275. By the 13th century, it fell to the Turks, and in 1455 it was annexed by the fledgling Ottoman Empire. Both Foças were controlled by Greece during the Greco-Turkish war of 1919-1922, which explains the wealth of Greek architecture.

Sights

While the remains of **Ancient Phocaea** are minimal, there are a few destinations around town worth checking out. About 15 kilometers from Eski Foça on the Foça Yolu is the **Persian Mausoleum,** an odd-looking tomb dating to the 4th century BC, believed to be the burial chamber of a Persian king. On arriving to the town you'll see the ruins of 19th-century windmills, used until the 1960s. After winding past the windmills, turn left at the junction to reach the center of Eski Foça. Just past the junction is the newly uncovered **theater,** dating to 340-330 BC and believed to be the most ancient theater in Anatolia.

Another of the town's oldest ruins is the Genoese fortress of **Beşkapılar** (Five Gates), facing the Large Sea. The Ottomans repaired its fortifications in 1455 and added the watchtowers. The castle's boathouse now serves as an open-air theater. The fortress houses the 15th-century **Kayalar Cami** (Mosque of the Rocks), which beckons with its 200-year-old lighthouse-like solitary minaret. Its rectangular base and the flat wooden roof are interesting in that they predate Ottoman architecture's domed roofs and square bases. The *şadırvan* (ablution fountain) stands due west.

The wooden walkway near to the Five Gates connects to the Small Sea. Along the way are the sites of the **Cybele Open Air Temple,** dating to 580 BC, and the **Temple of Athena.** Statues and relics of the Anatolian goddess Cybele, as well as smaller niches for lanterns, suggest this was an important place of worship, particularly for sailors who could honor the temple from the water. Above the Cybele Temple, excavation teams working to uncover the Temple of Athena in 2005 discovered sculptures of a griffin and a horse's head thought to date to the 5th century BC. Excavations continue today.

The dilapidated **Dış Kale** (External Castle) was built in the 17th century to guard from seaborne invasion along the tip of the peninsula that delineates the town's southwestern point. Stone cannonballs found during underwater archaeological research may have been hurled from catapults at this location to deter approaching enemy armadas.

North of the shores of Foça lie the volcanic Siren Rocks, described in Homer's *Odyssey*. The legend is that sailors lost their way and crashed into these rocks after hearing the mesmerizing voices of the Sirens, the mythological winged women.

Cruises

To reach the legendary Siren Rocks, take a boat trip with **Delphin Boat Tours** (0232/812-5011, May-Sept., 35TL). Cruises depart from either harbor for a seven-hour tour that winds through the various isles.

Accommodations

While Foça is a recommended lunch stop for travelers, the town brims with B&Bs in renovated Greek and Ottoman mansions made popular by Turkish tourists. Once you've seen the sites, there's not much to do but lie in the sun on the boardwalk and eat seafood on the esplanade. If that's appealing, these lodgings are ideal.

The only boutique hotel in town is ★ **Bülbül Yuvası** (Knightingale Nest, 121 Sk. 20, 0232/812-5152, www. bulbulyuvasi.com.tr, from 200TL). Muvaffak and Selma Bülbül's award-winning hotel boasts sophisticated rooms—including one with its own hamam—and a delectable breakfast, promoting Aegean produce, served above the Large Sea.

For those on a budget, the youthful meeting spot **Iyon Pansiyon** (198 Sk. 8, 0232/812-1415, www.iyonpansiyon.com, from 120TL) offers 10 sparsely furnished rooms with private baths in the Tutar family's renovated Greek stone mansion, a block from the shore. Book in advance; this charming place is popular.

Food

Most of Foça's eateries are located around the bay of the Small Sea, with prices traditionally listed at the entrances. Fish is the only exception, as the catch, and its price, vary—sometimes widely—from day to day. Some of the best Foçan dishes revolve around fish, but determine the price per serving prior to ordering to avoid any misunderstanding.

Try your luck eating the catch of the day along the esplanade, or skip the uncertainty of fish prices by venturing over to Büyük Deniz to ★ **Fokai Restaurant** (121 Sk. 8, 0232/812-2186, 20TL). Cradled between Greek homes one street up from the shore, Fokai dishes out a generous menu of fresh seafood, mezes, pastas, and pizzas—all at set prices. The ambiance is serene, with the twinkling Aegean in the foreground and a meal served in the comfort of a Greek stone patio.

For a quick haggle-free bite around the

small bay, **Kale Cafe** (Aşıklar Cd. 1, 0232/812-1989, 12TL) gets thumbs up from the locals for its Foça cheeseburger with fresh herb sauce and its frozen lemonade.

On especially hot days, cool down with a scoop of any of the 28 flavors of *dondurma* (ice cream) at **Nazmi Usta** (0232/812-5471) along the esplanade, and catch some rays on the boardwalk nearby.

Information and Services

Located diagonally across the street from the *otogar* is the **tourism information** office (Değirmenlik Cd., 0232/812-1222, 8:30am-5:30pm Mon.-Fri., 10am-7pm Sat. June-Sept., 8am-5pm Mon.-Fri. Oct.-May). Banks, the PTT (post office), and ATMs line Reha Midilli Caddesi, the main cobbled street that runs from opposite the *otogar* to the Küçük Deniz.

Getting There and Around

The İzmir *otogar* has a **dolmuş** operating to Foça *otogar* almost every hour (9TL, 1.5 hours). However, from central İzmir, the faster route is via the metro and suburban **IZBAN Trains** (www.izban.com.tr). Get the metro to Halkapınar, then change to the IZBAN Train toward Aliağa. Travel for about 45 minutes to the Hatundere, where municipal bus 744 goes direct to Foça Otogar (35 minutes). Trains and buses operate every 10-20 minutes. Buy tickets for the entire journey (8.50TL) from the departure station or, departing from Foça, from the driver when boarding the bus.

Foça is located at the end of the Foça Yolu, 26 kilometers from the E87/D550 highway. The distance from Pergamum to Foça and İzmir to Foça is about 70 kilometers, about 45 minutes by car.

If flying to **İzmir Adnan Menderes Airport** (ADB, 0232/274-2626, www.adnanmenderesairport.com), pick up the IZBAN Train at the Airport (Havalimanı station) and travel direct to Hatundere (1.5 hours) to transfer to municipal bus 744 for Foça Otogar.

İzmir

Turkey's third largest city, İzmir, formerly Smyrna, extends along a 56-kilometer-long gulf ringed entirely by beautiful mountains—a natural inheritance that has lured conquerors since its Neolithic origins circa 6000 BC, and according to Aristotle, witnessed the birth of Homer around 900 BC.

In the 17th century the Ottomans promised special tax breaks and benefits that enticed a mosaic of ethnicities called Levantines (wealthy European immigrants) to call İzmir home alongside Turks, Greeks, and Armenians. Living side by side, they transformed the multicultural city into cosmopolitan port. The city still exhibits the architecture and memory of these grand days.

İzmir enjoys mild weather year-round (with the exception of hot, dry summers), a healthy tourism sector, and an agricultural industry based on tobacco, figs, and raisins. It's the country's second-largest port and home to a bustling economy. With a population three million, İzmir's importance is also reflected by a hefty annual calendar of international trade expositions.

The city's boom, however, has had its downside. Three decades of unchecked housing and industrial development has led to an urban wasteland. On the outskirts, run-down ghettos teem with the screech of auto repair shops and sweatshops cranking out knockoff Gucci jeans. But thanks to municipal beautification and restoration efforts, wealthy coastal areas like the Kordon—a lushly landscaped esplanade on the banks of the Aegean—as well as the historical neighborhood of Aslancak to the north, with its age-old Greek and Ottoman mansions, draw visitors.

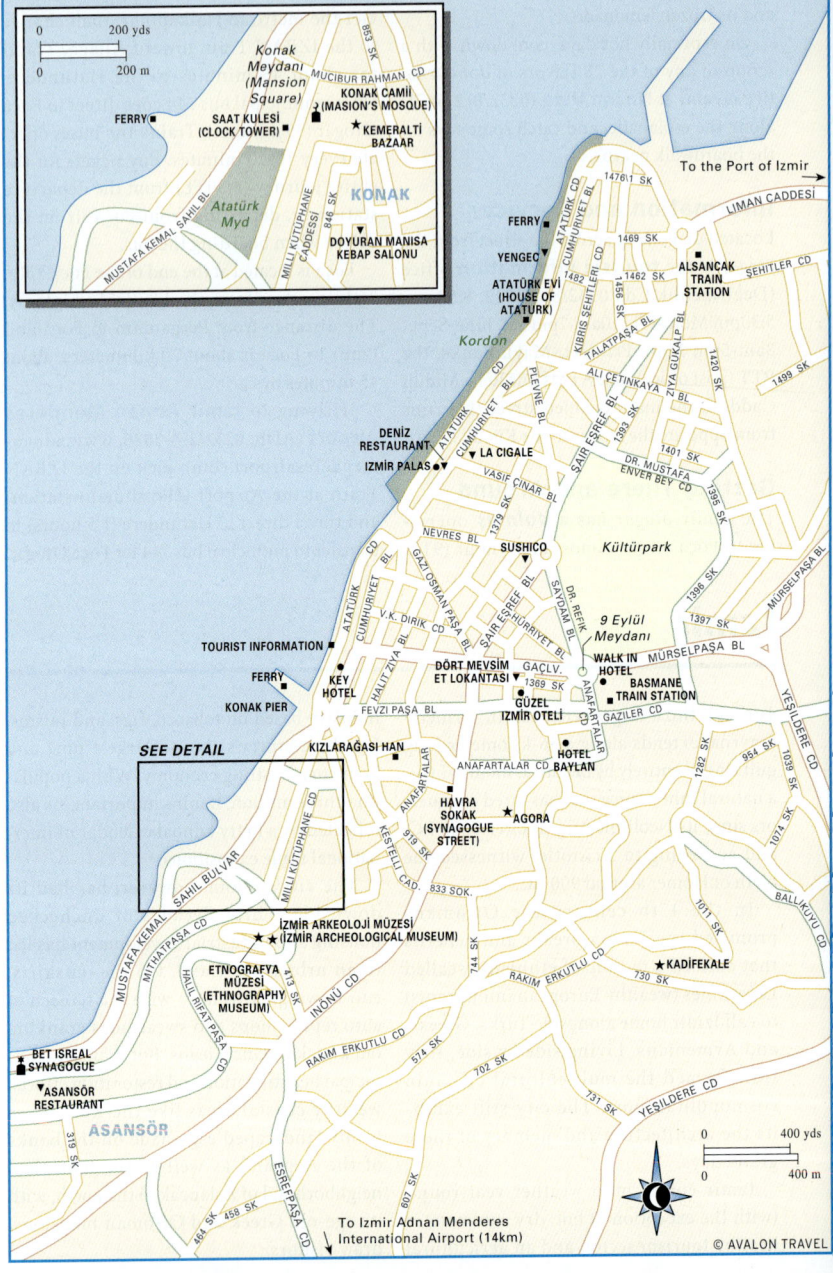

HISTORY

Ongoing excavations at Yeşilova Höyük in İzmir's Bornova district have dated the city's beginnings back by at least three millennia to 6500 BC, the Chalcolithic Period. But theories of İzmir's first settlers vary. Some historians maintain that a warring Amazon queen—most probably a Hittite priestess—by the name of Myrina settled the city and used a corruption of her name to come up with Smyrna. Local historians, however, place İzmir's first settlement at about 3000 BC, according to ongoing archaeological research being conducted at a site in modern-day Bayraklı. By the 16th century BC, the city fell under the rule of the central Anatolian Hittite Empire. By then, Smyrna's population—the Luwians—used an advanced cuneiform system and the polytheistic rituals of their rulers.

Two centuries after the fall of the mighty Hittite Empire in 1200 BC, Ionians flooded their previously controlled colonies in western Asia Minor. Under their tutelage, Smyrna exploded as a cultural metropolis, much like its contemporary, Troy. Around this time, according to Herodotus, Homer was born along the banks of Smyrna's Meles River. But prosperity attracted the neighboring Lydians, who battered the city around 600 BC, and the Persians, who arrived decades later. Even these mighty warriors proved no match for Alexander the Great, who arrived in 334 BC in Smyrna, by then a mere village. Shortly thereafter, Alexander commissioned a new city atop Mount Pagus—today's Kadifekale—at the request of Smyrnians. This truly Hellenic metropolis was absorbed shortly thereafter by General Lysimachos's Pergamum in 323 BC. Two centuries later, King Attallus III's, more interested in growing tomatoes than ruling his state, forfeited the region to the Romans. As part of Rome's Asian realm and under the subsequent Byzantines, old Smyrna was resurrected with magnificent buildings while remaining largely independent in political affairs. Its maritime trade was revitalized, and with it came a vast cultural expansion, until a massive earthquake in 178 BC flattened the city.

Smyrna was annexed by the developing Ottoman Empire under Murat II in 1425 after centuries of power struggles between the Byzantines and the Selçuks. The city—by then renamed İzmir—became a haven for Jews fleeing the Spanish Inquisition. Thanks to a measure according sweeping trade privileges to foreigners, İzmir developed into the declining Ottoman Empire's most successful commercial center, attracting the Levantines to settle in the city. By the beginning of the 19th century, the city was home to a large Greek population and a myriad of religious structures serving Christians, Jews, and Muslims. After the Ottomans' defeat in World War I, the Greek military occupied İzmir for three years, hoping to annex the city and much of the Aegean to Greece. But a nationalist movement led by Mustafa Kemal Atatürk proved too massive for the Greeks. After the Turks gained control of the city on September 9, 1922, the Greeks burned the city's minority neighborhoods before retreating to mainland Greece in an event now called the Great Fire of Smyrna.

SIGHTS

İzmir sprawls over many districts, with most attractions near the shore in the Konak district, the northern entertainment and shopping area of Alsancak down to the old Jewish quarter of Karakaş in the south. Between these neighborhoods is Konak Meydanı, the bazaar streets of Kemeraltı, inland by 1.3 kilometers the gritty workers hub of Basmane, and the expansive inner city green space of Kültürpark. The most notable attractions, like the Agora and Kadifekale, are east of Konak Meydanı.

Konak Meydanı

Konak Meydanı (Mansion Square) is a large pedestrian plaza that owes its name to the yellow Ottoman gubernatorial mansion on its periphery. It was built in 1865 when the seat of the province of Aydın moved to İzmir. From

Konak's center soars **Saat Kulesi** (Clock Tower). It was commissioned in 1901 to the French Levantine architect Raymond Charles Péré to commemorate the 25th anniversary of artsy Sultan Abdul Hamid II's ascension to the throne. The 25-meter-tall marble structure was inspired by North African Moorish themes and features four fountains on its cardinal points as well as a mechanical movement given by Germany's Kaiser Wilhelm II. The other historical structure amid this aggressively modern square is the nearby mid-18th-century **Konak Camii** (Mansion's Mosque), whose facade is stunningly tiled in Kütahya faience.

Just north of the square is the **Konak Pier,** the 19th-century landmark designed by Gustave Eiffel, the same man who designed that tower in Paris. Restored in 2003, the pier is now home to some sophisticated pricey restaurants, reputable brand-name shops, and a cinema.

Asansör

In Karataş, a 15-minute stroll southwest of Konak Meydanı, stands the iconic **Asansör** (elevator). Look for a hill-hugging brick tower at the end of Dario Moreno Street, off Mithatpaşa Caddesi. Statues and tributes to Dario mark the street, a famous Turkish musician who once resided here. The elevator was built in 1907 to take wealthy Levantines to their plush mansions on the hill from the business hub below, replacing 155 steps. The tower features a recently refurbished elevator, that zooms up to an on-site café and restaurant with wide views of the Gulf of İzmir.

Kemeralti Bazaar

As the closest commercial center for İzmir's bustling textile and leather industry, **Kemeralti Bazaar** (9am-9pm Mon.-Sat. May-Sept., 9am-5pm Mon.-Sat. Oct.-Apr.) is well worth a few hours' foray for that perfect deal. Getting lost in this antique mall is half the fun. Stalls of pungent leather garments, overly flashy bridal wear, baskets piled high with spices, coffeehouses, and shops selling home wares crowd the dozen lanes that constitute this historical mall largely catering to bargain hunters. Ambling up its main artery, Anafartalar Caddesi, shoe and clothing vendors loudly bid for the next sale. Tucked just west of here is the covered two-story 18th-century **Kızlarağası Han**—the place to haggle for colorful carpets and silver. Of the 103 *hans* in İzmir, this is where jewelry is a tempting purchase.

Within the tangled streets of the bazaar are a number of historic mosques. İzmir's largest, the 16th century **Hisar Camii,** near the Kızlarağası Han, was built in 1597 by Aydınoğlu Yakup Bey and features İzmir's best examples of Ottoman Islamic architecture.

Agora

One of İzmir's last pre-Ottoman relics, the **Agora** (just south of Anafartalar Caddesi, 0232/425-5354, 8:30am-7pm daily, 5TL) lies in ruins at the bottom of İzmir's highest hill. This was old Smyrna's marketplace, commissioned in the 4th century BC by Alexander the Great. Thanks to reconstruction efforts conducted by Faustina, wife of Roman emperor Marcus Aurelius, the Agora was entirely rebuilt after the massive earthquake of AD 178. Of the several Corinthian columns that once delineated the Agora's northern and western flanks, only one colonnade, bearing the likeness of Faustina in one of its arches, still stands. The Altar of Zeus that once stood in the marketplace's center was lost, but the statues of Poseidon and Demeter believed to have been part of this altar are exhibited in the local archaeological museum. While exploring the Agora's ruins, watch for blocks from the four original gates—identifiable trading stalls, coats of arms, and gravestones dating from the site's stint as a Byzantine and later Ottoman cemetery.

The entrance to the Agora is off Gaziosmanpasa Bulvarı, so it's an easy walk from the bazaar or Basmane districts.

Kadifekale

Southeast of the Agora, the perpetually

floodlit **Kadifekale** crowns ancient Mount Pagus. This lofty location, chosen by Alexander the Great to reconstruct Smyrna in 334 BC after the Persians were driven from the city, now serves mostly as a playground for young soccer players and a busy sales point for women from Anatolia's remotest corners.

Today's Kadifekale (Velvet Fortress) is a product of Byzantine and subsequent Ottoman reconstructions of the Roman structure that was devastated by a late-2nd-century-AD earthquake. The fortress's ruins are disappointing after the journey to the site, but the sunset viewed from this location is stunning.

Hiking up the hill is not advised due to the maze of backstreets in a shanty neighborhood that may be unsafe. Avoid getting lost in these streets by using the safest transportation option, a taxi. Ask the driver to wait to avoid a hike back to town. Otherwise, to reach Kadifekale, hop on bus 33 from Konak bus station to its terminus, 350 meters from the fortress.

Kordon

Extending from Cumhuriyet Meydanı to the tip of the posh enclave of Alsancak, the busy three-kilometer **Kordon** is green space for long walks by the water. This strip is also noted for its string of alfresco restaurants where deep-pocketed *İzmirlis* hustle for tables to dine while gazing at the sunset. A nostalgic way to experience this esplanade is by horse-drawn phaetons from Konak.

Kültürpark

The 42 hectares of **Kültürpark,** located in the center of the city, contain over 8,000 trees donated from around the world, an open-air theater, and plenty of recreational space for walking, running, and in-line skating. The park is an area of the city destroyed in the 1922 fires.

Museums

İzmir Arkeoloji Müzesi (İzmir Archaeological Museum, uphill on Halil Rıfat Paşa, behind Konak bus station, 0232/489-0796, 8:30am-5:30pm Tues.-Sun., 8TL) houses Greco-Roman artifacts from the town's ancient Agora and Tepekule (Old Smyrna) as well as from Pergamum, Iasos, and Ephesus. The grounds include an array of Hellenic amphorae. In the lobby, maps detail the country's lengthy history. The floor above contains an ornately etched sarcophagus dating to 3000 BC, the head of the statue of Roman emperor

İzmir at nighttime, as seen from Kadifekale

Domitian from Ephesus, and a collection of ceramics, glass, bronze statues, and mosaics arranged chronologically in an effort to retrace İzmir's history. The lower floor has the statues of Demeter, Poseidon, and Artemis found during a Turkish-German archaeological excavation in the Agora during the 1930s.

Sharing the same courtyard as the Archaeology Museum, İzmir's **Etnografya Müzesi** (Ethnographic Museum, 0232/489-0796, 8:30am-5:30pm Tues.-Sun., free) complements the Archaeology Museum. It opened in the late 1980s in the converted late-19th-century Sainte Roche Hospital with four floors of accumulated folk exhibits. These shed light on local traditions and craftsmanship, including dioramas depicting the casting of *boncuks* (blue and white beads that ward off the evil eye); the manufacture of pottery and felt; and camel-wrestling. Before leaving, check out traditional İzmir housing, from the wooden Ottoman house to the posh Levantine townhouse of Christian and Jewish traders.

Farther up the hill is the **Oyun ve Oyuncak Müzesi** (Toys and Games Museum, Halil Rıfat Paşa 31, 0232/425-7513, www.izmiroyuncakmuzesi.com, 9am-5pm Tues.-Sat., donation), displaying some of the world's most important historic toys, some dating to the 19th century. The toys were collected by Turkish ceramic artist Umran Baradan, who also donated the mansion in which the museum is housed.

The adjacent Archaeological and Ethnographic Museums are a 10-minute walk southeast from Konak Meydanı up a short incline. The Toy Museum, along the same road near the top of the hill, is best accessed via taxi.

The **İzmir Museum of History and Art** (Kültürpark, 0232/445-6818, 8:30am-5:30pm Tues.-Sun., 3TL) is located inside Kültürpark. Three buildings house displays of precious stone works, ceramics, and more from the Roman, Hellenic, classical, and Archaic periods, dating back to 900 BC.

A number of new museums have opened in İzmir in recent years. The **İzmir Mask Museum** (Cumbalı Sk. 22, 0232/465-3107, www.izmirmaskmuseum.com, 10am-6pm Tues.-Sun., 4TL) set in an old Levantine home in Alsancak that exhibits a small collection of masks from around the world.

The former fire station, built in 1932 near Kültürpark, was converted in 2001 into the **Ahmet Piristina Museum of Metropolitan History and Archive** (Sair Eşref Blv. 1/A, 0232/293-3900, www.apikam.org.tr, 9am-6pm daily, free). The museum, named for a former mayor who died in 2004, displays photos, drawings, and historical information about İzmir and Smyrna, including images of the great fire of 1922.

A tribute to the father of the Turkish republic is at **Atatürk Evi** (House of Ataturk, Atatürk Cd. 248, 8:30am-5:30pm Tues.-Sun.), the headquarters for the Turkish army and where the president stayed to conduct private meetings and study from 1930 to 1934. The wooden townhouse, converted into a museum in 1941, offers an inner look at the sumptuous digs of the onetime local aristocracy. The museum is a preview of the few remaining 18th- and 19th-century mansions between 1469 and 1453 *sokaklar* that evaded the 1922 blaze.

Synagogues

İzmir's rich Jewish heritage thrived in its Asansör quarter from the time Jewish people arrived from Spain and Portugal in the 15th century. The **Bet Israel Synagogue** (Mithatpaşa Cd. 265, 0232/425-1628), built in 1907 in Asansör, is İzmir's largest. On the outskirts of the bazaar, three of the nine historical synagogues along 929 Sokak (originally Havra Sokak—Synagogue Street) are open to the public during services on Saturday mornings. Private guided tours of İzmir's Jewish heritage are offered through **Tutku Tours** (Gaziosmanpasa Blv. 3/303, 0232/441-8676, www.tutkutours.com).

Across the Gulf of İzmir

The neighborhood of Sasalı houses the **İzmir Doğal Yaşam Parkı** (İzmir Wildlife Park,

Ahmet Piriştina Caddesi, 0232/327-3016, www.izmirdogalyasamparki.org.tr, 9am-6:30pm Mon.-Fri., 9am-7:30pm Sat.-Sun. Apr.-Sept., 9am-4:30pm daily Oct.-May, 2TL). This expansive and impressive open-air zoo strives to care for tigers, lions, Asian elephants, birds of prey, and other wildlife in a natural habitat. It's a good day out for kids and adults alike. To get here, take a ferry from any port to Bostanlı (2TL with KentKart or up to 3.25TL with a 3-5 Bilet card, 20 minutes) and then bus 777 from the Bostanlı port. The Bilet card or KentKart can be bought at the port. If driving, follow the E87 highway to Ahmet Piriştina Caddesi. Free parking is available on-site.

While in the area, drive down the road beyond the zoo and turn right onto Kuş Cenneti Yolu to find **Birds of Paradise** (0232/482-1213, www.izmirkuscenneti.gov.tr, free), 8,000 hectares of protected land for species including Dalmatian pelicans and red-winged flamingos.

NIGHTLIFE

Party people barhop through Alsancak's Kordon and the narrow backstreets filled with Levantine mansions-turned-bars centered around 1953 Sokak. The lifespan of clubs and bars averages about two years, and what's in today may soon be outdated. Before joining the bar scene, join the Kordon crowd in the traditional evening stroll—the *passegiata*—İzmir's casual pedestrian parade along the Kordon inherited from its Italian ancestors.

Pick up a game of backgammon with the locals at **Passport Café and Bar** (Atatürk Cd. 140, Konak, 0232/425-3901). A puff of narghile (hookah) over *çay* or a heady stein full of Turkey's most popular beer, Efes, can all be found at this local hangout. For comforts closer to home, head to the northern end of the Kordon to **SPR** (Atatürk Cd. 370/1B, 0232/278-4243), an old English-style pub, also open for pub-grub lunches and dinners, complete with a red telephone box for added affect.

FESTIVALS

The first half of March, İzmir hosts the two-week **İzmir Avrupa Caz Festival** (İzmir European Jazz Festival, www.iksev.org) focusing solely on European jazz. From June 10 to July 20 every year, the **İzmir International Festival** celebrates classical and contemporary theater, music, and dance by Turkish and international artists. Kültürpark comes alive in late August with the **İzmir International Fair** (www.ief.izfas.com.tr), the oldest trade show in Turkey, and in mid-November is the **Short Film Festival** (www.izmirkisafilm.org), featuring filmmakers and works from all corners of the world.

ACCOMMODATIONS

İzmir, an international convention city, has five-star chains such as the Mövenpick and Swissotel around the central Cumhuriyet Meydanı. While a number of boutique hotels are emerging along the seaside and in Basmane, the city lacks cheap backpacker accommodations. Those on a tight budget should look for affordable lodging away from the coast near the 19th-century Basmane Train Station. The Basmane area feels rough, with its male-dominated streets and lines of shoe shiners and street vendors, so most prefer to stay in Basmane but dine in Alsancak. Save more on the prices below by booking via discount accommodations providers online.

Under 150TL

Located in 9 Eylül Meydanı, overlooking the main gate of Kültürpark, is the new ★ **Walk In Hotel** (9 Eylül Meydanı 2, 0232/402-2200, www.walkinhotels.com, from 140TL). Catering to business and leisure travelers, the hotel offers six types of rooms with light furnishings with blue trim. Suite and superior rooms have a pleasant view of the fountain in the middle of the square.

Established in 1989 but fully renovated in 2010, **Hotel Baylan** (1299 Sk. 8, 0232/483-0152, www.hotelbaylan.com, from 120TL) is a short walk from the Basmane Train Station and has more than the usual amenities of a budget hotel. With complimentary tea and coffee in the rooms and large ultra-clean rooms with mood lighting, Baylan is an unquestionably excellent value; families will appreciate the five-bed family room.

Backpackers searching online for discounted rooms will find several cheap places in Basmane, but the only one that is recommended, with a good location and cleanliness, is the **Güzel İzmir Oteli** (1368 Sk. 8, 0232/483-5069, www.guzelizmirhotel.com, from €48). The 30-room hotel provides small no-frills rooms with private showers. At these prices, check out several of the available rooms—a common practice in Turkey—before settling on one.

Over 150TL

The locally-owned **İzmir Palas** (Atatürk Blv., 0232/465-0030, www.izmirpalas.com.tr, from 230TL) is the oldest hotel in town. Built in 1927, the three-star Palas was entirely renovated in 2005, resulting in a mix of Old World style with groovy orange baths. Regardless of the look, it's located on the prestigious Kordon, so expect panoramic sea views from seaside rooms with balconies. Its sidewalk Deniz Restaurant is well regarded for its tasty regional fish dishes.

For boutique luxury and design-hotel panache, secure your standard, superior, or suite room near 9 Eylül Meydanı at **Met Hotel** (Gazi Blv. 124, 0232/483-0111, www.metotel.com, from €99). The plush lobby of modern lounges and elegant fixtures continues through to the large rooms decked out in fashionable gray and purple. One suite room comes with a private sauna and an enormous balcony.

The ★ **Key Hotel** (Mimar Kemalettin Cd. 1, 0232/482-1111, www.keyhotel.com, from €168) exudes modernity, VIP services, and high-class appeal. The rooms are smart-wired for remote control of all the electronic comforts, the on-site à la carte restaurant is gastronomic heaven serving up Aegean delights, and if that's not enough, order an airport transfer in their classic 1974 Rolls Royce or 1956 Mercedes.

FOOD

İzmir is renowned for its coastal seafood. Mussels are ubiquitous at finer restaurants—the safest place to try them—and from tray-balancing street peddlers. Choose from *midiye dolma* (mussel stuffed with spiced rice) or fried versions at finer establishments. Remember that buying from a street vendor during the hot summer months increases your risk of food poisoning. Typically Aegean, the *çipura* (gilthead bream) is a delicacy that's outrageously tasty when grilled. Another regional specialty is fried or grilled *barbun* (red mullet). The adventurous can try *tuzda balık* (fish cooked in salt) or even fish that's been simmered in milk. Meat lovers will delight in the local *çöp şiş* (literally "trash kebab"). But don't let the name scare you: It's simply grilled skewers of giblet-free leftover lamb.

For a regal meal among İzmir's elite, head to Kordon's brimming terraces. Or better yet, head farther north to the restored mansions of Alsancak, where you'll find cafés, bars, and restaurants.

There is no shortage of quick and easy cafés and fast-food chains around the bazaar, Konak Meydanı, and Alsancak's Kıbrıs Şehitleri Caddesi. Practically every second shop in these bustling areas is dishing out pizzas, sandwiches, kebabs, and Turkish cuisine. These locations are ideal for a no-fuss stop on a long sightseeing or shopping tour. For a quick snack during the day, early birds should try the bazaar's typical street fare of *pide* (flat bread) and kebabs. These close at 7pm, but the majority of İzmir's eateries remain open until well past 11pm.

Turkish

Hands down, the most exquisite Turkish restaurant is **Meshur Tavacı Recep Usta** (Atatürk Cd. 364, Alsancak, 0232/444-1978, 35TL). The prices may seem steep, but you'll be showered with included starters and desserts. This place is so good that even princes from Dubai eat here when they're in town. Chef Recep Usta is renowned for his *kaburga* *dolması*, lamb ribs stuffed with flavored rice and steamed until the meat falls off the bone. It's best shared with others.

For more affordable Turkish cuisine, **Servet** (Şehit Fethibey Cd. 78C, 0232/445-0478, www.servetcopsis.com, 15TL) between Alsancak and the bazaar, peddles regional kebabs in a modest setting. It's a good place to try the Aegean lamb dish *çöp şiş*, a specialty from Selçuk and Germencik, near Ephesus.

In the bazaar area, bustling tiny restaurants offering Manisa kebabs reign supreme. For this kebab, sliced *pide* is topped with thin slices of marinated meat and tomato and drizzled with yogurt, butter, and garlic. To try it, find **Doyuran Manısa Kebap Salonu** (866 Sk. 14-16, 0232/425-1263, 10TL) in Ali Paşa Meydanı overlooking a 500-year-old fountain. Leave the Kızlarağası Han at the exit closest to the seaside and turn left on 871 Sokak. Follow the street until you see a fountain in a square to your right. Owner Nurettin Bahaivan and his sons warmly welcome guests. Non-meat eaters will find other food options facing the fountain. After a meandering shopping spree, try the *fincanda pişen kahvesi* in one of the many coffee shops of the bazaar. Brewed from beans that are finely crushed in a stone mortar, the coffee is prepared in the cup, giving a richer aroma and smoother texture than coffee ground in a mill.

Staying in Basmane and don't have the energy to venture to Alsancak? Go to **Dört Mevsim Et Lokantası** (1369 Sk. 51/A, 0232/489-8991, from 10TL). Turks from as far as Ankara file into its packed quarters for a chance to reacquaint their taste buds with the house specialty, *köfte* (meatballs) served with chili sauce. It also features an *ocakbaşı* (open grill), which continually offers baked delicacies like stuffed-eggplant kebab.

International

For the best views of İzmir, head to **Asansör Restaurant** (0232/261-2626, 10-50TL) accessed via the historic elevator off Dario Moreno Sokak. There are two restaurants to choose from once you reach the lofty heights of the lookout with its European charm. The café on the right has café-style meals of pizzas, pastas, and sandwiches for under 15TL. The more formal restaurant on the left has a set menu (reservations are essential) with three dishes for 50TL pp. Choose fish, chicken, or lamb and enjoy the meal with mezes as the sun sets over the Gulf of İzmir.

Say *"oh, là là"* as you walk into the eclectic garden oasis of **La Cigale** (Cumhuriyet Blv. 152, 0232/421-4780, www.lacigale.com.tr, Mon.-Sat., 20TL), a hidden gem nestled in the side street of the Fransız Kültür Merkezi (French Cultural Center) where diners may forget what city they're in. The menu is naturally European with creamy pastas, gourmet pizzas, cheese platters, and steaks drizzled in French sauces, all at reasonable prices and catering for all tastes. Bon appétit!

Seafood

Deniz Restaurant (Atatürk Cd. 188/B, 0232/464-4499, 25TL, reservations required), considered one of the best eateries along the Kordon, is where Turkey's glitterati refuel. Try the specialty *balik kavurma* (roasted flaky fish served in a traditional earthenware pan).

Along the Kordon, the fish restaurant earning rave reviews for its exceptional service and location is **Yengec** (Atatürk Cd. 314/A, 0232/464-5757, www.yengec-restoran.com, 25TL). Owner Kerim Özsoydan greets guests on arrival to introduce both a small catch like red mullet and bigger specialties such as swordfish or groper. Like all fish restaurants in Turkey, negotiate the price prior to taking a seat, or choose from the prix fixe menu of steaks, chicken, and vegetarian dishes.

Located in the Efes Swissotel complex, **SushiCo** (0232/484-0070, Şehit Nevres Blv. 2/F, www.sushico.com.tr, 20TL) offers seafood in the form of sushi. Pad thai, curries, and many forms of sushi are prepared by Japanese chefs on-site, a break from fish restaurants and Turkish kebabs.

INFORMATION AND SERVICES
Visitor Information

Just north of Key Hotel, spanning Cumhuriyet Bulvarı and Atatürk Caddesi, is İzmir's main **Tourism Information Office** (1344 Sk. 2, 0232/483-5117, 8:30am-5:30pm Mon.-Fri.). There's also a **Tourism Information Kiosk** (0232/274-2214, 8:30am-5:30pm Mon.-Fri.) in the airport arrival hall.

One of the most reputable tour operators in İzmir is **Tutku Tours** (Gaziosmanpasa Blv. 3/303, 0232/441-8676, www.tutkutours.com). Multilingual staff specialize in day tours of İzmir, Sardis, Ephesus, Pergamum, and Pamukkale. An open-top hop-on, hop-off city tour (www.eshot.gov.tr, 9am-3pm daily, €10) operates when the luxury cruise ships are in town, three or four times a week in summer. The loop around the city lasts one hour, with pickups every half hour. Major stops include the Alsancak port, Atatürk Museum, Agora, and opposite Konak pier at the municipal bus stop.

Banks and Currency Exchange

Banks and 24-hour ATMs are located all around the city, with the majority on Cumhuriyet and Konak Squares, as well as along Fevzi Paşa Bulvarı. Exchange offices are also located along Fevzi Paşa Bulvarı.

Communications

For postal services, money transfers, and currency exchange, İzmir's main **PTT** (0232/464-0141, 8:30am-5pm, Mon.-Sat.) post office is on Cumhuriyet Square. Other PPT offices are in Basmane (Fevzi Paşa Cd. 170, 0232/425-3410) and Konak (856 Sk. 2/A, 0232/441-4438).

For foreign books and magazines in English, head to **Remzi Kitabevi** (Konak Pier, 0232/489-5325), and as with all cities and towns in Turkey, most hotels and cafés offer free Wi-Fi to guests to catch up on the latest news.

The **İzmir Metropolitan Municipality** (www.izmir.bel.tr) has a useful website detailing public transportation options and local events.

Emergency Services

The **American Consulate** (1387 Sk. 0232/464-8755) is located in Alsancak and can assist with emergencies. Its staff regularly refers U.S. citizens needing medical assistance to the local **American Hospital** (1375 Sk., 0232/484-5360).

GETTING THERE
Air

One of the country's busiest international and domestic airports, İzmir's **Adnan Menderes Airport** (ADB, 0232/274-2626, www.adnanmenderesairport.com) is served by Turkish charter airlines and Turkey's national airline, **Turkish Airlines** (0232/484-1220, Halit Ziya Blv. 65, Çankaya), **KLM** (www.klm.com), **Lufthansa** (www.lufthansa.com), **Germanwings** (www.germanwings.com), **Corsair** (www.corsair.fr), and **Condor** (www.condor.com).

From the airport, use the **IZBAN** and **metro rail** networks to get to central İzmir. Pick up the IZBAN going to Aliağa at Havalimanı station outside the airport. The IZBAN will stop at Alsancak and then Halkapınar. Switch to the metro at Halkapınar to get to Basmane and Konak (9TL). The whole journey takes about an hour. A **Havaş** (www.havas.com.tr, 10TL) bus departs the airport for every domestic arrival and terminates at Cumhuriyet Square. Eshot bus 202 also transports people to Cumhuriyet Square (4TL), near the Efes Büyük Swissotel, every hour daily until midnight.

Bus

Most travelers arrive in İzmir by coach or *dolmuş*. Roughly five kilometers northeast of Konak Meydanı, the city's *otogar* is one of the largest transit hubs in the nation. If you arrive at the main *otogar,* the coach company will have a free *servis* to 9 Eylül Meydanı, just a two-minute walk to Basmane train station for transfers to the metro. Otherwise, exit the *otogar* to find the municipal bus stop near the main rotary and take Eshot bus 54 or 191 to Konak. These buses also stop adjacent to the

Basmane train station on Gazi̇ler Caddesi. From Üçkuyular *otogar,* take Eshot bus 169 or 121 to Konak and Alsancak.

Most travelers also depart İzmir via coach or *dolmuş* from the *otogar*, where there are dozens of agents crowded shoulder-to-shoulder vying for the next customer. For intercity connections, don't be tempted to purchase the cheapest coach ticket or the earliest departure; opt instead to travel with one of the more reputable companies, which include **Ulusoy** (0232/444-1888, www.ulusoy.com.tr) and **Pamukkale** (0850/333-3535, www.pamukkale.com.tr), or others mentioned earlier. During the hectic summer months, reserve coach seats at least 24 hours ahead of departure and at least two days ahead for weekend travel. Sales offices for coach services are located in 9 Eylül Meydanı in central İzmir, or at the *otogar* on the top and lower floors. From the *otogar,* a fleet of *dolmuşlar* regularly head to Selçuk (1 hour, 9TL), Çeşme (1.5 hours, 15TL), Foça (1.5 hours, 9TL), Bergama (2 hours, 12TL), and Salihli (1 hour, 8TL), where you transfer to a minibus for Sardis. Buses from İzmir to Çeşme also run from Üçkuyular *otogar* southwest of the main *otogar*.

Train

Aegean regional trains from Selçuk (1.25 hours, 8 trains daily, 5.65TL) and Denizli (4.75 hours, 6 trains daily, 20TL) arrive at the **Basmane Garı** (train station, 0232/484-8638), while the historic **Alsancak Garı** (0232/464-7795) is reserved for intercity lines to Ankara (15.5 hours, 1 train daily, 37TL), Konya (11.5 hours, 1 train daily, from 35TL) and Bandırma (5.75 hours, 2 trains daily, from 22TL) where the IDO fast ferry bound for Yenikapı in İstanbul can be boarded (www.ido.com.tr). Visit the state railroad, **TCDD** (www.tcdd.gov.tr), for information about regional and intercity rail lines.

GETTING AROUND

İzmir has an extensive public transportation network that includes the **IZBAN** (www.izban.com.tr) suburban trains, metro, municipal buses, and ferries. Severe congestion makes walking almost a necessity. **Taxis** go everywhere and start the meter at about 3TL. A typical taxi from Alsancak to Basmane is about 15TL. The underground **Metro** (www.izmirmetro.com.tr, 6am-midnight daily, 2TL) zips from Basmane train station to Konak Meydanı in about 10 minutes.

İzmir's dependable Eshot buses depart from **Konak Otobus Istasyonu** (bus terminal) south of Konak Meydanı. There are two options for purchasing tickets. The first is the 3-5 Bilet, which costs 6.50TL for two credits, 9.40TL for three credits, or 15.20TL for five credits. Boarding public transit to travel within the general vicinity of the city will deduct one credit from the card; travel farther afield costs more. Bilet cards can be bought from the driver or at kiosks near public transit stations. If you intend to use public transit more than five times, then the prepaid İzmir KentKarts may be a better deal. They provide discounted fares (2TL-4TL) for all metropolitan buses, ferries, and train networks. KentKarts can be purchased for 5TL from kiosks near public transit stations. Simply add extra credit to cover the cost of your fares. Both cards are swiped as you board buses or enter the turnstiles for trains and ferries. Subsequent trips within 90 minutes of your first journey will be free. Visit **Eshot** (www.eshot.gov.tr) for fare information.

Ferries (www.izdeniz.com.tr) crossing the Gulf of İzmir and linking the jetties of Alsancak, Konak, and Pasaport are an enjoyable way to see the city from the water. Karşıyaka from Alsancak Port (2TL with a KentKart, 20 minutes) is the most popular route, taking visitors to the lively shopping district across the gulf.

Driving in İzmir can be nightmarish due to the city's heavy congestion. Patience is key when negotiating bumper-to-bumper traffic, particularly when the headache is compounded with İzmir's confusing one-way thoroughfares. Many hotels offer free parking for guests.

To explore farther afield, rent a car from **Avis** (Adnan Menderes Airport, 0232/274-1790, www.avis.com.tr, 24 hours daily), **Hertz** (Adnan Menderes Airport, 0232/274-3610, www.hertz.com, 24 hours), or **Europcar** (Adnan Menderes Airport, 0232/274-6420, www.europcar.com.tr, 24 hours daily).

★ SART (SARDIS)

Day trippers from İzmir will enjoy the ancient site of Sart, on the outskirts of the farming village of the same name, at the foot of the Tmolus Mountains, overlooking the fertile Hermus River Plain. Its origins are so ancient that its origins are unknown. A joint archaeological research team from Harvard and Cornell Universities claims that the site has been a major metropolis for at least four millennia. First-time visitors to the restored early-3rd-century-AD Lydian gymnasium are awed by its grandeur. The discovery of an adjoining 3rd-century synagogue stunned historians by revealing that Judaism was thriving during the Roman era. Sardis's ruins are an eye-popping experience for fans of archaeology and history.

History

The site is known variously as Sardis, Sardes, and Sardeis; Sparda in Persian; and Sart in Turkish. Academics agree that it was the capital of the Lydian Empire (8th-6th century BC). At its height the realm extended from the Aegean Sea well into central Anatolia. Noted for its fertile soil and rich deposits of gold and silver form the nearby Patolus Çayı (river), Sardis quickly became affluent. Lydian kings were the first to mint the electrum (silver and gold coins). The renowned King Croesus (563-546 BC) made a fortune from trade, facilitated by the newly minted coins that had replaced the barter system. But this prosperity caught the attention of the Persian King Cyrus the Great, who in 546 BC conquered Sardis after a 14-day siege in which Croesus was burned alive. Under the Persians, Sardis marked the last stop on an administrative route that began in Persepolis—today's Susa in Iran. Industry and commercial trade made Lydia one of the richest kingdoms of its time, with a lifestyle known for extravagance. During the Ionian Revolt (499 BC), the Ionian Greeks to the west launched a systematic rebellion against the tyrannical rule of the Persians, burning Sardis to the ground in the process. Any subsequent attempt to repel the Persians from Asia Minor proved unsuccessful until Alexander the Great's army successfully accomplished the feat in 334 BC. Sardis surrendered to Alexander. The great warrior tasked his architect with returning the former Lydian capital to its onetime architectural magnificence, but a massive earthquake in AD 17 devastated much of these marble structures. One of Sardis's important sculptures, a stone shrine to the mother goddess Cybele, survived the earthquake untouched. It's one of the earliest Ionic temples and earliest examples of Ionic architecture (6th century BC). During the ensuing Greek era, after the death of Alexander, Pergamum kings coveted Sardis's exotic wealth, and in 282 BC the city became the Seleucid capital and an independent Greek city-state. The colossal Artemis Temple at the site dates from this era. Under the Romans, the shrine was greatly enlarged with a bath-gymnasium complex.

Sardis continued to play a major role in religion. The seat of a Christian bishopric, Sardis's church was the third of the Seven Churches of the Revelation to receive an ominous letter from Saint John the Apostle in the 1st century AD. It also had a thriving Jewish community, which built one of the largest ancient synagogues outside of Palestine.

Sardis remained one of Asia Minor's major metropolises until the late Byzantine era. By the 11th century, various raids and conquests of the lush surrounding Hermus Valley by the Turks and the Christians had cut most vital routes to and from the city. Sardis's citadel fell to the advancing Turks in 1306, and less than a century later, Mongol warlord Timerlane destroyed the once grand capital; it never recovered.

Sardis was the capital of the Lydian Empire.

Sardis synagogue is the largest of its kind. Tiled columns and walls have historical information, and look for a plaque listing the mostly North American benefactors who've enabled the renovation process of this *havra* (synagogue).

Right next door to the synagogue is the site of a once impressive **gymnasium and bath complex,** destroyed by the Sassanian-Persians in AD 616. Beyond it stands an astonishingly tall and meticulously restored **Marble Court.** It may have been completed in AD 211 or 212, according to the dedicatory inscription that honors Roman emperor Geta, who only ruled for those two years. Beyond the structure's finely striated columns is an entrance that leads to the court's marble **swimming pool** and resting area. Judging from the magnificence of its forecourt, the bath was used to honor the imperial cult.

Current archaeological research has unveiled parts of **city walls** dating back to the Lydian era as well as a **Roman residence,** which sits atop an earlier Lydian structure.

Sights

The **Ruins of Sardis** (8am-7pm daily May-Oct., 8am-5pm daily Nov.-Apr.) are clustered in two main groups that are easily approachable from the main road. Informative signs lead visitors through the entire site. The first includes the stunningly restored gymnasium and adjacent synagogue, which are reached by following the **Roman Road** that leads past **Byzantine shops** and **Byzantine latrines.** The tunnels that drained these ancient communal toilets can still be seen along the shops' rear walls. These vertical partitions backed into the adjoining synagogue. Among the clearly marked businesses along this ancient commercial lane, the names of their owners, Sabbatio and Jacob, keep recurring. The former was a benefactor of the synagogue, while the latter may have been one of its elders.

A left turn at the end of the road leads to Sardis's **synagogue.** The floors of this 3rd-century-AD structure feature original mosaics; the ones on the walls, however, are replicas. At over 100 meters in length, the

TEMPLE OF ARTEMIS

Heading west from the synagogue, past the tea houses of the village of Sart—short for Sartmahmut—the **Temple of Artemis** (8am-5pm daily, 8TL) boasts the remnants of six 18-meter-tall columns. The construction of this impressive Roman temple began in 300 BC but was never finished. Researchers believe that a wall may have been planned as a division to allow each deity a separate chamber: The west-facing hall was meant to be shared by the goddess Artemis and Roman empress Faustina, while the east-facing chamber was allocated to Zeus and the exalted Antonine emperor. By the mid-4th century AD, the temple was "cleansed" of its Roman past and a **Byzantine church** was built among its ruins.

Before leaving the site, there are two ruins worth a detour. The first, the Altar of Cybele, lies in the center of the Sardis archaeological site, next to the Lydian gold refinery. It faces east and is flanked on either side by crouching lions—felines considered sacred to the Anatolian mother goddess Cybele. The mid-6th-century shrine was erected during the rule of Lydian King Alyattes. The second set of ruins, more than 100 burial grounds, is located on the right side, or north, of the highway leading from Sardis. The series of tumuli are saucer-like burial mounds that entomb Lydian royalty.

Getting There and Around

The best way to visit the Sardis ruins is with a regional agent from İzmir. If touring on your own, however, get the *dolmuş* to Salihli from İzmir's main *otogar* and transfer to the minibus to Sartmahmut, the town on the doorstep of ancient Sardis. For cars and buses it's a pleasant 90-minute, 96-kilometer ride along the E96 from İzmir.

ÇEŞME PENINSULA

Two decades ago, a trio of die-hard sailboarders "found" what they called paradise on earth: the beaches of Çeşme's windswept, scrubby coastal shores. A few years later Bodrum's summer residents rediscovered the location's cooler and drier climate and made the westernmost peninsula of Anatolia what it is today—a weekend escape for Istanbul's youthful elite. Some 74 kilometers southwest of İzmir, Çeşme is blessed with more than a dozen sandy shores and pristine waters. The Greek island of Chios looms 15 kilometers across the Aegean. The peninsula is a contradiction: Its ringed coast is a bastion for unchecked hedonism, while its inactive interior can be purely prosaic. Its agricultural landscape has noted mastic gum trees and fields of aniseed, sesame, and artichokes scattered with fig and olive trees. Its unspoiled bays provide sunbathers and swimmers absolute peace.

The peninsula is named after the fort town of Çeşme at its tip. The name Çeşme (Drinking Fountain) is from the myriad of Ottoman fountains that were built here atop natural springs. Discovered in the late 18th century, these springs were forgotten until recently. Turkey's tourism magnates are finally exploiting this natural richness with the opening of several luxurious spa resorts.

Summer sees a number of festival and events crowd the towns and beaches. The Çeşme Fortress is the setting for the Çeşme Sea and Music Festival (July), Ilıca hosts the International Çakabey Optimist Yacht Race (July), and surfers flock to the region with the Professional Windsurfers Association's World Cup (early Aug.) and the Red Bull Aegean Cross from Turkey to Greece (late Aug.).

You could spend a week exploring Çeşme's fine beaches and secluded coves, lounge in its exclusive haunts, and investigate its countryside, but 48 hours should suffice to visit the uniquely Greek village of Alaçatı and its nearby windsurfing paradise and the golden shores of Altınkum. Çeşme's international harbor is a great spot to take one of the daily ferries to the nearby Greek island of Chios.

Çeşme

A 14th-century Genoese castle, the **Çeşme Fortress,** looms over the handful of cobblestone lanes of the picturesque enclave of Çeşme. Shortly after conquering this Aegean outpost, Sultan Beyazit II (son of Sultan Mehmet the Conqueror of Istanbul) strengthened the fortress. It later served as a watchtower from which guards surveyed the horizon for marauding pirates. Unlike Bodrum's fortress, the citadel here is disappointingly barren, but it does offer a stunning panorama of the Aegean Sea and Chios. Its museum, **Çeşme Müzesi** (Çeşme Museum, 9am-6:30pm Tues.-Sun., 5TL), however, boasts wonderful artifacts discovered at the nearby ancient village of Erythrea. Just outside the castle lies the statue of Cezayirli Gazi Hasan Paşa, a naval commander of the Battle of Chesma (1770) who later became grand vizier. The lion he's caressing represents his infamous pet. Also nearby is **Öküz Mehmet Paşa Kervansaray,** a *han* commissioned in 1528 by Süleyman the Magnificent. For centuries, this trading post marked the end of the transcontinental Silk Road for the many

Çeşme Peninsula

caravans that made their way from the Middle East into the arid steppe of central Anatolia and beyond. From this point, Asian goods were unloaded from camels and exported to Europe. While today it has been converted into the Kanuni Kervansaray Hotel, its solid stone architecture is intact and its courtyard provides a nice location to escape the blazing heat of summer.

Amid Çeşme's backstreets is the 19th-century Greek Orthodox **Church of Agios Haralambos** (Inkılap Cd., free) that now serves as an art gallery. On its doorstep, Inkılap Caddesi, the main shopping street, leads up to the *dolmuş* stop on Atatürk Caddesi and down to the seaside. Stroll the seaside promenade and the **marina** of the breezy harbor to take in the views to Chios.

ACCOMMODATIONS AND FOOD

The all-inclusive ★ **Piril Hotel Thermal and Beauty Spa** (İnönü Mahallesi,

0232/444-0232, www.pirilhotel.com, from 360TL) proves that a full-service resort doesn't necessarily have to be an eyesore. A compilation of pleasing glass, concrete, and pools, this structure boasts 140 sunlit rooms that tend to be on the small side. As its name suggests, many luxurious treatments are available in its 370-square-meter mind-and-body retreat.

Getting the nod mainly for its central location is **Ridvan Otel** (Cumhuriyet Meydanı 11, 0232/712-6336, www.ridvanotel.com, from 150TL). This harborside hotel has large rooms with balconies that overlook the square. The public areas of this five-story hotel are a little dated, but the rooms have modern amenities.

Owner Emre Kurtbay says his **Nese Hotel** (3025 Sk. 37, 0232/712-6345, www.neseotel.net, from 140TL) isn't fancy, but the excellent breakfast served in a Mediterranean courtyard makes up for the basic rooms. Emre's obliging personality has made this 15-room hotel popular for independent travelers searching for clean and comfortable accommodations. Emre also owns affordable hotels in Çeşme and Alaçatı.

For the best dining in town, Turks return year after year to ★ **Imren Lokantasi** (Inkılap Cd. 6, 0232/712-7620, 10TL). The Kadagan sibling quartet has been serving simple yet spectacularly good traditional Turkish entrées and veggie appetizers since 1953. Head to the back of the eatery to sit by the soothing water feature in the pleasant garden atrium. Try the specialty *Karnıyarık* (meat-stuffed eggplant) for a traditional meal.

Along the waterfront are lines of fish restaurants marketing an excellent deal of *levrek* (sea bass) with salad (18TL), but for a broader menu with sea views, head to **Medcezir Cafe** (3057 St. No. 7/1, 0232/712-7286, 15TL); with its menu of international cuisine such as steaks and curries, it's a hit with Turkish and international visitors alike.

For a change of scenery, drive up to Dalyan Harbor to dine at the fish restaurants. Prices are a little more expensive, but feasting by this harbor is a fashionable thing to do in Çeşme. Which fish restaurant to choose? The locals recommend **Cevat'in Yeri** (Liman Cd. 161, 0232/724-7045, www.dalyanrestaurant.com, 25TL).

★ Alaçatı

There are a number of beachside locations on the peninsula, but the place to see and be seen is, strangely, a town away from the beach. **Alaçatı** has been transformed into a platform for country living and a year-round weekend

Alaçatı is gourmet paradise.

escape for Istanbul's and İzmir's elite and ambitious. It was a pleasant Greek village replete with gorgeous 19th-century stone abodes until one was turned into the upscale hotel Taş Otel in the mid-1990s. This B&B proved so popular that a number of copycats followed suit. Then came the trendy restaurants and cafés, whose cosmopolitan and Turkish menus merit a trip to the peninsula. Due to strict building regulations, the town's antique architecture remains intact, at least in the town center, where cobblestone streets are lined with art galleries and tiny souvenir and antiques shops. Although the tourist season is longer every year, most hotels and restaurants are open mid-May to mid-October and on school and year-end holidays. Hotels reservations are strongly advised.

ACCOMMODATIONS AND FOOD

An abundance of boutique hotels in Alaçatı offers highly rated five-star services in luxury home-style abodes. If you're willing to pay extra for food and accommodations, Alaçatı is the prettiest place on the Çeşme Peninsula to stay. The one that started it all, **Taş Otel** (Kemalpaşa Cd. 132, 0232/716-7772, www.tasotel.com, from €170) transports guests from the streets of rural Turkey to the opulence of an English-style manor. Every room has romantic curtains hung from high ceilings with elegant cottage-style furnishings. The outdoor area features an inviting pool and garden that hosts complimentary breakfasts and afternoon teas, introducing guests to the specialty of the house: oregano and lavender honey.

Ultra-stylish inside and out, the eight-room **Vintage Boutique Hotel** (3046 Sk. 2/1, 0232/716-0716, www.vintagealacati.com, from €150) exceeds all expectations. The garden is peppered with classy outdoor European decor and the rooms are large and full of über-chic features. Concierge services are available in both hotels, and both are close to the action of Alaçatı but quiet enough for relaxation.

Alaçatı is growing in gastronomic attractions, with a Saturday farmers market; the Herb Festival the first week of April has gastronomes whipping up dishes blended with fresh regional herbs. Don't fret if you miss the event because **Asma Yaprağı** (1005 Sk. 50, 0232/716-0178, www.asmayapragi.com.tr, 20TL), open year-round, specializes in Aegean dishes with ingredients bought directly from local farmers. Owner and chef Ayşe Nur Mıhcı changes the menu of 14-15 family recipes often, but the meals cooked on-site in a quaint Turkish kitchen come highly recommended by many businesses in town. Reservations for lunch and dinner are a must.

Another sought-after gastronomic treat is high above the town at **Alancha** (1036 Sk. 1, 0232/716-8307, www.alancha.com, 155TL pp). The prix fixe tasting menu is experimental, using only local produce cooked on a wood fire. Prices are high, like the views, but perfect for an opulent special occasion. For more affordable options, many reputable restaurants line the main Kemalpaşa Caddesi, offering contemporary menus for around 30TL pp. Do watch for *kuver*—a fee some restaurants charge per head for bread, olives, and water. Ask up front if they charge this before deciding to take a seat.

Finally, perhaps the most fashionable meal on the peninsula is the most affordable: *kumru* sandwiches. Best served at **Şevhi** (café, many locations), these sandwiches have cheese, tomato, sausages, ham, pickles—basically anything on the counter.

Sports and Recreation

Some of Turkey's finest beaches sparkle on the Çeşme Peninsula. **Pırlanta Beach,** southwest of the Çeşme town site, scores high among the country's top-10 best. It earns its name, which means "diamond," from the 1.5-kilometer strip of sand that glitters in the sun's rays. Located southwest of Çeşme, this public beach faces north toward the peninsula's craggy shores and features winds ideal for kite surfers. Farther along this stretch of the peninsula is **Altınkum Beach,** consisting of a series of pristine undeveloped beaches and coves with several beach clubs offering sun beds and umbrellas for rent (10TL) and restaurant facilities. Those into windsurfing, parasailing, kiteboarding, and the like will also find equipment rentals at **Fun Beach** (www.funbeachclub.com, 40TL, not including equipment rental) on the road to Altınkum Beach. The club also has restaurants and bungalows for anyone wishing to make the most of a coastal holiday.

The white sandy beaches of **Ilıca** and **Sifne Bay** in the north are famous for their healing thermal springs that seep through the seabed, believed to remedy an assortment of ailments. Whiste, about five kilometers south of Alaçatı, is superb for sailboarding, although the strong winds can be a nuisance for sunbathers.

Çeşme is renowned as one of the world's top four windsurfing destinations, so eager beginners by the hundreds try to get their balance with this demanding sport in Alaçatı. **Alaçatı Beach Resort** (0232/716-0101, www.alacatiwindsurfokulu.com) employs knowledgeable instructors for windsurfing classes. Adjacent to the resort, beachgoers can also rent Jet Skis (100TL), wakeboards (100TL for 15 minutes), canoes (20TL per hour) and more from **Borcın Su Sporları** (www.alacatiborcinsusporlari.com).

For those seeking more relaxing water activities, **day cruises** depart every morning from the Çeşme marina and provide roughly seven hours of snorkeling, swimming, or simple sunbathing fun. These cruises range from the typically crowded music-blasting boats to private day cruises with lunch included.

Deep-sea diving around the several shipwrecks that line Çeşme's seabed is another possibility with **Dolphin Land** (0232/337-0161, www.divecesme.com) in Dalyan. This outfit offers fully certified diving instructors and provides full-day diving trips as well as refresher courses and PADI certification for those itching to earn their fins in this underwater sport.

Party people who prefer to sleep all day and dance all night should head to the beach clubs along Alaçatı beach and Ayayorgi Koyu in the late afternoon to party well into the evening. Clubs are seasonal and often change names; ask the locals which clubs are the hottest this year.

Information and Services

In Çeşme, the **Tourism Information Office** (Iskele Meydanı 6, 0232/712-6653) is adjacent to the rotary near the fortress. Most banks, ATMs, tour offices, and taxi stands are between this office and Cumhuriyet Meydanı, Çeşme's main square. The **PTT** (3053 Sk. 24, 8am-5pm Mon.-Fri.) post office is located along the esplanade, just north of the ferry port.

Getting There

All coach connections from major cities to Çeşme run via the İzmir *otogar*. In summer, Çeşme Seyahat **shuttle buses** to and from İzmir Üçkuyular and Çeşme *otogarlar* depart every 15 minutes (6:30am-10pm daily, 15TL); in winter they run less often. Çeşme's *otogar* is inland, about 15 minutes' walk from the marina, but there are stops in Alaçatı *beledeysi* (municipality) and in Çeşme, at the rotary connecting Atatürk Bulvarı and Inkılap Caddesi. A **Havaş** (www.havas.com.tr) bus links Çeşme *otogar* directly to İzmir's Adnan Menderes Airport (20TL) in one hour.

The *otoyol* (expressway) E881, a toll road, links İzmir to the Çeşme Peninsula in less than an hour by **car.** The D300 highway also links İzmir to the peninsula without a toll.

Car-and-passenger ferries link Çeşme to the Greek island of Chios. The service runs twice daily in high season and four times a week in winter. It generally departs Çeşme at 9:30am and at sunset, with departures from Chios at 8am and around 6pm. View timetables and purchase tickets from **Ertürk Travel Agency** (Beyazıt Cd. 6, 0232/712-6768, www.erturk.com.tr, €21 round-trip, vehicles from €125). Ferries that once ran to the Italian ports of Brindisi, Ancona, and Bari are no longer operating. The dock is less than a 15-minute walk from along the bay from Çeşme's marina.

Getting Around

Getting around the peninsula is easy, with a network of convenient minibuses serving the towns and beaches from Çeşme. The *dolmuş* to Pırlanta, Fun Beach, and Altınkum (3.50TL) departs every half-hour south of Çeşme's *turizm danışma* (tourism office). The last bus returns to Çeşme following the same route at sunset. To reach Alaçatı, jump on the *dolmuş* at the stop near the rotary on Atatürk Caddesi (3TL). It will first pass through Ilıca Beach before reaching a park opposite Alaçatı Belediyesi. This is the stop for the town. The *dolmuş* runs every 10 minutes until midnight. Adjacent to the *belediyesi,* the *dolmuş* to Alaçatı marina and beach (3TL) departs every 30 minutes.

The Southern Aegean Coast

The Ephesus Region 214
Pamukkale 238

The southern Aegean coast has the world's densest concentration of antiquities per square kilometer. One of Turkey's most fertile regions, it sprawls over the lush deltas formed by the Küçük and Büyük Menderes Rivers. From their banks spread fields of tobacco, grains, and cotton, while fir and olive groves unfurl as far as the eye can see. So valued were these rivers in antiquity that their twists and turns inspired early Greek lexicographers to coin the word *meander*.

This natural abundance, combined with comfortable topography and close proximity to the Aegean, produced some of the world's earliest civilizations. Greek islanders later colonized the coast, creating the mighty Ionian realm and some of the first advancements in science, history, and art.

In addition to Sardis and Pergamum, the crown jewel of Turkey's ancient cities is Ephesus, with less-visited but worthwhile cities—Miletus, Didyma, Priene, and gorgeous Aphrodisias—nearby and packed with ruins. Rebuilt stele by stele, Priene stands high on a hill overlooking the lush delta with breathtaking views of the fields. Its Acropolis is second in importance to Delphi in Greece. The Ephesus region also features Meryemana (House of the Virgin Mary); the small ruins of the Temple of Artemis, one of the Ancient World's Seven Wonders; and other dazzling sites from early Christianity.

Other destinations include the small village of Şirince, renowned for its fruit wines, picturesque architecture, and starring role in the 2012 film *Mayan Apocalypse*. Selçuk, in the middle of the major sites, provides an idyllic, peaceful place to relax after hours of absorbing so much history. The nearby coastal resort of Kuşadası, with its many massive vacation resorts and nightlife, satisfies those seeking full-on partying and entertainment with their sightseeing.

The area is more than just the coast and its many attractions: A three-hour drive inland from Selçuk leads to Pamukkale, where surreal snow-white outcrops of calcium jut from the earth, creating majestic ledges pocked with shallow thermal pools. These mineral-rich springs are believed to be therapeutic. This

Previous: Pamukkale's white travertines; Hierapolis. **Above:** the Temple of Hadrian at Ephesus.

Look for ★ to find recommended sights, activities, dining, and lodging.

Highlights

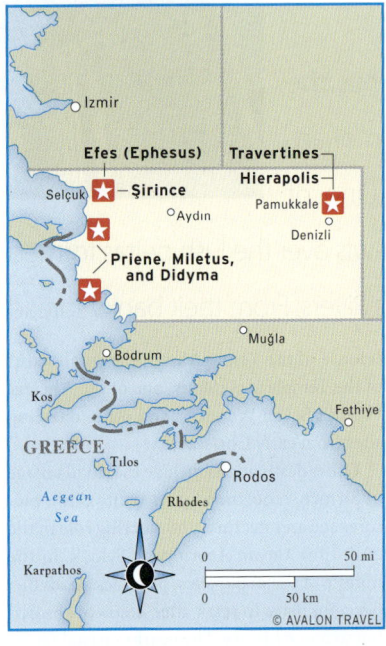

★ **Efes (Ephesus):** In this ancient Ionian metropolis, stroll by such spellbinding monuments as the Library of Celsus (page 215).

★ **Şirince:** Bask in the preserved Greek beauty of this elevated village, renowned for its orchards, mountain herbs, and fruit wines (page 228).

★ **Priene, Miletus, and Didyma:** From sweeping views to the impressive ruins of the Temple of Apollo, this trio of ancient cities is certainly worth the day trip from Selçuk (page 236).

★ **Travertines:** A barefoot walk on these calcified travertines reveals splendid views of the valley below (page 239).

★ **Hierapolis:** Take a dip in the lily-white travertine pools of this surreal mineral-laden spot in the Roman ruins in Pamukkale (page 239).

Şirince

The Southern Aegean Coast

must-do day trip and many others provide a getaway in an area brimming with sights.

PLANNING YOUR TIME

Set aside at least four days to visit this region, but for a three-day trip, base yourself in pretty, blue-collar Selçuk. This allows for a variety of half- or full-day side trips to Ephesus, Şirince, the Temple of Artemis, the House of the Virgin Mary, and the PMD (Priene, Miletus, and Didyma) excursion. A visit to farther-off Pamukkale is also an option. If large resorts or partying into the morning are your cup of tea, consider staying 20 kilometers away in lively Kuşadası. Tours, taxi excursions, and public transportation are readily available in both towns, but renting a vehicle allows for more independence and is a more relaxing option than the sometimes rushed schedules of tour companies.

The southern Aegean is best enjoyed during the months of May and September, when temperatures are mild and tourism drops to a trickle. Perhaps the worst time is at its busiest, during summer, when this stretch is assaulted with busloads of visitors and daily high temperatures over 38°C. Beaches, hotels, and restaurants are packed, and the Kuşadası bars are hopping. Some revel in this brouhaha; others find it dreadful. If you're traveling in peak season (Apr.-Oct.), enjoy the more famous sites in the late afternoon when the tour buses have left and temperatures are cooler.

The rest of the year (Nov.-Mar.) has a quiet atmosphere. Some hoteliers and restaurateurs, particularly in Kuşadası, synchronize their clocks with the official summer season and may close up shop for the off-season, so plan ahead for your accommodations.

The region's sought-after Mediterranean climate makes any season ideal for touring, but winter temperatures can dip to 2°C, and even in summer temperatures can be as cool as 16°C.

TOURS

Contact **Anker Travel** (İnönü Blv. 14, Kuşadası, 0256/612-4598, www.ankertravel.net) to arrange tours, transportation, lodging, and entertainment around Ephesus. Management and staff have more than two decades of experience: book a cruise to the Greek islands, rent a car (€43-99 per day), request airport transfers from İzmir, or book a side-trip. The popular regional excursions include Pamukkale (daily, from€65 pp includes lunch and entrance fees); Ephesus (daily, from €54); and Priene, Miletus, and Didyma (Wed., from €54). Departure dates and prices may change depending on the size of your group, so confirm details at the time of booking.

When searching for a tour to your chosen destination, confirm if the schedule includes compulsory shopping stops to peruse carpets, onyx, or other arts and crafts. Browsing the goods at these dealers can be tedious if you're not an enthusiastic shopper, so look for a tour that suits your interests.

The Ephesus Region

What was once the ancient Ionian territory sits atop verdant land once covered by the Aegean Sea. The sea gradually retreated due to silting but left watery remnants. Settlements were founded by migrants from mainland Greece and its islands. Later, metropolises like Ephesus, Priene, and Miletus became centers of the arts and sciences thanks to early philosophers like Thales and Miletus, "the Father of Science," as well as the famed architect Isidore. It was also in this region that Christianity's early structure coalesced. Saint John brought the Virgin Mary here from Jerusalem in AD 41. Just a decade later, Saint Paul riled local officials by preaching the gospel to local pagans.

It wasn't until the 1980s that mass tourism discovered the area. Tour buses started trickling in, and the nearby fishing village of Kuşadası slowly transformed into the pub-laden mecca for Northern Europeans that it is today. The town's renewed boardwalk and splendid beaches please those with a few hours to spend among the throngs. Selçuk is also capitalizing on the onslaught of vacationers with an influx of boutique hotels and tour companies offering daily excursions. The region is also home to the mountain village of Şirince, known for its splendid fruity wines and pastoral homes, just a short *dolmuş* (communal taxi) ride from Selçuk, and the marvelous Dilek Peninsula National Park, near Kuşadası, with its wide wooded expanses that plunge dramatically into the sea. A hike to the park's isolated shale beaches may provide glimpses of wild boars, wild horses, and the rare Anatolian leopard.

★ EFES (EPHESUS)

One of the highlights of the ancient world, **Ephesus** (0232/892-6010, 8:30am-7pm daily Apr-Oct., 8am-5pm daily Nov.-Mar., www.muze.gov.tr/ephesus-archaeological, 30TL) is the best-preserved ancient city in the Eastern Mediterranean. It played a key role in the development of Western thought and of Christianity. About 40 points of historical, archaeological, and religious interest are within this large open-air museum. A brisk tour of the ancient city can be accomplished in as little as two hours; a full tour can take a full day. Summers are extremely hot and crowded, so stock up on water and wear comfortable shoes, or visit first thing in the morning or later in the day when the tour buses have left. The sun sets behind the Library of Celsus, so photos of the famous library are best taken in the morning.

To learn more about this city's role in antiquity, consider taking a tour booked through your hotel or **Anker Travel** (www.anker-travel.net), or hire one of the eager and competent licensed guides at the gates (200TL for a 2-hour tour). This price can vary depending on the guide's experience and the duration of tour, so confirm the details before sealing the deal. Another option is to rent the self-guided multilingual **audio guide** (15TL) available from stalls near the ticket booths at both entrances.

Tours can start at either the lower (north) or upper (south) gate, with most choosing to start from the upper gate, as the 1.3-kilometer path through Ephesus gently winds downhill between the State Agora and Library of Celsus. There are no vendors inside the gates of Ephesus, so buy enough water for your tour before entering.

History

Myths surrounding the founding of Ephesus abound. Some say the Amazon women were here first; others claim that in the 10th century BC, Androclus, son of Athenian King Crodus, followed a prophecy of Apollo pinpointing the exact location of his next great Ionian colony: a place where the boar meets the fish.

Fables aside, Ephesus was already a prosperous trading center under the Mycenaeans in the 11th century BC. Word of this wealth reached rich Lydian King Croesus, who invaded and annexed Ephesus in 560 BC. The Persians, seeking access to the Mediterranean, toppled Croesus's reign less than two decades later, thus incorporating all of Asia Minor's cities into their growing empire. The Ephesians rebelled against Persian rule by joining in the Ionian Revolt in the Battle of Ephesus in 498 BC. Ionians gained their independence, but greater Anatolia was only liberated from Persian control about 150 years later, when Alexander the Great defeated the Persians in the Battle of Granicus in 334 BC. After Alexander's untimely passing, Lysimachus, one of his generals, ruled over much of Asia Minor, and Ephesus was moved two kilometers from Mount Ayasuluk near present-day Selçuk to its current site between Panayır Dağı (Mount Pion), where the Great Theater is, and Bülbüldagı (Mount Koressos).

Ephesian daily life didn't change much with the changes in power. Immigrants

Ephesus and the Birth of a Religion

The Temple of Artemis, one of the Wonders of the Ancient World, lies in ruins near Ephesus. This temple to the Anatolian goddess of fertility and the hunt drew pilgrims from around the Greek empire. As the Greeks colonized the western coast of Anatolia, they adopted the cult, as did the Romans in the 3rd century BC.

As minority religions, such as the cult of Isis and Mithraism, arose throughout the Roman empire, it lost stability. The Christian apostles Paul and Peter allegedly ministered at Ephesus in the AD 30s and 40s, and the city became a leading Christian pilgrimage site. Peter is said to have brought the Virgin Mary here and built her a house.

The Nicene Creed, the yardstick of Christian belief, was ratified by the First Council of Ephesus in 431. The city remained one of Christianity's capitals, and church elders considered it the epicenter from which the Gospel was spread to the Roman Empire. Bishops were once installed from here throughout Asia Minor, extending east to the great city of Antioch.

Unfortunately, the natural buildup of silt from a nearby river, the rise of Constantinople under Christian emperor Constantine the Great, and the Muslim westward push ended Ephesus's role as a center of the ancient world. Today, archaeologists report that only about 15 percent of this once massive city has been unearthed.

---

easily assimilated, and education and trade were at the forefront. The cult of the goddess Artemis, which drew pilgrims from throughout the ancient world during the classical period, was a symbol of women's rights. Women artists thrived, according to the writer Pliny, who later wrote of having seen a depiction of the goddess Diana (Artemis) by the Ephesian painter Timarata.

By the end of the 3rd century BC, the Syrian King Seleucus I Nicator bloodily removed Lysimachus and absorbed Ephesus into the expanding Seleucid Empire. An ensuing struggle between the Egyptian Ptolemies and the Seleucids lasted for over a century before the city finally was absorbed by the Romans in 133 BC. Ephesus became the capital of Asia Minor in 27 BC under Emperor Augustus. With a reported population of over 250,000, Ephesus grew to be the largest metropolis in the empire after Rome, thriving thanks to trade with the Middle East.

During the 1st century AD, as the cult of the goddess Artemis slowly declined, a budding Christian movement centered around Ephesus began to take root. Saint Paul, who preached Christianity and converted many Ephesians during his three-year stay in the city from AD 53 to 56, was largely responsible.

Even the Virgin Mary, led by Saint John the Apostle in AD 41, allegedly settled and lived the rest of her days in Ephesus.

The constant deposit of dirt and sand creeping into Ephesus saw a gradual decline in trade and power. Despite attempts during the reigns of Nero and Hadrian to divert the flow of the Menderes, the harbor—now five kilometers inland—silted up. Now landlocked, Ephesus began its long decline, though it still ranked as a center of Christianity; Emperor Theodosius even chose the city's Church of Mary as the setting for the Third Ecumenical Council in 431.

Sights
TOMB OF SAINT LUKE

Before entering Ephesus via the upper gate, visit the purported **Tomb of Saint Luke,** located behind the souvenir shops on the other side of Meryem Ana Yolu. The remains of Luke the Evangelist, the author of the Gospel of Luke and the Acts of the Apostles, were said to be buried here under the circular structure of the former 5th-century Byzantine church. A pillar depicting a cross and bull—the symbol of Saint Luke—led researchers to believe Saint Luke was interred here before his remains were transported to Istanbul's

Church of the Holy Apostles, where the Fatih Mosque now stands.

STATE AGORA

The first set of ruins near the upper (south) gate are those of the **Bouleterion-Odeon.** This small theater, with a capacity of 1,500, held meetings of the *boulea* (senate) and also functioned as a concert hall. Dating from the 2nd century AD, the building's benefactors were the wealthy Ephesians Publius Vedius Antoninus and his wife, Flavia Papiana.

Farther on, the scattered ruins of the **Prytaneion** come into view. The building was dedicated to Hestia, the goddess of the hearth, and contained Ephesus's perpetually burning sacred flame. The pit, once the center of the Prytaneion, marks the spot of the flame. All of Ephesus's religious and official ceremonies were held here from the time Lysimachus ordered its construction in the 3rd century BC. Today's ruins, however, date from a renovation undertaken during the reign of Augustus in the 1st century AD. Two statues of the Ephesian Artemis were discovered in the Prytaneion; they're housed in the Ephesus Museum in Selçuk.

The path eventually forks, with **Domitian Square** to the left and the **Memmius Monument** to the right. The square is named for its central **Domitian Temple,** built to honor 1st-century-AD Roman emperor Domitian. The monument commemorates the noted Roman orator Memmius. Also located near this junction is a pillar depicting the snake on a staff, the symbol of Asclepius, the god of health—suggesting a medical center once operated here. Look across the junction to see the reaching winged goddess of victory, **Nike,** and the nearby **Polio Fountain,** which distributed water to the city from aqueducts through a clever system of terra-cotta pipes.

The **Hercules Gate** marks the start of Curetes Way. Named after the large Herculean reliefs on its posts, the gate is believed to have arrived at its current location in the 4th century AD.

CURETES WAY

One of Ephesus's three main thoroughfares, the sloping and sometimes slippery **Curetes Way** connects the State Agora to the Library of Celsus. Early-20th-century archaeologists named the road according to an inscription found on one of the stones that referred to the Curetes or priests of Artemis. In its heyday, statues, shops, fountains, and monuments lined both sides. Most structures, particularly the colonnades, were damaged by one of the many earthquakes that struck the city. Blocks and other columns salvaged from Ephesus's other buildings were used in their reconstruction.

The **Fountain of Trajan** once stood on Curetes Way. Unfortunately, not much remains of the towering statue of the early-2nd-century-AD emperor, aside from a single marble foot. The awesome statues of Dionysus that beautified this monument are now at the Ephesus Museum.

Along the Curetes Way, you'll notice the **mosaic floor,** followed by the **Terrace Houses** (8am-5:30pm daily Apr-Oct., 8am-5pm daily Nov.-Mar., 15TL) on the left on the rise of Bülbül Dağı (mountain). This is the proverbial jewel in Ephesus's crown, a definite must-see for visitors. The city's ruling class lived in these residences during the 1st to 7th centuries AD. The impressively colonnaded and tiled interiors were impeccably preserved thanks to the alluvial silting that buried them over time. They are reached by a steep flight of stairs behind the shops on Curetes Way. More than others in this region, these buildings put historical rhetoric aside to show, in stunning detail, the lifestyle of the period.

The most stunning structure along this stretch is the **Temple of Hadrian.** Built around AD 120 by Publius Quintilius, a relatively unknown bourgeois person of the time, the temple was dedicated to Emperor Hadrian, Artemis, and the Ephesians. The facade's four Corinthian columns bolster a curved arch, which features a relief of the goddess of victory, Tyche, in its center. The side colonnades are square, and the monument's interior bears four friezes that depict the various myths related to the creation of Ephesus. The inscribed pedestals fronting the temple facade bear the names of Galerius, Maximianus, Diocletianus, and Constantius I, suggesting that the statues of these imperial men might once have stood above them.

Ephesus's **latrine** was built in the 1st century AD. Use of these men-only communal toilets wasn't free. A closer look beneath the carved marble shows that the system was rather advanced for its time, with a gutter below that had constantly running water. The bench was covered by a roof, while the public room's center remained open to the elements. A sunken pool in the center caught rainwater; the rest of the floor was tiled in mosaics.

At the intersection of Curetes Way and the Sacred Way stands Ephesus's **brothel.** Funny how the mere mention of this structure evokes concern among modern visitors; in its heyday, visiting it was as common as going out for a jug of olive oil. The lobby to the west of the entrance has a colorful mosaic floor that captures the four seasons. The main bath next to it has an elliptical pool with a pretty mosaic featuring a trio of women eating and drinking, a server, and a couple of house pets nibbling on crumbs. The chambers on the second floor were used to entertain clients. A statue of the overly endowed Hellenic fertility god Priapus was discovered near this structure. Scandalous rumors suggest there was a tunnel leading from the library to the brothel for the privacy of highbrow Ephesians.

LIBRARY OF CELSUS

The **Library of Celsus** is Ephesus's most memorable building. Astonishingly well preserved, the library was constructed in AD 117 by the Consul Julius Aquila as a mausoleum for his father, Roman governor of the Asian provinces Julius Celsus Polemaeanus. Celsus's grave remains beneath the ground floor, across from the entrance. A statue of Athena, the goddess of wisdom, once stood guard over his remains; the statue's current whereabouts are unknown. The library's

the reconstructed Library of Celsus, Ephesus

collection, an estimated 12,000 scrolls, constituted the world's third-largest collection after Alexandria and Pergamum. The scrolls were kept in cupboards in wall niches with double walls behind them to temper the effects of atmospheric conditions, particularly humidity.

The two-level facade, which actually hides a three-story book repository, consists of three entrances interspersed by statues. These are copies of the originals, which somehow found their way to the Ephesus Museum in Vienna in 1910. The goddesses of wisdom (Sophia), knowledge (Episteme), intelligence (Ennoia), and valor (Arete) symbolized Celsus's virtues. A fire ravaged most of the library's interior; its exterior was redeemed centuries later with the addition of a monumental pool.

SACRED WAY

So named because it once led to the Temple of Artemis beyond Panayır Dağı (Mount Pion), the **Sacred Way** today runs from the Grand Theater to the Library of Celsus. The Marble Road (its other name) was originally laid in the 1st century AD but was rebuilt 400 years later. Its western flank delineates the Commercial Agora's wall, upon which a higher platform was constructed during Nero's reign to accommodate pedestrians. Look for the footprint next to the ridge; it leads to the brothel and may constitute history's first advertisement.

The **Commercial Agora** was the shopping district, arguably one of the largest in Asia Minor. Built in the 3rd century BC, today's ruins date from the reign of the murderous Caracalla (AD 211-217). The 110-square-meter marketplace was surrounded by columns and had three gates: one leading to the theater on the northeast, one facing the harbor to the west, and a third opening to the Library of Celsus. Its northern wall was wide open, while a portico with rows of bustling shops ringed its remaining perimeter. A sundial and water clock were featured in its center.

ARCADIAN WAY

The **Arcadian Way** is an 11-meter-wide pedestrian lane situated between the Harbor Baths and the Grand Theater. Traders and sailors entering the city from the harbor first set foot on this once magnificently marbled street. This includes the Egyptian queen Cleopatra and Mark Antony, who rode in procession here in 41 BC. Lofty colonnades were added along the 530-meter-long stretch during the reign of Emperor Arcadius (AD 395-408). Shops and galleries lined both sides. At its height it was one of only three lighted avenues in the Roman Empire, along with avenues in Rome and Antioch. Some 50 lights lit the colonnades; sewers ran along its length beneath the marble flagstones.

Ephesus's **Grand Theater,** on the slopes of Panayır Dağı (Mount Pion), sits at the eastern end of the Arcadian Way. Built during the reign of Lysimachus (3rd century BC), it was greatly enlarged by the Romans three centuries later. It's the largest of its kind in Anatolia, with a seating capacity of 25,000. It took excavators about six decades to recover this arena from the side of the hill. Sixty-six rows of seats are divided by two *diazomas* (aisles), forming three horizontal sections. The lower section's marble seating with sweeping backs was reserved for dignitaries; the Emperor's Box is nearest center stage. The rest of the populace entered from the top. Reliefs, statues, and niches once ornamented the facade of the three-story-high stage building. During its heyday the theater hosted major events such as sermons, philosophical discourses, and gladiator fights. Saint Paul delivered a sermon condemning pre-Christian religions on its stage in the 1st century, riling shopkeepers who profited from the cult of Artemis. Climb to the upper *cavea* (tier) to check out the striking view of the archaeological park, and if you have any voice talent in your group, have them sing to hear the acoustics of the theater.

Exiting the theater, the first building on Arcadian Way is the impressive ruins of the two-story **Theater Gymnasium.** This structure was mainly used as a sports arena. The four-story **Harbor Baths,** located at the opposite end of the street, were built in AD 2. Nicknamed the Baths of Constantine on account of the restoration that was undertaken by that Roman emperor in the mid-3rd century, this was the lane's largest building at 160 meters wide and 170 meters long. A peristyle forecourt led to a central bath-gymnasium complex, with rooms of various sizes for cultural and spiritual instruction.

DOUBLE CHURCH

This 2nd-century-AD Roman cultural and educational center was known as the Hall of the Muses. When Christianity was adopted as the official religion of Rome, the 260-meter-tall structure became the Church of the Virgin Mary, its name taken from one of the two aisles inside, which was dedicated to the Virgin Mary; the other was dedicated to Saint John. The church's baptistery is the best preserved in Asia Minor.

Emperor Theodosius II held the Third Ecumenical Council in this church in AD 431; some 200 bishops attended the multiple-day debate that culminated in defining the double nature of Christ as a god and a man, and Mary as the mother of God. It also denounced as heresy the teachings of the Archbishop of Constantinople, Nestorius, who rejected the divine nature of Christ and claimed Mary was not the mother of God but the mother of a human being.

GYMNASIUM OF VEDIUS

The first ruins beyond the lower gate are those of the ancient gym and stadium. Built in the 2nd century AD for wealthy Ephesians Publius Vedius Antoninus and his wife, Flavia Papiana, the **Gymnasium of Vedius** is dedicated to the goddess Artemis and to Emperor Antoninus Pius. Its eastern entrance leads to a *palaestra* (courtyard) encircled by tall marble pillars. Along the walls of the Imperial Hall, notice the statues of the gym's benefactors above floors intricately inlaid with mosaics.

Traditionally, gymnasiums were where youth were taught the arts, sports, literature, drama, and speech. At its height, this gym housed a *frigidarium* and a *tepidarium* (cold and warm baths, respectively); the *frigidarium* pool was filled with a large amphora held by a statue of the god of the Cayster (Menderes) River.

GROTTO OF THE SEVEN SLEEPERS

An unmarked paved road leads east about 800 meters from the Gymnasium of Vedius to the **Grotto of the Seven Sleepers.** As legend has it, seven young Christian boys, fearing the Decian Persecution (AD 250), fled to the cave in an attempt to sidestep Roman guards; being Christian at the time was a serious crime. Once the guards reached the grotto, they callously barricaded the boys inside. The septet fell asleep for what seemed a night, and woke up to an earthquake that miraculously reopened the cave. Famished, the boys walked to town only to realize they were strolling through 5th-century Ephesus. In the two centuries that had elapsed, their religion, once condemned, was now the common faith. The Seven Sleepers, who later died of natural causes, were buried in the grotto. The story of the Sleepers also appears in the Koran, where the boys, accompanied by a dog, slept for 309 years. A church made of crypts was built above this grotto. Christians fleeing Roman persecution built similar structures throughout Anatolia. A rural wooden restaurant serving *gözleme* (Turkish pancakes) and *ayran* (a yogurt beverage) mark the entrance to the grotto.

Arcadian Way, Ephesus

Festivals

In May, the antique Grand Theater, Library of Celsus, and Odeon provide a sublime outdoor setting for enjoying the opera, ballet, and orchestral music as part of the **International İzmir Festival** (www.iksev.org). The program changes annually, but previous festivals have hosted legends like José Carreras, Elton John, Sting, and Ray Charles.

Getting There and Around

If you haven't opted for a tour or a rented vehicle, a **dolmuş** (2.50TL, 5 minutes) from Selçuk *otogar* (bus station) runs every 20 minutes the three kilometers from Ephesus's lower (north) gate during the site's open hours. Arriving via *dolmuş* requires an easy walk to the entrance, and later a minor ascent up the Curetes Way to the State Agora. To return to Selçuk via *dolmuş,* walk the 1.3 kilometers back through the archaeological site to the lower gate. Those traveling from Kuşadası via *dolmuş* (5TL, 30 minutes) must first travel to Selçuk *otogar* and transfer to the Ephesus *dolmuş,* or ask to be dropped off at the intersection to Efes Yolu to walk about one kilometer to the lower (north) gate.

Many hotels will take guests to Ephesus for free, but be aware that this is illegal under the current tourism laws. **Taxis** are available at both entrances of Ephesus for a one-way transfer to Selçuk (approx. 15TL, 5 minutes). A three- to four-hour private excursion via taxi can also be arranged from Selçuk *otogar* (40TL) or Kuşadası (€45). Bear in mind this includes a small fee for the driver to transfer you to and from the site, travel between gates, and wait for you to finish your tour. Deals are also available with taxis to combine Ephesus with the House of the Virgin Mary or other destinations.

If you're **driving,** the upper gate is off Meryem Ana Yolu. Parking here is free. However, you need to walk back to the upper gate once the tour is complete. The lower gate entrance to Ephesus is located just south of Dr. Sabri Yayla Bulvarı, off Efes Yolu. Walking is the only way to get around inside the site.

SELÇUK

Selçuk could be mistaken for just the transportation hub for the spectacular ruins of Ephesus, three kilometers west. But there's more to this small leafy rural town than meets the eye. Selçuk's tranquil vibe welcomes guests to stroll through the historical and shopping attractions. On Saturday, the area around the *otogar* boasts a busy, colorful street market (check out the ridiculously cheap fake designer clothing). Events like the centuries-old camel wrestling festival bring pomp and pageantry to the streets in January. In April, white storks bask in the serenity of the town as they nest atop the ancient Byzantine aqueducts and the broken minaret of the Isabey Camii (Mosque of Jesus).

Ruin-wise, the Ephesus Museum is stunning; it houses the important archaeological finds from Ephesus—at least those that weren't ruthlessly carted off to European museums. The House of the Virgin Mary, the 6th-century Basilica of St. John, and the Temple of Artemis—one of the Seven Wonders of the ancient world—are also popular sights in and around Selçuk. Ayasoluk Fortress, with its 15 commanding towers, is set high on a hill above the town and dates back to the Byzantine, Ottoman, and Aydınoğulları (14th century) dynasties. While there are rumors that the fortress may one day open to visitors, the doors remain shut as excavations continue in the area where Ephesus once stood before 300 BC. Adrenaline junkies can skydive or hang glide over the ancient world below. Information about aerial activities, as well as exhaustive information about Ephesus and Selçuk, can be found at the user-friendly website www.selcukephesus.com.

Sights
EFES MÜZESİ (EPHESUS MUSEUM)

The **Efes Müzesi** (Uğur Mumcu Sevgi Yolu, 0232/892-6010, 8am-6:30pm daily Apr.-Oct. and 8am-5:30pm daily Nov.-Mar., 10TL) had a complete face-lift in 2014 and is brimming with Ephesian relics dating from prehistory through modern times. What holds

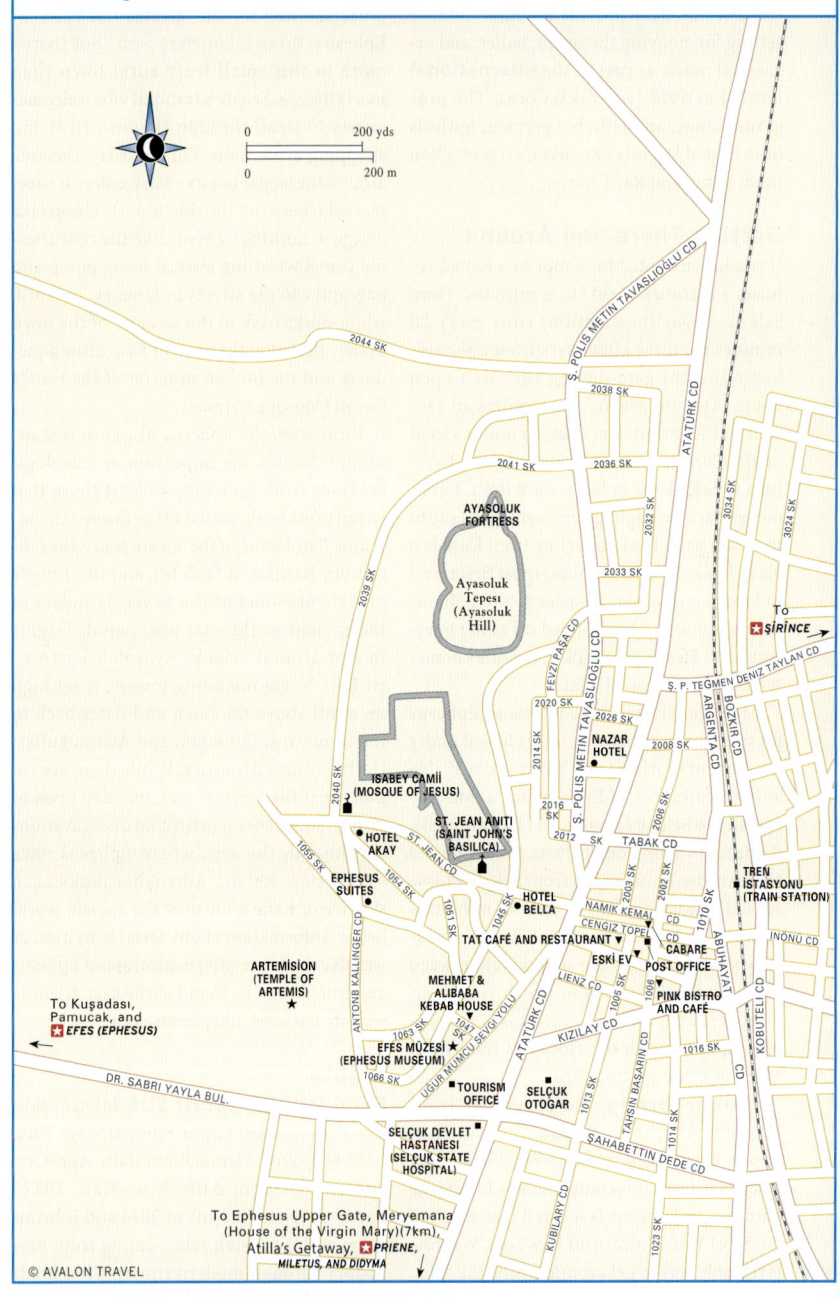

the attention of most visitors, however, are the artifacts that date from Artemisian, Roman, and Byzantine eras. Allow at least 90 minutes to walk through the displays, preferably after a visit to Ephesus, as you can appreciate where the relics were discovered.

Artifacts from the Terrace Houses, whose Roman relics have been gradually unearthed over the last 50 years, are on display. These include plans of the hillside houses of Ephesus's privileged class and photos of the excavations. Several showcases contain medical and cosmetic artifacts as well as religious and cult items. A statue of Artemis the Huntress and a 3rd-century-AD fresco of Socrates were retrieved from one of these upscale abodes, attesting to the importance of philosophy and spirituality in everyday Roman life. Also exhibited is the 2nd-century-AD bust of Roman emperor Marcus Aurelius, along with statuettes of the virile Greek god Priapus and Egyptian deity Bes. Despite their enormous phalluses, neither god was esteemed for their manhood; rather, Priapus was a guardian deity who thwarted the evil eye. The ugly, stumpy Bes protected households, particularly keeping an eye on mothers and children. The pièce de résistance, however, is the large bronze statue *Eros with Dolphin,* once a centerpiece of a 2nd-century-AD fountain, and a copy of a Roman statue of Eros by Greek sculptor Lysippos (4th century BC).

The museum has relics from the Pollio, Trajan, and Laecanus fountains at Ephesus, including the bust of Zeus and a headless statue of Aphrodite, both dating to the 1st century AD. Statues of Greek mythological deities Odysseus and Polyphemus, which adorned the Pollio Fountain near Ephesus's Domitian Square, can be found along with two impressive and stunningly carved statues of Dionysus, the Greek god of wine. The first is with a satyr, a male companion versed in poetry; the other is his dazzling marble likeness flanked by the imperial family. There's also the enchantress Aphrodite with her trusty oyster shell, among a variety of other statues. The series of busts once belonged to the statues gracing the Laecanus Bassus Fountain.

Ephesian discoveries unearthed in the last decade include Byzantine relics amid collections of coins and jewelry. There are a few pre-Roman Ephesian coins depicting the city symbol and a bee on one side and Artemis's deer on the other. Theater masks fashioned of leather, which were recovered inside Ephesus's Grand Theater, are among the treasurers here, as is the stunning ivory frieze excavated from an upper terrace of one of Ephesus's hillside houses; it details a war scene involving Roman emperor Trajan and his soldiers fighting eastern barbarians.

Exhibits depicting Anatolian burial customs are perhaps the most telling exhibit in this museum. The small relics, found in a grave in front of the Basilica of St. John, date to the Mycenaean age (13th century BC) and attest to Ephesus's long history.

Perhaps the most striking displays are focused on the mother goddess Artemis. The 1st century AD statues found in Ephesus's Prytaneion, the town's religious and ceremonial center, are displayed. Both, the Great Artemis and the Beautiful Artemis are covered with rounded protrusions. These were once believed to be additional breasts, but scholars now believe these mounds may have been sacrificed bull testicles, further emphasizing this most venerated goddess's role in fertility.

ARTEMISION (TEMPLE OF ARTEMIS)

One of the Seven Wonders of the Ancient World, the ruins of the **Artemision** (just off Dr Sabri Yayla Blv., free) are dismal. Just a column and the scattered fragments remain of this surreal monument, one of the largest constructions of antiquity. Financed by the wealthy Lydian king Croesus, it took 120 years to erect the marble monument; Cretan architect Chersiphron and his son Metagenes did the initial design and construction. The original temple was built in 550 BC, with just 36 columns, each about four meters in height.

According to Roman author Pliny the Elder (AD 23-59), this marshy site was specifically selected for the monument due to its softer ground; the wisdom of the time ran that the soil's softness would absorb seismic activity. Others believe that the Temple of Artemis was erected on this site, already sacred to Cybele, the ancient Anatolian mother goddess, to carry on a cultic tradition.

The temple was constructed and destroyed several times and was a key feature of the pre-300 BC site of Ephesus. It first fell prey to a mad arsonist and later toppled during a massive earthquake at the beginning of the 4th century BC. Within a century, a new and improved Artemision was erected atop its previous location. This newer structure contained 127 columns, each a whopping 18 meters tall, delineating a space 115 meters in length and 55 meters wide—four times the size of Athens's Parthenon. It stood for six centuries before being razed by the Goths in their furious assault of the region in AD 262. Two centuries later, as the majority of Ephesians were converted to Christianity, the Temple of Artemis lost its allure and became a source of construction material for local churches. Today, you can drop in on the way to or from Kuşadası or Ephesus's lower gate. Most people visit for less than 15 minutes to get a photo with the column in the distance; you can also sit and absorb the peaceful energy of the location and imagine the enormity of the structure back in its heyday.

ST. JEAN ANITI
(BASILICA OF ST. JOHN)

After bringing the Virgin Mary to Ephesus in AD 41, Saint John the Apostle spent the last years of his life in the region, preaching the gospel and writing some of his momentous texts. He was buried on the southern slope of Ayosoluk Hill. During the 4th century, a small chapel was constructed over the grave to commemorate the 300th anniversary of his death. The building was enlarged into the magnificent **St. Jean Anıtı** (St. Jean Cd., 0232/892-6010, 8:30am-6:30pm daily Apr.-Oct., 8am-5:30pm daily Nov.-Mar., 10TL) during the reign of Emperor Justinian (527-565). The monumental church was constructed of stone and brick in the shape of a cross and topped by six domes. Rather than the typical square base crowned with cupolas, this layout was a rarity for its time. Saint John's marble tomb, in the center of the sanctuary beneath the lofty central dome, was exalted as one of Christianity's most sacred sites during the Middle Ages. During the 7th and 8th centuries, ramparts were erected around the structure to fend off constant Arabian attacks. By 1330, the Selçuk Aydınoğlu Emirate had conquered Selçuk and the basilica was converted into a mosque. Tamerlane's fearsome Mongols razed the building in 1402. Whatever was left of the basilica's original stones was pillaged in the subsequent centuries for use as construction material.

Some on-site exhibits are worth checking out, including the columns in the courtyard, which bear the monograms of Emperor Justinian and his wife, Theodora. There's also a 5th-century baptistery, located north of the nave; the interior has 10th-century frescoes that depict Saint John and Jesus. If you're with children, be on the lookout for the small basilica tortoises that often rest under the shade of the ruins.

ISABEY CAMII
(MOSQUE OF JESUS)

The **Isabey Camii** (intersection of St. Jean Cd. and 2040th Sk., dawn-dusk daily, free) is the most ornate example of extant Selçukian architecture, conceived by the master Syrian architect Ali, son of Mushimish al-Damishki, in 1374. The mosque features stones and columns culled from Ephesus's great monuments. Its asymmetric interior design was highly unorthodox for its time; none of its windows, doors, and domes were designed to match. But a mosque it is, down to the geometric carving and Koranic calligraphy etched in stone that adorn its lofty marble entrance. Inside, the dome, tiled in turquoise and blue tiles, seemingly floats above a *mihrab* (niche in the wall pointing to Mecca) and pulpit, both sculpted of marble.

MERYEMANA (HOUSE OF THE VIRGIN MARY)

It's believed that Saint John brought the Virgin Mary, the mother of Jesus, to Ephesus in the mid-1st century AD and later built her the small **Meryemana** (Meryemana Yolu, 8am-7pm daily Apr.-Oct., 8am-5pm daily Nov.-Mar., 15TL, parking 8TL cars, 25TL minibuses, 40TL coaches) atop lofty Bülbül Dağı, seven kilometers from present-day Selçuk. Pilgrims visit the house believing this is where the Virgin Mary lived until her Assumption, as Roman Catholics call it, or Dormition, as it is known in Orthodox doctrines. Missionaries from İzmir discovered the four dilapidated walls that upheld the small stone abode in 1891, following German nun Anne Catherine Emmerich's visions more than 50 years earlier of Mary's final whereabouts. The İzmir missionaries further learned that the Christians of Ephesus visited the site annually on August 15—the date of the Virgin Mary's death. This yearly service continues to this day. Although the Vatican has yet to officially recognize its authenticity due to the lack of compelling evidence, three popes, including John Paul II and Benedict XVI, have visited the site.

The House of the Virgin Mary is considered holy for Muslims as well. Christ was referred to as a great prophet in the Koran, and his mother is the only woman referred to by name in the Islamic scriptures. Muslims also make pilgrimages to this house, marking their visit with scraps of cloth or paper pinned to a wishing wall on the path below the house. A wish is made during the process, with the strong belief that the sanctity of the site will assist in its materialization. Pack a pen and tissue paper to add your wish to the collection, and take an empty water bottle to fill with the purportedly healing waters of the home's natural spring.

Mass at the House of the Virgin Mary is held at 10:30am every Sunday. Additional services take place at 7:15am and 6pm Monday-Saturday. The woodsy grounds include resting areas ideal for picnicking and the pleasant **Café Turco** (0232/894-1010, from 7TL), which serves a variety of special coffees as well as salads and sandwiches.

The House of the Virgin Mary is located seven kilometers from the center of Selçuk, and it will take no more than an hour to visit. Since there's no *dolmuş* serving the site, hiring a return cab from Selçuk (60TL) or Kuşadası (€58) is the best way to go if you don't have a tour or your own wheels. Combine the excursion with your visit to Ephesus to save some lira. The upper gate is on the road to Mary's House, so the driver can drop passengers off here after visiting the house. Travelers staying in Selçuk can then pick up the *dolmuş* or another taxi (15TL) back to town from the lower gate. Kuşadası travelers pay €65 for private transfers to the two sites.

Entertainment and Events
FESTIVALS

Every year in mid-late January, **Camel Wrestling Festivals** are held along the Aegean littoral. Selçuk is considered one of the centers of this centuries-old tradition, in which hundreds of spectators watch colorfully garbed 900-kilogram stags parade through the streets of Selçuk before the wrestling in a field close to Pamucak Beach (3rd Sun. in Jan.). Make sure to arrive early since there's no seating. Bring a garbage bag to sit on, as well as adequate clothing for cold and rain.

The town also comes alive in the first two weeks of September with the **Selçuk/Efes Festival** showcasing a variety of traditional Turkish and worldwide folk songs and dance performances. It's also an arts expo, with artisans displaying their mastery in carving, weaving, pottery, and ceramics. The event translates into a great opportunity to purchase truly indigenous art.

Touted as the festival where "the world meets the sky," the **İzmir Hot Air Balloon Fiesta** lifts off in mid-September. Over 180 pilots and balloons from around the world take flight from Selçuk Airport, dotting the skies above Ephesus with surreal layers of color and rivaling the beauty of ballooning in Cappadocia.

NIGHTLIFE

Downtown Selçuk is small enough to bar-hop to find a casual drinking scene suited to you. Most bars are located along Cengiz Topel Caddesi and Siegburg Caddesi, two streets that run parallel off Atatürk Caddesi. The vibe of the bars depends on who's in town attracting a crowd on any given night, but for most, a late night out always involves heading to **Pink Bistro and Café** (Siegburg Cd. 24, 0232/892-9801), Selçuk's oldest pub, where Efes beer seems to grace every table on the crowded street terrace.

Accommodations

To avoid Kuşadası's mass tourism scene, or if Şirince's charming B&Bs seem too far away from the sightseeing, the hotels in Selçuk are the best option—and inexpensive to boot. In recent years, boutique-style abodes have flourished alongside family-owned inns, with many owners now managing two or more lodgings catering to differing tastes and budgets. A favorite in the mid-range category is ★ **Hotel Bella** (St. John Cd. 7, 0232/892-3944, www.hotelbella.com, from 130TL). Just across from Basilica of St. John, the vine-covered Bella excels with its cozy traditional Ottoman decor that features handcrafted dark wooden furnishings, colored Iznik tiles and decorative ceramics, and wooden floors dressed with handwoven kilims (Turkish carpets). This unpretentious style of the 11 guest rooms continues through the charming rooftop terrace and café, where guests can view the basilica, Ayasuluk Fortress, and the white storks nesting atop the Byzantine aqueducts while dining on seasonal soups, grilled kebabs, and homemade desserts created from local produce. A gift shop downstairs boasts some of the most intricate ceramics you'll see in town.

The owners of the popular **Nazar Hotel** (Sehit Polis Metin Tavaslıoglu Cd. 34, 0232/892-2222, www.nazarhotel.com, from €40) are former tour guides who speak Turkish, Spanish, French, and English and are on call to answer questions about the local attractions and the rest of Turkey. Their newly renovated small hotel has spacious basic rooms with ceiling fans and air-conditioning, welcome in Selçuk's summer heat. Take a dip in the inviting pool and enjoy sweeping views of Ayasuluk Fortress on the rooftop terrace. In the evening, enjoy sunset while dining on homemade Turkish dishes like fresh mezes and succulent kebabs. The hotel is situated in a traditional Turkish neighborhood, where tractors display the pick of the day from the orchards and where elderly men gather to play *okey*.

Take the peaceful ambiance of a former natural therapy space and blend it with an intimate leafy courtyard enclosed by an ornate stone building. From the courtyard, walk into a homely abode and be welcomed by elegant furnishings set in enormous rooms with housekeeping like that of a five-star hotel. The **Ephesus Suites** (Anton Kallinger Cd. 1057 Sk. 1, 0232/892-6312, www.ephesussuiteshotel.com, from 200TL), nestled in the quieter streets of town, offers this boutique style and service just 200 meters from the Artemis Temple. The lodging may not have the rooftop restaurants that other larger hotels have, but with just four immaculate suites, it would be difficult to find a more elegant and private lodging in Selçuk. Families will appreciate the two family suites and the rooms named after the children of the owners, the Özkan family.

A longtime favorite for small tour groups and independent travelers is **Hotel Akay** (1054 Sok, 0232/892-3172, www.hotelakay.com, from €50). Four generations of owners have nurtured Akay into what it is today—a mid-range hotel with its original 15-room main building and an annex of nine rooms that offer a little more luxury, with wooden ceilings and floors, tasteful decor, and a balcony overlooking the welcoming pool. The highlight of the hotel, other than its proximity to the Isabey Camii and Basilica of St. John, is the lunchtime and evening meals, cooked fresh and served on the rooftop terrace with views of the basilica. After dinner, recline on the open-air divan (Turkish couch) and look up to the night sky to count shooting stars.

Lugging your worldly possessions on your back is exhausting, so when you reach Selçuk, relax and lay your backpack down at the backpacker resort **Atilla's Getaway** (Acarlar Koyu, 0232/892-3847, www.atillasgetaway.com, from €8). Australian-Turkish Atilla and his family built this inexpensive oasis for travelers in the green hills near ancient Ephesus, two kilometers from Selçuk. They cater to campers, backpackers, and budget travelers with poolside sunbeds and comfy lounges in a garden with fresh country air. Choose from campsites, dorms, and bungalows with shared facilities, or rooms with private en suite baths. The rates are for lodging only, but for just €5 more Atilla and his crew will prepare breakfast and dinner. A free shuttle to town, a pool flowing with natural spring water, and happy hour at on-site Bar 81 are just some of the other features that make this an iconic getaway for backpackers.

Food

Selçuk is a bastion for simple traditional meals of farm-fresh meat and cold veggie dishes. The best place to people-watch and taste the local *çöp şiş* (roasted skewered lamb) is ★ **Tat Café and Restaurant** (Cengiz Topel Cd. 9, 0232/892-1916, 18TL), in the center of town. The Daşdemir family excels at friendly service and welcomes you to sit inside or streetside in their comfy retro-rattan chairs by one of the town's busiest streets. You can choose mezes from the kitchen window (try the mushrooms stuffed with cheese) or order from the menu. There isn't much they don't offer, but in addition to the *çöp şiş*, the sizzling *karvuma* (chicken sautéed in vegetables) and *pides* (Turkish pizza) baked in a wood oven are recommended.

Eski Ev (Old House, 1005 Sk. 1/A, 0232/892-9357, 15TL) provides a serene rural setting in the heart of town. This family-run restaurant is set in an old house with an attached courtyard, filled with the cackle of birds and rich with fruit trees and blooming perennials. Grab one of the chairs out back and order the house's much-lauded Old House kebab, sizzling chicken or lamb with tomato and peppers served over a warming flame.

Located near the Ephesus Museum, **Mehmet & Alibaba Kebab House** (1047 Sk. 4A, 0232/892-3872, www.kebabhouseselcuk.com, 12TL) is praised for attentive service and generous servings of standard *gözleme* and kebabs with rice, fries, salad, and bread. The *köfte* (meatballs) are juicy, the chicken kebab is succulent, and Mehmet will gladly offer complimentary mezes of *haydari* (creamy yogurt with garlic and dill) and *ezme* (spicy pepper and tomato) as starters as well as a fresh glass of *çay* (tea) to finish.

For a change in the local culinary scene, head to **Cabare** (Cengiz Topel Cd. 18, 0232/892-6200, www.cabarerestaurant.com, 10TL) which offers a tasty Mediterranean menu of pastas and salads in addition to the tried-and-true Turkish classics. Despite looking like a modern pricey venue with white table settings, it's anything but expensive. For under 15TL you can order overflowing salads, fettuccine alfredo, spaghetti bolognaise; even the mixed grill is just 20TL. You'll also appreciate the affordability of set menus for breakfast, lunch, and dinner, and if you're traveling with children, the kids menu with 5TL meals will surely entertain the little ones.

Information and Services

Selçuk's **Tourism Office** (Uğur Mumcu Sevgi Yolu, 0232/892-6945, 8:30am-noon and 1pm-5:30pm daily May.-Sept., 8am-noon and 1pm-5pm Mon.-Fri. Oct.-Apr.) is located directly across from the Ephesus Museum. The local state **hospital** (Dr. Sabri Yayla Blv., 0232/892-7036) employs multilingual staff and houses modern diagnostic equipment. Banks and ATMs are located on Namık Kemal Caddesi.

The **PTT** (Cengiz Topel Cd. 13, 0232/892-3119, 8:30am-5pm Mon.-Fri.) post office provides services such as currency exchange, money transfers, and faxing.

Getting There
AIR
Located 60 kilometers from Selçuk, İzmir's **Adnan Menderes Airport** (ADB, 0232/274-2626, www.adnanmenderesairport.com) is the point of arrival for daily domestic flights and some flights from Europe. The easiest way to get to Selçuk from the airport is to board the TCDD train bound for Denizli. Transfer to Selçuk will take one hour (4.50TL, 8 times per day). Tickets can be bought at the airport station at the front of the terminal. Hotels will offer to collect you from the Selçuk station or arrange a private transfer from İzmir's airport with a taxi (about €50). The **Selçuk-Efes Airport** on Dr. Sabri Yayla Bulvarı is for light aircraft and private planes.

BUS AND TRAIN
Both long-distance coaches and *dolmuşlar* arrive and depart at Selçuk's *otogar*, located along Atatürk Caddesi across from the Tourism Office. Contact your hotel ahead of time to arrange pickup from the *otogar*.

TCDD (www.tcdd.gov.tr) train services link Selçuk's *tren istasyonu* (train station, end of Cengiz Topel Cd., 0232/892-6006) to İzmir's Basmane train station (5.75TL, 80 minutes 8 times per day) and İzmir's Adnan Menderes Airport (4.50TL, 60 minutes, 8 times per day) in the north, and to Denizli (14.50TL, 3 hours, 7 times per day) for transfer to Pamukkale in the east.

Getting Around
Commuting within Selçuk is a snap. The majority of the sites are within a small walkable area. **Taxis** can be taken for sites outside the city center like Ephesus, the House of the Virgin Mary, and the Grotto of the Seven Sleepers. The ***dolmuş*** services to Ephesus (2.50TL, 10 minutes), Kuşadası (5TL, 30 minutes), Şirince (3TL, 20 minutes), and Pamucak (3TL, 20 minutes) depart and terminate regularly at Selçuk's *otogar*.

Şirince village

★ ŞIRINCE
One of the most attractive villages on the Aegean coast, Şirince—meaning "cute"—is set amid sprawling peach orchards and olive groves in a bowl at 300 meters above sea level. It's surrounded by pine-blanketed hills and boasts 100 or so historic residences, all commanding spectacular views of the lush valley below. Whitewashed stucco houses with red-tile roofs are a throwback to the 19th century, when the town was predominantly Greek. So cute was this place that until 1924 village folk called it Çirkince (rather ugly) to preventing outsiders from spoiling it.

After the name changed, Şirince began to charm the domestic entertainment industry, which featured the idyllic setting in films and soap operas. Curious crowds followed, and local tourism started to thrive. The village became internationally prominent in 2012, when some believers of Mayan apocalypse lore said ancient Mayan hieroglyphs predicted that Şirince would be one of two places on earth to survive the December 21, 2012, apocalypse, making this hillside settlement a temporary doomsday hot spot.

Ephesian Christians retreated to Şirince when the Islamic Selçuks conquered the Aegean in the 13th century. The local *Şirincelis* were later displaced to the Greek Macedonian town of Kavala during the population exchange of 1924. In turn, Muslim Kavalans trickled into Şirince, bringing their Baltic winemaking skills. Thanks to this rich heritage, the town has earned historic preservation status.

Today, Şirince, with its rustic charm, is enjoying tremendous popularity. Its narrow streets and town center teem with village women peddling tatted lace, homemade jam, and olive oil to the busloads of visitors. Local fruity wines draw hordes to **Artemis** (0232/898-3240, www.artemisrestaurant.com, 20TL), a restaurant housed in the village's most eminent building—an adeptly restored 19th-century schoolhouse. Also worth a look are the fading frescoes of the **Church of St. John the Baptist,** built in 1832 restored after years of vandalism.

Given its proximity to Selçuk, spending two to three hours here allows time to browse the village produce, shop for indigenous jewelry and art, sample the locally produced fruit wine, and enjoy a hearty homemade meal while gazing at the terraced Greek houses that flow down the valley. Those with limited mobility may find it difficult to explore the upper part of the town due to the haphazardly placed stones in the streets around the Church of Saint John the Baptist. If you have time, wander up the paths to the local homes to appreciate the view and the simplicity of life here. Some entrepreneurial Şirincelis may ask for a small tip to photograph their humble homes with their endearing faded color, crumbling stucco, and timeworn woodwork.

Accommodations

While there are a few roads in Şirince, they're not named, and most hotels are located off the warren of unmarked pathways; phone your lodging ahead of time for directions.

If you do fall for Şirince's charm and decide to stay overnight, there's no better spot than ★ **Nişanyan Eveleri** (follow signs from the town entrance, 0232/898-3208, www.nisanyan.com, 120-540TL). Host Sevan Nişanyan converted several properties into a series of inns, houses, and cottages that appeal to all budgets, from the barest of rooms to the two-bedroom two-story houses. The inexpensive rooms are in the seven-room Kilisealtı (Tower) house, with prices higher for the other rooms, including the five charming Ilyastepe cottages around a shared kitchen and terrace, the quirky five-room Nişanyan Inn, and the three premium houses, large enough for two couples or a family. With each room done in a unique style reminiscent of a cozy rural cottage, most guests find it hard to peel themselves away from the ambiance and energy of the property, which also features an on-site restaurant, a pool, and a Turkish bath.

To put a little color and life back into your holiday digs, rest your head at the charismatic **Şirince Nana Pansiyon** (0232/898-3100, www.nanapansiyon.com, from€50). This old Greek home has been converted into an inn with five quaint rooms, each with their own color theme, that open onto an Aegean-style courtyard overlooking the village. The breakfast is homemade dishes from fresh vegetables and herbs of the village.

Food

Most of the culinary treasures in town are hidden off the pathways leading up to the Church of Saint John the Baptist. These restaurants draw on the region's Baltic, Hellenic, and Ottoman roots and serve meals with fresh produce from mountain farms, prepared on-site in tiny cottage kitchens. Expect herbs, vegetables, mezes, meat grills, and *gözleme* to rule the menus here. **Can Restaurant** (0232/898-3074, www.canrestaurant.com, 10TL) has a ground-floor terrace surrounded by village greenery, but for an extra treat, take the flight of wooden steps to dine in the treetop platform above the restaurant. The stairs are steep and the *şark köşesi* (lounges) at floor level can be difficult to get up from, but the views are spectacular. Try the *etli arap saçı* (roasted meat with herbs), Şirince *mantası* (small ravioli), or *keşek* (stewed lamb with barley), normally a ceremonial dish in the Middle East. The restaurant is on the main path up to the Church of St. John the Baptist, just up from the undercover market area.

Homemade baklava, *çiçek dolma* (flavored rice-stuffed flowers), and *sarmos* (stuffed grape leaves) are just a few of the dishes on offer at **Gülgün Ablanın Yeri** (cell tel. 0531/842-1599, 10TL). Owner Gülgün serves delicious homely meals to guests in her open-air restaurant perched high above the village. You can choose to sit at the tables and chairs or higher up under the drying peppers on the divans. The restaurant has the best views in town for photographing the Greek homes on the hillside. Foodies will appreciate the tiny tour of Gülgün's cottage kitchen. To find the restaurant, first locate the gates of the old schoolhouse on the main road into the village, then take the path opposite into the village. You'll find Gülgün on the right about 50 meters from the main street.

Getting There

A *dolmuş* (3TL, 20 minutes) connects to the village from the Selçuk *otogar,* seven kilometers away, every 30 minutes. If **driving,** take the Şehit Pilot Teğmen Deniz Taylan Caddesi off the main D550 highway, then turn left onto Şehit Er Yüksel Özülkü Caddesi, which runs up the mountain to the village entrance. Parking (5TL) is available at the village entrance.

KUŞADASI

Local farmers remember a pristine Kuşadası with no high-rises, no massive vacation resorts, not even a paved road. But that was in the 1970s; since then, zealous developers have constructed massive holiday resorts and plots of summer housing for Northern Europeans. Some foreign visitors purchased vacation homes; others loved it so much they chose to live year-round at Kuşadası's warm, golden coast.

Despite its reputation as a package-holiday playground, unrestrained growth, and slightly British cachet, Kuşadası (Bird Island) still beckons crowds of overseas travelers. Its year-round population of 50,000 soars to nearly 500,000 in summer. This popularity is partly due to the busy port, where mammoth cruise ships dock. The town's subdued Turkish feel, great beach resorts, rambunctious nightlife, splendid coast, and the availability of countless archaeological and cultural excursions all make it a full summer trip for families or partiers. If you're willing to overlook its consumer-centric aspects, Kuşadası is a great all-inclusive base for exploring this incomparable slice of Turkey. For more information about the town, see www.kusadasi.com.

Sights

Kuşadası sprawls inland on either side of its central causeway, which leads to Güvercin Adası (Pigeon Island). Aside from inspiring the town's name, the popular island is home to a diminutive **fortress.** The stone structure is usually closed, but its appeal is more in its history than whatever relics it contains. During the 16th century the pirate Khair ad-Din—the feared Barbarossa—based his operations, which ran throughout the Mediterranean, at this point. Later he led Sultan Süleyman the Magnificent's Ottoman navy.

The town centers around the **Öküz Mehmet Paşa Kervanserai,** a 12-meter-high Ottoman inn built in 1618 by Sultan Osman II's vizier to accommodate overseas trade. That same year he commissioned the **Kaleiçi Cami,** nearby hamam (bathhouse), and **city walls,** which were all financed through proceeds from the caravanserai. A thorough restoration in the 1960s led to the caravanserai's grand opening as Club Karavanserai, a hotel and restaurant. Slightly southwest of this ancient inn are a handful

Kuşadasi

19th-century timber townhouses in the regional architectural style of the period.

The **Grand Bazaar** is home to roughly 1,000 stalls, where virtually anything Turkish—ornate carpets, knockoff designer purses, watches, and clothing—sells cheaply. Shopaholics will also delight in the weekly Friday bazaar (across from the *dolmuş* station), when villagers from the region flock to town with their carts of fruits and vegetables, towels and lace, and locally made clothing.

The town is also rife with **organized tour providers** with tours to the major attractions of Ephesus, the Temple of Artemis, and the House of the Virgin Mary (€45, full day), Pamukkale (€45, full day), Priene, Miletus, and Didyma (€40, full day), Şirince (€25, half-day), or the Greek island of Samos (€40). You can also saddle up for the horseback ride (€30) or all-terrain vehicle safari (€35) on Pamucak Beach, or simply soak and scrub in a humid Turkish bath (€20).

Beaches and Water Sports

After a day of traipsing through ancient ruins and visiting museums, soak in the Aegean's clear waters. Unfortunately, the crowds of visitors and unchecked development has rendered the area around Kuşadası and much of the coast unpleasant for anyone seeking relaxation on a public beach. The tiny municipal stretches of **Merkez Plajı** (Downtown Beach) and **Kadınlar Plajı** (Women's Beach)—named in the past when vacationing women went topless—are two options, but there are better beaches near Kuşadası, including **Uzun Plajı** (Long Beach), six kilometers south of town. Here you'll find cafés and restaurants, chaises longues and parasols, and water-sports equipment for rent. The **Kuştur and Pygale Beaches,** five kilometers north of town, offer a kilometer-long sandy shoreline with facilities, warm limpid waters, and heavy crowds on summer weekends.

You won't go wrong laying your towel at one of the beach clubs, where prime seaside space allows for maximum hedonism, water sports, dancing, and bass-thumping DJs day and night. Kuşadası's coast is dotted with them; a good choice for its location is **Papaz Hammamı Beach Club** (just left of the Pigeon Island causeway, 5TL umbrella, 5TL sunbed) or **Miracle Beach Club** (Women's Beach, 0256/614-5090, www.clubmiracle.com, free). These are more affordable than the nearby Saint-Tropez style **Jade Beach Club** (Yılancıburnu, 0256/612-7220, www.jadebeachclub.com, €10), which is also worth

Kuşadası port

checking out. Entry fees may vary depending on the program of events for the day.

If you have kids or just love water playgrounds, head to **Aqua Fantasy** (Pamucak Beach, 0232/850-8500, www.aquafantasy.com.tr, €17 ages 4-9, €24 over 10). With over 20 pools, thrill rides, slides, and other attractions, you're sure to have a good day out. Race your friends down the Proracer slide, try the world's first sphere waterslide, float in the lagoon, or relax by the adult or kids pool. Take a tube and sail down the Lazy River that drifts the weary around the park.

Nightlife

If you're fond of rowdy inebriated crowds, raucous Irish pubs, tattoo parlors, and cheesy karaoke dives, head to Barlar Sokak. For a more laid-back vibe, walk down to Kuşadası's old town to the grid of narrow streets between Barbaros Hayrettin Bulvarı and Kışla Sokak. The night scene doesn't get going before midnight mid-March to mid-November; the rest of the year, it's practically nonexistent. The top pick is the **Orient Bar** (Kışla Sk. 14&17, 0256/612-2736, www.orientbar.com), a hidden sanctuary for acoustic music fans. The venue has two bar areas; one is in the open-air courtyard of an old Turkish home where, at the right time of year, you could munch on the grapes hanging from the vine above. The second, just across the small lane, is a cozy barn-like bar with low, dark wood ceilings on which you can etch your name. The whitewashed walls are covered in musical instruments, Turkish trinkets, and other memorabilia, and unlike most bars there is an easygoing vibe for all ages.

A trip to Turkey wouldn't be complete without an evening folkloric show, and **Club Caravanserail** (Atatürk Blv. 2, 0256/614-4115, Tues. and Fri., €40), is one of the best places to experience the cabaret-type festivities. Attendees line up at a gigantic banquet table, filled with innumerable appetizers, just as the show starts in the historic caravanserai. A basic main course arrives as a variety of folk dances from the various regions of Turkey are performed. There are also glittering belly dancers and percussionists as well as international music.

Accommodations

Lodging in Kuşadası runs the gamut from economical inns to pricey five-star all-inclusive resorts; at last count there were more than 400 properties from Pamucak Beach in the north to Women's Beach and Long Beach in the south. Only about a quarter of these are open year-round; the majority operate only April-November. To find additional properties and useful discounts of up to 20 percent, visit **Kuşadası Hotels** (www.kusadasihotels.com).

Lodging in the center of town may seem like a smart way to save time commuting, but the din of the nightlife means light sleepers may be uncomfortable. If you're not immune to noise, look to lodgings just out of town, such as the ★ **Bakkhos Guesthouse** (just above Kirazli Köy Yolu, 0256/622-0337, www.bakkhos.com, €17.50-35). It's a typical Turkish country house that has been transformed into a picturesque 12-room inn near Kirazli village, a community famous for cherry orchards. It is four kilometers from Kuşadası, but booking with the Özbaşes, a Turkish-Dutch couple who own the property, has its merits. All rooms boast Mediterranean porches surrounded by blooming gardens and lofty palms; interiors ooze country charm and simplicity. Common areas promote amity with an oversize pool and wraparound sofas perfect for a late-afternoon cup of tea with friends. The Kuşadası *dolmuş* conveniently passes by, so a private vehicle is not required.

Right near the main cruise-ship terminal and tourism office, conveniently located close to the Grand Bazaar and restaurants, is the adored **Mr. Happy's Liman Hotel** (Kıbrıs St., Buyral Rd., 4, 0256/614-7770, www.limanhotel.com, €50). Rated highly by independent travelers, each of the 14 rooms are basic but spacious and tastefully decorated, with most sporting a balcony facing either the seaside or a back street. With the motto, "Come as a guest, leave as a friend," everything oozes genuine Turkish hospitality, from owner Mr. Happy's accommodating personality to the rooftop terrace that serves inviting home-cooked meals. Travelers return repeatedly for the hotel's location and service. Make sure you dine on the rooftop to watch the majestic sunset behind Pigeon Island.

While the buzzword around town is "boutique," most venues with that moniker fall short on style and luxury. The **Efe Boutique Hotel** (Güvercinada, 0256/614-3662, www.efeboutiquehotel.com, €100), on the waterfront, does provide ultra-chic panache in its 40 rooms. Completely refurbished in 2011, standard and deluxe rooms feature crisp white bedding and aquamarine walls all atop white wooden floors that provide a spacious, fresh feel. All rooms face the sea, and most rooms, except those on level four, have private balconies. For added luxury, book into the suite room, a classy apartment with a lounge and kitchenette decked out in black and white.

For peace and serenity in the heart of town, the ★ **Villa Konak** (Yıldırım Cd. 55, 0256/614-6318, www.villakonakhotel.com, €60-70) is a welcome retreat from the bustling streets nearby. The Enderin family offers 17 rooms in old Turkish houses that look out to the inviting pool area and a plush garden of grass and fruit trees—rarely seen in hotels here. Keeping with its homey theme, the spacious rooms are decorated with kilims on wooden floors and regional handicrafts reminiscent of a Turkish country manor rather than downtown Kuşadası. Complimentary breakfast and afternoon tea are served by the pool.

For a truly unique experience, bask in Ottoman history at the **Hotel Caravanserail** (Atatürk Blv. 2, 0256/614-4115, www.caravanserailhotel.com, €85). This 400-year-old *han* (caravanserai), commissioned by an Ottoman vizier in 1618, features immaculately clean rooms bearing centuries-old detailing and inset stone fireplaces. The inner courtyard, where breakfasts and dinners are served in summer, is magically transformed with a live Turkish dinner show on Tuesday and Friday in summer.

Food

Kuşadası's culinary offerings are a mixed bag of dishes tailored to the Northern European palate. You shouldn't necessarily rely on the ratings on well-known travel websites; the top-rated restaurants on these sites can be run-of-the-mill fast-food cafés that dish out fries with every meal. If you'd rather avoid that kind of food, there are some worthwhile alternatives. Be aware that food prices here are significantly higher than in nearby Selçuk, İzmir, or Şirince, as restaurateurs cash in on the short tourism season and have to cover the cost of importing ingredients to reproduce foreign favorites.

Soaring tourism in Kuşadası lured families from around Turkey to set up restaurants to share their regional specialties with an international crowd. One such eatery is ★ **Öz Urfa** (Cephane Sk. 9, 0256/612-9881, www.ozurfakebabs.com, 20TL). The Zorlu family's first restaurant was opened by the current owner's great-grandfather in 1959 in Urfa, in Turkey's southeast. In 1977 the family moved to Kuşadası, where today guests can enjoy meals in their pleasant courtyard or informal indoor restaurant filled with photos from their hometown. Öz Urfa means "the real Urfa," so expect real Turkish and Kurdish hospitality paired with complimentary mezes and generous portions of Urfa's favorite dishes, such as eggplant kebab, liver kebab, and kebab with pistachios—all cooked in the wood oven and barbecue on-site. Steaks, pizzas, and other Turkish regional kebabs are also available.

Turks vacationing in Kuşadası love the fish entrées at ★ **Kazım Usta Restaurant** (Liman Cd. 4, 0256/614-1226, 25TL). Open since 1956, Kazım is the oldest restaurant in town and is considered Kuşadası's finest locale for grilled fish. Try the house specialty eggplant salad, followed by a locally caught *çıpura* (gilthead bream), cooked superbly on a charcoal grill. This fine meal, combined with the marina atmosphere, is a memorable outing.

The family-owned **Avlu** (Cephane Sk. 15, 0256/614-7995, 20TL) has remained a local favorite for decades, and thanks to sated guidebook writers, getting a table at lunchtime seems harder these days. Simplicity and consistency are key here. The meals of the day are on a counter waiting for the next in line to pick one, so get in early. Veggies rule, but the house's *ezme* (chili pepper meze) and juicy chicken and lamb kebabs are sought after.

Hidden in the streets of the old bazaar is the truly international **Saray Restaurant** (Bozkurt Sk. 25, 0256/612-7088, www.sarayrestaurant.com, 25TL). The stylish modern decor seems a little out of place in the antiquated bazaar area, but the food and entertainment is what people come for; there is something for everyone—steaks, traditional Turkish, Indian, Thai, Chinese, seafood, and even Mexican cuisine. This place is brimming with people celebrating birthdays and special occasions because it's an instant party with Turkish Night (Wed.), Cabaret Shows (Fri.), and live music. Call ahead to make a reservation, and take advantage of the pickup and drop-off service from Kuşadası hotels.

Information and Services

Kuşadası's **Tourist Information Office** (Iskele Meydanı, 0256/614-1103, 8am-noon and 1pm-5pm daily May-Oct., 8am-noon and 1pm-5pm Mon.-Fri. Nov.-Apr.) offers town maps and plenty of information. **PTT** post offices are in several locations, but the one with the longest hours is on Zeki Aydinli Sokak (0256/612-3311, 9am-8pm Mon.-Sat.); it provides all postal services, currency exchange, and money transfers as well as a faxing and phone calls. **Banks** and 24-hour ATMs are located along the Barbaros Hayrettin Paşa Bulvarı.

Kuşadası's new private **Universal Hospital** (Rıza Saraç Sk. 1, 0256/612-7200) is located in the heart of town, near the seafront and marina.

Getting There
AIR
The closest airport is İzmir's **Adnan Menderes Airport** (ADB, 0232/274-2626, www.adnanmenderesairport.com), with international and domestic flights. At the İzmir airport is the train station for **TCDD** (www.tcdd.gov.tr) trains bound for Denizli. Disembark in Selçuk (4.50TL, 1 hour, 8 times per day) and either organize a transfer from your hotel, a taxi (65TL, 20 minutes), or walk five minutes to the *otogar* to transfer to the Kuşadası *dolmuş* (5TL, 20 minutes) that departs every 15 minutes. Taxis also offer private transfers from the airport to Kuşadası (€55, 1.5 hours).

CAR
From İzmir (100 kilometers, 90 minutes) travel south along the region's main toll highway (E87) to the Selçuk-İzmir connector (D550). Drive the D550 through Selçuk and turn right onto the westbound Aydın Bulvarı. This road leads into Kuşadası. Via Bodrum (160 kilometers, 2.5 hours), take the D330 that leads directly from Bodrum, and after 48 kilometers, turn left onto the D525. Follow this road north until the town of Söke, and turn left onto the D515, which leads west to Kuşadası.

BUS
Kuşadası's central *otogar* (Kahramanlar Cd., 0256/614-9571) is located less than one kilometer from the town center. Tickets for the usual Aegean coach companies can be found here, including **Kamil Koç** (444-0562, www.kamilkoc.com.tr) and **Pamukkale Turizm** (0850/333-3535, www.pamukkale.com.tr), however the offices of major coach companies are also located along İsmet İnönü Bulvarı; these provide convenient shuttle services to the *otogar*. From the *otogar*, coaches run to Istanbul (70TL, 11.5 hours), Bodrum (25TL, 2.5 hours), and other destinations, more frequently in summer. Although there are many *dolmuşlar*, hailing a taxi is the best way to get to your hotel.

BOAT
Ferries run from the port of Kuşadası to the Greek island of Samos (www.feribot.net, 75 minutes, daily Apr.-Oct., €35 one-way,

€40 same-day return, €55 open return). Departures to Samos are at 9am. An additional service departs Kuşadası at 5pm Tuesday-Thursday and Saturday-Sunday. The return boat departs from Samos at 5pm daily. There is an additional ferry from Samos to Kuşadası at 8:30am Tuesday-Thursday and Saturday-Sunday. Purchase tickets online or via reputable travel agents like **Anker Travel** (Inonu Blv. 14, 0256/612-4598, www.ankertravel.net/en). Passports are checked at each port prior to boarding, so arrive at least 45 minutes ahead of departure.

Getting Around

Commuting in Kuşadası on the cheap is easy by hopping on one of the numbered *dolmuşlar* (1.75-2.75TL). These leave from the *garaj* (station) on Adnan Menderes Bulvarı but can also be boarded anywhere in town. Route details are posted on the windshield. *Dolmuş* number 1 (Efes Princess) runs north to Kuştur-Pygale Beaches, while the number 6 (Sahil Siteleri) travels south to Long Beach, six kilometers from downtown Kuşadası. The popular coastal number 5 *dolmuş* travels along Atatürk Bulvarı and Güvercin Ada Caddesi, making stops at Kadınlar Denizi (Women's Beach) south of the ferry terminal. The *dolmuş* for Selçuk (5TL) departs about every 15 minutes from the station and passes along Dr. Sabri Yayla Yolu within one kilometer of the lower gate to Ephesus.

DILEK MILLI PARKI (DILEK PENINSULA NATIONAL PARK)

Dilek Milli Parkı (8am-7pm daily summer, 8am-5pm daily winter, 3TL, cars 10TL, vans 40TL) is one of Turkey's most pristine natural reserves, where nature is juxtaposed with a heavily militarized buffer zone between the Greek island of Samos and the Turkish mainland. This 113-square-kilometer park is a hilly extension of Samsun Mountain, cloaked with pine and indigenous fauna until it naturally juts into the Aegean Sea. Here, protected fauna like the rare Anatolian leopard and even rarer sea turtles and monk seals may be glimpsed. The beaches and picnic areas of the park beckon sun-seeking eco-travelers April-October. Trekking and climbing opportunities abound deeper in the woods and up to the park's highest point, Dilek Tepesi (Dilek Hill, 1,237 meters). The park extends from Guzelcamli village to Doganbey.

Day tours to the Dilek Peninsula, 23 kilometers south of Kuşadası, are offered in the form of Jeep safaris by most travel agencies in town (€35) and includes swimming stops at the beaches, lunch, and a drive up Samsun Mountain. Independent travelers can catch the *dolmuş* service (6TL) that departs from Kuşadası's *otogar* every 30 minutes, or by private vehicle.

Just beyond Dilek's entrance is the refreshing swimming spot called the **Cave of Zeus,** a small cave with cool water. If it's too cold, head onto **İçmeler Köyü,** a shaded sandy beach less than one kilometer away. It's usually blanketed with sunbathers, so travel onto the less crowded shingle beaches of **Aydınlık** and **Kavaklı,** five and seven kilometers from the park entrance. A large track, signposted as **Kanyon,** snakes up to the summit of Dilek Hill. Dilek's farthest beach, **Karasu Burun,** is worth the trek; it is a pebbly strip straight across from the Greek isle of Samos. Each beach has public amenities and snack bars open in high season.

★ PRIENE, MILETUS, AND DIDYMA

Called "PMD" by people in the local tourism sector, Priene, Miletus, and Didyma are among the best-preserved ancient cities of the Ionian realm in Anatolia. While these historical locations are minor compared to the magnificence of nearby Ephesus, a visit is worthwhile, even for the views of the lush Büyük Menderes Valley from Priene's heights alone. All three sites have the same **hours of operation** (8am-7pm daily summer, 8:30am-5:30pm daily winter) and **entrance fees** (10TL). Detailed maps and history guides are sold at each park's entrance.

the Temple of Athena at Priene

difference between the two Ionian cities. The area today has some ruins of Miletus's prominence, which lasted for 14 centuries (700 BC-AD 700). Some of its natives inspired new schools of thought at a time when mainland Greece was in its bleak cultural Dark Ages. Chief among Miletus's luminaries was the pre-Socratic philosopher Thales of Miletus, one of the Seven Sages of Greece and also considered the father of science for his breakthroughs in astronomy and geometry. There was also Hecataeus of Miletus (550-446 BC), the first historian of ancient Greece; he actually coined the word "history." Even Miletus's alphabet was adopted by ancient Greece as its official alphabet. The ruins, including the striking 15,000-spectator **Roman Amphitheater** and the **Baths of Faustina,** mostly date back to a Roman beautification project in the 2nd century BC.

Rounding out the archaeological outing is **Didyma** (0256/875-5206). The impressive 6th-century-BC **Temple of Apollo,** constructed entirely of alabaster marble, was fronted by 120 columns, each 20 meters high. The temple's oracle was chief among those of ancient Greece, rivaling Delphi, and the largest monument of its time. Priests waited just beyond the colonnaded entrance to communicate queries to and answers from the oracle. A walk through the stone rubble reveals a colossal **Head of Medusa.** The road that connects Didyma to Miletus today is directly on top the 1st century AD Sacred Way, once graced with spectacular sarcophagi, sphinx, and lion statues.

From its lofty location, it's hard to believe **Priene** was once a port city, with its lowest level at the mouth of the river. It offers sweeping views of the Aegean from its acropolis atop the city. Priene was built on a military-inspired grid plan, essentially duplicating the innovative city design of Miletus. It rose to fame in the 4th century BC as an entertainment center and member of the mighty Ionian League of Cities. Much of what can be seen today are remains of the sweeping monuments constructed to bolster its political status during the rise of Asia Minor. These include the theater, the once wooden-roofed bouleuterion (senate house), parts of its seven-meter-thick city walls, sprawling private houses, gymnasium, and stadium. The most prominent monument is the **Temple of Athena,** built by Pythius of Halicarnassus, the architect of the famed mausoleum in Bodrum.

After Priene's sublime views, the marshlands surrounding the ruins of **Miletus** (Balat Köyü, 0256/875-5206), once also on the edge of the Aegean, reveal the stark geographical

Getting There

Dolmuş services are available from Söke but are infrequent. Instead, plan a day to walk around these sites by joining one of the myriad tours offered by local travel companies, or by renting a vehicle. Most hotels in the area provide tour arrangements through contracted agencies; ask them to schedule the **PMD tour** when you make the hotel reservation, keeping in mind that the availability and frequency of tours are greatly reduced in the off-season. If you **drive** the PMD route from Kuşadası, head south on the D515, following the signs for Söke (25 kilometers), or from Selçuk, take the D550 before turning right onto the D525 to reach Söke (42 kilometers). Continue along the D525 and take the road to the town of Güllübahçe.

Priene is the first site reached via this town, about 14 kilometers south of Söke. Miletus is another 22 kilometers due south through the vast cotton fields on either side of the Menderes River near Balat *köyü* (village). The ancient site of Didyma is another 19 kilometers south of Miletus.

Pamukkale

The travertine pools at Pamukkale command attention from far away. These sparkling white cascading terraces are one of a kind; the outcrop is known among Turks as the world's eighth wonder. The terraces sprawl over 200 meters up the Çaldağ Mountain chain from the Curuksu Plain. This dramatic geological anomaly is the result of eons of calcium-laden accumulation brought forth by hot springs spurting from rifts in the earth, created over time by seismic activity. Scientific data aside, this once magnificent outpost has been Anatolia's ultimate spa resort since antiquity. Roman imperials bathed in the colonnaded Sacred Pool corralled in a plateau halfway up a cliff. From its pine-blanketed flanks unfurl the ruins of the ancient city of Hierapolis and its 2,000-year-old ruins.

It's hard to believe that these ruins, and the integrity of the entire locale, in fact, almost didn't survive the force of developers. By the late 1980s the pools at Pamukkale (Turkish for "cotton castle") were brown from sewage runoff from hotels atop the travertines, and local tourism had all but stopped. Baffled as to how to reinvigorate the site's popularity, local authorities called in the United Nations. A UNESCO designation followed in 1988, leading the way for the displacement of the hotels to the local town of Karahayıt and a major cleanup of the area's springs. The site today is just a fraction of its original size, but Pamukkale merits a visit nonetheless.

A trip to the ruins at Hierapolis inevitably involves a soak in its thermal pools. The typical day-trip option, offered through travel agencies from Kuşadası and Selçuk, allows for no more than a three-hour swim and tour, as there's six or seven hours of commuting involved. These tours are enjoyable, but it's even better to set aside a day or two en route to or from the Mediterranean to fully explore Hierapolis, enjoy a longer soak in the thermal pools, and take in the nearby ancient city of Aphrodisias. Those who stay in the plush yet dirt-cheap resorts of Karahayıt, just five kilometers north of Pamukkale, will find thermal baths, but these are unimpressive in comparison. These springs, known locally as Red Pamukkale, are considerably warmer (42-56°C) and slightly tinged red due to the iron content of the village's springs.

The best time to plan a stopover in Pamukkale is any time outside the mad tourist rush and searing heat of summer, preferably during the months of May and October. To catch Pamukkale's annual arts event, visit in September during the monthlong International Music and Culture Festival, when concerts are held in the restored Hierapolis amphitheater. This festival features Turkish musicians and international acts, regional gourmet food, and homemade crafts and wares.

SIGHTS

The starting point for exploring the **travertines** and **Hierapolis** (0258/272-2077, 8am-7pm daily, 25TL entry covers both sights) depends on which gate you enter—there are three in the perimeter around the sights. Most visitors enter the Main Gate from Pamukkale town and walk up via the travertines, reaching the Pamukkale Archaeology Museum first, followed by the Sacred Pool—which today doesn't look so sacred, with a 1980s building marking the entrance. Reaching the north and South Gate requires a vehicle. Enter the North Gate, closest to Karahayıt town, and walk the necropolis of Hierapolis first, or from the South Gate, see the gymnasium of Hierapolis before reaching the Sacred Pool.

★ Travertines

Besides the beautiful calcified landscape that leaves visitors wide-eyed and gaping, the amount of flesh on display may raise the eyebrows of more modest visitors. Aside from the crowds of tourists with barely-there swimsuits, a barefoot walk up the hillside **travertines** is magnificent, with spectacular views of the valley. The rough calcium path provides natural foot exfoliation, while the shallow cascading waters are refreshing in the heat of the day. Along the easy 800-meter trek are artificial travertine pools for wading.

★ Hierapolis

Sprawling over two kilometers long, the ruins of **Hierapolis,** Greek for "Sacred City," attest to the importance the ancients placed on the site and its potent springs. From its founding in 190 BC by Eumenes II, king of Pergamum, Hierapolis was centered around the temple of Hiera. This monument predated the city by at least 200 years and may have been the inspiration for its name. Incidentally, Hiera was the gorgeous wife of Telephus, son of Hercules, grandson of Zeus, and mythical founder of the kingdom of Pergamum. Ancients firmly believed that the Greek god Apollo was responsible for Hierapolis's wild outcrops, while the odorous sulfur fumes emanating from the pools were linked to the god of the netherworld, Pluto.

But it wasn't until the 2nd century AD that Hierapolis experienced its heyday. Its spa was its main claim to fame, but textiles, particularly wool and dyes, also made the city commercially significant. By the time Roman emperor Hadrian visited, Hierapolis's infrastructure badly needed an overhaul after a series of earthquakes; buildings like the theater were added. After the advent of monotheism, the metropolis was home to a large Jewish community as well as an important Christian center. In the 5th century, the Byzantines added a handful of churches and the large Martyrium of St. Philip the Apostle.

The ruins of Hierapolis are a startling

Pamukkale's white travertines are an ethereal geological anomaly.

collection of ancient city's historical pedigree and an amalgam of religious sites that relate the advent of faith through Anatolia, from its early pagan roots to the dominance of Judaism and Christianity. Most of the site's archaeological treasures were discovered over six decades by a team of Italian researchers led by archaeologist Paolo Verzone, who worked on site for more than 30 years.

Most tours of Hierapolis start at the Sacred Pool. Behind the Sacred Pool is the **Nymphaeum,** a monumental fountain that distributed water throughout the city. It was built in the 4th century AD with three walls surrounding a bowl of water to which steps led on the open side. Beyond this are the remains of the **Temple of Apollo,** the sun god and principal deity who ruled over the city during Hellenic times. In the same complex as the temple is the famed **Plutonion.** Essentially a small cave about 10 meters in length, the Plutonion is a death chamber filled with lethal carbon dioxide emanating from an open fault below. In those days, only eunuchs serving the **Temple of Cybele** with up to four layers of cloth wrapped around their heads were able to withstand the noxious fumes during the animal sacrifices that were conducted in this rock chamber. The emissions are still potent, but the chamber is sealed today to avoid injury to visitors who venture too close.

The **Roman Amphitheater,** farther uphill, is the third-largest of its kind in Asia Minor and arguably the best preserved. Originally built by Titus Flavius Vespasianus in AD 60 on the slope of Hierapolis's hill, the grand amphitheater's size was increased by Hadrian in the mid-2nd century. A century later Septimius Severus extended the seating by another tier of 25 rows to a capacity of 15,000. Intricate busts, statues, and reliefs depicting the myths of Dionysus, Apollo, and Artemis were discovered in the two-story proscenium (raised stage). These are on display at the Pamukkale Archaeology Museum.

As you exit the amphitheater at its highest point, you can see a path leading uphill to the **Martyrium of St. Philip the Apostle.** This is where St. Philip's remains are thought to be buried. One of the original 12 apostles, Philip, according to the Christian Bible, was crucified upside-down in Hierapolis. Although no evidence has been discovered to attest to the whereabouts of his tomb, researchers have determined that this octagonal basilica dates from the 5th century. A blaze ravaged the structure just a few decades later; its columns still bear scorch marks.

Hierapolis

Heading back down toward the Sacred Pool, head to your right (north) to reach the 5th-century **Byzantine Gate,** which was built as an outpost to guard the city from Arab invaders. This gate led to the colonnaded street called the **Plateia**—Hierapolis's main drag. It ran 800 meters from the current North Gate to the monumental **Domitian Gate** in the south, built around AD 83 by Julius Frontinus, the Roman proconsul of Asia Minor in AD 84-86. Originally two stories high, the once-massive towers, connected by three arches, were the entrance of Frontinus Street. This was central Hierapolis, with covered walkways on either side for shops and ateliers, known as the agora. Not much remains of this commercial area, but beyond it is the former **Suburban Theater.** Look closely to make out the remaining seating on the left side of the hill.

The last stop before reaching the necropolis is the restored 3rd-century-AD **hamam** (baths) where visitors to the city had to bathe before mixing with the city folk beyond the agora. The structure, displaying the arches and vaulted ceilings characteristic of Roman architecture, was converted to a Byzantine basilica when Christianity took hold of the city in the 5th century.

Continuing toward the North Gate is the massive **Necropolis,** one of the largest and best preserved ancient cemeteries in Asia minor. Among the 1,200 tombs, mostly constructed of local limestone, are ornately etched sarcophagi used for VIPs, circular tumuli for kings entombed during the Hellenic period (1st century BC), and 2nd-century-AD tall mausoleums used and reused by wealthy families. Both locals and those who visited for medical reasons were interred here, explaining the variety of burial structures designed according to tradition and rank. This whopping 1.5-kilometer-long cemetery does question the validity of the curative powers ascribed to the Sacred Pool.

Continuing north leads to the North Gate, where the half-hourly *dolmuş* runs back to Pamukkale; a shuttle service transports visitors back to the pools (2TL) every 15 minutes. To fully experience the 10 or so ruins of Hierapolis, devote at least half a day. Most tours whisk you through in under two hours, but those interested in religion or history require as much as an entire day. Significant ruins have signs explaining the relevance of the site. No matter how time is allotted, finish with a dip in the Sacred Pool; it will reward you for the often sweltering hike through the ancient metropolis.

Sacred Pool

It's not hard to see why visitors barely wait for their buses to stop to join other bathers in the crystalline thermal pools of this snowy-white natural wonder. The place to jump in is the **Sacred Pool** (Pamukkale Thermal, 0258/272-2024, 8am-7pm daily, 32TL adults, 13TL ages 6-12, free under age 6, locker 5TL), preferably early in the morning when everyone is gorging on the all-you-can-eat breakfast or in the late afternoon after the tour buses have gone. The waters are slightly radioactive, are rich in calcium, magnesium sulfate, bicarbonate, and carbon dioxide, and have a pH of 6.

The water filling the pools along the travertines spills from this ancient bathing spot, which is inside the only modern structure that escaped relocation to Karahayıt more than 20 years ago. The pool is decorated with fluted Roman columns and marble drums—reminders of Hierapolis's historical significance—perfect for a Pamukkale glamor shot.

Note that the entrance fee is charged only to those who bathe in the pool. Guest can also enjoy the on-site café and shaded seating among the verdant gardens. "Doctor" fish are also on call to tend to the weary feet of travelers (40TL, 20 minutes), and a kitschy multimedia installation will entertain those who want to "fly" on a magic carpet over Pamukkale through the magic of a green screen.

Pamukkale Arkeoloji Müzesi

Between the travertines and Sacred Pool lies the **Pamukkale Arkeoloji Müzesi**

(Archaeology Museum, 0258/272-2034, 9am-6:30pm daily, 5TL). Housed in the former baths, this outstanding museum covers the long history of Hierapolis and other towns of the Lycos (Çürüksu) valley. There's an outstanding collection of statues and reliefs along with artifacts such as coins, sarcophagi, medical objects, and jewelry, most dating to Roman times.

ACCOMMODATIONS

Considering all the larger hotels are five kilometers out of town, the family-run B&Bs within a short walking distance from the ruins and pools are the smarter choice. Traveling through the town will reveal the age of most hotels, but thankfully some owners continue to revitalize 1980s venues for modern-day travelers. Two such visionaries are husband and wife Mehmet and Ömmü Güleç, who experienced so much success with their first 19-room B&B that in 2013 they opened a second lodging, ★ **Melrose Viewpoint Hotel** (Çay Sk., 0258/272-2250, www.melroseviewpoint.com, from €41), a 17-room hotel closer to the heart of town with spectacular views to the cotton castle from the second floor bedrooms and the enormous rooftop terrace. The clean, light, and bright rooms with modern en suite baths are all beautifully decorated by Ömmü. After a long trek to Hierapolis, chill out in the poolside garden or sample the family's famous home-cooked meals (try the roast chicken) on the terrace as day turns to night and the travertines illuminate the Pamukkale sky.

The **Venus Hotel** (Tahsin Cd. 16, 0258/272-2152, from €41) is traditional Turkish, all the way down to the patterned lounges in the lobby. The quaint continental flair continues in the large rooms, some of which offer balconies. There's a pool and plenty of relaxing spaces, including a wraparound patio restaurant where traditional Turkish fare is on the menu. The main entrance to the springs and ruins is a 10-minute walk, but owner Recep Orhaniye will gladly arrange transfers and other side trips.

Budget travelers and families will adore Lola and Ömer's **Hotel Beyaz Kale** (Oguzkaan Cd. 4, 0258/272-2064, www.beyazkalepension.com, 60-150TL). Among the budget contenders, this "white castle" is open year-round and excels with authentic hospitality and clean rooms decked out with kilims, simple furnishings, and light colors. The hotel pool is brimming with water streamed from the thermal pools atop Hierapolis. From the rooftop, enjoy Lola's hearty meals and the vista of Pamukkale's white slopes.

FOOD

The majority of restaurants in town are located along Atatürk Caddesi, just down from the main entrance to the travertines, so they're ideal for lunch before or after visiting the ruins. They do struggle to compete with the convenience and quality of on-site hotel dining, however, so expect a bit of jovial hustling on the street as they tempt diners to take a seat inside.

If hunger hits in the center of town, head to **Mehmet's Heaven** (Atatürk Cd. 25, 0258/272-2643, 15TL). Walk in and sink into a cotton şark köşesi (floor-level sofa) inside the village-style wooden cabin, or continue out to the panoramic terrace for dining tables that look out to the travertines. Both have plenty of continental village character: The outdoor space echoes the sound of cascading water from the hillside, and the indoor setting, enveloped in kilims spread across the floor and walls, displays rural trinkets. The food goes with the atmosphere, excelling in village cuisine such as gözleme, vegetable dolmas (stuffed vegetables), and köfte. It's also a laid-back location to try the rich aromas of a narghile (water pipe) in the evening.

Due to the high number of Korean and Japanese travelers, it's possible to find restaurants that offer Asian cuisine in addition to Turkish specialties. One such reputable location is **Kaya's Restaurant and Bar** (Atatürk Cd. 3, 0258/272-2267, 15TL). The restaurant offers an assortment of noodles, pasta, and kebabs. But before deciding on the order, check out the cheap bites listed at the back of the menu. The open-air dining area by the bar is pleasant—under the shade of a leafy patio that offers respite from the heat of the day.

INFORMATION AND SERVICES

Pamukkale's **Tourism Information Office** (0258/272-2077, 8am-5pm Mon.-Sat.) is at the South Gate of Hierapolis. The ATMs are all lined up on Mehmet Akif Ersoy Bulvarı, near the shops that face the travertines, and the **PTT** (Sultan Selım Cd. 4, 0258/272-2895) post office is a five-minute walk from the central Atatürk Caddesi.

GETTING THERE

Day trips to Pamukkale can be arranged with most travel agencies in major cities and towns, including Kuşadası, Selçuk, Bodrum, İzmir, and Antalya. But traveling by bus from any of these points to the travertines takes six to eight hours round-trip, leaving at most three hours at the site, including a one-hour stop for lunch. If Pamukkale is in your plans, try to stay nearby. Day trips are also available from Istanbul, with flights and transfers to Denizli included in the price (€225).

Bus

A new Denizli *otogar* has been built opposite the train station on İzmir Bulvarı in the heart of the city. Regular coaches from Selçuk (25TL, 3.5 hours), Bodrum (30TL, 4 hours), Antalya (30TL, 4 hours), and Istanbul (55TL, 10 hours) all travel to Denizli *otogar*, the largest local town, 25 kilometers south of Pamukkale. From here a *servis* shuttle bus transports passengers to Pamukkale. In the peak season **Pamukkale Seyahat** (www.pamukkale.com.tr), **Metro Turizm** (www.metroturizm.com.tr), and **Kamil Koç** (444-0562, www.kamilkoc.com.tr) may have direct coaches to Pamukkale, which means not stopping at the Denizli *otogar*. Always confirm the final destination on the ticket. Passengers from Fethiye will arrive aboard the 24-seater buses of **Fethiye Seyahat** (www.fethiyeseyahat.com) that terminate at the Denizli *otogar*. From the *otogar,* jump aboard the *dolmuş* (4TL, 20 minutes) that departs for Pamukkale every 30 minutes. The service continues onto Karahayıt. Taxis are also available between Pamukkale and Denizli (50TL).

Pamukkale does not have its own *otogar*. Instead travelers arriving in town can be dropped off anywhere along Mehmet Akif Ersoy Bulvarı below the travertines. To leave Pamukkale, coach companies organize a *servis* to the Denizli *otogar,* where the coach to your next adventure awaits.

Train

The **Pamukkale Ekspressi** from Istanbul has been suspended for several years as the line is being upgraded for fast train services. Regional **TCDD** (www.tcdd.gov.tr) trains run from İzmir Basmane Gar (train station, 20TL, 4 hours 15 minutes), İzmir Adnan Menderes Airport (18.75TL, 4 hours), and Selçuk (14.50TL, 3 hours) seven times per day, terminating at the Denizli Gar (İzmir Bulvarı, 0258/268-2831). Timetables are available in Turkish on the TCDD website. To reach Pamukkale, exit the train station and cross İzmir Bulvarı. Walk to the left to find the bus station where the *dolmuş* to Pamukkale and Karahayıt (4TL) departs every 30 minutes.

GETTING AROUND

The Hierapolis ruins, Sacred Pool, and travertines are all contained within three gates: The **Main Gate,** in the center of Pamukkale town just off Mehmet Akif Ersoy Bulvarı; the **North Gate,** 2.5 kilometers from town, closest to the necropolis; and the **South Gate,** accessible via Yeniköy Yolu. The north and South Gates (parking 5TL) are atop the travertines on either side of the Hierapolis ruins, two kilometers apart. The sights are all within walking distance of these three gates. There is also a **shuttle** every 15 minutes between the North Gate and the Sacred Pool (2TL).

The most pleasant outing is to enter and exit the sites via the Main Gate. This means walking 800 meters up the travertines, and after visiting the various sights, descending to Pamukkale town via the same watery path. Those staying in Karahayıt or parking at the North Gate can use the **dolmuş** in Pamukkale town that runs back to Karahayıt (2TL) every half hour. Some hotels offer a free **shuttle** up to the South or North Gates, enabling guests to wander the ruins before walking down to Pamukkale town. **Taxis** are also available from Pamukkale town to South Gate (15TL), North Gate (20TL), and Karahayıt/Red Pamukkale (25TL).

APHRODISIAS

Visiting Pamukkale, don't miss a trip to Aphrodisias—it makes an excellent day trip. One of the finest archaeological sites in the Mediterranean region, Aphrodisias, adjacent to the city of Geyre, is an often-missed treasure trove of some of the best-preserved ruins, detailing 7,000 years of history. Thanks to the archaeological teams from of New York and Oxford Universities, the landscaping is sensational and the entire site is virtually free of rocks. If you have your own vehicle, don't miss it. If you don't have a private vehicle, hotels can book this excursion for you. Avoid Monday, when the on-site museum is closed.

History

Aphrodisias was associated with a fertility cult and may date as far back as the 5th millennium BC. From the accumulated ruins rose its central acropolis (8th century BC) and, in time, its nearby temple devoted to Aphrodite, goddess of love. The outpost grew into a significant town around the 2nd century BC, known for its Aphrodisian sculptures, which were facilitated by the marble quarries of nearby Babadağ mountain. Pilgrims flocked from the coastal regions for the Temple of Aphrodite. When Julius Caesar overnighted in Aphrodisias with his troops in 47 BC, he lavished the temple with a golden statue of Eros. Soon after Caesar's visit, the temple earned a reputation for its unruly fertility rites and orgies. When Christianity took hold, the temple was converted into a church and its marble blocks were used to build a delineating wall. To ensure that the town was rid of its lurid past, Aphrodisias was renamed Stavropolis (City of the Cross) in AD 350. The town prospered under the Byzantines but finally succumbed to repeated attacks from the Selçuks. Ancient Aphrodisias became the muse of Turkish American archaeologist Kenan Erim, who excavated most of the ruins visible today from 1961 until his death in 1990. Erim's book, *Aphrodisias: The City of Venus Aphrodite,* recounts his life's work.

Ruins

The entire site of **Aphrodisias** (0256/448-8003, 8am-7pm daily Apr.-Oct., 8am-5pm daily Nov.-Mar., 15TL) covers some 520 hectares and comprises 14 main sites, the majority of which date from the 2nd century AD. Naturally, the first stop has to be the **Temple of Aphrodite.** It was built in the 1st century BC and converted into a Christian basilica around the 5th century AD. Its lofty columns intersperse the rubble of this once amazing shrine to the goddess of love.

Near the park entrance, the stunning **Tetrapylion**—Aphrodisias's monumental gate—greeted lovelorn pilgrims to the city with true Ionic architecture. To the left is the grave of Kenan Erim on a beautifully landscaped plot. Following a cobblestone path, the impressive **Stadium of Aphrodisias** was one of Asia Minor's largest in its heyday. Measuring 262 by 59 meters, it accommodated 30,000 spectators. Seating was arranged according to guilds, as some of the inscription in the marble tiers reveals. After a particularly damaging earthquake during the 7th century AD, part of the stadium underwent a renovation to accommodate the public events that had previously been staged in the theater. The 7,000-seat **Theater** was entirely crafted of alabaster marble. Taking time to walk between the tiered seating, you'll notice chiseled renderings of a menorah, gladiators, even the name Nikoforos—a seemingly important thespian who commissioned a small dressing room next to the stage. The **Museum** (Tues.-Sun.) displays objects found in the ruins dating back to 5000 BC and the Bronze Age, as well as the relics from the Archaic, Classic, and Hellenic periods. You can also appreciate the iconic Aphrodite statue uncovered in the Temple of Aphrodite.

Getting There

Aphrodisias is 120 kilometers south of Pamukkale. For a carefree visit, the only option for those without a private vehicle is to book a **return transfer** through a hotel in Pamukkale (30TL pp). These transfers are available for groups of five or more people and are booked from hotels in and around Pamukkale. Pickup is around 9:30am, followed by a 1.5-hour journey to the Aphrodisias site. Just over two hours of self-guided sightseeing are included, and you arrive back in Pamukkale at around 3pm. Lunch is not provided; pack a sandwich or two for the trip back, or visit the café close to the ruins. **Driving** from Pamukkale, head south to Denizli, then to Tavas via the D585 highway. Follow the signs leading to Karacasu, and then to Aphrodisias. It's also possible to visit Aphrodisias driving from Selçuk, as the D585 also connects with the main E87 in the north.

The Turquoise Coast

Bodrum 249	Kalkan 297
Marmaris 265	Kaş 301
Dalyan 274	Olympos, Çıralı, and Chimera ... 309
Fethiye 280	Antalya 312

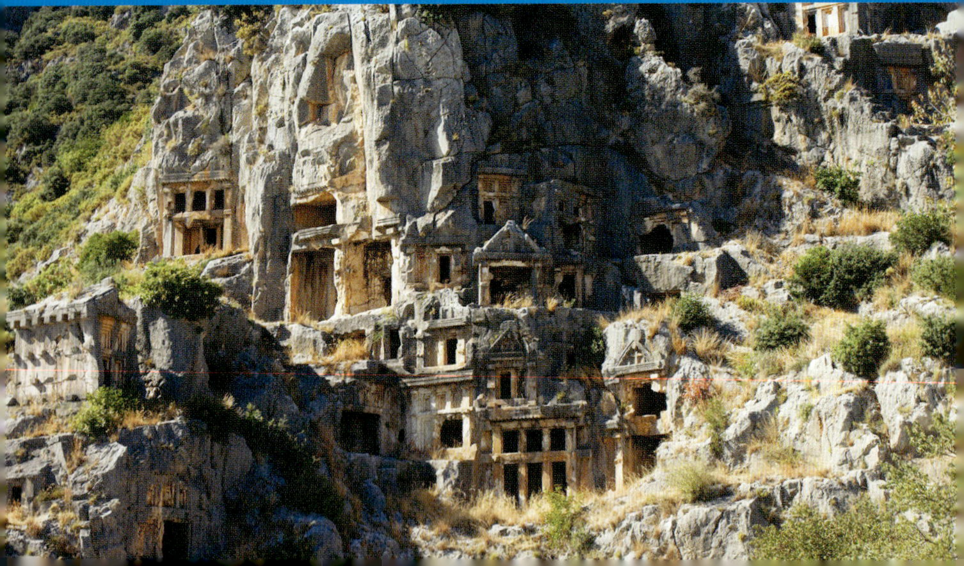

Aptly named for its deep blue Mediterranean waters, the Turquoise Coast is a paradise of hidden coves, bays, and isles set against the magnificent jagged cliffs of the western-most crags of the Taurus Mountains. The landscape is dramatic:

Conifer-filled canyons drop steeply into the sea in some places and give way to tiny sand and pebble beaches in others. This southern slice of Turkey lures millions of domestic and international visitors to the various land and water-based summer attractions along the 650-kilometer coastline from Bodrum to Antalya.

Just past Bodrum, the second of two sinewy peninsulas mark the start of the Eastern Mediterranean—a premier sailing mecca for the much-loved Turkish Blue Cruise. Here are tourism towns and postcard-perfect villages decorated with magnificent ruins, including the imposing Lycian rock-cut tombs that date back to the 5th century BC.

Outdoorsy types find the Turquoise Coast particularly appealing. Swim in crystal-clear bays from boat cruises that depart daily from major marinas; scuba-dive underwater canyons and wrecks in Kaş; kayak over the sunken Lycian city of Kekova; paraglide above Ölüdeniz's Blue Lagoon; or fight the chilly cascading waters of the Taurus Mountains as you walk the Saklıkent Gorge near Fethiye. Hikers love the serpentine 509-kilometer-long Lycian Way between Ölüdeniz and Hisarcandir, 20 kilometers from Antalya; and mountain bikers revel in riding downhill through the pine forests of the Taurus Mountains above Demre. Along the coast are the nesting grounds of loggerhead turtles at Dalyan, Patara, and Çıralı beaches; wild and captive dancing dolphins; and fishing aplenty in lakes, rivers, and the Mediterranean. If that's too much activity for one holiday, submerge your limbs in an authentic hamam (Turkish bath) or dip into the healing springs and mud baths near Dalyan.

The Turquoise Coast is an ideal vacation destination for all types of travelers. Attractions are served by modern roads and efficient public transportation. Expect to see narrow streets awash with designer bag-toting city slickers, luxury yachting enthusiasts,

Previous: Temple of Apollo, Side; the 1st century theatre at Myra. **Above:** Duden Waterfalls, Antalya.

Look for ★ to find recommended sights, activities, dining, and lodging.

Highlights

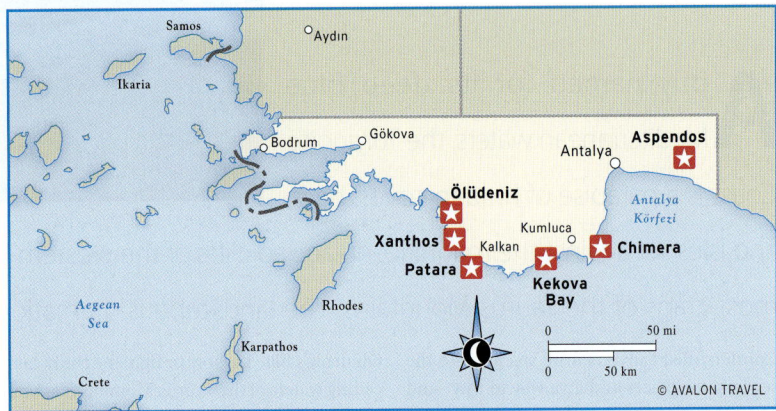

★ **Ölüdeniz:** Glide above, or laze on, the white sands of Turkey's very own Blue Lagoon (page 290).

★ **Xanthos:** Investigate the Lycian League's 3,000-year-old ruins (page 295).

★ **Patara:** Walk amid seaside ruins along one of the Mediterranean's longest sandy beaches (page 296).

★ **Kekova Bay:** Float by the sunken city of Kekova by boat or kayak and climb to Kaleköy's small fortress for spectacular views of the Mediterranean (page 306).

★ **Chimera:** Take a sunset hike through a pine forest to this eternally-burning flame (page 311).

★ **Aspendos:** Take in the ambiance of this 2,000-year-old Roman theater—the best preserved in Asia Minor—during the classical concert and ballet season every summer (page 317).

harem pant-wearing backpackers, families, and romantic honeymooners—all holidaying alongside hardworking Turks harvesting the freshest produce served up in hospitable hotels and restaurants.

PLANNING YOUR TIME

Spend at least a week to really enjoy this area's many sights and relaxing idylls. A two-week itinerary is recommended, however, with at least a couple of days in both Bodrum and Antalya as bookends to this scenic journey. Set aside four days for the Blue Cruise between the evergreen Olympos village and sun-soaked town of Fethiye. Book your itinerary around your cruise departure day to make the most of your time.

The region's mild temperatures make any season ideal for touring. Average summer low temperatures hover around 19°C, but perhaps the worst time is the busiest summer season, when the region is assaulted with busloads of travelers and highs above 40°C. Hotel rates follow the same arc to maximize income during the short season; come November 50 percent of hotels and restaurants shut down until mid-March. Some visitors revel in the summertime brouhaha while others find it dreadful. The Turquoise coast may be best enjoyed during spring and fall when temperatures, like the hotel prices, are milder, and tourism diminishes to a trickle. Coastal waters remain warm and cafés still have outdoor-seating with complimentary pashminas to cuddle when the evenings turn cool. Winter temperatures can dip to 9°C during the day and 3°C in the evening with northerly and easterly breezes dropping the temperature further in January-February. From November, expect to see the Taurus Mountains capped with snow. When the weather heats up again in spring, places like Butterfly Valley and Olympos offer nature-lovers a unique chance to check out butterflies hatching from their cocoons among displays of wildflowers and herbs that paint and scent the Mediterranean.

Bodrum

Bodrum, meaning "basement," takes its name from the town's location deep within Turkey's southern Aegean Coast. The town can largely owe its popularity to Turkish scribe Cevat Şakir Kabaağaçlı, who was exiled to Bodrum's Castle of St. Peter in 1924 for three years for writing a provocative political article. Local legend holds that when he arrived at the fortress, the local governor, an admiring fan, set Kabaağaçlı up in a house overlooking the gorgeous Aegean, where the author, later nicknamed the "Fisherman of Halicarnassus," waxed poetic about the scenery and the sweet life of what was then a small fishing community. He romanticized Bodrum and coined the term *Mavi Yolçuluk* (Blue Cruise), which has become the commercial name for the trendy nautical voyage along the Turquoise Coast. By the 1950s, Turkish intellectuals were sold on Bodrum through Kabaağaçlı's writings, and many moved here for the summer. A few decades later, the peninsula's tourism industry boomed.

Today's Bodrum looks nothing like the sea-lapped outpost Kabaağaçlı immortalized in prose, but the blue of the water remains, as does the friendliness of the anglers by the port. Now the Bodrum Yarımadası (peninsula) is one of the ultimate summer destinations for Europeans, Turkey's own version of ritzy Saint-Tropez, luring celebrities, luxury yachters, and middle-class sun soakers. The peninsula's other allure, aside from some 65,000 hectares of rolling hills, is the long Aegean shore. Dozens of unique villages, comprising blocks of whitewashed low-rises, are draped in showy fuchsia-colored bougainvillea. The idyllic setting outdoes the Greek islands and is celebrated as the Turkish dolce vita. Unlike similar high-end resorts Kuşadasi

The Turquoise Coast

and Marmaris, which are overrun with Northern European tourists, Bodrum has retained much of its Turkish aura and charm, attracting visitors who are more interested in culture and history.

The proof of Bodrum's modern-day popularity is in the numbers: The peninsula's permanent population of about 136,000 swells to one million in the summer. High season is July and August, and by November the peninsula clears out until late March, when tourism restarts.

What grabs visitors is the unrivaled excitement of the harbor town Bodrum, with the medieval Castle of St. Peter commanding the cape between downtown Bodrum's yacht-filled harbors. Near this looming fortress are the remains of the Halicarnassus Mausoleum, one of the Seven Wonders of the Ancient World. Both offer plenty to keep sightseers busy during the day along with the streets of shops and cafés catering to travelers'

needs. Come nighttime, the port roars to life with a laser light display letting everyone know where the party's at. And that's usually at Halikarnas Club, once the loudest and largest nightclubs on the Mediterranean, or Club Catamaran, a floating disco that sails every evening until the wee hours of the morning. Nowadays the lineup of international DJs at these mega clubs contend with a slew of blaring bars and lounges on the harborside promenades.

But Bodrum is not all about partying. If relaxation is your goal, take to the turquoise waters aboard a one-day cruise on a *gület* (motorized wooden sailboat), or linger longer on an eight-day Blue Cruise exploring the Gulf of Gökova. From the foot of the castle you can also take day trips in peak season to Turkey's Datça peninsula and the Greek islands of Rhodes, Kalymnos, or Kos.

During summer Bodrum's center is the eye of the tourism storm, with an unrelenting

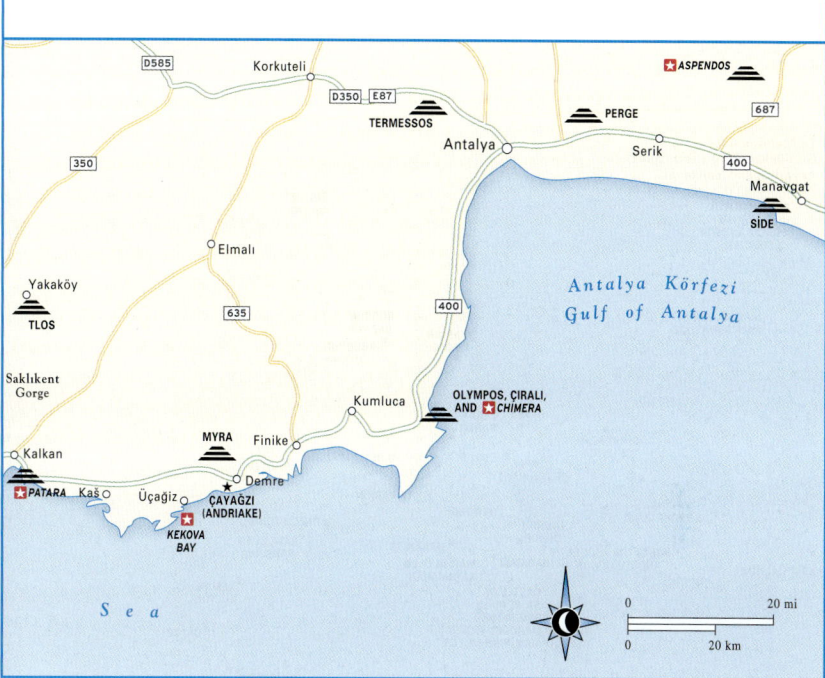

whirlwind of cruise boats, yachts, and tour buses. If you thrive in the middle of the action, this place is for you. You might also enjoy the lively enclave of Gümbet, a beachside village popular for its youthful bar scene and international restaurants. Otherwise, base yourself elsewhere on the peninsula and take a *dolmuş* (communal taxi) back to the center for sightseeing. Bodrum hosts a plethora of festivals most months of the year. These celebrate international and Turkish dance, music, culture, and recreation, and hotel prices will vary depending on the calendar of events. For more information about Bodrum, visit **Bodrum Life** (www.bodrumlife.com).

HISTORY

The history of Bodrum—called also Halicarnassus by the ancient Greeks and Halikarnas in Turkish—is deeply entwined with its port. The first Hellenic colony to capitalize on the strategic seaside outpost were the Dorians in the 11th century BC. The strategic location didn't elude the Persians, who stormed Asia Minor in the mid-6th century BC and used Bodrum as the capital of the Carian satrapy (province), a title that allowed a significant amount of autonomy for the locals, particularly when it came to the wealth of the prominent local boat-building and trading guilds. It wasn't long before the area spawned the likes of Artemisia I (the first female fighting admiral in the 5th century BC) and the great ancient Greek historian Herodotus of Halicarnassus (484-425 BC), known as "the father of history."

The Mausoleum of Halicarnassus, built in the 4th century BC, became a tribute to the wealth and love of siblings and lovers Carian princess Artemis II and Mausolus. The ruined foundations of this impressive Wonder of the Ancient World is just a couple of blocks inland from the fortress.

The Persians lost control of the town in

Bodrum

334 BC to Alexander the Great after the battle of Halicarnassus. By the 11th century, the Selçuk Turks ruled the Aegean city, only to relinquish it to the Knights of Saint John in 1402 as compensation from Sultan Mehmet Celebi for losing their stronghold of Smyrna. These chevaliers built the Castle of St. Peter atop a diminutive Selçukian fort with stones from the nearby mausoleum. The knights provided the lone Christian refuge in Asian Minor for over a century within the walls of the castle, which withstood attacks from Sultan Mehmet II (conqueror of Istanbul) in 1453 and 1480. When Sultan Süleyman the Magnificent set his sights on Rhodes, a six-month campaign ensued, handing Rhodes and Halicarnassus to the victorious Ottomans in 1523. The Italians occupied the town during World War I until the subsequent Turkish War of Independence in 1921 handed Bodrum to the Turkish Republic.

Bodrum's 15th-century Castle of St. Peter sits between two bays of crystal clear water.

SIGHTS

Visiting most of Bodrum's outdoor sites will require walking up hills and steps that have minimal shade. Bring water and wear sunscreen and a hat.

As you explore the peninsula, keep an eye out for the white low-rise domes that can be seen from major roads. These structures are Ottoman water cisterns, once used to collect and store water for livestock and irrigation.

Castle of St. Peter

Bodrum's main attraction, the **Castle of St. Peter,** is one of the largest and best preserved castles of the Knights of St. John, and handsdown the world's best archaeology museum for underwater artifacts. The garrison, also referred to as Bodrum Castle, lies atop an earlier Selçukian fort on what was once the island of Zephyria, named after Zephyros, the Hellenic god of the western wind. This spot was chosen by the knights and bankrolled by their various European duchies and the Vatican for a new garrison after they lost their foothold in İzmir to Tamerlane and his rapacious Mongol troops in 1402. According to historians, the knights were handed free reign of the littoral by Ottoman Sultan Mehmet Celebi, who also feared the wrath of the Mongols. Pope Callixtus III, intent on renewing a crusade against the westward-marching Turks, personally appointed German knight and architect Heinrich Schlegelholt to launch the project. The pontiff even went as far as to guarantee laborers eternal life in heaven for their holy "participation." It took decades for the fortress, originally a set of moats and fortifications, to reach its current size. In 1522, just months before the mighty Ottoman army of Sultan Süleyman the Magnificent captured most of the eastern Mediterranean, the knights uncovered Mausolus's burial chamber and its treasure while searching nearby for additional stones to strengthen the garrison. The fortress became a prison under the Ottomans, and storage space for numerous undersea finds after Mustafa Kemal Atatürk's rise to power in 1923. The 600-year-old castle has remarkably withstood time and repeated earthquakes. With more than 240 coats of arms, varied inscriptions, and armor along the garrison's five towers, the interior and exterior spaces make the fortress a leading example of medieval European history.

Since 1963 the looming structure has been open to the public as the **Bodrum Sualtı Arkeoloji Müzesi** (Museum of Underwater Archaeology, 0252/316-2516, www.muze.gov.tr/bodrumunderwater, www.bodrum-museum.com, 8am-noon and 1pm-7pm Tues.-Sun. summer, 8am-noon and 1pm-5pm Tues.-Sun. winter, 25TL, audio guide 10TL). It is an impressive repository for the countless treasures collected from nine offshore shipwrecks, some dating as far back as the 14th century. Aside from vast collections of barnacle-crusted amphorae, stunningly ornate gold, silver, and glass jewelry, oil lamps, and copper tools, shipwrecks are perfectly reconstructed as they appeared underwater when sponge divers discovered them. One of these exhibits is the 3,400-year-old Uluburun Shipwreck. Its cargo included a gold chalice and a remarkable gold scarab inscribed with the name of the ancient Egyptian queen Nefertiti.

Aside from historical artifacts, the fortress's grounds feature samples of Mediterranean flora and fauna, with most linked to information placards about local myths and legends. For example, take note of the myrtle tree in the main court. Dedicated to Aphrodite throughout history, the tree was sought by royalty for its health-promoting benefits. Be on the lookout also for the resident peacock around the grounds of the castle; he's a sure-fire photo opportunity for families.

Plan at least a couple of hours to tour this gem while on the peninsula, but note that most exhibits close from noon to 1pm. The self-guided tour of the exhibition halls is clearly marked by red and green arrows signifying a long and short tour, respectively. The main difference is that the short tour bypasses the steep descent to the dungeons where infamous Captain Oruç (a.k.a. Barbarossa) was held for three years by the Knights of St. John.

Mausoleum of Halicarnassus

When the Carian satrap (governor) Mausolus grew tired of having to answer to his higher-ups in the Persian capital of Persepolis in 362 BC, he revolted and moved the ancient seat of the Carian satrapy from Mylasa (Milas) to Halicarnassus—today's Bodrum. From this new coastal seat he invaded Lycia and Ionia, accompanied by his wife and sister, Artemis II. The duo spared no expense to beautify their new capital and in the process devised a burial ground called the **Mausoleum of Halicarnassus** (Turgutreis Cd. 93, 8am-7pm Tues.-Sun. summer, 8am-5pm Tues.-Sun. winter, 10TL) that would attest to their accumulated riches for ages to come. Unfortunately, Mausolus died at the age of 24 in 353 BC, leaving his sister and widow with the task of completing the site. Artemis obliged by seeking out the best architects and sculptors; the final product was a massive marble cube 45 meters high that was divided into three equal parts. The base featured bas-reliefs of lions and demigods; a colonnaded terrace encircled a marble tomb; and a pyramidal roof supported a colossal horse-drawn chariot containing the grander-than-life statues of Artemis II and Mausolus. The term *mausoleum,* meaning monumental grave, derives from Mausolus. Despite various pirate raids in the mid-1st century AD, the tomb stood pretty much intact for 1,500 years until a series of devastating earthquakes destroyed most of its roof around the end of the first millennium. The 36 columns that surrounded the grave and the structure's base were used for construction of a Selçukian fortress in the 12th century. The Knights of St. John took whatever remained to build the Castle of St. Peter.

The remains of the Mausoleum are strewn haphazardly in a pleasant landscaped courtyard. These include some fluted columns, marble drums, one of the grave's grand stairways, and rubble culled from its chambers. Of note, however, are fragments of friezes that appeared on the base of the mausoleum and a collection of models illustrating the enormity of the 2,300-year-old structure.

Bodrum Antik Tiyatrosu (Bodrum Antique Theater)

The **Bodrum Antik Tiyatrosu** (Kıbrıs Şehitler Cd., 0252/316-8061, 8:30am-5pm Tues.-Sun., free) has a capacity of 13,000 and doubles as an outdoor music hall during the concert season. From its location high atop Bodrum's hillside, the views of the marina and the Greek island of Kos are reason enough to visit. Historically, the theater is another 4th-century-BC legacy of architectural aesthete Mausolus and one of the oldest theaters in Anatolia. The Romans later enlarged and enriched it in the 2nd century AD, leaving clues etched in stone pertaining to the wealthy benefactors who contributed to the makeover.

Myndos Gate

When Mausolus made Halicarnassus his capital in the 4th century BC, he built a seven-kilometer city wall with the Mylasa Gate in the east and the monumental **Myndos Gate**

Around the Bodrum Peninsula

(off Büyük Iskender Cd., free) in the west. Recently restored, the reconstructed western gate is the only gate to remain; it is named for the ancient city it faces (now Gümüşlük). According to Greek historian Arrian, a seven-meter-wide defensive moat in front of the gate resulted in mass causalities during the brutal siege of Halicarnassus in 334 BC when Alexander the Great captured the Persian city. Myndos Gate is a 30-minute walk from the port. The view from the gate and the opportunity to retrace Alexander's mighty steps intrigue many travelers.

Bodrum Deniz Müzesi (Bodrum Maritime Museum)

In the heart of the old town, opposite the PTT (post office), is the **Bodrum Deniz Müzesi** (Eski Bedesten Binası, 0252/316-3310, www.bodrumdenizmuzesi.org, 11am-10pm Tues.-Sun. Jul.-Oct., 10am-6pm Tues.-Sun. Nov.-Jun., 5TL). Opened in 2011, the museum preserves documents, artifacts, and valuables from Bodrum's rich seafaring past. In addition to 54 model boats and exhibits celebrating the local boat-building and sponge-diving industries are a collection of works by essayist Cevat Şakir Kabaağaçlı and 4,500 seashells amassed from around the world by Turkish conchologist Hasan Güleşçi.

Around the Bodrum Peninsula

Most people will enjoy the shopping vibe in the whitewashed old Bodrum town with its labyrinth of pedestrian alleyways and streets lined with white pebbles and glass mosaics of butterflies and the nazar (evil eye). Here you'll find boutiques and run-of-the-mill tourist shops selling textiles, clothes, shoes, knockoff perfumes, watches, and other merchandise.

MARKETS

For serious bargains, head to Turgutreis on Saturday for the peninsula's largest **farmers market.** If you miss it, there's a *pazar* (market) every day of the week in various coastal and inland towns. Tuesday sees creative locals in Bodrum and Milas selling textiles and handicrafts. On Wednesday, Gümüşlük and Ortakent host their own farmers market, which spills in to Bodrum proper, Akyarlar, and Yalıkavak on Thursday. The fruit and vegetable options expand with Bodrum's biggest *Cuma Pazar* (Friday market), which also peddles spices, knockoff designer clothes and shoes, textiles, home wares, and trinkets.

SIGHTS

Beyond the castle, amphitheater, and mausoleum of Bodrum are the ruins of other ancient Carian and Lelegs cities. A popular destination for experienced hikers is the 7th-century-BC **Pedesa,** also known as Gökceler Kalesi, located on the highest points of the peninsula near the village of Cirkan. Opposite the beach of Gümüşlük is tiny Tavşan Adası (Rabbit Island), home to **Myndos**—the city cited in Shakespeare's *Julius Caesar* for having sheltered Brutus and Cassius after they led the assassination of Caesar in 44 BC. Current excavations are uncovering over the 2,500 years of history relating to this ancient city, and there are plans to set up an archaeological park in the future to protect the uncovered relics.

When out exploring the peninsula near Yalıkavak, it's worth stopping by **Dibekli Han** (Yakaköy Çilek Cd. 46/2, cell tel. 0532/527-7649, www.dibeklihan.com, 10am-7:30pm daily May, 10am-1pm and 4pm-11:30pm daily Jun.-Sept., 10am-9pm daily Oct.). Resembling a stone fortress, the historical building now doubles as an art and cultural center where you can browse traditional crafts and jewelry by local artisans and enjoy one of many evening cultural performances throughout the high season.

ENTERTAINMENT AND EVENTS

Bodrum is reputed for its high-end nightlife, and its gaudy haunts vie for prominence with the jet-set magnets of Göltürkbükü (enclaves of Gölköy and Türkbükü north of Bodrum) that keep the paparazzi on their toes when the latest starlets hit town. Generally, Bodrum's nightlife starts along the terraced diners, bars, and booths selling trinkets on the narrow, packed Dr. Alimbey Caddesi in Bodrum. It then flows along the broader Cumhuriyet Caddesi (Bar Street), where British pubs share space with sophisticated dens catering to most lifestyles and musical tastes. Dance clubs and bars get going around 11pm with last call around 2am around the peninsula. The *rakı*-fueled fun can continue well into the wee hours in Bodrum. No matter the location, entertainment is not restricted to night; seaside bars and beach clubs guarantee a generous flow of beer, big-screen TVs, and boisterous games of backgammon all day long.

Nightclubs

A trip to Bodrum by jet-setting party people warrants an evening at the legendary **Halikarnas** (Cumhuriyet Cd. 132, 0252/316-8000, www.halikarnas.com.tr, Apr.-Oct., Sun.-Thurs. 40TL, Fri.-Sat. 50TL, includes 1 drink). With four clubs within a club, glittering chandeliers, elegant whitewashed columns, and Vegas-like shows right on the shores of the Aegean, it's no wonder celebrities like Mick Jagger, Claudia Schiffer, Pamela Anderson, and Yves Saint Laurent have all partied here. The recently opened Secret Garden restaurant, designed by Jade Jagger, is the place to be seen with a decadent French-style set menu of seafood and truffles (125TL), which includes a glass of champagne and entrance to the club. Check the website, which touts the schedule of events for the club, including theme nights and upcoming international guest DJs and stars.

The biggest floating disco in Europe **Marine Club Katamaran** (Dr. Alimbey Cd., 0252/313-3600, www.clubcatamaran.com, 10pm-4am daily Apr.-Oct., 40TL, includes 1 drink) is *the* place to party on the Aegean Sea. The enormous catamaran, with a capacity for 2,000 guests, sails nightly and boasts five bars and a glass-bottom dance floor that has guests and go-go dancers bopping to house, Turkish pop, and R&B music from the DJ decks. The first cocktails are poured at the marina at 10pm before revelers set sail at 1:30am. If your sea legs can't handle the pace, speedboats shuttle guests to and from the marina every 10 minutes.

The newest glamour club on the Bodrum scene is Flavio Briatore's **Billionaire Club** (Palmarina, Çökertme Cd., Yalıkavak, 0252/385-4356, www.billionairelife.com, from 11pm Thurs.-Sat.). The fifth club of this international chain is situated in the epitome of billionaire playgrounds—on a private island alongside Turkey's largest marina that can berth 34 megayachts. While entry is free to the club, expect to pay premium for drinks and cuisine from the club's exclusive Cipriani and Sait restaurants.

Bars

Stroll any of the harbors in the evening and see there is no shortage of bars in Bodrum. You won't need to go into the beach clubs or nightclubs to enjoy a cocktail or two because you can literally barhop on Cumhuriyet Caddesi (known locally as Bar Street) or venture west to Neyzen Tevik Caddesi to enjoy a range of evening entertainment offerings on the harborside promenade. Those looking for sports bars won't have to venture too far either, as most venues sport big-screen TVs and ice-cold beer.

The bar responsible for launching Bodrum's night scene more than 30 years ago is **Hadigari** (Dr. Alimbey Cd., 0252/316-0048). Located just left of the castle in a converted power plant, Hadigari—meaning "let's go, folks"—lures foot traffic with gigantic torches flanking its harborside entrance. This all-in-one space does dining best from 7pm onward, although it doubles as a busy bar and upscale nightclub after hours. Nearby is **NewOld** (Kale Sk. 29, www.newold.com.tr), in a 300 year old open-air tavern where R&B, house, and 1980s favorites spin from the decks.

Along Dr Alibey Caddesi, a former sponge depot is now the sophisticated **Mandalin** (cell tel. 0549/226-48448, www.mandalinsound.com). The bar by the sea hosts local and international artists playing blues, jazz, Turkish pop, and Latin tunes. Walk farther east along Cumhuriyet Caddesi and find bars with indoor dance floors and seating that sprawls onto the pebble beach. Take your pick of seating locations and take in Bodrum's nightlife, including the laser show emanating from Halikarnas.

Head to Neyzen Tevik Caddesi to find another smorgasbord of nighttime venues. While here, pay homage to Mehmet Helvacıoğlu at his bar, **Helva** (www.helvabodrum.com). Mehmet is credited for being one of the pioneers of the Bodrum nightlife scene, having started Hadigari and later Club Catamaran. He now manages his own bar, conveniently located a few doors up from another nightspot, **Fink Bar** (0252/316-4716). Set in a 19th-century building with a palm tree planted by the Fisherman of Halicarnassus, this bar is popular with young vacationers on long summer nights. Farther along the street, the **Marina Yacht Club** (0252/316-1228, www.marinayachtclub.com) is a supreme meeting point in town. Gaze at the castle from the rooftop bar or chill out to jazz, Latin, or nostalgic Turkish tracks in one of four bars in the club.

The party scene also kicks on until the early hours of the morning in nearby Gümbet, and don't forget the trendy beach clubs and bars in Göltürkbükü, Yalıkavak, and Turgutreis—worth a visit to absorb Bodrum's nightlife.

Festivals and Events

The last two weeks of August herald the **International Ballet Festival** (0312/231-8515, www.bodrumballetfestival.gov.tr). Held at the Castle of St. Peter, the event highlights Turkey's top ballet stars in modern and classical performances.

Every year in August the **Bodrum Yacht Festival** at Turgutreis Marina showcases the latest fads, accessories, and activities related to boating, including a key accessory—demure and luxury yachts. Also on the yachting theme, the **Wooden Yacht Regatta** (www.

The Blue Cruise

Imagine spending three days or more with nothing but fragrant pine-clad mountains to break the interminable blue of the sky and calm azure waters; hours reclining in the Mediterranean sun; and falling asleep looking at the Milky Way curled up in a blanket on deck. That's what's on offer on a **Mavi Yolculuk** (Blue Cruise).

This unique journey aboard a *gül022 (wooden motorized sailboat) was made famous in the 1920s when the poet and travel writer Cevat Şakir Kabaağaçlı, known as Bodrum's "Fisherman of Halicarnassus," wrote about it. Since then, the nautical jaunt has become the highlight of a trip to Turkey that allows travelers to visit places that are only accessible by boat. This popular sea trip comes in all sizes, shapes, and itineraries, so it pays to be informed about what's on offer.

Larger and wider than most watercraft, a *gület* offers spacious decks, large public areas, and private cabins with showers and modern amenities. A typical *gület* with a crew accommodates 8-12 people. Day-trip boats can carry up to 30 or more and generally have floatation devices for inexperienced swimmers.

There are several options for a Blue Cruise. Experienced sailors can choose a bareboat charter, meaning a boat without a crew. Chartered captained boats, on the other hand, have a crew but do away with other passengers, leaving you to chart the course. Chartering a cabin on a scheduled cruise is the most popular option. The typical sailboats used for cabin charters are sometimes the oldest models of an operator's fleet and have the bare essentials and antiquated cabins. Spending a bit more money will add finer touches to your cabin and amenities, but you'll spend more time in the sun and water then belowdecks anyway.

The favorite eight-day Blue Cruises from Bodrum to the Gulf of Gökova or Gulf of Hisarönü combine plenty of opportunities for swimming and lazing on the deck in secluded bays. Other trips from Bodrum head to the north (Kos, Kalymnos, and Patmos) or south (Rhodes and Simi) Dodecanese Islands, adding visits to these irresistible Greek Islands. Most first-timers opt for the popular four-day Olympos to Fethiye cruise, which departs from Demre (with land-based transfers to Olympos) or Fethiye passing Kekova, Kaş, Gemiler Island, Butterfly Valley, and Ölüdeniz. Multiple-day Blue Cruises are also available from Antalya, Kaş, Göcek, and Marmaris, visiting nearby idyllic bays and ruins.

Blue Cruises sail generally April to December, weather permitting, although the peak summer months (June-Aug.) are best for swimming and sleeping under the stars. Booking ahead with a local or international travel agent can pay off because it allows them enough time to match you with travelers of a similar demographic. Cruises depart almost every day, and prices are generally listed on the websites of operators. *Iyi yolculuklar* (Have a nice trip)!

---

bodrumcup.com) in the third week of October commemorates the official end of the sailing season, attracting hundreds of domestic and international sailors.

Divers and cyclists are not forgotten in May with the **Diving Festival** hosted by the Marina Yacht Club and the **Bodrum Bicycle Festival** organized by the Bodrum Nature Sports Club to promote the use of bicycles instead of cars. No festival program is complete without an **International Film Festival,** held annually in September with screenings in the castle. Gümüşlük and Turgutreis also present their own classical music festivals in July and August, respectively. Visit the website **Destination** (www.mydestination.com/bodrum) for up-to-date event details.

SPORTS AND RECREATION

With a landscape so stunningly varied, at least a day should be set aside to fully experience Bodrum by trekking through its countryside. In addition to the must-do ridiculously hip daylong boat tours, you'll also find Jeep safaris, horseback riding, diving tours, fishing trips, and rafting. You can also rent a scooter for a self-guided trip on the peninsula. Walk through Bodrum's center and along the harbor to realize the myriad touring possibilities.

Owned and operated by brothers Metin and Hüseyin Aydın since 1990, **Onelli Tour** (Üçkuyular Cd. 7B, 0252/316-0569, www.bodrumtour.com) can assist with tour, transportation, and recreational needs. Their Jeep safari tour (€25) east to Mazı takes groups through the Bodrum forest to see breadmaking in a local village and swimming at Yalıçiftlik Beach. Their rafting tours (€60) paddle on the Dalaman River near Dalyan, and they can organize horse riding tours (€30), fishing trips (€40), and even tickets to a Turkish bath (€7), Dedeman Aquapark (€15), Club Catamaran (€16), and Halikarnas (€16). Book day-trips here for €25 to explore Pamukkale (4 hours away), Dalyan (3 hours away), Ephesus (2.5 hours away), and the Greek islands of Kos, Rhodes, and Kalymnos. If your bucket list includes swimming with dolphins, you can do so in Bodrum for €55, but it only lasts seven minutes.

Bodrum has a number of golf courses near the Aegean sea. The largest, **Vita Park Golf Resort** (Boğaziçi Köyü, Tuzla Ova Mevkii 23, 0252/524-5333, vitaparkgolfresort.com, from €45 for 9 holes), is in Milas, with a driving range and two 18-hole par-71 champion courses that have stunning mountain views and waterfalls. You can rent clubs here.

Boat Tours

To join the requisite day cruise, head for Bodrum's westernmost harbor the evening before you plan on cruising. Here you'll find handfuls of deckhands and captains peddling the standard seven-hour cruise. The price will depend on the number of people aboard, the lunch menu, itinerary, and type of vessel, so it pays to shop around to find the boat, meal, and crew suited to you. Typically departing around 10:30am and returning by 5:30pm, wooden *gületler* run a cookie-cutter itinerary, stopping at five favorite swimming locales, among them offshore caves, scenic bays, and a therapeutic mud bath at **Karaada** (Black Island). If comparison shopping at the marina seems like a lot of work, travel agencies sell all-inclusive cruises for around €20 (including lunch and drinks) or €10 for the cruise and lunch only. These are usually with large groups and sometimes are more of a party boat than a relaxing day cruise, so ask what the vibe of the boat is like before forking out the cash. VIP boat cruises for 15 people (€10, lunch included) are also available from travel agencies in town.

For the extended Blue Cruise, whether a two-week trip through the Greek islands, the venerated seven- or eight-day Blue Cruise, or even custom itineraries, there's a company to oblige. One notable cruise and charter company is **Ege Yat** (Aegean Yacht, Yokusbasi Akdeniz Cd. 4, 0252/313-2655, www.aegeanyacht.com). A favorite with the media, Aegean Yacht leads the pack of yacht service providers in Turkey thanks to a varied fleet of boats with 2 to 10 cabins and an impeccable safety record. Take your pick of itineraries, yachts, and prices from the information on their website, and call or email for bookings. Multiple-day cruises can depart from Bodrum, Marmaris, and Göcek, near Fethiye.

Horseback Riding

Country Ranch (Turgutreis Piren Cd., Turgutreis, 0252/382-5654, www.countryranch.com, 50TL) in Turgutreis offers three horseback-riding itineraries through the hills, valleys, and beaches around Turgutreis. They also have a cafeteria and a mini zoo onsite sure to entertain families with little ones.

Water Sports

Bodrum is a mecca for activities that involve water. The sea beckons scuba divers to explore the superb fauna and flora as well as underwater reefs, islands, and caves. For underwater exploration, **Aşkın Diving** (Kibris Şehitleri Cd., Ataman Is Merkezi E/3, cell tel. 0532/323-2997, www.askindiving.net) is *the* diving provider of choice. Owner Aşkın Canbazoğlu is an archaeologist who was affiliated with the Museum of Underwater Archaeology for eight years before going commercial. A range of daytime and evening diving outings are available, including full-day dives (€50) that include the use of equipment, a boat trip, and lunch. Also on offer are a range of professional courses such as the four-day PADI certification to obtain an international diving license for €385.

Kitesurfers and windsurfers breeze over to **Fener Windsurf** at Fener Beach between Akyarlar and Turgutreis. Owners Jimi and Jale have a team of competent instructors for lessons and surfing equipment for rent from €27 per hour. A one-hour starter lesson is €40, or take a full beginner course from €170. The surfing season runs April-early November with mild winds in the morning that pick up dramatically by mid-afternoon. Book in advance to secure lower rates for hourly or multiday lessons and equipment rentals.

Beaches and Beach Clubs

Most of the beaches along the Bodrum peninsula are "free"—unless they're managed by a nearby restaurant or a beach club, where you have to pay an entrance fee. A restaurant beach requires only that you purchase refreshments from the restaurant in exchange for a chaise and parasol. This option is far more affordable then the beach clubs and is often quieter. These are also often regarded as blue-flag beaches, meaning they are among the best beaches in the world for safety, cleanliness, and environmental management.

To find Bodrum's best beaches, travel to the southern side of the peninsula, stopping at **Akyarlar.** It even appeared in Forbes magazine's "15 Best Sandy Strips in the World." It owes its reputation to the powdery sand and the string of traditional Greek stone houses that line its tiny concave bay. **Karaincir**'s long sandy stretch, just next door to Akyarlar, is also popular, as is **Bitez,** a beach that mixes shallow depths, ideal for children. **Ortakent, Bardakcı,** and **Bağla,** nearby, are also recommended, as is the up-and-coming enclave of **Gümüşlük,** with its coffee-colored sand and laid-back beachside accommodations and dining.

Numerous swanky Saint-Tropez- and Ibiza-style beach clubs embellish the peninsula, with the most elite located in the north at **Göltürkbükü.** Clubs are open from mid-morning and usually charge an entry fee between 50TL and 125TL or more per day. This entitles guests to a sun lounge, umbrella, and unlimited music till late. Be aware that some clubs issue a club credit card to purchase food and drinks from on-site bars and restaurants. Your bill is deducted from the entry fee, so if you spend more than the entry fee, you'll need to pay more. Check your beach club's payment system on arrival to avoid any surprises. It's a system that guarantees an income for the clubs in the very short season (usually July-Aug.), largely determined by the vacations of celebrities who visit Bodrum's VIP lounges to mingle with fellow glitterati. By mid-September they are back filming the latest soap operas, and most of the beach clubs close. One of the elite clubs at which to rub shoulders with the celebs is **Maki 29 Beach** (Mimoza Sk. 10, Göltürkbükü, 0252/377-6105, www.makihotel.com.tr). **Xuma Beach** (Küdür Mevkii, Yalıkavak, 0252/385-4775, www.xuma.com.tr) is also popular for enjoying water sports and massages. New clubs open most years, so ask the locals for recommendations for the hottest clubs of the season.

ACCOMMODATIONS

Finding quiet lodging in the center of town can be difficult. Inn owners swear by the efficacy of double-glazed windows, but the nightly hubbub around both marinas may keep light sleepers counting sheep until 2am. If you'll be cutting a rug until the wee hours anyway, by all means, stay in central Bodrum and the young party scene of Gümbet. Otherwise, opt for a serene B&B in Gümüşlük, Bitez, Ortakent, or Akyarlar; apartments and villas in Turgutreis and Gündoğan; or at any of the sleek resorts, beach club hotels, and boutique lodgings along the peninsula in Yalıkavak or Göltürkbükü. Several all-inclusive hotels and resorts are found in Torba and Turgutreis. Note that most hotels are closed November-April, opening for the two-week New Year holiday.

Opened in 2013, the delectable ★ **Sade Butik Pansiyon** (Üçkuyular Cd. 6, 0252/316-4768, www.bodrumsadebutikpansiyon.com, from €85) is an Aegean dream with its cobalt blue decor, whitewashed stone walls, and blushing bougainvillea. Breakfast is a highlight, with fresh bread, local olives, and white cheeses served gourmet-style in the leafy courtyard lined with bright rooms that are on the doorstep of the shopping and restaurant strip Cumhuriyet Caddesi. Revel in the inn-style lodging that exudes more luxury and cleanliness than most, and when you leave, you can leave a note of appreciation on a river stone for owners Ebru and Cenk Akkaya to add to their garden's collection.

Situated between the *otogar* (bus station) and castle is the admired **Kaya Pansiyon** (Eski Hukumet Sk. 10, 0252/316-5745, www.kayapansiyon.com.tr, 100-180TL). Mustafa Kaya manages this family-run inn that has been greeting international guests since 1987 and is renowned for its friendly service and excellent location. Breakfast is served on the rooftop terrace, and there's a ground-level courtyard to recline in and relax. Rooms are small but have some creature comforts like wide-screen satellite TV and air-conditioning. There is even a two-room apartment with a kitchenette.

One of most charming escapes in Bodrum is **Güleç Hotel** (Üçkuyular Cd. 18, 0252/316-5222, www.hotelgulec.com, €70). The 18 units provide bare but immaculately clean amenities with views of the hotel's lush garden. This family-run inn also serves a breakfast of local produce in the last remaining tangerine orchard in town, filled with blooms and birds of every color. It's a little oasis just 50 meters from the shore.

A recommended mid-range boutique hotel in Bodrum is ★ **Aegean Gate Hotel** (Guvercin Sk. 2, Bodrum, 0252/316-7853, www.aegeangatehotel.com, May-Oct., €120), a retreat among gorgeously landscaped grounds high on a rocky mound above Bodrum. Taking time to meet with each guest, Irish owners Rory and Gary are another plus; they're a virtual gold mine of information when it comes to the peninsula. The Aegean has only six rooms with a pool. Be quick to book; rooms go fast.

Another gem tucked away on a bougainvillea-lined alley in the heart of town is **Asmin Hotel** (Türkkuyusu Cd. Alibaba Sk. 1030/9, 0252/316-7989, www.asminhotel.com, from €110). Rated highly for its cleanliness and services, Asmin has largish modern rooms around an inviting pool with a paddling area for kids. An in-house hamam is included in stays of three or more nights, and a tour desk removes the headache of organizing travel plans. You'll enjoy the complimentary afternoon tea and the hotel's proximity to the castle, restaurants, and *otogar*. It's one of the rare hotels in town open year-round.

If you're looking to snare a billionaire from the Billionaire's Club in Yalıkavak, stay nearby at the darling of the national media, the **4reasons Hotel+Bistro** (Bakan Cd. 2, 0252/385-3212, www.4reasonshotel.com, from €150). Open year-round, this chic boutique hotel is set high above the long bay of Yalıkavak. The four reasons why guests swoon over this property, according to its owners, Esra and Ali Akin, are serenity, design, quality, and attitude. You'll find all of those things and gorgeous island views, lush fruit orchards, and white-on-white spacious rooms that exude easygoing yet refined charm. Add the eclectic Middle East-meets-French cuisine offered at the upscale on-site bistro, and you won't want to dine anywhere else.

For unbridled luxury, head to the secluded five-star ★ **Kempinski Hotel Barbaros Bay** (Kızılağaç Köyü, Yalıciftlik, 0252/311-0303, www.kempinski-bodrum.com, from €263), just a 10-minute drive east from Bodrum town. One of Bodrum's top resorts, the Kempinski's guest rooms are modern in design, each with balconies and an endless array of amenities. But what truly surprises here are the grounds: The pool features sunken replicas of minarets and domes, and the decadent 5,500-square-meter spa facility offers detox and Asian therapies. Top-notch, five-star restaurants, lounges, grand deluxe rooms with 180-degree sea views, and even a marina to dock luxury yachts are some of the extra indulgences here.

FOOD

Bodrum's cuisine revolves around the plentiful Aegean seafood, fruit from the orchards, and oil olive reaped from groves dotting the peninsula. Due to Bodrum's popularity with foreign guests it's also a great place to rekindle your love for international cuisine; expect to pay a little more in most restaurants because of the large numbers of wealthy visitors. But you also don't need to spend a fortune or live like a celebrity to enjoy a meal in Bodrum. The most affordable eateries line the traffic thoroughfare of Atatürk Caddesi, where meals are touted for under 15TL. For a more pleasant view by the busy seaside promenade, aim for Cumhuriyet Caddesi, where it's possible to find pizzas, salads, and pastas for less than 20TL. Menus are posted at the front of restaurants, so there is no need to be seated until you've decided on your meal.

La Pasion (Atatürk Cd. Uslu Sk. 8, 0252/313-4594, www.lapasion-bodrum.com, 25TL) is an international restaurant specializing in Spanish cuisine served in the courtyard of a stone house that's oh-so-romantic with candlelit ambiance. The theme is sharing, with a good selection of tapas and paella for two, although you can also dine on individual entrées. The extensive international wine list will please connoisseurs with Chilean, French, Italian, and American vintages, or for the total Spanish experience, try the sangria. Reservations are advised.

Earning rave reviews for its European style and affordable yet decadent three-course lunch menu (17TL) is a little French place called **Evimiz** (Sehit Yusuf Can Sevdi Sk. 18, 0252/316-3005, Mon.-Sat.). The restaurant can be hard to find, but it's certainly worth the search. This small shabby-chic restaurant has a dozen tables inside and out in a courtyard, secluded and intimate. The menu by French chef Stephane changes every day, so there's an excuse to return for more treats on more than one occasion.

The front of the menu for **Leman Kültür** (Cumhuriyet Cd. 161, 0252/316-5316, www.lmk.com.tr, 20TL) says "The menu which makes you think while you are laughing, and while you are laughing you eat." This quirkiness runs throughout this comical, colorful restaurant with inventive meals like "Poor chicken is now a schnitzel" and "A strange pizza-something with beef." There is something for everyone's taste and budget with a choice of dining on the pebble beach, inside, or on a terrace with views of Bodrum Bay and the castle. If you enjoy the menu and food, you can find Leman Kültür in most major cities in Turkey.

When it comes to seafood, Turkish visitors recommend **Orfoz** (Cumhuriyet Cd. 177B, 0252/316-4285, www.orfoz.net, 150TL pp). Brothers Çağlar and Çağrı Bozçağa own and operate this small, modestly decorated seafood tasting restaurant near Halikarnas. Individualized flavorsome dishes like groper soup, stuffed mussels with lemon and garlic, chili clams, and oysters with parmesan are presented one after another. The dishes will keep arriving until you confess to Çağlar, *doydum* ("I'm full"). Allow a few hours to work your way through the menu and match it with one of the Turkish wines on offer. Two tables at the front offer views of the castle, so book in advance to get these sought-after seats.

Closer to the castle in the western harbor is the iconic **Körfez Restaurant** (Neyzen Tevfik Cd. 2, 0252/313-8248, www.korfezrestaurant.com.tr, 25TL). The 1923 population exchange saw Cretan Ali Subaşı move to Bodrum, where he worked and cooked on merchant ships in the Mediterranean. His passion for dishing up tasty Cretan cuisine soon had fellow mariners promoting his cooking as the best on board. Encouraged by this feedback, Ali established Körfez in 1930. Today, his son Hasan and grandson Ali offer a diverse menu, including Cretan seafood specialties like scorpion soup and inked squid. Eat outside by the harborside promenade to watch the wooden boats and luxury yachts sail in with the majestic castle in the background.

A trip to Bodrum is not complete without an evening meal on the beach in Gümüşlük, and there's no other place like ★ **Soğan-Sarımsak** (0252/394-3087, cuisineol@aol.com, 25TL). Mother and daughter foodies Hümeyra and Sevinç turned the family's beachside stone holiday home into one of Bodrum's best-loved Turkish restaurants, the name of which means "onion-garlic." In a tiny homey kitchen they prep and dish out a small selection of Turkish cuisine from their grandmother's turn-of-the-20th-century recipes. Don't leave without trying the fruit or pear treacle tart. Dinner is served on the veranda or on the beach with views to ancient Myndos.

Melengeç (Gümüşlük beachfront, 0252/394-4858, www.melengecgumusluk.com, 35TL), with its white-on-white wooden canopy entwined with colorful pumpkin lanterns is earning a good reputation for its delicious fresh seafood served on candlelit tables decorated with vibrant bougainvillea on the water's edge. It's a wonderful place to relax and enjoy groper marinated in garlic and lemon.

INFORMATION AND SERVICES

Bodrum's main **Visitor Information Office** (Dr. Alim Bey Caddesi, 0252/316-1091, 8am-noon and 1pm-5pm daily) is located in the square in front of the castle and obliges with helpful maps and brochures. The **PTT** (0252/316-1212, 9am-7:30pm Mon.-Sat.) post office and the majority of currency exchange offices are located along Cevat Şakir Caddesi, south of the *otogar,* while banks line the main Kıbrıs Şehitleri Caddesi and in the old town on Kale Sokak. ATMs are located here and along Cumhuriyet Caddesi.

GETTING THERE
Air

The airport serving Bodrum is **Bodrum-Milas International Airport** (BJV, Bodrum-Milas Havalimanı, 0252/523-0101, www.milasbodrum.dhmi.gov.tr). The two terminals at are about one kilometer apart and welcome charter flights daily in high season from Europe as well as domestic flights on **Turkish Airlines** (0212/444-0849, www.turkishairlines.com), **Pegasus Airlines** (0850/250-0737, www.flypgs.com), **Atlas Jet** (0850/222-0000, www.atlasjet.com), **Anadolu Jet** (0850/333-2538, www.anadolujet.com), and **Onur Air** (0850/210-6687, www.onurair.com.tr). Thanks to fierce competition among these carriers, tickets from Istanbul can usually be purchased well ahead of time for less than 100TL—even cheaper during the shoulder seasons.

Havaş (0252/523-0040, www.havas.com.tr, 10TL) shuttle buses are the pain-free mode of transportation to and from Bodrum, as most hotels cannot do transfers. The Havaş shuttles leave from Bodrum's *otogar,* stopping on the main highway at Torba, two hours before departure times of regular domestic Turkish Airlines, Anadolu Jet, Onur Air, and Pegasus Airline flights. Check the airport's website for departure times. The journey takes 45 minutes, and seating on shuttles is first come, first served. Atlas Jet has a free shuttle for their passengers to and from the airport and Bodrum, Turgutreis, Bitez, Gümbet, and Konacık for every flight. Alternatively, the convenient **Taxi Coop** (at the airport, 0252/523-0024, www.bodrumairporttaxi.com) shuttles passengers directly into town (100TL) or to any of the villages around the peninsula (100-130TL) any time of day or night.

Car

The Bodrum Peninsula is connected to the Bodrum-Milas airport (48 kilometers) by the D330 highway. Traveling on the D330 away from Bodrum also connects to the D525, which leads toward Selçuk and Ephesus; or continue on the D330 to reach highway D550, which connects to Aydın and the Trans-European Motorway (E87) to İzmir (250 kilometers) and Istanbul (710 kilometers). The D550 also connects south to the Mediterranean coastal D400 via Akyaka.

Bus

Most travelers still arrive at Bodrum by coach with the usual dependable coach companies **Ulusoy** (444-1888, www.ulusoy.com.tr), **Kamil Koç** (444-0562, www.kamilkoc.com.tr), and **Pamukkale Turizm** (0850/333-3535, www.pamukkale.com.tr). This mode of travel is often the cheapest way to get to the peninsula from anywhere in the country. To reach Marmaris (20TL, 2.5 hours), Ortaca (for Dalyan), or Fethiye (35TL, 4 hours), **Marmaris Koop** (0252/313-0835, www.marmariskoop.com) has small coaches departing regularly. All coach and bus services depart from the **Bodrum Otogar,** centrally located on Cevat Şakir Caddesi, less than one kilometer northeast of St. Peter Castle.

Boat

Daily round-trip boat services from Bodrum connect to the Greek islands of Kos (€17, 45 minutes, June-Oct.), Kalymnos (€35, 1 hour, June-Sept.), and Symi and Rhodes(€52, 2.5 hours, June-Sept.), as well as the Turkish town of Datça (30TL, 2 hours, June-Oct.). Purchase tickets right at the dock or through any of the travel agents in town. Arrive at least 30 minutes ahead of boarding time for passport formalities, more if tickets need to be purchased. Travelers must check their visa requirements for entering ports in the European Union, of which Greece is part, and arrange for visas if these are needed. Tickets purchased in Turkey include port fees, while port costs are paid up front when you arrive in Greece. For those traveling to Datça, bus transfers from the port in Körmen to the town are included in the fare. Ferries for all journeys depart from the foot of the castle at 9:30am and return in the late afternoon. For more information and timetables, contact the **Bodrum Ferryboat Association** (Kale Cd. 22, 0252/316-0882, www.bodrumferibot.com).

GETTING AROUND

Bodrum's center, with its web of narrow cobblestone streets, is small enough to cover by foot. Another option is the popular scooter, which can be rented quite cheaply; it allows for quicker transit and easy parking. For those staying outside of Bodrum's center, frequent *dolmuş* (2-5TL) services connect the peninsula's bays and villages from the Bodrum *otogar*. Signs at the front of the *otogar* show how frequent they are, and every *dolmuş* is conveniently color-coded with its terminal station written on the vehicle's hood. In peak season some *dolmuş* routes run until 5am, but always recheck schedules, as these change throughout high season without notice. **Renting a car** for a day or two will give you more freedom to explore the peninsula. Travel agencies in town rent small vehicles from around €25 per day.

Another unique way to discover Bodrum town is a **Segway tour** from Gümbet with **Aegean Gingers** (Adnan Menderes Cd. 48/B-7, cell tel. 0542/366-4592, www.aegeangingers.com). A guide will train you how to use the two-wheeled stand-up vehicle before you take off on a 150-minute tour of the major sites, including the castle, Myndos Gate, the amphitheater, and the harbors.

Marmaris

Marmaris has grown into one of the most popular resorts for Northern Europeans on Turkey's west coast, and tourism is the city's main industry. Much like its sister cities, Kuşadası and Antalya, Marmaris has fallen prey to a huge population explosion and overbuilding to accommodate the summer influx of European travelers. Its year-round population of 20,000 explodes to 350,000 come summer. Whether by coach or boat, travelers come on cheap package tours in June-September, turning the town into more noisy blight than peaceful summer escape. Interestingly, Marmaris is one of only a handful of towns in Turkey where improprieties like public drunkenness and skimpy clothing aren't derided but rather are expected. It's great for people-watching!

While it's true that the town is just a shadow of the fishing backwater it once was, it has striking topography, surrounded by the steep pine-covered Taurus Mountains and sitting at the end of a long azure inlet. Its spectacular harbor is home to one of Turkey's largest and most modern yacht marinas as well as a castle built long ago by the crusaders. The tree-lined promenade and traffic-clogged commercial side streets are primarily geared to satisfy the needs of tourists. Expensive designer knockoffs and Turkish knickknacks are for sale everywhere. Town eateries capitalize on British staples like fish-and-chips, meat and chips, pasta and chips, and curry and chips rather than trying to win over fickle palates with Turkish or gourmet fare.

To imagine what the former Marmaris looked like, explore the coastline jutting from the overgrown harbor town. A day-trip to the Hisarönü and Reşadiye Peninsulas provides an antidote to the mass commercialization. Interlaced bays backed by lushly forested mountains reveal sandy beaches touched only by the bluest waters. Farther out, the peninsulas unfurl like gnarly fingers, divulging sleepy hamlets and the architectural footprint of the ancient Greek islanders who colonized the coast.

The old town of Marmaris, with its tiny alleyways, delectable cafés, medieval castle, and panoramic views of islands and peninsulas, is worth a visit, as is the marina, lined with good-quality restaurants. The boat cruises from Marmaris are also some of the prettiest trips along the Mediterranean. But away from the old town and the marina is a world that has largely lost its Turkish charm. Party people and package tourists may love Marmaris for its nightlife and the familiarity of home for a night or two, but if you want Turkish culture, choose instead the nearby peninsulas, Dalyan, and beyond.

SIGHTS

Marmaris Castle now functions as the **Marmaris Müzesi** (0252/412-1459, 8am-5pm Tues.-Sun., 8TL). Plan an hour to visit the bastion's five separate displays, most of which focus on the region's archaeological discoveries from the Archaic period (650-480 BC) to the Ottoman era (1299-1923). There's an archaeological trove of amphorae, altars, earthenware, glassware, and coins excavated from the nearby ancient Dorian cities of Knidos, Burgaz, and Hisarönü. The exhibits were revamped in 2013 and have excellent basic descriptions about well-known artifacts found along the Mediterranean, often lacking in other museums. Two of the most impressive exhibits are the detailed late Hellenic bronze hand and a sword sheath from statues unearthed in Knidos, near Datça. The view of Marmaris and the islands beyond alone is worth the price of admission.

According to the ancient Greek historian Herodotus, there has been a castle on Marmaris's hill since 3000 BC. Around the time Alexander the Great swept through Asia Minor to repel its Persian occupiers (334 BC), the town's 600 inhabitants realized they were no match to Alexander's 40,000 troops and retreated to the hills, but not before burning their valuables inside the castle and destroying the structure. An entire overhaul of the fortress was commissioned in 1522 by Süleyman the Magnificent in order to proceed with his scheme to invade the Greek island of Rhodes.

In 1914 the castle was devastated by shelling from a French battleship, and it has slowly been restored since 1979. On the way down from the castle to the bazaar area, look out for the **Hafize Sultan Caravanserai,** an Ottoman inn built in 1545, named after Sultan Süleyman's mother. Caravanserais were built throughout the Ottoman lands to accommodate and provision weary travelers carrying goods long distances; now the historic inn is a souvenir shop for modern visitors searching for bargains in the lackluster bazaar, which resembles a retro shopping arcade rather than the charming antiquated bazaars found elsewhere in Turkey.

NIGHTLIFE

Marmaris's vibrant nightlife is legendary and rivals Bodrum and Antalya. The local *Barlar Sokak* (Bar Street), located along narrow Hacı Mustafa Sokak (a.k.a. 39th Sokak), gets going by 8pm, and truly hits its stride at midnight, lasting until 4am. Atypical for a party town is Marmaris's lack of entrance fees and the range of music that includes house, rock, R&B, and traditional *alaturka* tunes. Bar-hop down 39th Sokak to find the music and happy hour to your liking. Dress codes are nonexistent; shorts, tube dresses, and one-size-fits-all sundresses are the norm. The vibe is party as you like. This is also the general theme for bars along the beachfront (207 Sokak) heading to İçmeler and along the marina on Barbaros Caddesi.

If the 20-something ruckus is not appealing, head for the infinitely calmer nighttime entertainment options at the **Netsel Marina** (0252/412-2708), just east of the Old Quarter, or for the best views in town and a relaxed vibe, climb up the narrow stairs to the top of the old town to **Castle Bar** (37 Sk. 59, 0252/412-7528)—an old Ottoman home with a charming warren of divans (Turkish lounges) sprouting from the house on three levels.

Families will also enjoy the dancing fountains at the 19 May Youth Square along Ulusal Egemenlik Bulvarı. It's not quite on the scale of the Bellagio in Las Vegas or the Burj in Dubai, but it's still pleasant entertainment

view of the majestic Reşadiye Peninsula from the Marmaris Müzesi, formerly Marmaris Castle

on a hot summer night. The show starts at 8:45pm nightly.

SPORTS AND RECREATION

The Datça-Marmaris region is served by many travel agencies, but one agency that earns good reviews from travelers year after year is **Ago Travels** (Mareşal Fevzi Çakmak Cd. 1/B, Kumtas Plaza A Blok, 0252/417-2588, www.agotravel.com), which can arrange for an all-terrain vehicle, horseback riding, Jeep tours, boat cruises, hamams, and tickets to the Aquadream water park as well as introduce you to genuine Turkish hospitality and culture on a village tour. Prices are listed on the website, and like most services in Marmaris are quote in British pounds due to the popularity of the region with British travelers.

Boat Tours

The cookie-cutter boat excursion through the region's wealth of flora and geological splendor is highly recommended. A variety of boat-charter companies provider Marmaris's coastline, where the Aegean meets the Mediterranean, with generally two run-of-mill itineraries. One traditionally sets off aboard a *gülel* at around 10:30am and returns by 5:30pm. The cruise includes stops at the popular seven bays, including Turunç, Kumlubük, Kadirga, Aquarium, and Phosphorous Caves. The other cruise includes a half-hour drive followed by a sail to Cleopatra's (Sedir) Island, where Mark Antony is said to have imported white sand from the Egyptian desert as a token of his love for her. It's possible to haggle for a private charter at the marina or book a public tour through a travel agency. The price will change depending on the season, with the shoulder seasons more expensive due to the fewer passengers on board. Expect to pay 40-50TL for the public cruises around Marmaris. Chartering catamarans, monohulls, *gületler*, and luxury yachts for longer cruises is also possible through highly reputable **Pupa Yachting** (0252/413-1853, www.pupa.com.tr).

Mariners operate the Marmaris cruise season from May to October.

Day cruises to Dalyan are also available on a 450-passenger vessel called the **Orca** (0252/413-3001, www.orcamarmaris.com, 25TL), moored by Barbaros Caddesi near the tourism office. The fare includes lunch, swimming breaks en route to Dalyan, and an excursion on a river boat that passes the magnificent Lycian rock-cut tombs on the way to the mud baths.

Diving

Diving takes on a whole different meaning in Marmaris's splendid underwater landscape. While there's no coral, there is plenty of sealife and underwater caves to explore. Experienced divers will prefer the dive spots farther east off Kaş, and trial dives for beginners are the rule at Marmaris. For a day of snorkeling or undersea exploration, **Paradise Diving Center** (Namık Kemal Cd. 248 Sk. 1, cell tel. 0531/708-0496, www.paradisediving.net) offers a range of day dive tours (2 dives 90TL), as well as three-day diving courses for newbies (800TL) and specialty courses for qualified divers. The company's yellow-hulled dive boat departs from the marina near the Atatürk statue, and helpful crew members are available at the boat to answer any questions you have about the dives available.

Beaches

Downtown Marmaris is short of palatable beaches, making the day cruises popular. But like Bodrum, you can laze on a beachside sunbed along 207 Sokak for "free" if you purchase goods from the restaurant that maintains the peppery-colored patch of sand. Otherwise, the closest sandy idylls are **İçmeler,** eight kilometers south of the town center, and **Turunç,** farther away on the Hisarönü Peninsula. The pleasant sea taxis that depart from Kordon Caddesi in Marmaris take people to these coves (10TL). Otherwise, the frequent *dolmuş* from Ulusal Egemenlik Bulvarı and Atatürk Caddesi shuttle people to İçmeler (2.50TL, 10 minutes) every few minutes. The *dolmuş* to

Turunç (6TL, 1 hour) leaves from Orgeneral Mustafa Muğlalı Caddesi and the *otogar,* just outside town, every 30 minutes.

ACCOMMODATIONS

Marmaris proper has some decent hotels, but if you seek peace and a pristine coastline, opt for the charming country B&Bs on the Hisarönü Peninsula, just 20 kilometers south of town. From the Hisarönü Peninsula, nightlife and shopping in Marmaris town is still just a short car or *dolmuş* ride. If you want to stay in Marmaris close to the action on Bar Street and the marina, the following lodgings are worth checking out.

Backpackers should head to 66 Sokak, where they can find a number of simple furnished backpacker-style inns with very cheap rooms (under 40TL). One such place is **Maltepe Pansiyon** (66 Sk. 9, 0252/412-1629, www.maltepepansiyon.com). The rooms here are a bit dated but they're clean and passable for a night or two. When the weather heats up, you can hang out in the leafy courtyard with the very popular house cat, Nuriye—the biggest cat in Marmaris, maybe even Turkey. Friendly manager Mehmet is also happy to help out with tour bookings and subsequent travel plans.

A few streets back from the beach is **Otel Dost** (Org. Mustafa Muğlalı Cd. 74, 0252/412-1343, www.oteldost.com, from €60). Part of the Marmaris hotel scene for 25 years and refurbished in 2012, this hotel offers 19 bright standard rooms, a suite, and a top-floor two-bedroom apartment, close enough to walk to the old town, the beach, and the *dolmuş* stops. Sunbeds line an inviting pool area, creating an ideal retreat for hot summer days, and there's no need to refuel outside, with a restaurant and snack bar all located on-site. If you're a light sleeper, though, opt for a room away from the main street to enjoy a good night's rest.

A British favorite closer to the old town than most lodgings is **Öztürk Apart** (Ulusal Egemenilik Cd., 85 Sk. 14, 0252/413-3050, www.ozturkapart.com, €60-70). The location isn't pretty, tucked away in an average-looking suburban side street about 10 minutes from the beach, but you'll love sprawling out in your own spacious apartment, each with a lounge and kitchen area separated from the bedroom, providing maximum privacy for those sharing with kids or friends. An extra room is available in the form of a private balcony or terrace area. The pool, bar, and restaurant are relaxing and the friendly hosts, Hüseyin and his nephew Mehmet, take care of all your needs.

FOOD

None of Turkey's top culinary prizes have ever been awarded to chefs in Marmaris, and it's a town where review websites like Tripadvisor can't be trusted if you're into gourmet food. The town is overrun with eateries with big-screen TVs dishing out fries with every meal—an essential ingredient for good reviews from some tourists. But like the lodging options, it is possible to find some hidden gems if "fries with everything" is not your thing, and Marmaris does have a few specialty dishes to try. These include *sura doldurması* (oven-roasted lamb stuffed with rice, raisins, and pine kernels, made for festivals); *pirinçli balık* (fish sautéed with vegetables and rice); and *kıstırma* (lamb and rice in eggplant) to name a few. As in any city along the coast, fish dishes reign supreme; head for the marina. Expect to pay more for restaurants here than in most towns, as the prices rise wherever northern Europeans dominate the coast.

For cheap food options, head for an authentic Turkish meal around the hole-in-the-wall eateries and cafés off Ulusal Egemenlik Bulvarı near the castle and bazaar. You'll also find two fast food chains flanking the main square on the same road. Walk over to **Netsel Marina,** close to the cruise boat terminal, where a range of high quality restaurants serve up seafood and Turkish fare.

The cream of the Turkish crop is the reputed **Ney** (26 Sk. 24, 0252/412-0217, 22TL), a 250-year-old Ottoman home that has served as one of the town's tiniest restaurants for over

20 years in the narrow alleyways between Bar Street and the castle. Expect delightful Turkish treats and views of the marina from the cozy rustic dining area upstairs, or dine downstairs among the collection of trinkets from years gone by. The Aegean-themed restaurant, with cobalt blue and stucco white, is barely wide enough for two rows of tables, so reservations are essential to guarantee a view. Recommended dishes include the cowpeas with a selection of cold mezes, finished off with thin skewer kebabs. There are also hearty casseroles and steaks on the menu.

Liman Restaurant (40 Sk. 38, 0252/412-6336, 25TL) is *alaturka*: traditional Turkish music, sumptuous Turkish cuisine, and positioned within the maze of the bazaar, perfect for the hungry bargain hunters. Open for lunch and dinner, Liman's courteous staff serve up an assortment of mezes, salads, kebabs, and seafood highly recommended by the locals. In the evening this modest Turkish restaurant doubles as a hangout for local men who indulge in Champions League soccer games.

Sporting plenty of style and sophistication without the hefty price tag is ★ **Bono** (207 Sk. 4/C, 0252/412-2148, www.bonobeach.com, 20TL). Right by the Mediterranean shore, Bono looks like a classy Hamptons beach shack offering an extensive menu of international cuisine for lunch or dinner. Gourmet hamburgers, pizzas, pastas, and Asian noodles are on offer. In the evening Thursday to Saturday, a DJ spins tracks to accompany your meal, and the comfy cushioned benches will have you lingering longer to people-watch the beachside promenade. During the day, pull up a Bono sunbed on the beach and work your way through the menu.

A legend in the local food scene is **Dede Restaurant** (Barbaros Cd. 15, 0252/413-1711, www.dederestaurant.com, 25TL). Ali Denizelli, a letter carrier who delivered mail by sea to Rhodes and Marmaris, started this restaurant in 1973. Originally a café, the seafood-infused menu was slowly developed and refined over the years by mixing modern and traditional cooking techniques. Today, Ali's grandchildren provide attentive service to guests from the marina, with house specialties such as fish pie, sea bass roll, and salt fish for two, a slow-baked fish buried in rock salt. The restaurant's name means "grandfather," keeping Ali's passion for the sea and cuisine alive. It must be healthy food—he lived to the age of 104.

INFORMATION AND SERVICES

The **tourism information office** (end of Kordon Cd., 0252/412-1035, 8am-6pm Mon.-Fri., 10am-2pm Sat.-Sun. June-Oct., 8am-5pm Mon.-Fri. Nov.-May) is full of up-to-date information and brochures for Marmaris and environs. Several **PTT** (44 Sk. 5/1, 0252/421-0011, 9am-5:30pm Mon.-Sat.) post offices exist in Marmaris, with the main depot located near the tourism office and bazaar area. **ATMs** and **banks** line Ulusal Egemenlik Caddesi and Atatürk Caddesi.

GETTING THERE

Air

Marmaris is served by the modern **Dalaman Airport** (DLM, Dalaman Havalimanı, 0252/792-5291, www.dalaman.dhmi.gov.tr), 95 kilometers east of Marmaris. **Turkish Airlines** (0212/444-0849, www.turkishairlines.com) operates at least two daily flights to Dalaman from Istanbul year-round. **Bora Jet** (0212/465-2878, www.borajet.com.tr), **Onur Air** (0850/210-6687, www.onurair.com.tr), and **Pegasus Airlines** (0850/250-0737, www.flypgs.com) also fly to various points in Turkey. Foreign airlines **Easyjet** (www.easyjet.com), **Thomson** (www.thomson.co.uk), and **Thomas Cook** (www.flythomascook.com) fly into Dalaman as well.

To reach Marmaris, there are several options. **Havaş** (0252/792-5077, www.havas.com.tr, 15TL) shuttles passengers the 90-minute journey from Dalaman Airport to the Marmaris *otogar* every two to three hours, or **taxis** (www.dalamanairporttaxi.com) provide rides into Marmaris (150TL, 1 hour) 24 hours a day. Alternatively, consider renting a car at Dalaman Airport from **Avis** (0252/792-5118, www.avis.com.tr), **Budget** (0252/792-5150, www.budget.com.tr), or **Europcar** (0252/792-5414, www.europcar.com.tr).

Bus

Close to the main highway, the Marmaris *otogar* is three kilometers north of the town center. Long distance coaches to and from Istanbul (90TL, 13 hours) and Ankara (70TL, 10 hours) depart at least twice a day. It may be worthwhile taking an overnight coach for these journeys to save on lodging. Buses to Antalya (40-50TL, 5 hours) depart a few times a day and travel the *Yayla Yolu* (express route) instead of the longer D400 coastal route via Kaş and Kalkan. Buses to İzmir (41TL, 5 hours) depart more regularly. **Kamil Koç** (444-0562, www.kamilkoc.com.tr) and **Pamukkale Turizm** (0850/333-3535, www.pamukkale.com.tr) provide the most frequent coach services to a range of destinations. Bus ticketing offices are located on Orgeneral Mustafa Muğlalı Caddesi or at the *otogar*. Some bus companies provide a *servis* (free shuttle bus) to and from the *otogar* and their office in town. If not, the green *dolmuş* bound for the *şehir* (city) leaves from the *otogar* (2TL) regularly in high season and travels down Ulusal Egemenlik Caddesi and Atatürk Caddesi.

The **Marmaris Koop** (0252/413-5543, www.marmariskoop.com) minibuses to Bodrum (20TL, 2.5 hours), Ortaca (for Dalyan, 12TL, 1.5 hours), and Fethiye (20TL, 2.5 hours) depart at least every 90 minutes year-round. Pay the driver when requested or at the end of the trip.

Hiring a cab from the *otogar* may be a smarter choice for those with heavy luggage, but know how far your hotel is from the *otogar*, as Marmaris taxi fares vary widely due to the expansive size of the town.

Boat

Catamaran services run by **Yeşil Marmaris Tourism & Yacht Management** (Barbaros Cd. 13, 0252/412-1033, www.yesilmarmarislines.com, €37 one-way, €39 same-day round-trip, €55 open round-trip, includes port taxes) ply the route between the Greek island of Rhodes and Marmaris twice daily mid-April to October. The service departs from Marmaris at 9:15am and 5:30pm and leaves Rhodes at 9am and 5pm. Reserve online or purchase tickets from any travel agent in Marmaris.

Passengers leaving Turkey are required to arrange their European Union visas in advance, if required; show their passports to ferry personnel; and arrive at least 60 minutes prior to departure for passport control.

It's also possible to connect to Bodrum via Datça with **Bodrum Ferryboat Association** (Kale Cd. 22, 0252/316-0882, www.bodrumferibot.com, 30TL one-way, 50TL round-trip, vehicles from 90TL one-way). The car ferry departs from Körmen Harbor, nine kilometers from Datça, at 9:30am and 5:30pm. A transfer from Datça to Körmen is included in the price. Also from Datça, the **Dodekanisos Express** (www.ferriesingreece.com, €12 one-way) takes a 20-minute voyage to the Greek island of Symi; the service only operates on Saturday afternoon, so day trips to the island are not possible.

GETTING AROUND

Taxi fares in Marmaris and İçmeler are expensive in comparison to other Turkish towns, so commuting around Marmaris on public transportation is recommended. There are ***dolmuş*** services that vary in color to signify their route. Of the five separate routes from the town center, the popular green and blue services hit various intercity spots; the orange line heads north to İçmeler; and the pink minibuses head south to Yalancı Bay. Destinations and fares (1.50-3TL) are posted on the windshield. Check with your hotel as to which *dolmuş* runs closest to the hotel, and flag them down at the designated bus stops. The Turunç *dolmuş* (6TL, 1 hour) and Datça minibus (14TL, 1.5 hours) depart from the *otogar*.

To explore destinations farther afield, such as Datça and the various coves around Marmaris, consider **renting a vehicle.** Hotel concierges can negotiate a cheaper rate for a Jeep, scooter, or car rental than the walk-up rates at vehicle rental companies. To avoid any misunderstandings, secure the model of the vehicle and its rate prior to delivery.

NEAR MARMARIS
Gökova and Akyaka

The traditional Ottoman town of **Gökova** (Heaven's Plain) is 35 kilometers north of Marmaris on the road to Muğla. Gökova is a small town with a shale beach and a river backed by towering forested cliffs. It's home to traditional Muğlan architecture, the wooden two-story arcaded townhomes made famous by the prize-winning Turkish architect Nail Çakırhan. Don't leave before venturing to nearby **Akyaka** to enjoy Halil Usta's tempting Aegean and seafood cuisine at **Halil'in Yeri** (İnişdibi Cd. 69, 0252/243-5622, 20TL), by the river. Blue Cruise veterans disembarking in Gökova head straight for this 40-year-old diner, also renowned for its farm-fresh breakfast.

Hısarönü Yarımadası (Hısarönü Peninsula)

On a day trip from Marmaris, head south toward the fiercely protected **Hisarönü Yarımadası;** the first stop is usually the sheltered bay of **İçmeler.** This revered mooring spot on the Blue Cruise is also a base for trekkers on the 20-kilometer trail that winds westward, and uphill, to the charming forest village of Değırmanyanı.

Two kilometers south of İçmeler is the village of **Turunç.** Thanks in part to its isolation, Turunç retains its rustic roots despite its increasing appeal with vacationers. The journey by car takes about 25 minutes from İçmeler and winds around the mountain separating the two attractive bays. Long transplanted from Marmaris, locals clad in traditional colorful şalvars (Anatolian pants) are here, hawking irresistible handmade goods like tatted lace, scented olive oil soaps, and some of the most fragrant honeys.

The road to the cape's heights runs 20 kilometers farther southwest to the fishing outpost of **Selimiye.** Perhaps the loveliest outpost on the peninsula, the economy of this Yörük (nomadic herder) settlement is in boat-building, fishing, and almond production. From here you can see the beauty of **Kameriye,** the small islet that bears the remains of a Greek monastery, just across the bay.

From Selimiye, either continue to the tip of the peninsula to the centuries-old traditional boat-building settlement of Bozburun (6 kilometers) or make your way back slowly toward **Orhaniye.** En route, get refreshed at the waterfall at **Turgutköy** before walking on Orhaniye's Kızkumu sandbar beach. You can rest and revive with a succulent fresh seafood meal at a restaurant by Orhaniye Bay.

ACCOMMODATIONS

The recently renovated, all-inclusive **Martı Resort** (İçmeler, 0252/455-3440, from 290TL pp) was the first resort in Turkey, opened in 1967. A collection of wooden and stone buildings meld into the surrounding pine woods with grounds that feature burbling fountains and verdant gardens extending down to a long blue-flag beach. The five-star property's 280 rooms and villas boast either a balcony, a French balcony, or a terrace; deluxe villas have the added luxury of a jetted tub and a kitchenette. It's a one-stop vacation spot, with a popular nightclub, a spa, a mini club for kids, six dining options, and bars. Don't leave without enjoying a drink at the Orient Bar with its panoramic view of the islands and the bay.

Farther from İçmeler in Kumlubuk village is **Villa Florya** (0252/476-7553, www.villaflorya.com, 300TL-850TL). The villas and rooms are situated high atop a limestone headland that bisects the three-kilometer sandy strip of Kumlubuk. To its rear, a cluster of farmhouses and inns dot a secluded and undeveloped bay. The three-story building boasts 13 colorfully stylish and roomy units, each with a splendid sea view. The beach welcomes with bright overstuffed cushions and a traditional Turkish restaurant.

Reşadiye Yarımadasi (Reşadiye Peninsula)

Anyone looking for yet another reason to leave the rowdiness of Marmaris behind need look no farther than the sinewy **Reşadiye Yarımadası.** Seemingly untouched by time and development, the peaceful cape, also called the Datça Peninsula, is actually the boundary between the Mediterranean and Aegean Seas. Aside from its geography, the cape is venerated throughout the country for its three B's: *balık* (fish), *badem* (almonds), and *bal* (honey). It's also known internationally for the historical vestiges at the ancient site of Knidos on the headland's tip.

The cape's natural wealth and its central location are why the Dorians colonized this spot. What little remains of **Knidos** (0252/726-1011, 8:30am-7pm, www.muze.gov.tr/knidos, 10TL) was, in fact, part of the Dorian Hexapolis—a federation of six ancient cities. The ancient Greek historian Strabo (64 BC-AD 24) described Knidos as "a city that was built for the most beautiful of goddesses, Aphrodite, on the most beautiful of peninsulas." Knidos gained prominence in the 4th century BC as a center for Doric art and culture. The stepped headland gives way to the site's double harbor: one in the Mediterranean and the other in the Aegean. An agora, two amphitheaters, a sundial, and an odeum as well as temples and sanctuaries honoring Dionysus, the Muses, and Apollo were all unearthed here. Most of the architectural wealth, mainly statues, has made its way to museums in London and the Vatican.

Adding to this coastal beauty is the main port town of **Datça** and a couple of nostalgic hamlets nearby. On the road south to Körmen from Datça (7 kilometers) is postcard-perfect **Eski Datça** (Old Datça). Its narrow cobblestone paths flanked by stone dwellings and colorful ornate doors decked in stunning bougainvillea hark back to decades past when this tiny hamlet was entirely populated by Greeks. Aside from the superb Greek architecture, one of the cape's best kept secrets, homemade silk needlework, can be purchased at souvenir shops in the Saturday street market. Regular *dolmuşlar* transport people the four kilometers to Eski Datça from the main square of Datça on Atatürk Caddesi (2.25TL, 15 minutes), just down from the harbor.

Travelers could easily spend a few days on the peninsula to visit Knidos, where legend says Aphrodite once swam; wander Eski Datça for an hour or two; or sunbathe on any of the day cruises that explore some of the 52 remote bays nearby. There is a **tourism office** (0252/712-3163) near the main square on Atatürk Caddesi, but it is rarely open, so it's best to ask your hotel for information about touring the region.

ACCOMMODATIONS

Should you choose to stay on the cape for dinner or the night, there's a handful of little-known oases that provide dining and lodging facilities. With tons of charm and Ottoman decorative ceilings and original furnishings is **Konak Tuncel Efe** (Atatürk Cd. 55, 0252/712-4488, www.konaktuncelefe.com, 300-350TL), a mansion right on the bay of Kumluk Beach in Datça with 20 uniquely decorated rooms. Ten of the rooms face the sea, with four attic style lodgings large enough to accommodate four people. The hotel and restaurant, managed by brother and sister duo, Serkan and Selma Ünal, is open year-round and is within five minutes' walk of the harbor.

Around from the bay but also on the waterfront in Datça is the friendly **Fuda Otel** (Turgut Dündar Cd. Hastane Yanı., 0252/712-8188, www.fudaotel.com, 160-180TL). Yalçın Kaya's family-run hotel features several simply decorated sea-facing rooms with large balconies perched above the Med. These light and bright rooms are near Turkey's first blue-flag beach, which meets stringent criteria for safety, cleanliness, and environmental management. Full-moon dinner parties at the hotel with local wine, meat, and fresh seafood will certainly satisfy; ask Yalçın about his special discounts for longer stays and shoulder seasons.

Way off the beaten track, but well worth its remoteness, is the ★ **Golden Key Bördübet** (Bördübet Mevkii, 0252/436-9230, www.bordubet.com.tr, from €300). This property, split by a rivulet that trickles through the surrounding pine forest, is 30 kilometers from Marmaris on lush grounds. Aside from a cantankerous family of geese and meandering tortoises, this chalet-like hotel is sublimely peaceful. The balconied rooms evoke a Zen-like atmosphere with decadently appointed custom-made country furnishings. The Golden Key's very private cove can be accessed by a free shuttle service, by bicycle, or via a pleasant 20-minute walk through the woods. The restaurant serves authentic, superior Turkish cuisine with a long wine list.

FOOD

Food prices seem to drop the moment you drive away from the tourism precinct of Marmaris. In Datça you can enjoy fish restaurants at the harbor and around Kumluk Beach, but also savor the sumptuous Turkish home-cooked food at **Zekeriya Sofrası** (Zekeriya's Table, Iskele Cd. 60, 0252/712-4303). It's ridiculously good and inexpensive, and you can take a peak in the kitchen to see what's cooking.

It's *salute* ("cheers" in Italian) down on Kumluk Beach as the wine and amazing Italian dishes pour out of the European chic **Mayistry** (Kumluk Yolu Sk. 14, 0252/712-2822, 20TL). The many delicious options include antipasto plates, gnocchi, gourmet pastas, and pizza. Buon appetito!

On the higher end in both location and price is the highly recommended **Culinarium** (Liman Mevkii, 0252/712-9770, www.culinarium-datca.com, 25TL), owned by husband and wife Faruk Dinç and Ulrike Böhmer-Dinç. Faruk utilizes the region's best produce to create perfectly presented meals consumed while gazing at the wonderful views from the harbor. Dine on juicy beef fillets and gourmet fish dishes, or order the duck à l'orange for two (125TL) a day ahead of dining to get the best dish in the house. Choose to sit downstairs in the cozy indoor dining saloon or the rooftop's contemporary open-air terrace. Advance reservations are advised.

GETTING THERE AND AROUND

Tickets for the long-distance **Datça Koop minibus** (14TL, 1.5 hours) are available from Pamukkale Turizm at the Marmaris *otogar* and depart every hour 6am-1pm daily, and then less often until 10pm. The service terminates at the Pamukkale Turizm office on Atatürk Caddesi in the heart of Datça. In a **private vehicle,** the 71 kilometers from Marmaris to Datça takes about an hour via the D400 highway. Keep the camera ready, as the first 30 kilometers offer some of the most stunning panoramic views of the islands and two peninsulas stretching out to the Mediterranean.

The 38-kilometer, 45-minute road from Datça to Knidos is basic, but picturesque. A *dolmuş* transfers Knidos explorers from Datça twice a day, at 10:30am and noon. **Boat cruises** (45TL) also depart from the Datça harbor, taking three hours to reach Knidos, passing the splendid coves of **Palamut Bükü, Ova Bükü, Hayıt Bükü,** and **Akvaryum** that line the peninsula's southern flank. These bays are remote enough to deter mass tourism and maintain some of the purest and bluest waters in the Mediterranean.

Dalyan

Another gem of the Mediterranean that's managing to maintain its rural charm is the old river town of Dalyan—a bastion of serenity in the sea of packaged-tourism resorts along the coast. Its appeal lies mostly around the spectacular wetlands of the Dalyan Çayı (Dalyan River), a natural channel connects Köyceğiz Lake in the north to the Mediterranean Sea in the south. The riverside cafés and hotels are the heart of Dalyan come summer, when the local population explodes with boatloads of tourists arriving from Marmaris and Fethiye. They come to gawk at the stunning temple tombs hewn from the steep rocks that rise from the marshes as well as the ruins of the antique Lycian port at Kaunos. There's also the open-air mud baths to the north and the thermal baths of Köyceğiz Lake farther upstream. Iztuzu Beach, the natural sandbar at the mouth of the Dalyan River, protecting it from the Mediterranean, is one of the few remaining nesting grounds for the graceful loggerhead turtle.

Dalyan actually owes its tourism popularity to this gentle endangered reptile, whose dwindling numbers earned the beach high protection status after a well-publicized dispute between developers and environmentalists in 1986. Thanks to international vigilance and the influence of local Yörük people, the village of Dalyan has also managed to retain its quaint hamlet feel, making this spot a great base from which to explore the region's ecotourism opportunities on foot, bike, kayak, Jeep, or boat.

SIGHTS

Most sights can be explored within a day by hopping on one of the boats awaiting passengers at Dalyan's riverside docks. Skip the tourist traps and opt for the ride offered by **Dalyan Deniz Tekne Kooperatifi** (0252/284-2094, www.dalyanteknekoop.com, 30TL, includes lunch). The excursion typically departs at 10:30am daily and visits the mud pools for an hour of beautification, followed by a swim at the Köyceğiz Lake, with two hours to laze on sandy Iztuzu Beach. The tour passes by the prominent Lycian rock tombs of Dalyan and allows guests an hour to roam the ancient ruins of Kaunos. Pack a sweater in addition to your swimsuit and sunscreen, as the late afternoon can be chilly.

A whole range of day and moonlight boat cruises (from €17), tours for canyoneering (€35), sea kayaking (€35), sea fishing (€22), trekking (€32), diving (€65), paragliding (€95), and go-karting (€24) can be booked through the reliable team at **Kaunos Tours** (Dalyan Main Square, 0252/284-2816, www.kaunostours.com). Drop in and see their range of tours and services, which also includes outings to the Köyceğiz Monday Market via riverboat (€15), airport transfers, and car rentals (from €30).

Kaunos

Facing Dalyan halfway along the river, ancient **Kaunos** (Caunos, 0252/614-1150, 8:30am-7pm daily Apr.-Oct., 8:30am-5pm daily Nov.-Mar., 10TL) was, according to the 5th-century-BC historian Herodotus, the capital of the region between Lycia and Caria. Its steep slopes were first settled by native Anatolians around 3000 BC, but Kaunos didn't gain prominence as a major trading port until the 6th century BC. More than 40 years of archaeological excavations have revealed a dual harbor, which included a pier for commerce (mainly salt and slaves) and another for military purposes.

According to the 1st-century-AD Roman poet Ovid, Kaunos's namesake founder was the son of Miletos and the water nymph Kyane who fell in love with his twin sister, Byblis. This illicit affair was the reason Kaunos fled home to found a city in a place far enough away that she would never find him. All the

Leisurely riverboat cruises pass the 2,400 year-old Kaunos Lycian tombs.

empires in Asia Major, from the early Persians (600 BC) and Carians to the Egyptians and finally to the Romans (AD 200), influenced Kaunian culture and architecture. But no building reflects the Lycians' strong Eastern influence more than the rock-cut tombs, which, unlike their Carian neighbors, who buried their dead communally outside town, were not only integrated in the city but also beautified it. Kaunos's fate, like a good portion of its neighbors along the coast, was sealed when its port finally silted up with sediment from the Dalyan River. The bubonic plague of the mid-5th century AD killed more than half of its inhabitants and essentially ended already ailing trade.

Tour boats moor at the edge of the 15-meter-wide Dalyan River at a wooden *dalyan* (fish weir) near Kaunos. Independent travelers have to take a rowboat (4TL), powered by some of Dalyan's strongest women, from the small wooden jetty at the end of Yalı Sokak. On reaching the other bank, walk through the makeshift café to find a paved road, and follow this for one kilometer past the cemetery, pomegranate orchards, and fruit-juice vendors to the entrance of the ruins. You'll also have closer views of the rock-cut tombs as you walk to the site, but they can only be admired from afar, as climbing the tombs is prohibited. The main entrance to Kaunos is located atop the **Palaestra Terrace.** The towering ruins of the **Roman Baths** are located on the right of the entrance, while the path leading left travels to the 6th-century **Domed Church** and the remains of the marble **Circular Building,** thought to be a measuring platform to assist in designing the cityscape against the prevailing coastal winds. Beyond these structures is the commanding entrance to the 5,000-seat **Theater of Kaunos,** rebuilt five times between the 4th century BC and the 3rd century AD. From here you can see the **Acropolis** high on the hill that holds the ruins of a defensive sea wall; the sea has retreated more than five kilometers south since Lycian sentries stood guard here. The high vantage points of the Palaestra Terrace provide spectacular views of the Dalyan delta and the lower city, which includes the **Agora,** a 3rd-century-BC **Fountain** with ancient text on its walls, four **Hellenic and Roman Temples,** and the **Harbor,** now on the edge of Sülüklü Gölü (Lake). The lower city is accessible via a steep rocky path next to the Roman Baths. The significant ruins throughout the site are all signposted with illustrations and historical information. Allow two to three hours to walk through the entire city and admire the views of the landscape.

Çandır Kültür Evi

One kilometer beyond the main entrance to Kaunos is the tiny village of Çandır, nestled in a valley among fruit orchards on Ala Gölü (Lake). Just off the main road is Mehmet Varol's beloved **Çandır Kültür Evi** (Culture House, 0252/284-3329, donation). Mehmet, a Karamanlı Yörük (nomadic people) and writer, has collected thousands of pieces celebrating the nomadic culture of his ancestors and displays them in the courtyard of the

Looking for Loggerheads

Mediterranean loggerhead sea turtles, known in Turkey by their scientific name *Caretta caretta*, are solitary creatures that swim great distances to spawn. Those that nest along Turkey's Mediterranean coast return annually to lay their clutches of 70-150 eggs in the same place where they were born. The species is endangered; only about 60,000 egg-laying females have survived the greatest threats—poachers and the frequent unintentional capture in the nets and longlines of the world's fisheries.

The most common turtle in the Mediterranean, the reddish-brown loggerhead, prefers pristine, empty, and quiet sandy beaches to lay its eggs. But so do tourists, and the rise in development to accommodate the needs of vacationers during the 1980s and 1990s encroached on a large part of the turtle's spawning beaches. To make matters worse, just a few soft-shelled hatchlings ever make it to the sea. The baby turtles that make it past the lizards, crabs, and seabirds are often eaten by fish. Only one or two of the hatchlings from each nest is expected to survive.

The species and its breeding grounds along the Mediterranean coast now enjoy protected status in Turkey. Stringent schedules restrict sunbathers and swimmers from beaches frequented by the loggerhead, usually from dusk to sunrise May-October. Because these turtles bury their eggs deep in the sand, local scientists place string cages over the buried nests, helping to protect the nests from accidental human destruction.

Mature loggerheads live an average of 30 years, but their life span can extend to 50 years. At about 120 kilograms, an adult turtle measures about 90 centimeters. They feed on bottom-dwelling invertebrates and sea mollusks, easily crushing their shells with their powerful jaws.

Although the laying grounds for the loggerheads are most of the Turquoise Coast, Dalyan remains the best place to view the turtles. İztuzu Beach, downriver from Dalyan and about 80 kilometers south of Marmaris, is a favorite location for loggerheads and where you'll find the **Kaptan June Sea Turtle Conservation Foundation.** A few makeshift shacks are here to nurse numerous injured sea turtles back to health, along with excellent information on Captain June's efforts to conserve Turkey's loggerhead population.

---

home where he was raised. Be sure to check out the collection of kilims (carpets) from local clans, a donkey saddle used for traditional weddings, cooking utensils that travel with the nomads, an intricate Ottoman ceremonial lavender blouse, and his wife's wedding dress, all displayed in the type of tent his nomadic people would live in. Mehmet speaks only Turkish, but an inventory of the collection is available in English. Simply point to the pieces of interest and Mehmet will uncover its location. Complete the visit by snacking on a *gözleme* (Turkish pancake) and fruit picked from the orchard. If you're lucky, a plump warm loaf of Yörük bread may be fresh from the oven to taste with organic honey. *Afiyet olsun* (bon appétit).

Iztuzu Beach

With the tall reeds rustling in the background and pristine waters backed by some of the lushest hills, Iztuzu Beach is one the prettiest of its kind in the region. Endangered loggerhead turtles (*Caretta caretta*) return annually to this seven-kilometer-long sandy strip where they were hatched, one of only three remaining nesting grounds for the air-breathing sea reptiles in Turkey. Iztuzu Beach became headline news in 1986 when conservationists successfully fought an attempt to develop a luxury resort on the site to protect the turtles, which lay their eggs after sunset May-September. Beach access is therefore restricted between 7pm and 8am to avoid interfering with the turtles. When the beach is open, chaise longues and parasols are rented at the beach (12TL), and concession stands remain open throughout the day.

A *dolmuş* (8TL round-trip) makes the 20-minute journey between Dalyan and the southeastern point of Iztuzu Beach every 30 to 60 minutes. Alternatively, water taxis (10TL) wind down the canal through the marshes to land on the western end of the beach.

KAPTAN JUNE SEA TURTLE CONSERVATION FOUNDATION

One of the conservationists responsible for preserving Iztuzu Beach for the loggerhead turtles is a British woman affectionately called Captain June. After winning the 1986 fight against development, June Haimoff set up the **Sea Turtle Conservation Foundation** in 2011 to continue conservation work and to treat injured turtles. At Captain June's hut on the southeast end of Iztuzu Beach, you can read about her environmental efforts in Dalyan, including the Propeller Guard Project, and visit the gentle giants of the sea being nursed back to health. Some of them have been rehabilitated for over two years. Captain June is also working to protect the freshwater Nile turtle and sweetgum trees (*Liquidambar orientalis*), also found in Dalyan. Entry to the center is free, but donations are appreciated.

Sultaniye Kaplıcaları (Sultaniye Hot Springs)

There are two major mud baths in Dalyan. The first are the open-air public mud baths on the riverbank close to Dalyan, often the first stop on riverboat day tours. But the baths most locals will recommend are the mud baths and hot springs of **Sultaniye Kaplıcaları** (0252/266-0077, 4TL), said to rid bather of wrinkles—or at least Cleopatra thought so. Located on Köyceğiz Gölü (Lake), with its blue-and-white domed thermal spa, the 40°C hot springs gush the most radioactive waters in Turkey, high in calcium, sulfur, iron, potassium, and salts said to allay afflictions from acne to rheumatism. The baths in Dalyan hark back to the Kaunian era and have since lured the likes of thespians Dustin Hoffman and Jack Nicholson, and even Britain's Prince Charles.

A *dolmuş* boat departs for Sultaniye Hot Springs from Dalyan at least hourly. The price will vary with the number of people aboard. Excursions to the hot springs are also included in package tours with **Kaunos Tours** (0252/284-2816, www.kaunostours.com).

NIGHTLIFE

Dalyan's nightlife is more laid-back than its neighbors in upbeat Marmaris and Fethiye, but it's possible to have a nice evening in peak summer on Maraş Caddesi, where quiet lounges, karaoke saloons, rock bars, and beer joints reel in a mature European crowd. When the bars call last drinks, head to **Club Sweet** (Maraş Cd. 71, cell tel. 0530/694-6696), where you can groove until sunrise on the banks of the Dalyan River. The club has been pumping out beats for 20 years and hosts a variety of theme parties and DJs that keep revelers entertained through the summer.

ACCOMMODATIONS

Thankfully, Dalyan managed to prevent the invasion of mass tourism and all-inclusive resorts, and increasingly stringent protectionist regulations imply that it'll be some time before any large development. Family-run inns still thrive here despite the arrival of more boutique options along the riverbank. Overall, there are accommodations for every budget. Note that summer is Dalyan's dreaded mosquito season. Ask hotel staff where to buy Sinkov, an effective bug repellent.

Campers and backpackers have dibs on prime real estate on the river overlooking the Lycian tombs at the rustic **Dalyan Camping** (Maras Cd. and Kaunos Sk., 0252/284-5316, www.dalyancamping.com, 20-300TL). This campground feels like a colorful village within the town with its quaint bungalows (2 people, 70TL), large air-conditioned bungalows (2-4 people, from 90TL) and villas (300TL) that line a large grassy area, perfect for pitching a tent under the trees (from 20TL). Set up the RV (40TL) and relax by the fireplace in the wood-cabin restaurant from October to December or, in summer, sit on the deck over the river and gaze at the river boats and cliff-side tombs with a drink from the bar.

The ★ **Dalyan Pansion** (Kaunos Sk. 34,

0252/284-2370, www.dalyanpansion.com, Apr.-Oct., from 100TL) is one of the top budget choices among the two dozen properties that line the river. This 14-room family-run inn boasts a garden shaded by old pine trees and a welcoming deck where breakfast is served right on the riverfront with views to the rock-cut tombs left by the Lycians. There is ample landscaped space for little ones to run around, and the adults can hang out in the hammock or join Dalyan's turtle population in a refreshing plunge in the river. The Nur family is happy to take care of all your travel needs during your stay, with moonlight cruises as well as day trips to Köyceğiz market every Monday.

Another inn with loads of charm near the center of town is the **Gül Rose Pension** (Caretta Sk., 0252/284-2467, www.dalyangulpansiyon.com, from 80TL). Sevdiye and Cemil Tekinay are the perfect hosts, with 20 rooms on three floors and a gorgeous rooftop terrace with views of the Lycian tombs. All rooms have a balcony and a small table and chairs, but the spacious attic rooms are the best. Rooms are simple but clean and decorated with wooden cottage-style furniture and fresh white linens. Guests will appreciate the proximity of the inn to the bars and restaurants of Maraş Caddesi, an easy two-minute walk.

The Osmanlı Hanı Apartments (Yılmazer Sk. 51, 0252/284-4498, www.ottomanretreat.com, from 205TL) is a stylish take on the old Selçuk and Ottoman *hans* of the Middle East where lodgings for travelers surround an *avlu* (central courtyard). The modern gray stone and white stucco Ottoman-inspired apartments have private patios, open-plan kitchens with dining areas, and separate bedrooms just one block from the Dalyan River. One-bedroom and two-bedroom apartments are available for self-catering travelers, who will also appreciate the large swimming pool and kiddie paddle pool in the expansive open garden. This oasis in the Turkish countryside is a 10-minute walk from the center of town along the tree-lined riverbank and is ideal for exploring the Dalyan area on an extended stay.

FOOD

Riverside dining has never been so good, particularly after sunset when the ancient cliff tombs are awash with mood lighting. The only problem is the relentless mosquitoes; bring along Sinkov bug repellent. Also note that most restaurants in Dalyan close from mid-November through mid-March.

Atay Dostlat Sofrası (Gürpınar Cd. 10, 0252/284-2156, 15TL) is one of the more unassuming restaurants opposite the main square that dishes out generous servings of delectable traditional Turkish fare. Pick from the affordable menu of pizzas, *pides* (gondola-shaped pizzas), and grilled meats or walk inside to point to dishes to mix and match a multiple-course meal with lentil soup, Turkish rice, moussaka, lamb casseroles, and *kuru fasulye* (white beans). This authentic setting, with dark-wood continental decor, looks more like a workers eatery, but it's ideal for enjoying a beer in the sun while people-watching on the square.

Venturing to Dalyan gives foodies the opportunity to try a seafood dish rarely seen in other regions of Turkey—*mavi yengeç* (blue crab). ★ **Ceyhan Restaurant** (0252/284-3977, 25TL), along the riverbank near the main square, is one of Dalyan's finest fish restaurants, offering a range of dishes with the delicate meat of this crustacean. At night the warm lighting on the rock tombs enhances the romantic ambiance of the waterfront deck; during the day diners can peer into the calm waters to spot freshwater Nile turtles and gray mullet. The menu boasts Turkish and seafood cuisine, including mezes, kebabs, and casseroles for those averse to seafood.

INFORMATION AND SERVICES

There is a **Tourist Information Office** (Main Square, 0252/284-4235, 8am-noon and 1pm-7pm Mon.-Fri. Nov.-Apr., 8am-noon and 1pm-5pm Mon.-Fri. May-Oct.) but you'll be lucky if it is open. **ATMs** line Maraş Caddesi near the central **PTT** (Beledeyi Sk. 12, 0252/284-2212, 8:30am-5:30pm Mon.-Sat.) post office.

GETTING THERE

There are no direct public transportation options to Dalyan from the regional **Dalaman Airport** (DLM, Dalaman Havalimanı, 0252/792-5291, www.dalaman.dhmi.gov.tr), 35 kilometers away. The **Havaş** (0252/792-5077, www.havas.com.tr, 15TL) shuttle bus to Marmaris drops passengers at Ortaca *otogar*, about 12 kilometers from the airport. From here, a *dolmuş* (4TL) departs every 30 minutes for Dalyan (16 kilometers). Alternatively, opt for a door-to-door **taxi** (70TL) between the airport and Dalyan, or arrange a transfer via your hotel or through **Kaunos Tours** (0252/284-2816, www.kaunostours.com).

Intercity coach companies do not have direct services to Dalyan. The only option is to travel to Ortaca *otogar* from major cities by coach or, if you're traveling from Marmaris (12TL, 70 minutes) or Fethiye (10TL, 1 hour), book your ticket with **Marmarıs Koop** (0252/413-5542, www.marmariskoop.com) or **Fethiye Seyahat** (0252/614-6785, www.fethiyeseyahat.com), which also stops at Ortaca *otogar*. From here catch a **cab** (45TL) to Dalyan or board the *dolmuş* that departs every 30 minutes and terminates in Dalyan's main square (4TL).

GETTING AROUND

Dalyan town is small enough to walk around, but the best way to reach surrounding attractions is via water taxi and *dolmuş* services run by local cooperatives. **Water taxis** depart at the riverside docks in front of the main square once a certain number of passengers have boarded, or if you have enough guests, consider chartering a private cruise. Prices for destinations are listed at the jetty. *Dolmuş* services for Köyçeğiz town (30 minutes), Iztuzu Beach (20 minutes), and Ortaca (15 minutes) depart from Dalyan's main square and cost 4TL one-way.

GÖCEK

The splendid Bay of Göcek, at the northern tip of the pine-clad Gulf of Fethiye, has long been the exclusive mooring station of the Mediterranean's moneyed mariners. The arrival of a couple of upscale holiday resorts transformed this superbly scenic fishing hamlet and its celebrated marina into a secluded playground for yachters. Thanks to strict laws regarding development, it seems that Göcek's allure won't be blemished any time soon by cookie-cutter resorts like its sister cities along the coast. Some call Göcek sophisticated; others call it pretentious, but either way this idyllic marina town is worth a visit to gain another perspective of the Turkish coast, where the likes of Rod Stewart, Shakira, Tina Turner, and Bruce Willis have all holidayed. The town is small enough to see in a couple of hours and is perfect for a lunchtime or dinnertime excursion from Dalyan or Fethiye. In peak summer, the marina is brimming with luxury boats and yachts.

Accommodations and Food

The sophisticated **D-Resort Göcek** (Cumhuriyet Mahallesi, 0252/661-0900, www.dresortgocek.com.tr, May-Oct., from €195) is swankiest hotel in the bay. In a previous incarnation was as the Swissôtel, one of the hotels to ignite Göcek's popularity. Today, the resort at the tip of the bay screams opulence with beige and white tones throughout, Turkish baths, the D-Spa, two world-class restaurants, and a private beach—the only one in town—with white sand imported from Egypt. You only need to spend a moment at the Sundowner restaurant, right on the waterfront, with the Mediterranean breeze in your hair to realize that Göcek is one of the best-kept secrets of luxury living on the Mediterranean coast.

Most of the exclusive hotels have their own restaurants, but if hunger strikes when you're out exploring the shops, stop by the popular **West Café and Bistro** (Seashore, 0252/645-2794, www.westcafegocek.net, 20TL) right by the marina. Locals and boaters flock here for a diverse menu of international cuisine and the collection of foreign newspapers. The large indoor-outdoor dining area has a laid-back feel surrounded by greenery and homey touches, but dining under the enormous rubber trees by the pedestrian thoroughfare is ideal for people-watching and checking out the assets out on the water.

Getting There and Around

Göcek is located just off the D400 highway between Dalaman Airport (23 kilometers) and Fethiye (30 kilometers). The **Fethiye Seyahat** (0252/614-6785, www.fethiyeseyahat.com) minibus and a *dolmuş* service from Fethiye's main *dolmuş* station takes passengers from Fethiye *otogar* to a bus stop on the D400, about one kilometer north of the Göcek marina (5TL, 30 minutes). Travelers from Ortaca and Marmaris *otogarlar* can also stop at the same bus stop with **Marmaris Koop** (0252/413-5542, www.marmariskoop.com). The marina, restaurants, and shopping precinct are neatly packed together, so walking around the town is a cinch.

Fethiye

Fethiye is picture-perfect with idyllic topography of piney mountains outlined by the most beautiful bays of beige sand and gleaming water. With this backdrop, places like Ölüdeniz—Turkey's spectacular Blue Lagoon—elicit inertia, while the rocky cliffs beyond and the offshore isles and relics of the Lycian era beg to be experienced and their ancient history explored.

Fethiye is tucked into the southeastern coast of its namesake bay, in the center of a region of abandoned villages, remnants of civilizations past, and unsurpassed vegetation that covers some of the eastern Mediterranean's sheerest cliffs. The town has a long history, but a massive earthquake in 1856 severely damaged its previous incarnation, the ancient Lycian port Telmessos, as did another powerful temblor in 1957. Today's Fethiye is modern and, aside from its pretty harbor sheltered by Şövalyie Adası (Chevalier Island) and a long coast, offers a handful of attractions amid plenty of tourist fare and shopping opportunities. If you happen to be in town on Tuesday, check out the fresh produce at the market that sprawls over the streets near Cahit Gündüz Caddesi.

Fethiye's environs were home to ancient Anatolians known as the Lycians, who left ruined cities, rock tombs, and other monuments. There's also the ghost town of old Kayaköy, an open-air museum in a lush valley eight kilometers south of Fethiye. And hidden 50 kilometers east among the cliffs along the coast are the rushing torrents of icy cold water that have cut the narrow Saklıkent Gorge. Also here is Turkey's tourism poster-child, Ölüdeniz, a sun-drenched cape that majestically halves the splendidly turquoise still waters of the Mediterranean's very own blue lagoon. Just before Kalkan and near Fethiye are the ancient ruins of the once grand cities of Xanthos and Letoön. With a private vehicle or by *dolmuş*, travelers can also venture to quaint villages like Üzümlü, which hosts its own mushroom festival every May.

This natural abundance laced with history makes the Fethiye region attractive, and it is one of the Blue Cruise's top destinations. Innumerable bays, most accessed only by sea, and the cliffs behind them host active pursuits like paragliding, diving, trekking, sea kayaking, and mountain-biking. For more recommendations and tips on Fethiye, visit **Turkey's for Life** (www.turkeysforlife.com), an informative website managed by Julie and Barry, a British couple who are local experts.

SIGHTS

Among the buildings saved from centuries of seismic calamities are a handful of monuments that attest to each of Fethiye's most illustrious

Fethiye

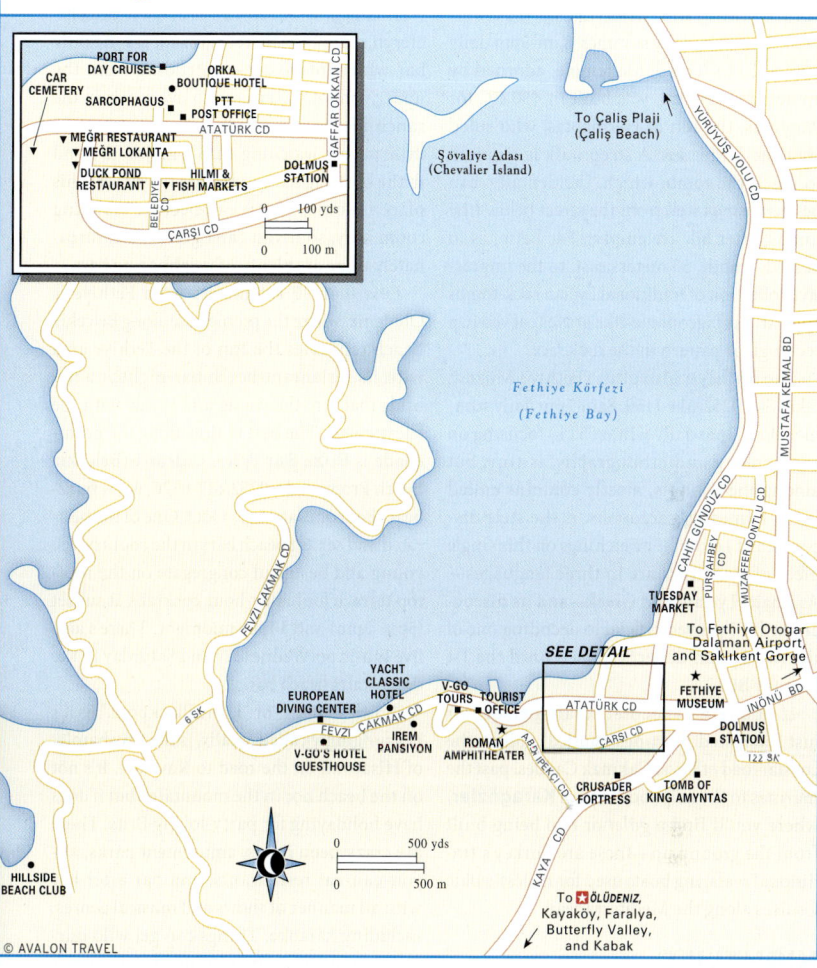

eras as the ancient town of Telmessos. Those arriving from the sea get an eyeful of the **Roman Amphitheater,** built in the early 2nd century BC to accommodate 5,000 spectators, while those passing between the PTT post office on Atatürk Caddesi and the harbor will see the impressive 2,500-year-old Lycian **Sarcophagus.** The two sides of its Gothic-style lid bear carvings of war scenes, while its two-story facade's etchings resemble square wooden joists. Long stripped of their contents, there are burial chambers like this one all over town, both in public and private spaces.

The hills that surround Fethiye have more historical sights. Behind the town is the **Crusader Fortress** (free), built by the Knights of St. John in the late 15th century atop what is thought to be the remains of a Hellenic acropolis. The fort stands where the city was first founded some 2,400 years ago; the walls surrounding it date from the 11th century.

Fethiye's heights are dotted with Lycian rock-cut tombs, the most impressive being the **Tomb of King Amyntas** (135 Sk., 0252/614-1150, 8am-7pm daily summer, 8am-5pm daily winter, 5TL). This Ionic temple, adorned by an arcaded portico, was built in 450 BC for Amyntas, the son of Hermapias, who ruled Hellenic Telmessos. A steep walk is required to reach the tomb, which, incidentally, can be seen just as well from the street below (the tombs, after all, are empty). Far better is to head downhill, 50 meters east, to the impressive collection of traditional Lycian rock-tombs and various pigeonhole-like graves carved in a rectangular pattern in the rock face.

The **Fethiye Museum** (Fethiye Müzesi, Okul Sk., 0252/614-1150, 8am-7pm daily summer, 8am-5pm daily winter, 5TL) focusing on archaeology and ethnography, is tiny, but among the exhibits, mostly columns culled from Telmessos's acropolis, is the stele discovered at Letoön. The etchings on this single piece of stonework are in three languages—Aramaic, Lycian, and Greek—and its discovery in 1973 proved crucial to decoding one of the two Lycian dialects spoken until the 1st century BC.

If you're a carpenter, craftsperson, or just interested in things nautical, follow the coastal road of Fevzi Çakmak Caddesi past the marinas to the neighborhood of **Karagözler,** where you'll find a *gül8t* or two being built from the ground up—these are Turkey's traditional seafaring boats used for majestic Blue Cruises along the Mediterranean.

NIGHTLIFE

Fethiye and a few nearby hamlets have a lively bar and nightclub scene worth checking out. Fethiye's old bazaar quarter has a good variety of restaurants and bars tucked in narrow lanes where merchants take advantage of the heavy foot traffic at night to sell home furnishings, designer knockoffs, and kitschy baubles until at least midnight. You'll find the heart of the evening entertainment in Fethiye town along Hamam Sokak, located behind the entrance to Fethiye's lukewarm touristy Turkish bath. Here you'll find the hip and happening granddaddy of the town's bar scene, **Car Cemetery** (Hamam Sk. 8, 0252/612-7872, www.carcemeterybar.org). Easily recognized, it's the only bar with vintage cars protruding from the upper windows. Rock out to live music in the ranch-like bar area indoors, or partake in a little people-watching with a mojito in hand in the bustling seating area on the street. This place is so popular it can become standing room only, so if you can't get a table, fortunately there are plenty of neighboring bars.

Less than 15 kilometers from Fethiye is Ölüdeniz, where the promenade along Belcekiz Beach replicates the fun of the Fethiye area with its restaurant-beach bar-nightclub hybrids that lure the young and rowdy with the latest music. The best option along the promenade is **Buzz Bar & Restaurant** (Belcekiz Beach Promenade, 0252/617-0526, www.buzzbeachbar.com, late Apr.-Oct.). One of the best-rated and sexiest beach bars in the country, the young and beautiful congregate on the rooftop terrace for happy-hour cocktails at sunset (5pm-8pm) and 10pm-midnight. There's also live music on Wednesday and Saturday in the downstairs beach bar.

"Little Britain" or "Little Blackpool," as it's begrudgingly called locally, is the tiny hamlet of Hisarönü on the road to Kayaköy. It's not on the beach nor in the mountains but it does have holidaying for party-loving Brits. There are crazy neon lights, amusement parks, all-you-can-eat restaurants, and bar after bar with all manner of shows and musical genres, including karaoke. Things can get wild during summer, especially at one of Hisarönü's most popular night spots, the **Time Out Bar** (Hisarönü, cell tel. 0553/505-0455), where bar staff dance to cheesy music to the howls of the crowd. It won't take long to realize that happy hour never ends in Hisarönü.

SPORTS AND RECREATION
Beaches

Ironic as it may seem, the nearest beach to Fethiye is named **Çalış** (work), five kilometers north of downtown along Fethiye Bay. It may have been named because its three-kilometer length makes a long walk. It actually comprises two strips of gray sand and pebbles: The touristy strip at Çalış gives way to the surf haven **Koca Çalış** at its northern tip. The main beach has the expected array of hotel resorts and shops touting sunscreen and beach balls, while the wind-battered Koca Çalış remains too wild for mass tourism and has a lovely unblemished natural setting where film director Sam Mendes shot part of Skyfall in 2012—specifically the scenes when James Bond is recuperating by the beach after plummeting from a rail bridge (Turkey's Varda Viaduct).

Çalış Beach can be reached from Fethiye in 35 minutes by the water taxi (5TL) that departs every half hour from Fethiye's marina. There's also the frequent *dolmuş* (2TL) that connects Çalış from Mustafa Kemal Bulvarı to the minibus station in 10 minutes, stopping in between to pick up passengers.

The pristine cove of **Gemiler Beach** is worth visiting after an outing to the museum-village of Kayaköy. Untouched by development, this beach boasts picturesque mountains in the distance and the possibility of swimming or boating to **Gemiler Adası** (Boat Island), also affectionately called Santa Claus Island because it's home to the ruins of the 1,300-year-old Byzantine **St. Nicholas Monastery** (8TL). The monastery is named after the benevolent saint who once lived on the Mediterranean Coast. Back on the beach you'll find a boat rental booth and a makeshift café known for its fish fare. To reach Gemiler Beach, board the Gemiler *dolmuş* (6TL) that departs every hour from Fethiye's smaller *dolmuş* station at the intersection of 97 and 101 Streets. The *dolmuş* winds through Hisarönü and Karaköy and terminates at the beach.

For immaculate sands worth the attention of sunbathing aficionados, plus an impromptu walk through Byzantine ruins, board the water taxi from Fethiye's marina to **Şövaliye Adası** (Chevalier Island). And don't forget the beach resort of **Belcekız Beach** and the Blue Lagoon nearby at **Ölüdeniz** for the best coastal scenery in the eastern Mediterranean.

Cruises

Join the hyped one-day **12-Island Tour** (around 50TL, lunch included) by booking through your hotel or visiting the Fethiye marina near Ataturk Caddesi to find a boat, group size, and program suited to you. This mini Blue Cruise can be booked the day before departure and includes 12 stops at six islands. Take a dip in the turquoise waters just off Yassicalar Adası (Flats Island) and Tersane Adası (Shipyard Island), and snorkel above the sunken Byzantine baths at Hamam Bay, a.k.a. Cleopatra's Bath. A therapeutic mud bath at Kızıl Ada (Red Island) is the last stop on the itinerary. Expect to pay a little more November-April as crowd dwindle. Cruises normally depart around 10am and return to Fethiye marina at 6pm.

If you'd like to extend the seagoing adventure beyond the eight hours of a day cruise, consider booking a short four-day, three-night version of what most consider the "best of" the Blue Cruises along the Turkish Coast. There's a panoply of travel agencies and even boat captains who offer this shortened option from Fethiye. The itinerary typically includes the ports of Ölüdeniz, Gemiler Island, and the formidable Patara Beach before switching for the land portion of the tour at Demre-Myra by bus to the last stop at Olympos. Among dozens of travel agencies with similar tours, the Turkish-Belgian owners of **V-GO** (Iskele Meydanı, below Dedeoğlu Hotel, Fethiye, 0252/612-2113, www.bluecruisesturkey.com) are multilingual and highly recommended by the national tourist association and some of the largest European tour operators. Cruises are priced at €229 pp July-September, €179 pp April-June and October-November. The fares include hotel transfers to the boat, all meals, harbor fees, and the use of snorkeling equipment. It does not cover drinks on board or tips for the crew, which, for good professional service, is normally 5TL per crew member per day per passenger.

Round-trip four-day, three-night sailing trips from Fethiye that explore the bays to Göcek are also available through the reputable and ecofriendly **Before Lunch Boast Cruises** (cell tel. 0535/636-0076, www.beforelunch.com, from €250 pp). The company prides itself on taking more time to explore the coves and islands with wind power (where possible) than their competitors, who motor around the coast to Olympos. The vessel, the *Ros*, named after the Australian seafarer who owns the business with Turkish skipper, Ahmet, carries 16 to 18 passengers and sails to a variety of bays depending on where the wind is, allowing for land based exploration of several temples and tombs. Evenings are spent moored in the calm waters of picturesque bays where you can tuck into delicious meals, all made on board, before enjoying a nightcap and falling asleep on deck. Itineraries, longer cruise programs, and private charters are available via the website.

Tours

There are numerous ways to enjoy the pine forests of Fethiye, its countryside, and its beautiful coast. **V-Go Tours** (Iskele Meydani, below Dedeoğlu Hotel, Fethiye, 0252/612-2113, www.bluecruisesturkey.com) organizes Blue Cruises and can also arrange land excursions. Wander through Fethiye's back mountain roads on three-hour horseback riding tours through the ghost town of Kayaköy (60TL) or above the astonishing Blue Lagoon of Ölüdeniz (60TL). If the lagoon impresses on horseback, try paragliding to see it from above, launching from the sheer 1,969-meter Mount Babadağ. The tour (180TL) includes an hour-long mini Jeep safari to reach Babadağ's summit from Ölüdeniz, followed by a 40-minute flight down to Belcekız Beach.

Jump aboard an open-top 4WD vehicle for an exhilarating **Jeep safari** (70TL, lunch included) on dirt roads in Fethiye's backcountry that begins with a stop at the rock temples at Tlos. After an open buffet feast at Yaka Park Trout Farm, the ride continues to Saklıkent Gorge, where the convoy will follow the river to Xanthos to explore the ruins. The excursion ends at Patara, one of Turkey's longest sandy beaches. It gets grimy, dusty, wet, and muddy; appropriate clothing is advised. For a slower pace, take the same route to the gorge with a bus instead of a Jeep (70TL, lunch included) or ride on a camel through the ghost town of Kayaköy (€20) before lunching on *gözleme* in the village.

There are also day tours farther afield to explore Pamukkale (110TL, 3 times per week), or sea kayaking over the sunken city of Kekova (€40). Check V-Go's website for more adventurous ideas, itineraries, and prices.

Water Sports
DIVING
There are more than 20 dive sites around the Gulf of Fethiye for scuba divers of any experience level. In fact, the area's underwater caves are world-famous for their unparalleled scenery. Thanks to shallow depths—less than 30 meters—and large entrances, daylight filters in easily. Colorful mollusks, large fish, and colonies of seahorses and shrimp by the million reside alongside 3,000-year-old amphorae littering the seabed. The latest star attraction is the 150-ton wreck of the *TCSG-121*, an old coast guard ship 27 meters down. Dives to Fethiye's underwater treasures and a range of scuba courses can be organized with **European Diving Center** (Fevzi Çakmak Cd. 133, Fethiye, 0252/614-9771, www.europeandivingcentre.com). This British-owned company was established in 1989 and is the most reputable diving center in Turkey, with branches in vacation destinations throughout the littoral.

SURFING
Of the handful of surfing schools that have opened, **Fethiye Surf Center** (0252/622-0753, www.fethiyesurfcenter.com), in Çalış Beach is the top pick. It's run by a trio of siblings including national kitesurfing champion Taner Aykurt. Instructors specialize in

windsurfing and kitesurfing, offering options like an hour-long introductory kitesurfing session (€35); a three-lesson basic windsurfing course (€70); and the advanced international VDWS license windsurfing course (€170). Board rental is also available by the hour (€12-20), day (€45-55), or week (€210). Fethiye Surf Center's on-site café, used in the filming of *Skyfall*, makes a great outing for the entire family, with comfy oversize cushions for lounging and great Turkish fare cooked by Taner's mom.

ACCOMMODATIONS

As the center of the region, Fethiye is hard to beat for accommodations if you want to be near transportation, entertainment, dining, and extensive shopping opportunities. The town is packed with activities and day trips, and as the departure point for the four-day must-do Blue Cruise, Fethiye offers the ideal base for a pleasingly varied vacation. While Caliş Beach offers a range of inns and B&Bs, hotels closer to the heart of town are better for making the most of the town's attractions and network of *dolmuş* services.

Dock your boat at the door and take a dip in your private jetted tub on the deck of your deluxe room at the ★ **Yacht Classic Hotel** (Fevzi Çakmak Cd. 24, 0252/612-5067, www.yachtclassichotel.com, from €150). Fethiye's first boutique hotel has been fully renovated with plush decor and the finest touches of gold, white, and blue throughout. In addition to the stunning deluxe rooms, five enormous villas, each with their own Turkish bath, and standard rooms with velvet tufted feature panels, have all attracted international guests to this bit of luxury on the marina. The contemporary setting combined with the hotel's inviting layered infinity pools have lured A-list celebrities, including Daniel Craig and Bond girl Bérénice Marlohe, who stayed here during the filming of *Skyfall* on Çalış Beach.

For friendly service and clean budget rooms, **Irem Pansiyon** (Fevzi Çakmak Cd. 45, 0252/614-3985, www.irempansiyon.com, from 60TL) is a pleasant family-run inn with 21 basic rooms for singles, couples, friends, and families, all within five minutes' walk of the old bazaar, restaurants, and bars. Six rooms have marina views and eight have a balcony, but the recently refurbished rooms are the nicest; these are found in the Polat block to the left of the entrance. Breakfast is served under a shaded patio overlooking the street with glimpses of the marina. It's one of the few inns in town that's open year-round.

Backpackers have an extravagant option in Fethiye. Weary travelers bound for a Blue Cruise or ongoing journey along the Mediterranean can stay at a guesthouse with harbor views and a pool at **V-Go's Hotel Guesthouse** (Fevzi Çakmak Cd. 109, 0252/612-5409, www.v-gohotel.com, from €13). With a coed dorm as well as single, double, and triple rooms (from €22), you won't get a better deal or nicer facilities if you're traveling on a budget. You can walk to town from here in 10 minutes or take the Karagözler *dolmuş* in less than five minutes. Barbecue is served every night for guests to make new friends, and remember, V-Go doubles as a booking agent for tours and boat cruises, so it's easy to organize your next adventure in Turkey.

Wake up to breakfast right on the marina in the heart of town at the **Orka Boutique Hotel** (Kordon Boyu Başlangıç Mevkii 1, 0252/614-5010, www.orkaboutique.com, from €85). Open year-round, this new hotel offers splashes of carnival colors in its restaurant and 23 stylish standard, deluxe, and superior rooms. Every room has complimentary tea and coffee and features bold artwork, light wooden floors, and crisp white linens. Given its proximity to the marina, the hotel is an ideal base for exploring Fethiye and is an easy five-minute walk to the *dolmuş* station and Fethiye Museum. Some of the best rooms offer views of the marina and surrounding islands.

One of Fethiye's most exclusive resort hotels, the remote all-inclusive ★ **Hillside Beach Club** (Kalemya Koyu, 4 kilometers west of Fethiye, 0252/614-8360, www.hillsidebeachclub.com, €299 pp full board) is run by Alarko Tourism Group, Turkey's premier developer. The upscale touch is pervasive here, with superior spa facilities, large rooms, and either a seaside terrace or balcony, making the most of this massive property's private cove. Oodles of sporting activities are included, including all the water activities like otherwise pricey sailing instruction, and there's a "festival" of food offered on buffet tables at the three restaurants and four bars on-site.

FOOD

Fethiye has its fair share of street food, from *dürüm* (wraps with meat) and *pide* to the highly popular corn doused in salted butter substitute. These might come in handy when enjoying a day at the beach or on a stroll, but it won't satisfy foodies who like to indulge in local culinary scenes. Most of the locals now head to the long stretch of restaurants that line the waterfront along Cahit Gündüz Caddesi. Anyone of these restaurants come highly recommended by the locals, but to make the most of the region, venture out of Fethiye toward Kayaköy or Ölüdeniz for the gourmet masters of the Fethiye area.

The quintessential dining experience in Fethiye is to wander over to the ★ **Fish Markets,** located a short walk from the old bazaar. The modern brown brick single-story *han*-like structure houses a large courtyard overflowing with farm-fresh produce, restaurants, and vendors peddling fresh fish. Octopus, calamari, sea bream, sea bass, shrimp, blue crab, and if the season is right, anchovies can all be bought from the market directly and then cooked by the chefs in the restaurants lining the courtyard. For 6TL, **Hilmi Seafood Restaurant** (0252/612-6242, www.hilmi.com.tr) will cook your fish to your liking and serve it with bread and a green salad. You can also choose a meal from their menu, but you can literally pick the catch of the day from the market yourself. Throughout the night, be entertained by musicians playing Turkish popular music. If they play at your table, you can wave them off before they get into a song; otherwise it's customary to tip them for their work.

Meğri Restaurant (40 Sk. 10, 0252/614-4046, www.megrirestaurant.com, 25TL) is a Fethiye staple. In the center of Fethiye, hidden in the streets of the bazaar, Meğri actually comprises three venues: a corner café, an unassuming traditional *lokanta* (diner), and the original restaurant, which consistently impresses. During the summer, the tables of this homely restaurant spill out into the square, creating a jolly atmosphere to enjoy a succulent and crafty mix of French, Mediterranean, and Turkish cuisine. The fish is the house specialty, with calamari headlining the menu. For affordable Turkish meat grills without the pomp, try the nearby **Meğri Lokanta** (Çarsi Cd. 26, 0252/614-4047, www.megrilokantasi.com, 25TL); you'll still get to enjoy dinner under the stars in the lively courtyard on summer evenings.

Northern Europeans are not the only ones to fly to Turkey for the country's therapeutic natural springs. The **Duck Pond Restaurant** (0252/614-7429, 20TL) in the old bazaar is a haven for migratory ducks and white geese who bath and nest in the bazaar's natural spring in summer. Meals are served by the pond, where a water fountain and the occasional round of quacking provide a pleasant location to dine on pizzas, seafood, and kebabs. The restaurant was opened in 1990, probably to capitalize on the natural entertainment that frequently draws a crowd, and has attracted a loyal following ever since. With the avian activity on the pond, it's ideal for families with children.

INFORMATION AND SERVICES

In Fethiye, the **Tourist Information Office** (0252/614-1527, 8am-noon and 1pm-6pm Mon.-Fri., 10am-4pm Sat.-Sun. summer, 8am-noon and 1pm-5pm Mon.-Fri. winter) is located across the marina next to the antique theater. The **PTT** (Atatürk Cd. 21, 0252/612-4446, 8:30am-5:30pm Mon.-Fri., 10am-3:30pm Sat.) post office, banks, ATMs, and currency exchange booths are also located on Atatürk Caddesi.

GETTING THERE
Air

Fethiye is served by the **Dalaman Airport** (DLM, Dalaman Havalimanı, 0252/792-5291, www.dalaman.dhmi.gov.tr), 55 kilometers northwest of town. Many airlines and charters serve Fethiye, including domestic carriers **Turkish Airlines** (0212/444-0849, www.turkishairlines.com), **Onur Air** (0850/210-6687, www.onurair.com.tr), and **Atlas Jet** (0850/222-0000, www.atlasjet.com). International carriers include **Pegasus Airlines** (0850/250-0737, www.flypgs.com), **Easyjet** (www.easyjet.com), and **Thomas Cook** (www.flythomascook.com).

Transferring to Fethiye from Dalaman is easy with the **Havaş** (0252/792-5077, www.havas.com.tr, 10TL) shuttle bus that waits for passengers just outside Dalaman Airport's terminal. The white Havaş buses are labeled with their terminus, and tickets are bought aboard the bus. Passengers for Fethiye (1 hour) are shuttled to the Fethiye *otogar*. A **taxi** from Dalaman Airport will set you back 140TL for door-to-door service, and vehicles can be rented from car-rental companies at the airport.

Bus

Pamukkale Turizm (0850/333-3535, www.pamukkale.com.tr) has various routes from Istanbul via Izmit (80TL, 13 hours) or through Bursa, İzmir, and Ortaca (14 hours), picking up passengers along the way. **Ulusoy** (444-1888, www.ulusoy.com.tr) also runs from Istanbul (12.5 hours, 75TL). Both companies connect from various cities around Turkey, but to connect from Denizli (from Pamukkale, 25TL, 3.5 hours), Bodrum (35TL, 4.5 hours), or Marmaris (20TL, 2.5 hours), you can take a minibus with either **Fethiye Seyahat** (0252/614-6785, www.fethiyeseyahat.com) or **Marmaris Koop** (0252/313-0835, www.marmariskoop.com). **Batı Antalya** (0242/836-3677, www.batiantalyatur.com.tr) minibuses travel between Fethiye and Antalya (35TL, 6.5 hours) along the coastal D400 highway, with pickups anywhere along the winding road and major stops at the *otogar* of Kalkan (13TL, 1.5 hours), Kaş (16TL, 2.5 hours), and Demre (22TL, 3.5 hours), as well as the highway minibus stations for transfers from Xanthos and Patara (10TL, 1 hour), and Olympos and Çıralı (32TL, 5.5 hours). There is also an express route from Antalya via the D350 highway, which shaves up to three hours off the journey with Batı Antalya and any of the major bus companies that run the Fethiye to Antalya route (25TL, 3.5 hours).

All intercity coaches terminate at the Fethiye *otogar,* which is about 1.5 kilometers east of the town center. To get closer to town, flag down the frequent Ölüdeniz and Kayaköy *dolmuş* services at the Carrefour supermarket on Ölüdeniz Caddesi in front of the *otogar*. These will stop at the *dolmuş* station (2TL) at the intersection of 97 and 101 Sokaklar (streets). The station is more like a bus stop on the side of the road, but nonetheless it's where you'll pick up the *dolmuşlar* for Fethiye and environs on your stay. A taxi will cost 15-20TL for the same route. There is also a larger *dolmuş* station on Çarşı Caddesi, but most visitors will not need to travel that far. One last tip: In summer, it pays to buy intercity coach and minibus tickets in advance to avoid travel delays. Fares for the *dolmuş* services, however, can be paid to the driver when you board.

Boat

Many travelers will arrive by boat, either aboard a Blue Cruise or via the daily ferry from the Greek island of **Rhodes** (Apr.-Oct., €60 day trip, €50 one-way, €75 open roundtrip). Tickets can be purchased from **Yeşil Dalyan Travel** (Adnan Menderes Blv. 45A, 0252/612-8686, www.yesildalyantravel.com). Voyages to Rhodes depart Fethiye harbor at 9am and 5pm daily, while ferries from Rhodes set sail at 8:30am and 4:30pm daily. Travelers are advised to be at the port an hour before departure to deal with passport formalities.

Car

You can reach Fethiye via the D400 highway from Datça in the west, passing all the major coastal towns on the Mediterranean to Antalya. From İzmir and Denizli in the north, follow the E87/D585 to the D350. The D350 is the express route between Antalya and Fethiye that connects to the D400 about 25 kilometers northeast of Fethiye.

GETTING AROUND
Car

A good way to explore the areas around Fethiye is to rent a car from **Circular Car Hire** (Atatürk Cd. 132/A, 0252/612-0751, www.circularcarhire.com.tr), which rents compact economy vehicles for as little as 73TL per day. You can also book a vehicle online with either **Avis** (www.avis.com) or **Hertz** (www.hertz.com) at Dalaman Airport.

Dolmuş

Fethiye's main *dolmuşlar* station is at the intersection of 97 and 101 Sokaklar near Fethiye's only mosque, between Atatürk Caddesi and Çarşı Caddesi. More like a bus stop than a station, the *dolmuşlar* here are clearly marked with their destinations and run regularly in summer between Fethiye and Çalış Beach (2TL, every 15 minutes), Ovacık/Hisarönü (3.50TL, every hour), Gemiler Beach (via Hisarönü and Kayaköy, 6TL, every hour), Kayaköy (via Hisarönü, 4.50TL, every 30 minutes), Ölüdeniz (5TL, every 30 minutes), and Faralya/Kabak (6.50TL, every 2 hours). Timetables are available from Ölüdeniz Minibus Cooperative (www.oludenizmnb.com). The Taşyaka-Karagözler *dolmuş* (2TL, every 10 minutes) that runs along the marina in Fethiye can be hailed along Atatürk Caddesi.

NEAR FETHIYE
Kayaköy

Romanticized in a mesmerizing novel, the village of Kayaköy was author Louis de Bernières's pick for an Anatolian locale for his 570-page best-seller *Birds without*

Panaghia Pyrgiotissa in Kayaköy

Wings, about an interethnic love affair during the decline of the Ottoman Empire and the ensuing World War I battle at Çanakkale. The historical epic's vivid descriptions of Eskibahçe—Kayaköy's fictitious name in the book—prepare the reader for the village's haunting scenery.

While the town was originally founded by the Lycians as Carmylessus, it wasn't until the 17th century that Greeks resettled it as Levissi. **Kayaköy** (0252/614-1150, 8:30am-6:30pm daily Apr.-Oct., 8:30am-5pm daily Nov.-Mar., 5TL) is the name of the ghost town today. It stands as a grim reminder of the impact of the population exchange between Greece and Turkey in 1923. After Turkey gained independence, both nations agreed to swap Turkey's Ottoman Orthodox Christians for Greece's Muslims. Scores of people were uprooted and "sent home" to a country most had never visited before. In the case of Levissi, its former Christian population of over 6,000 founded the town of Nea Levissi in the Athens suburbs. Most of their Muslim counterparts from

Greece shunned the inland village, by then renamed Kayaköy (Stone Village), to "repatriate" along the coast.

Kayaköy's 300 buildings were severely damaged during a series of earthquakes, most notably in 1957. The ghosts of churches, schools, workshops, and homes, all built in the 19th century, were left roofless and crumbling. A long-term restoration effort launched in 1988 by Turkey's Association of Travel Agencies and its Council of Architects is slowly returning the hillside village's single-story buildings back to a state worthy of exposition. Built to have spectacular views of the green valley below, the buildings have a golden glow as the sun sets. The town's two churches have long been denuded of their gilded icons but still retain enough of their original friezes and mosaic flooring to warrant a visit. The largest, Panaghia Pyrgiotissa, is in the village, while the church of Taksiyarhis is higher up on the slope.

ACCOMMODATIONS

"Kaya," as the locals call it, is a gorgeous setting for those who thrive on waking up to farm animals and fresh country air. Despite its proximity to bustling Hisarönü and Fethiye, Kaya is a serene place for a calm vacation, with plenty of B&Bs and hotels around the village; some require a car or *dolmuş* to access.

Delight in the serenity and laze by the pool at the recently opened **Han Pension** (Belen Cd. 3, 0252/618-0203, www.hancamping.com, 120TL), on a large farm with chickens and a rooster, just 10 minutes from the ghost town. Han has plenty of space for RVs and camping among the property's fruit trees. Decent-size wooden bungalows with private en suite baths and air-conditioning are available in the garden or, for bricks and mortar, rent a room in the rustic yet elegant village house. As the sun wakes the Kayaköy valley, breakfast is served in the garden, where nonguests can also partake in the restaurant's farm-fresh mezes and other local produce for lunch and dinner.

Kaya Cottages Kayaköy (Kayaköy, 0537/579-2050, www.kaya-cottages.co.uk, €335-480 per week) appeal to self-caterers, with two cottages that each accommodate up to four adults. Located two kilometers from the Kayaköy ruins, these once-crumbling farms were transformed into alluring vacation dens, including the addition of a pool. The larger unit, the Smokehouse, boasts high-beamed ceilings, a modern bath, a full kitchen, a balcony, and a patio.

FOOD

★ **Levissi Garden Winehouse & Restaurant** (Kayaköy, 0252/618-0173, www.levissigarden.com, 30TL), at the base of the ghost town, is set in the restored 400-year-old stone cottage of a Levissian town sheriff. The original stables now house a large cellar where more than 10,000 bottles of wines are stored; Greek lunch and dinner are served in the house. Start the night tasting a range of domestic wines in the cellar, then dine on the terrace on *kleftiko*—lamb shanks slow-cooked in a furnace. The views of the eerily lit-up ghost town are mesmerizing. Relax on a bean bag in the garden after dinner to polish off the bottle of wine, and try a fruity narghile (water pipe). Levissi provides complimentary transfers to your hotel.

Approaching Kaya on the old Fethiye-Kaya Road, look for the charming **Jazibe Restaurant** (Keçiler Köprüsür Yanı, 0252/618-0505, www.jazibe.com, 20TL), an old Greek stone farmhouse in a large garden. The kids can run around on the lawn while the adults work through a contemporary menu of excellent Mediterranean cuisine. Owned by Australian Lauren Gallagher, this shabby chic-meets-al fresco place serves brunch, lunch, and dinner. Some evenings Jazibe (meaning "charm") plays to its moniker when local musicians perform live acoustic sets that echo through the valley. It's definitely a place to recharge and seek a little serenity away from the hustle of the coastal towns nearby.

GETTING THERE

A *dolmuş* runs to Kayaköy from Fethiye (4.50TL, 8 kilometers) on the half hour during the summer, and almost hourly November-April. Visitors from Ölüdeniz can take the frequent *dolmuş* to Hisarönü (2.75TL, 4 kilometers) and transfer to the half-hourly *dolmuş* bound for Kaya (3TL, 5 kilometers). If **driving,** take the old Kaya Road behind the Crusader Fortress and wind you way over the hill to the valley (7 kilometers), or travel via the newer Fethiye-Ölüdeniz highway through Hisarönü before arriving in Kaya via Cumhuriyet Caddesi (15 kilometers).

Alternatively, **hikers** can take the **Likya Yolu** (Lycian Way, www.lycianway.com) behind Fethiye's fortress to hike nine kilometers over a large hill to Kayaköy. It's about two hours' walk, best done before 10am to avoid the blazing afternoon sun. Pack plenty of water and snacks, as there's nothing but pine forest, the old Kayaköy road, and panoramic views between the two towns.

★ Ölüdeniz

If heaven was an earthly place, one contender for its location is the beach at **Ölüdeniz** (Dead Sea). This large, splendid sandbar bisects the tiniest of the country's innumerable bays is reason enough to visit Turkey. If you pass through the party towns of Hisarönü and Ovacık (labeled "Ölüdeniz" on maps) and continue along the main road over the pine-covered mountains, the scenery eventually opens up to reveal the bluest water marked only by the long sandy arm of Belcekiz Beach, which shelters the calm turquoise waters of the all-natural Blue Lagoon.

On reaching the town, follow the crowd to **Belcekiz Plajı** (Belcekiz Beach), the landing site for daring paragliders who jump off the nearby summit of **Babadağ** (Father Mountain). This popular beach has hotels, resorts, restaurants, and a nascent entertainment scene in peak season that will rival anything in Fethiye. You'll also find many water and land-based tours and spectacular white sands lining iridescent waters that on occasion conjure a few waves for bodysurfing. A sun lounge and parasol can be rented for 12TL

Ölüdeniz lagoon

per day, but the high tide can make the water a little rough for children.

Follow the long arm of Belcekiz Beach to the northwest to find the protected pebble shoreline and calm water of the Blue Lagoon in the **Ölüdeniz Tabiat Parkı** (Ölüdeniz National Park, Ölüdeniz Cd., 8am-8pm daily, 6TL). Although it's protected from development, you'll find lounge chairs and parasols as well as water sports, food stands, toilets, and showers to ensure a pleasant day by the lagoon. Be sure to arrive before 10am to claim a waterside chair in this sun-kissed national park. Families love the entire region for its warmer waters, but the Lagoon's shallower sea makes it particularly irresistible for those with smaller children. A couple of beach clubs also line the lagoon for those who want a musical soundtrack to their sunbathing.

Ölüdeniz has a privately run **Tourism Development Cooperative** (Belcekiz promenade, 0252/617-0438, www.oludeniz.com.tr) that operates like a tourism information center, assisting travelers with queries about lodging, transportation, boat tours, beach clubs, and excursions around the Ölüdeniz and Fethiye area. Check their website for all the activities on offer along this heavenly coastline.

ACCOMMODATIONS AND FOOD

Be aware that some hotels and inns advertise their locations as Ölüdeniz, but in reality they are in Ovacık and Hisarönü, four kilometers up from the beach. Do confirm the lodging's location prior to booking. Unless you want to be immersed in British comforts, you could forgo these inland locations and head to the beach resorts and the handful of charming boutique hotels on Belcekiz Beach. Leading the pack is ★ **Jade Residence** (30 Sk. 1, 0252/617-0690, www.jade-residence.com, from €110). Undoubtedly named for the color of the sea just beyond this beachfront property, the Jade can't be beat for its friendly staff and calm clientele—no boisterous boppers here. The 10 spacious rooms add to the serenity of the place with tasteful furnishings and French windows overlooking a tropical garden. There is even a refreshing pool with an elegant timber deck to laze on when the beach gets too crowded or rough. At the end of the day, gaze at a breathtaking sunset over the rugged Fethiye landscape while savoring regional mezes and grilled fish on the terrace of the highly regarded beachfront on-site Jade Restaurant.

The all-inclusive **Club Belcekiz Beach** (Ölüdeniz, 0252/617-0077, www.belcekiz.com, from 475TL) provides a no-fuss vacation, particularly if you have kids in tow, at the very tip of Belcekiz Beach, with Babadağ looming in the background. Club Belcekiz Beach has a slew of guided outdoor trips organized daily as well as on-site facilities that include immense pools, a full range of spa treatments, a traditional hamam, and a Kids Club, all in a property with beautifully manicured gardens. Rooms have modern tiled baths and a patio or a balcony and are identical in either section of the hotel. There is also a nightclub with floor shows. Reserve far in advance.

LykiaWorld Ölüdeniz (0252/617-0400, www.libertyhotelslykia.com, from 725TL full board) is one of the largest all-inclusive holiday villages in Turkey, nestled in the pines three kilometers from Ölüdeniz. Lykia boasts 888 rooms and a 2.2-hectare Children's Paradise that includes a water park, eight swimming pools, water slides, and playgrounds such as Treasure Island, Pirate's Forest, and Hidden Caves, and even a beach. Meanwhile, parents can get massages at the hands of Balinese and Turkish specialists at the Manolya Spa. Lykia's beach is Ölüdeniz's best, and so are its host of outdoor activities, including mini golf, archery, tennis, diving, and a three-hole golf course. There are 19 pools on the premises and nine restaurants with widely varied cuisine.

If you're down on Belcekiz Beach when hunger strikes, pick up some cutlery at the casual California-themed **Help Bar & Lounge** (Belcekiz Beach promenade, 0252/617-0650, www.helpbeachlounge.com, 20TL). This place, the brainchild of Erkin Koçak, has colorful decor complete with a hot pink Apache Chevrolet as the DJ box. During the day, you can wander up from the beach to gorge on nachos, burgers, and pizza while reclining on the huge wooden couches, or at sunset savor a cool beverage and stuffed mussels as the last of the paragliders land in front of the restaurant. Food is served for breakfast, lunch, and dinner, and happy hours are 5pm-8pm and 10:30pm-midnight. Have a traditional, strawberry-infused, or mango-and-peach mojito—cheers!

GETTING THERE

The Ölüdeniz **dolmuş** (5TL, 15 kilometers) departs from Fethiye's *dolmuş* station at the intersection of 97 and 101 Streets every 30 minutes in high season, and at least twice hourly November-April. The *dolmuş* also passes by the Fethiye otogar (opposite Carrefour Supermarket), Hisarönü, and Ovacık, picking up and dropping off passengers anywhere along the route before terminating at Belcekiz Beach. **Driving** to Ölüdeniz

Faralya, Kelebek Vadisi, and Kabak Koyu

For an excursion that will satisfy ecotourists, outdoorsy types, and the spiritual, head to the ancient Lycian town of **Faralya,** high above the protected natural reserve of **Kelebek Vadisi** (Butterfly Valley). This stunningly beautiful dale, lined by pristine beaches, owes its name to the 35 species of butterflies that paint its skies June-September. In addition to the year-round presence of some 40 nocturnal moths, it's also a hatching spot for the rare cherry-red Jersey tiger butterfly in April-May. The heady scents emanating from the 350-meter-deep valley's abundant Mediterranean flora—mainly mint, jasmine, and thyme—is what draws these winged creatures.

Two trails lead from the beach of Butterfly Valley into the gorge. The path on the left is a 30-minute hike into the valley along a densely vegetated trail to a refreshing 60-meter-high waterfall (5TL). Take the rocky path to the right from the beach that leads uphill through the canyon to the headland where the village of Faralya sits. Be sure to follow the trail, part of the Lycian Way, which is marked. A sturdy rope has been added to help on the steeper and narrower inclines. This route to Faralya takes about an hour for adults with good mobility and fitness. Wear sturdy hiking shoes and bring water.

Farther along the Lycian Way, eight kilometers south of Faralya, is the up-and-coming free-spirited haven of **Kabak Koyu** (Kabak Cove), where the main attraction is pure solitude and serenity by the Mediterranean's azure waters. It's also an ideal spot for hikers, yoga enthusiasts, and people who enjoy the outdoors.

ACCOMMODATIONS

Faralya and Kabak barely had a road until a few years ago. Today, it's booming with New Age retreats, organic produce, and mediation and yoga sessions. One of the most popular lodgings is the summer home of the earth-friendly family who run the **Yuva Eco-Holiday Center** (Faralya, 0417/675-5888). *Yuva* translates as "den," which is what founder Atilla Sevilmiş created by offering soul-nurturing yoga, reflexology, and detox programs in a spectacular unblemished wilderness. With the turquoise sea just a hike away and traditional Turkish country cuisine, the seven-day program (all meals, activities, lodging, and group airport transfers included, €550 pp) helps reconnect you to yourself and to nature.

Mentioned in the writings of many journalists and bloggers is the iconic **George House** (Faralya, 0252/642-1102, www.georgehouse-faralya.com, 35TL-120TL). Established in 1995 about 300 meters above Butterfly Valley for environmentalists and hippies to thrive in nature, George House offers campsites, bungalows, dorms, tree houses, air-conditioned cabins, and even an apartment—some with private baths—for solo travelers, couples, friends, and families. Breakfast and dinner is included in the rates. Once you've hiked the valley and photographed the flora, fauna, and views, there's not much to do but lie by the pool, read a book, or share travel tales with other like-minded people.

GETTING THERE

Most Blue Cruises and boat cruises from Ölüdeniz stop at Butterfly Valley for a short time, but for an extended stay, board a **water taxi** (20TL round-trip, 30 minutes) that leaves from Belcekiz Beach six times daily June-September and three times daily (9:30am, 1pm, and 5pm) October-May. The return service departs from the valley at 11am, 2pm, and 6pm daily, more often in summer. Keep your ticket safe for your return trip. Alternatively, a *dolmuş* (6.50TL, 25 minutes) departs for Faralya and Kabak from Fethiye (32 kilometers) by way of Ölüdeniz every two hours daily in summer, less often in winter. Reaching Kabak requires a short hike downhill to your lodging. It's best to call your host

No trip to Turkey is complete without a Blue Cruise.

ahead of time so they can advise on how best to reach them.

Tlos and Saklıkent

The spectacular Lycian ruins of **Tlos** (Saklıkent Yolu, 0252/614-1150, 8:30am-8:30pm daily, 5TL) on Ak Dağı (White Mountain) and the cool cascading waters of the Saklıkent Gorge are within 15 kilometers of each other, making a combined visit to these attractions a pleasant day trip just 45 kilometers east of Fethiye. Begin the excursion with two hours exploring Tlos, one of Lycia's major cities. Tlos was also Lycia's oldest and most commanding city, thanks in part to its defensible location high above the Xanthos Valley. Inscriptions in recently unearthed Hittite records reveal that Tlos was founded well before 2000 BC. When the Hittite Empire was absorbed by the Lydians in the 12th century BC, Tlos became part of Lycia, and was absorbed by the Romans about a millennium later. According to archaeological excavations, Tlosians were divided into three *demes* (districts) named for Greek mythological heroes Bellerophon, Iobates, and Sarpedon. A Jewish populace made up yet another subdivision with its own political representatives. The city was an important bishopric under the Byzantines and, interestingly enough, one of the very few to thrive well into the 19th century under the Ottomans.

From its towering seat at the eastern end of the Xanthos Valley, Tlos flows down the cliff from the ancient city's acropolis. Tlos has remarkable examples of temple-like rock caves carved into the sheer northern cliff. Several freestanding sarcophagi nearby leave an indelible impression. All other ruins are from monuments dating to a mid-2nd-century AD reconstruction of the city, commissioned by two Roman philanthropists, following the massive earthquake of AD 141. If you can bypass the flocks of curious goats grazing around the entrance of the theater, you'll be able to read the ancient carvings on its stage walls. Much like other Hellenic arenas, this one was built on a slope with 34 rows of seats, supported by an intricate structure of underground vaults. Climbing farther up the hill leads to the city's walls, which were added by the Byzantines and later fortified by the Ottomans. These last occupiers added a large garrison in the late 14th century atop the summit to keep an eye on the wide Xanthos Valley below; February-May you can view hectares of blooming flora, including wild orchids and poppies.

Uphill from the ancient city of Tlos lies the traditional farming village of **Yakaköy,** an ideal lunchtime pit stop before hiking Saklıkent. Driving uphill through the village leads past a couple of Yaka Park signs, but ignore these; they're imposters trying to cash in on the **Original Yaka Parkı** (Yakaköyü, 0252/634-0391, 20TL) success. Instead, look for the stone archway and the sign for the original restaurant. This long-established restaurant is a trout farm whose owners have ingeniously opened an entertainment park and popular restaurant. The farm, with its old mill and trout pond, offers visitors an opportunity to play with a fish before ordering it for lunch. Also interesting is the bar, filled with tiny trout and cackling ducks. The staff will dare guests to try the on-site pool, but do so at your own risk, since it's filled with freezing runoff from Ak Dağı. Lounge on an oversize cushion on Yaka's soft rolling hill or pick one of the terrace tables shaded by adult pines. The mezes are great, but the crispy grilled trout is even better.

Rounding out the day trip to the ruins of Tlos is an exhilarating hiking expedition through **Saklıkent Gorge** (8:30am-9pm daily, 5.50TL May-Oct., free Nov.-Apr.), also known as the Canyon of the Hidden Valley. Eons of torrential runoff from Ak Dağı have formed a 500-meter-deep natural crevasse. Getting to the hiking section of the gorge is not for the faint-hearted; it requires wading through waist-high water from the Gökçesu and Ulupnar Rivers that merge on their way down from Baba Dağı. The canyon is so steep and narrow that the sun barely hits the stream, and the 18-kilometer-long gorge renders even mid-August temperatures chilly—so cold you'll go numb after just five minutes. You don't need to hike the whole gorge; there is the opportunity to wade the waters and hike one kilometer of the canyon with a recommended on-site guide (25TL) who knows the terrain well and will get you through part of the gorge and back safely. A word of warning, though: Wear clothing that you can get wet and walk in comfortably, and make sure personal belongings are stored in watertight bags. Plastic shoes that can grip slippery rocky surfaces are also a must and can be bought near the entrance. Also know that the rocky trail can get steep at times, requiring scooting on your backside to maneuver through the gorge. If this all sounds like too much, opt out of the hike and simply dangle your feet in the water after walking the narrow 150-meter-long catwalk attached to the gorge's cliff face. Alternatively, try river rafting (20TL, 30 minutes) near the **Saklıkent Gorge River Restaurant** (0252/659-0074, www.saklikentgorge.net, 15TL) across the river from the entrance. This eatery is a nice open-air place to savor traditional "wintery" oven-baked dishes, seated on mats around low tables with rushing water just an arm's length away. The restaurant's owners, the Ulutaş brothers, also own the nearby **River Bar and Tree Houses,** where 20-somethings hang out for days of endless fun in kayaks by daylight and narghile parties by night.

GETTING THERE

Tours by air-conditioned minibus or Jeep safari head daily for Saklıkent Gorge during summer, with stops at the ruins of Tlos and lunch at the Original Yaka Parkı. Book a tour by contacting one of Fethiye's premier travel agencies, **V-Go Tours** (Iskele Meydani, below Dedeoğlu Hotel, Fethiye, 0252/612-2113, www.bluecruisesturkey.com, 70TL). The excursion includes lunch and transfers as well as a guide and park entry fees.

For independent travelers, a *dolmuş* (10TL) leaves Fethiye's *dolmuş* station at the intersection of 97 and 101 Sokaklar every 15 minutes for the 42-kilometer drive east to Saklıkent (30 minutes). There is no scheduled *dolmuş* service to Tlos, but if you leave early, be on the lookout for enterprising *dolmuş* drivers who will sell day trips for small groups to Saklıkent (10-15TL pp) with stops at Tlos, the trout farms of Yaka Park, and a couple of their family-run businesses. It can be a pleasant surprise if you have the time to see all these sites, but the time to explore Tlos and Saklıkent is rushed. Clarify your itinerary before jumping aboard a *dolmuş*, as some visitors have been duped into a day trip rather than an express trip to the gorge.

Hiring a **car** and driving offers maximum flexibility in your itinerary. Follow the D400 highway toward Antalya and continue onto the D350 upon reaching the major junction with traffic lights. One kilometer after the junction, turn right onto the Tlos Saklıkent Yolu. The turnoff for Tlos and Yaka Park is on the left, eight kilometers farther; or continue along the Tlos Saklıkent Yolu for 12 kilometers to reach the doorstep of Saklıkent Gorge.

ruins of theater and sarcophagi in Xanthos

A *dolmuş* also connects Saklıkent from *otogarlar* in Kalkan (12.50TL, 40 kilometers) and Kaş (15TL, 60 kilometers).

★ Xanthos

As Lycia's oldest city, dating to the 8th century BC, and its capital, **Xanthos** (near Kınık village, 0242/845-4799, 9am-7pm daily Apr.-Oct., 8am-5pm daily Nov.-Mar., 10TL) played a major role as a center of culture and commerce for the Lycians as well as the Persians, Macedonians, Greeks, and Romans who later governed it and other cities in the Lycian League. The most striking events attesting to the fierce independence of the Lycians are two suicide missions undertaken by the men of Xanthos after killing their wives, children, and slaves and destroying their own acropolis in 540 BC and again in 42 BC to escape submission to the Persians and Brutus's Roman troops, respectively. Only the 80 families who were out of town during the onslaught survived when the Persians invaded. This UNESCO World Heritage site, along with 17 others around the valley, was discovered in 1838 by British archaeologist Charles Fellows, who dismantled the city and shipped its most stunning monuments to the British Museum in London a few years later.

Two of the site's most impressive monuments actually lie on the road to Xanthos from the greenhouse village of Kinik. The **Xanthos Gate,** which was built during the Hellenic era, is on the right, and to the left rises an arch dedicated to the Roman emperor Vespasian—a gift from the locals, largely in thanks for his philanthropic interest in Xanthos. Farther to the right are the sporadic remains of the magnificent **Nereids Monument;** the prized pieces are now on display in the 7th hall of the British Museum. Heading left toward the town's **Original Acropolis,** you'll see the 2nd-century-AD ruins of a **Roman Theater.** Next to it are Xanthos's most memorable monuments: the 5th-century BC **Harpies' Tomb** (named after the sirens who carried off the souls of the dead, whose images were carved on the original marble frieze that stood atop the column tomb); the **Lycian Tomb;** and the unique **Roman Pillar Tomb.** Farther back, the tall **Obelisk,** with its Greek and lengthy 250-line Lycian inscription, was critical in deciphering the enigmatic Lycian tongue. Across the road is the newer **Acropolis,** home to a **Byzantine Basilica,** whose only remains are its magnificent mosaic flooring. Nearby, an untended path follows an ancient wall to the **Necropolis.** Take the time to visit this often-overlooked site, where, through a scattering of sarcophagi, you'll find three intricately carved tombs: the 4th-century-BC Belly Dancer Sarcophagus, the Lion's Tomb, and a 2,400-year-old tower tomb.

GETTING THERE

The Antalya Batı **minibus** from Fethiye *otogar* travels into the town of Kınık (9TL, 1 hour). Tell the driver you're going to Xanthos, and they will stop at the correct spot, less than 200 meters from the entrance to the ruins, just outside the Kınık town center. ***Dolmuş*** services from Kalkan (3.50TL, 19 kilometers), and Kaş (7.50TL, 46 kilometers) also travel to Kınık. **Driving** to Xanthos requires drivers to leave the D400, where a brown sign marks the turnoff to the ruins.

Letoön

Just 10 kilometers south of Xanthos, the ancient city of **Letoön** (9am-7:30pm daily, 8TL) is a UNESCO World Heritage Site. It's situated in a fertile plain by a quiet farming village whose ravenous flocks of sheep are often grazing at the site. Rising from waterlogged terrain, the ruins are a refreshing escape during the hot summer months.

Xanthos and Letoön were closely linked, with the former governing the latter. Letoön was Lycia's center for a sacred cult and the realm's primary sanctuary. It was founded to honor the three main Lycian deities, Leto and her twin children Apollo and Artemis, whom she bore during a love affair with Zeus. The 4th- and 5th-century-BC temples honoring each deity stand at the center of the site. A frog-filled **Nymphaeum,** used for baptismal services, and a recently discovered mosaic floor delineate a 6th-century **Byzantine Basilica.**

GETTING THERE

Hikers will be happy to walk the distance from Xanthos and Letoön, via the Lycian Way, in this area a series of signposted roads. Alternatively, the Kumluova-Karadere **dolmuş** with the red front departs from Fethiye *dolmuş* station (7TL) every 20 minutes. Tell the driver your destination, and they'll drop you about one kilometer from Letoön's entrance. Follow the signs to Letoön. A brown tourism signpost shows the turnoff to the ruins for drivers along the D400.

★ Patara

Patara (0242/843-5018, 9:30am-7pm daily, 5TL) was Lycia's main port city until its location at the mouth of the Xanthos River silted up and its marshes became infested with malaria-carrying mosquitoes. Today, Patara is a national park noted for its rich birdlife and stunning 12-kilometer-long **Patara Beach,** one of the world's top beaches.

Much of Patara's old city remains undiscovered, buried in the shifting sand brought by fierce winds. According to legend, Patara was founded by Patarus, son of Apollo, sometime in the middle of the 1st millennium BC. It was noted in antiquity for its temple and oracle of Apollo, second only to that of Delphi in Greece. Patara's high priestess interpreted omens only during the six months of summer, since Apollo is thought to have spent summer here and the rest of his time at Delphi.

Patara's more recent fame, however, is as the birthplace of Saint Nicholas, bishop of Myra—a.k.a. Santa Claus. Saint Paul stopped here during his second missionary journey in AD 49-51. He helped launch Patara as an important Christian center, but by 600, continual pirate attacks, the silting up of its harbor, and malaria virtually decimated the city.

Through ongoing excavations of layers of sand, parts of the ancient city beyond Patara's imposing main gate—the triple-arched **Triumphal Gate of Modestus** (1st century AD)—are being discovered. One of these discoveries is the Lycian League's **Bouleuterion** (senate), whose rows of seats form a semicircle much like the arrangement found in the U.S. Congress. Another recent find is believed to be the world's oldest lighthouse.

Patara Beach is located at the end of the road to the ruins, about one kilometer south of the entrance. At 50 meters wide and 12 kilometers long, this sandy strip is by far the country's longest and one of the most beautiful. The only drawback is that the dark sand can get scorching hot in the summer, and the absence of trees means there is no shade. Thankfully, you'll find beach umbrellas and sun lounges (10TL pp) and a restaurant offering refreshments. Also note that Patara Beach is a nesting ground for sea turtles; it closes at dusk when the reptiles begin their approach.

The sleepy village of Gelemiş—a haven of family-run inns, ideal for budget travelers who want to laze by the beach—is three kilometers from the beach, halfway between the D400 highway and the entrance to the ruins.

GETTING THERE

Antalya Batı (0242/331-4081, www.batiantalyatur.net) minibuses that depart the *otogar* of Fethiye (10TL, 75 minutes), Kalkan (6TL, 20 minutes), and Kaş (7TL, 1.5 hours) every 90 minutes shuttle visitors to a stop on the D400 near the turn off to Patara. A half-hourly local *dolmuş* also travels from Kalkan (6TL, 18 kilometers) and Kaş (8TL, 45 kilometers), also stopping on the highway where passengers transfer to another *servis dolmuş* that connects the D400 to Gelemiş, the ruins, and Patara Beach. Passengers are expected the pay the 5TL pp entry to Patara in addition to the transportation fares. **Drivers** will find the exit to Patara less than 10 kilometers from the turnoffs for Xanthos and Letoön along the D400.

Kalkan

Reminiscent of the Italian Riviera, Kalkan has gone through more transformations than any other resort along the coast. Its classical Greek Ottoman charm was all the rage with glitzy Turks looking for a remote getaway in the 1960s. Word got around, and by the mid-1980s wealthy Europeans were arriving en masse. The construction of a tiny yacht marina followed, and unfortunately, so did development. But thanks to lack of space in Kalkan town, these sprawling holiday complexes have been built on the outskirts. Today, German and British expatriates, particularly retirees, are the majority of the high season population, which doubles the winter population of 3,200. British travelers rule in summer; in fact, English may be the only language you hear all day. The locals, who earn their livelihoods mainly from tourism, don't seem to mind.

The seaside village sprawls steeply downward from the main D400 highway onto rows of street-side and rooftop terraces that overlook a diminutive postcard-worthy harbor. Along the streets are the traditional Kalkan houses: two-story whitewashed stone town houses with contrasting woodwork on the shutters and balconies. During the high season, the narrow lanes are abuzz with vendors touting silver trinkets and the colorful kilims of the region.

Kalkan became important as a trading port in the mid-19th century, with maritime trade surpassing Fethiye and Antalya. Then known as Kalamaki, the town was both Greek and Turkish and thrived from the trade of regionally produced charcoal, silk, olive oil, cotton, and wine as well as lumber from the cedar and pine forests. In the population exchange of 1923, Kalkan's Greeks were moved to the nearby Greek island of Meis (Castellorizo).

While Kalkan's mixed Bohemian-upmarket feel offers loads of romanticism, its proximity to a host of historical sites and stunning beauty also makes it a convenient base on the western Mediterranean coast. For more information on hotels and activities, visit Kalkan's exhaustive website at www.kalkan.org.tr.

NIGHTLIFE

Kalkan twinkles come nighttime with lights around its harbor and in its web of streets, with atmospheric rooftop cafés and bars on Greek houses. You'll find the odd Turkish-themed clubs with belly dancers, gypsy bands, and folkloric music as well as narghile cafés and even bars where you can watch sports—like **Moonlight Café & Bar** (top of Mustafa Kocakaya Cd., 0242/844-3043) where there's a view of the Mediterranean and live soccer that always draw a crowd. The excitement extends to the breezy harbor front, where some upscale restaurants often turn into a dancing fest well into the evening.

Among the bars located on or near the marina are a couple of standouts. House music, cocktails, and VIP treatment (with a VIP card easily obtained from the staff) can be found halfway up Mustafa Kocakaya Caddesi at **Mojito Lounge and Club** (0242/844-3985). This is where the party people mingle in the club's white überchic lounges until late. Adjacent to the harbor is the more chilled out **Sandal Bar** (Iskele Sk. 0242/844-2453, www.sandalinkalkan.com). With its limestone Roman arches and tropical palms, it offers a romantic location with plenty of seating looking out to the harbor. Follow the wafting aroma of waffles cooking on the marina to find **Fener Café Bistro** (0242/844-3752), sometimes referred to as Lighthouse Bar. It's perfect for sunset beverages while the kids tuck into an ice cream. Check out the beach and people-watch as you sit in a *köşk* (elevated covered Turkish lounge). But like any summer town in Turkey, the most popular night venue can be determined by who's in town or what event is on. Before planning a big night out, ask the locals where the place to be is this summer. Kalkan is small enough to walk to any place they recommend.

BEACHES

Kalkan is one of the few Mediterranean enclaves with an attractive public beach right near the town's action. Located just east of the marina, the white pebbles of the town's blue-flag beach illuminate the calm, clear water that's pleasant for swimming and snorkeling. Umbrellas and parasols are available to rent, or laze on your own towel by the shore.

Much like Bodrum in the west, visitors here revel in the Mediterranean beach clubs to soak up the Turkish summer sun and partake in some adrenaline-pumping water activities. Most do not actually have a beach, but rather have piers over rocky outcrops with ladders leading directly to the sea. Facing the sunset over western Turkey, one kilometer from town is the **Palm Beach Club** (Komurluk Mevkii, 0242/844-3987, www.palmbeachkalkan.com). It's one of seven or so beach clubs in town that provide free water taxis from the Kalkan lighthouse, transfers to and from your hotel, restaurant and bar facilities, and activities for the whole family. The sun beds sit atop a wooden pier over the water, so you won't have to venture too far to cool down. It's one of the more family-friendly clubs, with trampolines, a private bay for kids, and loads of water sports such as waterskiing, Jet Skis, and wave skiing. On arrival, a tab is set up to pay for your activities, food, and sun beds (10TL pp).

Adults and couples may prefer the Likya Residence Hotel and Spa's more sophisticated **Yali Beach Club** (Sumbul Sk. 1, 0242/844-1055, www.likyakalkan.com). The club, atop a craggy bay, is just five minutes down from the hotel and offers top-quality cuisine from its restaurant and bar, stepped timber decks adorned with white umbrellas that shade 60 comfortable day beds, and a chilled-out Ottoman lounge where you can read a book and breeze through the cocktail menu. Expect to pay a little more for food and drinks, but the day beds are similar in price to other clubs on the coast (10TL for nonguests).

Beyond the beach clubs of Kalkan, travelers can also lay down a towel at Patara and Kaputaş Beaches farther out. Both stretches of sand have plenty of sun and mild surf on the open sea, just 18 kilometers west and 10 kilometers east of Kalkan, respectively.

ACCOMMODATIONS

Kalkan offers a wide array of inexpensive, romantic B&Bs and self-catering villas on its heights or just outside town. Those listed here are far enough from the marina's high-decibel-pounding cafés and bars to ensure a restful stay. And with less than 15 units to rent, most still offer facilities, including a pool and at least an on-site café, for a fraction of the price of hotels elsewhere along the coast. If you prefer the grand all-inclusive resort hotels, look in Kalamar Bay, accessible through a convenient water taxi service. One-, two-, and three-bedroom apartments, some with private pools, can be viewed and booked through UK-based websites like www.ownersdirect.co.uk.

At the very top of one of Kalkan's narrow lanes is ★ **Türk Evi** (Yalıboyu Mah., 0242/844-3129, www.kalkanturkevi.com, €50-60). The Turkish-Norwegian owners have imbued this family-friendly B&B with the charm and warmth typical of Turkish hospitality. Share truly memorable complimentary breakfasts or mingle with other guests over a barbecue dinner on the rooftop terrace with views to the Mediterranean. Türk Evi features nine large rooms, each with their own style and color-coded decor reflecting the comforts of a humble Turkish manor. Five of the rooms are air-conditioned, and evening meals can be prepared on request.

The cleanest and brightest inn in town goes to **Kleo Pension** (Yalıboyu Mah., 0242/844-1633, www.kleopension.com, €55). Tucked away on a side street just up from the harbor, this inn has received rave reviews for its location, friendly service, and five spacious suites that have wooden floorboards and a small lounge that steps down to the bedroom. The rooftop terrace is where breakfast is served a short distance from the glistening Mediterranean. This inn has such style and space it's in a league of its own for budget accommodations in town.

Family suites, apartments, seaside rooms, and sumptuous evening meals dished out from a rooftop restaurant are on offer at **Zinbad Hotel** (Mustafa Kocakaya Cd. 26, 0242/844-3475, www.zinbadhotel.com, from 150TL). Established in 1985, Zinbad is one of oldest in town and is open year-round. Rooms are tastefully decorated with dark wooden furniture and crisp white linens, some with balconies or sea views. Guests will appreciate the hotel's proximity to the restaurants and narrow shopping lanes that stretch up from the harbor. Breakfast is served in the rooftop restaurant, and a meal here as the sun sets over the sea is a truly memorable experience.

A commanding presence along Kalkan's diminutive gulf is the opulent **Likya Residence** (Sumbul Sk. 1, 0242/844-1055, www.likyakalkan.com, from 515TL), limited to guests over age 16 and with 34 stunning rooms, three pools, a world-class restaurant, several bars, and a day spa that offers a full range of therapies. There is also an on-site travel agency. Deluxe and master deluxe rooms have natural stone walls complementing blue hues and white wooden furniture. Rooms on the first floor have large terraces with sun lounges, while those on the second floor boast balconies with views to the bay or the sea. Check into room 100 and you'll have private access to the infinity pool via your private terrace. Luxury villas are also available nearby.

FOOD

Kalkan boasts more upmarket restaurants and bars per capita than any other resort on Turkey's Mediterranean coast, and most of the mid-size and larger B&Bs offer sumptuous Mediterranean cuisine at their restaurants, which are open to nonguests. But since chefs only buy food based on reservations, you'll need to reserve at least a day in advance. Note that most restaurants close from late October until early April.

Local restaurateurs have been quick to set meal prices according to what their predominantly European guests can afford. This means you'll be paying a lot more to eat in the village than almost anywhere else along the coast. One affordable Turkish-grill restaurant is **Hunkar Ocakbaşı** (Şehitler Cd. 38/E, 0242/844-2077, 12TL), with simple, delectable meals that won't ruin your budget. An *ocakbaşı* simply means a restaurant that offers meals grilled over a charcoal fire, so expect various kebabs from around the country, *lahmacun* (Turkish pizza) with minced lamb, parsley, onion, and chili, and *pides*—practically any Turkish dish that's cooked over flame.

A great choice for a sophisticated informal dining experience is ★ **Agora Restaurant** (halfway up Mustafa Kocakaya Cd., 0242/844-3716, www.kalkanagorarestaurant.com, 25TL). It's Kalkan's friendliest restaurant and gaining popularity for abundant portions and comical waiters with great customer service. Decked out in elegant white wooden furniture, the restaurant is on three floors, including a terrace with plenty of space with views of the Mediterranean. The generous menu caters to all tastes with international dishes like paella and steaks embellished with French sauces, contemporary entrées such as apricot chicken with avocado, and flavorsome mezes, kebabs, and the catch of the day.

Korsan Fish Terrace (Atatürk Cd., 0242/844-3076, www.korsankalkan.com, 25TL) is one of Kalkan's most celebrated fine-dining establishment for fish. Since his father opened the original restaurant in 1979, owner Uluç Bilgütay and his wife Claire have added this fish restaurant to please both fish fans and carnivores. The original **Korsan Meze** (0242/844-3622) is located in front of its little sister restaurant and offers tantalizingly modern versions of its namesake dishes. Both have stunning views of the Mediterranean and exquisite food, with prices to match. Incidentally, *korsan* means "pirate," so find a bounty of meticulously sautéed seafood at Fish Terrace or dine on contemporary East-meets-West fare built on traditional recipes at Meze.

Touting "something different with exclusive wine and exclusive food" is **White Table** (Atatürk Cd. 13, 0242/844-2926, 20TL). With its chic white decor and relaxed ambiance, this small eatery just a street up from the marina produces meals unlike any other restaurant in Turkey. Gourmet burgers like the curry apple chicken and smoked basil beef burgers team up with eggplant and mint bruschetta. The entrées and pastas are just as intriguing thanks to the owners' creative flair for mastering contemporary fusion from traditional recipes. If the mystery of the food isn't alluring enough, know that the wine list is one of the most affordable in town.

In the tiny village of **Islamlar,** nestled high on a mountainside eight kilometers from Kalkan, is **Mahmut'un Yeri** (Mahmut's Place, 0242/838-6344, 20TL). Mahmut Arga's restaurant was the first to start the trend of trout diners in the village that's situated on the freshwater İslamlar Spring. With splendid views of the turquoise Mediterranean in the distance, guests can dine on the region's peppery arugula, pan-fried halloumi cheese, and soft eggplant salad over a glass of the local vintage before an entrée of perfectly grilled trout. A three-course set menu (€18 pp) is available, or choose items such as the slow-roasted lamb. Mahmut's is the first restaurant on the right as you enter the village.

INFORMATION AND SERVICES

Kalkan does not have a tourism office; instead, the municipality runs a website (www.kalkan.org.tr) that features exhaustive information about the town. The **PTT** (0242/844-3004, 8:30am-5:30pm, Mon.-Fri.) post office, banks, and ATMs are located on Süleyman Yilmaz Caddesi.

GETTING THERE AND AROUND

Kalkan is served by the **Dalaman Airport** (DLM, Dalaman Havalimanı, 0252/792-5291, www.dalaman.dhmi.gov.tr), 120 kilometers southwest of town. Transfers are available by **taxi** (180TL one-way, 250TL round-trip), but a less costly option is to take the one-hour **Havaş** (0252/792-5077, www.havas.com.tr, 10TL) shuttle bus to Fethiye *otogar*, and from there take the 90-minute **Antalya Batı** (0242/331-4081, www.batiantalyatur.net, 13TL) minibus to the Kalkan *otogar*. The minibuses depart every 90 minutes and travel along the D400 highway, stopping for five minutes at Kalkan *otogar* (at the top of the hill) and every major coastal town to Antalya (28TL, 5 hours). The smaller *dolmuş* service also connects to Kalkan from Kaş (6TL, 28 kilometers) and Patara (6TL, 18 kilometers) every 30 minutes. Night coaches direct from Istanbul (80TL, 13.5 hours) and İzmir (50TL, 7 hours) are also available through **Pamukkale Turizm** (0850/333-3535, www.pamukkale.com.tr) and **Kamil Koç** (444-0562, www.kamilkoc.com.tr).

Once in Kalkan, your feet can do most of the work up and down the steep hill connecting the *otogar* to the harbor. Consider staying by the harbor to avoid the ominous hike uphill, or hire a car (€32 per day) with one of the many travel agencies peddling the usual tour and airport transfers (€73 to Dalaman Airport), Jeep safaris of Saklıkent (€36), paragliding above Kaş (€120), and water-based activities.

KAPUTAŞ

Most visitors to Kalkan and Kaş venture to Kaputaş, a thimble-size beach dusted with sand and pebbles and backed by a massive gorge, just 10 kilometers east of Kalkan and 18 kilometers west of Kaş along the D400. In peak season sun beds and parasols are available to rent, and the local women will gladly sell you affordable *gözleme* packed with white cheese and spinach. About 500 meters east of the beach is **Mavi Mağara** (Blue Cave), named for its luminescent interior. The cave is on the open sea that laps onto a jagged rock face, and there are no lifeguards, so proceed with caution.

Getting There

The narrow enclave of Kaputaş sits below a section of the D400 highway and can be reached by local ***dolmuş*** from Patara Beach (6TL, 28 kilometers) and the *otogarlar* of Kalkan (3TL, 10 kilometers) and Kaş (5TL, 18 kilometers) every 30 minutes. It drops passengers off by the highway railing above Kaputaş, which leads down to the beach via a steep stairway.

Kaş

Backed by lofty pine-clad mountains, Kaş sits on a small bay within sight of the small Greek island of Meis (Castellorizo). Like Kalkan to the northwest, Kaş was a small fishing enclave with whitewashed stone houses lining the cobblestone lanes that jut from a small harbor. But unlike its neighbor, Kaş maintained most of its original charm and relaxed atmosphere thanks to domestic tourism and the absence of major European package-tour operators. There are no mammoth holiday resorts; instead find charming B&Bs and excellent restaurants, praised among Turks for simplicity and lack of pretense. By day, the action revolves around the harbor, where boat cruises depart and fisherfolk tend to their boats. Visitors and locals mingle in restaurants and a *çay bahçesi* (tea garden) lining the main Cumhuriyet Meydanı (square) by the harbor, which features a commanding statue of Mustafa Kemal Atatürk, father of modern Turkey. Come nightfall, Kaş's cobblestone lanes are thronged with middle-class Turks and foreign travelers vying for space in the alleyway bars and terrace tables of lively restaurants.

Kaş grew among the ruins of the ancient Roman port city of Antiphellos, and during the Ottoman era it was a place of exile for political dissidents. With more than 300 days of sunshine and clear warm water, it's not a bad location to serve time. Today, its drawback, some say, is also its savior: Kaş's lack of long sandy beaches makes it less appealing for beachgoers than other resorts along the coast. But it redeems itself with a coast that's peppered with alcoves and in close proximity to the region's major recreational attractions. Kaş is the best base to partake in outdoor activities such as mountain bike riding, hiking, kayaking, and paragliding. The variety and quality of diving sites make it one of the best places in Turkey for scuba diving. It's also an ideal and restful base to tour the coast, starting with an excursion to Kekova and its sunken city, Patara Beach, the Xanthos Valley with its Lycian ruins, and Demre, a town with the Lycian tombs of Myra and the legend of

Saint Nicholas (a.k.a. Santa Claus). Like Ölüdeniz's Mount Babadağ to the north, Kaş has its own mountain—albeit much smaller, at 500 meters high—in the form of Yatan Adam (Sleeping Man). Here, extreme sport enthusiasts paraglide off the top for a bird's-eye view of the postcard-perfect coastline and Meis island.

SIGHTS
Antiphellos Ruins

The sparse remains of Kaş's ancient Roman antecedent, Antiphellos, attest to the village's lengthy history as a Hellenic center. The **Amphitheater,** 500 meters west of the main square, is the most impressive monument still standing. It's free to enter, as is nightly show starring the Mediterranean sunset, best savored with your own cheese, crackers, and a glass of wine.

The **Lions Tomb** takes its name from the lid of this handsome sarcophagus, which is embossed with lions. You'll find it located at the end of the slippery Uzun Çarşı Caddesi, lined with traditional houses, just northeast of the main square. While the city was once filled with a variety of burial chambers, the other remaining examples are those carved into the hillside above the town that are illuminated in the evening.

ENTERTAINMENT AND EVENTS
Festivals

Every year in June the three-day **Kaş Lycia Festival** is in full swing with Turkish and foreign folk dancing troupes displaying their culture and artistry. There is no website for the event, and dates are announced annually, so ask your hotel or the Kaş municipality (0242/836-1020) for schedules.

Nightlife

Much like Kalkan, Kaş's nightlife begins at 7pm and goes well into the night. Bars are scattered around the tiny town, most hidden in back streets and gardens around the main square. The dress code is relaxed, much like the vibe, so shorts and T-shirts are acceptable.

The **Hideaway Café & Bar** (Cumhuriyet Meydanı 16/A, 0242/836-3369) deserves its name because it's removed from the street in the rear garden of a restored Greek house just west of the town square. If you blink you'll miss the entrance. Here you can listen to relaxing blues and roots music and feel a little lost in the serene mood lighting. The quality of the cocktails depends on who mixed them, so to play it safe with beer and wine, coffee, and other beverages that can accompany a dessert. On Sunday the garden hosts brunch (22TL) with farm-fresh regional fare.

At the small, cozy **Hi-Jazz Bar** (Zümrüt Sk. 3, 0242/836-1165), it's all about jazz and the occasional Turkish tune. Owner Yilmaz, a retired New York cabbie who discovered his passion for music in New Orleans, chose to return home to set up this relaxing spot, tucked in a back alley. The live music goes on nightly, starting with smooth grooves at 5pm. Seating is available inside and out on the alleyway, where you can drink well into the early hours of the morning.

For people-watching and rock music, head to the main square and look east for the multicolored chairs of **Mavi Bar** (0242/836-1834). It's the oldest bar in town and a hangout of choice. For years its nightly summer party has extended onto the harborside promenade because, starting as early as 9pm, there's often not even standing room inside.

SPORTS AND RECREATION
Beaches

Just 1.5 kilometers south of the town center, a pleasant 10-minute stroll, Kaş's solitary beach is the picturesque **Büyük Çakıl Plajı** (Big Pebble Beach), aptly named for its large pebbles and because it is larger than its neighbor **Küçük Çakıl Plajı** (Small Pebble Beach), which accommodates a couple of rows of sun lounges and a few restaurants where staff vie for food and drink orders. Closer to the center of town is **Leymona Beach and Restaurant** (Hastane Cd. 33, 0242/836-2647, www.leymona.com), a beach club with no sand but where you can laze in sun lounges among the lemon trees that line the deck out to the water.

Straight across the bay is **Limanağızı,** a pebble-covered beach with transparent water and beach clubs with wooden platforms, oversize cushions, and outdoor eateries. A water taxi from Kaş harbor (12.50TL round-trip) departs every 15 minutes 9am-6pm daily. The taxi will drop you off at a jetty close to one of the more modest beach clubs, but you can follow the shore to reach others with a little more luxury. Sun lounges are generally free if you dine in the on-site restaurant.

Boat Trips and Tours

Kaş may lack sandy acreage, but its beauty in the Kaş-Kekova Marina Protected Area begs to be discovered. Jagged mountain cliffs, small islets, protected bays, and a few coral cliffs provide the perfect backdrop for outings. While there are a dozen ways to explore the region around Kaş, the most popular is a day trip to Kekova and Üçağız, which includes numerous stops to explore a range of ruins and to swim. For a private cruise with up to six people, charter Captain Ergun's modern 15-meter yacht, the *Gülşsah 1* (Kaş marina, cell tel. 0542/731-2358, www.boattripturkey.com, 1,000TL per day includes meals). The captain and his first mate Merve, his wife, excel in tailor-made day and overnight tours to explore the seascape off Kaş.

Alternately, venture down to the marina to charter a boat suited to your group size and budget, or book a spot on a public cruise (50TL pp) with any of the travel agents in town. One such reputable company is **Bougainville Travel** (Çukurbağlı Cd. 10, 0242/836-3737, www.bougainville-turkey.com). Owned by a Turkish-British trio of adventure travel and outdoor activities specialists, Bougainville has a kayaking excursion (€30) to the sunken city of Kekova Bay, canyon trips (€50) through the gorges of Saklıkent (experienced canyoneers only), or Kibris Canyon (for amateurs), paragliding (€90) off the mountains above Kaş, and mountain bike riding through mountain villages above Demre (€40) among other outdoor trips. They can also take care of bookings for scuba diving courses, dives (from €25), and trial dives (€35) for beginners. All day trips include lunch, a guide, and transfers to and from Kaş. Check the website for a full listing of tours and attractions.

The round-trip to the Greek Island of Meis

the harbor of Kaş, a preferred holiday destination for locals

(Castellorizo) used to be a popular trip for foreigners to renew their three-month Turkish tourist visas in a few hours. The visa conditions have changed—there's no quick renewal anymore—but a daily 20-minute cruise to the colorful harborside village of the island is still possible with **Meis Express** (Hükümet Cd. 16, 0242/836-1725, www.meisexpress.com). Meis has a couple of attractions, such as the Red Castle and Blue Cave, and even a couple of rare endangered monk seals, but just having lunch in a café looking back at the Turkish coast is a memorable experience. Make sure you have your passport with your valid Turkish tourist visa as well as your EU visa (if needed) for departure from Kaş harbor.

ACCOMMODATIONS

Kaş teems with lodging options that are within easy walking distance of shops and restaurants. Perhaps the only downside is that many of the hotels do not have elevators. Five kilometers due west, the tranquil Çukurbağ Peninsula, a four-kilometer-long spit of rock with steep cliffs that descend to pristine waters, offers a handful of boutique hotels. The sea is all around and it has a stunningly deep, rich color. The Greek island of Meis is a mere two kilometers from the Turkish coast at this point. Rather remote, unless you have your own wheels, Çukurbağ's cape is reached by turning right from Kaş's central rotary, right before the harbor.

With friendly Turkish-Belgian hospitality by owners Ahmet and Marie, 20 contemporary rooms and 180-degree uninterrupted views of the Mediterranean are on offer at ★ **Hideaway Hotel** (Anfitiyatro Sk. 7, 0242/836-1887, www.hotelhideaway.com, from 140TL). The highly sought rooms, all with small balconies, were recently refurbished in different themes of light and bright colors, with high-quality finishes throughout the bedrooms and en suite baths. When temperatures rise in summer, lie by the pool downstairs or head up to the spectacular terrace for complimentary tea and coffee all day long and happy hour at sunset. Buffet meals are also prepared on the terrace in the evening—with the best views in town. The quality of service and the standard of the rooms are in great demand, so book well in advance.

A favorite for backpackers and those on a budget, just west of the center of town is **Ateş Pension** (Yeni Camii Cd. 3, 0242/836-1393, www.atespension.com, 40-110TL). Established in 1985 and open year-round, no other inn matches the price and million-dollar views offered from the rooftop lounge. Basic rooms are in two buildings; the back building offers slightly larger abodes, and the front building has a four-bed dorm. The hosts prepare a homey breakfast on the terrace every day, and for an extra 25TL, a barbecue dinner with eight mezes. The terrace also features a small book exchange and plenty of divans to put up your feet and read your novel.

The **Gardenia Boutique Hotel** (Hükümet Cd. 41, 0242/836-2368, www.gardeniahotel-kas.com, €110-175) is all about art and immaculate design. Owner Ömer Caglar has an eye for style, and as an architect, he's traveled the world collecting pieces of art that adorn the walls. It might take you a while to walk to your room as you stop to gaze at some of displays of color and life from Asia and South America. The 11 rooms have top-class amenities like rain showers and quality dark furnishing decorated with crisp white linens. For larger rooms, opt for the junior suite, with its private terrace, or sea front rooms, which look to the Greek island of Meis. A full Turkish breakfast is served on the hotel terrace that shares amazing views of the sea. The hotel is located across the road from the beach clubs surrounding Küçük Çakıl Beach, so a refreshing dip in the sea is only a few steps away.

For an affordable lodging close to the restaurants, shops, and bars, check into **Hotel Ferah** (Hükümet Cd. 33, 0242/836-1377, €35-60). The Muslu family own and operate this inn, with a pool at the foot of 20 rooms, all with balconies. There is no rooftop terrace, but sea-view rooms on the upper floor look out on the Mediterranean and Meis. A huge buffet breakfast with plenty of farm-fresh options is served by the pool daily.

Out on the Çukurbağ Peninsula, **★ Hadrian Hotel** (Doğan Kaşaroğlu Sk. 10, 0242/836-2856, www.hotel-hadrian.de, €140-370 half board) is a bright B&B that hugs the end of the rocky Çukurbağ Peninsula. The sunny courtyard, which centers on a large, sophisticated saltwater pool, and the pavilion below are covered in magenta bougainvillea and open to superb views of the entire bay. Stairs lead to the hotel's rocky beach platform below, which is located above water so deep that it's ideal for diving and snorkeling. The Hadrian offers 14 roomy units, including two-room family suites (€180-370).

FOOD

Kaş is overrun with fine-dining establishments. It's a fierce environment with quick turnover; what's "in" this season might not be around the next. You can't go wrong with any of the gourmet Turkish restaurants along Süleyman Sandıkçı Sokak, nestled above the street in beautiful gardens. There are a couple of fish restaurants, but be wary of the typical price tampering methods that can happen in fish restaurants around Turkey. Closely review the prices on the menu and make sure they match the bill. Before ordering, confirm the price of dishes that are not listed, and scrutinize the bill before paying to ensure there aren't any extra charges.

Erkal Mavış, the chef-proprietor of **★ Ratatouille** (Cumhuriyet Meydanı 10, cell tel. 0531/724-5846, 25TL), travels to local markets to select the best produce of the day, picks the herbs he uses from his garden, and greets guests at the end of their meals, because, he says, "I want to treat guests like my family." The seasonal menu changes regularly, but expect a complimentary soup on arrival, along with a small but flavor-packed menu of gourmet fare that can be enjoyed while overlooking the main square. Book ahead and let Erkal know if you have any food intolerances; he'll gladly prepare a dish suited to you.

Çınarlar Pizza & Pide (Ibrahim Serin Sk. 4, 0242/836-2860, 20TL) is a popular choice for those on a budget or wishing to enjoy a no fuss pizza or *pide* cooked in a *taş fırın* (wood oven). This family-owned and operated business sprawls over two venues. The first is a small café where you can watch the pizzas served straight from the oven; the second and more popular spot is across the street in an open-air garden courtyard, sporting decor typical of an Italian pizzeria. Kebabs, fish, and salads are also available.

A *meyhane* is a traditional Turkish tavern were guests down aniseed flavored alcohol called *rakı* while grazing through a menu of scrumptious mezes, seafood, and meat dishes while listening to live Turkish music. In Kaş, the *meyhane* to go to is Nuri Kocakanat's **Hayta Meyhane** (Zümrüt Sk. 5, 0242/836-3776, 20TL). Tucked away in an vine-covered alley beyond the main square, Nuri woos his guests with the soulful serenade of his *oud* (Middle Eastern mandolin) while Hayta, his golden retriever, casually greets the guests. The restaurant is so popular with the locals it can get crowded, so reserve ahead to secure a table. To order your meal, simply point to what's written on the chalkboard in the alleyway, or pick out some mezes from the counter inside.

INFORMATION AND SERVICES

The **Tourist Information Office** (Cumhuriyet Meydani 5, 0242/836-1238) is located on the main square. The **PTT** (Bahçe Sk. 5, 0242/831-4100, 8:30am-5pm Mon.-Fri.) post office is available for mail and currency exchange. Banks and ATMs line the main drag of Atatürk Caddesi.

GETTING THERE

Kaş is on the D400 highway about 150 kilometers southeast of **Dalaman Airport** (DLM, Dalaman Havalimanı, 0252/792-5291, www.dalaman.dhmi.gov.tr). There aren't many options for transfer to Kaş except a costly cab ride (210TL) or private transfer (€160 for 1-3 people). A cheaper but longer option is to board the one-hour **Havaş** (0252/792-5077, www.havas.com.tr, 10TL) shuttle bus to the Fethiye *otogar*, and from there take the **Antalya Batı** (0242/331-4081, www.batiantalyatur.net) minibus that departs every 90 minutes and travels along the D400 highway, stopping at major towns on the way to Antalya, including the *otogar* in Kaş (16TL, 105 kilometers, 2.5 hours).

Night and daytime **coaches** by **Pamukkale Turizm** (0850/333-3535, www.pamukkale.com.tr) and **Kamil Koç** (444-0562, www.kamilkoc.com.tr) run from Istanbul (80TL, 14.5 hours) and İzmir (55TL, 8 hours) to the Kaş *otogar,* located on Atatürk Bulvarı, less than 700 meters from the harbor. Local **dolmuş** services also leave every 30 minutes from Kaş *otogar* westbound for Kaputaş (5TL, 18 kilometers), Kalkan (6TL, 28 kilometers), and Patara (8TL, 45 kilometers). From Kaş, the **Antalya Batı** east to Demre (8TL, 1 hour), Olympos and Çıralı (18TL, 3 hours), and Antalya (24TL, 4 hours) departs every 30 minutes.

The best way to transfer safely to a hotel with luggage is to take one of the **taxis** at the *otogar* for less than 20TL, or call your hotel; they may provide pickup service. Once your luggage is stowed at your hotel, roam the small town on foot.

★ KEKOVA BAY

Before hitting the high seas, take time to explore sleepy Kekova Bay, home to fishing and farming villages and the sunken city of Kekova. Just 34 kilometers east of Kaş is **Üçağız,** the first village you come to and which has a collection of stunning Lycian tombs, located at the rear of the village. Easily accessible by boat, the submerged tombs of **Aperlai** and the spectacular acropolis of **Apollonia,** due west of Üçağız, are two well-preserved ancient sites that are worth an hour's side trip.

Frozen in time, the nearby village of **Kaleköy**—antiquity's Simena—is a popular tour destination for day-trippers from Kaş.

ruins in the ancient village of Kekova

The only way to reach it is by boat or sea kayak or via a path from Üçağız that's inaccessible to cars. Kaleköy's harbor is overshadowed by the **Byzantine Fortress of the Knights of St. John** (5TL). Interestingly enough, the knights built the castle's perimeter walls around a tiny Hellenic amphitheater, rather than taking it apart during construction. No roads cross this village, just dusty lanes lined with decrepit stone houses that lead to rock-hewn Lycian tombs and three-meter-tall sarcophagi. Kaleköy's jetty is lined with great fish restaurants, offering grilled fish fare that begs to be enjoyed while relaxing at a terrace table overlooking the gently lapping waves. Spend an afternoon swimming off a couple of the sandy spots around the village. You can also spend the night in one of the air-conditioned rooms with balconies at the waterfront **Sahıl Pansiyon** (Kaleköy 145/A, 0242/874-2263, www.sahilpension.com, from 195TL).

Over the water from Kaleköy is **Kekova Adası** (Kekova Island). Topping the list of archaeological sites here is Lycia's **Batık Şehir**

(Sunken City), which lies submerged six meters beneath the clear water of Kekova Bay, on the northern tip of the island. The most stunning relics are those of city walls and private homes that were once in the residential area of ancient Simena; these became submerged during a massive earthquake in the 2nd century AD. To preserve the integrity of the site, boats are forbidden from getting too close, and swimmers and snorkelers are restricted from exploring the stairways, terraces, and amphorae beneath the water.

Getting There

While there is a *dolmuş* service from Demre and one service via **Antalya Batı** (0242/331-4081, www.batiantalyatur.net, 28TL) daily from Antalya, once here, you would need to negotiate boat prices to visit the sites. A far better option is to book a **boat trip** (from 50TL, including lunch and guide) that departs usually around 10am daily from the Kaş harbor. The excursion stops four times along the way to Kekova with lunch on board and an hour-long excursion to the village of Kaleköy. The excursion includes an optional climb to Kaleköy's Byzantine fortress and stops to swim or snorkel in the warm waters of the Mediterranean. Sea kayaking tours that allow you get up close to the sunken city and Kaleköy also depart from Kaş daily (€30), with the nine-kilometer kayaking trek starting from Üçağız.

By **car,** follow the D400 highway and turn off at Kuşcağız Yolu to travel through some greenhouse villages before arriving in Üçağız. The route is well signposted.

DEMRE

Not a major or scenic destination, Demre has become something of a cult hit for Santa Claus fans; the legend of the man from the north pole actually began here.

Arriving from Kaş, the main road descends through the rocky slopes of Mount Alaca to the fertile alluvial Demre plain. The structures in the area are greenhouses—masses of them—growing citrus fruits, pomegranates, and vegetables. Demre is still an agricultural town, but it's fast becoming a pit stop for tourists traveling between Fethiye and Antalya.

Before it became Demre, the city was known as the Roman town of Myra and was situated 1.5 kilometers north of its current boundaries. The Christian apostle Saint Paul stopped on his way to Rome from Caesaria in AD 60. Of the many bishops who worked in Myra, Saint Nicholas—Santa Claus—became celebrated for his generosity.

The restored Basilica of St. Nicholas is located just off the same road as the Demre *otogar*. This church, which sits below today's ground level, still bears some of its original frescoes and mosaics and is Demre's major sight. Myra, a five minute drive north of town, attests to its lengthy Lycian past with a magnificently preserved set of rock-hewn Lycian tombs set high on the steep cliff flanking its ancient amphitheater.

Busloads of visitors, mainly Greek and Russian Orthodox pilgrims, swing through the town in three hours to visit the two sites. Restaurants serve kebabs around the basilica, and lodging can be found, but Demre is largely a gritty working area set back from the coast. Sleeping in nearby Kaş and coming here on a day trip is a much more pleasant option.

Sights
AYA NICOLA KILISESI (CHURCH OF ST. NICHOLAS)

The **Aya Nicola Kilisesi** (Müze Cd., 0242/871-6820, 9am-7pm daily Apr.-Oct., 8:30am-5:30pm daily Nov.-Mar., 15TL, 10TL audio guide) was built just after the death of Saint Nicholas in the mid-3rd century AD. Badly damaged during the earthquake of 529, the building was later reconstructed as a grand basilica by Emperor Justinian, with the addition of two domed chambers. The church was reconstructed twice more, following pillaging at the hands of marauding Arabs in the mid-9th century and again in 1034. Emperor Constantine ordered its restoration in 1043, ordering that a monastery be built alongside the sanctuary. As for the saint's remains, the

The Legend Of Santa Claus

Canonized just decades after his death in AD 343, Nicholas, the bishop of Myra (modern-day Demre), was born into wealth, a Greek from the Lycian city of Patara when Asia Minor was under Roman rule. Young Nick was so devout that he was said to have rigorously observed the Coptic fasts every Wednesday and Friday. He he eventually became a reader, a priest, and finally a bishop.

Legend has it that on Christmas eve, Nick used a large inheritance to bestow secret gifts on villagers by dropping coins and gifts in their shoes left on doorsteps. Another legend says he saved three young poor women from prostitution by throwing satchels of gold to be used as dowries through their window. Another account even claims he resuscitated three boys whose bodies had been left to "cure" in brine by a malevolent butcher who wanted to sell them as pickled meat during a famine. No text attests to his being rotund or bearded, but his crimson outfit is indicative of his position in the church.

Nick's ornate tomb, gaping hole and all, can still be seen inside his namesake cathedral in Demre. His remains were taken without permission of the church by Italian sailors in 1087, despite outrage from local Orthodox monks. Myra was then ruled by Muslim Selçuks, so their concerns were not addressed, and Saint Nick's bones arrived in Italy soon after. Some called the sailors thieves and pirates; others claimed the act was justified by a vision of Saint Nicholas personally pleading to have his remains carried away from impending doom and saved for posterity.

When alive, Nick stated the desire to be buried in the church he commissioned in the city of his birth, but continued requests of the Vatican to return his relics to Turkey have gone unanswered. Nonetheless, the fact that Saint Nicholas—the American Santa Claus, the Dutch Sinterklaas, and the Italian San Nicola—was born by the sunny beach of Patara astounds travelers to this day.

Vatican claims that they were taken by Italian merchants to Bari, Italy, where they were enshrined in a cathedral. The basilica was renovated most recently in the mid-19th century at the order of Czar Nicholas I, this time adding the belfry. This church is one of the few that escaped conversion to a mosque when the Ottomans took over.

Despite the wrath of nature and humans, some of the original mosaic floor has fared well. Albeit faded, the wall and dome frescoes are still visible. The empty tomb Saint Nicholas is located in an alcove between two pillars and behind a screen to protect it from the masses of visitors. The sarcophagus, which still has the hole made by the Italian merchants, dates from the Greek era, and was obviously reused; Saint Nicholas died penniless.

MYRA RUINS

Two kilometers due north of the Church of St. Nicholas are the ruins of **Myra** (0242/871-6820, 9am-7pm Apr.-Oct., 8am-5pm Nov.-Mar., 15TL). Of the structures that have withstood time are a mid-1st-century-AD Hellenic amphitheater and a well-preserved pseudo-tenement of Lycian tombs. Intricately carved stage masks litter the theater area. Befitting the status of a Greek temple, the nearby cliff-side tombs were carved out of the rock face, with supporting columns and pediments, in the 4th century BC. British archaeologist Charles Fellows wrote that when he discovered the ancient city of Myra in 1840, these funeral chambers were "a riot of color, colorfully painted red, yellow, and blue." Saint Nicholas may have ordered the demolition of Myra's Acropolis and its once grand Temple of Artemis to prevent the locals from practicing their older religions.

Due to effluvial silting, Myra, like much of its neighbors on the western littoral, gradually became landlocked during the Byzantine era; it now sits five kilometers from the Mediterranean coast.

ÇAYAĞZI (ANDRIAKE)

Just a four-kilometer *dolmuş* ride west of town, today's **Çayağzı** (Stream Mouth) is a mere collection of ruins. It was once Andriake, a

the 1st-century theater and masks of Myra

natural harbor town annexed by the city of Myra, which stood where the Demre Creek flows into the sea. Andriake's most important ruins are an eight-room triangular granary, built in the 1st century AD during the reign of Roman emperor Hadrian. The site also contains the ruins of two Byzantine basilicas, a harbor street, a necropolis, a bath, and aqueducts, all straddling the stream (in summer; in winter it is a marsh).

The ruins extend widely on either side of the river, whose mouth forms Çayağzı Plajı (Çayağzı Beach). A handful of boatyards and fishmongers, as well as a decent restaurant, make up this fishing port. The sea's particularly shallow waters are ideal for families with smaller children; the restaurant makes an even better location to experience the minutiae of rural life.

Getting There

Demre is 48 kilometers east of Kaş and 145 kilometers southwest of Antalya along the D400 highway. Coach services, and the more frequent **Antalya Batı** (0242/331-4081, www.batiantalyatur.net), connect Demre to Fethiye (22TL, 3.5 hours), Kalkan (12TL, 2 hours), Kaş (8TL, 1 hour), Olympos and Çıralı minibus stations on highway D400 (12TL, 2 hours), and Antalya (18TL, 3 hours) every 30 minutes.

Olympos, Çıralı, and Chimera

Perhaps the top location in Turkey for nature lovers and backpackers, **Olimpos Beydağları Sahil Milli Parkı** (Olympos Bey Mountains Coastal National Park) is one of the region's less visited idylls. Nestled in a valley in the foothills of Tahtalı Dağı (Timber Mountain), also called Olympos, Greek for "Great Mountain," is the ancient Lycian city of Olympos, flanked by the more modern treehouse haven of Olympos village in the southwest. Just a 10-minute walk through the ruins from the village is a postcard-perfect pebble beach with a rugged lush green cliff face rising up from the water. Continue an awkward 15-minute walk along the shoreline, battling the pebbly terrain, past two restaurants to find Çıralı beach and its sprawling laid-back town. Like Dalyan and Patara, this beach is one of the Mediterranean's few remaining nesting grounds for the endangered loggerhead turtle, so access to the shore is limited in the evening. Beyond the inns and narrow roads of Çıralı is the natural eternal flame of Chimera, set high in the pine forest above the town, best visited at night.

Choosing where to stay comes down to your interest in partying. Çıralı is the more mature setting of the two settlements and has the same stunning scenery as Olympos down the road. Olympos, on the other hand, is close to the ruins and is a favorite place for backpackers to party all night. At either location you can rent a room in an inn offering half board, but Olympos is where the tree houses are at—although most are bungalows close to the ground rather than up among the branches and leaves. The Olympos Bey Mountains Coastal National Park is the best place in the region to completely unwind in nature, take a rejuvenating yoga class, or ease into natural therapies such as Thai massage and aromatherapy. And if you haven't guessed by now, organic food and natural living thrive here. You won't regret spending a night or two here to recharge.

OLYMPOS

The ancient Lycian settlement of **Olympos** (0242/892-1325, 9am-7pm daily Apr.-Oct., 8am-5pm daily Nov.-Mar., 5TL), set in a verdant coastal valley straddling the Ulupınar Çayı (Great Spring Stream), enters recorded history in the 2nd century BC. One of the six main cities of the Lycian federation, Olympos, according to Roman philosopher Cicero (1st century BC), was a city filled with great culture and extensive riches. With the Chimera flame close by, it's no wonder Olympos grew as a pilgrimage center honoring Hephaestus—a.k.a. Vulcan, the god of fire—until the advent of Christianity in the 2nd century AD. During the Middle Ages, Genoese and Rhodian Crusaders erected a pair of fortresses along the coast, but by the turn of the 15th century, Olympos was abandoned. The vast site is overgrown and scattered with fragmented ruins, so make sure to get the map, available at the ticket booth. If you're not interested in seeing the ruins, come to see rare Mediterranean flora—splendid wild orchids, oleanders, and lavender—or to pick wild figs from the hundreds of fruit trees that line the burbling stream.

Accommodations line the single dusty street of the village that leads up to the entrance to the ruins. Walking is the main way to get around, meaning that the beach is a 20-minute hike away. Bikes can be rented to make getting around a little easier in the heat of summer. Some of the best places to stay are located farther away from the entrance, including ★ **Kadir's Treehouses** (0242/892-1250, www.kadirstreehouses.com, 30-140TL half board). It's *the* place to stay in Olympos for several reasons. Friendly owner Kadir Kaya is the original Robinson Crusoe of Olympos and can recall the days when this remote valley had no roads or accommodations, when the only shelter was in a tent or trailer with no running water or electricity. When Kadir built his first wooden tree house in 1986, it became such a popular hangout that other houses followed, and after a 1991 BBC documentary, the treehouse phenomenon spread and tourism boomed. Despite a devastating fire in 2007 that destroyed 95 per cent of Kadir's property, he's fully operational again with capacity for 300 people in 100 bungalows, 15 cabins, and 10 dorm rooms. There are three bars and restaurants made completely of cedar wood and the remnants of wagon wheels and other detritus; it has to be seen to be believed. The artwork is impressive, as is the diamond-in-the-rough Bull Bar. There's Wi-Fi, air-conditioning, and people to provide yoga classes and tours on water and land. The team here also organizes the four-day **Rock-Climbing Festival** every October.

ÇIRALI

A few steps north from the point where the Ulupınar stream meets the sea is **Çıralı Plajı** (Çıralı Beach), one of Turkey's few beaches to remain entirely undeveloped. It extends almost four kilometers, and the roads along its sands have several fine family-run inns. If you're considering a remote setting to base yourself in the region, Çıralı may be the answer. Atop the list of sublimely rural hotels is Turkey's first boutique hotel, the ★ **Olympos Lodge** (0242/825-7171, www.olymposlodge.com.tr, €150-225). Cross the bridge when you enter town and turn right to see the white fence of the lodge, which opens up to flowers, neat lawns, and fragrant thickets. A hammock here, a pond there, and the calls of chickens, geese, and a peacock add surprising touches to this remote escape, which also features a romantic honeymoon suite. Some 15 elegantly spare rooms are Zen-inspired in swatches of linen and white, and all feature cedar flooring and large modern baths. Wednesday and Saturday feature a barbecue buffet for guests and nonguests to graze through a huge selection of mezes, meats, fish, and delicious desserts in a romantic setting with mood lighting hanging from mature palms and bowing trees, just meters from the beach.

For yummy farm-fresh produce and yoga, revel in an organic spiritual retreat at **Myland Nature** (0242/825-7044, www.mylandnature.com, from 226TL). Engin and Pınar, pals from university, saved money for a decade to purchase six hectares of mostly clearings and fruit orchards to build their dream inn, which opened in 1999 as Myland. Set back 100 meters from the beach to protect the adjacent nesting ground of loggerhead turtles, the property features 13 timber cabins, each with a veranda with a hammock and deck chairs. Many activities are provided for guests, including the daily free yoga class led by owner Pınar. If you're planning to come in May, ask about the annual yoga and meditation festival.

★ CHIMERA

The Chimera, or *Yanartaş* (Burning Rock) in Turkish, is a series of flames once thought to have been a mythical fire-breathing monster that roamed the Olympos mountain spitting flames from its three heads. Part goat, part lion, and part serpent, Homer's legendary behemoth was so feared among ancient Anatolians that the rocky slopes of Olympos were to avoided until Greek geographer Strabo debunked the site as just a natural combustion phenomenon. Actually, this earthly marvel is attributed to methane gases rising from deep beneath the earth through a fissure and igniting at a precise point where the serpentine hills rise from the limestone shelf. Chimera is seven kilometers, a one-hour hike, uphill from the village of Çıralı. As you approach, don't be surprised by the barbecue odors emanating from the site; a couple of sly entrepreneurs are roasting kebabs and boiling water for tea right atop the flames.

GETTING THERE AND AROUND

Situated about 110 kilometers south of Antalya, the Olympos and Çıralı-Yanartaş exits are one kilometer apart on the D400 highway. The **Antalya Batı** (0242/331-4081, www.batiantalyatur.net) minibus connects to Demre (12TL, 2 hours), Kaş (18TL, 3 hours), Kalkan (22TL, 4 hours), and Fethiye (30TL, 5.5 hours) in the west and Antalya in the east (12TL, 1 hour) every 30 minutes. It stops at the Çıralı-Yanartaş exit and at a highway restaurant for transfers into Olympos. From May to November, the Olympos *dolmuş* (6TL) leaves every half hour from the restaurant until 7pm daily, and the service to Çıralı departs from the junction less frequently—usually when the minibus fills up.

If **driving** to Chimera, take the turnoff for Çıralı-Yanartaş which leads to a bumpy road that follows a lush riverbed for about six kilometers, eventually leading to a bridge. Cross the bridge leading into Çıralı to reach the inns and the "official" entrance to the mountain footpath leading to the Chimera (1.5 kilometers).

Bikes and **cars** are available to rent in both settlements, with some hotels offering bikes for free, a welcome perquisite given the size of these expansive villages.

Antalya

Inside a long gulf (Antalya Körfezi), Antalya sits on an enormous travertine plateau formed over eons by the innumerable springs flowing toward the Mediterranean from the Taurus Mountains. The beauty of this once Roman-Ottoman port, with its lengthy history and lengthy sun-kissed beaches, is only eclipsed by towering snow-capped Beydağları (Gentleman's Mountains) just beyond its periphery.

The city of Antalya is the center of Antalya province, which stretches all the way northwest to Kalkan and east to Alanya. This strip, known as the Turkish Riviera, boasts more sandy acreage and resort hotels than the coasts of Italy and Spain combined. The surge of wealthy Russians choosing the city as their summer escape, and the Russion developers who've come to build upscale accommodations, have redefined Antalya as one of the sexiest, most luxurious resorts along the Turkish coast. The US$1.5 billion Mardan Palace resort in the megaresort area of Lara Beach has outpriced some of Las Vegas's most upscale lodgings. But don't expect to find slot machines here; casinos and gambling have been banned in Turkey since 1998.

If you thought that Antalya is just about the sea, sun, and nightclubs, note that its peripheral mountains have gushing waterfalls, deep gorges, trickling streams, and lush plains. Canyoneers, white-water rafters, long distance hikers and cyclists, golfers, and divers revel in the region's outdoors. There's also a good day's stroll through the well-preserved Kaleiçi quarter (old town), a web of cobblestone alleys that has delineated Antalya's center and harbor since the Roman era. The award-winning Antalya Archaeological Museum is home to innumerable artifacts found in the region's ancient settlements of Perge and Aspendos. In addition to recreation and museums, there are numerous drinking and fine dining establishments for gourmets.

A short walk west of historic Kaleiçi is the decidedly modern enclave of Konyaaltı, with a wide shale beach fringed by a palm tree-lined promenade, where you'll find an outdoor mall perfect for the family to spend the day: Adults can dine while the young ones shoot paint balls or climb the monkey bars at the kiddie park.

If time allows, an overnight stay in Antalya is sufficient to explore the old town, visit the impressive Antalya Museum, and treat yourself to a hamam. (The unisex 700-year-old hamam on Balık Pazarı Sokak is the most authentic hamam in the Old Town, but has only male attendants. Ladies wear bathing suits for modesty). Otherwise, if resort holidays are your thing, there are many options in Lara Beach, an hour's drive in traffic or closer to the old town in Konyaaltı. With a major *otogar* and an international airport, Antalya is transportation hub for the Mediterranean region and north to Konya and the moonscape of Cappadocia.

HISTORY

The Greeks couldn't have chosen a better name when they called the 115-kilometer coastal area between ancient Lycia and Cilicia—today's Antalya province—Pamphylia, meaning "all tribes." Throughout history, starting with the prehistoric nomads who roamed Antalya's mountainous periphery some 52,000 years ago through today's modern Turks, a long list of civilizations either settled or traveled through this province.

While the Hittites and various Greek colonies settled the region, Antalya doesn't officially enter historical records until the 3rd century BC, thanks to the accidental discovery in 2008 of a necropolis and its 361 graves during construction excavation in Doğu Garajı. This find is particularly interesting because Antalya's foundation can no longer be attributed to Pergamum's King Attalus II,

Antalya

THE TURQUOISE COAST
ANTALYA

who named the settlement Attaleia after his father, Attalus I. It's safe to say that the city is younger than its sister metropolises of Perge, Termessos, and Aspendos by at least seven centuries. The reason Antalya still thrives while the others are in ruins may be due to its location at the end of an easy-to-defend gulf. At least Attalus I thought so, and his harbor town continued to flourish well after his son bequeathed it, along with the entire empire of Pergamum, to the Romans in 133 BC. A spectacular triumphal gate was built 260 years later to honor the momentous visit of Roman emperor Hadrian.

After the arrival of the Selçuk Turks in 1207, Attaleia was renamed Antalya and the Yivli Minare (Fluted Minaret) became its symbol, to commemorate Attaleia's conversion to Islam. In 1391, Antalya was absorbed by the Ottoman Empire. After World War I, the Ottoman Empire dissolved and Antalya was transferred to the Italians. Mustafa Kemal Atatürk's armies drove out the Italians in 1921 after winning the War of Independence and reclaiming the former Ottoman port, now Turkey's largest city on the Mediterranean coast.

old harbor in Antalya

SIGHTS
Kaleiçi (Old Town)

Kaleiçi is where most travelers choose to stay in Antalya—which is highly recommended—so you won't need to plan specific trips to explore. Make sure you visit the impressive entrance of the old town by checking out its most impressive monument, **Hadrianus Kapısı** (Hadrian's Gate). Built in AD 130 to honor the visit of Roman Emperor Hadrian, this triumphal gate—also called Üç Kapısı (Three Gates)—gets its name from the trio of arches that connect to the ancient city walls on either side. It's located on Atatürk Caddesi at the end of Hesapçı Sokak, one of the main pedestrian thoroughfares of Kaleiçi.

At the northern end of the Kaleiçi is **Kale Kapısı Meydanı** (Fortress Gate Square). On its western flank are the 2nd-century-AD city walls and the **Saat Kulesi** (Clock Tower)—a timepiece that was probably added during the 19th century. It graces one of two watchtowers (only one remains) built by the Selçuks to protect the gate.

Directly south of the square, just off Uzun Çarşı Sokak, is the **Tekeli Mehmet Paşa Camii,** a petite mosque with particularly intricate Koranic inscriptions on colorfully tiled panels. Its commissioner, Mehmet Paşa, was one of Sultan Mehmet III's illustrious public servants who began his 60-year career as a sergeant major in the Ottoman army and ended up serving as the governor of Van in 1616.

Up on Cumhuriyet Caddesi, along the north edge of Kaleiçi, is the **Yivli Minare** (Fluted Minaret), built in true Selçukian architectural style alongside, not atop, the adjoining mosque by Sultan Alaeddin Keykubad in 1225. The fluted thick brick structure has come to symbolize the city of Antalya. At 38 meters tall, the minaret's 90 steps were climbed five times a day by the *müezzin* who sings the *ezan* (call to prayer). The adjoining **Alaeddin Camii** is a converted Byzantine church; it gained its six-domed appearance during a mid-14th-century reconstruction. You can enter the mosque to see this unique structure from the inside, but respect local worshippers and only enter if you're dressed modestly—for women this includes covering your head and shoulders. Also in the mosque complex is the former **Mevlevi Tekke** (Whirling Dervish Monastery), built in 1255. In the complex's lush gardens are two tombs, one of Sufi sheikh Zincirkıran Mehmet Bey (1377) and the other Nigar Hatun, wife of Ottoman sultan Beyazıt II.

Wandering southwest toward the harbor, the busy old quarter of Kaleiçi is lined with Ottoman houses serving as inns, B&Bs, and touristy shops that were restored during an award-winning project launched in the late 1970s. Continue walking downhill to find the ancient Roman harbor, punctuated by imposing cliff faces on either side. Numerous vendors vie for customers for one-hour cruises to *Yapay Şelale* (Little Waterfall, which you can see from the harbor) and the larger Düden Waterfall, accessible on a two-hour cruise. Prices vary depending on the size of the group; expect to pay more in shoulder seasons.

Above the harbor, Kaleiçi's southern section is more peaceful and features a handful of interesting sights. One of them is the ruined **Kesik Minare Kulliyesi** (Broken Minaret Mosque, Hesapçı Sk.). Built in the 13th century, this single-galleried Selçukian minaret was the Byzantine Basilica of Panagelia in the 5th century AD, transformed into a mosque in 1467 by the Turkish sultan Korkut. The minaret earned its name after losing its crown in a fire in 1896, and today its remarkable interior prayer hall still bears the church's original twin sections in the shape of a double cross. While entrance to the complex is restricted, you can walk around the building to see the Byzantine influence, an arched gate, and marble columns that depict the building's original function.

Crowning a rocky ledge at the end of Hesapçı Sokak is the 14-meter-tall **Hidirlik Kulesi.** Also known as the Red Tower, this 2nd-century-AD fortress was originally part of the city walls and functioned as a lighthouse. Continue left on the seaside path to hang out with the working-class folk at Karaalioğlu Parkı, a large park that often hosts cultural events and stunning views of Mediterranean sunsets.

Kaleiçi Müzesi (Kaleiçi Museum)

Located in the center of Kaleiçi, the **Sunan-İnan Kıraç Kaleiçi Müzesi** (Kocatepe Sk. 25, 0242/243-4274, www.kaleicimuzesi.com, 9am-noon and 1pm-6pm Thurs.-Tues., 3TL) comprises two buildings that were meticulously restored in the mid-1990s. The first, a traditional Ottoman mansion, features typical ethnographic recreations of daily rituals and the rites of passage of the Ottomans and describes the interesting design features of an Ottoman home to cope with the hot climate of Antalya. The other structure, the former Greek Orthodox church of Aya Yorgo (1863), contains an extensive collection of Turkish ceramics and displays an entertaining photo exhibition of the 19th-century street vendors of Antalya.

Antalya Müzesi (Antalya Museum)

The **Antalya Müzesi** (Konyaaltı Cd. 1., 0242/241-4528, 9am-7pm daily, 20TL) is Turkey's second most important archaeological museum, after Istanbul's, and definitely deserves a two-hour visit. Located two kilometers west of Kaleiçi, it is a repository for the bulk of the relics excavated in Antalya province—one of the world's richest cultural centers. Over 5,000 archaeological artifacts are displayed in chronological order in 14 exhibitions halls. It opens with a prehistory hall that includes a mind-blowing collection of artifacts excavated from the Karain Cave at Burdur. The longest continuously inhabited cave in Turkey, Karain contained tools and figurines that were over 50,000 years old. These are displayed chronologically from the Paleolithic era to the late Bronze Age.

Even for those not interested in statues, the Hall of the Emperors and Empresses truly amazes with its dedication to larger-than-life mortals such as Roman emperors Hadrian and Trajan. But what steals the show is the sculpture of a dancing woman carved of white and black marble that dates to the 2nd century AD, uncovered in the 1970s during excavations of Perge and Aspendos. Next, the Hall of the Gods and Goddesses impresses with 16 gods from Greek mythology, including incredibly well-preserved statues of Zeus, Apollo, Aphrodite, and Athena.

One of the highlights of the museum, the Gallery of the Perge Theater contains enormous marble statues of gods and emperors uncovered in excavations of the 1st-century-AD Roman theater.

The Hall of Burial Culture, which retraces funeral rites from the 2nd century AD, contains the tomb of Hercules, the most prominent of the finely carved wall burial chambers on display. Near the impressive collection of sarcophagi is the museum's current pride and joy, a marble copy of the bronze *Hercules Farnese* sculpture, cast by Lysippos of Sikyon around 330-320 BC. The bust of the statue was smuggled from Perge to the United States in 1981 and returned to Turkey in 2011 as a goodwill gesture. Reunited, the bust and lower fragments of the statue are now displayed in full among red velvet drapes.

The remaining halls are considerably smaller but no less stunning, with exhibits of Byzantine religious icons; pre-Hellenic coin collections; and Selçuk and Ottoman ceramics, carpets, and Koranic texts, among a plethora of household articles.

DAY TRIPS

The Province of Antalya spans 115 kilometers of coastline and extends 45 kilometers inland. With so much geography to cover, picking the ideal day trip can be daunting, especially considering that more than two dozen outings—outdoorsy, archaeological, cultural, or just plain fun—are available from the town center. The ones to consider are excursions east to the ancient cities of Aspendos and Perge, or west to the mountaintop fortress at Termessos. Renting a car is the best means of transportation, but day tours in air-conditioned minibuses or Jeep safaris are also possible. Antalya's well-organized *dolmuş* cooperative also makes it simple and economical to tour the sites without having spending hours in transit. A safe and trouble-free alternative is to prearrange a tour before you arrive; check out **Dos Plumas Tours** (0242/321-3105, www.gotourturkey.com), owned by Americans Jim and DeAnne Reynolde and specializing in customized tours. They can access the best and most qualified guides to show you the highlights of Antalya as well as other parts of Turkey. Travel companies in town also offer cultural day trips to Perge, Aspendos, and Side (€50), Termessos and Düden Waterfalls (€45), and farther afield to Pamukkale (€55) and sites along the Mediterranean.

Perge, Aspendos, and Side

Adding the ancient cities of **Perge** and **Side** to an outing to must-see **Aspendos** extends a three-hour jaunt into an eight-hour day trip. You can explore Aspendos's magnificent theater and also get a decent bird's eye view of the whole of ancient Pamphylia and its ruins-packed ancient cities. A little farther east along the Mediterranean are a couple of magnificent pit stops to refresh at the gushing waterfalls of Manavgat and to bask in Side's irresistible sunsets. Although this itinerary seems busy, the farthest point is only about 80 kilometers east of Antalya. Getting an early start and spending an hour or so at each stop will still get you back to Antalya by evening.

PERGE

The ancient Pamphylian capital of **Perge** (Hwy. D400, Aksu, 0242/426-2748, 9am-7pm daily Apr.-Oct., 8am-5:30pm daily Nov.-Mar., 20TL) is 17 kilometers east of modern Antalya. Entirely relegated to history, the ancient city was settled by the Hittites and called Parha in the 15th century BC. Christian Saints Paul and Barnabas evangelized here on their missionary journeys to Antioch in AD 42. The ruins are widely scattered but still impressive enough to warrant a visit. Not much remains of the Bronze Age acropolis, one of antiquity's oldest, but Perge has a stunning stadium—one of Asia Minor's best preserved arenas after Aphrodisias near Pamukkale. It accommodated 12,000 spectators in its 2nd-century-AD heyday. Below the rows of seating were a total of 30 chambers, and every third chamber was used as an entrance or shop; the arcades still bear the engravings of the shopkeepers' names. The amphitheater is purely Greco-Roman, as evidenced by its position on the hillside, and the stage area features ornate reliefs of mythological scenes.

★ ASPENDOS

Not much remains of **Aspendos** (off Hwy. D400, Belkis, 0242/735-7337, 9am-7pm daily Apr.-Oct., 8am-5pm daily Nov.-Mar., 20TL), originally settled in 1000 BC by the Argives, colonists from the Peloponnesian city of Argos, but its one remaining monument, the **Aspendos Theater,** is worth the 48-kilometer trip from Antalya. It's by far the best-preserved theater complex in Asia Minor thanks to periodic maintenance and reinforcements provided by the Selçuks of Rum, who converted its stage into a palace at the end of the 1st millennium and a caravanserai by the mid-1300s. The best way to experience this monument is to try to coordinate a visit with one of the nighttime performances during the national opera and ballet festival from mid-June to early July.

SIDE

On a one-kilometer-long peninsula, the ancient metropolis of **Side** (off Hwy. D400, 0242/753-1542, 8am-5pm daily, 15TL) overlooks a contemporary, yet picturesque, summer resort 75 kilometers east of Antalya. In just 30 years this once idyllic fishing hamlet, with its unspoiled white sandy beaches and spectacular Roman ruins, has become a tourism powerhouse. While most of the visitors are Turks and Brits more interested in sunshine than history, Side's main claim to fame are its ruins. The most spectacular is the **Temple of Apollo** (southwestern tip of the harbor), which has crowned a hill overlooking the Mediterranean since the 2nd century AD. It's magnificently well-preserved, and along with the adjacent **Temple of Athena,** is arguably Turkey's most enchanting ruins. Exploring it at dusk with the sounds of the crashing waves and spotlights is

Aspendos Theater

a truly memorable experience. Side's **Roman Theater** was Pamphylia's largest, with a capacity of 20,000 spectators. Since Side lacks a hillside, this massive 2nd-century-AD structure was constructed in the Roman style, using an arch plan to support the sharp verticals, rather the typical Greek style of hollowing out a hillside. Other buildings include an agora, a library, and a 6th-century Byzantine basilica. The building blocks of most of these are so unstable that the park has had to install fencing to restrict access. Before leaving the site, stroll through the Roman baths that now house the **Side Museum** (0242/753-1006, 9am-7pm Tues.-Sun. Apr.-Oct., 8am-5pm Tues.-Sun. Nov.-Mar., 10TL). It's a small yet impressive repository of the statues and sarcophagi found intact at the site.

Side is a perfect place to linger. The town has excellent restaurants, all with sea views and phenomenal sunsets. Near the beach, one of the most popular for its quality and overall casual atmosphere is **Soundwaves Restaurant** (Barbaros Cd., 0242/753-1059), with jovial and attentive owners and staff and a nautical theme. The menu offers something for everyone, but the best picks are the fresh seafood, including garlic prawns, swordfish kebabs, or a mixed platter of calamari, prawns, and the catch of the day.

Just eight kilometers northeast of Side, the **Manavgat Waterfalls** (Manavgat Şelalesi, 3TL) provides another popular and refreshing escape from the scorching temperatures along the coast. This touristy spot, which can be underwhelming for some due to its small scale, is at the point where the Taurus Mountains' waters form the Manavgat River. Plenty of riverside diners offer grilled or baked fish. To reach the falls, head four kilometers west from Side to Manavgat, then another four kilometers north to the park.

Termessos

The citadel city of **Termessos** (0242/423-7416, 9am-5pm daily Apr.-Oct., 8am-5pm daily Nov.-Mar., 5TL) crowns a lofty mountaintop in the center of the rugged **Güllük Dağı Milli Parki** (Güllük Mountain National Park). With an elevation of 1,050 meters, even the mighty Alexander the Great couldn't conquer the walled city he later referred to as "an eagle's nest"; the Termessians—a fierce indigenous people of this former Pisidian metropolis—bravely defied his valiant efforts. Perhaps this is why the Seleucids, and the Romans after them, reluctantly complied with Termessos's desire to remain an independent ally.

Termessos is an impressively preserved ancient site, ideally situated high amid sheer cliffs and dense pine forests. Its most stunning ruins—both for historical value and mind-bending views of Antalya—is the **Roman Theater.** Like most of what remains of this magnificent, expansive city, the theater dates to the 2nd century BC and was crafted from boulders cut from the surrounding peaks. Also of note are a collection of magnificent rock-cut tombs and the pair of sarcophagi—those of Alexander's general Alcates and ancient Greek geographer Agathemerus.

Exploring Termessos can be tricky; the site is steep, vast, and exposed to the elements. Plan on arriving early with plenty of water, comfortable hiking shoes, sunscreen, and a hat. Site maps, provided at the ticket booth, will assist you in navigating the 14 points of interest. Follow the signs toward the tombs along the long, sometimes steep and narrow footpath that snakes past rock-hewn tombs, part of the upper city walls, and the odd sarcophagus. After accomplishing the site's most intense climb, turn back and go down to Termessos's center, where the theater and 90 percent of the ruins are located. A quick early-morning visit shouldn't take longer than two hours. It will take longer in the more crowded, hotter afternoon.

Termessos is 35 kilometers north of Antalya, about 10 kilometers southeast of the Antalya-Denizli highway (E87). Visiting on your own with a vehicle is possible, but an excursion with a knowledgeable guide is highly recommended. Contact tour agency **Nirvana Travel Service** (Hesapçı Sk. 3, Antalya,

0242/244-3893, www.travelantalya.com) to book this day trip (€45), which also includes a visit to the picturesque and refreshing **Düden Şelalesi** (Duden Waterfalls). All entrance fees, lunch, an English-speaking guide, and air-conditioned transportation are included.

ENTERTAINMENT AND EVENTS
Nightlife

There are several options for nighttime outings in Antalya. You can to take to the streets of Kaleiçi for a stroll winding through the souvenir and carpet shops, stopping at an ice cream parlor, and ending the evening at a bar at the old harbor or Paşa Camii Sokak. Another choice is to head to Konyaaltı's Antalya Beach Park, where clubs and restaurants spill onto the sand on the beachside promenade, and convivial *meyhaneler* (taverns) line the other side. To find the local flavor of Antalya, check out the pricier bars and restaurants lining Atatürk Kültür Parkı, just one kilometer from the old town. If you're keen to party all night with an Eastern European crowd, try the hot nightclubs in the resorts of Lara Beach, 17 kilometers from the city center. Don't forget the Turkish or *Arabian Nights* evening shows touted by most travel agencies in the area. There's no enforced dress code, but since Antalya has more Eastern Europeans than the resorts to the west, you may be more comfortable dressing up more than, say, at clubs in Fethiye and Marmaris, where beachwear is standard.

In the heart of Kaleiçi, the übercool **Public** (Hesapçı Sk. 47, 0252/244-2196, from 4pm) bar fills street-side tables every night of the week in summer with a trendy crowd of locals and travelers. House music plays indoors and outside at this restored Ottoman abode, and live music is featured inside on occasion.

If you're staying in the old town, a more convenient nightclub option than Lara Beach and Konyaaltı is **Ally's** (Sur Sk. 4/8, 0242/244-7704, www.ally.com.tr). This 4,000-square-meter facility, atop the ancient city walls, boasts 10 elegant bars and restaurants. Ally's is one of Antalya's entertainment trademarks for its laser shows and lineup of Turkey's top singing acts and Europe's reigning DJs. With white tables and fuchsia accents, Ally's welcomes guests dressed in their finest attire nightly during the summer.

For an evening out in Kemer, 45 kilometers west of Antalya, head to the coast's largest—and trendiest—clubs after Bodrum's Halicarnassus, **Club Inferno** (Deniz Cd. 1, Kemer, 0242/814-5332, www.infernoclub.net). This megaclub is known for its themed parties and racy cabaret acts. But be warned: The atmosphere here is more like a strip club than a dance club. At capacity, you can dance the night away with 3,000 mostly Russian guests.

Festivals

Every year in the first week of October, Turkey's movie stars and journalists head to Antalya for the **Altın Portakal Film Festivalı** (www.altinportakal.org.tr). Showings of full-length movies and short films around town and an awards ceremony celebrate the best national and international talents in filmmaking.

Also of note is the **Lara Sandland** (www.larasandland.com, May-Nov.) festival that features the talents of dozens of the world's top sand sculptors as they create temporary architectural masterpieces along the beaches of Antalya's Lara quarter. In 2013, the theme was "Empires." In 2009 the theme "Mythology" saw five artists molding 1,000 tons of sand into a Chinese dragon, a creation that entered *Guinness World Records* as the largest sand sculpture. A complete list of festivals in Antalya can be found at www.antalyafestivals.org.

SPORTS AND RECREATION
Beaches

The entire province of Antalya is lined by a long sandy strip along the Mediterranean, so snatching a good spot to catch some rays won't be difficult. Right in the center of town, the Konyaaltı quarter boasts a 1.5-kilometer pebbly beach with world-class amenities aimed to entertain families. The **Beach Park** (0242/249-0900, www.beachpark.com.tr) includes the kid-tailored **AquaLand** (28TL pp ages 7-11, 47TL pp over age 11), one of Turkey's largest water parks, and **DolphinLand** (27TL ages 3-11, 40TL over age 11). Otters, white whales, and bottlenose dolphins thrill spectators during one-hour performances scheduled twice daily in summer; for an extra 200TL, you can swim with dolphins—although only for five minutes. Also of interest to families in Konyaaltı is **Antalya Aquarium** (Dumlupinar Blv., 0242/245-6565, 10am-8pm daily year-round, www.antalyaaquarium.com, €25 adults, €19 children). With 40 exhibition spaces, this giant amusement center has the largest underwater aquarium tunnel in the world and a swimming reef where the kids can get up close to harmless rays and sharks in a shallow pool. Don't miss having a snowball fight in Snow World, either—it's definitely fun for the whole family.

Of the seven beach clubs currently in operation, **Eleven** (Beach Park 11, 0242/249-0922, www.elevenbeach.com, 10TL) commands the largest crowds for its luxurious parasol-covered couches in the sand and its tasty menu of grills and fresh salads. No matter which beach club you choose, each features its own restaurant and water-centric or fashion- and music-filled activities—some even organize boat tours—along with the expected beachfronts outfitted with comfy lounges, umbrellas, and bathing facilities. As day turns to night, these beach clubs turn into upscale outdoor nightclubs.

The Antalya Beach Park is located three kilometers west of Kaleiçi and can be accessed by riding the tram to the Müze stop. A 200-meter stroll westward leads to the main entrance.

The second beach option is the long sandy strip of **Lara Beach,** 17 kilometers east of Kaleiçi, but it can take up to an hour to get there aboard municipal bus KL09 (2TL) through city streets, so the prospect of spending the day here after visiting Konyaaltı's beachy amusement mall is less than inspiring.

Unique to Antalya are the icy springs that find their way from high up in the Taurus Mountains to the sea, creating some stunning scenery in the process and plenty of soaking opportunities for the brave. The best spring is **Aşağı Düden Şelalesi** (Lower Duden Falls), where the torrential water cascades into the Mediterranean. It's located 10 kilometers east of Antalya, right before Lara, and is best

Aşağı Düden Şelalesi cascades into the Mediterranean.

reached by boat. Or head north 10 kilometers to **Yukarı Düden Şelalesi** (Upper Duden Falls), where you'll find teahouses and cafés.

Another glacial spring is just east of Kaleiçi harbor at a point called **Memerli Plajı** (Marble Beach). Accessed through **Memerli Restaurant** (Kaleiçi Banyo Sk. 25, 0242/248-5484, 11TL), this small beach is separated by Antalya's ancient city walls. Due to its proximity to the old town, this tiny sun-kissed stretch gets busy in summer, so claim your sunbed early.

Cruises

The Phaselis and Three Islands day cruise from Kemer provides a pleasant option for visiting Antalya's fantastic coast. Prearrange the cruise with local agent **Nirvana Travel Service** (Hesapçı Sk. 3, 0242/244-3893, www.travelantalya.com). This particular trip stops first at Phaselis, the ancient port founded by Greek pirates in 674 BC, and moves on to picturesque Ayışığı Bay and Pirates Cave. Others cruises, particularly those setting off from the Antalya's old harbor, are varied and include one- and two-hour excursions of the Gulf of Antalya (from €10). The two-hour cruise to the Lower Düden Waterfalls is by far the better option, as the highlight of the one-hour tour is the waterfalls seen from the harbor. Other cruises have much longer itineraries that might include stops as far north as Demre, Olympos, and even Kaş. The size of the group and the type of lunch (which ranges from a sandwich to a three-course meal) served on board affects the price of a cruise, as does the type of vessel—at the harbor in Kaleiçi you can board anything from a 10-meter fishing boat to a full-scale replica pirate ship.

Diving

The Gulf of Antalya's seafloor is littered with the remains of two French World War II ships and fighter planes. The wrecks provide another dimension to diving among the area's kaleidoscopic display of flora and fauna, which include giant sea sponges, rare Mediterranean Monk seals, and glittering schools of bluefin tuna. Mild winds and shallow caves also make this bay ideal for discovery divers.

Diving schools and services are provided at major resort hotels from Kemer to Belek (past Lara Beach) in the east. Courses and individual dives are popular, so it may be smart to book in advance. Antalya's outfitter and instruction facility of choice is **Yunus Diving School** (Konyaaltı Beachpark 5-6, 0242/238-4486, www.yunusdiving.com). Led by Cumhur Tuğ, the founder of the Antalya Underwater Sports Association, Yunus offers two-hour dives and weeklong certification programs, starting at 65TL (not including equipment rental).

Golf

Ensconced among the surrounding peaks of the Taurus Mountains, the bulk of golf schools, resorts, and clubs are situated in Belek, 47 kilometers east of Antalya. As Turkey's premier destination for golfers, the region now boasts over 10 championship golf courses and in 2013 hosted the inaugural US$5.3 million Turkish Airlines World Golf Tournament at the **Antalya Golf Course** (Belek, 0242/725-5970, www.agc.com.tr), where Tiger Woods drove and putted around the courses designed by European Golf Design and David Jones.

Another reputable property is **LykiaWorld & Link** (Köprüçay Mevkii, 0252/754-4343, www.lykiagroup.co.uk). Designed by acclaimed course architect Pete Dye, this demanding 18-hole course is the only links course in Turkey and the only one hugging the Mediterranean. It features loads of pot bunkers, rye grass, elevated tees on curvaceous sand dunes, and shifting Mediterranean winds to challenge the seasoned golfer along its par-72 course.

Hiking

Turkey's first long-distance waymarked trekking route, the **Lykia Yolu** (Lycian Way), and the more recent **St. Paul Yolu** (St. Paul

Hiking the Lycian Way

Brainchild of hiker extraordinaire Kate Clow, a British expatriate residing in Antalya, the Lycian Way winds its way along ancient Lycia. Clow cleared and marked this path that swoops through the Tekke Peninsula, a headland that juts dramatically into the Mediterranean, and she continues to maintain it. The mountains soar from the pined coast forming pygmy coves, astounding vistas, and excellent trails. Along the way, the Lycians' impressive burial chambers in their ancient architectural style can be explored along with a myriad other ancient sites.

A 509-kilometer marked trail, the Lycian Way loops from Fethiye to Antalya. It's graded medium to difficult since it's not level, ascending and descending as it approaches and swerves away from the sea. The trail consists of footpaths and mule trails and tends to be hard-surfaced in limestone and coarse gravel. The going is easy near Fethiye and gets more difficult as it winds southward. Spring (Feb.-May) or fall (Sept.-Nov.) are the best seasons to hike. Stay away in summer, as temperatures can hover around 40°C with high humidity. Hotels and inns pepper the start of the route around Patara, Kalkan, Kaş, Myra, Finike, Adrasan, Olympos, Çıralı, and Tekirova. Village houses and camps dot the rest of the way. Camping does not require any special permission.

Some of the features of the trail include dazzling walks along the slopes of Babadağ, with paragliders soaring above; the spectacular slope into Faralya from the cliffs of the protected Butterfly Valley; Patara's 12-kilometer-long beach; the pebbly coasts of the resorts of Kaş and Kalkan; the Genoese Castle, harbor, and sunken Hellenic city near Üçağız; Myra's stunning theater masks and the church of the Angel Gabriel in the hills above; the exhilarating trek on the mountain ridge leading to Finike; the views from Cape Gelidonia; the rough climb up Mount Olympos (2,388 meters); wading through the canyon at Göynük; and the ruins of out-of-the-way Lycian cities—along with meeting gregarious villagers, old country houses, and lush green forests along the snow-white rocks and the startling blue of the Mediterranean.

There's lots of information online at **Trekking in Turkey** (www.lycianway.com) or in the highly recommended book *The Lycian Way* by Clow and avid hiker and photographer Terry Richardson. Solo travel is safe, although you can arrange a guided tour for 8 to 16 people with **Middle Earth Travel** (Cevizler Sk. 20, Göreme, 0384/271-2559, www.middleearthtravel.com), which has three Lycian Way tours ranging 7 to 14 days, as well as a range of hiking itineraries around Turkey. The eight-day Pirates Coast Trek runs from Antalya to Cape Gelidonia (€680), while the easier seven-day Seven Capes Trek runs from Kayaköy to Patara (€570). Tours include airport transfers, accommodations, a guide, most meals, and luggage transfers from one stop to the next.

Trail), were realized by British expatriate and avid hiker Kate Clow. Along with Terry Richardson, she spent years signposting these spectacularly scenic courses. The 509-kilometer Lycian Way winds through ancient Lycia, from Fethiye to Antalya, along rocky footpaths and mountainous mule trails that never stray far from the sea. This medium-to-difficult course involves several steep climbs and descents, accentuated by summer's blistering heat. The second path leads northeast from Perge (10 kilometers east of Antalya) over the Taurus Mountains to ancient Antioch in Pisidia, in the stunning Eğirdir lake region. This more rigorous 500-kilometer route partly covers Saint Paul's first missionary journey through Asia Minor. It involves 2,200-meter climbs, with two optional 2,800-meter ascents for more seasoned trekkers.

Clow created an extensive website, **Trekking in Turkey** (www.lycianway.com), and penned two companion books with detailed maps. The best time to hike either trail is February-May and September-November. And while the Lycian Way is generously signposted, the Saint Paul Trail only has officially approved white and red waymarkers.

ACCOMMODATIONS

For most international travelers, the prettiest and most convenient place to stay is Kaleiçi, and thankfully there are numerous tried-and-true boutique, five-star, and inn properties for all budgets. The old town is ideal for a stay of a night or two, but if a weeklong vacation by the beach is in the cards, check into one the hotels and resorts in Konyaaltı or Lara Beach.

Kaleiçi has a wealth of historical Ottoman mansions lovingly restored into family-run inns. Most of these have their own pint-size luxuries with rarely more than a dozen cozy rooms lining a landscaped courtyard or a pool. The size of some smaller rooms is due to the fact these lodgings were designed as homes rather than modern hotels, though some owners have mastered the art of renovating historical digs while maintain the abode's former glory. In the evening these hotels transform into romantic dining settings from which to savor succulent Turkish fare. And with the ancient harbor just steps away, you'll be within walking distance of Antalya's old town bar and restaurant scene.

Under €100

Boasting a mid-range traveler's dream setting is ★ **Hotel Alp Paşa** (Hesapçı Sk. 30, Kaleiçi, 0242/247-5676, www.alppasa.com, €80-1,500). This hotel oozes with charm and luxury in its 150-year-old collection of *konaks* (residences) that once belonged to wealthy Ottoman merchants; two of the original structures—the *selamlık* and *haremlik* (men's and women's quarters)—were painstakingly scoured clean of layers of paint and cement. Carved doors, intricate ceilings, and building stones dating from Roman and Byzantine times were discovered underneath. Inside, the rooms are ample and sparsely decorated with Ottoman touches and have individual air-conditioning units and tiled baths. Some feature canopied beds, others whirlpool tubs. Outside, a time-worn pond surrounded by an original mosaic-tiled courtyard became the perfect spot to add a small pool. An overflowing breakfast buffet welcomes guests every morning, while two à la carte restaurants also offer high-quality dinners for guests and nonguests.

Mavi Konak Guesthouse (Tabakhane Sk. 1, Kaleiçi, 0242/248-2558, 42-130TL) is a two-story Ottoman abode with fresh blues and whites decorating the rooms and common areas, creating clean and inviting ambiance. Male and female dorm rooms are available, and basic rooms provide privacy. The guesthouse is just off the main pedestrian thoroughfare of Hesapçı Sokak, where a good variety of restaurants and bars can be found; guests can also relax in the trendy open-air courtyard adjacent to the house.

It would be hard to find a friendlier host than Yaman Yılmaz, the manager of ★ **Dantel Hotel & Pansion** (Zeytin Geçidi 4, Kaleiçi, 0242/247-3486, www.dantelpension.com, from €45). Yaman goes above and beyond to ensure guests enjoy this homey eight-room inn. Nestled a street back from the Red Tower on one of the side streets of Kaleiçi, it is within 10 minutes' walk to the ancient harbor. Big rooms with bold colors sport modern baths, air-conditioning, and even wide-screen TVs. Breakfast is served in the courtyard, but venture up to the rooftop to take in the scenery of Antalya's coast. This inn is excellent value for the money.

Villa Tulipan (Kaledibi Sk. 6, Kaleiçi, 0242/244-9258, www.villatulipan.com, €45-75) comprises eight spacious rooms, two of which are suites that have separate lounges decked out with Dutch artwork and continental decor honoring Kaleiçi's Old World charm. Four of the rooms have balconies, but the Istanbul suite is the one with breathtaking views of the glistening Mediterranean from a sizeable balcony. If you miss out on the suite, there's always the Turkish apartment, with its own Turkish bath, kitchen, and dining area. The rooftop terrace also has panoramic views of Antalya's rugged coast, and the courtyard at ground level will appeal with its vegetable patch and olive and citrus trees. It's not a bad place to read a novel in peace and quiet just five minutes from the harbor.

€100-200

Tuvana Hotel (Karanlık Sk. 18, Kaleiçi, 0242/244-4054, www.tuvanahotel.com,

€95-350) is a 46-room B&B that far surpasses its competition in the old town of Kaleiçi. Located on a quiet side street, sheltered from the fray of touristy boutiques, Tuvana comprises the four mansions of Abdi Effendi, a high Ottoman officer who threw lavish parties for visiting dignitaries during the first half of the 18th century. Today, his descendants continue that hospitality. The B&B's main house features simple guest rooms with opulent drapery and bed linens as well as the owner's prized antiques. The deluxe rooms are located in the other buildings and feature flat-screen TVs, Ottoman-style gold-leaf ceilings, and crystal lighting. Outside, the walled courtyard welcomes with a full-size swimming pool. Orange, tangerine, banana, plum, and pomegranate trees offer fruit for the picking, but if real hunger strikes, head to one of the three good on-site restaurants.

The best hotel near the harbor is the **Puding Marina** (Mermerli Sk. 15, 0242/244-0730, www.pudinghotels.com, €120). With 74 rooms in seven historical mansions, you'd expect Ottoman intricacies and antique allure in the heart of Kaleiçi, but this salubrious special boutique hotel is very chic. Modern decor of rich purples, beiges, and whites embellish standard, deluxe, and suite rooms, while family rooms with the same decor come in a single-story or two-story design. Guests all have access to a gym, luxury spa center, and Saint-Tropez-inspired outdoor pool area. At the end of the day, enjoy dining at the Patio Restaurant either poolside or on the busy slate lane with its exclusive international dishes, such as smoked salmon and rich pastas. Puding Marina is ideal for couples and families to make the most of the harbor and Mermerli Beach, just two minutes away.

The **Marmara Antalya** (Eski Lara Yolu 102, Lara, 0242/249-3600, www.themarmarahotels.com, €124-303) is the quirky addition to the Marmara Group's list of exclusive hotels. Located toward Antalya's Lara quarter, just five kilometers from central Kaleiçi, it commands spectacular views of the bay. The 232 superior rooms are bright and contemporary, and well worth the rates, but plan to spend a little more for one of the 24 doubles on the three-level "Revolving Loft." Its floating apparatus is unique in the world in that it slowly revolves in its own pool. The result is constantly changing scenery of mountains, the sparkling Mediterranean Sea, and the hotel's vast grounds. Aside from an award-winning spa facility, the deluxe amenities feature a lily-white beach deck, an immense outdoor pool, and a 300-meter-long kayaking canal that crisscrosses the property. Rounding out the list of amenities are a stunning Turkish bath and sauna, tennis courts, four café-bars, a golf course, and the Marmara Group's celebrated Tuti restaurant.

Over €200

Mardan Palace (Kundü Köyü, Oteller Mevkii, Lara, 0242/310-4100, www.mardanpalace.com, €336-1,440) successfully blends Istanbul's historical landmarks with the pomp of Las Vegas's Caesar's Palace. With a total of 560 rooms, including two Royal Suites with private pool and butler (€14,000 per night!), the US$1.4-billion Mardan comprises three buildings and a series of garden villas that surround a sparkling five-acre pool, this insane property's version of the Bosphorus. In its center, the bridge, inspired by Da Vinci's original plan for the Galata Bridge, also spans a gondola track devised to transport guests on a 30-minute ride across the pool. Within the pool is a sunken aquarium with 3,000 fish; it doubles as the decor for the underground Aquamarine, the exclusive fish restaurant that shares acreage with 23 other high-end wining and dining facilities. The list of amenities goes on: a Jack Nicklaus signature golf course; a 7,500-square-meter full-service spa; toddler and teenager clubs and spas; and a dramatic Greek-style amphitheater. While the Mardan is touted as the most expensive resort on the Mediterranean, the Anatolian Wing's stunning superior rooms, at €336 per night, are not that exorbitant, considering their palatial decor, velvety Hermès linens, marble baths with rain showers, and sumptuous views.

Hotel SU (Dumlupinar Blv., Konyaaltı, 0242/249-0700, from €200) brings Miami Beach to Antalya's posh Konyaaltı neighborhood. A vision in white, from white floors and walls to the thick linens gracing the stainless steel bathroom racks, SU is far from stark. Its *Saturday Night Fever*-inspired lounge, featuring four gigantic disco balls, large welcoming atrium, and whimsical red accents throughout, makes up for the lack of color. The bonus of the sizable rooms (253 doubles, 41 suites) are the relaxing lounge beds provided on balconies that either open to splendid views of the Mediterranean or the Taurus Mountains. From its single (yes, it's white) tower, the property sprawls along perfectly clipped lawns. A blue-flag beach, a sparkling teak-decked pool, and Sushi, one of Antalya's best Asian-themed restaurants, round out its outdoor facilities. Other amenities include a full-service spa and gym, six international restaurants, three bars, and an indoor pool.

FOOD

Antalya can be considered Turkey's second culinary capital, after Istanbul, not for any particular food tradition but for its sheer number of restaurants. Included in the calculations are the industrial buffets and the eateries featured in the hospitality behemoths along the coast. Only Antalya's sought-after eateries and time-revered establishments are included here. It's a good idea to change out of the shorts and wear long pants, and reserving a table ahead of time will guarantee space and seating arrangements. If it's local flavor you're after, head to *lokantalar* (canteen-style restaurants) on the outskirts of Kaleiçi along 2 İnönü Sokak, near the corner of Cumhuriyet and Atatürk Caddesi. This pedestrian street shot to stardom in 2013 as "Umbrella Street," named after the 600 colorful umbrellas suspended over the laneway lined with inexpensive eateries.

Turkish

Gizli Bahçe (Dizdar Hasan Bey Sk. 1, Kaleiçi, 0242/244-2828, 20TL) doesn't stray from its Anatolian roots by going continental; regional appetizers like yummy *şakşuka* (a garlicky appetizer of sautéed eggplant, zucchini, and tomato) and *tahinli piyaz* (white bean salad in tahini sauce) are reasons enough to dine here. The fish *köfte* (meatballs) served on arugula and the Ottoman Special—stewed lamb served on caramelized eggplant and unexpectedly drizzled with orange juice—are delectable entrées. Gizli is located up on the ramparts overlooking the sea. In the evening, enjoy this romantic setting with Antalya's lights twinkling along the coast.

International

Perched high above the Mediterranean on the cliff face of Atatürk Culture Park is **Nar Beach & Bistro** (Konyaaltı Cd. 55, 0242/247-6868, www.narbeachbistro.com, 15TL), a classy café where, in summer, you can recline in comfy cedar beach chairs under enormous white umbrellas and order your pasta, pizza, or burger from an iPad. The outdoor deck is popular during the day, but in the evening the indoor dining area comes alive with Turkish live music Thursday to Saturday. The café is an ideal stop for those returning to Kaleiçi from the Antalya Museum. Simply get off the historic tram at Barbaros to find Nar (Turkish for "pomegranate") at the eastern end of the park.

Castle Bar & Restaurant (Hıdırlık Sk. 48, 0242/248-6594, www.kaleicicastle.com, 20TL) is a casual two-level open air venue right on the cliffs of the Gulf of Antalya near the Red Tower in Kaleiçi. This prime location translates to dining by the Mediterranean while gazing over the stunning scenery of the Taurus Mountains. And because the restaurant faces west, grab a table for sunset to capture fantastic photos of the day's end over the rugged coastline. The menu touts the usual fare found at Turkish restaurants that combine international cuisine with kebabs and plenty of steaks, salads, pasta, and seafood. Being in close proximity to the hotels of the old town makes it quite convenient to linger in one of the canvas deck chairs with a beer, wine, or cocktail in hand before turning in.

A number of the boutique hotels in Kaleiçi have restaurants open to both guests and nonguests, but expect to pay a little more than usual for the privilege of dining with a sophisticated set. One restaurant that's worth a visit is **Il Vicino Pizzeria** (Paşa Camii Sk. 13, 0242/247-6015, www.ilvicinopizzeria.com, 25TL). As part of the Tuvana Hotel complex, this petite pizzeria complete with red-and-white checkered placemats, barebones wood seating, and a wood-fired pizza oven that will transport you to Florence. No wonder: chef Alessandro Paoletti is a Florentine. Standard pizzas and delicious antipasti plates are available for under 25TL, but the setting warrants trying Alessandro's signature or folded calzones, prepared and cooked before your eyes. Perhaps the best part of the night is polishing off the meal with an authentic Italian dessert such as *panna cotta* or tiramisu. *Si*, that's *amore!*

Seafood
Club Arma (Iskele Cd. 75, 0252/244-9710, www.clubarma.com.tr, 30TL) is located in a refurbished 19th-century gasworks on a small bluff at the north end of Antalya's ancient harbor. Long gone are the sacks kept here when the building was later used as a silo; in their stead, tables dressed in white linens occupy a setting that evokes European dining at its best. The fish and meat dishes on the menu are grilled to perfection, but Arma's seafood—from grilled lobster to the jumbo prawns and avocado appetizer—is succulently addictive. By 10pm, Arma earns its "Club" prefix by welcoming hundreds of partygoers on the outdoor platform adjacent to the restaurant.

INFORMATION AND SERVICES
Antalya's **Tourism Information Office** (Cumhuriyet Cd., 0242/241-1747, www.antalyakulturturizm.gov.tr, 8am-7pm daily) is located less than 100 meters west of Kaleiçi clock tower, on the sea side of the street. Flyers, maps, and brochures are available at this location, but reputable maps and information can also be found at travel agencies and hotels. For an exhaustive Internet resource about Antalya and its districts, **Antalya Guide** (www.antalyaguide.org) has up-to-the-minute information about weather and happenings around town.

Run by English-speaking Kemal, the **Owl Bookshop** (Kocatepe Sk. 9, Kaleiçi, 0242/243-5718, 10am-7pm daily) has secondhand English books available for purchase or exchange in two rooms.

There are no banks, ATMs, or currency exchange offices in the old town. They're located on Kazım Özalp Caddesi, just north of Cumhuriyet Caddesi, and ATMs are also at the southern end of Atatürk Caddesi. The main **PTT** (Atatürk Cd., 600 Sk. 1, 0242/229-2811, 7am-11pm Mon.-Sat.) post office is situated in Konyaaltı.

GETTING THERE
Air
Antalya Airport (AYT, Antalya Havalimanı, 0242/330-3030, www.antalya.dhmi.gov.tr) has more than 200 flights daily during summer, so finding a connection from anywhere in Europe is a breeze. Domestic carriers **Turkish Airlines** (0212/444-0849, www.turkishairlines.com), **Pegasus Airlines** (0850/250-0737, www.flypgs.com), and **Sun Express** (444-0797, www.sunexpress.com) provide domestic and international flights to and from Antalya daily. Other domestic airlines that may have lower fares include **Atlas Jet** (0850/222-0000, www.atlasjet.com) and **Onur Air** (0850/210-6687, www.onurair.com.tr). British charter airline **Thomas Cook** (www.flythomascook.com) flies nonstop from London's Gatwick, and **Swissair** (www.swissair.com) flies nonstop from Zurich.

Antalya's airport is located 17 kilometers east of the city center. The **Havaş** (0242/330-3800, www.havas.com.tr, 10TL) shuttle buses run hourly to and from the airport, Antalya *otogar*, and the 5M Migros Shopping Mall in Konyaaltı. Unfortunately, the shuttle doesn't pass close to Kaleiçi; therefore a taxi (35TL) from the airport or a 20-minute **AntRay** (light rail) journey (5TL with a KentKart) from the *otogar* is advised to reach hotels in the old town. The nearest AntRay stop is Ismetpaşa, a five-minute walk north of the entrance to Kaleiçi.

Car

The airport has a dozen rental agencies, including **Avis** (0242/330-3073) and **Hertz** (0242/330-3848). Cars (80TL per day), scooters (60TL per day), and bicycles (25TL per day) are also available for rent in Kaleiçi from **Özbaylar Antalya Rent A Car** (Hesapçı Sk. 65, 0242/248-9723, www.antalyacityrentacar.com).

Traveling from towns east or west of Antalya means following the coastal D400 highway; from the northwest, follow the E87 to the D350 (the express route from Fethiye). The roads are all well signposted once you reach the city. Parking in Kaleiçi is free if you have accommodations within the old walls.

Bus

With one-hour flights priced occasionally as low as 85TL, traveling up to 14 hours cross-country by coach for about the same fare doesn't make much sense. Nonetheless, Antalya is still a huge hub for coach companies; at last count there were more than 150 serving regional, cross-country, and international routes.

The largest coach providers serving Antalya are **Ulusoy** (444-1888, www.ulusoy.com.tr) and **Kamil Koç** (444-0562, www.kamilkoc.com.tr). Fares vary slightly among companies, but here are some rough estimates: Istanbul (710 kilometers, 70TL, 11 hours), İzmir (465 kilometers, 45TL, 5 hours), Ankara (555 kilometers, 55TL, 7 hours), and Nevşehir (for Göreme and Cappadocia, 525 kilometers, 55TL, 9 hours). **Metro Turizm** (444-3455, www.metroturizm.com.tr) also has coaches to Mavagat (75 kilometers, 19TL, 1 hour) and Alanya (135 kilometers, 18TL, 3 hours) east of Antalya.

Coach travel is just about the only means of getting around the region inexpensively. The best way to travel along the Mediterranean coast is with **Antalya Batı** (0242/331-4081, www.batiantalyatur.net) minibuses from Fethiye via the express highway D350 (200 kilometers, 25TL, 3.5 hours) or via the slower, winding D400 (222 kilometers, 35TL, 6.5 hours) stopping anywhere along the route, including major towns like Kalkan (28TL, 5 hours), Kaş (24TL, 4 hours), Demre (18TL, 3 hours), and Olympos and Çıralı (12TL, 1 hour).

Antalya's *otogar* is a massive dual terminal situated just eight kilometers northwest of the old town on Dumlupınar Bulvarı. The easiest way to get to town from the *otogar* is with the light-rail **AntRay** (5TL with a KentKart). Ticket offices are at the station, just a short walk from the *otogar*; follow the signs from the bus terminals. The closest AntRay stop to Kaleiçi is Ismetpaşa. Taxis are also available at the *otogar*.

GETTING AROUND

If your base is Kaleiçi, you can walk to most of the historical sites within 15 minutes. For destinations just outside this historic district, a convenient **historical tram** (1.50TL) stops at 14 locations along the coast and inland. Starting west at the Antalya Museum, just a few hundred meters from the entrance to Konyaaltı's Beach Park, it winds its way inland along Cumhuriyet Caddesi, stopping near the clock tower, and continuing southeast along Atatürk Caddesi.

Antalya's center is gridlocked with traffic from morning till night. Commuting by car or taxi is not a good idea. Clogged one-way streets make it horrendous for those not used to the city. Even walking the two kilometers west from Kaleiçi to Konyaaltı may prove faster (30 minutes) and much cheaper than by car or taxi.

Cappadocia and Central Anatolia

Cappadocia 332
Konya 356
Ankara 365
Hattuşaş (Boğazkale) 377

Much of central Anatolia remains unknown to foreigners, perhaps with the exception of the capital Ankara and the Cappadocian region's fairy chimneys—the phallic-shaped monuments of soft volcanic ash carved by the wind. This region is a steppe, a large area of flat, unforested grassland. But shake any notions of windswept wastelands. This massive elevated plain, roughly 300 meters above sea level between Turkey's two mountain ranges, the Pontic Mountains to the north and the Taurus Mountains to the south, is anything but bland.

There's history that still remains buried deep in the earth's layers. Suffice it to say that this strategic corridor, stuck between the East and the West, was the center of trade routes for eons. First, the Assyrians were lured by the wealth of ancient Anatolians around 2000 BC. Then came the Persians, the Greeks, the Romans, and the Selçuk emirates; each group left its cultural mark. Places like Hattuşaş, Cappadocia, and Konya are imprinted with traces of the ancients. Atatürk's famed capital, Ankara, is a perfect mix of old and new, as found in the pre-Hittite Citadel district and its spectacular mid-20th-century buildings.

Cappadocia's spectacular landscape may be central Anatolia's pearl, but the rest of the region is worth a look to appreciate Turkey's history and diversity. You will find the lunar landscape of Cappadocia; the sheer amount of history and culture; the country's adoration for Atatürk; and the region's exclusive haunts absolutely stunning.

PLANNING YOUR TIME

A decent exploration of the Cappadocia region requires at least three days. If you're also visiting Konya and Ankara, take six days. Base yourself in Göreme or pricier Ürgüp. The best time to visit arid central Anatolia is in the off-season, spring and fall. Summer in the unshaded valley is hot—often over 40°C—making a visit too exhausting. Cappadocia's cave hotels are the recommended accommodations, since these remain cool throughout summer and warm in winter. There's also a significant difference between day and night

Previous: tomb of Rûmî at the Mevlânâ Museum, Konya; hot-air balloons over Cappadocia. **Above:** colonnade at Atatürk Mausoleum, Ankara.

Highlights

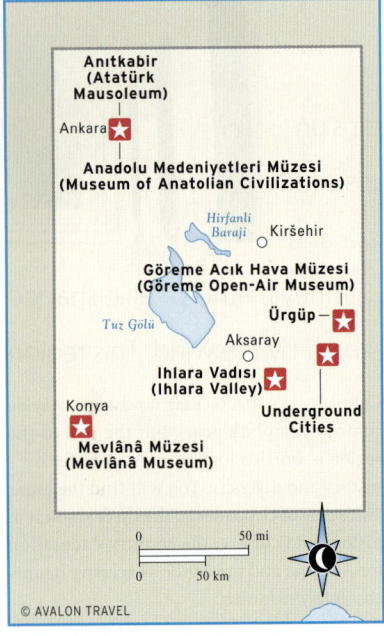

★ **Göreme Acık Hava Müzesi (Göreme Open-Air Museum):** Explore this immense outdoor park's collection of 10 rock-hewn churches and their remarkably well-preserved frescoes (page 335).

★ **Ürgüp:** Experience Cappadocia's rich wine history and five-star cave accommodations (page 347).

★ **Underground Cities:** Probe underground at Derinkuyu, Kaymaklı, and Özkonak, three subterranean cities that date back to the Hittites (page 351).

★ **Ihlara Vadısı (Ihlara Valley):** More than 100 rock-carved churches await discovery in this valley along the lush banks of Melendez River (page 353).

★ **Mevlânâ Müzesi (Mevlânâ Museum):** Pay your respects to the legendary Sufi mystic and poet Rûmî by visiting the 13th-century mausoleum built in his honor (page 358).

★ **Anıtkabir (Atatürk Mausoleum):** Join the legions of Turks who visit the massive mausoleum in the heart of Ankara, built to commemorate founding father Mustafa Kemal Atatürk (page 368).

★ **Anadolu Medeniyetleri Müzesi (Museum of Anatolian Civilizations):** Take a walk through Anatolia's past, where a parade of civilizations marches from the Paleolithic era through the Greeks, Romans, Selçuks, and Ottomans (page 370).

Cappadocia and Central Anatolia

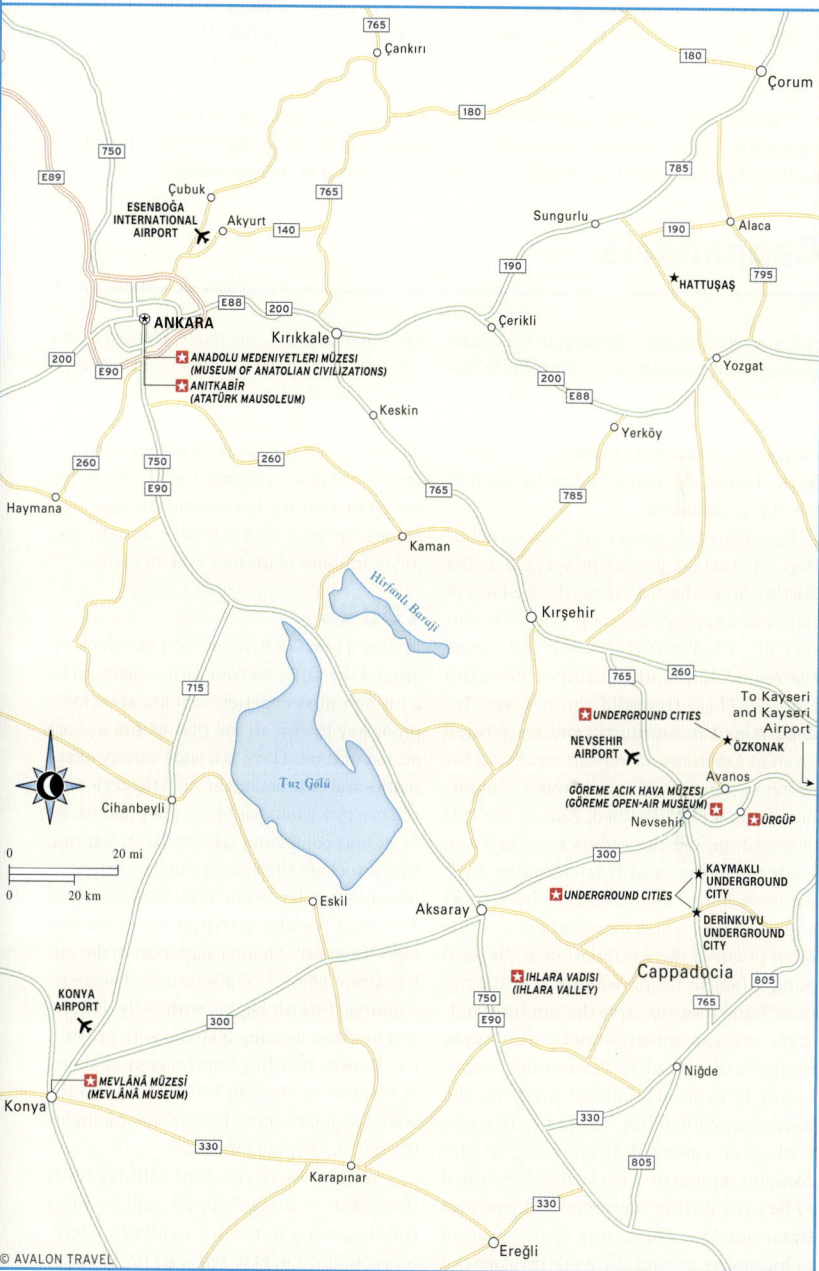

temperatures, sometimes as much as 20°C. The winters in the Anatolian heartland are freezing, with an average temp of -2°C December-February. The plus side, however, is that the already magical scenery gets even better with a thick cover of snow, up to 30 centimeters. This climate in no way hinders sightseeing; it gets even better when Mount Erciyes (Argeus), east of Cappadocia, opens for skiing and heart-pounding all-terrain vehicle touring.

The Konya Whirling Dervish Festival in mid-December is a great time for Rûmî fans to visit. Ankara comes alive for Victory Day, August 30, marking Turkey's victory over the Greeks in the Battle of Dumlupınar in 1922, one of last defining battles of the 1919-1923 Turkish War of Independence.

Cappadocia

Ask any government official as to the actual geographical boundaries of Cappadocia and they'll be hard-pressed to come up with an answer. Its eastern and western boundaries are unclear, but we know it's bordered to the south by the Taurus Mountains and to the north by the Pontic Mountains.

Its history, however, is not as nebulous. Historians generally agree that the Hittites were the first to settle the land of fairy chimneys sometime in the 18th century BC. The Persians followed and named the region Katpatuka (Land of Beautiful Horses). These fine wild equines were indeed famed in antiquity, and were often given to Assyrian and Persian royalty. In the center of Anatolia, this area was an important stop on the Silk Road. Rule of the area changed among the region's eastern and western empires and finally among Arab warlords before the advent of the Selçuks and Ottomans. These incessant power shifts often involved the annihilation of the local population, so it's no wonder that the natives found a way to carve the soft tufa landscape to create underground hideaways to escape hostile invaders. Persecution continued in the name of religion; Christians who were deemed heretics before Christianity took over enlarged these refuges into complex monastic cities that continued to be used during the somewhat peaceful Byzantine Era. These once again reverted to hideaways during the Arab invasions of the 7th century. Conversely, Cappadocian Christians were free to practice their religion under Muslim rulers.

The region's importance waned over time, its rock-hewn treasures forgotten until the arrival of French explorer Paul Lucas in the early 18th century. Lucas thrust this geological marvel back into scientific annals, and today, millions of tourists visit annually.

TOURS

Joining a tour is a better option than looking around the valley on your own, which can be a hit-and-miss experience; tours are a foolproof way to visit all the sites within a short period of time. There is a wide variety of activities and destinations around the region, so you can pick a tour based on your preferences. Most tour companies sell similar itineraries, which include site visits as well as activities like cooking classes and belly dance courses. The most popular activities are horseback treks (from €40, 2 hours); Jeep tours of the valleys (from €65); ATV adventures (from €35, 2 hours); Turkish Nights with belly dancers and folkloric dancing (€40-50, with or without dinner); Whirling Dervish evening shows at Saruhan or Dervish House (€25) and the wildly popular sunrise hot-air balloon flights (€175-250, discount for cash).

There are three standard full-day tours (from €50, 9:30am-5:30pm) sold by most travel agencies in town. Essentially, operators combine forces to sell seats on 16-seater

The Cappadocia Region

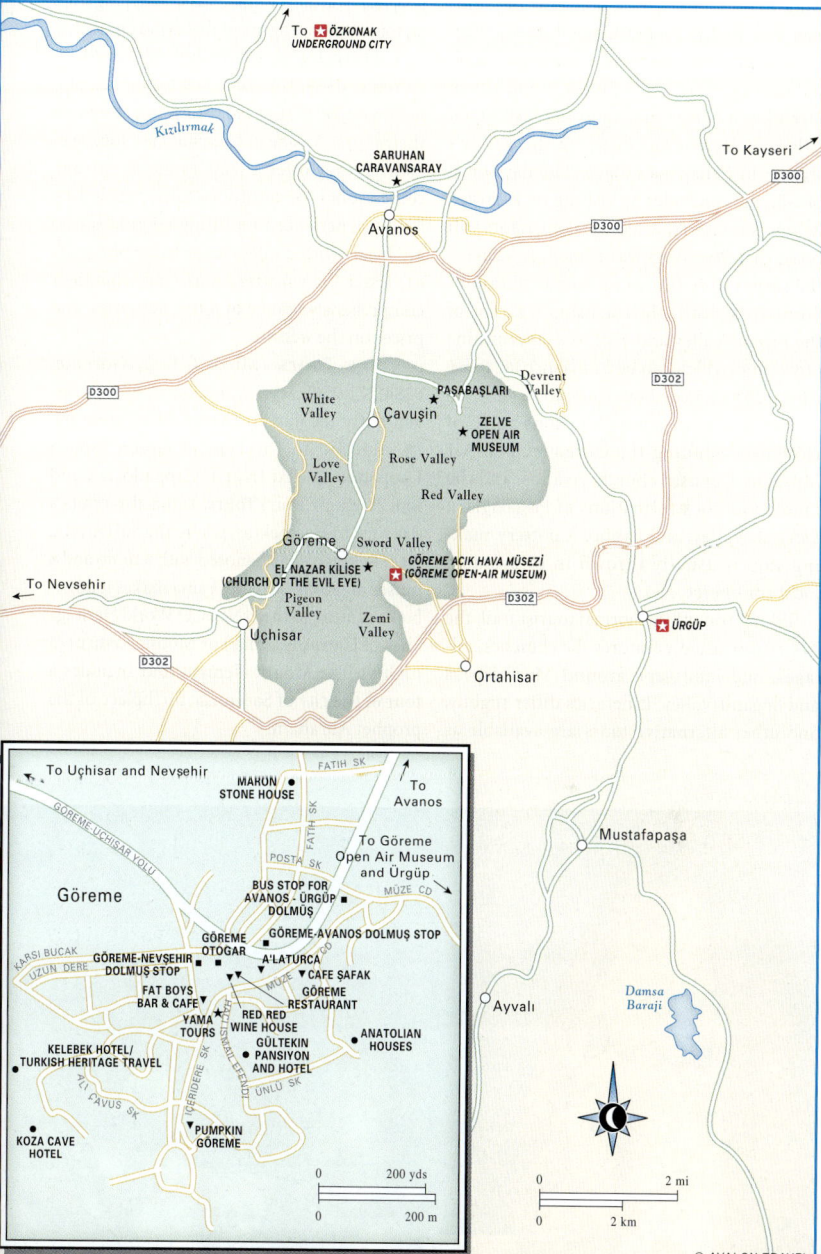

minivans with one English-speaking guide as the host. When one minivan sells out, they work to fill another. Best taken during summer and highly recommended, the **Green Tour** transports you from a panoramic look out near Göreme to the underground city of Derinkuyu before hiking in the lush green Ihlara Valley, with lunch by the valley's stream in Belisırma village. The day south of Göreme concludes by visiting rock-carved Selime Monastery, where local operators will boast that *Star Wars* was filmed; it wasn't—the scenes were filmed in similar terrain in Tunisia. Typically the final stop is a view of the Pigeon Valley and visit to a labyrinthine onyx shop, which can be a nuisance for those who aren't excited about shopping.

The **Red Tour** covers locations north of Göreme, including the Göreme Open-Air Museum, Çavuşin church, Avanos, and the mushroom rock formations of Paşabağları, Devrent Valley, and Ürgüp. A pottery-making stop is usually thrown in to promote local commerce.

Taking you off the normal tourist trail, the **Blue Tour** usually features the churches, villages, and landscape around Mustafapaşa and Soğanlı Valley. Itineraries differ slightly, and other alternative tours are available as companies try to offer something unique, but you can be sure the tour will have less than 15 people. If you don't want to make shopping stops on tour, there are agencies that avoid doing this.

Turkish Heritage Travel (Yavuz Sk. 1, Göreme, 0384/271-2687, www.goreme.com) is one outfit that avoids shopping stops on their tours. As one of Cappadocia's tour specialists, they offer a wide range of custom, recreational, or outdoors tours, all led by highly experienced multilingual guides who are locals with endless knowledge of the area's lesser-known attractions. Check out their comprehensive range of tours, activities, and prices on the website.

Yama Tours (Müze Cd. 2, Göreme, 0384/271-2508, www.yamatours.com) is conveniently located in the heart of Göreme. In addition to the typical Green (South Cappadocia), Red (North Cappadocia), and Blue (Soğanlı Tour) Tours, Yama also offers a day tour to Hacıbektaş, where the Sufi mystic Hacı Bektaş Veli is honored with a tomb and a museum. From Göreme, Yama makes it possible to venture to the UNESCO World Heritage Sites of Hattuşaş (1 day) or Mount Nemrut (3 nights). The Mount Nemrut tour includes a tour of the city of Şanlıurfa, birthplace of the prophet Abraham.

Cappadocia at dusk

GÖREME

Göreme is a small village, the massively popular original heart of Cappadocia, with a high density of tall fairy chimneys and rock-carved dwellings, some of which are still inhabited by local people. Small churches appear unexpectedly on the 1.5-kilometer stroll from Göreme to its main attraction, the Göreme Open-Air Museum. But what makes Göreme truly unique is its hiking along sometimes steep trails amid the striking landscape.

When compared to the nearby luxury hotel-packed hamlets of Ürgüp and Uçhisar, Göreme offers more variety and vibrancy for mid-range and budget travelers who want to explore the region. Restaurateurs and hoteliers have slowly refurbished dated cafés, homes, and barns into cozy eateries, and formerly abandoned caves now mold beautifully with modern structures, creating appealing B&Bs and hotels. These features, along with the abundance of shops, travel agencies, and the network of coaches and *dolmuşlar* (communal taxis), make Göreme the best base for exploring Cappadocia. Staying here also means being close to the action, with the moonscape of white fairy chimneys soaring up around the town's maze of paved streets, reminiscent of *The Flintstones* or the planet Tatooine in *Star Wars*. Walk up to **Sunset Point** (via Aydınkırağı Sk.) to watch sunset over the valleys, or if you're an early riser, come to watch the hundreds of hot balloons at sunrise. The changing colors of the landscape at dawn and dusk make wonderful photo opportunities.

★ Göreme Acık Hava Müzesi (Göreme Open-Air Museum)

Cappadocia's most noted site is the **Göreme Acık Hava Müzesi** (Müze Cd., 0384/271-2167, 8am-7pm daily Apr.-Oct., 8am-5pm daily Nov.-Mar., 20TL). While you'll find plenty of cave-dwelling scenes, much more striking are the collections of frescoed cave churches, carved out of the soft volcanic rock and embellished with light-reflecting frescoes by Orthodox Christian monks during the Middle Ages.

The Open-Air Museum is a testament to the piety of early Christians including Saint Basil the Great, who partly founded eastern monasticism and prescribed communal life that emphasized poverty, piety, liturgical prayer, and manual labor; and his followers, who opted for the pious life in the honey-combed rock dwellings of Cappadocia over the hedonistic life in the coastal cities. The museum includes a collection of 30 churches and chapels as well as rectories, abodes, and religious schools; the buildings form a roughly circular monastic complex carved entirely in the tufa. From the diamond-shaped rotary just past the entry, look for the clearly signed path that'll take you through the park and the sights on a counterclockwise route.

The frescoes are stunning despite minor damage caused by the elements. A few were badly marred during the Byzantine Iconoclasm during the 8th century, and most of the eyes were gouged out by Muslim locals fearing the evil eye.

First on the itinerary is **St. Basil's Church.** Its rectangular nave has niches and a trio of arches. The narthex, or lobby, features tombs in the floor, which interestingly have been left open. The north wall bears frescoes depicting Saints George, Basil, and Theodore. Check out the three Maltese crosses on the nave's vault; these are thought to represent the Holy Trinity.

Dating from the mid-11th century, **Elmalı Kilise** (Apple Church) owes its name to the red orb clenched by Saint Michael the Archangel in a fresco near the entrance. Michael is usually portrayed holding a red shield, not an apple. The frescoes inside depict saints, bishops, and martyrs. Another boasts a Last Supper scene with a large fish, the codified symbol of Christianity.

Just behind the rock that houses the Apple Church is the **Azize Barbara Kilisesi** (St. Barbara Chapel). It has a cruciform layout, with three apses embellished with simple red figures on white plaster. On one wall a giant locust, representing evil, faces two crosses on the opposite wall.

The **Yılan Kilisesi** (Snake Church) is named for the dragon that Saint George is seen slaying in one of its murals. Beyond the barrel-vaulted narthex, renditions of the hermit Saint Onuphrius, fronted by a sapling, can be seen, along with one depicting the church's founder, Saint Basil, holding a book in one hand.

The most impressive of the rock-carved churches is **Karanlık Kilise** (Dark Church). An extra 10TL fee is required to view its frescoes, which are the best preserved in Cappadocia. Thanks to its hidden location, this church escaped the wrath of the Iconoclasts, leaving intact most of its murals. The lack of direct sunlight in the inner halls also preserved the vivid frescoes from discoloration.

Azize Katarina Kilisesi (St. Catherine Chapel) rises from a Greek-cross floor plan, with a domed central crossing and barrel-vaulted transepts. Interesting for the number of graves on-site, the chapel has four beneath the floor and two in niches. The chapel, built by a donor named Anna, dates to the 11th century.

Çarıklı Kilise (Church with Sandals) earns its moniker for the pair of footprints in the narthex, right under the Ascension scene. Inaugurated in the early 13th century, this space is relatively new compared to the others, and its frescoes are much more elaborate. Look for the inner fresco of Christ Pantocrator with the busts of angels, right below the central dome.

Tokalı Kilisesi (Church with Clasp) is just outside the museum; a ticket to the museum grants visitors access. Of all the rock churches in Cappadocia, Tokalı boasts the greatest number and most detailed paintings narrating the life of Christ. The complex sprawls over four chambers, with a barrel-vaulted, single-nave 10th-century Old Church leading to the rectangular New Church. There are three vertical sections painted in bands of vivid green, reds, and indigo depicting Saint Basil and other saints.

The paintings and decorations represent a flowering of a uniquely Cappadocian artistic style, while the Byzantine architectural features of the churches, including the arches, columns, and capitals, are interesting in that not one of them is structurally needed.

El Nazar Kilise (Church of the Evil Eye)

If time permits, one of the most interesting rock-cut churches, **El Nazar Kilise** (Zemi Valley, 8am-7pm daily Apr.-Oct., 8am-5pm daily Nov.-Mar., 5TL), is an 800-meter walk from the Open-Air Museum. With frescoes and paintings dating to the 11th century, this church is famous for being cut into a solitary fairy chimney in a crucifix form. Two artists are responsible for the depictions of the life of Christ, from birth to the Passion, and the portrayals of saints and prophets of the Old Testament on the arches between the vaults and the main dome. When gazing at these frescoes, remember they were done at a time when books did not exist; they preserve the stories of the Christians who worshipped here a millennium ago. For an extended excursion, ask the custodian to reveal the whereabouts of the nearby Hidden Church.

Sports and Recreation

If there ever was a region that's best explored through nontraditional methods, Cappadocia is it. Gliding over the tufa in a balloon at sunrise, hiking or riding horseback through the myriad of easy-to-medium trails, and taking a safari in a Jeep or ATV through the entire valley, camera on standby, guarantees a memorable trip.

HOT-AIR BALLOONS

Hour-long hot-air balloon rides start at sunrise when you take off in a gigantic wicker basket dangling from a colorful balloon to reach a maximum height of 460 meters. In season, a veritable aerial ballet can be seen over the region as balloons by the dozen sail along the prevailing winds in colorful splendor.

Heading out before sunrise isn't fun, but that is easily forgotten once you're off the ground and gliding high above the landscape.

Early-morning takeoffs are best since winds are typically calm and cool, ensuring gentle and stable flight, mild landings, and maximum lift. This time of the day is also ideal for photography as sunrise enhances the valley's colors. Here is what to expect from a traditional flight: hotel pick-up before sunrise, snacks or breakfast before a 60-minute flight, a balloon basket accommodating up to 20 people, ceremonial champagne upon landing, and drop-off at the door of your hotel afterward. Deluxe 90-minute flights in a smaller basket, for up to 12 people, are available at higher cost. Private flights for couples or special groups can also be arranged at higher cost. Reservations are required prior to all flights; in season, book at least a week in advance by phone or online. And wear warm clothes; even in summer a sweater and cap will make for a more comfortable flight. Pants are ideal attire for both men and women, since passengers have to climb up into the basket.

Under new management since 2009, **Kapadokya Balloons** (Nevşehir, 0384/271-2442, www.kapadokyaballoons.com, €175-250, discount for cash) was the first hot-air balloon company established in Cappadocia in 1991. A slew of others followed, but Kapadokya is still one of the most experienced, with a staff of highly trained pilots who have worked all over the world. Flights are fully insured and run year-round, weather permitting.

When Martha Stewart (and my mother) toured Cappadocia, they took to the skies with **Royal Balloons** (Dutlu Sk. 9, Göreme, 0384/271-3300, www.royalballoon.com, €175-240, discount for cash), which uses silver Lindstrand balloons, known for their quality and safety; Royal is the only company in Cappadocia to use them. Royal also provides top insurance coverage and welcomes guests with a full buffet before the flight.

Many travel agencies and hotels have arrangements with balloon companies that make them likely to push sales for one company over another. Feel free to buy a ticket through them, as their commission is greatly valued, but confirm Royal and Kapadokya's services against what's on offer before agreeing on the sale.

HIKING

Even for those not fond of athletic shoes, Cappadocia's pastel-colored dunes make for a dreamy stroll. By day or night, particularly guided by a full moon, through summer's floral splendor or winter snow, meditative types will revel in wandering through the dozen little valleys with names like **Rose Valley** (Güllüdere I & II, 4 kilometers), **Red Valley** (Kızılçukur), **Pigeon Valley** (Güvercinlik, 4 kilometers), **Sword Valley** (Kılıçlar), **Zemi Valley** (5 kilometers), **White Valley** (also called Honey Valley, 6 kilometers), and the phallic **Love Valley** (Bağlıdere Vadisi). These valleys have relatively easy trails, most littered with rock-hewn churches too numerous to list, and take anywhere from one to three hours to walk. If you have an entire day earmarked for outdoor exploration, you can easily do a couple of these hikes, since most trails are interconnected.

One of the most striking outings is Red Valley, which extends from Çavuşin to the entrance of Ortahisar, passing various rock formations and rock-cut chapels. Pigeon Valley is another easy stroll through magnificent dovecotes; it starts on the south side of the Uçhisar Castle and ends at Göreme village. Avid hikers love the challenge of the White Valley hike, which runs about six kilometers from Uçhisar to Çavuşin village and winds through local gardens and Love Valley.

To be safe and comfortable, wear athletic shoes and a light coat for evening, when temperatures drop. Carting water and a picnic in a backpack is also a good idea if you want to dine under the ubiquitous Cappadocian apricot trees, but you can also stop at any of the makeshift cafés along the way for tea, freshly squeezed orange juice, or a game of *tavla* (backgammon). A word to the wise: Signs lead to the trails, but there are few markers once you're en route, so having a local guide is advised, especially if you're traveling solo.

For a no-hassle hiking experience on Cappadocia's trails, secret caves, and churches, Göreme native Mehmet Güngör of **Walking Mehmet** (0384/271-2064 or 0532/382-2069, www.walkingmehmet.net, €60 half-day, €80 full-day) is both an exhaustive resource of local knowledge and a die-hard hiker; he's clocked more than 1,350 kilometers guiding 8,000 guests on foot tours of the area. You can contact him through his website year-round or meet him and discuss plans for hiking the valleys at his Café Noriyon, by the amphitheater behind the *otogar* (bus station).

HORSEBACK RIDING

Cappadocia inherits its name from the Persian *katpatuka,* meaning "land of fine horses." Equines were bred in the valley from as early as 1500 BC. Cappadocia was renowned throughout the classical period for its stables, and honoring local landlords with horses became a tradition. You can saddle up with horses trained by Ekrem Ilhan, locally known as the Turkish cowboy and a bona fide horse whisperer. As the owner and operator of the **Dalton Brothers Ranch** (Müze Cd., 0384/271-2840, www.cappadociahorseriding.com), Ekrem and his team of guides offer two- and four-hour tours (100-200TL) daily through the valleys closest to Göreme, including Rose, Red, Honey, and Love Valleys. These tours are for beginners or experienced riders and can be taken morning and afternoon, but a trot at sunset is the best, as temperatures drop and the ambiance of the serene valleys are magical. Full-moon rides and multiple-day tours with camping as far afield as the Taurus Mountains near Antalya are also possible.

Accommodations

More than 80 percent of Göreme's hotels offer inexpensive and excellent accommodations; the remainder are some of the most exclusive hideouts in the entire valley. But however romantic the idea of staying in a cave might be, the lack of light and ventilation in some can result in a musty smell. The remedy is to book accommodations outfitted with a window and plenty of space for air circulation. No matter what the comforts of your room are, be prepared to be woken early by the sound of balloon pilots igniting their burners above Göreme. The Islamic morning call to prayer follows, echoing among the rocks of Göreme.

The town's top-end boutique hotel is ★ **Anatolian Houses** (Cevizli Sk., 0384/271-2463, www.anatolianhouses.com.

Cappadocia's blush-worthy Love Valley

tr, €150-240). Tucked at the end of a winding lane, the inconspicuous gate of this surreal property opens to a stunning outdoor-indoor pool. Upper-level rooms, "carved" into the soft bedrock, are lit either by skylights or clever floodlit recesses. Also deserving a nod are the collections of antiques and artifacts from Nevşehir Museum displayed in niches throughout the property. Luxury amenities include a sauna and hamam, as well as the highly recommended Rasoi Indian Restaurant located close by.

Göreme's best bargain accommodations are ★ **Kelebek Hotel** (Yavuz Sk. 1, 0384/271-2531, www.kelebekhotel.com, €55-180). This family-owned B&B offers a large assortment of lodging, from cave and traditional arched rooms to a duo of private fairy chimneys. The spacious suites are bright—a rarity in the region—and appointed with locally handmade furniture and fabrics; the en suite baths boast marble walls and unique hamam basins, power showers, and hot tubs. Kelebek's forte is in providing a full-service experience with a variety of tours, a pool, a restaurant that specializes in Cappadocian cuisine, and a fully-staffed Turkish bath.

Families looking for a cave dwelling of their own will love the spacious family suite (room 13) at **Gültekin Pansiyon and Hotel** (Roma Kalesi Arkası, 0384/271-2785, www.gultekinmotel.com.tr, 100-250TL). This gem of a budget to mid-range lodging is conveniently located one street back from the main thoroughfare, making it a great location for popping out for dinner or shopping. The lower floor has three cave rooms, while the second floor has a small courtyard lined by homey limestone rooms with colorful wooden ceilings, Anatolian rugs, and village-embroidered bedspreads. A buffet breakfast is served on the rooftop, which offers expansive views to the fairy chimneys surrounding the town. Get a seat early enough to watch the hot-air balloons drift above the valleys.

The all-natural **Koza Cave Hotel** (Cakmakli Sk. 49, 0384/271-2466, www.kozacavehotel.com, Mar.-Nov., €70-175), owned and operated by the Dural family, is a home away from home among the fairy chimneys. With views of Uçhisar to the west and Rose Valley to the east, Koza (meaning "cocoon") wraps visitors in luxury high above Göreme in ancient caves decked out with modern comforts and Anatolian touches. There is an on-site tour booking service, an à la carte restaurant, and personalized touches such as spas and private terraces attached to some rooms. Be warned, though, it can be difficult to leave this cocoon.

Bunk beds and dorms (from 30TL) for backpackers are found in a handful of hostels around town, but **Maron Stone House** (Göreme Kasabası 9, 0384/271-2535, www.maronstonehouse.com, €12-80) has quality rooms and bath facilities as well as a garden where guests are welcome to enjoy complimentary tea and coffee throughout the day. Located in the residential area of Göreme, it's not a cave, but the natural stone walls, wooden ceilings, and Anatolian decor, along with the terrace views to Rose Valley, will put some Cappadocian magic in your vacation.

Food

Göreme eateries offer menus based on a delectable Cappadocian cuisine, rich in meat and veggies from the fertile land. Two local dishes that must be experienced are *mantı* (tiny lamb- or beef-filled ravioli drenched in garlicky yogurt sauce) and platters of beer-battered Anatolian crispy fried cheeses. The most spectacular central Anatolian dish is the flaming *testi kebabı,* a kebab of chicken or beef in vegetables cooked for hours in a sealed clay pot and served by a waiter who cracks it open above roaring flames by your table. Many restaurants around the country serve this casserole dish on request, but at Cappadocia you can try the authentic version. You can pair these meals with local vintages from Cappadocian wineries as well as feted local potatoes and capers. For a heads-up on the local viticulture, the white narince and emir grapes and the red boğazkere, kalecik karası, and öküzgözü are some of the most popular Cappadocian varieties. Reservations are a must at the better eateries during the summer and on major Turkish holidays.

The **Pumpkin Göreme Restaurant & Art Gallery** (Iceri Dere Sk. 7/A, Göreme, 0384/271-2066, 30TL) is one of the newest and most innovative in the local restaurant scene. Oğuz Kaya, a lovable chef from Kayseri, handpicks organic produce from the Nevşehir market every day for the tasty five-course set menu. The restaurant is nestled in a former Cappadocian barn that Oğuz personally renovated with Melo Eroğlu, the artist responsible for the gorgeous colorful pumpkin lanterns that give the restaurant its soothing ambiance. If you have the time, ask Melo for a pumpkin lantern-making workshop to design your own as a memento of your time in Göreme.

★ **A'la Turca** (Gaferli Mah. 20, 0384/271-2882, www.alaturca.com.tr, 35TL) attracts travelers and locals with their simple yet delicious contemporary meals, served in a dressed-up country atmosphere that's purely Anatolian, with loads of handwoven fabrics and rich wooden furnishings. An upstairs dining area with two terraces gives diners a view of the town and the landscape beyond. In summer, retreat to the garden bar after dinner for serenity in the heart of town, or when the weather turns, relax by the ground-floor fireplaces and work your way through the offerings of local wine from the cellar.

There is so much to like about the Cingitas family's **Café Şafak** (Müze Cd. 28, 0384/271-2597, http://inekelam.wix.com/cafesafak, 10TL), which gratifies guests with excellent Italian coffees and cheap meals like the award-winning lentil soup, judged the best in Cappadocia at the annual Göreme food festival, held at the end of September. Hikers can also make a stop en route to the valleys to buy a take-out picnic of a sandwich, snacks, dessert, and a drink, all for 10TL. If the warm welcome at this cozy Melbourne-style café leaves you wanting more, you can join the owner, Fatima Cingitas, for a Cappadocian cuisine cooking class (from 60TL) in the cave kitchen of the family home.

The local Serinsu family converted their home into the well-liked **Göreme Restaurant** (Müze Cd. 18, Göreme 0384/271-2183, 15TL), a traditional eatery that has both Cappadocian and world cuisine. Sit at a table and chairs or choose to dine like Anatolians in the village-style lounges and low tables surrounded by trinkets portraying Göreme's bucolic personality. Once sated, head next door for a nightcap at **Red Red Wine House.** This tiny bar, with a low arched ceiling and a good collection of Cappadocian wines, was renovated from a stable. The families at both venues are a wealth of local knowledge, but if you want a conversation starter, ask them about Carlos Santana, who entertained locals here in the 1980s.

Late-night bars and clubs were once a feature of the town, but ongoing issues with rowdy behavior has curbed the entertainment options. Instead of partying till late, most travelers will find themselves reclining in the cushions out front of **Fat Boys Bar & Cafe** (Belediye Cd. 22, Göreme, cell tel. 0536/936-3652, 15TL). It's centrally located, and the international menu has nachos and a couple of Australian snacks that lure an Aussie crowd keen to devour a meat pie far from home. The bar has a great friendly vibe day and night for people of all ages and nationalities. Those looking for a spectator-sports fix will also appreciate the big-screen TVs playing major games from around the world.

Information and Services

Göreme is a bustling burg centered around its *otogar*. A range of ATMs are located near the *otogar* on Belediye Caddesi and along Müze Caddesi. The **PTT** (Bılal Eroglu Cd. Sağlık Sk. 4, Göreme, 0384/271-2420, 8:30am-12:30pm and 1:30pm-5pm Mon.-Fri.) post office provides telecommunications services as well as currency exchange.

Göreme's Tourism Society (*otogar*, 0384/271-1111, www.goreme.org) was created by area merchants and hoteliers. The service steers visitors to its member businesses, so gathering tips from local hotel concierges or B&B owners, or the helpful staff at the many travel agencies, is also advised.

Getting There
AIR
The most inexpensive flights to Cappadocia arrive at **Kayseri Erkilet International Airport** (ASR, Kayseri, 0352/337-5244, www.kayseri.dhmi.gov.tr), about 80 kilometers, an hour's drive, from Göreme. The newer **Nevşehir Airport** (NAV, Nevşehir, 444-2407, www.kapadokya.dhmi.gov.tr) is closer, with a 35-minute travel time, but the airfares are generally more expensive and less flights are offered. Flight time from Istanbul is about 80 minutes. Local travel agencies and shuttles waiting for passengers heading to major destinations in Cappadocia provide airport transfers for 20-25TL; some hotels run a similar shuttle service that may be complimentary, depending on the length of your stay.

BUS
When booking travel with coach companies, make sure your ticket says Göreme, not Cappadocia or Nevşehir, as your *varış yeri* (destination); otherwise you may not arrive at the Göreme *otogar*. If you are unceremoniously left at Nevşehir *otogar* and left without a *servis* (free transfer), phone your hotel, which may be able to pick you up, or board the *dolmuş* (2.50TL) that departs every 30 minutes for the 12-kilometer trip to Göreme. Taxis are also available. **Metro Turizm** (444-3455, www.metroturizm.com.tr), **Nevşehir Seyahat** (444-5050, www.nevsehirlilerseyahat.com.tr), and **Süha Turizm** (www.suhaturizm.com.tr) run various domestic coach routes to Göreme from Istanbul (85TL, 10.5 hours), Ankara (40TL, 4.5 hours), Fethiye (70TL, 12.5 hours), İzmir (75TL, 12 hours), and Antalya (50TL, 10 hours). Check the departures a day before leaving, as some coach routes run only once a day, early in the morning or late at night.

TRAIN
From Istanbul, take the **Yüksek Hızlı Tren** (high-speed train, www.tcdd.gov.tr, 80TL, 3 hours) to Ankara Gar, then walk 10 minutes to the Tandoğan Ankaray Train Station to transfer to the enormous Ankara Şehirlerarası Otobüs Terminalı (AŞTI, city bus terminal) in five minutes and then catch a coach to Göreme. Tickets for Ankaray can be bought at the Tandoğan station (3.50TL).

Getting Around
Primarily flat and rather small, Göreme is an ideal walking town. Cars, ATVs, scooters, and even bicycles are available through the travel agencies and rental agencies in town to explore farther afield.

Two *dolmuş* companies offer services to nearby locations. **Göreme Transport** (0384/271-1111, 2-3TL, timetables at Göreme's Tourism Society) runs a half-hourly Göreme-Nevşehir *dolmuş* (7:30am-6pm daily) passing within one kilometer of Uçhisar Castle via the Göreme-Uçhisar Yolu. The Göreme-Avanos *dolmuş* departs from outside the Göreme *otogar* on the Göreme-Uçhisar Yolu every hour (8am-6pm daily) and travels past Çavuşin, Paşabağları, and Zelve en route to Avanos. While Göreme Transport's Göreme-Ürgüp *dolmuş* departs every two hours, the **Ürgüp VIP Seyahat's** (0384/341-8118, 3TL) Avanos-Göreme-Ürgüp *dolmuş* is hourly and also passes Zelve, Paşabağları, Çavuşin, and the Göreme Open-Air Museum on its route. All services to Ürgüp depart from the corner of Müze Caddesi and Göreme Yolu in Göreme. Timetables for the Ürgüp VIP Seyahat services are posted at the bus stops.

Taxis (*otogar*, 0384/271-2527) are available for trips between towns and also offer the full-day Green and Red Tours (without a guide or lunch) for 250TL and 150TL, respectively.

ÇAVUŞIN
Between Avanos and Göreme is tiny Çavuşin, a town that sits in the shadows of its towering cavernous ancient village that can be seen

from the main Göreme highway. The caves were abandoned in the 1950s after erosion and rock falls made the conditions unsafe for residents. Today, the modern villagers welcome sightseers with friendly greetings, potted products, and freshly squeezed orange juice at the start of hikes to the Rose and Honey valleys. The village also has two churches of local significance that many come to explore. The first is the 5th-century-AD **Church of St. John the Baptist** (top of the village, free), reportedly the oldest and biggest cave church in the Cappadocian region and resembling a Swiss cheese-like structure with three naves separated by ornate archways. While the frescoes have faded, the columns and Christian motifs carved into the rock show the remnants of an important place of worship. The lower church, **Nicephorus Phocas** (8TL), has beautifully preserved frescoes depicting biblical scenes over a nave and three apses and dates to the 10th century. Although impressive, the local consensus is that if you visit the Open-Air Museum and the churches of the Ihlara Valley, don't bother with the lower church here.

Getting There

Çavuşin is three kilometers north of Göreme, reachable via the Göreme Yolu. Most hikers catch the hourly **Ürgüp VIP Seyahat** (0384/341-8118, 3TL) Avanos-Göreme-Ürgüp *dolmuş* or the **Göreme Transport** (0384/271-1111, 3TL) Göreme-Avanos *dolmuş* to Çavuşin and hike back to Göreme following the Rose or Honey Valleys. ATV tours come to the village, although photo opportunities of the rock-carved former village are only possible with the time given. The popular Red Tour includes a short guided tour of Çavuşin.

ZELVE AND PAŞABAĞLARI

The community of Zelve, like hundreds of others in western Anatolia, was once inhabited by Greeks. In fact, it's one of the earliest monastic settlements in Anatolia. The rock-hewn monasteries and their adobes remain; the Anatolian Greeks, who inhabited this settlement, were removed in 1922 to Greece during the compulsory population exchange, to be replaced by Ionian and Thracian Turks. **Zelve Open-Air Museum** (0384/271-3535, 8am-7pm daily Apr.-Oct., 8am-5pm daily Nov.-Mar., 10TL) is located on the outskirts of the village of Aktepe, 10 kilometers from Göreme. Zelve was emptied of its inhabitants when they moved to Aktepe in 1952 because the dwellings of this UNESCO-listed national park were deemed unsafe. Today, Zelve's monasteries, some built as early as the 9th century by Christians who fled the Persian and Arab invasions of the Middle Ages, stand eerily empty.

While it's true that the chapels and monasteries may not be as striking as those of the Göreme Open-Air Museum, the land is dramatic, to say the least. These hills are peppered with housing of all types. Walking though the cliffs to explore this historic park's nooks and crannies is for the fit. To guard against invaders, the settlement was built like a maze: foothold-only entrances, long concealed tunnels, and underground paths. A full exploration of Zelve takes about four hours and requires climbing and hiking ability. Since navigating the settlement and terrain can be tricky, with some of the structures crumbling, it's best to book a private tour or the full-day Legend Tour with **Argeus Travel** (Istiklal Cd., 7 Ürgüp, 0384/341-4688, www.argeus.com.tr, €100). The tour includes a visit to Avanos, Paşabağları, Uçhisar Castle, and the Dervent Valley with its impressive camel rock formation.

Formerly known as Monk Valley, **Paşabağları** (adjacent to Zelve, free) has the most striking earthen pillars in the middle of a vineyard. Some of these tufa formations—there are hundreds of them—dramatically split into smaller cones midway through. Incidentally, these chimneys are called mushrooms. Some of history's most severe Christian stylites (ascetics who live atop pillars) built their monastic communities on these sometimes double- or triple-headed chimneys.

pottery shop in Avanos

AVANOS

The ubiquitous pottery displayed throughout Cappadocia usually comes from Avanos, nine kilometers north of Göreme's center. Like towns throughout the region, Avanos (pop. 13,210) is entirely hewn from volcanic rock; but unlike the others, it is the only one along the banks of the Kızılırmak (Red River), Turkey's longest. This waterway, which separates Avanos from the rest of Cappadocia, gets its name from the red sediment that tints it. From this abundant silt, ceramic clay is formed to produce the pottery so unique to Cappadocia.

The practice dates back before the Hittites, according to their 3,500-year-old records. Once predominant, the craft was practiced by every inhabitant of Avanos: Children collected silt and adults ran pottery wheels in a workshop attached to every household. Today, Avanos thrives on clay products for commercial sale, like roof tiles and building blocks. There's also a variety of household pottery, such as the traditional Avanos handled urn, for sale in some three dozen shops around town. Some shopkeepers invite onlookers to try molding at the kick wheel, a tactic that always guarantees a sale. Be prepared to haggle for that perfect piece; once acquired, have it shipped rather than risk damaging it on the way home. Aside from terra-cotta pottery, alabaster and onyx trinkets and handwoven rugs are also produced locally.

To get a piece of terra-cotta, or just learn the tricks of Avanos's master potter, head to **Chez Galip** (www.chezgalip.com). Galip's bric-a-brac in his workshops confirms that he's all about the art of pottery—and all about hair; his peculiar collection includes millions of strands of hair from customers during his five-decade career. It's a little eerie but somewhat fascinating that so many have parted with their locks in his cave of pottery products.

While plenty of inns and boutiques thrive in this burg heavily patronized by French tourists, I don't recommend spending the night in Avanos. It's just too far away and

In fact, Simeon monks mirrored the ascetic existence of their patron, Saint Simeon, here during the 5th and 6th centuries. A three-level chapel dug out of a 15-meter-tall cone was dedicated to Simeon. Inside, the rooms boast five-meter ceilings and walls adorned with frescoes depicting his life and the self-imposed hardships he withstood when he decided to live in seclusion atop a 2-meter (and later a 10-meter) platform in Aleppo.

Getting There

To get to the Zelve Open-Air Museum and Paşabağları, travel north along Göreme Yolu for five kilometers and turn right onto Zelve Yolu, where you'll first pass Paşabağları before reaching the parking lot of Zelve, one kilometer later. The **Ürgüp VIP Seyahat** (0384/341-8118, 3TL) Avanos-Goreme-Ürgüp *dolmuş* and the **Göreme Transport** (0384/271-1111, 3TL) Göreme-Avanos *dolmuş* pass both sites, dropping off and picking up passengers up along the way.

feels a bit cheap; a few hours looking around the pottery shops should suffice. If you've come this far, there's no reason not to continue another five kilometers southeast to the spectacular **Saruhan** (Yeni Kayseri Yolu, 0384/511-3795, www.sarihan1249.com), a caravanserai that is the last, and perhaps the finest, built by the Selçuks, in 1249. Its finely ornamented architecture adheres to tradition, except that its mosque appears over the gateway and not in the courtyard. The *sema* (whirling dervish ceremony) is performed here at 6pm daily. Tickets (€25) for the hour-long rite and transportation can be secured through most travel agencies in the region.

Getting There

To reach Avanos, drive north along Göreme Yolu, or hop on an hourly *dolmuş* with **Ürgüp VIP Seyahat** (0384/341-8118, 3TL) that departs from the Ürgüp *otogar* or the corner of Müze Caddesi and Göreme Yolu. **Göreme Transport** (0384/271-1111, 3TL) plies the same route hourly and departs outside the Göreme *otogar* on the Göreme-Uçhisar Yolu.

UÇHISAR

Traveling eastward from Cappadocia's capital town of Nevşehir, an eerie landscape unfolds in a series of dust bowls pocked by soft yellow and pink dunes, cones, and fairy chimneys. The mighty **Erciyes Dağı**—the once-active volcano responsible for this mad lunar landscape—stands guard at 3,920 meters tall, extending well into the clouds. This fantastic scenery means arriving in Uçhisar is imminent.

Uçhisar is an old-time Cappadocian village with plenty of lore and a small valley of fairy chimneys between the main highway and the castle. It's far more peaceful than the bustle of Göreme and more down-to-earth than upscale Ürgüp, and is a preferred destination for southwestern Europeans.

Uçhisar's stone fort is the highest volcanic outcrop in Cappadocia; its apex, reached via 225 steps, is a favorite panoramic destination, particularly at sunset. **Uçhisar Kalesi** (Uçhisar Castle, 0384/219-2618, 7:30am-7pm daily, 5TL) is bisected below ground by artificial tunnels, and its faces are pocked by hand-cut lookout windows. Ottomans in the 15th and 16th centuries and the Selçuks before them utilized these natural formations in conjunction with similar chimneys in Ortahisar, Ürgüp, and Çavuşin, both as observation and defense points. Guards used a system of mirrors to warn about invaders, sending messages in relay all the way to the

the fairy chimneys of Uçhisar

Cappadocian Wine Heritage

Cappadocia's famed vineyards, first tilled and tended by the Hittites, are extremely productive due to the region's fertile volcanic soil and soft rock, where ideal underground cellars were easily carved out. Outside the Kavaklidere, Turasan, and Kocabağ wineries, viniculture is more a household undertaking than an industrial one. The rather small size of vineyards (16-28 hectares) and arable terrain wedged between Cappadocia's profusion of hills may have a lot to do with this.

Wine production is a family affair. Villagers apply skills handed down through the generations. The traditional öküzgözü (ox-eye) grapes intended to be used at home are either eaten whole (55 percent of production); boiled down to produce the grape syrup called *pekmez* (35 percent); or are made into a medium-bodied dry red wine (about 4 percent). The tilling, replanting, and harvesting are left to the older folks, who can often be seen in horse carriages on the way to their vines early in the morning. Collection starts early in the day from early September to the beginning of October. The first fruits are black and intended to be consumed whole or used for juice. The end of the season is the white grape harvest, with the finest variety, emir, picked from mid-September on for the production of sparkling wine or a medium-body wine with a hint of apple.

The *Vitis vinifera* grape species is also used to produce red wine. While more than 1,500 grape varieties are cultivated in Turkey, only 1,100 are indigenous. In Cappadocia, well-known grapes like cabernet sauvignon and and chardonnay are cultivated alongside subtle and unique domestic varieties like öküzgözü, emir, and dry narince. **Kocabağ** (www.kocabag.com), an internationally heralded boutique winery located in Üçhisar, is the preferred producer, according to oenological experts. Their öküzgözü varietal—from grapes originating in the eastern Turkish city of Elaziğ—is applauded for being simple, crisp, and fresh.

Other varietals worth sampling are boğazkere, meaning "throat-burner." Also from Elaziğ, this red grape imbues a rich hue to the juice, and when fermented produces a well-structured wine with strong overtones of dried fruit and figs. Kalecik karası is a dark indigenous grape known for its deep ruby color. Its rich, well-balanced structure provides a strong aroma of red fruit, vanilla, and cocoa, with a finish that's light, fresh, and elegant. Among the white grape varieties, the narince is a soft, gently spicy peer of other white varieties cultivated only in Turkey such as sültaniye and emir. For more information about Turkish wines, visit **Wines of Turkey** (www.winesofturkey.org).

---

empire's capital at Istanbul. From the top you can marvel at the valley's colors and rock formations in all directions, even to Erciyes Dağı (Mount Erciyes) in the east.

The valley that encircles Üçhisar reveals the geological tale of the entire Cappadocian region, with rock formations in various states of disintegration. Upon closer inspection, rocky channels can be explored along the valley's ridge; below, the Pigeon Valley reveals myriad pigeon houses, all painted white to lure the winged animals and their precious droppings—a potent fertilizer for agriculture.

Winery

Little known even to Turkish oenophiles is the winery in Üçhisar, **Kocabağ** (0384/219-2979, www.kocabag.com), where wine lovers throughout Cappadocia come for the internationally recognized vintages, among the top five in the country. Kocabağ only produces 300,000 liters per year, making the three floral and fruity whites and four intensely fruity reds highly sought-after. The most distinctive wine is the Kalecik Karası, an elegant, lightly spicy claret with rich pomegranate, plum, and cherry undertones.

Accommodations

Accommodations range from bed-and-breakfasts to superb cave hotels that put Istanbul's five-star establishments to shame. A trip to Cappadocia, however, should be spent outdoors, visiting the valley, not in a room fit for a sultan. Go for a clean bed and shower and an organic farm-fresh breakfast.

Shop online for a cave room at **Kaya Pension** (Tekelli Mah. 1, 0384/219-2441, www.kayapension.com, 135-210TL) and settle into a room featuring wood floors, colorful Anatolian tapestries, and an open fireplace. Some rooms sport private terraces overlooking the valley. A full buffet breakfast on the rooftop reflects the homey charm of this inn, integrated into the natural Cappadocian landscape, hence the name Kaya (rock). It is excellent value and ideal for families, who will appreciate the garden and playground.

From the top-floor rooms of ★ **Has Konak** (Goreme Cd. 59, cell tel. 0535/719-0205, 180-240TL) you can gaze out to a Cappadocian morning sky full of hot-air balloons. The family that own this stone mansion are earning rave reviews for their hospitality, local knowledge, and breakfast served on the rooftop terrace on the edge of Uçhisar. Request room 5 to get a balcony to enjoy the view.

As the name suggests, **Kale Konak Cave Hotel** (Kale Sk. 9, 0384/219-2828, www.kalekonak.com, €120-150) is a *konak* (historical mansion) adjoining a complex of 1st-century caves situated atop the town close to the *kale* (castle). This translates to wonderful views from their rooftop restaurant and refined elegance in the rooms and suites. Couples will find the ambiance romantic, amplified by medieval-style pointed stone arches. After a strenuous hike in nearby Pigeon Valley, guests can relax in the courtyard or be rejuvenated in the hotel hamam.

The ★ **Museum Hotel** (Tekeli mah. 1, 0384/219-2220, www.museum-hotel.com, €300-2,500) defies classification—in fact, the label "hotel" underrates what the property really is. If the sultans of yesteryear had built palaces in this ethereal valley, this property and its lavish interiors would have fit their requirements. Immediately striking is the collection of textiles and antiques from owner Ömer Tosun's private collection, amassed during his previous life as a fine carpet and fabric dealer. True to its name, the property's impressive pieces are found in the 12 double rooms in the form of 6th-century Roman jars, antique brass beds, and antique Selçuk and Ottoman rugs. The Khayyam Suite, named for the 11th-century mathematician, poet, and astrologer, boasts his quatrain poems and books, all rarities, and an awe-inspiring bath replete with a fine marble whirlpool tub and shower combo with a window that overlooks a gigantic Cappadocian boulder. Amenities fit for royalty include the award-winning Lil'a restaurant, adjoining cross-golf driving range, a state-of-the-art wellness center, a mosaic-tiled infinity pool and a rooftop panoramic terrace.

Food

A dressy alternative among the string of small and inexpensive cafés lining the village center, ★ **Elai** (Eski Göreme Cd., Uçhisar, 0384/219-3181, www.elairestaurant.com, 25TL) replaced a nicotine-tarnished *çayhane* (Anatolian teahouse). Today, it's a swanky restaurant boasting high wood-beamed ceilings and a cavernous interior. A terrace of local stone offers an ideal place to watch the setting sun over a glass of local wine. The food leans heavily toward classical Anatolian cuisine and the imperial dishes of Istanbul, but the style is unabashedly simple. European classics featured on the menu include rack of lamb and duck à l'orange.

Getting There

Uçhisar is only four kilometers southwest of Göreme, but the castle is set back from the main road and not within direct reach of public transportation. The half-hourly Göreme-Nevşehir *dolmuş* (2.50TL) travels along the Göreme-Uçhisar highway and can drop passengers at a tourist stop, complete with a camel photo opportunity, that looks over the small valley and the castle. From here, you can walk down into the valley for some great photos and follow the unmarked dirt tracks uphill, keeping the castle on the right, until you reach the cobbled Göreme Road in the village. Walk uphill on this road until signs lead to the castle entrance. You'll have to walk back to the main highway to catch the *dolmuş* to Göreme or Nevşehir.

ORTAHISAR

Ortahisar (Middle Castle) is the up-and-coming destination in Cappadocia for highly rated inns and boutique hotels. Despite its central location, it's one of the last major villages in Cappadocia to cash in on tourism. That said, the village is an excellent choice for independent travelers seeking a quieter vibe among floral-scarfed Anatolian women and portly men wearing newsboy caps who continue their rural farming life around the tourism trade. The town itself has a prominent 86-meter chimney rock called **Ortahisar Castle** that was once a settlement and defensive fortress to spot potential invaders, similar to Uçhisar Castle to the east. The valley below is littered with numerous **churches** and rock-carved storage spaces used to stockpile vegetables and citrus fruit imported here from the Mediterranean.

The celebrated **Culture Museum & Restaurant-Cafe** (Cumhuriyet Meydani 15, 0384/343-3344, www.culturemuseum.com, 9am-7pm daily, 5TL), near the castle, was started by a group of young entrepreneurs who are now Turkey's youngest museum managers. This 1,500-square-meter ethnography museum has a range of dioramas portraying Cappadocian industries of weaving, agriculture, and molasses production alongside depictions of important community events and rituals.

Accommodations

Travelers with boutique tastes will appreciate any one of the highly rated hotels in quiet Ortahisar, but for personalized friendly service, reserve early at **Lamihan Hotel** (Cami Sk. 15, 0384/343-3316, www.lamihan.com, from 185TL). There are only four rooms, each with a terrace, in this 300-year-old restored mansion.

Cozy and rustic and within walking distance of the castle is **Antique House Pension** (Bahçe Sk. 12, 0384/343-3313, www.antiquehousepension.com, from €50). A garden and à la carte restaurant complements the relaxed vibe of this 200-year-old cave dwelling.

Getting There

Cumhuriyet Meydani, the main square of Ortahisar, is 1.5 kilometers off the main Nevşehir Ürgüp Yolu, approximately five kilometers south of Ürgüp and five kilometers from Göreme via the Müze Caddesi, which winds past the Göreme Open-Air Museum. A half-hourly *dolmuş* from Ürgüp travels to Cumhuriyet Meydani (8am-5pm daily, 2TL) terminating near the castle and museum. The more regular Nevşehir-Ürgüp *dolmuş* can also be hailed on the main highway every 15 minutes. The Red Tour booked through most travel agencies also includes a tour of Ortahisar.

★ ÜRGÜP

Just nine kilometers east of Göreme, Ürgüp is an ideal base for a Cappadocian holiday, with superior hotels, fine restaurants, lively nightlife, and high-end shopping—although it is more expensive than anywhere else in the valley. Tourist numbers are soaring and revenues are skyrocketing from the luxury tourism niche. Ürgüp has become a bastion of boutique hospitality, with every crumbling shack reborn as a five-star cave hotel or upscale restaurant. This growth, for the time being, has yet to whitewash the town of its indigenous Anatolian culture.

Sights
TEMENNI HILL

To get a sense of the lay of the land, scale the highest point, **Temenni Hill** (a.k.a. Wishing Hill), a 100-meter-tall column that towers over the town's piazza and serves as a marker separating the modern structures of the new town from the cave dwellings of the old. This natural rock formation, reinforced by a layer of concrete after a massive rockfall in 2006, is home to two interesting monuments. The first is the *türbe* (tomb) of Selçuk sultan Kiliçarslan IV, who dodged an assassination attempt by poisoning in Aksaray only to be caught and killed in Ürgüp in 1266. His remains were later relocated to the Selçuk Empire's capital at Konya, and a shrine to him was built there in 1863. Nearby, an Ottoman-era library features a neat teahouse and an interesting photo collection detailing Ürgüp's past.

The entrance to Temenni Hill faces the old town and is a 10-minute walk northeast of the *otogar*. The easiest way to get to the top is to follow the base of the hill, keeping it on your right. You'll eventually see signs leading up a steep path to the entrance.

ÜRGÜP MUSEUM
The shop and restaurant-lined thoroughfare of Atatürk Bulvarı gives way to a pleasant tea garden that doubles as a hub for visitors to recharge and check in with the tourism information office. The small **Ürgüp Museum** (9am-noon and 1pm-5pm daily, free) has an assortment of artifacts from the Bronze Age, Hellenic, and Roman periods as well as ethnographic items from the town's Ottoman era. A display of 10-million-year-old marine fossils and elephant tusks uncovered near Mustafapaşa, however, is the most fascinating indication of what the Cappadocian landscape has seen through the ages.

SARICA KILISESI (SARICA CHURCH)
The restoration of the **Sarıca Kilisesi** (in Kepez Valley), one of the oldest Byzantine churches in Cappadocia, dating to the mid-6th century, was undertaken by the private company Vasco Travel in 1997, at a time when the then Turkish government supplied little or no funding to restore historical sites. For centuries the basilica was damaged by erosion and the accumulation of pigeon droppings, during its spell as an aviary and guano storage facility. When work began in 2001, crews had to scour off layers of dung to reach the artwork on the walls and floors of this magnificent rock-carved basilica. What they found were elaborate mosaic floorings and frescoes on ocher walls. The architectural details are even more striking, such as intricately carved niches, arched vaults, and lofty columns. What originally seemed like another far-fetched undertaking paid off a decade later when project manager Cengiz Kabaoğlu won the 2007 European Union Prize for Cultural Heritage.

Sarıca Kilisesi is located on the way to Mustafapaşa, three kilometers south of Ürgüp, off Ürgüp Yolu. It can also be accessed on foot when hiking the valley of Ortahisar.

WINERY
Cappadocia's history has been bound to wine-making for millennia, and several wineries in the region show their wares. **Turasan Şarapevi** (Turasan Winery, Tevfik Fikret Cd. 6A-B, 0384/341-4961, www.turasan.com.tr) is one of the country's largest wine producers and welcomes guests to their cellar in Ürgüp. Founded in 1943, Turasan features a collection of the area's finest vintages and offers a good affordable selection of reds, whites, and rosés. Come for wine-tasting at sunset to enjoy the spectacular view.

Tours
A number of travel agencies specializing in Cappadocia are available to help organize tours, airport transfers, balloon flights, and other transportation. **Argeus Travel** (Istiklal Cd. 7, Ürgüp, 0384/341-4688, www.argeus.com.tr) rates highly as a comprehensive travel agent for day tours of Cappadocia and beyond. Their attention to detail, much smaller group sizes, unwavering customer service, and overall professionalism has earned them recommendations by Turkish Airlines.

Another highly respected outfit for international travelers is **Euphrates Tours** (Istiklal Cd. 59/9, Ürgüp, 0384/341-7485, www.cappadociatours.com), owned by travel specialist Süleyman Çakır. Off-the-beaten-track day trips are this outfit's specialty, including Cappadocia's Underground City and Traditional Villages tour, which allows momentary immersion in a rural life that hasn't changed for centuries.

Accommodations
A restoration project supported by UNESCO and the World Heritage Center in Ürgüp's

historic first neighborhood of Kayakapı is creating a complex of lodgings called ★ **Kayakapı Premium Caves** (Kuscular Sk. 43, 0384/341-8877, www.kayakapi.com, €110-1,080). This rocky outcrop with a honeycomb of caves once housed mansions of wealthy Ottoman *ağas* (landowners) during the 18th century, one of which accommodated Saint John the Russian—a saint of miracles—who spread his Christian Orthodox teachings among the predominantly Muslim residents of the neighborhood. The neighborhood has a long and interesting history, but today, travelers will be spellbound by the 29 suites, rooms, and mansions, some of which have private heated indoor pools, courtyards, and Turkish hamams. Staying here is made extra special with an à la carte restaurant, Bistro Manzara; views over the region; and a free shuttle to the center of town.

4ODA Cave House (Esbelli Sk. 46, 0384/341-6080, www.4oda.com, €110-135) launched restorations in the Esbelli quarter. This cave-dweller lodging boasts five delightful rooms that highlight the Greek heritage of the region. The sitting room, whose ceiling is probably the highest in Cappadocia, is both homey and artsy, with a personal collection of classic books and musical instruments ready to be strummed, along with reproductions of paintings by European masters. 4ODA is known for its big included breakfast—more like a brunch—that has a huge variety of cheeses, homemade jams, and pastries. Discounts for cash payment and stays of three nights or more provide more reason to choose a standard room or suite here.

★ **SerInn House** (Esbelli Sk. 6, 0384/341-6076, www.serinnhouse.com, Apr.-Oct., €110-130, discount for cash) has five cool, monochromatic caves that are sparsely furnished in luxurious, colorful modern pieces, creating spaces that are utterly relaxing yet grown up enough for today's discerning traveler. Colorful shag rugs highlight black lacquer four-poster beds and metal chairs that come in lip-smacking colors in a *Flintstones*-meets-Guggenheim setting. The property is really "cool"—also what the hotel's name translates to—among a backdrop of properties that highlight the area's Anatolian heritage.

History abounds at the centrally located **Hotel Cave Konak** (Dar 2 Sk. 5, 0384/341-4322, www.cavekonak.com, €48-100). Underground caves, cut some 1,000 years ago, have been transformed into cozy rooms along with aboveground lodgings that feature either stone arches or wooden ceilings reflecting the style of Ottoman times. The hotel's location, just minutes from restaurants, major attractions, and the *otogar,* along with its rooftop terrace and pillared balcony for relaxing, ensures the hotel's top rating.

Ürgüp has its share of mid-range to luxury hotels, but those traveling with backpacks can find a dorm or an affordable private room at the stone house of **Dede Hostel & Pension** (Dereler Sk. 18, 0384/341-8969, 30-90TL). Get in quick to request a room with a private balcony or terrace, where you can chill out between visits to nearby Göreme or Mustafapaşa. Breakfast is not included, though a communal kitchen and the proximity to cafés make it easy to get your own meals.

Food

Şömine Café & Restaurant (Cumhuriyet Meydanı 9, 0384/341-8442, www.sominerestaurant.com, 25TL) offers alfresco and indoor dining. As the name *şömine* (fireplace) suggests, you'll find a large ornate hearth, which provides warmth during Cappadocia's cool nights. Marble floors and linen-covered tables complement a menu packed with Turkish cuisine. The house special, slow cooked *testi kebab,* is highly recommended, as is the delectable *beğendi kebab*—tender stewed lamb or beef served over a cheesy eggplant puree. Call ahead for reservations on weekends or during summer.

★ **Ziggy's Shoppe & Café** (Tevfik Fikret Cd. 24, 0384/341-7107, www.ziggycafe.com, 20TL) is a modern take of an ancient caravanserai that sprawls over three rock-hewn terraces with table-and-chair or couch-and-coffee table seating. The menu is light, with pasta and salads, and there's a long drink menu that's great for sunset aperitifs or an after-hours hangouts. Try the mezes and the innovative fresh pasta with *pastırma* sauce—a sun-dried spiced beef dish.

Another recommended dining destination in Cappadocia is **Dimrit Café & Restaurant** (Tevfik Fikret Cd. 40, 0384/341-8585, www.dimrit.com, 20TL). Expect an all-out Turkish feast in this renovated stone adobe, high on one of Ürgüp's loftiest hills. A second-floor terrace boasts chic white tabletops and a 270-degree view of dusty rolling hills, while interior barrel-vaulted alcoves offer an ideal setting for couples.

Talented home-style cook Emine prepares different dishes every day with the freshest produce at ★ **Zeytin Café & Restaurant** (Atatürk Blv., 0384/341-7399, www.zeytincafeurgup.com, Mon.-Sat., 10TL). There's nothing fancy here, just good quality home-cooked Ürgüp food piled high. *Zeytin* means "olive," inspiring the green walls and unassuming cottage-style decor on the way to Temenni Hill; this is a must-do pit-stop for breakfast, lunch, or dinner.

Information and Services

Ürgüp's **Tourism Information Office** (Atatürk Blv., 0384/341-4059, 8am-6pm Mon.-Sat.) is in the park next to the museum and provides the usual maps and pamphlets, although hotel staff and travel agents are better at answering queries.

A couple of small bank branches, a regional hospital, a police station, and a **PTT** (8:30am-5pm Mon.-Fri.) post office are near the eastern base of Temenni Hill, just off the town's main thoroughfare, Atatürk Bulvarı.

Getting There and Around

The town has two bus stations side-by-side along Güllüce Caddesi. The western (main) *otogar* is where the **Ürgüp VIP Seyahat** (0384/341-8118, 3TL) Avanos-Göreme-Ürgüp *dolmuş* terminates and departs every hour on the hour (8am-5pm daily). The Nevşehir *dolmuş* departs every 15 minutes from here also, while the *dolmuş* to Kayseri departs every hour on the hour 7am-10am and then every two hours until 6pm. The local **bus** to Mustafapaşa (8am-7pm daily, 2TL) departs from the neighboring *otogar* every half-hour. Confirm timetables ahead of time, as they can change with the seasons.

Walking around Ürgüp by foot is highly recommended, but be advised that the town's Esbelli neighborhood is up a rather steep hill. Walking it during the heat of summer can be unbearable, so hiring a **taxi** may be a better option; also check with your hotel, which may have a shuttle service for guests.

MUSTAFAPAŞA

A sleepy and often forlorn-looking village near Ürgüp, Mustafapaşa was once a vibrant community called Sinasos (City of the Sun) where Christian Greeks, Turkish-speaking Christians (Karamanlides), and Muslim Turks lived and worshipped. In 1923, after the signing of the Treaty of Lausanne, the Greek-Turkish population exchange occurred, and the Christians of Sinasos was sent to Greece in exchange for the Muslims of Kastoria (now western Macedonia). Today, the remnants of this once flourishing 19th-century community remain, with fine masonry, churches, and elegantly carved wooden doors. Stroll for an hour with your camera to capture the ornate features of this quiet sunny town of 1,700 people. You'll be charged 5TL to look inside the empty 18th-century **Constantine and Helen Church** (town center). The ticket buys you entry to the **Sinasoss Church** one kilometer away, accessible via a desolate road, so go with other people; otherwise consider the entry fee to one church as donation to local tourism efforts.

If you're curious to see inside one of the stone buildings, visit the **Old Greek House** (0384/353-5306, www.oldgreekhouse.com, 15TL) and take a seat to enjoy the menu of Greek, Anatolian, and Ottoman dishes in the open foyer. A favorite filming location, this 200-year-old Greek mansion—featured in the hit Turkish TV series *Asmalı Konak*—was purchased in 1938 for 10TL by the Öztürk family. A few generations later, Süleyman and Fuat Öztürk converted the property into a hotel-restaurant. Recommended dishes include *karnıyarık* (eggplant stuffed with stewed ground lamb), *mantı*, and *köfte* (meatballs).

Getting There

Mustafapaşa is six kilometers south of Ürgüp en route to Soğanlı Valley via Ürgüp Yolu. Blue tours offered by Cappadocian travel agencies usually stop here to see the churches and masonry. Independent travelers can catch a *dolmuş* to Mustafapaşa (2TL) from the eastern Ürgüp bus station every half hour.

AYVALI

An example of Anatolia at its purest is the village of Ayvalı (pop. 1,200), which remains untouched by modernity and unchanged for centuries. The village is bisected by the İçeridere River, which crosses the valley to Golgoli Tepe (Golgoli Mountain), with a seven-kilometer hike through ghostly caves and rock-hewn chapels. In the village you will find a multiple-domed Selçuk mosque (open except at prayer times) and a myriad of caves and houses hewn out of stone.

Run by the Yazgans family, the ★ **Aravan Evi** (0384/354-5838, www.aravanevi.com, €75) is a charming boutique hotel that boasts five highly affordable standard rooms, irresistible local dishes on its veranda restaurant, cooking classes, and Turkish hospitality that has made this hotel one of the most popular in the region. Donkeys or a Jeep are available to venture to the family's garden and pastoral Ayvalı; just allow enough time to drink *çay* (tea) in the cave homes of the villagers you meet on your way—that's how friendly the folks in this tiny valley are.

The only other hotel in town is the ★ **Gamirasu Cave Hotel** (0384/354-5815, www.gamirasu.com, €205-2,013), housed in an ancient monastery and seven exquisitely restored houses on the edge of a creek in a verdant valley. Managed by the local Gamirasu family, the hotel has 33 unique rooms of regal luxury fused with Anatolia-style handmade cotton mattresses and colorful carpets, also available in barrel-vaulted monk's cells.

Getting There

Ayvalı is 10 kilometers south of Ürgüp, past Mustafapaşa. Hotels will pick up guests from the airport with enough notice. A regular *dolmuş* also travels to and from Ürgüp.

★ UNDERGROUND CITIES

The history of Cappadocia's 200 famed subterranean communities is as nebulous as their deepest levels, which remain closed to the public. Based on Hittite artifacts found in the vicinity of the caves, the general assumption is that these ancient Anatolians may have carved the top levels to hide from Phrygian invaders around 1200 BC. These caverns were subsequently inhabited by early Christians fleeing Roman persecution during the 1st and 2nd centuries, and were later expanded into complex cave-dwelling cities by later generations fleeing the Arab invasions of the 7th and 8th centuries.

Inconspicuous entrances belie complex underground metropolises that, in the case of Derinkuyu, extend 85 meters below ground and may have been populated by as many as 50,000 people. Numerous secret passageways leading from these discreet portals allowed for a quick retreat underground when invading armies marched through. While the actual number of cities remains a mystery, their interconnectedness was revealed by these tunnels. From above, millstones were used ingeniously to both conceal and seal off each key entrance. A tiny hole in the center of these hefty circular stones, which can measure up to 1.5 meters in diameter and weigh as much as half a ton, provided a lookout to the outside world. Beneath, a similar closing aperture further sealed every floor's main access points. An ideal system of defense, these underground caves provide a chilling look at the ingenuity and tenacity of early Cappadocians.

Those with claustrophobia should be wary about visiting; although the caves are well ventilated, at times the rooms are small and some tunnels require crouching to get through. If you know you'll suffer in these confined spaces, there's plenty of shopping and cafés aboveground to pass the time while your companions take the tour.

Derinkuyu

Derinkuyu means "deep well," and **Derinkuyu Yeraltı Şehir** (Derinkuyu Underground City, 0384/381-3194, 8am-7pm daily Apr.-Oct., 8am-5pm daily Nov.-Mar., 20TL) is the deepest and most expansive subterranean settlement discovered to date in Cappadocia—though not all levels are open to the public. Derinkuyu exhibits the typical amenities of other underground complexes: cellars, wine and oil presses, stables and storage rooms on the upper floors, kitchens, chapels, and hundreds of private dwellings. Derinkuyu has a couple of unique features, including a vast gallery used as a seminary. This large barrel-vaulted room is located on the second floor and is flanked on the left by small cells thought to have been used for study. On the lowest level, the cruciform church is also one of a kind, entered through a vertical stairway between the complex's third and fourth levels. A massive ventilation shaft extending 55 meters aired out the levels beneath and also appears to have been used as a well. This reservoir provided water to villagers aboveground and to the subterranean dwellers when the world outside was sealed off.

A network of wells, storage rooms, and air shafts—the majority of which extend 30 meters down—gave locals the possibility of hiding from the outside world for months at a time. Ranging 185 to 650 square meters in size, each floor had an entrance that could be sealed with a doughnut-shaped millstone.

Kaymaklı

While Derinkuyu's sheer size is impressive, **Kaymaklı Yeraltı Şehir** (Kaymaklı Underground City, 0384/218-2500, 8am-7pm daily Apr.-Oct., 8am-5pm daily Nov.-Mar., 20TL) offers a much better understanding of how a cave-dwelling community actually functioned. Still in use today for storage, the nearly 100 tunnels—all smaller in height and width and more steeply inclined than those in Derinkuyu—crisscrossing this complex connect to at least one of the dwellings beneath. The city's layout is also unique in that each space is near a ventilation shaft, making both dwellings and public spaces dependent on the location of air vents. The first floor has a

the underground city of Kaymaklı

stable that is so small it has led archaeologists to believe that Kaymaklı may have had other similar rooms in sections that have yet to be excavated. To the left of the stable, a millstone entrance leads to a tiny chapel and confessional; to the right are some rooms believed to be living quarters. The second level comprises a church with a nave and two apses as well as a baptismal font. Along the walls are seats carved right out of the soft rock. Interestingly enough, names of individuals appear both on graves inside the church and engraved in an area just outside, pointing to the possibility that the people interred here may have been the church's benefactors or possibly religious leaders. The entire structure's depth has been estimated at 20 meters, with the capacity to house upward of 15,000 people for months at a time.

Clues pointing to Kaymaklı's possible role as a regional commercial center include its large number of storerooms, wine and oil presses, and a greater number of kitchens. These are located on the third floor and extend to the fourth floor, where yet another large number of rooms were used to store clay jars stockpiling oil and wine. Also of interest is an immense hollow block of textured andesite, a dark volcanic rock prevalent throughout the cave complex, that was utilized as a vat in which copper was melted. The sides of this cauldron-like fixture have 57 holes, each about 10 centimeters wide; the semi-molten metal would be placed in each of these holes to facilitate molding.

Elaborate systems of communication and engineering are also apparent. Small holes carved into the floor allowed the transmission of messages with the occupants above. This came in handy when each floor was sealed off with the hefty millstone. The air shafts, which extend well beyond the last level of the complex, ventilated the entire compound and also allowed for the dissipation of kitchen smoke.

Özkonak Underground City

Slightly different in design to its southern subterranean neighbors, the **Özkonak Underground City** (Özkonak Village, 0384/513-5168, 8am-7pm daily Apr.-Oct., 8am-5pm daily Nov.-Mar., 10TL) is a complex of four halls, 10 rooms, eight water wells, a winery, and four tombs connected by tunnels that can be closed off with millstone doors. Unique to this city are the five-centimeter narrow horizontal holes between rooms, used for communication and ventilation, rumored to support 60,000 inhabitants. The holes in the ceilings above the millstone doors once functioned as channels to spear or pour hot oil on would-be invaders. The city was discovered in 1972 by a farmer curious to see where his water supply was disappearing.

Getting There

Kaymaklı and Derinkuyu are located 20 kilometers and 30 kilometers south of Nevşehir, respectively, on the Nevşehir-Niğde Road (D765). The best way to visit Kaymaklı or Derinkuyu is to join a **day tour** that includes the magical valley of Ihlara. Tour companies in Göreme have guided day tours starting at €65 pp, mostly to Derinkuyu and its pastoral and archaeological surroundings. If the itinerary doesn't suit you, organize a private tour by taxi or travel agent, or rent a car and visit any of the cities on your own schedule. A *dolmuş* from Nevşehir *otogar* to Niğde will stop in Kaymaklı and Derinkuyu (3TL) every 30 minutes, but you have to get to Nevşehir first using the regular *dolmuş* services (2-3TL) from any of the Cappadocian towns.

Özkonak Underground City is 14 kilometers north of Avanos via the Özkonak Bucağı Yolu that runs off the main Avanos Gülşehir Yolu. A half-hourly *dolmuş* from Avanos will drop passengers about 500 meters from the entrance; ask the driver to drop you at the underground city.

★ IHLARA VADISI (IHLARA VALLEY)

Located about 120 kilometers southwest of Göreme, **Ihlara Vadısı** (four entrances, 0382/453-7701 8am-6:30pm daily, 10TL) is a dramatic gorge carved out of volcanic Cappadocian rock by the Melendez River. The calming landscape is unparalleled, and greenery unique to the region stretches up from the babbling stream that splits the valley. Friendly ducks and other wildlife inhabit the valley's relatively untouched serenity.

Ihlara is a testament to religiosity, with about 105 rock-hewn churches and eerie monasteries, tiny chapels, austere hermit caves, and thousands of cave dwellings, some dating as far back as the 6th century. Today, village life continues along the banks of the Melendez; goats scurry on its flanks as boys play street soccer among the dusty lanes that lead from the stream. Once known as Peristrema, the Ihlara Valley is a 14-kilometer-long canyon with walls in some spots as high as 100 meters. It snakes along the contours of the sometimes rushing stream below. The banks of the Melendez are lush with poplars, neat rows of pistachio trees, and vineyards and are populated by croaking amphibians, colorful butterflies, and birds.

Hiking through Ihlara Valley can take as little as two hours or as long as a day. For the shortest tour, enter through **Ihlara Vadisi Turistik Tesisleri** (Ihlara Valley Touristic Facility, Güzelyurt İlçesi Center, Aksaray) along the valley's western perimeter, two kilometers north of Ihlara Village. Here you'll find a grueling 360-step staircase into Ihlara Valley National Park. It's a rather difficult entry point, but since it's located closest to the sights, it allows for the quickest tour between the end of the staircase north to Belisırma (3.8 kilometers, 3 hours) or south the Ihlara Village (3.2 kilometers, 3 hours), the southernmost point of this national park. Organized tours from Göreme avoid climbing back up the stairs, starting the valley at the staircase and hiking to Belisırma—the canyon's midpoint—where vehicles can drive to the banks of the stream to pick up hikers. The northernmost point of the valley is Selime village, another seven kilometers from Belisırma.

Sights

The churches of the Ihlara Valley near Aksaray are a testament to time and constant erosion. Some date back to the mid-8th century; the frescoes gracing their inner walls, however, were added later during the 10th and 12th centuries. The churches vary in architectural style: Those clustered around Ihlara Village reflect the Coptic style of Egypt and later Syria, while the churches in the village of Belisırma are strictly Byzantine.

The **Ağaçaltı Kilisesi** (Church under the Tree) is the first religious building on the route from the bottom of the staircase; it's the cross-vaulted structure hidden behind a mound of rocks on the left side of the stream. Also nicknamed Church of Daniel for the fresco of biblical Daniel flanked by two lions on the wall facing the main entrance. This church was actually consecrated to Pantanassa, a religious icon typically depicted in the hands of the Virgin Mary; modern Orthodox Christians believe that it has the power to cure cancer. The crude muted frescoes and the geometric shapes—checks and rosettes—reflect the Eastern Coptic style of architecture.

Continuing to the right of the stairway, Ihlara's two other noteworthy churches, **Pürenli Seki Kilisesi** (Church with the Heather Terrace) and the **Kokar Kilisesi,** house additional religious frescoes.

The **Eğritaş Kilisesi** (Church with the Crooked Stone) is about 500 meters past the old wooden footbridge on the stream's eastern bank. Thought to be a funerary chapel and the valley's oldest and most ornate church, Eğritaş consists of a vaulted chapel with an apse and burial chambers below. The ceiling is covered by a gigantic gilded Greek cross with three rows of chiseled frescoes on either side. The Crooked Stone moniker refers to the church's eroded state, not for any fault in construction. Again, this structure reflects Arab influence in its composition and is a prime example of early Eastern Christianity's pre-Iconoclasm art.

Heading north from the staircase to Belisırma leads to the 10th-century **Yılanlı Kilisesi** (Church of the Serpents), named from the fresco showing adders in the act of admonishing four female sinners. A popular theme in early Christian art is the punishment of women, who were thought to be the root of temptation and sin.

Aptly named for the hyacinths in the fields that surround it, the **Sümbüllü Kilisesi** (Hyacinth Church) is on the stream's western bank. This two-level structure's facade of pillars and arched niches hewn from the surrounding rock is unique and recalls the ornate tombs made popular by the Lycians. Adjoining the many cells are chapels bearing some relatively unmarred frescoes, including a Byzantine reproduction of the Annunciation—when the archangel Gabriel announced to the Virgin Mary that she would conceive Jesus.

One kilometer north of staircase and 50 meters from the river's west bank, the **Kırk Damaltı Kilisesi** (Forty Checkered Church) is also known as the Church of St. George, the valley's newest church. The wall paintings are a reflection of the religious and cultural mix present during the structure's construction in the late 13th century. Of particular interest is the dilapidated fresco of Georgian princess Thamar and her husband Basil Giagupes, a Greek minister who ruled the region during the reign of Selçuk Turkish Sultan Mesud II, presenting a model of the Church of St. George. Thamar funded the vineyard attached to the monastery and the frescoes within—gifts, which at the time entitled her to the status of sole benefactor and creator. Basil is shown cloaked in a Selçuk caftan and headdress, and the title *amirarzes* (emir) suggests that he was granted a fief, with the caveat that he would supply troops to assist the Selçuks whenever necessary. This panel is regarded as an expression of Christian gratitude for the tolerance of the Selçuks.

Bahattin'in Samanlığı Kilisesi (Bahattin's Granary Church) is 300 meters farther past Kırk Damaltı Kilisesi. It is named for the local grain gatherer who stored straw in this small barrel-vaulted church, which dates to the 11th century. Its apse is adorned with niches and some 20 portraits depicting the life of Christ.

At the end of the shortened tour is Belisırma. Before the arrival of Selçuk Sultan Kılıçarslan II in 1156, this village was an ancient center of medicine. The medical school, which focused primarily on a process of mummification that was widely practiced in the valley, was transferred later to the Selçuk Sultanate capital of Aksaray.

Food

Belisırma offers dining options right on the water to satisfy the trail-weary. The riverside **Belisırma Restaurant** (0382/457-3057, 9am-10pm daily, 12TL) juts over the Melendez River. Settle in at a table on the second-story terrace overlooking the family of dabbling ducks, or lounge on the tiny wooden piers outfitted with cushioned sofas. House specialties are baked in earthenware; the lemony trout is particularly succulent.

Getting There

Visiting Ihlara Valley is best done with a **guided tour.** You'll save time this way and get a greater appreciation of the valley's history when you hear it told by a professional guide. It's difficult to accurately grasp the region's background and the historical and architectural nuances between churches while hopping over the stream for kilometers trying to get your bearings from a map. Arriving with a group by bus has the additional benefit of a drop-off by the main entrance. **Driving** to Ihlara means parking at either end of the 14-kilometer canyon, in Belisırma or Selime, which means an additional hike up or down the gorge to get back to your vehicle. Parking at the main entrance at Ihlara Valley Touristic Facility is also feasible but includes a hike back to the car via the dreaded 360-stair climb.

If you're game to hike the Ihlara Valley solo, plan for an entire day out. The drive alone is about 90 minutes from Ürgüp or Göreme. To get there from central Cappadocia, follow the Nevşehir-Aksaray Road to Aksaray, which leads to Ihlara. The main entrance is located two kilometers north of the village. Using public transportation isn't advised because it wastes too much time, with three changes required just to reach the valley. Save yourself a headache and drive, or take the Green Tour.

Taxis in Cappadocia can also provide a private full-day tour following the Green Tour itinerary for around 250TL.

Konya

The administrative center of its namesake province—Turkey's largest in terms of area—Konya is a dichotomy, at once fervently conservative and one of the country's economic powerhouses, yet also one of the country's largest consumers of alcohol. After its Turkification by the mighty and religious Selçuk Empire in the 12th century, Konya became the capital of the Sultanate of Rûm for about 150 years. Its changing political status over the years welcomed Islam's most venerated leaders, one of whom was the great Sufi mystic Mevlânâ Celâleddin-i Rûmî (simply known as Mevlânâ or Rûmî), who settled here and founded the Mevlevi Order and the dance of the whirling dervish.

Today, Konya connects to its colorful past through its extensive Selçukian and Ottoman architectural legacies, with ornate hamams, caravansarais, and *medreseler* (Islamic schools), most of which have been converted to museums or cafés. These stunning architectural feats are spread around the city among the 3,046 mosques that serve a population of 1.1 million. Such enormity in the number of places of worship (Istanbul has the most mosques, with 3,113) makes Konya one of the most religious societies in the country. Traveling from the relaxed "anything goes" vibe of the Mediterranean, expect to come face-to-face with a more conservative atmosphere that still provides the friendly hospitality seen elsewhere in Turkey.

While Konya is not high on the traditional traveler's map, the museum containing the tomb of Rûmî remains a pilgrimage site for millions of Muslims and spiritual aesthetes. To fully appreciate some of Konya's sites, one should learn about the exceptional poet and scholar and his spiritual companion, Şems-i Tebrizi (Shams-i-Tabrizi) before arriving. *Forty Rules of Love* by acclaimed Turkish author Elif Şafak, and *Me and Rûmî: The Autobiography of Shams-i Tabrizi*, by William C. Chittick, are both recommended. The highlight of Konya is visiting on Saturday to experience the *sema*—a Sufi meditative whirling ritual, initially created by Rûmî and Şems and evolved by Rûmî's followers and son, Sultan Veled. The ceremony is held at the Mevlânâ Kültür Merkezi (Mevlânâ Culture Center, Aslanlı Kışla Cd., 0332/352-8111, 8pm Sat., free).

Staying a few hours or a night in Konya offers one of best culinary treats in Turkey. The surrounding fertile lands and the richness of centuries-old roasting and baking legacies from the Selçuks, Ottomans, and the Mevlevi Order are worth a lunchtime stop en route to Cappadocia or Antalya. Due to the religious nature of the city, it's rare to find a restaurant that offers alcoholic beverages.

Lingering another day in Konya will allow ample time for half-day side trips to the ongoing excavations of Neolithic-era Çatalhöyük (www.catalhoyuk.com), the former viticulture neighborhood of Meram, Kilistra (Gökyurt), or Sille—the latter two home to churches and caves characteristic of the Cappadocia region. Ask your hotel or the tourist information office for more details.

HISTORY

Recent archaeological findings suggest that this region may have been inhabited as early as the 8th millennium BC. By the mid-1st century AD, Konya had grown into such a regional commercial hub that Saints Paul and Barnabas visited on their missionary journeys around Anatolia. Their repeated visits made

Konya

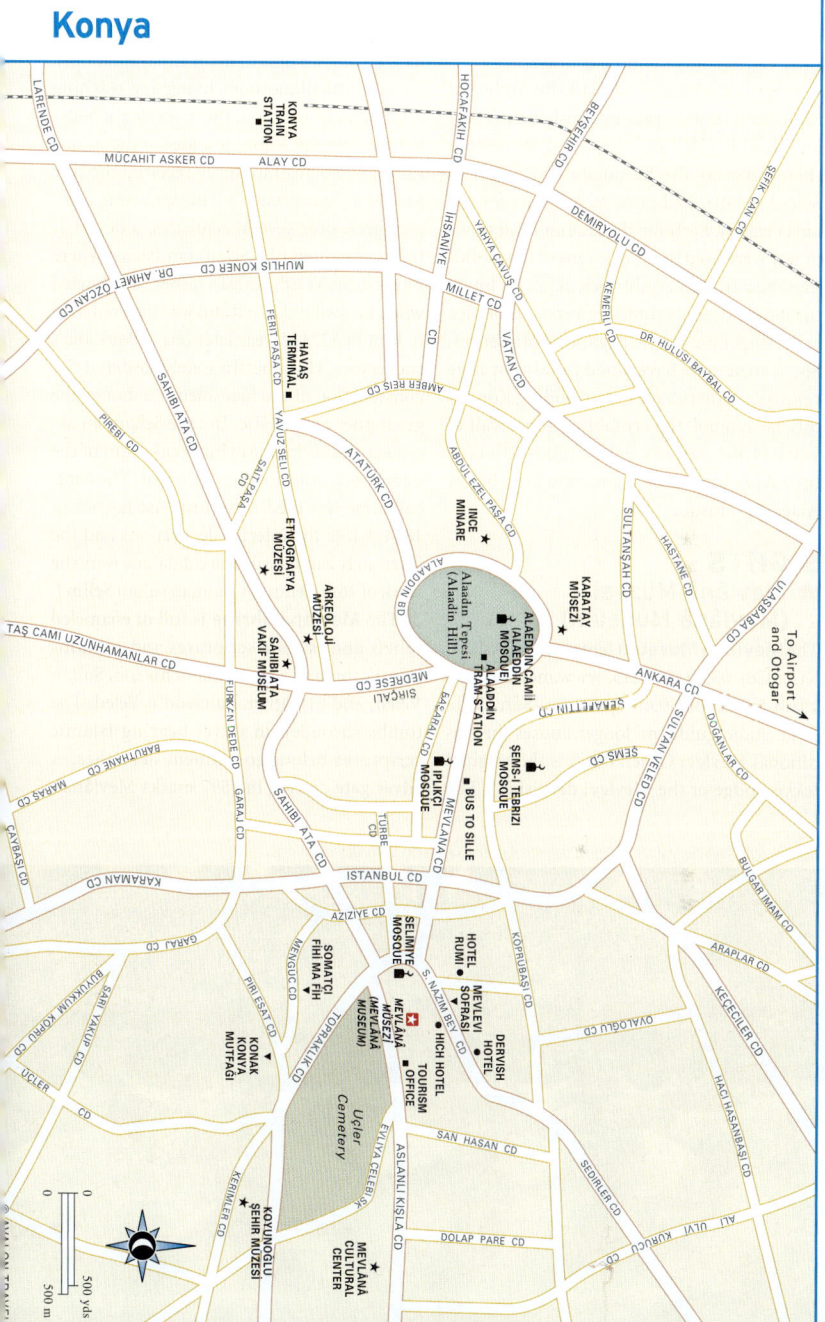

Iconium one of the early Christian communities, leading to its selection as the site of one of early Christianity's church councils.

Once the Selçuks crushed the Byzantines at Manzikert in 1071, they established their seat on Alaeddin Hill in Konya and reinvented themselves as the Sultanate of Rûm. The Selçuks controlled most of Anatolia for the next century. Early on, the accumulated spoils of war were used to fund dozens of fine buildings, boasting an erudite Selçukian architectural style strongly rooted in Persia while also reflecting more ornate Byzantine influences. Some structures have stood for almost nine centuries; others have not, including Konya's official symbol, the crumbling stone wall of Sultan Kılıç Arslan's Palace (mid-12th century AD), braced by a concrete arch below Alaeddin Mosque.

SIGHTS
★ Mevlânâ Müzesi (Mevlânâ Museum)

The **Mevlânâ Museum** (entrance off Aslanlı Kışla Cd., 0332/351-1215, www.mevlana.net, 10am-5pm Mon., 9am-5pm Tues.-Sun., 5TL, 10TL audio guide) no longer houses the traditional Mevlevi Order, but it is the original *tekke* (lodge of the Mevlevi dervishes). The 18,000-square-meter complex comprises a *semahane* (open room for the whirling ritual), a *şadırvan* (fountain for ritual ablutions), a *mescit* (small mosque), living and teaching quarters, a library, and the mausoleum housing the tomb of Rûmî, founder of the mystical sect who posthumously received the title Mevlânâ ("our master"). This sprawling complex grew over several centuries; it began as the rose garden of a Selçukian Palace where Bahaeddin Veled, Rûmî's father, was buried when he died in 1231; Rûmî was interred next to him in 1273. A year later one of Mevlânâ's successors, Hüsamettin Çelebi, ordered the construction of the mausoleum to honor the great poet and mystic. In true Selçukian architectural form, the cylindrical drum of the dome once rested on four columns. The conical dome was tiled with turquoise faience in 1854, while the interior decorations and the intricately carved wooden catafalque were the work of 16th-century Ottoman sultan Selim I.

The **Mevlânâ Shrine** is full of enameled reliefs and Islamic scriptures and contains Rûmî's tomb as well as that of his son, Sultan Veled, and his father, Bahaeddin Veled. The tombs shrouded in velvet bearing Islamic scriptures belong to eminent dervishes. A silver gate crafted in 1597 marks Mevlânâ's

Konya's whirling dervishes perform the ritual of the *sema* on Saturday evenings.

tomb, the largest in the complex. Notice the hierarchy in which Veled's tomb stands next to Mevlânâ's, a sign of respect.

Adjacent to the shrine is the *semahane*, followed by the mosque, both of which were added in the 16th century by Süleyman the Magnificent. Beneath the crystal lamps donated by Selim I in the late 16th century are a collection of Mevlânâ's robes and the oldest original copy of Mevlânâ's greatest works, Mesnevi—some 26,000 verses of poems in six volumes written in Persian for fellow Sufis. Under the mosque are the oldest and largest Korans in the museum, dating to the 9th and 16th century. Be on the lookout for the smallest Koran in the collection, less than three centimeters high, and line up to see the Sakal-i Şerif, a mother-of-pearl box containing tufts of Prophet Mohammed's beard. Outside the mausoleum, you'll have to jostle to get a view of the tiny cells and *matbah* (kitchen) of the Mevlevi. All exhibits have excellent background information explaining the lifestyle and characteristics of the order.

In September 1925, Atatürk banned all religious sects throughout the country to further his vision for a secular republic. But the mystical Sufi sect survived as a religious order; special permission was granted by the Turkish government in 1957 to the Mevlevi Order (also known as the Mawlawi Order) of Konya to perform their ritual whirling dances for visitors for two weeks each year during the commemoration of Mevlânâ's death in December.

The **Selimiye Camii,** located in the park across from the museum's entrance, is a traditional Ottoman mosque. Construction was completed in 1587 and funded by prospective sultan Selim II during his training as the governor of Konya. Farther down the road on Mevlânâ Caddesi is the **Iplikçi Mosque,** built in 1201. The unremarkable Selçukian rectangular structure once housed a *medrese* where Mevlânâ conducted his early teachings. Northeast of here is the **Şems-i Tebrizi Mosque and Mausoleum,** a place of worship for many who respect the teachings and influence of Şems on Mevlânâ and the creation of the Mevlevi. While mystery surrounds Şems actual resting place, this mosque and the velvet-cloaked sarcophagus attract many pilgrims retracing the Sufi path.

Access to all these sites requires the removal of your shoes and covering your legs and shoulders. Women are also required to wear a shawl over their hair.

Alâeddin Camii (Alaeddin Mosque)

Konya's second most important building is the **Alâeddin Camii,** built by a Damascene architect in 1221 to commemorate the reign of Alaeddin Keykubat. This plain-looking Selçukian edifice sprawls over Alaeddin Tepesi (Hill of Alaeddin), Konya's original acropolis. Past its restrained stone entrance, the mosque's interior is a surprising collection of marble pillars crowned by Roman and Ionic capitals, most probably quarried from the collection of churches that the Selçuks razed on their arrival. Of special note are the intricately carved wooden *minbar* (pulpit); an antiquated marble *mihrab* (niche indicating the direction of Mecca), adorned with typical black and blue Selçuk Islamic calligraphy; and one of the two *türbeler* (tombs) said to contain the remnants of eight Selçuk sultans.

Alaeddin Hill's *çaybahçeler* (tea gardens) are the preferred hangout of students attending the local university. It's not a bad place to watch the hustle on the streets below.

Other Museums

The museums of Konya are a little lackluster in comparison to other cities and struggle to draw crowds in the shadows of Konya's main draw, the Mevlânâ Museum. Nonetheless, a handful of collections may be of interest if you have time to explore the archaeology, history, and arts of the region. Certainly the museums in restored *medreseler* are worth a visit sımply to see the architectural legacy of the Selçuk and Ottoman empires. Two such examples are situated within 100 meters of each other, across from Alaeddin Hill. First, **Karatay Müzesi** (Karatay Museum,

Whirling Dervishes and the Legacy of Rûmî

So few texts suggest acceptance and tolerance like the verses etched on the tomb of Mevlânâ Jelaleddin Rûmî:

> Come, come, whoever you are.
>
> Wonderer, worshipper, lover of leaving.
>
> It doesn't matter.
>
> Ours is not a caravan of despair.
>
> Come, even if you have broken your vow
>
> A thousand times
>
> Come, yet again, come, come.

Born in 1207 in modern-day Afghanistan, Rûmî became one of liberal Islam's most celebrated poets and philosophers. Mevlânâ came from a noted family of poets and jurists. Like his teacher-father, he wrote and ministered in Persian, then the literary language of the Selçuks. After finally settling in Konya in 1228 at the behest of Sultan Alaeddin, Mevlânâ earned the name Rûmî, denoting that he was "of Rûm," the formerly Roman lands of Anatolia and the Balkans.

Perhaps most critical in Rûmî's prose and inspiration was his friendship with renowned Sufi mystic Shams-i Tabrizi. Considerably older than Rûmî, Shams introduced him to spiritual dance, music, and poetry. But within three years of his appearance, Shams vanished. Some say he may have been killed by Rûmî's jealous acolytes. Rûmî was bereft and withdrew for years, penning 50,000 verses during this hiatus, some of which expound on his deep loss and even refer to Shams as his soul mate. His collected works are known as the Mesnevi, a set of five tomes written in Persian.

Rûmî lived another 25 years, and he was often seen whirling through Konya in sheer ecstasy. On December 17, 1273, a night known as *Seb-i Aruz* (wedding night with God), Rûmî finally went to meet his maker.

THE MEVLEVI ORDER

The Mevlevi Order, a Sufi (Islamic mystic) sect, was founded by Rûmî's son Sultan Veled to carry on the master's teachings and practices. For 700 years the sect has been led by Mevlânâ's direct descendants. The current Çelebi (Mevlevi leader), Faruk Hemdem, is the 20th great-grandson of Mevlânâ and the 33rd Çelebi. Mevlevis welcome people of all faiths. Their main task in pursuing their 13th-century master's teachings is to bring love and compassion to the lives of all.

Throughout their history, the Mevlevi sect and the Osmans (the Ottoman empire's founding family) were irrevocably intertwined, and when the descendant of Sultan Veled, Devlet Hatun, married Sultan Beyazıt I in 1450, both families were forever tied by blood. Their son, Sultan Mehmet I Çelebi, elevated the order to become the most respected in the empire and bestowed the sect with many gifts. Some dervishes even rose to fame with their poetry and music, including Sheikh Ghalib, whose literature and songs greatly influenced the empire during the 17th century through his friend Sultan Selim III. Known

---

Ankara Cd., 0332/351-1914, 8:30am-5:30pm daily summer, 9am-5pm daily winter, 5TL) is a tile museum in a *medrese* built in 1252 by Selçuk Emir Celaleddin Karatay, with a collection of rare Selçuk tiles and descriptions of the different production methods. There are also star-shaped tiles recovered from the 13th-century summer palace of Selçuk Sultan Kubadabad. At the museum entrance, take a moment to look at the intricately carved Islamic scriptures on its circular stone gateway. Follow Alaeddin Bulvarı south to see another superb facade on the 13th-century **Ince Minare** and its minaret decorated with

among Mevlevi ranks as Galip Dede, the Sufi poet was indoctrinated at the Galata Mevlevihanesi, the first Mevlevi monastery to be built in Istanbul in 1491. As the Ottoman Empire spread, so did the order, reaching as far west as Bosnia and extending east and south into Syria and Egypt. Mevlevis are still active in these two countries, where their sect retains the Arabic name Mawlawi.

As the new secular Republic of Turkey was being formed, Mustafa Kemal Atatürk issued an order to close all sects, including Mevlevi *tekkes* (dervish lodges), on December 13, 1925. Mevlevi assets were confiscated and all ceremonies thenceforth banned. Two years later, the Mevlânâ Mausoleum in Konya was allowed to reopen, but only as a museum. But by the 1950s, the Turkish government had again permitted the order to hold its annual whirling performance in Konya to commemorate the death of its master.

THE *SEMA*

The Mevlevis are also known as *semazens* (whirling dervishes), or those who practice the *sema* (whirling dervish ceremony). Mevlevi historians believe *sema* was created by Rûmî. The story goes that one day, as the master was ambling through Konya's marketplace, he heard the rhythmic hammering of goldbeaters. Their chants in praise to Allah so enthralled him that he stretched out his arms and began spinning.

The modern performance is based on this movement from the marketplace, accompanied by traditional music, and consists of seven distinct parts that follow a prescribed ritual that bring the dervishes toward perfection and enlightenment. Dervishes wear a white gown, symbolizing the ego; a black cloak, signifying the world; and a conical headdress, representing the ego's tombstone. They spin in circles around their sheikh (the order's elder), who is the only one to revolve in place. Whirling begins on the left foot with their arms crossing their torso, a movement representing their testament to their bind with god. The arms are slowly stretched out with the right palm turned to the skies to receive god's blessings, while the dervish looks at his left palm, which faces the earth and passes the benediction to those on Earth. Revolving occurs counter-clockwise, from right to left, around the heart, embracing all of humankind and creation with affection and love.

The first part is the eulogy of *Nat-I Serif*, in which the Prophet Muhammad, who represents love, and all the prophets before him, are praised. *Naat* follows with a chant in praise to Muhammad, accompanied by the beating of the drum. Third is *Taksim*, or the playing of the reed *ney* (flute), which signifies the divine breath, or the first breath that gives life to everything. *Devr-i Veled* ensues, with each dervish bowing his head to his peers to acknowledge the divine breath that each of us receives, as the sounds of the *peshrev* symbolize their souls greeting each other from beneath their earthly bodies. The dervish then cast off into their spin with *Four Selam* forming the centerpiece of the *sema*. The *semazen* represent the moon, spinning just outside of the sheikh, who personifies the sun. The four *selams* (salutations) performed represent the entire spiritual journey that every Mevlevi goes through: the first recognizes the existence of god, the second acknowledges the existence of his unity with all, the third one represents the ecstasy experienced in a state of total surrender; and the fourth involves the sheikh joining the dance as a symbol of peace having achieved uniting with the divine. After another *Taksim* is performed, the ceremony concludes with recitations from the Qu'ran and a prayer by the sheikh.

turquoise tiles. Inside is the **Museum of Woodwork and Masonry** (Alaeddin Blv., 0332/351-3204, 8:30am-5:30pm daily summer, 9am-5pm daily winter, 5TL), seven rooms displaying ornate stone scriptures and carvings from the Selçuk and Ottoman eras, including some remarkable wooden doors and window shutters from both periods. It's a tiny collection but carpenters and craftspeople should not miss it.

South of Alaeddin Hill are three museums near each other in gritty narrow backstreets. A 10-minute walk from the hill, these are easily explored within 90 minutes. The first and best presented is the **Sahip Ata Vakıf Müzesi** (Foundation Museum, Uzun Harmanlar-Taş Camii Cd. 4, 0332/353-8718, www.vgm.gov.tr, 8:30am-5:30pm daily summer, 9am-5pm daily winter, free) in a former *hangâh* (dervish convent) attached to a complex comprising a mosque (built in 1258), a tomb (1276), and double hamam. Several guards are posted inside to protect the relics, which include another venerated tuft of the Prophet Muhammad's beard (Sakal-i Şerif), artifacts from the Şems-i Tebrizi Mosque, original Korans collected from the various mosques in Konya, and kilims and carpets dating to the 17th century that once adorned the Alaeddin Mosque. Next is the rather tired-looking **Arkeoloji Müzesi** (Archaeological Museum, Sahibiata Cd., 0332/351-3207, 8:30am-5:30pm daily summer, 9am-5pm daily winter, 3TL) just around the corner. If you don't have time to visit the Neolithic settlement of Çatalhöyük, 50 kilometers southeast of Konya, this museum presents finds from the ongoing archaeology digs as well as a small array of Roman sarcophagi and artifacts from before the Bronze Age and the Hittite and Byzantine periods in three small galleries. Since you're in the neighborhood, venture over to the **Etnografya Müzesi** (Ethnography Museum, Sahibiata Cd., 0332/351-8958, free), just a block away, to see one room devoted to costumes, jewelry, carpets, and some nasty-looking weaponry from the Ottoman period.

If you have time, there's also the **Koyunoğlu Şehir Müzesi** (Koyunoğlu City Museum, Kerimler Cd. 25, 0332/351-1857, 8:30am-5:30pm daily, free) south of Uçler Cemetery. This museum lacks explanations for its exhibits but contains the restored home and personal collection of A. R. Izzet Koyunoğlu—a prominent Konya businessman. Expect to find more ethnographic items such as clothing, photography, coins, and a library of 30,000 books as well as stuffed animals and birds.

Ince Minare

FESTIVALS

One of Islam's most anticipated commemorations is Konya's annual **Mevlânâ Festival** (Dec. 7-17), a 10-day observance celebrating Mevlânâ, who taught complete tolerance, awareness of God through love, and union with the divine through dance. The festival concludes on Seb-i Aruz, the "wedding night" (Dec. 17) that commemorates Mevlânâ's final breath in 1273—considered his ascension to heaven and his ultimate union with God. For schedules and tickets to festival *sema* performances, contact **Konya Il Kültür & Turizm Müdürlüğü** (Konya Provincial Cultural and Tourism Directorate, Aslanlı Kışla Cd. 5, 0332/353-4020, www.konyakultur.gov.tr, €10).

ACCOMMODATIONS

Konya's hospitality scene runs the gamut from the barest accommodations to well-known high-class five-star hotels like the Rixos and Hilton. That said, most visitors stay only one night, so nothing beats staying close to the Mevlânâ Museum in the old town—ideal for access to the sights and transportation options. Be aware, though, with the enormous number of mosques, it's almost impossible to escape the early-morning call to prayer that may wake you from your slumber.

Dervish Hotel (Sehit Nazim Bey Cd. Güngör Sk. 7, 0332/350-0842, www.dervishotel.com, €55-90), an elegant 150-year-old former home of the Çelebi family, who are direct descendants of Mevlânâ, has been transformed into a beautiful hotel just five minutes' walk from the Mevlânâ Museum. Owner Mehmet and his team warmly welcome guests and have an abundance of local knowledge and hospitality. The seven rooms are perfectly appointed with the traditional Ottoman flair of original wooden trim and flashes of regal red. The *dolmuş* to most locations around town stops right out front, making it a great base for exploring the city.

Hotel Rumi (Durakfakih Sk. 5, 0332/353-1121, www.rumihotel.com, €40-80) has a great location across from the Mevlânâ Museum; it's hard to miss in the old town's maze of streets because it's painted aqua blue. This business hotel has 33 immaculate rooms, including three suites, each with modest yet modern furnishings with black-on-white tiled baths. As a plus, the top floor terrace looks out into the rose garden of the Mevlânâ Museum and the rooftops of the city. In summer you can bask in the morning sun here while savoring the buffet breakfast. A sauna and hamam as well as an indoor gym and billiard room round out the facilities.

It's no surprise the ★ **Hich Hotel** (Celal Sk. 6, 0332/353-4424, www.hichhotel.com, €60-150) rates highly with international travelers with 21 well-appointed classy rooms and suites, just minutes away from the Mevlânâ Museum. The special touches of complimentary tea and coffee, iPod docks, and a courtyard with views to the Mevlânâ's rose garden please many of the guests who walk through the stain glass doors of this concept boutique hotel. Note the quaint use of old and new throughout the three refurbished Selçukian mansions, with handcrafted Anatolian rugs and vibrant contemporary artwork to create a homey ambiance.

FOOD

If religious and spiritual pilgrims come to Konya for Mevlânâ, foodies should trek to Konya for ★ **Somatçı Fihi Ma Fih** (Mengüç Sk. 36, 0332/351-6696, www.somatci.com, 20TL). Head chef Ulaş Tekerkaya, regarded as *emir-i çaşnigir* (chief taster in Selçuk times), toured the dervish lodges of Turkey to find Mevlevi recipes referred to in Mevlânâ's works. What Ulaş created is a stunning menu of the greatest Mevlevi dishes, which traditionally combine almonds or fruits with meat and vegetables. Ask for half portions of dishes to sample more of the treats on offer, and partake in a sip or two of the *sirkencübin şerbert* (sherbet drink) for full effect. The Pan Kebab with lamb soaked in a sauce of spices will have you wiping the plate with the freshly baked bread, while the meat and figs are perfectly cooked to melt in your mouth.

Mevlevi Sofrası (Amil Çelebi Sk. 1, 0332/353-3341, www.konyamevlevisofrasi.com, 15TL) is located next to the Mevlânâ Museum and offers several interior dining rooms oozing with Anatolian kitsch: colorful halls juxtaposed against even more vibrant chintz, carpets, and bric-a-brac. Outside, several terraces lure diners with views of the museum's Selçukian domes and Ottoman minarets just beyond splendidly tended flower beds. As expected for this region, meat-and-bread concoctions highlight the menu. Try the traditional *tirit*—chunks of tandoor-roasted lamb and bread served with homemade yogurt and drizzled with melted butter. The drink menu comprises strong teas, Arabic sherbets, and *ayran* (slightly salted watered-down yogurt drink).

Konak Konya Mutfağı (Piriesat Cd. 5, 0332/352-8547, www.konakkonyamutfagi.com, 10TL) has been a favorite since it opened in 1994. A darling of international food critics, Konak moved to a larger location to accommodate its increasing clientele and changed its name from *köşk* (chalet) to *konak* (mansion).

The house also expanded its excellent meaty offerings, but drink choices have remained limited (no alcohol). Sample the homemade yogurt set served in a clay bowl before diving into the house specialty Konak Kebap—stewed lamb on the bone, topped with fresh tomatoes, creamy feta, and veggie juice laced with tamarind, cinnamon, and other secret spices.

INFORMATION AND SERVICES

Konya's streets extend from the circular one-way road that wraps around Alaeddin Tepesi. Mevlânâ Caddesi runs from here east for about one kilometer to the Mevlânâ Museum; along this road are the government buildings, ATMs, banks, and the police station. The **Tourist Office** (Aslanlı Kışla Cd. 5, 0332/353-4020, 9am-5pm Mon.-Sat.) is just east of the entrance to the Mevlânâ Museum.

GETTING THERE
Air
Konya Airport (KYA, Vali Ahmet Kayhan Cd., 0332/239-1343, www.konya.dhmi.gov.tr) is 16 kilometers northeast of the city center and hosts international and domestic airlines, including **Turkish Airlines** (0212/444-0849, www.turkishairlines.com) and **Pegasus Airlines** (0850/250-0737, www.flypgs.com), which have several domestic flights a day.

Havaş (0332/239-0105, www.havas.com.tr, 25 minutes, 10TL) airport shuttle buses run for every departure and arrival to and from the airport and the junction of Atatürk Caddesi and Ferit Paşa Caddesi. On the way into town, the shuttle stops several times, including on the western side of Alaeddin Hill, where you can take a turquoise-colored *dolmuş* to Mevlânâ (1.75TL), where the recommended hotels are, or walk for 10 minutes east along Mevlânâ Caddesi to reach the same location. A taxi traveling the same distance costs about 10TL.

Bus
Konya's *otogar* is located 10 kilometers north of the town center. National and regional coach companies such as **Ulusoy** (444-1888, www.ulusoy.com) and **Metro Turizm** (444-3455, www.metroturizm.com.tr) connect to all domestic destinations, including Istanbul (75TL, 10 hours), Ankara (30TL, 3.5 hours), Antalya (45TL, 6 hours), and Göreme (30TL, 4 hours). Take a taxi from the *otogar* to Mevlânâ (25TL, 20 minutes) or opt for a *dolmuş* (2TL, 25 minutes) to Mevlânâ from the street outside the *otogar*. The municipal tramway (outside the *otogar*, 1.50TL, 30 minutes) only goes to Alaeddin Tepesi, where you'll have to walk or take a *dolmuş* to Mevlânâ.

Train
Traveling from Ankara's *gar* (central station, 25TL, 2 hours, 8 times per day 7am-8:30pm) is possible with the **Yüksek Hızlı Tren** (high-speed train) network. This network will also eventually connect to Istanbul, enabling rail services between Konya and Istanbul in less than six hours. The train terminates at Konya's *gar*, three kilometers southwest of the Mevlânâ Museum, in the suburb of Meram.

Car
If you are based in Cappadocia, Konya makes an excellent day trip. Via the D300 highway, the trip runs through 230 kilometers (3 hours) of open country, where you can see the landscape change from the moonscape around Göreme to the flat plains and rolling hills of central Anatolia. From Antalya, the coastal D400 heading east connects to the northbound D695 and D696 heading to Konya in four hours (320 kilometers). Reaching the city center from any of Konya's outlying highways can take up to 45 minutes and will require a good map; maneuvering through and parking along the web of antiquated roads running perpendicular to Mevlânâ Caddesi will require some patience and skilled navigation.

GETTING AROUND
Since most sights of interest to visitors are located in close proximity to Mevlânâ Museum, walking around town is easier than taking taxis. A stream of *dolmuşlar* runs the length

of Mevlânâ Caddesi between the museum and Alaeddin Tepesi. If you want to use the **tram** or **municipal buses,** an **Elkart** (swipe card) is required to pay the fares (1.50TL per journey). These can be bought from the small gray booths at tram stations and bus stops around the city. The area between Mevlânâ and the Archaeology Museum make up the bazaar district. Unlike the exotic bazaars of Istanbul, this area is a rather unkempt-looking working-class area where extra care should be taken to maintain your personal safety.

Ankara

Even after nine decades as Turkey's capital, Ankara remains in the shadow of Istanbul. This metropolis has grown in the last decade concurrent with the rule of the Justice and Development Political Party (AKP). Ankara has a dynamic spirit, most evident in its growing number of suburbs, its thriving café culture, and even a nascent culinary scene. It's a modern city that's not as friendly as others, as it home to rather serious civil servants and foreign diplomats, politicians, and the businesses that serve them. On the cultural front, the presence of the State Opera and Ballet, State Theater, and the Presidential Symphony Orchestra ensure that the city continues to beckon Turkey's artistic youth. Ankara has all the trappings of a capital city, but its lack of beauty and its secondary status to Istanbul prevent it from being as memorable as its European peers.

Paris or London it's not, and most travelers snub it all together for the fairy chimneys of Cappadocia and the coasts. But there is still plenty here to keep you entertained for 48 hours, including Atatürk's evocative mausoleum (Anıtkabir) and the exceptional Museum of Anatolian Civilizations. It won't take long to realize that Ankara's streets and museums throb with palpable nationalist pride, with exhibit after exhibit dedicated to the country's beloved Atatürk and the founding of the Turkish Republic. In fact, it can feel like anything he touched has turned to gold and is now on display somewhere in the city. Busts and statues of Atatürk adorn most public spaces. The Victory Monument in Ulus Square, for example, stands as a reminder of the three million lives lost during the country's War of Independence. This all makes the city feel more a site for domestic pilgrims and somewhat culturally fascinating for foreigners, but nonetheless experiencing the outpouring of love for Turkey's founding father is essential to understanding Turkish patriotism.

Venues like the ancient citadel bring the late Bronze Age to life, and plenty of pamphlets available from the tourism offices can direct you to the 68 museums and monuments across the city. From railroad and aviation museums, former prisons, the Cer Modern Art Museum (www.cermodern.org), and even museums dedicated to meteorology and postal services, there's likely to be something to entertain the hobbyist. Keep your eye out for the many parks and newly renovated historical neighborhoods like Hamamönü, named "Elite Destination of Europe" in 2011, with traditional Ankara houses converted to trendy cafés.

HISTORY

Ankara lies at a trade crossroads in the center of Anatolia, an area first settled some 5,000 years ago. After the Hittites invaded the region in the 2nd millennium BC, the city received its first name, Akuwash. Later, this important trading center was successfully ruled by the Phrygians, the Lydians, and subsequently the Persians, who were ousted by Alexander the Great's troops in 333 BC, paving the way for the Pontus Greeks from the Black Sea coast. At the end of 3rd century BC the city saw its first expansion as a commercial center where goods were traded between the Black Sea ports and Crimea to the north;

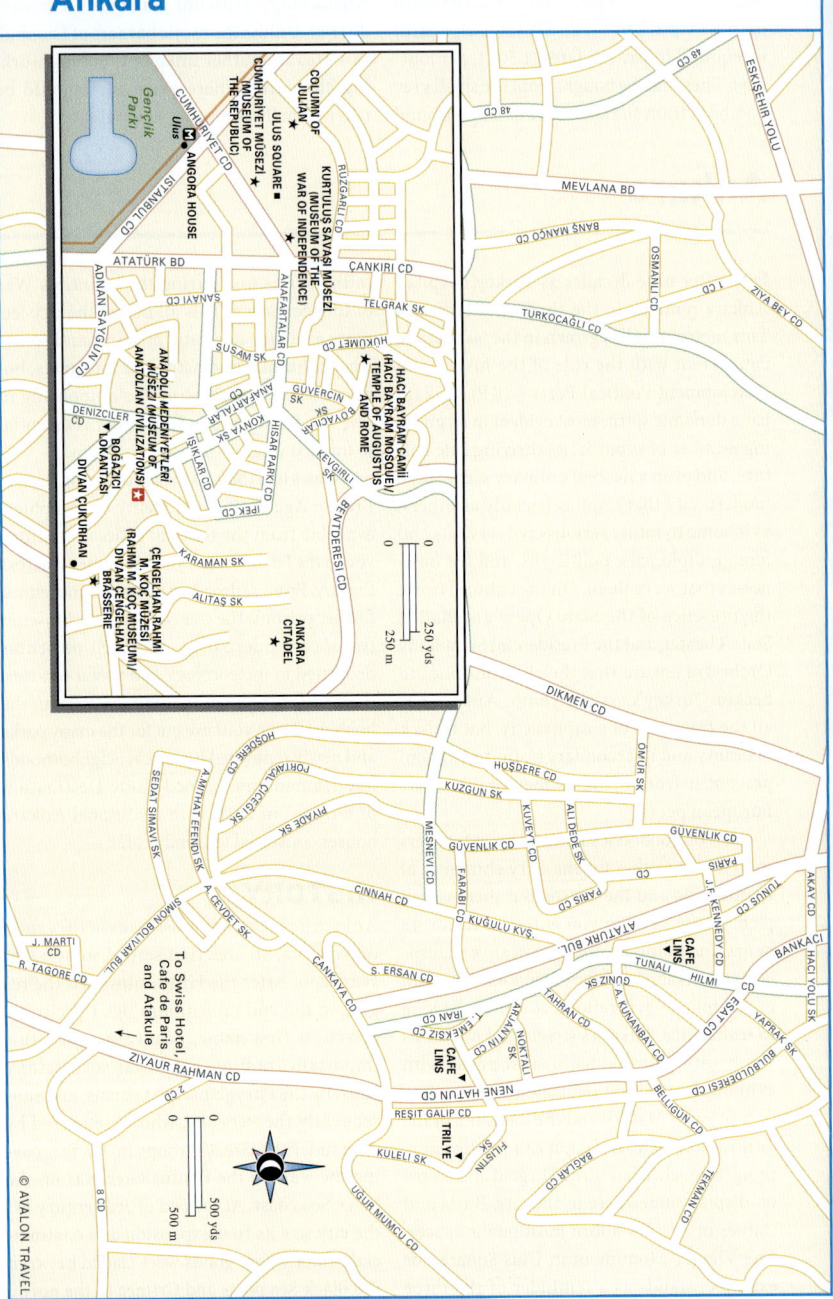

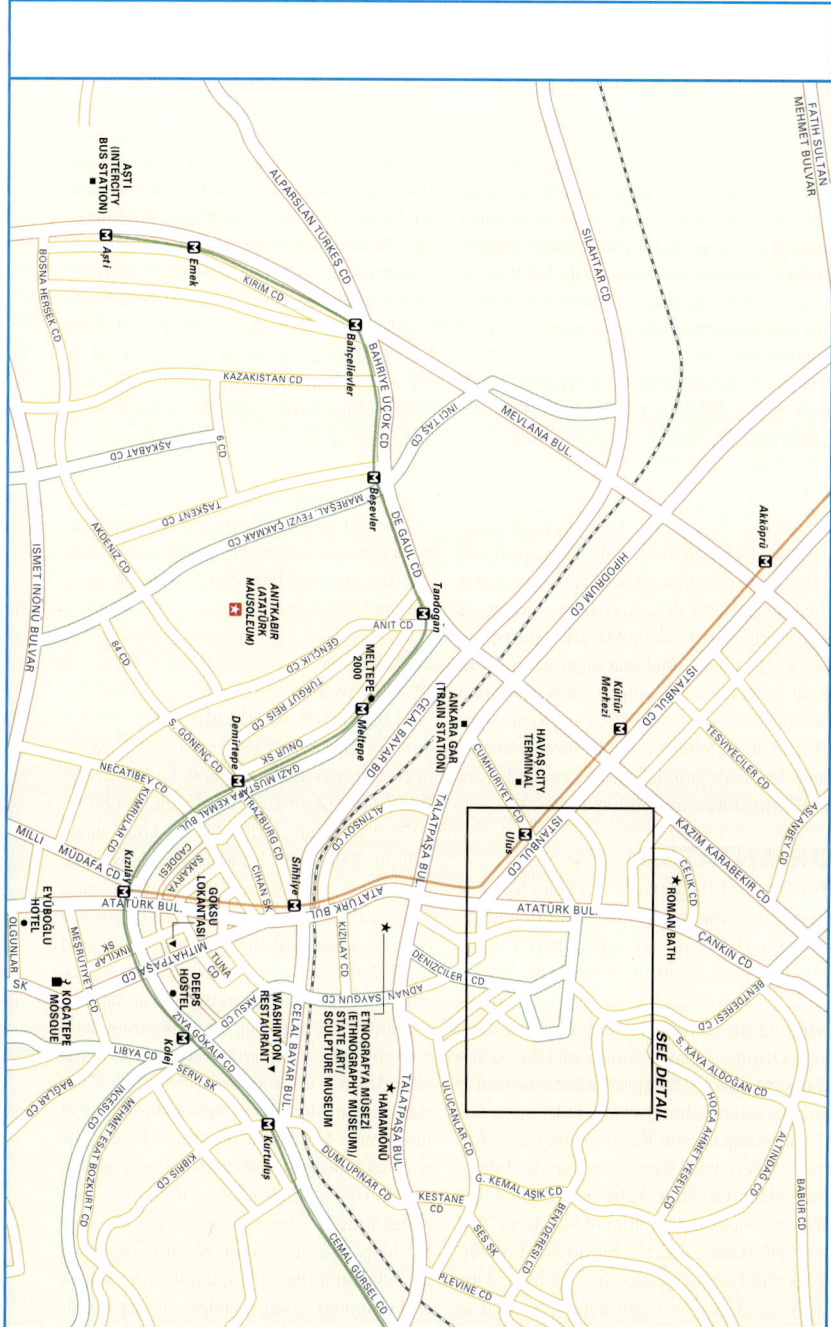

Assyria, Cyprus, and Lebanon to the south; and Georgia, Armenia, and Persia to the east. The Pontus Greeks aptly named this important commercial post Ànkyra (anchor). The city's first stint as a capital came under the Galatians, a Celtic race who migrated west from Thrace in the mid-3rd century BC. But they only ruled for two centuries until Augustus Caesar vanquished them, immediately annexing Ankyra and its 200,000 inhabitants to the Roman Empire and making it one of three administrative centers in central Asia Minor.

The Byzantines held on to the city until 1071, when the Selçuk Turks literally bulldozed the city, which subsequently was renamed Enguriye. The westward expansion of the Ottoman Empire left most of central Anatolia unsupervised. Ankara's population declined to 5,000; the grand trading post was left as mere pastureland for Angora goats. But the tide turned a decade after the Ottomans lost World War I, when Atatürk selected the city as the provisional seat of government in 1920. After the War of Independence, Ankara became the capital of the fledgling Republic of Turkey on October 29, 1923. Since its founding, Ankara's population has swelled from 35,000 to almost five million today.

ORIENTATION

Two areas of the city are worth a visit. The first is the more traditional and often gritty Ulus quarter in the Altındağ district in the north, with ancient buildings, the citadel, and classic Ankara houses that line narrow winding streets dating to Roman, Byzantine, and Ottoman times. South of Ulus is the Çankaya district that sprawls from the trendy Kızılay neighborhood and includes upmarket Gaziosmanpaşa and Kavaklıdere, which feature modern wide streets, theaters, and shopping malls. Çankaya is also where you'll find five-star hotels, government buildings, foreign embassies, and the presidential palace. Ulus and Çankaya are connected by Ankara Bulvarı, Ankara's main artery, as well as the underground M1 metro that terminates in Kızılay. From Kızılay you can board the Ankaray subway to travel to Tandoğan to visit Anıtkabır, or stay aboard to reach the ATŞI (Ankara's major station for intercity coaches).

Most museums are located within walking distance of Ulus Meydanı (Ulus Square). The city's Roman Bath and other remnants are located 500 meters north of the square, and the citadel quarter is a slow uphill walk 1.5 kilometers east. Get to the citadel directly by following the uphill slant of Hisarparkı Caddesi from the square, and turn right onto Ipek Caddesi; the end of this street marks the entrance of the Museum of Anatolian Civilizations. Farther uphill via Gözcü Sokak is the Rahmi M. Koç Museum, opposite the towering walls of the old city and citadel, one of Ankara's landmarks.

You can easily walk around Ankara; renting a car is not necessary unless you're considering visiting Hattuşaş or the outskirts of the capital.

SIGHTS
★ Anıtkabir (Atatürk Mausoleum)

Foreign dignitaries visiting Ankara are expected to pay their respects to Atatürk at **Anıtkabir** (Anıt Cd., Tandoğan, 0312/231-7975, 9am-5pm daily May 15-Oct., 9am-4:30pm Feb.-May. 14, 9am-4pm Nov.-Jan., free). They join the millions of Turks who travel to the capital annually to honor the man who founded the country. Completed in 1953 after nine years of construction, the memorial stands overlooking the capital. The colonnades dominating the structure strictly abide by the Turkish architectural style of the period, which utilized strong symmetrical designs and unadorned cut stone in the design of monument-like public buildings. Inside, the **Hall of Honor** houses a 40-ton red marble sarcophagus, under which a tomb room encloses Atatürk's remains, which are not open to the public. The tomb room is based on an octagonal floor plan, duplicating Selçuk and Ottoman building styles, with a pyramidal ceiling inlaid with gold tiles and mosaic walls that recall Anatolia's various empires. While standing in the Hall of Honor, look up to the 17-meter-high mosaic ceiling. Outside, a gallery wraps around the main building and leads to various exhibition areas, including the **Museum of Atatürk and the War of Independence,** which houses Atatürk's clothing, gifts, library, and political legacies bookending murals, tributes, and audio visual recreations of the battle fields of World War I and the War of Independence. In the **23 Nisan** and **Baris Towers** are Atatürk's boat and official automobiles; the **Zafer Tower** displays the gun carriage that carried Atatürk's remains from Dolmabaçhe Palace, Istanbul, where he died in 1938. The symbolic sarcophagus at the opposite side of the square facing Atatürk's resting place is that of **İsmet İnönü** (1884-1973), a former military officer, prime minister, and Turkey's second president. At each corner of the building stands a guard; stick around to experience the impressive **Changing of the Guard** ceremony, which takes place every half hour.

Ankara Citadel

Ankara's original acropolis dominates the city's tallest hill in the old town (off Gözcü Sk.), and was either built by the Galatians or the Hittites. The *kaleiçi* (inner walls) date to the 6th century AD, while the outer walls were commissioned 200 years later by Byzantine emperor Michael II to provide an extra layer of fortification.

Inside, the tiny **citadel district** sprawls along narrow winding lanes, flanked by traditional two-story wooden Ankara houses whose large wooden gates open to pebbled courtyards and fragrant gardens. Like a pearl within its oyster, the citadel is a traditional Turkish village in the heart of an important capital. The majority of the houses are now craft stores and cafés, so take your time to freely explore the mosques, towers, and homes with a coffee break in between. If you wander off track, the residents who still keep houses here will point you in the direction you need to go. A tourism office at the end of the main Kale Kapısı Sokak can also assist with information about Ankara and the citadel.

Çengelhan Rahmi M. Koç Müzesi (Rahmi M. Koç Museum)

Ankara's north-south and east-west trade routes stopped at the Çengelhan during the 16th and 17th centuries, but today this former inn houses the impressive **Çengelhan Rahmi**

Atatürk Mausoleum is a fine tribute to the father of modern-day Turkey.

M. Koç Müzesi (across from the Citadel entrance, Depo Sk. 1, Altındağ, 0312/309-6800, www.rmk-museum.org.tr, 10am-5pm Tues.-Fri., 10am-6pm Sat.-Sun., adults 6TL, children 3TL). Completed during the reign of Süleyman the Magnificent in 1522, this caravanserai was a gift to the sultan's daughter from her husband, Damat Rüstem Paşa. It was meticulously restored by Turkish business magnate Rahmi M. Koç for his father, Vehbi Koç, who had begun his career in 1917 at a small grocery store inside. The 26-room inn opened as a museum dedicated to Rahmi M. Koç's passions in 1995. Displays include engineering, rail, road, and maritime transportation, technology through the ages, and scientific instruments; there are lots of interactive exhibits to thrill the little ones. There may be 68 museums in Ankara, but this one has little bit of everything.

★ Anadolu Medeniyetleri Müzesi (Museum of Anatolian Civilizations)

Ankara's **Anadolu Medeniyetleri Müzesi** (Gözcü Sk. 2, 0312/324-3160, 8:30am-5:30pm daily, 15TL, 10TL audio guide) alone warrants a trip to the city. This archaeological museum, one of the finest of its kind in the world, takes up most of one of the oldest and largest Ottoman *hans* (caravansarais). This 15th-century covered bazaar—a fireproof *bedesten* (marketplace) where valuable metals and jewelry were traded—was completed during the reign of Mehmet the Conqueror. Since it opened in 1968, the museum inside this double-domed structure continues to detail the history of the region and the evolution of civilization in Anatolia, with the best artifacts collected throughout the country.

The museum is arranged like most museums of its kind in Turkey, with displays starting at the right of the entrance and continuing chronologically counterclockwise. At the start, remains dating to 2.5 million years ago to 8000 BC, discovered inside Antalya's Karain Cave, one of the oldest subterranean cities ever found, detail cave-dwelling hunter-gatherer life with tools carved of stone and bone.

The Bronze Age collections relate to the Hatti tribes that populated Anatolia during the 3rd-2nd millennia BC. On display is a recreation of a burial ceremony that includes solar discs, deer-shaped statuettes, and loads of gold jewelry that emphasize the importance of religion during the Bronze Age.

The Southern Hall gives way to the

Houses in the Ankara Citadel are transformed into a street bazaar of antiques and other goodies.

Assyrian Trade Colonies (1950-1750 BC). This era saw the rise of trade and writing in Anatolia. More than 20,000 Assyrian clay tablets, inscribed in cuneiform, relate to business deals and law. According to deciphered tablets, goods were exchanged for silver and gold.

The Great Hittite Empire collection (1750-1200 BC) centers around the impressive relief of the God of War, which was taken from the King's Gate at Boğazköy (ancient Hattuşaş). Near the reconstructions of Hittite religious rites and the King's Gate is a tablet inscribed in Akkadian scripts (1275-1220 BC), which constitutes what is perhaps the most important artifact relating to the period: correspondence from Egyptian queen Nefertari, wife of Ramses II, to Hittite queen Puduhepa, wife of Hattusili III, written after the Treaty of Kadesh, history's first peace treaty.

Exhibits in the central *bedesten* (marketplace) section vary, but mostly involve the latest archaeological finds of Anatolia. Displays on the lower level relate to the classical Hellenic, Roman, and Byzantine eras and provide a rundown of Ankara's historical highlights.

Haci Bayram Camii (Haci Bayram Mosque)

Completed in 1428 by Haci Bayram, founder of the Sufi Bayrami sect, who was also a poet and hymnodist, the **Haci Bayram Camii** (Sarıbağ Sk., Ulus) has a traditional Selçuk floor plan. The modest lines and decor of Selçukian style were revamped with the ornate touches of the illustrious Mimar Sinan in the 16th century.

This is by far Ankara's prettiest and most significant mosque, both for its combination of design styles and its benefactor. A hexagonal rosette, framed by six rows of flowered borders, dominates a large ceiling constructed entirely of wood. Kütahya tiles were added above the windows in the 18th century; hand-carved palm fronds border the faience.

Much like Rûmî's tomb, Sufi pilgrims visit the **Haci Bayram Türbesi** (Haci Bayram Mausoleum), adjacent to the mosque's *mihrab*. Bayram died in 1429 and his remains lie beyond the marble facade of a diminutive square building, topped by a stone octagonal drum, crowned by a lead dome. The structure's original wooden exterior and interior entrance doors are now on display at the Ethnography Museum.

If you want to go inside, you'll have to abide by the usual protocols of covering exposed skin and removing your shoes at the separate male and female entrances; women also must cover their hair.

Temple of Augustus and Rome

Attached to the Haci Bayram Mosque, the **Temple of Augustus** was built by the Galatians in AD 10 as a tribute to their commitment to Roman emperor Augustus, and reconstructed during the 2nd century by the Romans. Like most ancient monuments from the classical period, this one was built from the remains of a temple honoring the Phrygian god Men and goddess Cybele. Just before his death, Augustus penned the document *Res Gestae Divi Augusti* (Deeds of the Divine Augustus) in both Greek and Latin. A will of sorts, it contains four sections, each detailing a different aspect of his regal career. He instructed his senate to dispatch the document throughout the empire to be displayed carved in stone on monuments and temples. Many of these have survived, but Ankara's copy is the only one that is nearly complete; it can be seen on the walls of the temple.

The Column of Julian

Known by locals as the Belkis Minaresi, the **Column of Julian** (Ulus Square, free) was built to honor Emperor Julian in AD 362. The 15-meter-tall column is topped by a Corinthian capital, thought to have been added two centuries later.

Roman Bath

The **Roman Bath** (Çankiri Cd., Ulus, 8:30am-12:30pm and 1:30pm-5:30pm daily, 5TL) was built during the reign of Roman emperor Caracalla (AD 211-217) in honor of the god of medicine, Asclepius. What remains of this once large building are the three rooms typically found in public baths during the era: a *frigidarium* (cool room), a *hepidarium* (warm room), and a *calderium* (hot room). Ongoing excavations revealed a swimming pool and a dressing room adjoining the *frigidarium*, as well as a *sudatorium* (sweat room) in the *calderium* section. An underground heating system, courtyards, fireplaces, and areas for attendants and storage were other amenities.

Kurtuluş Savaşı Müzesi (Museum of the War of Independence)

The name of this war museum, **Kurtuluş Savaşı Müzesi** (Cumhuriyet Cd. 14, Ulus, 0312/310-7140, 9am-5pm daily, 1TL), is a little misleading as it displays the building's former life as the first home of the Turkish Grand National Assembly (1920-1924) rather than a war museum. The displays, only explained in Turkish, include Atatürk's office, the table where the Treaty of Lausanne was signed, and the original Assembly Hall where the Turkish Republic was formulated.

Cumhürriyet Müzesi (Museum of the Republic)

The building housing **Cumhürriyet Müzesi** (Cumhuriyet Cd. 22, Ulus, 0312/310-5361, 9am-5pm daily, 5TL) was the second home of the Grand National Assembly of Turkey, 1924-1960. It opened to the public in its current incarnation in 1980. The Assembly Hall in the center of the building is built entirely of wood and girded by corridors that connect to outside rooms. The senate's interior decoration bears homage to both the modesty of Selçukian design and the intricacies of Ottoman style. There are also documents relating Atatürk's vision for his new republic, as well as some of his personal possessions. The legends affixed to exhibits are in Turkish, so ask for a complimentary audio guide on arrival.

Etnografya Müzesi (Ethnography Museum)

Etnografya Müzesi (Talat Paşa Blv., Türkocağı Sk. 4, Sıhhıye, 0312/311-3007, www.etnografyamuzesi.gov.tr, 9am-5pm daily, 10TL) is the best ethnography museum in the country. The building was commissioned by Atatürk and completed in 1926 as Turkey's first state museum, situated on sacred Namazgah Hill, site of a former Selçuk burial place and religious ceremonial ground for the Ottomans. Several salons now boast dioramas depicting important cultural events such as preparations for weddings and circumcision ceremonies. The favored continental handicrafts such as ceramics, weaving, and woodwork are also shown with artifacts collected from around the country. One of the most interesting displays is the series of photographs of Atatürk's final journey in 1938 from Dolmabaçhe Palace, where he died, to the foyer of the Ethnography Museum, where he was interred until his mausoleum was completed in 1953. Next door to the Ethnography Museum is the State Art and Sculpture Museum, which displays fine art dating back to the 19th century.

Kocatepe Mosque

With room for 24,000 worshippers, **Kocatepe Mosque** was once the largest mosque in Turkey; it took two decades to build (1967-1987). Today, its four 88-meter minarets can be seen from most rooftops in the city, making it one of the most impressive buildings in Turkey. Inside is just as grand, with six levels of stained glass windows that shed light on blue and red decorative tiles that surround a central crystal chandelier measuring over five meters in diameter. If the design looks familiar, it is—it's based on the Blue Mosque of Istanbul.

ENTERTAINMENT AND EVENTS
Performing Arts

As the capital of a quickly emerging country, Ankara is ripe with a performing arts scene that rivals those of its European counterparts. The **Presidential Symphony Orchestra** (Talatpaşa Blv. 38, Opera, 0312/309-1343, cso.gov.tr) hosts concerts on a regular basis, while the **State Opera and Ballet** (Opera Sahnesi, Atatürk Blv. 50, Opera, 0312/324-2210, www.dobgm.gov.tr, tickets 10TL) showcases its talented performers at 8pm nightly through classical operas and ballets (from 12TL). The **Devlet Tiyatroları** (Turkish State Theaters, www.devtiyatro.gov.tr) runs Ankara's theaters and their programs, which feature the works of international and Turkish playwrights. **IF Performance Hall** (Tunus Cd. 14, Kavaklıdere, 0312/418-9506, www.ifperformance.com) is also a popular venue for the local arts scene. Tickets for events can be purchased through the organizations' websites or **MyBilet** (www.mybilet.com).

Nightlife

Central Ankara's night scene caters heavily to politicos and diplomats, with highbrow English pubs, jazz clubs, cafés, and a string of coffee shops open till the wee hours. Arjantin Caddesi in the Gaziosmanpaşa quarter has a group of irresistible cafés nicknamed "Ankara SoHo," but for more youthful—and cheaper—venues, head to Kızılay's Sakarya Caddesi, where Bilkent University's students hangs out. Here you'll find Inkılap Sokak, where you can barhop through the popular and casual live-music bars that line the street, including **Telwe** (0312/433-5454), **Biber Alternatif Café and Pub** (0312/430-0717), and **eSkiyEni** (0312/433-0701). Interestingly, almost on the doorstep of Kocatepe Mosque is Olgunlar Caddesi's nightlife precinct, which overflows with a mix of bars, Irish pubs, and traditional *meyhaneler* (Turkish taverns). Just south, on Bestekar Caddesi in Kavaklıdere, are more bars and even the odd wine bar.

For five-star entertainment, head to **Murphy's Dance Bar** (Tahran Cd. 12, Kavaklıdere, 0312/466-0054) at the Hilton Hotel. Each night the theme changes, from 100 percent Turkish pop and Latin to rap, hip-hop, and karaoke. The best thing about Murphy's is its clientele, which ranges through all ages.

Festivals

Ankara's abuzz with festivities year-round, and the largest event is **Victory Day** (Aug. 30), when the capital pulls out all the stops to commemorate the day the Turks repelled a Greek invasion in 1922. April marks Ankara's **International Music Festival** (0312/427-0855, www.ankarafestival.com), when Turkey's top musicians and dancers unite with their international peers for a monthlong program of events. The capital's **International Film Festival** (0312/468-3892, ww.filmfestankara.org.tr) occurs in June during a 10-day-long showcase of Europe's best indie films. On April 23, galas and televised concerts featuring children from all over the world mark the celebration of **International Children's Festival.** Atatürk dedicated the day on which Turkey's Grand National Assembly was established to the children of the world.

ACCOMMODATIONS

It's all about the battle of the titans in Ankara: the bigger the hotel, the better; the more the amenities for business travelers, the sweeter it is, though the downside is that there are few reputable budget and mid-range hotels in convenient locations. Trying to find good-quality affordable accommodations among the well-known five-star hotel chains is difficult. Staying in Ulus puts you close to the museums, but the area has a gritty underbelly because it's a bazaar district; if you're traveling alone, staying in Çankaya is a better option. Being close to the Ankaray or metro train stations will also keep costs down, although a taxi from one end of town to the other will cost no more than 20TL.

Under €100

★ **Maltepe 2000** (Gülseren Sk.4, Maltepe, 0312/231-8170, www.maltepe2000.com, €55-110), with enormous black-and-white photos of Hollywood and Turkish film icons, is stylish, fun, and affordable. The bold use of black and white stripes with flashes of red is striking in 35 standard, deluxe, and suite rooms that step up the boutique ambiance. Added bonuses include a huge buffet breakfast and complimentary tea and coffee in the guest rooms. It's located opposite the Maltepe Ankaray Station, so you can commute to the ATŞI or Ulus in less than 15 minutes or by taxi to Anıtkabir in 5 minutes.

If you're backpacking, reserve early to get a bunk at **Deeps Hostel** (Atac 2 Sk. 46, Kızılay, 0312/213-6338, www.deepshostelankara.com, €12-35). Large dorm rooms and private rooms with bright colors are accented by Ikea decor; it's close to the Ankaray Kızılay Station and near the bars and affordable eats of Sakarya Caddesi. Rooms go fast, as this is the only hostel in town, so reserve well ahead of time.

Located in the center of town, **Eyüboğlu Hotel** (Karanfil Sk. 73, Bakanlıklar, 0312/417-6400, www.eyubogluhotel.com, €49-79) is affordable but features five-star pillow menus, an on-site restaurant and cocktail bar, 24-hour room service, and 56 deluxe and standard rooms that are modern and full of little touches of luxury. This hotel is an excellent value and just 500 meters from Kızılay Square.

To sample the lifestyle in the old Ankara houses of the citadel, check into **Angora House** (Kale Kapisi Sk. 16, Ulus, 0312/309-8380, www.angorahouse.com.tr, €70-120). With just four doubles and two suites, this hotel is small, intimate, and oozing with Ottoman features. Expect high wooden ceilings with handcrafted antique furniture and fittings draped in continental fabrics. It's like staying in fairy-tale cottage designed with Grandma's homey flair, yet with all the amenities of a boutique hotel. Angora is an excellent choice for exploring the Ulus quarter; just pack a good map or GPS device to navigate the winding streets of the district.

€100-200

★ **Swissôtel** (Jose Marti Cd. 2, Yildizevler, 0312/409-3000, www.swissotel.com, €95-210) is eight kilometers south of Ulus but has impeccable service and luxurious amenities, beckoning the harried traveler with appealing restful spaces and a slew of opulent facilities, including a health club that overlooks the indoor topaz swimming pool, a sauna, and a hamam. The rooms boast satellite LCD TVs and personal CD players, dual electrical sockets (120 and 220 volts), espresso machines, and luxurious baths with rain showers.

The Çankaya district is full of high-rise five-star hotels, but if you have five-star tastes and a desire for a holiday in a charming location, retreat to Ulus at the **Divan Çukurhan** (Depo Sk. 3, 0312/306-6400, www.divan.com.tr, €120-400). The setting is stunning: a restored brick, stone, and wood caravanserai dating back to the 16th or 17th centuries. Prominent Turkish businessman Rahmi M. Koç saw the potential in this beauty when it was listed on the World Monuments Fund's Watch List of 100 Most Endangered Sites. From 2007 to 2010 it was restored while retaining the architectural character of the building that once served as an inn for Ottoman traders, near an old horse market. The hotel has deluxe rooms and suites with the usual personalized touches.

FOOD

Increasingly hip Ankara is receiving quite a bit of attention from gourmets. The touristy thing to do for an evening meal is to head to one of the "in" restaurants in Çankaya, or for snack-on-the-go options, try *simit* (Turkish bagels) filled with cream cheese and olive paste, or fresh-boiled corn from food carts; of course, there's always the *döner* (sliced roasted lamb) sandwiches from hole-in-the-wall cafés throughout the city. Despite it being a capital with many foreign visitors, English is not widely spoken, so be patient with the service.

Ottoman and Turkish

★ **Boğazıcı Lokantası** (Denizciler Cd. 1, Ulus, 0312/311-8832, www.bogazicilokantasi.com, 15TL) is synonymous with Ankara and great food. Original owner Mehmet Recai Boyacıoğlun has run the kitchen since this blue-collar restaurant opened in 1956. His secret for longevity is providing consistently excellent quality, and to achieve that he must be superhuman, considering his menu includes about 45 new dishes every day. Try the seasonal *zeytinyağlıs* (veggies cooked in olive oil and served cool) with any of the meat dishes.

Looks can be deceiving, especially at ★ **Göksu Lokantası** (Bayindir Sk. 22/A, Kızılay, 0312/431-2219, 20TL). This eatery looks pricey from the outside, but inside is a retro bistro complete with a golden glowing Hittite sculptures. Look past the decor and straight at the menu of Turkish favorites and Anatolian and Black Sea specialties. The menu at the front is just a summary of the oodles of dishes available. It's located just a five minute walk from the Kızılay metro station.

International

Café de Paris (Abdullah Cevdet Sk. 30/A, Çankaya, 0312/440-5123, www.cafedeparis.com.tr, 30TL) is a modern bohemian bistro with decor oozing with nostalgia for Paris's artistic past. Quite chic, but far from pompous, the rather small dining room is romantic with the traditional banquet listed on one wall. But unlike a typical French bistro, this one is missing the white tablecloths and the curt service; you'll find nothing but friendly hospitality here. Come on weekends for the signature Café de Paris filet, served with crispy french fries, perfect when enjoyed over live French music.

Divan Çengelhan Brasserie (Depo Sk. 1, Ulus, 0312/309-6800, www.divan.com.tr, 30TL) oozes atmosphere thanks to its location inside the 16th-century caravanserai it occupies along with the Rahmi M. Koç Museum. Part of the conglomerate Koç Holdings, whose current owner spent millions to renovate this historic building, the Divan hotel and restaurant chain replicated the quality and culinary innovation that's earned it a coveted membership in the acclaimed international gastronomic society, La Confrérie de la Chaîne des Rôtisseurs.

For a culinary change from the usual kebabs and Turkish fare, peruse the menu of the stylish **Café Lins** (Kader Sk. 9, Gaziosmanpaşa, 0312/428-5467, www.cafe-lins.com, 25TL). This shabby-chic restaurant is decked out in rustic grays and pastels with a tufted seating and has a menu of international dishes like pastas, steaks, crepes, and soups. The dessert, wine, and cocktail menu will see you through to last call, especially on Wednesday nights when jazz and Latin tunes accompany your meal. A second Café Lins with an enchanting garden can found at Bestekar Sokak 84 in Kavaklıdere.

★ **Washington Restaurant** (Muhsin Yazıcıoğlu Cd. 1436 Sk. 3/A, Çukuramba, 0312/311-4344, www.washingtonrestaurant.com.tr, 30TL) is Ankara's landmark haunt for politicians, international leaders, and foreign diplomats. Its no-nonsense dedication to quality and service is as steady as it was in 1955 when two brothers from Rize returned from a stint as Turkish diplomats in Washington DC. The menu reflects exactly what these bureaucrats are after: delectable entrées, a superior wine list, and an ambience that's classy but not over-the-top.

Seafood

No one in their right mind would consider eating fish in the nation's capital; Ankara's at least three hours from the nearest sea. But that all changed when a highly creative food-loving couple named Üzmez introduced seafood to traditional Turkish recipes and began showcasing the results at their ★ **Trilye Restaurant** (Hafta Sk. 11/B, Gaziosmanpaşa, 0312/447-1200, www.trilye.com.tr, 25TL) in the swanky Çankaya district. Its reputation lives up to its slogan: "The freshest fish from any of Turkey's coasts can be found here," and all these treats are served in an elegant and typically packed room of international foodies. Dine on the terrace; it's infinitely more inviting.

INFORMATION AND SERVICES

Ankara's **Tourist Information Offices** are located at the airport (0312/398-0348) and in Tandoğan (Gazi Mustafa Kemal Blv. 121, 0312/231-5572, www.kultur.gov.tr). Smaller offices are also found inside the ATŞI (ground floor) and the citadel (Kale Kapısı Sk.). Banks and ATMs are around Çankaya's Kavaklıdere and Altındağ's Ulus neighborhoods. There are over 60 **PTT** post offices in Ankara, so ask at your hotel for the nearest one. At these offices you can exchange currency in addition to the usual postal services.

GETTING THERE
Air

Ankara's **Esenboğa International Airport** (ESB, 0312/590-4000, www.esenbogaairport.com) opened in 2006 to accommodate the increasing number of domestic flights. Domestic airlines such as **Turkish Airlines** (0212/444-0849, www.turkishairlines.com) and **Pegasus Airlines** (0850/250-0737, www.flypgs.com) provide both domestic and international flights. International carriers Lufthansa, Qatar, and Borajet, among others, also serve the airport.

Esenboğa airport is 28 kilometers northeast of the city center. The Havaş shuttle bus runs two routes between the airport and the **Havaş City Office** (19 Mayıs Stadium, B Gate, Ulus, 0312/398-0376, www.havas.net, 10TL) and between the airport and ATŞI (ground floor). The trips take about 40 minutes and depart every half hour in both directions 2am-10pm daily. Outside these times, buses run if there are flights.

The much slower municipal **EGO bus** 442 (www.ego.gov.tr, 5.25TL) transports people from the airport to AŞTI and various stops in Çankaya and Altındağ, with the entire journey taking over 1.5 hours.

A trip to town with Esenboğa's **taxi coop** (0312/398-0897, www.esenbogataksi.com) will cost 75-85TL.

Train

The Turkish State Railways **Yüksek Hızlı Tren** (high-speed train, www.tcdd.gov.tr) between Ankara Gar and Istanbul (80TL one-way), via Eskişehir, travels the 533-kilometer distance in three hours. A 306-kilometer high-speed train also runs from Ankara Gar to Konya (25TL) eight times per day in less than two hours.

Bus

Ankara's **AŞTI** (bus station, 0312/207-1000) is eight kilometers southwest of Ulus and seven kilometers from Kavaklıdere. AŞTI is served by all major national coach companies and regional carriers. The largest, **Varan** (0212/692-9595, www.varan.com.tr), **Ulusoy** (444-1888, www.ulusoy.com.tr), and **Metro Turizm** (444-3455, www.metroturizm.com.tr), connect the most cities. There are, for example, over 45 coaches daily from Istanbul to Ankara (60TL). Traveling from Ankara to other Turkish cities is best done by checking schedules and fares online and booking ahead to ensure ticket availability and the lowest prices. While a taxi (15-20TL) is the fastest way to reach the center of town, there's also an Ankaray (A1, 3.50TL) train station in front of the *otogar* that connects to the M1 metro farther down the line in Kızılay every 10 minutes.

GETTING AROUND
Public Transportation

Ankara is quite adequately served by public transportation: *dolmuş* co-ops and EGO (www.ego.gov.tr) **bus** and **metro** services. These vehicles are marked with their destination on the front windshield and the passenger boarding side.

Ankara's main metro lines include the Ankaray (A1), which runs southwest-northeast from AŞTI to beyond Kızılay to Dikimevi; and the M1 metro east-northwest line, connecting Kızılay to Batıkent via Ulus. New lines M2 (Kızılay-Çayyolu), M3 (Batıkent-Sincan and Törekent), and M4 (Tandoğan-Keçiören) are under construction but are not likely to be of use to travelers.

Bus and metro fares use the **EGO card,** which can be purchased on buses and from ticket booths at all stations. Essentially the card costs 1.75TL, plus the cost of fares. If you intend to use public transportation more than once, buy multiple-ride passes for discount fares (3.50TL for 2 rides, 5.25TL for 3 rides, 8.75TL for 5 rides, 17.50TL for 10 rides). You just validate the pass in the machines found at turnstiles and on buses when boarding.

Taxis

Since Ankara's sights are located close together, hopping in a taxi won't break the bank. The base fare is currently 2.70TL, with an additional 2.40TL for every kilometer thereafter. Expect to pay at most 20TL for short trips in the city, even if the streets are clogged.

Hattuşaş (Boğazkale)

The UNESCO world heritage site **Hattuşaş** (0364/452-2006, 9am-7pm daily summer, 9am-5pm daily fall-spring, 5TL) is worth the three-hour trip from Ankara. For more than five centuries Hattuşaş was the capital of the Hittite Empire, and it is of great archaeological significance. A massive trove of tablets bearing cuneiform scripts was uncovered here; these early Anatolians recorded the minutiae of their daily lives, from birth and wedding announcements to trade and politics. They adopted the cuneiform script from the Assyrians, who, lured by the wealth and resources of the Hittites, arrived in droves to trade textiles and metals from the east. The records were stored in cavern-like libraries for posterity, and they have given us a good understanding of these Bronze Age people. In addition to the sights listed, take the time to visit the **Boğazköy Museum** (Boğazkale, 8am-5pm daily, 3TL) to view the artifacts uncovered from the sites, including the 3,500-year-old Boğazkoy Sphinx that was returned to Turkey by Germany in 2011.

HISTORY

As natural a citadel as any paranoid ruler might hope for, Hattuşaş may have been settled four millennia before what was once thought to be the original settlement by the Hatti civilization (2500-2000 BC). By the 19th century BC, Assyrian traders from Assur—who are credited with introducing writing in the form of cuneiform script to the region—founded a trading post and living quarters here. A sweeping fire appears to have ravaged the settlement around 1700 BC. King Anitta from Kussara in southeastern Anatolia claimed responsibility for the act and even put a curse on the city: "At night I took the city by force; I have sown weeds in its place. Should any king after me attempt to resettle Hattush, may the Weather God of Heaven strike him down."

Ironically, Labarna I—one of Anitta of Kussara's heirs—returned two centuries later to rebuild a city from the ashes. He named it Hattuşaş ("Land of the Hatti") and changed his own name to Hattusili in honor of his new capital. His descendants, more than 30 in all, expanded the city over four centuries to include most of Anatolia. This expansion didn't go unnoticed by the Egyptians, whose growing dominion had come to abut the Hittite realm in modern Syria. In 1279 BC, at the historic Battle of Kadesh, Egyptian pharaoh Ramses II marched into Hittite territory and battled Hittite king Muwatalli II and the battalions sent by his regional allies. The outcome is still a mystery; both rulers returned home claiming victory. But the importance of this titanic clash is the landmark peace treaty that followed, the first in recorded history. One of the original copies of the Kadesh Peace Treaty, inscribed in stone, was discovered in the Hattuşaş Palace Archives and moved to the Archaeological Museum in Istanbul. An enlarged replica also exists in the lobby of the United Nations headquarters in New York.

At the height of their power the Hittites ruled central and eastern Anatolia as well as northern Mesopotamia. In 1160 BC the empire collapsed under the stress of internal instability and opportunistic invasions by Thracians, Phrygians, and Assyrians. The eight centuries that followed are characterized as Hattuşaş's Dark Ages, when the city was all but abandoned, only to be resettled by the Phrygians around 800 BC and the Persians two centuries later.

Hattuşaş is strategically located on high rocky terrain overlooking a vast fertile valley. At its peak the city sprawled just under two square kilometers, with inner and outer sections girded by a massive eight-meter-high crenelated fortification system built by the great king Shupiluliuma I. The walls had two 12-meter-tall watchtowers, and several access gates were flanked by impressive lions and sphinxes carved in stone. The best remaining examples of these impressive statues are at the Museum of Anatolian Civilizations in Ankara.

SIGHTS
Büyük Tapınak (Great Temple)
A single entrance to the city remains today, and it leads straight to the Lower City and its walled **Büyük Tapınak.** At 15,000 square meters—twice the size of a football field—this temple was Hattuşaş's largest building, dedicated to the weather god Hatti and the sun goddess Arinna; only the king and queen, as the high priests of the land, and their personally handpicked temple priests could enter the innermost sanctuary. The inner court was open, surrounded by high walls, and paved with sizable flat stones. Some of these stones can still be seen in the rear (eastern) right corner. While its completion date is uncertain, foundation ruins show over 80 storerooms and dressing rooms believed to have been utilized by priests. The remains of hundreds of 2,000-liter vessels used to store foodstuffs attest that the temple was not only used for ritual purposes but also as a central part of daily life.

Büyükkale (Great Fortress)
From the Great Temple, walk up the road and turn left at the fork for **Büyükkale.** This royal citadel dominates the entire ancient city from a rocky pinnacle. Comprising 16 buildings enclosed by another set of fortifications, the palace housed the king, his court, and palace officials as well as providing shelter for the Bearers of the Golden Lances (the palace guard). The citadel's center offers fantastic views of the city and the valley to the north. Most of the clay tablets found in Hattuşaş were discovered in the three buildings located on the southern side of the palace. Original contracts, official documents, oracular prophecies, cult practices, folklore, legal decisions, and historical texts were all stored here on wooden shelves.

Nişantaş (Marked Rock)
Nişantaş (Northern Complex), located just above the Great Fortress, is another rock outcropping that once held a grand building adorned with massive sphinxes. There's an 8.5-meter-long inscription in hieroglyphic Luwian. The 11 vertical lines chiseled onto the smoothed rock have become so eroded that the text remains indecipherable. It dates from the reign of Shupiluliuma II, the last of the well-known great kings of Hattuşaş. It's highly plausible that the inscription refers to the construction of a monument the great king commissioned for his father, or details his long list of accomplishments, which included a bloody battle at sea followed by a landing on Cyprus.

Hieroglyphic Chamber 2
Across the road from Nişantaş, a path leads to **Hieroglyphic Chamber 2,** where Hattuşaş's best and recently discovered collection of reliefs are on display. These have weathered the test of time exceptionally well thanks to a mound of earth that kept them buried for centuries. A relief of a cloaked sun god, wearing slippers curled at the toe, graces the rear wall. The double-winged sun at the top of his head reveals his identity; his left hand holds a curved rod while his right holds a slightly modified version of an Egyptian ankh (symbol of life). The relief to the left represents Shupiluliuma II, who commissioned the construction of this

the Lion's Gate

chamber. Ever the warrior, he holds a sword in his belt, a lance in his right hand, and a bow over his shoulder. It's interesting that he chose to be portrayed wearing a pointed hat on his head, typically ascribed to divinities during the era, even though he was still alive when the building was created. And just across are six lines chiseled in hieroglyphic Luwian, explaining that through the blessings of the gods, Great King Shupiluliuma conquered several lands, including Tarhuntassa (an ancient city whose location is still unknown); established new cities; and made the appropriate sacrifices to the gods. The last sentence speaks of "a divine earth-road," which states that beneath the chamber is a symbolic passage into the underworld.

Kral Kapı (King's Gate)

At the city's southeasternmost point is **Kral Kapı**. It is the best preserved of Hattuşaş's five gates and is a mirror image of the Lion's Gate to the west. This gate is flanked by two towers, each measuring a whopping 10 by 15 meters and bearing its own arched entrance. The relief of a warrior on this gate faces the city, as opposed to decorating the exterior. The horns appearing on the helmet tell us that the warrior may well be Sharrumma (son of the weather god, Teshub, and the sun goddess, Hepat); the deity was the patron and protector of the great king Tudhaliya IV (1237-1209 BC), who may have commissioned this gate.

Ramparts and More Gates

Moving south along the 250-meter-long ramparts at **Yerkapi** (Earth Gate), one enters Hittite Temple District, where 30 temples have been found so far. The artificial ridge of Yerkapı is the southernmost and highest point of the city; it arches along the summit from the Lion's Gate in the west and the King's Gate in the east, connecting through the Sphinx Gate in the center. To get to the Sphinx Gate, you can either take the 70-meter-long postern (tunnel) or climb the narrow stone staircase. The **Sphinx Gate** is not flanked by towers, as opposed to those of great cities of antiquity, but passes unceremoniously through a single tower. It is named for the four sculpted sphinxes that once flanked the city's southernmost entrance. With a human head and the body of a lion, sphinxes are traditionally ascribed to the Egyptians, who used them to represent their kings. The Hittites adopted the symbol and softened the facial contours to represent the female. All that remains today is a chipped representation on the western wall. Moving westward, the **Lion's Gate** is still fairly intact, with well-preserved figures. These beastly felines were popular ornaments used on gates and temple entrances to protect the structures against evil.

Yazılıkaya (Inscribed Rock)

About two kilometers northeast of Hattuşaş, the shrine of **Yazılıkaya** is the most famous Hittite rock sanctuary. Two chambers, preceded by an impressive procession of gods of the Hittite pantheon, are edged by natural 12-meter-high rock faces. While both Chambers A and B were used for ritual purposes as early as the 15th century BC, the ornate reliefs of gods were commissioned by Hittite kings Tudhaliya IV and Shupiluliuma II. This holy site was used to celebrate the new year and the beginning of spring, and it has aptly been called the House of the New Year's Celebration. **Chamber A** is by far the most impressive, not only for the prowess of Hittite architects but for the sheer beauty of the rock-carved impressions and the amount of data collected about the mythical hierarchy of the ancient Anatolians. The left wall details a procession of male gods, wearing traditional kilts, curly slippers, and horned hats; the right wall depicts a parade of female deities wearing crowns and long skirts. Interestingly, the goddess of love and war, Shaushka (Mesopotamian goddess Ishtar), is shown on the male side with her two handmaidens. These lower deities are marching toward a central tableau, which depicts the pantheon's supreme deities: the weather god Teshub and the sun goddess Hebat, with their son Sharruma, daughter Alanzu, and granddaughter bringing up the rear. The wife of Hattusili III, Puduhepa, who was the daughter of a Hurrian priestess, was crucial in integrating Hurrian gods into the Hittite belief system. Such was the case with the Hurrian weather god Teshub. But other cultures' deities were assimilated as well, like the Mesopotamian god of wisdom, Ea (Enki), who appears in the male procession. And dominating the main relief is a 3.5-meter-high representation of King Tudhaliya IV, son of Hattusili III and Puduhepa.

Chamber B's reliefs are better preserved than those in Chamber A because the open-air room remained partly buried until the end of the 19th century. On the wall to the right is a procession of the gods of the underworld; on the left stands a depiction of Sharruma, the patron god of Tudhaliya IV. Flanking the relief is unexpected iconography of a large upright sword formed by two lions with the head of a god for its handle. It's attributed to Nergal, the god of the underworld. The last relief, a cartouche inscribed with the name and title of Tudhaliya IV, tells us that this chamber may have been a memorial to the great king and may have been erected by his son Shupiluliuma II.

ACCOMMODATIONS AND FOOD

For an overnight, the folks at **Hotel Aşıkoğlu** (Hitit Cd. 25, 0364/452-2004, www.hattusas.com, €30-65) offer 33 rooms with en suite baths, each with a balcony, a TV, and free Wi-Fi. There's also an on-site restaurant with an à la carte menu and a buffet to fill up on before the journey back to Ankara or Cappadocia. The hotel also acts as a useful tourist information center, providing maps, books, and historical anecdotes.

GETTING THERE

The 200-kilometer trip from Ankara to Boğazkale, site of Hattuşaş, by bus or *dolmuş* can take up to five hours; it's far wiser to **rent a car** or join a tour instead. The route is both scenic and easy to navigate. From Ankara, take highway D200/E88 east toward Samsun. Take the Çorum turnoff (D190) past Süngürlü, and continue another six kilometers east to Boğazkale, where signs lead toward the Tokat Yolu heading south. Another 20 kilometers of spectacular scenery leads to the archaeological site. Make sure to fill up the gas tank before departing, or at least before leaving the main highway (D200/E88), to avoid getting stranded along the way.

Those adamant on not driving can organize a private tour to the site from Ankara or Cappadocia with **Yama Tour** (Müze Cd. 2, Göreme, 0384/271-2508, www.yamatours.com).

Background

The Land 382	Government 403
Flora and Fauna 385	Economy 406
History 387	People and Culture 409

The Land

Straddling easternmost Europe and western Asia, Turkey's western coast extends south from the country's northern border with Greece and Bulgaria to the province of Anatolia. The coastline hugs the Aegean Sea, the Mediterranean Sea's largest bay, on its journey southward. To the north is Thrace, Turkey's European portion, delineated by the Black Sea to the east, the Bosphorus Straits, the Dardanelles, and the Sea of Marmara to the south, the Aegean to the west, and Greece and Bulgaria to the north. Thrace's southeasternmost point is Istanbul, Turkey's—and Europe's—most populous metropolis. Istanbul straddles the natural Bosphorus Straits, which link the Black Sea to the Sea of Marmara and also mark the continental divide between Europe and Asia. The city sprawls north of the Bosphorus as European Istanbul and southward as its Asian counterpart.

This book's coverage extends east to the major destination of Cappadocia, at the center of Turkey and the arid Anatolian steppe, and south to the Mediterranean Sea.

GEOGRAPHY

Turkey's western and central regions covered in this book encompass roughly 375,400 square kilometers and can be divided into four distinct regions: the Marmara region (67,300 square kilometers); the Aegean region (85,000 square kilometers); parts of the Mediterranean region (61,100 square kilometers); and central Anatolia (151,000 square kilometers).

Marmara

The Marmara region extends over Europe and Asia and is bisected by three bodies of water—the Bosphorus and Dardanelles Straits and the Sea of Marmara—that form a natural continental divide. The Thracian Peninsula extends over its northern section.

Istanbul is at the point of the continental convergence. The city's coasts sprawl along the Bosphorus, with luxuriant green groves pocked by centuries-old firs and colorful Judas trees. One of the world's most expansive and populated metropolises, Istanbul extends over 1,831 square kilometers. Its western and southern peripheries are delineated by the Sea of Marmara and even include an archipelago of dainty islands. Marmara's highest peak is Mount Uludağ (2,543 meters), a favorite winter destination for snow sports. At its foot lies "green" Bursa, whose densely forested mountains and verdant grasslands give the city its nickname. Dotting the region's southern quadrant are wide lakes and rivers visited by hundreds of migratory bird colonies.

Aegean

Bounded by the Marmara region to the north, the Mediterranean region to the southwest, and the central Anatolia region to the east, Turkey's Aegean territory takes its name from the sea that borders it. Crystal-clear waters lined with unspoiled beaches to the west and hundreds of kilometers of olive groves on rolling hills describe the northernmost territory, while the south gives way to a craggy coastline blanketed in pine forests. Its continuity of plains coupled with its unusually mild climate, fertile soil, and constant sea breeze make it a haven for vintners and farmers.

Western Mediterranean

Turkey's western coast occupies roughly 7 percent of the country's total area. Running

---

Previous: Galata Tower, Istanbul; decorative tiles in Iznik.

parallel to the coast are the lofty Taurus Mountains, a.k.a. the Beydağları range; the chain's highest peaks rise above 3,000 meters. These mountains sometimes jut dramatically into the Mediterranean's limpid waters or form narrow valleys before reaching the coast, disgorging their snow pack beginning in April, transforming tranquil streams into gushing rivers for white-water rafters. The remote plateaus boast serene lakes surrounded by the dense woods. This abundant mountain runoff, with Anatolia's fertile soil and the warm and humid Mediterranean climate, makes this region's plains agricultural powerhouses.

Central Anatolia

Central Anatolia is a plateau extending inland from the Aegean Sea between two mountains chains to the point where these ranges meet farther east. Accounting for 19 percent of Turkey's land area, it is the largest of the five regions. Its arid highlands are the heartland of the country. Ankara, Turkey's remote capital, sits in the middle of this elevated plateau. Similar to the steppe in Russia, central Anatolia is situated at elevations of about 600 meters in the west, climbing to 1,200 meters in the east. Its two largest basins are Konya Ovası and Tuz Gölü (Salt Lake). The north is mostly wooded, the south is rather barren, and the eastern area is characterized by the eerie Cappadocian landscape. The distinct and unique tufa cones that pepper this area's wide dusty bowls were formed 50 million years ago during the Tertiary period, when the surrounding volcanoes spewed out massive amounts of volcanic rock over the chimneys and craters that dot the terrain. Wind played a big part in the erosion of the chimneys to create the phallic-looking landscape of today.

CLIMATE

Turkey's four western and central regions all have different climates. The Marmara Region to the northwest, with its former Ottoman capitals of Edirne, Bursa, and Istanbul, enjoys a moderate climate. Average temperatures in winter and summer are 4°C and 27°C, respectively. But expect frost and even snow December to March. Summer's humid heat waves last for days, with temperatures of 35°C and higher, particularly in the crowded cities. Spring and autumn are typically mild but can change quickly. Lodos, a southwesterly wind, wreaks havoc on marine transportation year-round, and the northeasterly wind known as Poyraz brings the Black Sea's freezing temperatures to the Marmara Region in winter.

The climate of the Aegean is superbly mild. Summers are hot but rarely exceed 40°C, even during July and August. Spring and autumn are sunny, with blue skies and daily temperatures averaging in the high teens. Winters are mild with occasional precipitation. The many mountains that stretch both perpendicular and parallel to the coast contain the sea breeze, making this region ideal for agriculture. The Aegean cities beyond these hills enjoy a more continental climate. For sunbathing and water sports as well as mountain sports, the region's summer months can't be beat. Temperate spring and fall are ideal for traipsing through ancient ruins.

Turkey's western Mediterranean region enjoys a characteristically Mediterranean climate, with hot dry summers and moderately warm and rainy winters. Summer lasts nine months, but apart from midsummer, the coast is quite bearable. Sunny weather prevails 300 days of the year, and sea temperatures never dip below 15°C nor exceed 28°C. July and August temperatures can hover above the 40°C mark, making those heavily traveled months horrendous on unsuspecting visitors. In Antalya, the region's largest city, winter temperatures rarely dip below 15°C. On the other hand, temperatures have been known to rise above 40°C with humidity at 85 percent, demonstrating the climate's potential impact on the best-laid travel plans. The entire Mediterranean coast is protected from cold northerly winds by the Taurus Mountains.

Central Anatolia shows characteristics of a continental climate due to its elevation, but as you move south and east, it becomes a cold, semiarid climate. Averaging less than 25 centimeters per year, rainfall is sparse and typically occurs during fall and spring. Water conservation in cities like Konya and Ankara is often an issue, particularly during summer, and crops can fail during years of drought. Summers are bone dry and hot, with day temperatures averaging 29°C, falling to the mid-teens at night. Winters are cold and snowy, with daytime temperatures generally around 5°C and evenings at -2°C. The amount of winter snowfall is directly proportional to elevation.

ENVIRONMENTAL ISSUES

Turkey's main environmental angst relates to the lack of water, but its steady population growth coupled with the economic boom that began in the early 1990s has increased levels of pollution, putting the environment at risk. Developments to cope with population growth, such as new highways and Istanbul's third airport and Bosphorus bridge, have been criticized for the removal of green spaces and a lack of transparency in approving major construction projects. In June 2013, for example, Turkish citizens protested the government's plans to develop Gezi Park—a green space adjacent to Taksim Square—as a shopping mall.

Tensions against the ruling AKP party reached the boiling point at that time in many provinces as police used tear gas and water cannons at peaceful protest about environmental concerns. Prime Minister Erdoğan was quick to label protesters as drunks and *çapulcus* ("looters" and "marauders"). This fueled the protests and polarized the community for and against the prime minister. Eight fatalities and more than 8,000 injuries resulted from the clashes. One of the victims, a 15-year-old Alevi named Berkin Elvan, died after being in a coma for 269 days as a result of a police-fired tear-gas canister that hit his head. More demonstrations ensued in 2014.

Most believe that the Gezi Park demonstrations and Berkin's death were turning points in a fight for democracy for many Turkish citizens. What started as a sit-in to keep a park blew up into pro-democracy demonstrations about the government's creeping authoritarian rule, media blackouts, and a lack of transparency on a range of issues. But despite signing the Kyoto Protocol in 2009 and pressure from the European Union to improve environmental standards, there remain controversial plans to build new hydroelectric

Snow falls in Istanbul at least once a year.

plants in southeastern Turkey, four nuclear energy plants in the north, and moves to allow development in 40 national parks.

Some segments of Turkish society are becoming more conscious of protecting the environment. Government measures such as water restrictions, mass tree-planting projects, tougher fines for poachers, a zero-tolerance policy on chemical dumping, and the prevention of overfishing are signs that some improvements are being made. But littering is still a problem in some areas, and a lack of knowledge about the environment can be seen in the tourism sector. Tour operators in Dalyan, for example, sometimes feed endangered turtles for entertainment. Turtles that become friendly with the boats that feed them can lose their natural ability to hunt, and boat propellers can cause injuries that may takes years to heal.

Turkey still has a way to go on protecting its environment. The lack of waste and sewage treatment systems is one issue, as is air pollution from heating with coal and rising vehicle emissions. One of the biggest risks remains oil spills along the coast, particularly along the Bosphorus and Dardanelles, where more than 5,000 ships pass annually. Now that Turkey is a formal candidate for membership in the European Union, its environmental and power-generating efforts will be scrutinized even more.

Flora and Fauna

FLORA

You may be surprised to learn that tulips originate in Turkey, not in Holland. Turkey is the original home of other showy blooms, including crocuses, snowdrops, and lilies. Other indigenous plants that grow in various parts of the country include figs, apricots, cherries, sour cherries, almonds, hazelnuts, chickpeas, and lentils.

Anatolia is one of the world's pantries, with plants that have been cultivated for human and animal sustenance since prehistory. Two of those crops are wheat and barley, for which Turkey, along with its neighbors to the east, has become one of only four of the world's gene centers for the cultivated grain used agriculturally. More than 30 species of disease- and weather-resistant wheat, for instance, still grow wild on the Anatolian plateau. Over time, ideal genes will be transferred from the gene centers to various cultivars around the globe, preserving the species and retaining its quality. Aside from indigenous crops, Anatolia's climate enables the cultivation of many nonnative species, as in Antalya, where kiwifruit, native to northeast Asia, now thrive. Turkey is one of the few countries in the world to be self-sustaining in food production and still makes exports.

While 27 percent of Turkey's territory is forested, the remainder is home to seven species of cultivated trees, none more important that the olive, allegedly indigenous to Anatolia and which accounts for huge orchards and a billion-dollar industry. The wild maple, sycamore, bay laurel, pistachio, Turkish hazel, Cretan date palm, lime, and showy Judas trees are all indigenous to the Anatolian plateau.

Turkey's coasts are lush with vegetation. The Aegean and Mediterranean coasts host a multitude of species that thrive in the Mediterranean climate. Popular plants include showy oleanders, fuchsias, hydrangeas, jasmines, wisterias, and magnolias; fragrant bushes like rosemary, thyme, oregano, lavender, and juniper; imposing forests of oaks, pines, and cypresses; and fruit trees like lemons, oranges, and bergamots.

FAUNA

Turkey is a natural habitat for a wide variety of animals. Europe in its entirety is home to 60,000 species, while Turkey has 80,000, not counting subspecies.

Avian migrators fly north from Africa to Asia and Europe in spring and return in fall. The most spectacular migration is that of the showy stork, which flies above Istanbul's Bosphorus Straits in spring and fall. More than 250,000 have been counted as they glide through the clouds over the course of a few weeks. Birds of prey also have opted for this transcontinental route for eons, perhaps for the bounty and variety of fish species that migrate from the Black Sea to the warmer Sea of Marmara. The unspoiled wetlands peppering the country's Aegean and Mediterranean regions are ideal habitats for colonies of rare and endangered species of birds like the showy Dalmatian pelican, lustrous pygmy cormorant, the slender-billed curlew, fancy flamingoes, and chatty wild ducks and geese.

The shores of the Aegean and Mediterranean are a refuge for two near-extinct species: The shy Mediterranean monk seal, whose numbers have dipped to under 600 worldwide, prefers the finned bounty found near the tiny islands off the shore of Foça in the Aegean region. So far, 100 are known to survive in Turkey's waters. The gracious loggerhead sea turtle (*Caretta caretta*) chooses the warm sands found at specific sites along the coast of southwestern Turkey as its nesting grounds. The species and the breeding grounds are strictly protected, and efforts by teams of volunteers have been highly effective. İztuzu Beach and neighboring Köyceğiz, along the Mediterranean near Dalyan, have both been declared off-limits to development and designated Specially Protected Zones. Consequently there are more than a dozen sea turtle breeding grounds along the Mediterranean coast.

Indigenous to central Anatolia are a slew of quadrupeds that used to roam wild in the steppe and along the Taurus Mountains. The fallow deer, which was introduced to Europe in the late 1st century AD by the Romans, originates from the foothills of the Taurus Mountains just east of Antalya. This

Tulips are native to Turkey.

speckled ruminant was the preferred game of Paleolithic hunters more than 10,000 years ago, according to bones found at archaeological sites. Another native is the domesticated sheep, a direct descendant of the wild sheep *Ovis musimon anatolica*. The Anatolian leopard was the feline used in gladiator battles during the Roman era; in fact, 2,000-year-old tiger traps can still be seen scattered throughout the Taurus Mountains. The tiger is also from the central and eastern regions of Anatolia, and its modern name is derived from the Tigris River. The lion was a native of the Asian plain, as evidenced by Hittite statues found in modern Boğazkale.

The breeds of cats, goats, and rabbits that bear the name Angora are all indigenous to the region of the Turkish capital, Ankara, in central Anatolia. The rabbit is bred for its long silky hair; deep-piled fleece harvested once a year from the Angora goat, commercially referred to as mohair, a luxury fiber that is sought for its warmth, sheen, and durability.

History

Linking the Black and Mediterranean Seas, Asia, and Europe, Anatolia has been a crossroads since ancient times. The Greeks once called it Asia Minor, but today the Anatolian plateau is home to Turkey, whose realm extends northwest into the historically coveted Thrace. During the seven millennia since the earliest civilizations settled here, more than 20 empires have come and gone. From the early Hittites to the Assyrians, Persians, Greeks, Romans, Selçuks, Ottomans, and finally modern-day Turks, the land has witnessed the rise of numerous cultures, languages, art forms, and religions. This historical legacy in eight distinct eras affected many of humanity's beliefs and religions.

EARLY ANTIQUITY

Asia Minor's recorded history begins with the Hittites in 2000 BC. These warriors migrated from the Pontic Steppe in present-day Ukraine and were a fierce people who rivaled the Egyptians and Babylonians. For 800 years they recorded the minutiae of their daily lives on tablets with a Hurrian cuneiform writing system learned from the Assyrians. These precious stone relics, which only survive as copies, detail Bronze Age life and the major military campaigns of the era. The first to successfully smelt iron, the Hittites also thrived on agriculture, carpentry, and pottery. Silver, then found in massive deposits along the Taurus Mountains, was their currency in trade. They worshipped local deities that appeared in sets of local pantheons, headed by a fertility god responsible for the weather. The sun goddess, Hebat, ruled supreme as the mother of all living things, which suggests that a matrilineal system was used. A Hittite king served as high priest as well as supreme ruler, military commander, and high judge, but the opinion of his wife was also valued; the signatures of queens Puduhepa and Suppiluliumas I appeared on peace treaties along with those of their husbands.

The great Hittite Empire began its short, dramatic decline at the beginning of the 12th century BC. As the rise of seafaring peoples from mainland Greece threatened the coast, the Hittites moved troops west to protect their supremacy over the Aegean coast, and the Egyptians attacked Kadesh (now western Syria) in the hope of obtaining another coveted route across Mesopotamia. With troops guarding the western and southeastern fronts, the Assyrians took control of Mitani (now northern Syria). In the west, the seafaring peoples proved too numerous for the Hittites, and the entire Mediterranean and Aegean coasts fell just as the Assyrians and Egyptians were gaining on Hittite territory 1,000 kilometers to the east. The Hittites found themselves landlocked and vulnerable to attacks from all directions. By 1180 BC their capital, Hattuşaş, was burned to the ground in a collaborative assault not from the empire's enemies in the west and the east but from a coalition from the north of the Kaskians of the eastern Black Sea region and the Briges from the Balkans.

As the Hittites disappeared from history, several sovereign Neo-Hittite states sprang up in central Asia Minor. Most notable among them were the Urartu, the Carchemish, and the Milid, but they were absorbed by the Assyrians in the 8th century BC. By that time the Greeks were continuing their onslaught of the Aegean coast, forming small coastal states. According to the *Iliad*, the 8th-century-BC epic poem written by the legendary poet Homer, the first Greek victory was at Troy, the city-state they cunningly overtook with a mythological wooden horse. Thanks to *The Histories* of Herodotus (484-425 BC), regarded as the father of history, we have a record of Persian supremacy and consequent defeat by the Greeks in the first-ever systematic collection of research. *The Histories* has

Anatolian Timeline

It's crucial to think of Anatolia, or what the Greeks called *mikrá asía* (Asia Minor), as not only the buffer between East and West, but also as a land of such wealth that ambitious leaders from as far east as Mongolia to the West's Crusaders were green with envy for ages. With a whopping 30,000-year history, this steppe served as a crossroads for the most important civilizations of its time. This quick-reference guide will help you keep the civilizations and the timeline straight as you hop between ancient sites:

Age or Culture	Time
Neolithic Age	9000-5000 BC
Chalcolithic Age	5000-3000 BC
Bronze Age	3300-1200 BC
Hattians	2500-2000 BC
Akkadian Empire	2400-2150 BC
Assyrian Traders	1950-1750 BC
Hittites	1700-1220 BC
Ionian Collusion	1300-700 BC
Neo-Hittite Kingdoms	1200-800 BC
Phrygian Kingdom	1200-700 BC
Troy I-VIII	3000-700 BC
Aegean and Balkan Migration	1200 BC

been verified for its accuracy and also reads like a thriller.

LATE ANTIQUITY

During the mid-first millennium BC, a variety of indigenous sovereign states flourished in Anatolia, but none reached the level of Lydia. Its famous king and later emperor Croesus was celebrated for his wealth and lavished his capital, Sardis, with extravagant monuments and public buildings. The Lydians were the first to mint coins, using precious metals from the mines and silt of the nearby Pactolus River. Word of Croesus's lavish parties reached the Persian emperor Cyrus the Great, founder of the powerful Achaemenid Empire. The lure of Lydia's riches was so great that he launched an assault west toward Croesus's capital, conquering the whole of Asia Minor in the process in 546 BC. Lydia became a Persian province and its neighboring sovereign states in Asia Minor, except for Lycia, became Persian satrapies.

This lasted until Macedonian king Alexander the Great accepted the surrender of the Persian provincial capital and treasury of Sardis just weeks after conquering the Persian emperor Darius III's troops at the Battle of the Granicus near the Sea of Marmara in 334 BC. He went on to lay siege to the Ionians, first at Halicarnassus (modern-day Bodrum) and then all along the coast, forcing his enemies—the pirate Memnon of Rhodes and the satrap of Caria, Orontobates—to escape by sea. And so went his conquests all along the coast: First, Lycia's inner realm fell, followed by Pamphylia's and their coastal towns.

In 323 BC, Alexander's untimely death at age 32 from a fever, brought on by either poisoning or natural causes, forced the breakup of his immense empire. Asia Minor folded into a series of four Hellenic kingdoms that would be ruled by his successors, known as the Diadochi. Among them, the kingdom of Pergamum was allotted to Alexander's former general Lysimachus. A commander by nature, Lysimachus put his officer Philetaerus in charge of both the populace and the treasury in order to embark on military campaigns. After the death of Lysimachus, the impotent yet cunning Philetaerus, by then the sole ruler of Pergamum, went on to reinforce

Age or Culture	Time
Urartu Civilization	900-600 BC
Classical Antiquity	700-330 BC
Lydia, Caria, and Lycia	700-300 BC
Ionians	1050-300 BC
Persian Empire	559-331 BC
Kingdom of Alexander the Great	334-301 BC
Seleucid Empire	305-64 BC
Kingdom of Pontus	302-64 BC
Attalids of Pergamum	282-129 BC
Kingdom of Armenia	190 BC-AD 428
Roman Republic	133-27 BC
Roman Empire	27 BC-AD 330
Middle Ages to Today	AD 330-present
Byzantines	330-1453
Selçuk Sultanate of Rûm	1077-1307
Ottomans	1299-1922
Republic of Turkey	1923-present

the city and name his nephew Eumenes as his successor. Eumenes I became the first king of the Attalid dynasty, which lasted for 130 years. During that time, there was constant warfare among the Syrians, Achaean Greeks, and Seleucids of Antioch—a dynasty descended from another of Alexander's generals, Seleucus I Nicator. The kingdom of Pergamum found itself surrounded on all sides by enemies hungry to expand their empires, so Pergamum allied with Rome, which was slowly engulfing the Balkans. By 190 BC, Eumenes's fears were realized as the Syrians, after suffering an embarrassing loss to the Greeks the year before in east-central Greece, laid siege to the capital of his kingdom. The Romans, who had plowed effortlessly through western Asia Minor, fulfilled their part of the agreement by impressively defeating the Syrians at Magnesia. For their efforts, the Romans absorbed the entire territory of Asia Minor in 188 BC but allowed Pergamum sovereignty—until 133 BC, when the last Attalid king, the heirless Attalus III, bequeathed his kingdom to Rome. The city of Pergamum remained the administrative capital of Asia Minor under the Romans until Ephesus replaced it in 29 BC.

ROMAN ERA AND CHRISTIANIZATION

Around the end of the first century BC, trade and culture flourished in Roman Asia Minor. Roman emperors Augustus (63 BC-AD 14), Tiberius Julius Caesar (14-37), Trajan (53-117), and Hadrian (117-138) all traveled east from the empire's capital at Rome to assist in the development of the province of Asia Minor. Their ports of call, the great cities of Ephesus, Aphrodisias, Perge, and Aspendos, were all drastically improved. The first action was to lay down a complex road system to connect these early metropolises to the rest of the empire. Next, exquisite monuments and temples were erected throughout. Public facilities like libraries, fountains, and sewage systems were also added. Among the few structures to have survived the many earthquakes that have hit this seismically active region in the two millennia since, the almost intact Library of Celsus in Ephesus stands as evidence of the mastery of early Roman architecture. Culture was impacted as well; some of antiquity's important scientific and literary authorities originated in Asia Minor during this period. The geographer Strabo (64 BC-AD 24), who wrote the decisive *Geographica*, not only detailed the geography of his era but also its peoples.

The greatest change to sweep through Asia Minor under the Romans was the advent of Christianity. Immediately after the death of Christ circa AD 30, early Christians escaped Roman persecution in Jerusalem and fled to Asia Minor. They settled en masse throughout the plain in cities like Ephesus, Hierapolis, and Cappadocia, practicing their faith underground while the other residents still worshipped the Greek goddess Artemis. Some two decades later, missionaries like Paul the Apostle, who settled for a while in Ephesus to preach, as well as John the Evangelist, who allegedly wrote his Gospel there and brought the Virgin Mary to the city, propagated the Gospels and were key to the conversion of countless early Anatolians. By 380, Theodosius I had declared Christianity the official religion of Asia Minor and legalized the destruction of the temples of earlier religions. This development came just 55 years after the First Ecumenical Council, held in Nicaea (Iznik), in which 300 church elders under the direction of Roman emperor Constantine the Great defined the religion's basic tenets.

Meanwhile, the metropolises along the coast had been eclipsed by the city on the Bosphorus. Either following the prediction of an oracle or just understanding its strategic appeal, Constantine arrived in the colony of Byzantium and renamed it Constantinopolis. The new capital of the Eastern Roman Empire—the Byzantine Empire—became a center of learning, prosperity, and cultural preservation. The rest of this eastern empire prospered as well, albeit with less pomp, for the next few centuries. But while prosperity and expansion were constant, the Byzantines experienced internal religious divisions—like the bloody Nika Riots of 532—and recurring conflicts with their Arab neighbors to the east.

MEDIEVAL ERA

By the seventh century, Arab caliphates had launched the first of a series of wars challenging the Byzantines for control of Anatolia. These events, commonly referred as the Muslim Conquests, launched a chain of Christian counterattacks known as the Crusades. Between 634 and 718 the Arabs had twice tried unsuccessfully to capture Constantinople. But they were gaining elsewhere, securing—albeit momentarily—Roman Syria and Africa. After the impressive defeat of the Byzantines at Manzikert in 1071, the Selçuks swept across Anatolia and formed the first Turkic Empire.

The Selçuks, like other Turcoman peoples, had been pressured out of their homeland on the Asian steppes by the Mongols as early as 200 BC. By the 800s these able shepherds had migrated south to the watershed of Transoxania—today's Central Asian states, where contact with Arabs gradually led them to convert to Islam. Adept farmers and livestock breeders, some Turkish tribes came under central administration following the tenets of Islamic orthodoxy, which even included taxation. Others, like the Oğhuz Turks, remained nomadic, pursuing the *ghazı* tradition that sought to expand territory in the name of Islam while amassing huge riches in the process. Put simply, they had become Islamic mercenaries.

By 1080 the whole of Anatolia had fallen to the Selçuks. Along with the new rule came the gradual introduction of the Turkish language and Islamic religion. A century later, the Byzantines reasserted some of their rule in both western and northern Anatolia. The rest remained squarely in the hands of the Selçuk Sultanate of Rûm. In 1243 the Mongols vanquished the Selçuks in the infamous Battle of Köse Dağ in northeastern Anatolia and proceeded west to conquer the Selçukian capital of Konya. This resulted in turmoil for the whole of Anatolia, and the Selçuk state soon disintegrated. The Mongols, allied with Turcoman chieftains, bloodily took over central and eastern Anatolia in 1255 and retained their stranglehold from their garrison near Ankara until 1335.

By the early 14th century, the majority of Anatolia was controlled by a number of Turkish *beyliks*—or *ghazi* emirates. These somewhat autonomous states that had evolved from Turcoman tribes remained under the brooding watch of the Mongols. In 1330, Smyrna (modern-day İzmir), the last Byzantine stronghold, fell to the Turks, and Ottoman ruler Osman I emancipated his emirate by minting his own coins from his capital. In that era, according to Islamic convention, manufacturing currency was the exclusive right of sovereigns. So with Anatolia entirely under Turkish control, the Ottomans began to systematically acquire Anatolian Turkish *beyliks* from their capital in Bursa.

OTTOMAN ERA
A Budding Empire

Among the many Oğhuz leaders, the legendary Ertuğrul started a chain of events at the beginning of the 13th century throughout eastern and central Anatolia that paved the way for the rise of the mighty Ottomans. Founded in 1299, in the ensuing seven centuries this empire developed into a military powerhouse that drove through the entire Mediterranean region to absorb southeastern Europe and the Middle East, creating a rich cultural and spiritual legacy. But with the easy expansion of the empire, Western Europe feared that the wrath of the Turks would destroy the social and political fabric of the West, and with it, Christianity.

In 1220, Ertuğrul, flanked by 400 horsemen, joined the Selçuks in their quest westward. His military accomplishments against the Byzantines and other enemies so impressed Selçukian sultan Ala ad-Din Kay Qubadh I that the he ceded rule of the Kayı clan and Karaca Dağ, a mountainous region near modern Ankara, in 1227. From there, Ertuğrul conquered the village of Söğüt near the western Anatolian city of Bursa. By 1299, his eldest son, Osman, declared Söğüt the capital of his newly formed Ottoman emirate.

Osman I then pushed westward toward Bursa, which marked the southeastern frontier of the Byzantine Empire. In 1326, Bursa became the new Ottoman seat from which the protocol and tenets of this nascent political entity were founded. His plans were much broader, as he believed in a prophetic vision of an empire in the shape of a big tree whose roots spread through three continents and whose branches covered the sky.

The Ottoman expansion continued at the expense of the Byzantine Empire. With their eyes on Constantinople but not yet ready to assault the heavily defended Byzantine capital, they moved north into the Thracian Peninsula. In 1363 they swept and conquered Adrianople (Edirne). Administratively centralized, fervent in their mission, and militarily unchallenged, the Ottomans gained quick and sweeping support from great numbers of people who had until then lived through decades of conflict and uncertainty. While devoutly Muslim, Ottomans tolerated and even welcomed Anatolia's various creeds and religions. This new domain became a cultural hodgepodge of Greeks, Turks, and other minorities practicing either Islam or Christianity. Sultan Murat I even established a private corps of Janissary Guards—males culled from mostly Christian conquests.

Expansion

By the 1370s this nascent world power had plowed through the Eastern Mediterranean and the Balkans, and in 1389 vanquished Kosovo, quashing Serbian rule in the Balkans and paving the way for further expansion through Europe. But the integration of the fervently Christian Balkans demanded an entirely new system of governance; the *millet* system was established, granting the various minorities within the empire recognition and autonomy. The last and largest European attempt to defeat the Ottomans occurred at the Battle of Nicopolis in Bulgaria in 1396. This final massive crusade failed miserably and even served to galvanize the victorious Ottomans. By the beginning of the 15th century, the invincible Sultan Beyazıt had grown arrogant. While in Ankara in 1402, his public derision of Tatar commander Tamerlane led to his capture, the defeat of his troops, and the end of the Ottomans' early eastward campaigns.

Recovering from this damaging embarrassment and waiting for the Mongols' retreat eastward took about 10 years. To make matters worse, inner turmoil over who should take the throne raged among Beyazıt's nine sons. Mehmet I was victorious. Swiftly regrouping, he focused on enlarging the empire by first occupying the lands just vacated by the Mongols throughout Anatolia, sweeping through Greece, and launching a first attack on Constantinople.

The ascension of born warrior Mehmet II to the throne in 1451 regalvanized the empire's mission. Aged just 19, Mehmet remained untried, and he thought of the conquest of Constantinople as a rite of passage. For the next two years he schemed a strategy that first dealt with strengthening the Ottoman navy. Then he set out to systematically encroach on and starve the city, the last Byzantine stronghold. He cut off all sea access, including constructing the Rumeli Hısarı (fortress) on the city's European flank to face the existing Anadolu Hısarı on the opposite coast that had been built by his grandfather, Beyazıt I. From there, he blocked land access on either side of the straits and halted westbound sea traffic through the cunning use of a massive chain connecting both fortresses. In 1453 the siege of Constantinople began, with an army of more than 200,000 troops backed by a navy of over 300 vessels. Legend has it that he directed his fleet to line up side-by-side in the shape of a crescent at the western entrance of the Bosphorus, thus blocking eastbound supply lines from the sea. The Byzantines desperately pled for assistance from Europe, but their appeals went unheeded. The fall of Constantinople came on May 29, 1453, after a seven-week siege. This marked the end of the Byzantine Empire, and in an ironic twist, Mehmet even claimed the title of Roman emperor. His lineage included Byzantine imperials, since his great-grandfather Orhan had married a Byzantine princess. His claim was never recognized by Rome.

Mehmet renamed the city Istanbul and established it as the center of the Ottoman Caliphate. An erudite diplomat who spoke seven languages, he established universities throughout the city—many of which are still functioning; integrated Byzantine laws into the Islamic sharia system; erected grand mosques, mostly from the ruins of ancient ornate basilicas; and provided the template for the Ottoman *padishah*—harem—that would be emulated by his successors for more than 400 years.

But as culture flourished in the new capital, the Ottomans continued with the business of expansion. Mehmet, by then known as "The Conqueror," launched campaigns annually. From 1454 to 1463 he pushed to install a firm military defensive line along the Danube River and the Adriatic coast against Hungary and Venice. First Serbia, along with its substantial silver and gold mines of Novo Brdo, fell. Greece's northern regions followed in 1458, along with Athens months later, and the whole of Serbia within a year. In the summer of 1461 another successful campaign engulfed the Candaroğlu Beylik in Sinope, and the Orthodox Christian lands of Armenia under Uzun Hasan and the Empire of Trebizond. Meanwhile, the Ottoman navy saw various successes as well. Competition raged for strongly contested seagoing trade routes with the Italian city-states in the Black Sea, Aegean, and Mediterranean as well as the Portuguese in the Red Sea and Indian Ocean.

As the Ottoman Empire expanded, the Janissary also grew in influence. Young Christian recruits of various cultures flocked from every corner of the growing realm in the hope of securing a lucrative career. With that, the Ottomans created the largest military corps in Europe from highly trained and highly resolved legions of volunteers.

With the ascension of Sultan Selim the Grim in 1512, the Ottomans hastened their expansion to the east and south. During one of his first military campaigns, Selim I crushed Shah Ismail of Persia in the Battle of Chaldiran in August 1514. He went on to establish Ottoman rule in Egypt and along the Red Sea, competing for dominance in the region with the Portuguese Empire.

Selim's son, Süleyman I, became known as "The Magnificent" throughout Europe; his acute competence as a strategist and commander was as esteemed as it was feared by his adversaries. But at home, Süleyman gained the moniker of *kanûni*—the law-giver—for ordering the systematic codification of sharia law. He took Belgrade in 1521, and a year later he forced the Knights of St. John to abandon Rhodes. Five years later, an Ottoman victory at the Battle of Mohács resulted in the conquest of Buda on the Danube. Süleyman tried to capture Vienna in 1529 but failed. This marked the end of Ottoman expansion to the west. After regrouping the troops, North Africa was next. Lands up to the Moroccan border came under Ottoman rule during the early 1530s. For the first time, governors personally appointed by the sultan were installed in Algiers, Tunis, and Tripoli. The conquest of Mesopotamia ensued, forcing the Persians to retreat to their capital, Ardabil, in modern Azerbaijan. This victory yielded convenient access to the Persian Gulf.

The Fall of a World Power

Süleyman diverted from the ancestral tradition of maintaining and enjoying a harem of women by marrying. Until his death in 1566, he remained faithful to his beloved Hürrem Sultan. This manipulative Ukrainian concubine, who became known in the West as Roxelana, rose in influence by sheer determination. She was a master plotter and conspired with Süleyman's greedy political aides to have two of her husband's eldest sons assassinated to ensure the ascension of her own son, Selim.

Selim's competence was nowhere near his father's. Some historians believe that his ascension to the throne caused the decline of the Ottoman Empire. Unlike any other previous sultan, he was untrained in war and politics. In fact, Selim was so utterly disinterested in all things political that he earned the moniker "Selim the Sot" in the West. Muslims referred to him as "Selim the Drunkard" for his unbridled addictions to sex and alcohol. He relinquished all administrative duties and the rule of the empire to indulge in his other passions. But blaming him for the beginning of the Ottoman decline may be unfair, as his father, Süleyman, may have been responsible; in the 1560s Süleyman attempted military campaigns that failed—the unsuccessful conquest of Malta and a naval ploy to bypass the Portuguese domination of the Indian Ocean. Süleyman, weary from defeat and brokenhearted at the execution of his two beloved sons, relinquished rule to his chief vizier and withdrew inside Topkapı Palace's harem. So while Selim's rule may have lasted just eight years, his legacy of extreme indulgence established a precedent that would last until the empire's last days.

By the early 1600s the Ottoman Empire was still the most powerful state in the world, both financially and militarily. But the hands-on sultans of the past had been completely replaced by a sultanic government. Power shifted for a short time among four major players: the grand vizier, the *diwan* (Islamic treasury), the supreme court, and the Janissaries. By the early 1700s the Janissaries had claimed the upper hand, and for the next century slowly absorbed all military and administrative positions within the administration and, as the sultans had done before them, bequeathed these offices to their sons. Eventually the Ottoman government decentralized into a military feudal class, but politics also ruled the affairs inside Topkapı Palace: Beginning with Roxelana, the first courtesan to participate hands-on in political affairs, the harem's leader—typically the sultan's mother—brokered power to further the interests of her male progeny, sometimes at the empire's expense. Rebellion, assassination, confinement, and fratricide were common.

By the 1680s the majority of the Balkans

was ceded to Austria, and while cartographers still claimed Egypt and Algeria as Ottoman territories, they had all but claimed independence and would subsequently come under British and Napoleonic French rule. To the north the Austrian Hapsburgs and the Russians were pushing their eastern and southern boundaries just as aggressively. All the while, Western Europeans had regrouped as military powerhouses thanks to the riches flowing from their colonies in the Americas. Ottoman culture, which had grown dramatically during the empire's expansion, had all but faded. To make matters worse, Europeans had become leaders in industry and architecture. Their goods and craftsmanship became the envy of the culturally and scientifically stagnant Ottomans. Advances in engineering, including electrical technology and railroad systems, all had to be imported.

At the beginning of the 19th century, sultan Selim III launched a series of military reform efforts to modernize the army along European standards. But the empire's religious leaders and the Janissary corps, who had both become disorganized and rather ineffective, opposed the changes. The Janissaries successfully revolted, bringing an end to Selim's reign and his life. But his successor, Mahmud II, took the throne and avenged his father's murder by massacring the Janissary corps in 1826.

Meanwhile, the rise of nationalism that had swept through Europe also percolated into the Ottoman territories. With the birth of a national identity came an increasing sentiment for ethnic nationalism. This monumental shift in thought, the most significant of all imports from the West, forced the Ottomans—of many ethnicities and cultural backgrounds—to deal with nationalism both domestically and beyond the empire's frontiers throughout the 19th and early 20th centuries. Revolutionary political groups took hold, tempers flared, and rebellions ensued, rippling through the beleaguered empire. To deal with the encroaching pressures of ethnicization, a series of constitutional reforms assured equality for all Ottoman citizens regardless of their ethnicity and faith. Christian *millets* gained special rights. In 1863 the Armenian National Constitution, approved by the empire's Islamic leadership, provided a set of 150 articles drafted by the leading Armenian academics. And as European nations were being created along ethnic and cultural lines from the sweeping empires of the past, the Ottoman amalgam also sought independence from subjugation. Serbia gained its independence in two rebellions in 1804 and 1815. By the end of the 19th century, Greece, the whole of Serbia, Bulgaria, Romania, and Montenegro had gained independence.

Rising Nationalism

Defending against foreign invasion and occupation had proved too challenging for the empire. Its leadership allied with Western European countries—the Netherlands, France, Germany, and Great Britain—and Russia instead of persisting on its own. In the Crimean War of 1853, the Ottomans allied their efforts with those of Great Britain and Ireland, France, and the Kingdom of Sardinia against the Russian Empire.

Pressured by a group of Western-oriented Turks known as the Young Ottomans, who deemed that a constitutional monarchy would solve the empire's mounting social turmoil, Sultan Abdul Hamid was allowed to reign on the sole condition that an Ottoman constitution be enacted. The charter created a representative parliament and guaranteed freedom of expression and religious freedom. With his eyes squarely on the throne, Abdul Hamid created the first Ottoman parliament in 1877. A year later the increasingly dictatorial sultan demanded parliament's dissolution, the incarceration of the Young Ottomans' leader, Midhat, and his eventual execution.

Abdul Hamid II's tyrannical rule created unrest both among the ethnic masses and among the Western-oriented young Turks. Military cadets as well as students plotted against the sultan's despotic regime in cities outside Istanbul, where the Sultan had sworn to quell dissent in any form. A young officer named Mustafa Kemal, who later assumed the surname Atatürk, set up an underground circle with fellow officers in Damascus. This society soon joined forces with other nationalist reform groups to form the Committee of Union and Progress (CUP). Also known as the Young Turks, this organization aimed to reinstate the 1876 constitution and fuse the empire's various factions into a uniform state. In 1908, as army units in Macedonia revolted and demanded reinstatement of constitutional government, Abdul Hamid II granted parliamentary elections, and the CUP secured all but one of the Turkish seats under a system that allowed proportional representation of all *millets*. Despite this success, the Young Turks' momentum was weakened by rifts among its nationalist and liberal reformers, and threatened by traditionalist Muslims and by increasing demands for greater autonomy from non-Turkish communities. Abdul Hamid was left with no choice but to abdicate under the pressure.

As European powers in the mid-1800s through the 1950s began jostling for territory, the once-feared Ottoman Empire, already in dramatic decline, was swept up in these conflicts with ill-chosen alliances. Czar Nicholas I of Russia aptly labeled the Ottomans the "sick man of Europe" in 1853 when discussing his neighbor's increasing financial reliance on European powers and its massive territorial losses.

World War I

With political turmoil rife in Istanbul, foreign powers saw the opportunity to attack the empire's peripheral suzerains. Austria annexed Bosnia and Herzegovina shortly after the 1908 revolution, and Bulgaria declared its independence. Fearing the French would pounce first, Italy heeded a campaign started by its national press and invaded mineral-rich Libya in 1911. A peace treaty signed by the Ottomans yielded the Dodecanese Islands and Libya to Italy. Allied Greece, Serbia, Montenegro, and Bulgaria secured Ottoman-controlled Macedonia and Thrace in October 1912 in the First Balkan Wars. The Ottomans retreated to Europe's easternmost periphery.

Political change occurred swiftly in Istanbul. The liberal parliament, which had been reinstated in 1912, was overthrown a year later in a coup plotted by the ambitious nationalistic Enver Paşa. Hardliners among his nationalistic Young Turk organization assumed parliamentary control. At the head of this new administration stood a trio of highly motivated and powerful pashas—Enver, Cemal, and Talat—known as the triumvirate of power. Enver was appointed both general and Minister of War; Talat assumed the role of Minister of the Interior, and Cemal served as the Guardian of Istanbul.

Secretly plotting to regain the former capital of Edirne, Enver allied with Greece, Serbia, and Montenegro in the Second Balkan War when the bloc objected to Bulgaria's territorial greed. The campaign was a success, and Edirne reverted to Ottoman rule. This was the last victory for the empire, but ironically the tumultuous land gains by the Europeans in the Balkans and in the Mediterranean started the malaise among Western powers that would lead to World War I.

As Europe marched toward war, the leadership in Istanbul was torn as to what to do next. Enver, who as a military attaché in Berlin had grown to admire German culture and politics alongside the country's most notable academics, made no qualms about his sentiments for aligning with the German kaiser. He successfully lobbied the bureaucracy and the military by using fear tactics that involved the empire's penultimate enemy, Russia, who by then had joined Britain and France in the war. Despite the fact that Germany had been an ally of the empire during the Balkan conflicts, Talat and Cemal Pashas as well as the Porte (the Ottoman Court) were adamant on neutrality. On August 2, 1914, Enver secretly allied the Ottomans with Germany. The next day, mobilization commenced, and the empire was embroiled in World War I. To make matters worse, the Allies opened a Middle Eastern flank in an otherwise European conflict.

The first incident to rile the Allies occurred on August 16, 1914, when two German naval vessels that had escaped to a neutral Ottoman port at the time war had been declared in Europe were turned over to the Ottoman navy. The following October, the same two vessels, flanked by an Ottoman armada, bombarded strategic Russian naval bases, including Odessa, while flying the Ottoman flag. Russia declared war on the Ottoman Empire on November 5; Britain and France followed the next day. By April 1915, there were 800,000 Ottoman ground troops fighting on four fronts: Russia in northeastern Anatolia, Greece in Thrace, Britain in Arabia, and an Allied front at Gallipoli.

Toward the end of 1914, Enver launched an assault on the Russians in the Caucasus region, hoping a win would shore up support among Russia's Turkish factions against the czar's encroachment on eastern Anatolia. But this ill-prepared campaign resulted in the loss of thousands of troops and territory for the Ottomans, who had by then retreated to the Armenian-dominated Lake Van. The Armenians, seeing Russia as their liberator, conspired against the Ottomans. Convinced that an Armenian revolt was imminent and that the conspiracy extended well beyond eastern Anatolia into the empire, Enver ordered the systematic detainment and deportation of Armenians on April 24, 1915.

The Ottomans appeared to be losing on all fronts of the war, except at Gallipoli. In early 1915 the Allies launched naval and land campaigns in the Dardanelles, intending to take the Ottomans out of the war swiftly and blast their way through the straits to create an open supply route to Russia. But the strategic planning of the campaign's British command was no match for the genius of Ottoman commander Mustafa Kemal. He galvanized the frontline and ordered his men to hold the front and march to their deaths. The invading British and Anzac forces suffered shocking losses and failed to broaden their beachhead.

By early October 1918 the Ottomans had been defeated. In Istanbul the administration resigned, and the Young Turk triumvirate fled to Germany. Mehmet VI, who had just ascended the throne, petitioned for peace to the liberal-minded administration. An armistice engineered by the Allies was signed at Mudros on October 30, 1918. The peace agreement dictated the surrender of garrisons outside Anatolia and allowed the Allies control of the Dardanelles and Bosphorus Straits, with an addendum granting them the right to occupy the country "in case of disorder."

The greater Treaty of Versailles of 1919 officially reallocated the Ottoman territories of Syria to the French; Mesopotamia, Iraq, and Palestine went to the British; and Arabia to the Europeans. Anatolia's dismantling was contentious. Southwestern Anatolia went to Italy; the British took Istanbul and control of Marmara's straits; the French took the Hatay and various ports in Thrace and along the Black Sea; the Greeks took northwestern Anatolia and İzmir; and the Armenians, supported by a large Russian detachment, took most of northern Anatolia along the Black Sea. According to a secret prewar agreement with Great Britain and France, the Russians were to receive a variety of lands and ports in Thrace and Anatolia for their role in the Armenian revolt against the Ottomans. But the ill-timed Russian Revolution took the Russians out of the running to acquire these territories.

A year later, the Treaty of Sèvres settled all territorial disputes in Anatolia among the Europeans, officially created a kernel of land for the Ottoman Turks, and ensured Woodrow Wilson's plan for a Wilsonian Armenia. This final pact never came into force, as the Turks soon stood up to the imperialism of the European powers by fighting for their independence.

The Fight for Independence

With an impeccable military reputation despite the defeat of the empire, Mustafa Kemal returned to Istanbul a hero. A Turkish nationalist movement was slowly taking root in the Allied-occupied city, and he soon assumed control of it. Considered a threat by the Allies for his expressed opposition to the Allied occupation and his growing political popularity, he was sent to eastern Anatolia, supposedly to oversee the demobilization of Ottoman forces. As soon as he arrived in Samsun in May 1919, he marshaled not only public support for the nationalist movement but also volunteers for a nationalist army. Once the congresses in Erzurum and Sivas were held in the summer of 1919, the objectives of the national protocol were set forth, and the insurgency against the occupying forces progressed from guerrilla warfare to a massive offensive against the Greek army.

On April 23, 1920, Kemal inaugurated the Turkish Grand National Assembly and established a new interim government in Ankara. Meanwhile, the Greeks proceeded to pursue their dream of recapturing the former territorial grandeur of the Byzantines. They had solidified their foothold along the Aegean and aimed for Ankara. Confident from the ease with which they were quelling bands of Turkish freedom fighters, the Greeks launched two massive campaigns, one in Eskişehir and Bursa and the other in Sakarya, but they were bloodily repelled by an organized Turkish army under the command of Colonel Ismet İnönü. The Turks caught up with them at Dumlupınar as they were retreating to the coast. Surrounded, they were killed and captured; the Greeks who survived quickly retreated to İzmir. There too a revolt against Greek occupation—and against Greco-Turks—was underway. On September 9, 1922, the city forced out the invaders and the majority of its Greek residents. Months later, Anatolia's Greeks were "repatriated" to Greece, and Greco-Turks were sent "home" in the massive population exchange of 1923.

Once more, Kemal emerged as the hero of the Turks. He eradicated the sultanate on November 1, 1922, and in its place established a parliamentary government. The international ratification of the Treaty of Lausanne in 1923 legally recognized the independence of the new Turkish nation. More importantly, the pact gave credibility to a people who had been humiliated just three years previously by the Treaty of Sèvres.

BUILDING A NEW REPUBLIC

With Turkey's existence ratified internationally and still high on the success of the War of Independence, the charismatic Kemal parlayed his remarkable strategic and leadership skills to lead the newly established Grand National Assembly in Ankara, the nation's de facto capital, and was elected president in 1923. A new constitution was drawn up that promised unequivocal civil rights to all and, most importantly, set up a new protocol for the government. Mustafa formed his cabinet, selecting the national military hero responsible for ousting the Greeks from Anatolia, Ismet Pasha, as his prime minister. His goals of Westernization, modernization, and secularization were swiftly pursued.

Rallying a multiethnic and multicultural population devastated by decades of war proved to be difficult. Mustafa presided over his newly formed democracy with a compassionate iron fist to enact his reform program. Secularization, he deemed, was necessary not only to modernize the country after centuries as an Islamic theocracy, but also to align itself with the rest of Europe. In this vein, he ordered the closure of sharia courts and the secularization of all theological schools in 1924. This met with opposition from those who wanted an Islamic element in the government and from those Kemal riled with his authoritarian rule and ego. Opponents, which included disillusioned members of his cabinet, joined to form the Progressive Republican Party (PRP). To prove his dedication to free discourse and to the democratic process, Mustafa allowed the political party into government, going as far as replacing Ismet Pasha with the PRP's leader, Fethi Bey, in 1924. This party was short-lived, as their acceptance into the assembly was concurrent with an insurgency in the Kurdish southeast. The first large-scale Kurdish rebellion, often labeled by modern scholars as "a nationalist rebellion in religious garb," was led by Sheikh Said of the Nakshbendi Order of dervishes. And while it is true that he was keen on reinstating the caliphate, the Kurdish sheikh and the tribal rebels were first and foremost motivated nationalists. Kemal quickly quelled the uprising and issued the Maintenance of Order Act, which outlawed the PRP and returned Ismet Pasha to the post of prime minister in 1925. This incident demonstrated Kemal's hardline stance on dissidence and his commitment to secularism not only to the bureaucracy but also to the public; the sheikh and some 40 others were tried and hanged, and the press was shut down.

The secularization process included a widespread ban on dervish sects and prohibitions on tomb-side prayers and the use of honorific titles. Kemal considered banning women's veils entirely in late 1925, but decided against it, fearing that such an action would rile his religious opponents; instead, head coverings were discouraged. Turkish women in major cities began donning fashionable hats, but the unveiling of the rest of Turkey's women was slow to come. In 1925 the fez was also outlawed; this blue-tasseled red hat had signified orientalism since the days Mahmud II had universalized it in the early 1800s. In its stead, Kemal replaced it with the Panama hat, which he donned during a speech in Kastamonu, saying that the ban was a necessary step in Turkey's modernization process, adding that "civilized men wear civilized hats."

In 1926, civil, commercial, and penal codes based on European models were adopted. The new civil law ended Islamic polygamy and divorce by renunciation and instituted civil marriage. The once-revolutionary *millet* system ended, and the oversight of all provinces and all ethnic groups was centralized. More importantly, women received equal rights across the board. The right to education at the secondary and postsecondary level was also granted. That year, growing opposition against Kemal's cultural revolution came to a head, as a wide conspiracy to assassinate the president was uncovered; 15 individuals were tried and hanged. A few of them were part of the defunct PRP. Finally, in 1928, the Republic of Turkey's secularization process was completed with the passage of a constitutional proviso that removed Islam as the national religion.

In 1927 the first official systematic census was undertaken. The results showed that only 10 percent of Turkey's population over the age of seven was literate. Even worse, few children were attending school; reforms to instate an education system were launched. Language also presented a problem: In the 1920s more than two-thirds of the population spoke Arabic, French, or Persian. Other dialects included Greek, Hebrew, Armenian, and Kurdish. One language was required to unite the Turks, so the Language Revolution of May 1928 began, whereby Istanbul Turkish was accepted as the official language, despite the differing writing systems and languages of several ethnic groups. The impact was far-reaching. Families had to forgo traditional names for their children in their own language in favor of Turkish names. Numbers that had been written in Ottoman were replaced with their Arabic equivalents, those used in the West. Later that year the Grand National Assembly approved the introduction of a new Latin alphabet, but not without opposition from assembly members who campaigned for a transition period of years rather than the months Kemal wanted to shift from the Ottoman system. Once again, Kemal's plan for speed won out, and within months the writing system was switched to the Latin alphabet. To assuage dissent and to prove that his proposal was viable, Kemal, armed with chalk and a blackboard, embarked on a weeks-long journey through the republic's villages and schools to educate a people that had suddenly become completely illiterate. Even Islam was forced to abide with the linguistic change when a 1932 law was passed that the call to prayer had to be in Turkish instead of Arabic.

The 1930s brought other sweeping changes. In 1934, Turkish women were given the vote, and the Law of Surnames brought an end to the confusion of identifying people only by their first names. Kemal adopted the surname Atatürk (Father of the Turks), and Izmet adopted the last name Inönü to commemorate the site where he had vanquished the Greeks. Although the adoption of family names was mandatory, the choice of names was left to the individual. Artisans, craftspeople, and traders were inspired by their professions. Today, entire families are known as the son of the baker or the carpenter. But the titles of old, like *bey* (Mr.) and *hanım* (lady) are still used pervasively after a person's name to denote respect.

Atatürk's legacy still prevails in a set of founding principles known as "Six Arrows." Also referred to Atatürkism or Kemalism, these fundamental guidelines were the essential building blocks for the establishment of modern Turkey. The first part, "republicanism," set the bar for the sweeping political revolution from the multinational Ottoman Empire to the state of Turkey and the realization of a national identity. The scope of the second principle, Kemalist "nationalism," preserved the independence of the budding Republic of Turkey and aimed to aid its political evolution. Not based on race, nationalism honored a nation's right to independence and stood firmly against imperialism and caste systems. With these two firmly in place, Atatürk's "reformism" cemented the way forward to activate the sweeping changes required to modernize the country from its dated and traditional public institutions and ideologies. Since Turkey's modernization hinged on its economic and technological development, Atatürk's "statism" guideline ensured the regulation of the nation's overall economic activity and assumed its management if the private sector was unable to do so, was inadequate, or was not acting in the best interest of the country. Later on, the state not only emerged as the main regulator of economic activity but also as the de facto owner of the country's main industries. Kemalist "populism" stood against class privilege and distinctions and favored no individual, family, class, or organization above another. Although it was somewhat hypocritical, since the government was an elitist group at its inception, the ideology of populism was actually based on the value of Turkish citizenship or national pride. Atatürk believed that indoctrinating the Turkish citizenry in this fashion would elicit the psychological drive necessary make people work harder for the state and unify diverse peoples under a national identity. To that extent, the policy succeeded in revolutionizing the social fabric of Turkey, including suffrage for women and what Atatürk defined as the true rulers of Turkey, its villagers. Finally, "secularism" not only created a division between state and religion but also separated the latter from educational, cultural, and legal affairs. Only in this manner could independence and individuality of thought be gained. It also did away with the dominance of religious institutions. Kemalist secularism did not endorse atheism nor shun Islam; it is simply anticlerical in nature. It didn't reject Islam in any form but vehemently opposed an Islam that was against modernization.

In hindsight, Atatürk's achievements were many. His five-year plan to achieve economic independence, launched in 1934, reversed centuries of virtual nonproductivity that had characterized the Ottoman era. Development packages for industrial and agriculture productivity were inaugurated along with fostering confidence in domestic products. Tariffs on imports were raised, and foreign railroad easements were purchased to protect the domestic market. But in other ways, change was slow to come. The economy still lagged behind European standards, as did living standards. The Labor Act of 1936 addressed some of these issues by providing workers the rights they were seeking. Although strikes were banned, a mediation system was created; a new state insurance program was instituted that guaranteed compensation for unexpected death and accidents on the job, as well as income for seniors.

On the international front, Atatürk aligned his ideal of "peace at home, peace abroad" with a foreign policy of peace. Pacts were signed with all the country's neighbors in the region as well as with larger powers. For the first time in their history, Turks enjoyed peaceful relations with the rest of the world, ending centuries of hostile takeovers. By 1932 Turkey had joined the League of Nations.

At 9:05am on November 10, 1938, Atatürk's presidency came to an end when he succumbed to cirrhosis of the liver after years of alcohol abuse. He transferred control to İnönü, his partner in war and peace. In his 15 years as president, Atatürk had created a modern, relatively democratic republic from the ashes of a defunct dictatorial regime. For this the League of Nations perhaps best characterized his efforts after his death by calling him a "genius international peacemaker." Today, every November 10 at 9:05am, sirens and horns sound and people stop what they are doing for a minute of silence to honor Atatürk's memory.

To understand Atatürk's place in Turkish history, his sweeping achievements must be weighed against the bloody events in Europe in the first part of the 20th century. His sweeping reforms united a fractured people under one flag and rewarded them with autonomy, national pride, equal rights, and the promise of economic prosperity after one of the most tempestuous periods in world history. To this day, his strength of character, bold reforms, and charismatic persona continue to inspire new generations of Turks.

TROUBLE ABROAD AND AT HOME

Izmet İnönü, Atatürk's successor, was elected president by the Grand National Assembly on November 11, 1938, the day after Atatürk's death. Although the Turkish economy was still lagging far behind those of its European counterparts when he assumed office, an international calamity on a scale never seen before was to rock Eastern Europe and impact Turkey directly.

Once again, allegiances among the World War I blocs were renewed as Soviet Russia and Nazi Germany's zeal for territory threatened both the Balkans and the intercontinental Bosphorus Straits. Turkey's geographical position between the two emerging Eastern European powers made the threat even greater if conflict were to arise. İnönü carefully planned amicable nonaggression treaties with France, Great Britain, and Hitler's Germany. By early 1945, neutral Turkey found itself unscathed by the conflicts that had erupted just outside its borders—until it was required to declare war on Germany in order to join the 50 other nations at the San Francisco Conference, the predecessor to the United Nations. Turkey had become an ally of the United States and a foe of Russia by definition. Availing itself of Turkey's strategic position bordering the Soviet Bloc, the United States lavished Turkey with financial aid. Turkey kept its end of the bargain by joining the United States in its military campaign in Korea. For this it was rewarded with an invitation to join the North Atlantic Treaty Organization (NATO) in 1949.

On the domestic front, democratization of the Turkish government accelerated. The one-party rule that had dominated Turkish politics was brought to an end in 1950, when the Democratic Party (DP) swept a majority of the vote and gained control of the assembly. During the next decade the Democrats rolled back some of Atatürk's reforms. First to be reinstated was the call to prayer, which was allowed to be in Arabic. But as the press of the day joked, power turned the DP into despots, and their slogan "rule by the people for the people" was largely ignored. The DP's success at gaining a majority of seats in the National Grand Assembly galvanized Turkey's politicians to form a multitude of political parties, ranging from the extremist fascist nationalists to pro-Islamic parties. But while each Turk was represented by a party that mirrored his or her ideals, the sheer variety of political groups represented in the assembly made the government stagnant at a time when the lagging Turkish economy needed effective governance. A slew of ill-managed economic reforms forced the government to seek out foreign loans. Legions of unemployed Turks with no job prospects chose to look for employment beyond the country's borders.

Seeking to return to a one-party system, the then-DP prime minister Adnan Menderes launched a censorship campaign by outlawing public political meetings, invoking gag rules on the press, and mandating formal investigations into the political activities of opposing parties. Menderes's rule was widely popular, but Turkey's military machine and its Western-educated academics were opposed to it. Fearing a coup and harassed by spreading student riots, Menderes imposed martial law on April 29, 1960. The Turkish army, headed by commander Cemal Gürsel, retaliated and seized power in a nonviolent coup d'état on May 27. President Celal Bayar, Menderes, and hundreds of DP sympathizers were arrested and tried. Bayar received a life sentence, dying at the age of 103 in 1986, and Menderes was hanged for treason. The DP was once again dissolved, and the military took power despite commander Gürsel's fierce opposition to permanent military rule. His nationalism compelled him to stay in charge, forming the Committee of National Unity. After his election in 1961 as the fourth president of the republic, Gürsel played an integral part in cementing the way for a new constitution and a return to democracy after the coup. Former president İnönü returned to serve as prime minister. The next five years were characterized by unlikely coalition governments among the Kemalists of the Justice Party (JP), led by Süleyman Demirel; the social democrats of İnönü's RPP; the center-right Turkish Workers Party; and the communist Confederation of Progressive Trade Unions. Opposing ideals made for a stagnant assembly until 1965, when Demirel's JP won a majority of seats. Despite the JP securing a big percentage of the popular vote, the assembly suffered incessant quarrels along party lines as well as party defections. As Turks lost confidence in their government, the turmoil among politicians in Ankara was felt in the streets nationwide. The value of the Turkish lira was at an all-time low, and unemployment was at an all-time high. Civil anarchy raged in the form of student riots, with Leninists and Marxists chanting antigovernment slogans on the streets of major metropolises. Political terrorism in the form of political assassinations and kidnappings ensued. The army felt forced to step in once again to depose Demirel's centrist government in the military coup of 1971.

By 1973 power was returned to a newly formed assembly, but difficulties still raged as terrorists from the pro-Islamic National Salvation Party and the ultranationalist neofascist youth organization called the Turkish Nationalist Movement Party, known as the Gray Wolves, wreaked havoc among the populace on the streets. Turning a corner on the street could prove to be fatal if one's political affiliation didn't match that of the terrorists, who were on a mission to eradicate dissenters. This domestic unrest coincided with tensions on the island of Cyprus, following a coup d'état that saw the overthrow of the Greek government in Athens. In July 1974, Ankara, led by then-prime minister Bülent Ecevit, sent 30,000 troops the island to protect its Turkish minority, fearing further attacks from the Greek junta. The West condemned the invasion, which effectively divided the island into two political entities, which it remains to this day. Incidentally, the north, which accounts for one-third of the island, declared independence in 1983; the Turkish Republic of Northern Cyprus is recognized only by Turkey.

Turkey plunged into a political and economic quagmire. The military, led by army chief of staff General Kenan Evren, once again stepped in on September 12, 1980, a coup d'état was met with jubilation from Turks and many foreign states. Evren became head of state for the next two years of military rule. Following the adoption of a new constitution by public referendum, Evren became the seventh president of Turkey in 1982. On

November 9, 1989, the Motherland Party swept the popular vote; in its pro-Islamic leader, the respected economist and businessman Turgut Özal, the electorate saw the talent necessary to fix the country's ailing economy. And that he did, doing away with Atatürk's dated policy of statism; industry and agriculture were decentralized and subsequently privatized. Aside from Özal's sweeping economic and legal reforms, the 1990s were also characterized by mounting tensions from the Kurdish separatist movement, raging corruption, and the reinstatement of opposing political parties.

AN ISLAM-CENTERED ECONOMIC POWERHOUSE

Living up to its NATO obligations, Turkey played a major role in the Persian Gulf War of 1990, not only lending its military bases to the Allied effort but also its airspace. In doing so it strengthened its relationship with the United States. One thing Özal's government didn't anticipate was the 1.5 million Kurds fleeing the wrath of Saddam Hussein's supporters in Iraq. Some made it into southeastern Turkey, fueling the increasing tensions of the Kurdish secession movement there. Another unanticipated turn of events was the creation of a semiautonomous Kurdistan in northern Iraq in 1991, where the Kurdistan's Workers Party (PKK) allegedly trained terrorists. PKK terrorist activities came to a head in the mid-1990s, forcing the Turkish military to take a stand against uprisings in the southeast and imposing martial law. This continued until PKK rebel leader and founder Abdullah Öcalan was captured in Kenya in 1999 after eluding Turkish authorities for years.

Through the early 1990s Özal's notoriously corrupt center-right government was fodder for calls for a return to a morally sound regime, boosting the power of the Islamist movement. Strictly Sunni Saudi Arabia saw an opportunity to provide financial assistance, helping to launch bold social programs and indirectly sowing the seeds of religious fanaticism. After Özal's death in suspicious circumstances, the Welfare Party, led by Islamic prime minister Necmettin Erbakan, received the majority of seats in the assembly. A year later the Turkish military ousted Erbakan's government for allegedly following an Islamist agenda, an allegation that was corroborated by a court ruling in 1998 that called the party antisecular. They banned the party and its leader for "violating the principle of secularism in the constitution." Some of the Welfare Party's original members pressed on with their Islamic agenda by regrouping and forming the Justice and Development Party (Adalet ve Kalkınma Partisi, AKP) in July 2001. With a much softer message, a more moderate position, and the desire to operate within Turkey's secular framework, AKP swept 34 percent of the vote in the general election of 2002. Turks, unhappy with the previous government's clumsy handling of the 1999 earthquake disaster and its failure to enforce construction laws that allowed not only widespread corruption in the construction sector but also for the erection of more than 500,000 buildings that proved structurally unsafe during the earthquake, voiced their outrage at the polls. Their anger wasn't directed only at political profiteers; the message for change extended to the entire assembly for its failure to foresee Turkey's major financial collapse of 2001.

The AKP, led by Bülent Arinç and Abdullah Gül, effected change quickly, even without its ringleader, Recep Tayyip Erdoğan, who in 1997, during a stint as the mayor of Istanbul, had recited Koranic verses in public, which a court ruled was anti-Kemalist. He made the statement, "The mosques are our barracks, the domes our helmets, the minarets our bayonets, and the faithful our soldiers," which got him removed from his mayoral post, banned from participating in politics for a six-year period, and given a jail sentence of four months. Steering the AKP since 2003, Erdoğan got another boost at the polls when 44 percent of Turks rubber-stamped the party's general direction in the 2004 elections. But when

Erdoğan nominated Abdullah Gül for the office of president in 2007, the Turkish military voiced its disapproval. At issue wasn't Gül, per se, but his wife, Hayrünnisa, who wears a *hijab* (headscarf), at the time forbidden in public buildings, including Ankara's presidential palace. But Gül's nomination for the presidency stood and went on to be ratified in the general elections of 2007. Gül became Turkey's 11th president, and in 2013, after years of being one of the most contentious issues in mainstream Turkey, the "headscarf issue" was tested again when the AKP immediately introduced laws enabling women to wear their *hijab* in public and government buildings, which they promoted as a way to encourage women to take jobs in government or higher education while maintaining their personal choice in dress. This disagreement and others between the secular social progressives and the Islamic traditionalists continue to this day.

Despite reaching the economic stability and growth Atatürk once dreamed of, Erdoğan's increasingly authoritarian rule, heavily criticized internationally, alongside an alleged billion-dollar corruption scandal, is threatening his once-illustrious majority-rule powerbase. The general elections of June 2015 could be a defining moment in Turkish politics that tests the AKP's decade-plus rule. The only difference now is that people can oust a government in democratic elections, should they be dissatisfied with its performance, rather than rely on a military coup to do so. The AKP secured its position by successfully reforming the constitution via a referendum in 2010. The reforms removed the military's right to amnesty in coups d'état, meaning personnel can now be tried and imprisoned for plotting to overthrow a government. Further demotion of the military occurred when the highly controversial Ergenekon trial saw 254 people, including one in five Turkish generals, imprisoned in 2013 on allegations of plotting to topple the AKP. Alongside all of this controversy is Turkey's bid for full membership in the European Union—a process that officially began in the mid-1980s and may take another decade or more to complete.

Government

Since 2002, Turkey's government has been in the hands of its dominant party, the conservative AKP, which maintains 326 of the 550 seats in the assembly since obtaining 49.9 percent of the popular vote during the most recent elections in 2011.

Recep Tayyip Erdoğan has served as Turkey's prime minister since 2003, roughly a year after the party gained 34 percent of the vote in the general elections of 2002. Early on, Erdoğan's government was successful in introducing reforms to assuage the country's poor track record on human rights, particularly when it comes to the Kurdish minority. In 2009 the AKP instituted measures to align the rights of the Kurds with those of the rest of the country by lifting a ban on the use of the Kurdish language in public and allowing its broadcast and use during political campaigns. The AKP-led government also worked to reverse the deeply stagnant economy it had inherited by introducing bold macroeconomic schemes and luring foreign investment through the removal of most government regulation. Abroad, Turkey's AKP government maintained close ties with the United States and Europe.

Turkey serves as a nonpermanent member of the United Nations Security Council since being elected to the position by more than two-thirds of the 192 member states in 2008. Along with Austria, Turkey is tasked with protecting Western European interests. Oriented toward the West since its inception in 1923, Turkey is a founding member of the Council of Europe. Turkey applied for full membership in the European Union in 1987 and was granted associate membership in 1992. Full admission to the bloc may take many years yet. At issue is Turkey's copious size and population; if accepted, it would become the bloc's second-largest member nation in terms of population, between Germany and Great Britain, and largest in geographic size by far. The EU and Turkey have remained at odds over Cyprus. Its northern third was declared the de facto Turkish Republic of Northern Cyprus (TRNC) by Turkey after Turkish troops invaded the island in 1974 to protect its Turkish Cypriot minority from militant Greek nationalists. Turkey is the only nation that recognizes the TRNC.

Turkey's relationship with the United States determines much of the country's foreign relations. Close bilateral ties between the two countries have been continuous since the Soviet threat of the Cold War era. Turkey's military support and allegiance during the Cold War, and especially during the U.S.-led Korean War, galvanized its amity toward Washington. In return, Turkey earned full membership in NATO in 1952. After the dissolution of the Soviet Union and the end of the Cold War in 1991, Turkey's strategic importance shifted to the Middle East. The United States considered Turkey a primarily Muslim secular democracy, an example for developing Middle Eastern nations to follow, and also supported a crucial allegiance with Turkey's largely positive relations with Israel. Turkey continues to benefit from the overall support of the United States, particularly in its bid to join the EU and their joint goal of restoring peace in Syria by seeing an end to the Bashar al-Assad regime. Recent disagreements between the two nations, however, have included tensions over the official definition of the killing of Armenians in 1915. At issue is the massacre of over one million Christian Armenians by Ottoman Turks, which is being labeled genocide by an increasing number of states worldwide. Turkey recognizes the atrocities but is steadfast in its assertion that the mass slaying was part of war casualties and not a systematic ethnic cleansing, as the definition of *genocide* entails. Since mid-2013, and in light of antigovernment demonstrations initiated by protests to retain Istanbul's Gezi Park, a growing number of high-level foreign policymakers across the U.S. government have urged President Obama to denounce Erodoğan's increasingly autocratic outspoken style.

ORGANIZATION

The Republic of Turkey is defined as a secular parliamentary representative democratic republic. Since the republic's establishment in 1923, secularism has been a cornerstones of Turkish politics and its constitution. A prime minister serves as the head of government and of a multiparty system. The government follows guidelines established by the constitution, which a president enacts to "represent the Republic of Turkey and the unity of the Turkish Nation."

Ratified on November 7, 1982, after two years of military rule following the nonviolent coup d'état in 1980, Turkey's current constitution maintains that the state is a secular and democratic republic that acquires its authority from the Turkish people. Power is delegated to an elected parliament, known as the Grand National Assembly. The constitution also asserts that Turkey is a unitary nation-state by definition of its attributes: the exclusion of ecclesiastical control, social equality, equality before the law, the republican form of government, and the indivisibility of the republic and of the Turkish Nation.

Supervising the state in a largely ceremonial position is Turkey's president, the head of state. Presidents serve five years and can only be reelected once. The country's 11th president, Abdullah Gül, was able to serve a seven-year term due to a constitutional change in 2012. Presidents-elect must break ties with all political parties and resign from any duties within the assembly before assuming the presidency.

Executive power is held by the prime minister and his ministerial council. Almost always a member of parliament, the prime minister is elected by members of the assembly in a vote of confidence for the government he or she has presented.

The legislative power of the Turkish government is in its parliament, the Grand National Assembly of Turkey. This body of 550 members, elected to four-year terms from constituencies, represent 85 districts in Turkey's 81 provinces. Due to their large populations, Istanbul comprises three districts, and Ankara and İzmir have two each. A party must win at least 10 percent of the general vote in a parliamentary election to be represented in the assembly to avoid excessive political fragmentation or hung parliaments. Independents may also run if they've received at least 10 percent of the popular vote in their province.

As asserted by the Turkish constitution, the judicial branch is free and independent of any private or political organization or institution, although this independence has been tested in light of the 2014 corruption scandal allegedly involving allies of the AKP. The executive and legislative branches of government must submit to the high court's rulings, which must be based on constitutional provisions, existing laws, jurisprudence, and their personal judgment. There are no juries in the Turkish legal system; rulings are derived directly from judges, who are bound by law to render decisions after all pertaining facts have been presented by legal representation. Justices of the peace are tasked with civil complaints and misdemeanors; one judge oversees each court at this level. Felonies and major civil lawsuits are handled in a three-judge court. Turkey's High Council of Judges and Public Prosecutors ensures the judicial integrity at all levels nationwide, nominates judges, and oversees court assignments.

THE TURKISH ARMY

Ever since Atatürk founded the Turkish Republic in 1923, the country's armed forces have taken it upon themselves to maintain the values of its founding father. While Atatürk never envisioned Turkey's military coming head-to-head with its politicians, the reality is that his ideology of a secular state—known as Kemalism—wouldn't have survived if the armed forces hadn't intervened.

Since the latter part of the 20th century, the behavior of civil governments toward Turkey's military has ranged from respectful unease to containment, granting the armed forces either too much leeway or divesting it of its authority. On three occasions, in 1960, 1971, and 1980, the Turkish military stepped in with nonviolent coups d'état to assume power for a couple of years before returning it to a civilian government.

In 2007, army chief commander General Yaşar Büyükanıt expressed his anger over the ruling conservative Islamic AKP party's politics. At issue were the party's lifting of the headscarf ban at universities and the appointment of a president who had once been a member of a banned Islamic political entity. In a letter, Büyükanıt asserted that these measures ran against Turkey's secular tenets and warned that the Turkish armed forces stood ready to intercede in politics with "absolute" determination. Turkey's high court soon allowed the AKP to continue these policies despite the popular belief that intercession was imminent. Since this time the AKP has slowly eroded the power and authority of the military with constitutional reforms, which has led to charges, trials, and later imprisonment of many military personnel found guilty of trying to overturn the government.

POLITICAL PARTIES AND ELECTIONS

Turkey's multiparty system has been in place since 1945. Reflecting its occasionally turbulent history, the system continues to change. Some parties hardly grow past infancy. This was the case of the Kurdish Democratic Society Party, banned in late 2009 for its alleged ties with Kurdish separatist movements and the terrorist PKK group. The near shutdown of the AKP in 2007 for allegedly trying to compromise Turkey's secular character led the ruling party to unsuccessfully propose constitutional amendments that would make it more difficult to ban political parties.

In early 2014, there were almost 40 political parties in Turkey, of which three major parties and several independents were represented in parliament's 550 seats. These representatives range from the center-right pro-Islamist ruling AKP to Atatürk's center-left Kemalist Republican People's Party (Cumhuriyet Halk Partisi, CHP) and the ultranationalist Milliyetçi Hareket Partisi (MHP). Independents largely representing the Kurdish minority make up the rest of the seats, with the backing of the Peace and Democracy Party (Barış ve Demokrasi Partisi, BDP).

The last general election took place in June 2011, with the next planned four years later, per the constitution, in 2015. Out of 50.3 million registered voters, 85 percent came to the polls in 2011, which saw the AKP attain almost 50 percent of the votes (326 seats), earning them a third consecutive term. The CHP won 135 parliamentary seats and 25.9 percent of the votes, up 23 seats from the 2007 election. Losing popularity was the MHP, which won 54 seats, 17 less than previously held. The independents got 6.65 percent of the votes and 35 seats. The reason for AKP's popularity in the last election came down to their positive role in stabilizing the economy, developing public amenities for the increasing population, and improving the quality of life, particularly for the Kurdish people, who constitute almost 20 percent of the population. Late in their third term, it would appear the AKP has lost much support thanks to Erdoğan's growing autocratic rule and the resultant drop in the value of the Turkish lira, which has hit the pockets of many. A country polarized over the government's actions awaits the outcome of the 2015 election.

Under the constitution, the prime minister, Recep Tayyip Erdoğan, cannot serve a fourth term, and president Gül's tenure ends in 2014. Change is therefore afoot, although many reports suggest Erdoğan has his eye on the presidency with a view to installing a presidential system similar to that of the United States, without a prime minister. What happens next is anyone's guess. With accusations of vote fixing, a looming corruption trial implicating close allies of the AKP, a ban on Twitter, and even wiretapped recordings allegedly implicating Erdoğan in a range of morally questionable behavior, Turkey's political highs and lows are sure to continue in the lead-up to the centenary of the Turkish Republic in 2023.

Economy

Like the rest of the world, Turkey was affected by the global financial crisis of 2008-2009. Modern industry and the service sector are two of its largest income generators, and the country did experience business closures, dips in orders for domestically produced products, and a reduction in disposable income. That said, Turkey was the least affected country in Europe by the credit crisis and weathered the global recession better than other emerging economies. Tough regulations, few toxic debts, and limited mortgage schemes helped the banking sector stay afloat and remain profitable. The government didn't have to turn to state coffers to bail out banks, as in most Western nations; instead it launched tax-free incentives on big-ticket items like cars and home appliances to stimulate the domestic economy.

Turkey may be famous for its textiles, but it remains one of the world's largest producers of agricultural products, motor vehicles, ships, construction materials, consumer electronics, and appliances. Turkey is the European Union's 6th biggest trading partner, and in 2013 was the only country to increase exports to Europe, valued at €50.2 billion. Globally, Turkey ranks 17th in nominal gross domestic product and has been a member of the G-20 since 1999.

Turkey was on a path of serious and

Olive Oil

People of the ancient Mediterranean believed olive oil to have magical and medicinal characteristics, and some believed it to be the source of the fountain of youth and beauty. Homer referred to it as "liquid gold." The olive tree's leafy branch, while still considered the symbol of peace and abundance, once crowned triumphant conquerors after bloody battles. And ultimately, the three major Abrahamic religions—Judaism, Christianity, and Islam—ritually use the golden liquid and olive branches to bless and purify.

In 2013, Turkey became the fifth-largest olive oil producer in the world after Italy, Spain, Greece, and Tunisia. As much as 70 percent of unbranded exported Turkish olive oil is blended with lower-quality oils to produce less-expensive oil. The bulk of Turkish olive oil makes its way to Italy, where the mixing takes place; it's then exported to countries such as the United States. This trade between western Europe and Asia Minor, according to fossilized remains found in Spain, North Africa, and Italy, dates back to the 6th millennium BC.

What makes Turkish olives different than those cultivated in the rest of Europe is the sandy soil in which the trees grow, the prevalence of a sea breeze, and the sheer variety of the fruits. This makes for fruitier, lighter-tasting oil. The growing environment is organic, and the fruit itself is generally harvested by hand.

Olives and olive oil are produced throughout Anatolia, but the coastal west is king. The northwest area around the Sea of Marmara is noted for its black olives—the kind that end up on the Turkish breakfast table. The Aegean and Mediterranean coasts, however, produce the olives that make the best oil. The land surrounding the Gulf of Edremit, particularly around Ayvalık, is reputed to produce some of the best olive oil in the world.

---

sustained growth until the Turkish lira fell precipitously in 2014. When the financial crisis hit in 2008, many investors saw opportunity in Turkey, but today, as major economies recover, foreign investment in Turkey has dwindled as investors are spooked by ongoing antigovernment protests and the war in neighboring Syria. Since the government imports gas and oil, the daily cost of living for many in Turkey has risen, and many businesses are feeling the pinch of lower consumer spending.

AGRICULTURE

Turkey is agriculturally self-sufficient and has been able to feed its rapidly increasing population since the mid-1980s. It is now the world's largest producer of hazelnuts, dried figs, dried apricots, sultanas, and raisins. Turkey is also a leading producer of watermelons, cucumbers, chickpeas, tomatoes, eggplants, green peppers, lentils, pistachios, onions, and olives. Sugar beets, tobacco, tea, apples, cotton, and barley are also important crops. Crops yielded US$62 billion in 2010, up from US$24 billion in just eight years. Total exports (including processed foods) reached US$12 billion in the same year. The proportion of Turkish citizens working in agriculture grew from 11 percent in 2006 to 25 percent in 2010, and Turkey is now aiming to become the fifth-largest food producer in the world by 2023.

A slew of irrigation projects are planned or underway, including the Southeastern Anatolia Project (GAP), an ambitious and controversial development project to use the waters of the Euphrates and Tigris Rivers to sustain development for the roughly 10 million people in Turkey's southeastern region. The US$32 billion project will include 22 dams, 19 hydroelectric plants, and the irrigation of 1.82 million hectares of land.

The livestock industry remains stagnant, but related products like milk, eggs, and wool account for almost one-third of Turkey's agriculture. Fishing and forestry accounts for seven percent of the total agricultural production, but pollution and overfishing have led to a reduction in catches. The Turkish government has introduced measures in recent years to replenish fish stocks.

INDUSTRY

With China producing ever-cheaper goods, global manufacturers are losing interest in producing clothing in Turkey, though the textile and clothing industry accounted for more than 18 percent of Turkish exports in 2011. That same year, Turkish clothing manufacturers made almost US$13.5 billion in exports, making Turkey the sixth largest clothing supplier in the world. Oil refining, construction, and the production of food, chemicals, automotive products, and electronics are also the main part of the country's manufacturing sector.

Thanks to the Customs Union agreement adopted by the EU and Turkey in 1995, the lifting of customs restrictions between the two has helped Turkish manufacturers of electronics gain a significant share of the EU market. Production of electronics increased from US$7 billion in 2005 to over US$12 billion in 2011 of which there was over US$6 billion worth of exports to 200 countries. This includes products such as LCD and plasma TVs and other household electronics, telecommunication and fiber-optic cables, medical equipment, automotive electronics, and fire alarms and security systems, to name a few.

The Turkish automotive industry, located around the Marmara Sea region, has also grown rapidly. Producing more than one million vehicles domestically, Turkey ranked 16th among automotive manufacturing countries in 2010.

Shipbuilding in the Marmara Region is also one of the country's major industries, ranking in the top five worldwide in the production of leisure yachts, sailboats, oil tankers, and cargo ships.

In the construction and contracting sector, Turkey ranks second after China. Thirty-three Turkish construction firms were listed in the top 225 internationally in 2012, thanks to continued expansion into Asia, Eastern Europe, and the Middle East.

TOURISM

Tourism in Turkey has grown rapidly since the late 1990s. Anatolia's historical sites, spanning at least five millennia and some 22 cultures, make Turkey the country with the most archaeological sites worldwide. Turkey's sun-kissed coasts and exotic seaside resorts compete with other Mediterranean countries such as Italy and Greece for European travelers.

According to the World Tourism Organization, Turkey was the sixth most visited country in the world in 2011. With over 31 million arrivals, Turkey surpassed the United Kingdom in popularity. In 2013 tourism revenue was up 40 percent over 2012, reaching a value of US$4.9 billion. The Ministry of Culture and Tourism is now aiming for 50 million visitors annually by 2023 to make Turkey the fifth most visited country.

Developers have been quick to heed the growing interest from abroad. Luxurious and all-inclusive resorts in Turkey's top two tourism provinces, Antalya and Muğla, have increasing options. Antalya, for instance, boasts more than 170 luxury resorts. Revenues at the US$1.4 billion Mardan Palace, opened in 2009, have proved that an over-the-top Las Vegas-style resort in the Mediterranean region can fill a niche.

DISTRIBUTION OF WEALTH

Turkey's upper- and upper-middle-class profited dramatically in the late 2000s when the government offered interest rates on deposits in the high teens to reverse the economic crash of 2001. The ambitious move paid off for the government and for those with money.

The recent introduction of credit-based financial products created a new middle class. Mid-range and long-term mortgage and loan schemes enabled Turks to own homes, and credit card use has expanded.

By 2008, the wealthiest 20 percent of Turks earned half of the country's income, and the poorest 20 percent had access to only 6 percent. The difference is vast, with the top 20 percent earning an average US$9,750 per year, and the bottom 20 percent, typically from Turkey's southeastern provinces, earning just US$1,250. The true difference is likely greater as top earners routinely underreport their income.

People and Culture

DEMOGRAPHY

In 2012, Turkey's population was 73.9 million, with more than 70 percent in urban areas. Turkey is a youthful country; more than two-thirds fall in the 15-64 age group, with another 26 percent under age 15.

Ethnic Turks are 80 percent of the population, while Kurds account for nearly 20 percent. Since a Turk is constitutionally defined as anyone who maintains Turkish citizenship, regardless of ethnicity, enumerating the other ethnic minorities who became Turkish during centuries of Selçukian and Ottoman rule is virtually impossible, but they include Abkhazians, Adjarians, Albanians, Arabs, Assyrians, Bosnians, Circassians, Hamshenis, Kurds, Laz, Pomaks, Roma, and Zazas. Additionally, Greek, Armenian, and Jewish minorities were officially recognized by the 1923 Treaty of Lausanne. A small number of Levantines—Western European minorities of French or Italian descent—have been present in Istanbul and İzmir since the Middle Ages.

Education is compulsory until the age of 14. Enrollment for primary school from 2008 to 2012 was close to 100 percent nationwide, while rates decrease to around 80 percent for secondary school. Schools are free, but the quality and the limited scope of the education provided by the state increasingly motivate middle-class parents to seek private schooling. Students can only be admitted to private high schools and universities through rigorous examinations, which require years of serious preparation.

Ninety-eight percent of Turkish men and 90 percent of Turkish women are literate. According to a 2006 report by the BBC, the gender disparity results from the traditional customs of Arabs and Kurds in southeastern Turkey.

RELIGION

Ninety-eight percent of Turkey's population is Muslim. About 100,000 Turks are registered as non-Muslims; of these, 64,000 are Christians of the Armenian Apostolic, Assyrian Church of the East, and Greek Orthodox sects, and 26,000 are mainly Sephardic Jews. Atheists and agnostics account for slightly over 3 percent of the population.

Once a year, Istanbul and its mosques transform for the holy month of Ramadan.

Traveling During Kurban Bayramı

Visiting Turkey during **Kurban Bayramı** (sacrifice holiday) may be an intense experience for Westerners traveling to Muslim country for the first time. Known as *Eid el-Adha* or *Eid el-Kebir* in Arabic, this four- or five-day observance, which is the most revered Islamic religious festival of the year, commemorates Abraham's will to sacrifice his son on Mount Moriah in order to prove his total submission to God. (In the story, God stops Abraham just in time, and instead gives him a ram to sacrifice). The date of the festival is based on the Islamic lunar calendar, so it changes yearly. In the next few years it happens in September and early October.

On the morning of the first day of the festival, most Turkish households sacrifice a sheep. A feast is then prepared for the entire family, and a portion is donated to a family in need. If guests happen to be around, be forewarned that they too will take part in the spectrum of "festivities," which may require a strong stomach.

Traveling during the festival is difficult. Since Kurban Bayramı coincides with the hajj—the annual pilgrimage to Mecca—domestic travel and travel to and from Turkey is exceptionally busy. During this time, tickets involving layovers in Europe or the Middle East should be confirmed well in advance, as most flights serving those regions are generally overbooked. The same goes for domestic and international coaches and boats.

If you are visiting during this time, try to travel a couple of days before the holiday's official first and last days. Confirm the rooms, dates, and the number of guests after booking your hotels. Banks are closed during the festival, so make sure that either your ATM card is working or that a sufficient amount of cash is on hand. Museums and public sites may be closed on the first day of the holiday. Businesses and government offices are closed for the duration of the holiday; some villages in remote Turkey may even be away en masse.

Muslim Turks are largely Sunni, with a 15 percent Alevi minority (11 million people) and a small Shiite community. Despite Turkey's secular stance, one in five Turks considers themselves Muslim first and Turkish second. Another 65 percent think religion is crucial but in no way trumps citizenship.

This strong identification with Islam dates to the Selçuk invasion of Anatolia during the Middle Ages. Centuries later the advent of the Ottoman Caliphate, with Istanbul as the capital of Islam, galvanized the faith. At the time, the empire was a strict theocracy ruled by sharia law. Christian and Jewish minorities enjoyed a healthy amount of autonomy but ultimately answered to the sultan. Until the dissolution of the sultanate and the formation of the modern Republic of Turkey, politics were at least in part ruled by Islamic tenets. Recently, Turkey's ruling pro-Islamist AKP party has asserted itself as secular but remains staunchly rooted in Islamic ethical and moral principles. Their early overwhelming approval rate reflects the increasingly conservative convictions of segments of Turkish society.

Turkey's Religious Affairs Directorate is tasked with oversight of the 82,700 registered mosques in the country and the employment of imams. Interpreting Islam's Hanafi school of law, this office follows the oldest and most liberal of the four schools of Islam.

Spiritually, Alevi Muslims differ from their Sunni counterparts in several ways. Alevis worship in assembly halls rather than in mosques. Their ceremonies feature music and dance rituals (*semâ*) in which both men and women participate. The liturgy is in the local language rather than in Arabic. The tenets practiced by Alevis, the majority of whom reside in central and eastern Anatolia, may be construed as somewhat mystical because they approach and interpret Islam from a more spiritual point of view, called Sufism. On the whole they follow the teachings of Ali, the prophet Muhammad's cousin, said to have been the first Muslim.

The oldest centers of the Greek Orthodox

Patriarchate have been located in Istanbul since the 300s. Turkish authorities have never recognized the patriarch as the leader of Orthodox Christianity and continue to enforce strict regulations on the patriarchate. Occasional tensions arise, particularly in times of political tension with neighboring Greece. The state-forced closure of the Orthodox Theological Seminary on Heybeli in the Princes' Islands and the expropriation of patriarchate property remain contentious issues. The patriarchate also continues to refer to Istanbul by its Greek name Kōnstantinoupóleōs (Constantinople).

Jews are also an integral part of the history of Anatolia. Their presence in limited numbers dates back to the 4th century BC, but Anatolia's Jewish population swelled when they fled Iberia during the Spanish Inquisition of the late 15th century. Welcomed by Sultan Beyazıt II, they settled in the empire's largest cities. By the early 1600s there were 30,000 Sephardic Jews and 44 synagogues in Istanbul. Today, Turkey's Jewish community is estimated at 26,000, primarily in Istanbul and İzmir. The *hakkam bashi* (chief rabbi) leads the nation's Jewish community as he did under the *millet* governing system of Sultan Mehmet II. While anti-Semitism has historically been rare, anti-Jewish attacks by Islamic militants have occurred three times since the founding of Israel. There are over three dozen synagogues in Turkey, 20 of which are located in Istanbul. The Zulfaris Synagogue in Istanbul's Karaköy quarter serves as the Jewish Museum of Turkey, inaugurated in 2001 to commemorate the 500 years of Jewish history in Turkey.

LANGUAGE

As mandated by the preamble of Turkey's constitution, Turkish is the country's official language. There are no statistics on the distribution of other languages spoken around the country, but the largest ethnic minority—the Kurds—have been allowed to campaign and broadcast in the Kurmanji language since 2009. One of the TV channels operated by national Turkish Radio and Television (TRT) is broadcast in Kurdish, while TRT stations devote a few hours of televised or radio programming in other languages spoken in Turkey, including Arabic, Bosnian, and Kabardian, a North Caucasian language also known as Circassian.

Countless languages and dialects are spoken nationwide. In Istanbul, minorities that include Armenians, Greeks, and Turkic people from "The Stans"—Turkmenistan, Uzbekistan, and so on—communicate in their own tongues. Turkey's growing expatriate community has propelled the use of English, German, and Russian.

Turkish is an Indo-European language spoken by more than 80 million people worldwide. Its characteristics include vowel harmony, agglutination, and lack of grammatical gender, which is consistent within the Turkic family of Altaic languages spoken throughout Asia. Following Atatürk's linguistic reforms of the 1920s, the Turkish alphabet was romanized from the previous Ottoman system, a variant of the Arabic script. And while Turkic words replaced hundreds of loan words from Arabic and Persian in the previously used Ottoman system, a few have remained. Globalization has also had its effect on the Turkish dictionary in recent years, as an increasing number of English loan words are finding their way into its pages, particularly in business and technological fields. The standard dialect of Turkey is called "Istanbul Turkish."

LITERATURE

Postindependence Turkish literature emerged from the heavily Westernized written works created just before the foundation of the republic. The late Ottoman literary scene was deeply rooted in oral folk traditions and the ideology of modernization. The language and education revolution of 1928, in which the Arabic-based Ottoman script was replaced with an altered Latin alphabet, generated a sweeping literacy movement nationwide. Prose and poetry together with deeply rooted folk traditions would come to constitute Turkey's rich literary scene.

One name currently defines modern Turkish prose abroad: Orhan Pamuk, winner of the 2006 Nobel Prize in Literature, Pamuk is the author of a dozen richly complex novels that analyze Turkish identity through historically based plots. Contentious issues like modernism, secularism, Islamism, Turkic tradition, and the constant pull between East and West are also recurring themes. Vivid representations of cultural and societal clashes in modern-day Turkey were first explored by Ahmet Hamdi Tanpınar in *Huzur* (*A Mind at Peace*, 1949) and *Saatleri Ayarlama Enstitüsü* (*The Time Regulation Institute*, 1961). But the socialist realists also had a voice, boldly discussing society's lower levels and ethnic minorities. No one achieved this as well as short-story writer and poet Sait Faik Abasıyanık (1906-1954). His discussions of Istanbul's destitute and unprivileged classes drew much criticism from nationalist zealots, forcing him to move to Burgazada in Istanbul's Princes' Islands. But writers of the era didn't only portray life in the city. The *köy romanı* (village novel), works based on village life, grew popular among the newly literate generations. Writers of this now-defunct genre were numerous, and the best-known internationally is Yaşar Kemal (born 1923). His *Inci Memed* (*Memed, My Hawk*) made local stories into national epics thanks to the leftist political views he shared with his generation. The various styles of Turkish prose are deeply rooted in the Ottoman era's enchantment with realism and naturalism. This trend peaked in 1932 with the publication of Yakup Kadri Karaosmanoğlu's *Yaban* (*The Wilds*), a narrative that foreshadowed the popular social realism theme and the village novel.

As prose evolved from its roots in the romanticism, realism, and naturalism of the Ottoman era into a complex social commentary, so did poetry. By the 1930s poets like Ahmed Hâşim and Yahyâ Kemâl Beyatlı (1884-1958) were constructing conventional verse in the Ottoman tradition in the newly romanized script. Poems of the time were penned using *Beş Hececiler*, a syllabic metric style that fostered the patriotism of Atatürk's national literature reform. The arrival of Nâzım Hikmet Ran and his free-verse style not only liberated Turkish poetry from narrow syllabic forms but also applied itself ideally to the richly melodic Turkish language. The publication of Hikmet's prose was banned in Turkey, and his controversial communist-friendly ideals caused him to spend much of his adult life in prison, but his free-verse style was adopted by his Turkish contemporaries. To this day, nothing endears the Turkish spirit so deeply as Hikmet's poem *I Love My Country, 1936*, written from a prison in Istanbul. By the early 1940s, the publication of a collection of poems by various writers titled *Garip* (*Strange*) rocked Turkey's literary scene. This manifesto pleaded for a literary form that would mesh with the tastes and needs of a Turkish readership. Writers Orhan Veli Kanık (1914-1950), Melih Cevdet Anday (1915-2002), and Oktay Rifat (1914-1988) weren't the first to campaign against the status quo in the literary genres at the time; they were echoing similar ploys first utilized by French poet Jacques Prévert. Their verse was a corruption of Hikmet's free style, but unlike him they used the vernacular of the time to relate everyday themes popular to the commoner. As expected, the reaction was instantaneous and sharply split; the trio was reviled by the literati while the masses rejoiced. The works of this decade-long movement still sell today and have also found an audience in a new generation. Later Turkish poets are synonymous with Turkey's poetry movement, including Can Yücel (1926-1999), who not only wrote colloquially lyrical prose but also played an integral part in the translation of Turkish poetry, and İsmet Özel (born 1944), whose early leftist influence evolved in a powerful spiritual—to some extent Islamist—form of the genre.

DANCE

Much of indigenous Turkish dance revolves around traditional folk dances. Bar dance is accompanied by the *davul* (leather-lined drum) and *zurna* (shrill pipe) throughout much of Eastern Anatolia and performed by gender-specific groups who line up side-by-side and arm-in-arm. Another line-dance form is the Halay of the eastern provinces, performed to old songs accompanied by the *davul* and *zurna* mixed with the *kaval* (shepherd's pipe), *sipsi* (reed), *çığırtma* (fife), or *bağlama* (three double-stringed instrument). Native to the Black Sea region, the fast and rigorous Horon is a round dance done in close formation while the Zeybek of western Anatolia takes a much slower pace that includes the use of colorful accoutrements. Less formal but just as popular are the *karşılama*, *kolbastı*, *samah*, and the Mediterranean region's *kaşık oyunları* (wooden-spoon dance). Each of these folkloric dances is specific to a region but can still be seen throughout the country. As for belly dancing, the Turks have a unique style of their own. Egyptian dancers glide, while Turkish dancers strut. Egyptian dancers glisten; Turkish dancers sweat. Many artists fuse the two today in cabaret shows throughout the tourism precincts of Turkey.

MUSIC

Turkey's musical genres draw inspiration from Central Asian folk music, Arabic, Persian classical music, ancient Greco-Roman music, and modern European and American pop. The country's rich musical legacy evolved into Turkish classical music, which resembles Greek classical music, and into Turkish folk music.

During the 18th century, the robust sounds of brass and percussion instruments used by the *mehter* (Ottoman Janissary troops) inspired Joseph Haydn's Military Symphony, Beethoven's Symphony No. 9, Mozart's rondo "Alla Turca," and various other operas. From this time on, Turkish cymbals, bass drum, and bells found a permanent place in the symphony orchestra.

On the pop music front, handsome Tarkan is probably the most internationally known Turkish artist, along with songstress Hadise, who placed third in the popular Eurovision Song Contest in 2009. Sezen Aksu's trademark sultry voice and passionate lyrics have enamored generations alongside other popular modern singers, including Ajda Pekkan, Candan Erçetin, and Sertab Erener, the 2003 Eurovision winner. Turkish rock has also had its fair share of attention since coming to prominence in the early 1960s. A trio of artists, Cem Karaca, Erkin Koray, and Barış Manço, were critical in creating a genre that mirrored the global lyrical trend of speaking out for peace and democratization while blending traditional Turkish folk and Western-style rock music. Later, the rise of heavy metal and the Seattle sound in the 1980s and 1990s inspired other artists like Şebnem Ferah, Özlem Tekin, and Teoman. Turkey's diverse musical genres and interests play out in bars and major arenas around the country almost every night of the week.

Essentials

Getting There 415	Food and Drink 424
Getting Around 416	Travel Tips 427
Visas and Officialdom 421	Health and Safety 432
Accommodations 423	Information and Services 437

Getting There

AIR

Turkey's main international transportation hub is Istanbul's **Atatürk International Airport** (IST, 0212/463-3000, www.ataturkairport.com), 20 kilometers west of Istanbul's main tourism district of Sultanahmet; it serves more than 45 million passengers annually in the adjacent *dış hatlar* (international terminal) and *iç hatlar* (domestic terminal). **Sabiha Gökçen International Airport** (SAW, 0216/588-8000, www.sabihagokcen.aero) is Istanbul's second airport, hosting mostly European charter flights as well as some Turkish domestic airlines with generally cheaper airfares. The catch is that Sabiha Gökçen, on the Asian side of the city, is 45 kilometers from Sultanahmet and therefore not as convenient as the larger airport.

Turkey's other international airports are located in **İzmir** (ADB, 0232/455-0000, www.adnanmenderesairport.com), **Bodrum** (BJV, 0252/523-0101, www.milasbodrum.dhmi.gov.tr), **Dalaman** (DLM, 0252/792-5291, www.dalaman.dhmi.gov.tr), **Antalya** (AYT, 0242/330-3030, www.antalya.dhmi.gov.tr), **Konya** (KYA, 0332/239-1343, www.konya.dhmi.gov.tr), and **Ankara** (ESB, 0312/590-4000, www.esenbogaairport.com).

National carrier **Turkish Airlines** (0212/444-0849, www.turkishairlines.com) is part of the global Star Alliance and connects nonstop to many cities around the world, including London, Singapore, and Melbourne and several destinations in the Americas and Europe. **Delta Airlines** (www.delta.com) has flights from the United States to Istanbul. European carriers such as **Lufthansa** (www.lufthansa.com), **Swiss International** (www.swiss.com), and **KLM** (www.klm.com) have competitive fares to Turkish cities and offer direct flights from most European cities. Major Middle Eastern players like **Emirates** (www.emirates.com) and **Qatar** (www.qatarairways.com) also have regular flights to Istanbul connecting to Asia, Africa, and Australia.

BOAT

Car and passenger ferries from Greece arrive at several Turkish ports; **Ferrylines** (www.ferrylines.com) lists all routes to, from, and within Turkey with links to timetables and ticket purchase. During the summer, departures are scheduled regularly, often every day. Ferries to the Greek and Turkish islands tend to cease around September or October due to weather and low passenger numbers, starting up again in spring. Ferry connections from Turkey to the Ukraine and Russia can also be found on the Ferrylines website.

Also in summer, a flotilla of cruise liners docks at major ports like Bodrum, Kuşadası, İzmir, and Istanbul, enabling passengers to explore these cities en route from Italy, Croatia, or Greece. Start your search for a dream cruise via **Cruise Lines International Association** (www.cruising.org) or **Cruise Critic** (www.cruisecritic.com).

TRAIN

International train services to Turkey are not as frequent as they once were as domestic rail lines are upgraded to high-speed services, and countries like Greece recover from the financial crisis that saw rail services to Istanbul end. Daily departures to and from the Bulgarian capital Sofia (€19-28, 12.5 hours) and Bucharest in Romania (€38-56, 20 hours) are still possible with the *Bosphorus Express,* while the *Trans Asia* service to and from Tabriz (€24.80) and Tehran (€33.30) in Iran departs from Ankara Gar and Kayseri once per week. As high-speed railroads are upgraded, expect more services to international ports from major cities like Istanbul, Ankara, and Kayseri. Contact **Turkish State Railways** (0212/520-6575 212, www.tcdd.gov.tr) for updated services and itineraries.

CAR

You can drive in a private vehicle across the borders from Bulgaria, Greece, or any of Turkey's eight neighboring countries as long as you present your passport, International Driving Permit, car registration (with the owner's name and details of the car), and an international green card (insurance) at the point of entry. The car can stay in Turkey for a period of six months. Contact the **Turkish Touring and Automobile Club** (0212/282-8140, www.turing.org.tr) for information on obtaining the green card.

Getting Around

Depending on your destination, the best way to travel within Turkey is by air. Cheap fares—sometimes as low as US$35 one-way across the country—and short 45-minute flight times to anywhere in central and western Turkey eliminate the much longer, though pleasurable, road trip. Considering the cost of gasoline in Turkey—the highest in the world at 5TL per liter—the saving are obvious. The most expensive round-trip flights from Istanbul to the Mediterranean for two people, plus transfers, are almost half the price of driving privately once you account for car rental, insurance, and gas. But if road trips are your thing, there's arguably no better place to drive than Turkey. If you really want to go solo by car, avoid the long trips and choose short daily jaunts instead.

Bus travel gives first-time visitors the best of both worlds. It allows scenic views of the countryside without the high cost of driving. Bus travel is more time-consuming than flying, but domestic coach companies have top-of-the-line luxurious coaches with pursers to

Istanbul's Eminönü port, where you can board the Bosphorus ferry from Europe to Asia

attend to your needs. Coach fares tend to be similar in high season and off-season, unlike airfares, but they are a bit lower during summer. As high-speed rail lines are commissioned, it also makes sense to choose rail over coaches when the rail service exists.

AIR

There are plenty of reputable airlines in Turkey. Leg room can be limited, so upgrade to an exit-row seat if you can, or take solace in the fact the flight time is less than 60 minutes. The national carrier, **Turkish Airlines** (0212/444-0849, www.turkishairlines.com), is often the most expensive, but you can collect frequent-flyer miles with a long list of their partner airlines. This includes their budget airline **Anadolu Jet** (0850/333-2538, www.anadolujet.com), which is cheaper and has fewer flights per day to major domestic locations. **Onur Air** (0850/210-6687, www.onurair.com.tr) and **Atlas Jet** (0850/222-0000, www.atlasjet.com) also offer reduced fares, and like Turkish Airlines include a small complimentary snack no matter the flight time. **Pegasus Airlines** (0850/250-0737, www.flypgs.com), on the other hand, can require the purchase of additional meals and sometimes seat allocation on top of the advertised ticket price. Other domestic flights are available through **Bora Jet** (0212/465-2878, www.borajet.com.tr) and **SunExpress** (444-0797, www.sunexpress.com). Choosing a carrier comes down to several factors. First is the best flight times, then deciding on which airport to use if Istanbul is part of the itinerary. Istanbul's Atatürk Airport is much easier and quicker to access than Sabiha Gökçen on the Asian side if you're based in Sultanahmet. It pays to plan ahead, especially during religious holidays such as Şeker Bayramı (Eid ul-Fitr, right after Ramadan) and Kurban Bayramı (Eid al-Adha), when the demand for domestic travel is enormous and prices go up accordingly. If you're lugging heavy suitcases, also make sure your discount fare includes 20 kilograms for checked luggage; otherwise you will be charged extra at the airport. Better rates for excess luggage can be purchased from your airline's website prior to departure.

CAR

Congestion, along with one-way traffic infrastructure, manic drivers, and the extreme difficulty of finding parking in the largest cities, can make driving in Turkey stressful. But driving but will give you the flexibility to venture to sites that a *dolmuş* or coach cannot reach, and nothing beats driving through the Turkish countryside. Formerly shoddy highways and signage have been updated to European standards, and city streets—outside Istanbul, İzmir, and Ankara—are easy to navigate. Driving under the influence, once a common practice nationwide, has been virtually eradicated thanks to ubiquitous sobriety checkpoints. both provincial and municipal police strictly enforce speed limits.

An International Driving Permit is not legally required but will help smooth the experience. Major international car rental companies are located at all airports and at major city centers nationwide; vehicles can be reserved via their websites. Among them are **Avis** (www.avis.com), **National Car Rental** (www.nationalcar.com), and **Hertz** (www.hertz.com). **Budget** (www.budget.com) also has a small presence in Turkey. German giant **Sixt** (www.sixt.com.tr) has numerous locations nationwide, providing one of the largest fleets available along with budget prices. Promotional rates as well as roadside and medical assistance packages provided by some vendors may come in handy when driving in a foreign country. Towns and cities also have car rental companies with basic sedans from as little as 70TL per day.

Turkey uses the metric system, so distances and speed are measured in kilometers. Drivers sit on the left side of the vehicle and drive on the right side, as in continental Europe and the Americas, but the road rules here are considered merely a guide and are rarely taken too seriously. Keep your eyes ahead to watch for vehicles entering your lane; look left and right, too, because some drivers use emergency lanes and shoulders to pass; and watch the speedometer to avoid fines from the traffic police (*polis*). Crosswalks are ignored, and drivers rarely give pedestrians the right of way. If you stop for a crosswalk, a barrage of honking from other drivers will surely follow.

Expect lots of activity in traffic-clogged locations such as Istanbul, İzmir, and other large cities, where you might think the car horn was Turkey's unofficial second language. In Turkey, it's not considered rude to get enthusiastic with the horn. Drivers honk to say "hello," "thank you," "hurry up," and "coming through." Continual honking means a wedding is taking place or a young man is entering the military service; expect a convoy to follow.

Because of the heavy traffic and the stress of navigating narrow one-way streets, driving in big cities is not recommended. Avoid renting a car in the cities, or park it and walk or use public transportation. Outside the cities, the experience is more relaxing, with many reporting courteous driver behavior and highways in excellent condition. Rural roads between villages are less maintained, so watch for potholes and oncoming traffic on unmarked roads.

Toll roads exist outside the big cities and are marked red on maps with the letter O for *otoyol*. Highways marked green are multilane expressways sometimes doubling as toll roads, and blue signposted highways are a combination of single and multilane roads with no toll. The speed limits for these are clearly marked: 120 km/h for highways, 90 km/h for open roads, and 50 km/h in built-up areas. White signs indicate exits, and brown signs point to the location of tourism sites. The tolls you're likely to encounter in a standard vehicle or motorcycle are: Istanbul to Edirne (O-3, 7.25TL), Istanbul to Kınalı for Eceabat and Çanakkale (O-3, 3TL), İzmir to Çeşme (O-32, 2.25TL), İzmir to Aydın for Pamukkale (O-31, 3TL), and Istanbul to Ankara (O-4/O-20, 15TL). Crossing either of the Bosphorus bridges costs 4.25TL per vehicle. Fees increase as the size of the vehicle increases. To pay for the tolls, your car rental company will place an HGS toll card on the windshield that automatically registers payments as you pass through tollgates. Cash and credit cards are not accepted at gates so make sure your vehicle has an HGS card and confirm the system for adding credit with your car-rental company before driving out of their yard. As a backup, credit can be purchased at PTT post offices around the country. Finally, remember to drive through HGS gates for HGS cards and OGS gates for OGS cards to avoid fines.

Turkey's fuel costs are the highest in the world at 5TL per liter for unleaded, 4.75TL for diesel, and 2.75TL for LPG. Petrol stations are situated throughout the country and feature restaurants and other amenities.

Equip yourself with a good map. A satellite GPS navigator is provided by all the rental companies listed above, but GPS technology is not entirely reliable at detecting one-way streets. Keep your International Driving Permit, rental car papers, and insurance documents in the car with you at all times. In the event of an accident, do not move the car—this could be viewed as fleeing the scene of an accident. Call the traffic police by dialing **154,** and place reflector triangles stored in the trunk of the car in front and behind the vehicle to warn oncoming traffic.

For more information about highways and tolls, visit the **Directorate of Highways** (www.kgm.gov.tr).

BUS

All passenger vehicles display their point of origin and destination on the front windshield, either on an electronic display or with more basic signage. This includes the three types of bus services mentioned in this book: intercity coaches, municipal buses within cities, and *dolmuşlar* (communal taxis).

Domestic long-distance coach companies operate fleets of European-branded buses that must be updated every other year. Reputable coach companies in Turkey include **Ulusoy** (444-1888, www.ulusoy.com.tr), **Kamil Koç** (444-0562, www.kamilkoc.com.tr), **Pamukkale Turizm** (0850/333-3535,

Dolmuş—Ride-Sharing the Turkish Way

Translating literally as "stuffed," the *dolmuş*—communal taxi—is one of the main modes of transportation in Turkey. The convenience and reduced price are ideal, if you don't mind sharing a minivan or sedan with perfect strangers. Yes, it does sounds a little daunting, but go on—get in, take a seat, and get lost in the culture. You won't regret it for the savings nor the experience.

Although its popularity is declining, the *dolmuş* is still very much in use in the country's rural areas, operating to and from the railroad or bus station to villages, towns, and even city centers. This type of transportation provides an alternative to costly taxis and coaches and is more likely to go farther off the beaten track than municipal buses.

These communal taxis travel the streets between two defined stops, picking up and dropping off passengers on request. The rules of engagement are easy. Look for the *dolmuş* with your chosen destination written on its windshield or body and flag it down. There's no need to walk to a defined stop or chase one down (unless you're in Marmaris, which has designated stops). Generally, men should sit with men and women with women in more traditional areas, but often it's a matter of getting in first for a seat. As you would back home, give up your seat for an elderly person, pregnant woman, and women with children. Enable older couples to sit together if seating is limited.

By law, the fare (which is rarely more than 5TL pp) must be posted in plain view, usually on the lower right side of the windshield. Pay the driver in cash directly at any stage of the journey or when requested. If you're stuffed in the back, cash can be passed along between passengers to the driver, who can often be found maneuvering through traffic and collecting fares while talking on the phone.

Expect occasional odd looks in rural areas, especially if you're traveling solo. These folks mean no harm—they're usually curious to know why a foreigner would take the time to visit their hometown. When it's time to stop, just shout out to the driver *tamam captain* (OK, captain), which usually does the trick for a *yabancı* (foreigner).

Hotels, tourism offices, and coach companies can inform you of the *dolmuş* routes near you and where to flag them down. Hop on board like a seasoned traveler and enjoy the ride.

---

www.pamukkale.com.tr), **Varan** (0212/692-9595, www.varan.com.tr), and **Metro Turizm** (444-3455, www.metroturizm.com.tr), with the latter two offering international routes to Greece and Bulgaria. Most have individual LCD entertainment systems (in Turkish) and complimentary tea and coffee services; some even have Wi-Fi and USB ports, but none have toilets on board, so plan ahead for a comfortable ride. Stops are made every two hours or less for refreshments and toilet breaks. Roadhouses charge 1TL to use the restroom facilities, but this does not guarantee pristine conditions. Pack tissues and an open mind and don't be surprised if only squat toilets are available. Some general rules for passengers on coaches: Your ticket will have a seat (*koltuk*) number. Use this and know, if traveling alone, then men will sit with men and women with women; if you're traveling together, you can sit side by side. Children need an extra seat or can sit in your lap if you want to save on fares. Silence your phone, as many people asleep on long journeys and dislike being woken. Where possible, take night buses to save some money and time—just pack an inflatable pillow to sleep.

Fares for coaches to the same destination may vary among companies as they can take different routes between city *otogarlar* (bus stations). Buy your ticket beforehand from travel agencies or coach sales offices in cities or at the *otogar*—usually some distance out of town. Avoid online sales, as these can be problematic. Arriving at an *otogar* is an experience. First, an army of salesmen are likely to greet you and convince you that, coincidentally, one of their coaches is leaving momentarily for your destination. Since this is rarely true, if you don't have a ticket, take the time to visit several offices before committing yourself to a deal. A note about travel times: The larger carriers post both travel distances and estimated journey times on their websites. Be aware that an eight-hour drive by car, for example, can increase to 10 hours or more with a coach due to meal and toilet stops and lower speed limits.

Within the city centers, fares on municipal buses can no longer be purchased with cash. An electronic debit card is required, although if you happen to board a bus without a card, a helpful local will usually swipe their card for you. Just pay them the equivalent fare in cash. These cards can be purchased from kiosks near bus stops and in train stations, as described in the destination chapters.

The *dolmuş* is as historical, particularly in Istanbul, as it is convenient. These communal taxis, either sedans or minivans, depending on the city's style, carry multiple passengers and stop at any point along their specified route for a fare based on the distance traveled. Cheaper than a taxi and more expensive than a municipal bus, this transportation system is ingenious: If a *dolmuş* has empty seats, its driver will honk and approach the curb upon seeing a potential fare; if it's full, it'll just keep driving. Pay your fare on the *dolmuş*. Fellow passengers will pass cash from those sitting in the rear up to the driver, who will return the appropriate change. The timetable for *dolmuş* services around the country can change unexpectedly. If demand is low, they'll stop doing late-night runs, so it pays always to check when the last *dolmuş* will run to avoid getting stranded away from your hotel.

TAXI

Taxis are a great way to get around in Turkey, particularly for short hops. The benefits of this type of travel include door-to-door service and round-the-clock availability. Taxi fares in Turkey are inexpensive compared to those in Western countries, but there are a lot of shady characters driving these ubiquitous yellow vehicles. To avoid being scammed, follow these important tips.

If traveling from a hotel or restaurant, ask an attendant to call you a taxi. These businesses commit to a single taxi company in exchange for their honesty and timely pickup of guests. Hailing a taxi on the street is not advised for tourists, but if you have to, make sure to board only a yellow taxi with signage on the front doors that indicates the name and number of the taxi stand. Some 2,000 unaffiliated illegal cabs still roam the streets of major cities. These dubious drivers are almost single-handedly responsible for the bad reputation their trade has earned among visitors. Any taxi that does not display this signage on their doors is considered illegal. Many of these roam tourist-heavy areas seeking their next fare—or victim.

Other typical schemes include taking a meandering route that takes twice as long to get to your destination. There isn't much to do except wait until you've arrived to argue about the fare. Lastly, there's a couple of scams to be on the lookout for, including: You offer a 50-lira note to pay for the fare and the shady driver hands back a counterfeit 50-lira note, claiming that he doesn't have change after leafing through a large stack of money. Also, until 2013, the five-lira note was the same color as the 50, allowing some cabbies to confuse passengers unsuspectingly by claiming that you handed over a fiver instead. The five-lira note is now purple to prevent this from happening. As a rule, check the money you hand over, and carry small denominations to avoid this type of "misunderstanding."

Most taxis in the cities operate on the meter, so there is no need to negotiate a fare upfront. When boarding a taxi, check that the meter has been activated. Long distance journeys such as private tours and airport transfers will have a set fee outside city areas; these can be negotiated.

Visas and Officialdom

Most foreign nationals need a passport that's valid for at least six months and an e-visa to enter Turkey for tourism and trade. The official e-visa website (www.evisa.gov.tr) has a list of nationalities requiring an e-visa to enter Turkey. To obtain the e-visa, complete the online form and pay a fee with a credit card or debit card prior to your arrival. The fee for a 90-day single- or multiple-entry visa varies by country, but as a guide, in 2014 U.S. and British passport holders pay US$20, and Australians and Canadians pay US$60. The visa is emailed to you upon payment. Print it out and carry with you on your travels, presenting it to security officials when requested. The e-visa website has a comprehensive list of frequently asked questions for potential travelers. Read this information prior to applying to understand the system. Visas could once be acquired painlessly at kiosks just before passport control at Turkish airports and ports, but this system is being phased out. Overstaying your visa can result in a fine, deportation, or ban from reentering the country.

STUDENT, WORK, AND RESIDENCY VISAS

Foreign passport holders seeking to work or study in Turkey must first obtain a special visa from a Turkish embassy or consulate prior to arrival. Without this visa, foreigners are ineligible for employment or school enrollment. A residency permit will be required for anyone wishing to stay in Turkey for more than 90 days. This permit does not allow you to work, but can be obtained after arrival in a process that makes any expatriate shudder in fear, as the process is fraught with inefficiencies. Rumors abound that change is afoot; normally, the process involves making an e-*randevu* (appointment) online through the police department's Yabancılar Şube Müdürlüğü (Foreigners Branch Directorate, http://yabancilar.iem.gov.tr). At the appointment you present copies of your passport, e-visa, several passport-size photos, and proof that you have enough funds in your Turkish bank account to stay for the duration requested. The best way is to start networking on arrival via Facebook pages for foreigners in Turkey or post on **InterNations** (www.internations.org) to ask fellow foreigners what the current process is.

TURKISH EMBASSIES AND CONSULAR OFFICES

The Republic of Turkey maintains embassies and consulates all around the world, often in multiple cities in one country. They are responsible for processing new and renewed Turkish passports, registration of births and marriages, and requests for Turkish citizenship. For a full list of embassies maintained by the Republic of Turkey, visit www.konsolosluk.gov.tr.

FOREIGN EMBASSIES IN TURKEY

Your country's embassy or consulate in Turkey should be contacted immediately if you need emergency medical referrals, assistance with legal issues such as arrests, or passport renewal in the event of a lost document. Many nations maintain embassies in Ankara and smaller consular offices in Istanbul. You can contact embassies in the capital, Ankara: **U.S. Embassy** (110 Atatürk Blv., 06100 Kavaklıdere, 0312/455-5555, http://turkey.usembassy.gov), **Australian Embassy** (Uğur Mumcu Cd. 88, 7th Fl., 06700 Gaziosmanpaşa, 0312/459-9500, www.turkey.embassy.gov.au), **Embassy of the United Kingdom** (Şehit Ersan Cd. 46/A, 06690 Çankaya, 0312/455-3344, http://ukinturkey.fco.gov.uk), and **Canadian Embassy** (Cinnah Cd. 58, 06690 Çankaya, 0312/409-2700, www.turkey.gc.ca). A database with contact details for all embassies and consulates worldwide can be found at http://embassy.goabroad.com.

CUSTOMS

While luggage is rarely checked on entry, be aware that the Turkish government maintains a list of items that may be brought into the country duty-free. This includes gifts to the value of €300 for travelers over age 15, €145 for those aged under 15; tobacco products limited to 200 cigarettes, 50 cigars, and 200 grams of tobacco; one 1-liter bottle or two 700-750-milliliter bottles of wine or spirits, for travelers age 18 and over; five bottles of perfume up to 120 milliliters each; medications for personal use; and food products like chocolate (up to 1 kilogram), coffee (1.5 kilograms), or tea (500 grams). Unlimited amounts of foreign currency can be brought in. Carrying, using, or importing drugs considered illegal elsewhere is forbidden and strictly punishable by law. Certain weapons and associated military equipment, such as night-vision binoculars, aren't allowed into the country without an import license. Permission must also be obtained for filming professionally in Turkey.

In terms of exporting, to avoid complications on leaving the country, register valuables with no commercial purpose, such as jewelry, over the value of US$15,000 to customs on arrival so you can take them with you when you leave. If you purchased goods over this value in Turkey, keep the receipt to prove you made the purchase through legally exchanged currency. Receipts for any valuable items acquired during your stay may be requested at your departure. Large items such as expensive carpets require a valid official Certificate of Origin. This is not only necessary to export the item from Turkey but also to import it into other countries. Furthermore, Turkish law states that anything older than 100 years or dating from the late 19th century needs to be authenticated by a government or museum officials before receiving its travel papers. Dealers should provide the certificate or directions for receiving permission for export upon purchase. Don't try to export them without permission as customs officials worldwide are well versed in Turkish antiquities and valuables thanks to an international database. Minerals are exportable, but only with a special permit granted by the General Directorate of Mineral Research and Exploration (www.mta.gov.tr).

Global Refund (www.globalblue.com), the world's leading tax-refund company, offers tax refunds for nonresidents on purchased goods over 100TL from registered sellers. Refunds can be obtained in the departure hall of Turkish airports.

POLICE

Turkey is a relatively safe country. The main worry for visitors is personal theft. Be aware of your surroundings and personal belongings at all times. For immediate police assistance, dial toll-free **115** in cities and **156** for Jandarma assistance in country areas. For medical emergencies dial **112** or to get police to traffic accidents **154.**

The **Gümrük Muhafaza** (Turkish Police Force) is tasked with enforcing the law in the cities and supporting customs officers at airports and border crossings. Police officers wear navy-blue uniforms and caps; patrol vehicles are white with a blue horizontal stripe and the "Polis" logo on both front doors and the front hood. Motorcycle patrol officers have black shirts and pants with red trim. Police officers are required to present their ID when approaching citizens.

The second branch, the **Jandarma** (Gendarmes), is part of military law-enforcement and responds to incidents outside urban areas, including many tourism areas. These officers wear dark green trousers and light green shirts with red-and-blue markings on the collar. This branch also maintains a traffic division, known as **Jandarma Trafik,** which patrols country roads.

If you come in contact with any of these officers, respectfully present your passport. In the event of a traffic violation, present your passport, driver's license, and vehicle rental contract. Turkish police are authorized to collect traffic fines on the spot. While officers generally don't speak English, their command post can often provide someone who does.

Accommodations

Properties in Turkey are categorized using a system that rates them with stars or classes. Similar schemes are used in other countries, but they're not consistent throughout Europe. The amenities and services guaranteed by a five-star hotel in Paris might not be on par with one rated five stars in Turkey. An older hotel may receive a fifth star because it offers a pool, but a new seaside construction without a water feature will receive just four. The elusive fifth star applies to properties that provide conference space, pools, nightclubs, and so on. It does not take remodeling nor the age of a property into consideration. Most bed-and-breakfasts and historical inns are not rated by stars but are listed as "special class" or "a class" hotels. These are generally smaller than three- and four-star properties but offer a historical aspect or a certain charm and are worth booking.

Online booking agents such as Booking.com and Hostelworld.com are used extensively in Turkey. These websites contain all the information required for deciding on a lodging suited to you. Prices, amenities, photos, availability, rankings compared to nearby hotels, and reviews by guests are included. Tripadvisor.com should be used with caution, as anyone can post reviews and competing business owners have been known to sabotage competitors with fake reviews.

Booking through online agents is easy. You need to sign up and sign in, but this can eventually lead to further discounts if you book under the same account. Confirmed bookings don't need to be printed; just bring the booking reference number for your host to locate you in the system.

It pays to compare rates over the phone or email against online prices, as savings can often be found. Double-check specials and complimentary services, as these often go astray on Web bookings. Rates for the properties listed in this book are generally for standard doubles in peak season and include breakfast and taxes, unless otherwise stated. They should be used as a guide only for prices to know which hotels are aimed at budget, backpacker, and boutique travelers. Inns and other properties rated three stars or below have a couple of issues: First, expect basic amenities; most provide air-conditioning, but other comforts such as bar fridges, big-screen TVs, satellite TV, and shower screens in bathrooms may be missing. Additional comforts like complimentary tea and coffee services may also be hard to come by. Overall, though, the savings are worth it. Another advantage of these budget lodgings is the hospitality, including sumptuous rustic meals often prepared on-site by the family. Boutique hotels have the same genuine service but with more luxury than most and are often a better deal than five-star lodgings that can be outdated and remotely located.

Turkish lira and euros are used interchangeably to price hotels. Always confirm that currency when booking to avoid confusion.

Fewer hotels are available in winter, as some business owners shut down for the season.

Food and Drink

FOOD

The backbone of Turkish cuisine is Mediterranean in essence: seasonal fresh vegetables and fruits, dairy products, and meat and seafood. A traditional Turkish meal at home or in a restaurant is invariably the same: an array of cold then hot meze platters accompanied with copious amounts of freshly baked bread followed by the main meal, either grilled or stewed fish or kebabs. Salt, olive oil, lemon, dried oregano, parsley, chili peppers, and even pomegranate juice promote foods' natural flavors.

Novices to the Turkish table will find it hard to pace themselves when confronted with such a rich array of starters. Favorites among mezes include *patlican salatası* (pureed eggplant salad), *zeytinyağlı* (seasonal vegetables cooked in olive oil), *dolma* (herbed and spiced rice with pine nuts stuffed in grape or cabbage leaves), *sigara böreği* (cheese-filled rolled phyllo pastry), and *ezme* (spicy tomato and red pepper salad), indigenous to southeast Anatolia.

Ordering main courses is simple. *Kebab* means roasted meat or fish that hasn't necessarily been skewered. *İzgara* denotes grilling, while *buğlama* specifies the steaming process used in savory fish preparations. Among the most popular kebabs are the *döner kebab* (slices of layered lamb roasted on a spit), *İskender kebab* (slices of layered lamb stacked on chunks of *pide* bread, drizzled with tomato sauce, and a generous amount of melted butter with a dollop of yogurt), *Urfa kebab* (roasted ground lamb skewers), and *Adana kebab* (the spicy version of *Urfa kebab*). The blue-collar *köfte* is a meatball served with grilled tomatoes, chili peppers, and sometimes onions. Chunks of meat laced with handsome amounts of aromatic spices, root vegetables, tomatoes, and peppers create a perfect synthesis in *güveç*, a stewed dish. The same ingredients roasted tandoori-style is called *saç kavurma*.

Turks don't live on meat alone. The diet of western and central Anatolians revolves around produce, fish, grains, and an insatiable appetite for olive oil. Vegetables find their way into the traditional *mevsim salatası* (seasonal salad) or seared delicately in olive oil. Turks don't fear carbs in the least. The very Turkic dumpling dish *mantı*, doused in garlicky yogurt, is a must for pasta lovers. And while rice may be of Asian origin, pilafs are strictly Anatolian. Try the *perde pilavı*, a richly spiced, nutty rice in a crusty pastry shell. Turkish breads are an institution on their own: the oven-baked *pide*—the Turkish version of pita bread—as well as *lavaş* and the ubiquitous crunchy white bread found in ample volume on breakfast tables or halved and stuffed with tender slices of *döner* or *köfte*. The *lahmacun*—as popular in Turkey as the hot dog is in the United States—is a thin clay oven-baked pizza slathered with finely minced onions, peppers, and lamb. The *gözleme* (savory crepe filled with spinach, cheese, potato, or meat) and the *simit* (large sesame-crusted tea ring) are great for quick bites between sights.

"Eat sweet, talk sweet" is a popular Turkish idiom, and it's reflected in rich desserts. After-dinner sweets fall into two categories: dairy- or flour-based. Dairy-based sweets include the rich oven-baked *sütlaç* (rice pudding topped with hazelnut crumbs) and the simple yet sumptuous *irmik helvası,* which combines semolina, pine nuts, sugar, milk, and loads of butter. Flour-based desserts are crowned by the *baklava,* delicate layers of phyllo dough drenched in sugar syrup covering generous amounts of either walnuts or pistachios. Another sweet tidbit is the *lokum,* known in the West as the Turkish delight. This chewy candy is composed of cornstarch, sugar, and a variety of flavors, including rose and pistachio.

A couple of soups (*çorbalar*) round out Turkey's food. Club-goers swear that *işkembe,* a garlicky tripe soup, is a surefire hangover cure. *Cacık* is a cold soup made of diluted yogurt, finely diced cucumbers, garlic, mint, and dill. Lentil soup is served on most menus and is ordered at the beginning of a meal to start an authentically Turkish feast.

Food intolerances are largely unknown in Turkey, although international tourism businesses are becoming increasingly aware of terms like "gluten-free" and "lactose intolerant." Inform your host of your food allergies, and they will oblige with a dish gentle on your stomach.

BEVERAGES

Çay (tea) pervades the Turkish life and is enjoyed ritually throughout the day. It is served piping hot and strong in small tulip-shaped glasses with a tiny spoon to stir in the two sugars that accompany the glass on a dainty saucer. The elegant tea glass is narrower in the middle to ensure that the brew retains its temperature. Turkish tea is a form of black tea that originates from the Rize region on the Black Sea coast. A perfect serving of tea, brewed in a double kettle known as a *çaydanlık,* is one tablespoon per person topped with boiling water and left to infuse for at least 15 minutes. If the brew is too strong, request its more diluted version, *acık çay,* which has more water. *Elma çayı* (apple tea) is decaffeinated and tastes just like heated apple juice.

Sadly, Turkey's traditional coffee culture is slowly being overtaken by Western frappuccinos and cappuccinos; Starbucks and Kahve Dünyası have replaced the time-honored *kahvehaneler* (coffeehouses). The coffee tradition was once so pervasive in Turkey that its name made its way into the Turkish word for breakfast (*kahvaltı,* meaning preceding or during coffee time). Officially forbidden in 1511 by orthodox imams for its stimulating effects, coffee was soon so popular among Istanbul's Ottoman hierarchy that the general ban was lifted just a decade later by Sultan Selim I, with Mecca's Grand Mufti Mehmet Ebussuud el-İmadi's enthusiastic approval. A perfect demitasse begins with the finest coffee beans, ground almost to a powder before they are mixed with a cup of purified water. It can be sweetened at this point with sugar. Order it *sade* (unsweetened), *az şekerli* (lightly sweetened), *orta* (sweetened), or *şekerli* (quite sweet). The mixture then cooks slowly over a flame until it comes to a boil, generating thick foam, before it's tipped into the cup. Begin sipping when it arrives. Once you've finished it, cover the cup with the saucer and flip it over

the right ingredients for a feast for the eyes and belly

Turkish Coffee: A Disappearing Institution

Türk kahvesi, Turkish coffee, is an art and ritual that is slowly entering the history books. Coffee culture actually got its start in the streets of Istanbul's Tahtakale neighborhood around the mid-1500s. A couple of Syrians had brought coffee to Istanbul—the center of Islam at that time—and began serving it as a brewed beverage to mark an 11 o'clock coffee break enjoyed by the palace staff.

A perfect Turkish coffee is served in a demitasse, with about three millimeters of froth. Any bubble appearing along the top of the beverage is considered a *nazar* (bad omen), and popping it prior to drinking is a must. The quality of the brew depends on the grade of the coffee, its grind, and how long it is cooked over a low fire. It takes about one teaspoon of finely ground coffee mixed in with the amount of water that fills the cup. Together, the grounds and water are gently mixed inside a copper *cezve*—a small rimmed, long-handled pot with a heavy flat bottom—and slowly brought to a boil. When served, the dregs settle at the bottom of the cup.

Ordering a shot of stovetop-made coffee is as simple as stating your sugar preference: *sade* (unsweetened), *az şekerli* (lightly sweetened), *orta* (normally sweetened), and *şekerli* (sweet). The liquid is best sipped, not gulped. If that first taste transforms you from a skeptic to a believer, recapturing that experience at home is as easy as purchasing coffee paraphernalia and grounds from the right purveyor. Line up at **Kurukahveci Mehmet Efendi** (Tahmiş Sk. 6, Eminönü, 0212/511-4262, www.mehmetefendi.com) just outside the main building of the Spice Bazaar in Istanbul to grab the necessary items.

Divining coffee grinds is also an art. Some cafés hire fortune-tellers who read the strains left by the wet grounds that have trickled down from the bottom of an inverted cup and come to rest on the saucer. Who knows? The key to your future might just rest on the bottom of that next cup of Turkish coffee. For coffee readings in English, head to one of the soothsaying outlets of **Symbols Cafe** (www.symbolcafe.com). Their branch in Beyoğlu (Ayhan Işık Sk. 23, 0212/292-5354) is the closest for most in Istanbul, but book ahead to reserve an English-speaking reader.

to allow the remaining grounds to coat the inside of the cup. After it cools, look inside the cup. You may be able to tell your fortune from the shapes and ridges formed by the grounds.

By day Turks enjoy *ayran*, a refreshing, slightly salted yogurt drink. By night, locally brewed Efes beer and *rakı*—colloquially referred to as "lion's milk" and Turkey's national drink—reigns supreme in nonconservative areas. *Rakı* and *ayran* have been the source of an open debate of late with religious prime minister Erdoğan claiming *ayran* as Turkey's national drink, much to the displeasure of Turkey's secular society. Erdoğan's angst probably comes from the alcohol content of *rakı*. At 65 percent alcohol, this beverage is distilled from grapes and then redistilled with aniseed. It is imbibed neat or diluted with water over ice and is a great accompaniment to mezes, best sipped slowly and in moderation. *Ayran*, on the other hand, is nonalcoholic and made by watering down yogurt and adding a pinch of salt. Westerners are often reluctant to try it, unaware that yogurt can be just as delicious savory as it is when sweetened with fruit.

RESTAURANTS

There are several types of restaurants in Turkey: the canteen-style *lokanta*, where various prepared dishes are displayed behind glass; the Turkish tavern, known as the *meyhane*; and the *restoran*, which typically but not always means a more upscale eatery that either specializes in fish or meat, and sometimes both.

Turkish eateries don't always abide by a set menu; sometimes they don't even have one. Offerings at a *meyhane* are displayed in refrigerated cases at the entrance and on the meze platters whisked about by enthusiastic waiters. If something is to your liking, simply point to it and confirm the price. Ordering a main course after platters of mezes is not obligatory, nor is accepting all the mezes that are brought to the table. If you do opt for fish, ensure that the price is settled before ordering it. The cost of fish is measured either by its weight in kilograms or per portion. It's perfectly OK to order half a portion, or even to negotiate a lower price for the entire amount if you're paying cash.

Travel Tips

WHAT TO PACK

Pack a **wheeled suitcase,** as backpacks are easy bait for pickpockets and can be too bulky for public transit. Limit **clothing** to versatile, wrinkle-free pieces. T-shirts, jeans, and flat shoes are the way to go for both men and women. Five-star restaurant may require more formal attire, but generally, casual dress is the look for day and night around the country. Bar and nightclub attire ranges from casual to hip and fancy depending on the location, but high heels don't fare well on cobbled streets and may be best left at home. Coastal weather often changes quickly, so light jackets and pashminas are handy. July and August call for T-shirts and shorts in coastal towns, and reef shoes are great for those who intend to walk canyons or pebble beaches. Clothing in Turkey is also inexpensive enough to purchase on the go.

Women are only required to don headscarves when visiting Islamic places of worship. Long skirts are also ideal for women planning to visit mosques.

For **laptops** or **digital cameras,** an adapter for continental European two-pin sockets is necessary. If you bring devices with a motor like a **blow-dryer,** you'll also need a 220-volt converter. **Smartphones** can be handy to access the free Wi-Fi spots found all over Turkey. Finally, a **money belt** is essential to stash important items such as a copy of your passport, credit cards, transportation tickets, trip itineraries, currency, driver's license, and critical medical information.

HIRING A GUIDE

Deciding on a guide should involve a few checks on reputation and credentials. First, travel agencies in Turkey must be registered with TURSAB, an agency responsible for accrediting and maintaining the standards of Turkish travel services. Most companies will display their TURSAB number on their website to show they are accredited. Second, guides to historical attractions and museums must complete a three-year university course to qualify as an accredited guide. Once complete, they must wear a photo ID around their neck so government officials can quality-control tourism areas, penalizing those who are not accredited. This degree, however, does not guarantee excellent service, as some guides still fail miserably in entertaining the interests of their guests over the sound of their own voice. Learning who the best guides are through word of mouth or through websites like Tripadvisor.com will go a long way to securing the services of a guide that others have enjoyed. Like all other services, it pays to shop around to get the best price with the best guide possible. These days, most agencies will advertise their prices online, but custom tours require a quote, as the itinerary and add-ons will differ depending on the number in the group. For cheaper options, opt for walking tours where possible rather than bus tours, simply because you can rub shoulders with locals and avoid long delays in traffic.

ACCESS FOR TRAVELERS WITH DISABILITIES

Although facilities for physically disabled people have improved in the last decade, concessions for museum entry and public transportation for those with special needs are almost nonexistent. The government has installed ramps at most national museums and transportation hubs to facilitate wheelchair access, but uneven paths, high curbs, and cobbled streets can make the journey tough going. Parts of Istanbul, such as Beyoğlu, may be particularly difficult because they're built on steep inclines, while towns such as Bodrum, İzmir, Fethiye, Antalya, and those in Cappadocia are generally flat and ideal locations for wheelchair users. Newer buildings, including hotels and most metro stations, are equipped with elevators. Most of the buildings of historical interest, however, particularly in the big cities, are not built for such technology, so stair lifts have been installed to assist. Inside buildings, narrow corridors and doorways, lack of restrooms for wheelchair users, uneven flooring, and out-of-the-way facilities make for an arduous outing even for the fittest. Hotels, restaurants, and public transportation are getting better at catering to wheelchair access, and if needed, staff or passersby are often obliging to help get chairs up ramps. Some of the larger hotel chains have rooms catering to the needs of wheelchair users. In terms of getting to Turkey, contact Turkish Airlines to see if you and your companion are eligible for 25 per cent discount on your fares. For more information on tours, transportation, and hotels for visitors with a disability, visit **Sage Traveling** (www.sagetraveling.com). The Istanbul-based services mentioned on their website are likely to assist with traveling in other parts of the country.

TRAVELING WITH CHILDREN

Turks are infatuated with children. They even have an International Children's Day (Apr. 23), started by Atatürk, to recognize the valuable role children have in society. Traveling with tots in tow will bring extra attention and you'll often hear *çok güzel* (very beautiful) or, *çok şirin* (very cute) along with random cheek pinches, pats on the head, and maybe the odd cuddle from strangers. It's an interesting way to see local people at their affable best.

Generally, sites of interest are kid-friendly: fairy tale-like palaces, creepy underground cisterns, and numerous ancient sites that fill their history textbooks back home. Children under the age of 12 are able to enter government-run museums (www.muze.gov.tr) for free, while most hotels and some transportation options offer some form of discount. Kids under the age of eight can typically board public transportation for free, while older children will pay full fare. Turkish Airlines also have discounts for children and infants on international fares, but conditions apply.

Western kid-favorite fast food chains such as KFC, Burger King, and McDonald's are pervasive in city centers, but if you want to enjoy a local diet, stick with the affordable canteen-style restaurants (*lokanta*) where staff are likely to entertain the kids. Restaurants typically don't offer kids menus but can provide smaller portions or reduced-price dishes. In seaside resorts, opt for park-themed hotels; these provide innumerable athletic and other fun activities for all age groups as well as themed rooms and children's menus.

Any hotel can accommodate children of any age. Cribs, cots, and rollaway beds can be had for the asking. Affordable self-catering family suites boasting adjoining bedrooms with kitchenettes and separate baths have become the norm in seaside resorts; some can accommodate up to seven people.

Infant needs, such as disposable diapers and jars of baby food, can be purchased in an *eczane* (pharmacy), a *bakkal* (corner grocery store), or a supermarket. On the downside, public facilities are rarely equipped with baby-changing stations, so a little creativity comes in handy. Discretion is advised when nursing in public.

For kid and teen-friendly information on Turkey, visit http://kids.mfa.gov.tr to meet Can and Canan, who provide background information (albeit complicated for the little ones) related to Turkey's history and culture.

Top Tips for Traveling in Turkey

As an avid—and often solo—traveler in Turkey, I've picked up a few handy hints from locals and through my own experiences (and mistakes):

- Turkish lira and euros are used interchangeably to **price hotels and tours.** Always confirm the currency quoted to avoid confusion. If the lira is low against the euro in exchange rates, asking for quotes in Turkish lira may save you some money.

- Most lodgings provide a generous **complimentary Turkish breakfast** of tomatoes, cucumbers, cheeses, olives, bread, and boiled eggs to guests as part of the room rates. More upmarket lodgings offer omelets, fruits, yogurt, and pastries. As a Muslim country, don't expect bacon on the menu. When it comes to pouring the Turkish tea at the breakfast table, look like a pro and half-fill the glass with black tea and top it up with hot water; otherwise it's too bitter.

- The **water supply** is not up to standard for drinking. Use bottled water, or better still, bring a water bottle. You can ask to have it refilled at the desk of your hotel.

- **Mosques** are free to enter and are open from the first call to prayer before sunrise until the last call to prayer after sunset. Mosques are closed to tourists for 30 minutes directly after the call to prayer, which is sung by a *müezzin* five times a day. This is when the imam can be heard reading verses of the Quran to worshippers. Early afternoon Friday prayers are the busiest time for mosques; expect pedestrian and road traffic to increase as people make their way to mosques. Some businesses will also close around lunchtime for less than an hour as the owner attends prayers. Prayer times are listed at www.salah.com.

- Visit the **big-name attractions** like the Ayasofya, Topkapı Palace, and Ephesus either first thing in the morning or late in the afternoon to avoid waiting in the hot sun and the crush of large organized tours.

- **Night coaches** for intercity travel are a good way to save on accommodations and time. You won't get the solid sleep of a regular bed, but you can arrive in a new destination feeling rested. Coach companies offer complimentary tea and coffee, in-seat entertainment systems (in Turkish), sometimes Wi-Fi, comfy reclining seats, and a smooth journey. Purchase an inflatable pillow at the roadhouses for added comfort.

- **Crossing chaotic roads** in Turkish cities requires luck and Allah on your side. Drivers rarely stop at designated crosswalks, and giving pedestrians the right of way is almost unheard of. For your safety, use underpasses when they're available or the controlled crossings with stop lights that bring vehicles to a halt.

- Towns with a multitude of laneways like Bodrum, Ayvalık, and Çeşme, have **addresses** for businesses that are laden with names and numerical details. It can get confusing and frustrating when you can't locate your hotel or restaurant, especially on an empty stomach. Take the following fictional address, for example. "Fatih Mah. Cumhuriyet Cd. 11 Sk. N:10, Kat: 5, Ayvalık." Navigating is easier when you know what you're looking at. "Mah." stands for *mahallesi*, "neighborhood of." The second piece of information, "Cumhuriyet Cd.," is the main *caddesi* (road) closest to the location. Sometimes streets will have numbers as their name. In this case, "11 Sk." is the *sokak* (street) name, while the second number, "10," is the number of the building. "Kat: 5" means the business is on the fifth floor.

- Not all streets are labeled, so it pays to **ask the locals for directions.** Do stop often and validate directions, as many won't admit they don't know the location but will point off to a direction anyway simply to be "helpful."

WOMEN TRAVELING ALONE

Women touring Turkey solo are generally treated with the utmost kindness. Turks are unaccustomed to women traveling alone, as Turkish women tend to enjoy their leisure and social outings in small groups of friends. However, this guidebook was researched and compiled completely by a solo woman traveler, and the experience was nothing but memorable, with the authentic Turkish hospitality that makes this country so amenable for female travelers.

When dealing with the opposite gender in Turkey, it's hard, as a foreigner, to draw the line between genuine warmth and covert flirtation, and the amiability displayed by Western women is regarded by conservative Turks as unchaste. So toning down the friendliness and eye contact is the key to keeping out of trouble. It's completely OK to ignore the banter on the streets and walk past those making comments like "Can I tell you something?" and my personal favorite, "Did you drop something?...My heart?" Like other big cities of the world, women here have reported the odd grope on crowded public transportation too. Although rare, your best bet to avoid this is to back yourself into a corner so you can see everyone on the tram or train, or stand next to an older Turkish woman—the unsung saviors of society. Don't be afraid to call the culprit out, too, as Turkish people are just as disgusted by this behavior and are likely to shame to perpetrator.

Women rarely dine alone, and although the practice is becoming more natural in metropolitan areas, a woman enjoying a meal alone at a countryside eatery might find herself the only woman in the place. Expect people to be curious as to why you're dining solo.

Turkey's seaside resorts and tourist meccas have an underground gigolo industry. These crafty businessmen thrive on meeting the needs of foreign women wishing to "fully" experience the country. Looks don't matter to them as much as bank accounts, age, and nationality; these young men are particularly interested in well-established women age 35 to 55. Money is always the motive, but so is the prospect of gaining citizenship in a Western country through marriage. Highly adept in the art of attraction and persuasion, they spin tales of woe and financial need that can disarm even the most wary. This, however, should not tarnish the huge majority of men in Turkey, who are genuine and kind; just be cautious about overly attentive gestures. If he sounds too good to be true, he probably is.

Sexual assault is rare, but women traveling in Turkey should take the same precautions they would at home. Be sensitive to local customs and the prevailing attitudes, and avoid wandering too far off the beaten track by yourself, especially in central Anatolia, where attacks on foreign women have occurred in recent times.

SENIOR TRAVELERS

Turkey is an ideal destination for seniors. Hotel chains such as Best Western, Intercontinental, Hilton, and Ramada provide generous discounts to seniors, and the ease of using public transit means travel is easy on the purse strings. That said, those with mobility problems may find some of the uneven paths and stairs difficult, while the lack of elevators and the hazard of slippery bathroom floors in some budget hotels without shower screens may mean you'll need to look harder for suitable lodgings. Note that large group tours may rush you through sights, whereas small group tours or private tours are likely to go at a slower pace. Senior discounts for museum entry and public transportation are generally not provided for foreigners, although asking at the ticket sales counter may occasionally get you a discount. In Istanbul the purchase of a Museum Pass (www.muze.gov.tr/museum_pass) will also bring discounts for activities like a Bosphorus Cruise. Contact your local senior citizens groups for advice on travel and discounts.

Customs and Etiquette

The customs and etiquette of this modern yet relatively conservative nation may confuse foreigners. These pointers will help you fit in, make friends, and avoid coming across as rude by local standards.

- **Dress modestly,** especially in conservative areas and mosques. Cover your shoulders and thighs. For women, cleavage and miniskirts without tights might be OK in beachside areas but will earn the stares of every passerby in big cities and rural towns. When sitting down with jeans on, cover the bare skin of the lower back to avoid unwanted looks.
- **Women** are required to cover their heads, legs, and shoulders when entering any mosque. Bringing along a large scarf and dressing accordingly will save you from having to don a loaner shawl that has been used by thousands of others.
- **Remove shoes** when entering a home or mosque.
- Never walk directly in front of people who are praying.
- **Avoid overly attentive public displays of affection,** especially in conservative areas. Holding hands, hugs, and gentle kisses are fine. Fondling and tonsil hockey are not.
- Greet strangers with a handshake, and friends with two kisses—one on the left cheek and one on the right. This also goes for men, although most Turkish males understand that foreign guests may be more comfortable with a handshake.
- Understand the **gestures** for **"yes"** (gestured by nodding the head forward) and **"no"** (indicated by throwing the head back). A "tsk" sound with the raise of eyebrows can also mean "no." Touching the left side of the chest with the right open hand is also a polite way of saying "No, thank you."
- **Do not show the soles of your feet** to Turkish people—it's considered rude.
- Ask permission before **photographing people.**
- **Tip staff** that provide good service in restaurants, hotels, hamams, tours, and boat cruises.
- **Be discreet with food and drinks** in conservative areas during the month of Ramadan, as many residents will be fasting from sunrise to sunset.
- **Bring a gift** if you're invited to a Turkish family home. A box of baklava or sweets will be appreciated. Wine is not advised unless you know the host drinks alcohol.
- Do not insult **Atatürk** or the **Turkish flag;** doing so is considered very rude.
- Do not possess, sell, or export **Turkish antiquities**—it's against the law.
- **Be wary** of people who approach you, especially on the streets of Istanbul—unless you want to visit a carpet shop.
- Expect a chorus of calls from waiters, restaurateurs, and other vendors to entice you to spend your money at their businesses as you walk through tourism precincts.
- Expect Turkish people to be curious and sometimes overly inquisitive about your life. Questions about your weight, income, marriage, children—nothing seems off-limits.

GAY AND LESBIAN TRAVELERS

Turks are paradoxically and simultaneously conservative and liberal—a feature that can be intriguing for the first-time visitor. Men, in a sign of friendship, will sit or walk close together arm in arm and even kiss or touch heads twice on greeting—a platonic gesture that's foreign in the West. A cursory look around Taksim's Istiklal Caddesi reveals every permutation of the headscarf and the chador, the miniskirt with leggings and the two-piece suit, as well as men chatting with high-heeled cross-dressers showing a bit of skin. This benevolent acceptance stems from the political and social revolutions of the 1960s, when beloved singers like Zeki Müren and Bülent Ersoy changed gender. But while Ersoy entertains millions of Turks on her weekly reality show, Turks are still generally conservative, so discretion is prudent.

To find travel ideas and travel agents or tour operators specializing in LGBT travel, contact the **International Gay and Lesbian Travel Association** (www.iglta.org) or search for Turkey on **Passport** (www.passportmagazine.com) for travel options such as LGBT cruises. Istanbul's **Pride Travel** (Incili Çavuş Sk. 33/11, Sultanahmet, 0212/527-0671, www.travelagencyturkey.com) excels at providing LGBT-friendly city guides and travel tips as well as bookings for hotels, day trips, and regional tours. For the latest news for the LGBT community of Turkey, visit **Kaos GL** (www.kaosgldergi.com) or discover LGBT events and venues with **Time Out Istanbul** (www.timeoutistanbul.com).

Health and Safety

Turkey's medical sector offers up-to-date facilities, technology, treatment, and medical care in English. Should you have a medical emergency, dial toll-free **112;** for police assistance in urban areas call **155,** or **156** in rural areas. Alternatively, for medical issues, just hop in a cab and request to be the driven to the nearest *hastane* (hospital) *acil servis* (emergency room). Turkish people will drop what they're doing to help even a stranger in dire need, though most are not trained in first aid.

BEFORE YOU GO

Ensure that all your medical information has been updated before your departure. Carry all prescription medications in their original packaging, regardless of whether it needs to be packed in a carry-on or in a suitcase. Taking along a copy of the original prescription is also advised. Loose pills of any kind make customs officers suspicious, but having the packaging on hand makes it easy for pharmacists here to refill the medication with its Turkish or European equivalent. For those with serious illnesses, a copy of your medical records facilitates the work of doctors in case treatment is necessary. If you are carrying syringes, be sure to have a doctor's letter specifying their medical necessity. In the case of food allergies, have a translation of the allergen's name to communicate when ordering meals.

Health Insurance

As the saying goes, "If you can't afford travel insurance, then you can't afford to travel." Purchasing health insurance to travel to Turkey is recommended, particularly if you suffer from a chronic medical condition, are traveling with children, or are the intrepid kind. A wide range of insurers provides travel health insurance. Go with one that has competitive rates, including insurance for trip cancellations based on medical reasons, trip-interruption insurance, baggage and personal effects coverage, medical and dental expenses coverage, and 24-hour worldwide emergency assistance and evacuation. Most insurers will not cover injury during adrenaline-junkie activities, so check the fine print of your policy and purchase additional coverage or proceed with caution should you wish to partake in such daring escapades.

The assumption that your embassy in foreign countries provides emergency medical evacuation is incorrect. They can assist in making the arrangements, but payment is the responsibility of the traveler. Also, insured medical services rendered and medications purchased are oftentimes paid for up front by the traveler in the foreign country, and a claim for reimbursement is then submitted to the insurance company after returning home. Check what claims process your insurance company has before paying any fees upfront.

Vaccinations

No specific vaccinations are required to enter Turkey. The World Health Organization (WHO), however, advises that inoculations be up-to-date for diphtheria, tetanus, pertussis, measles, mumps, rubella, and polio as well as hepatitis A and B. Boosters for tuberculosis and rabies are recommended for individuals traveling to Turkey. Malaria is rare in coastal areas, but it's recommended to consult a doctor before travel to ensure your body is in good shape.

HEALTH CARE
Pharmacies

The local *eczane* (pharmacy), on almost every corner, is indicated by a square white sign bearing a red E. Pharmacies in Turkey generally operate 9am-7pm Monday-Saturday. After-hours and Sunday service is available through a designated *nöbetçi eczane* (on-duty pharmacy), whose address and phone number must be posted on the front door of all the pharmacies in the neighborhood. Alternatively, visit www.nobetcieczanebul.com or dial **118** to find a 24-hour pharmacy near your hotel.

For minor illnesses, pharmacists can provide advice and treatment and deem whether a visit to a physician is required. Most pharmacies have English-speaking staff, so always confirm the medication's instructions for use as the information inside the package is written in Turkish. Toiletries, particularly makeup and sunscreen, are sold in most pharmacies, but they are much pricier here than anywhere else; it's smart to purchase them before you arrive. Regular tampons can be found in most supermarkets or *ezcaneler,* though those with applicators are nonexistent. A travel medical kit always comes in handy. Products that can be bought inexpensively in Turkey include fever and pain reducers, antidiarrheal drugs, vitamins, antibiotics, calamine lotion, bandages, scissors, and the like—all without prescription and for a fraction of the prices elsewhere.

Hospitals and Clinics

The Turkish health system is growing and evolving. Private and state-run hospitals, outpatient services, and family health clinics are available to residents, but most travelers who need medical assistance are better to visit the nearest hospital. Private hospitals throughout Turkey, while recommended, can be expensive. The consultation alone can cost around 200TL, with tests costing extra. Although cheaper than most countries, travel insurance will come in handy to offset the final medical bill. Public hospitals are more available but may lack fluent English-speaking personnel at the front door. Visiting the emergency department in both settings will result in being triaged to the most appropriate and available medical staff on-site. And as we say in Turkey, if you do become unwell, *geçmiş olsun* (may it pass quickly).

HEALTH ISSUES
Drinking Water

Tap water is not safe for drinking. Stick to bottled water. You can ask to have your water bottle refilled at your hotel's front desk.

Insect Bites and Snakebites

Insects are a major problem during summer. Insect-borne diseases do occur in eastern Anatolia but not in the rest of the country. The

WHO reports that **yellow fever**—an acute viral hemorrhagic disease—and **malaria,** both carried by mosquitoes (*sivrisinek*), can be present in southeastern Turkey during the warmer months of May-October. If you are planning to travel through Turkey's southeastern provinces, the use of mosquito repellent is advised to prevent bites, along with the use of the antimalarial drugs.

Mosquitoes are not the only insects to watch out for; there are bees, wasps, and the rarer scorpion (*akrep*) in warmer areas along the coast. If you're allergic to the bites of any of these, carry antihistamines or an epinephrine autoinjector—the drug blocks anaphylactic and allergic reactions. To prevent bites, pack DEET-based mosquito repellent and wear long clothing. Relieve itching caused by bug bites with calamine lotion, hydrocortisone, or antihistamine creams available from pharmacies.

Turkey's humidity and heat make a perfect habitat for reptiles, and snakes are present. The rare highly poisonous horned viper, which measures about 60 centimeters long and is easily recognized by the brown patterned horn features on its back, enjoys sunning itself on rocks. To avoid an encounter, avoid walking barefoot and poking through dense bush, tall grass, under rocks, and in dark crevices. If you're bitten, request emergency medical assistance by dialing **112,** and rest with minimal movement, keeping the affected area below the heart. Bandage the limb tightly from the bite up the limb as far as possible. Do not carve or attempt to suck the venom out of the bite. Treatment consists of an antivenin injection.

Heat and Sun

Staying hydrated during summer, when temperature can soar above 38°C, is important. Always carry a bottle of water. Thirst and dry mouth are preliminary symptoms of dehydration, and dark urine, sluggishness, and headaches indicate your body's need for fluids. Drink water throughout the day, preferably totaling about two liters per day. Wear loose-fitting light clothing made of natural fibers, which allows perspiration to evaporate.

Hours of traipsing through archaeological wonders under the searing sun can leave you physically exhausted and trigger symptoms of heat exhaustion, including dizziness, headache, disorientation, fever, hot skin with no sweating, and a rapid heartbeat. If this occurs, the primary concern is to reduce elevated body temperature. Move indoors to a cool, ventilated area. Lay down, elevate the feet to promote blood circulation, then cool the skin with wet cloths and ice packs. This type of exhaustion can easily turn into heatstroke, a potentially life-threatening condition if left untreated. Hallucinations, seizures, and fainting are symptoms of heatstroke. Seek emergency medical treatment if symptoms set in.

Aside from drinking water throughout the day and wearing weather-appropriate clothing, you can avoid heat-related illness by planning outdoor excursions for the early morning or late afternoon avoiding the peak temperatures.

The summer sun in Turkey is intense, especially along the southern Aegean and Mediterranean coasts. Wear a high-SPF sunscreen every day. Wide-brimmed hats will protect your face and eyes. Sunscreen is widely available in pharmacies and supermarkets throughout Turkey.

Traveler's Diarrhea

Diarrhea can be contracted by drinking tap water. Unless it has been satisfactorily filtered or chemically treated, stick to drinking bottled water. Unwashed and unpeeled fruits and vegetables can also cause intestinal or stomach infection, and at worst, a parasitic infection. Wash your hands before peeling fruits that have been rinsed with plenty of water. Unpasteurized dairy products and food that has lingered too long on a steam table are also prime candidates for bacterial infections.

Diarrhea is treated with ample fluid intake. Turks also swear by *ayran,* a lightly salted yogurt drink that replaces lost minerals, rehydrates, and soothes upset stomach. Typical diarrhea involves four to five loose or watery bowel movements each day. Other symptoms include nausea, vomiting, abdominal cramping, bloating, fever, urgency, and overall discomfort. Most cases last 24 to 48 hours without treatment. If bowel movements prove more intense, more frequent, or the affliction lasts more than three days, a trip to the doctor is necessary.

Smoking

A national ban on smoking in airports, hospitals, and state offices took effect in 2008. In 2009 smoking was banned in all public places, including restaurants and bars.

SAFETY

Turkey is one of the safest countries in the world for travelers. Violent crimes, including crimes involving guns, are rare. Theft, however, is a problem for visitors and for locals. Terrorism is an ongoing issue throughout the country, and so is seismic activity. But the likelihood of either happening during your stay is next to none and should in no way deter you from planning a trip. For more information, register for regularly updated travel warnings issued by your government's foreign affairs department or embassy.

Street Crime

Theft and mugging are a concern in most large cities in the world. Maintaining constant awareness of your surroundings is the single most important factor in preventing this type of assault. Reduce the chance of being robbed by not attracting attention and by keeping your belongings on you at all times. Individuals traveling alone are more susceptible to crime, so make your excursions with others if possible. Commuting by taxi is recommended if you're carrying luggage or if you're out at night. Here are a few of the reported tactics used by criminals in larger cities and seaside resorts throughout the country.

Pickpockets thrive in crowded places like bazaars, trains, trams, boats, and at the entrance to amusement parks. Watch your handbag, wallet, wristwatch, camera, and jewelry, and stand close to others in your group.

Bag slashers and snatchers use scissors and razor blades to slash handbags and travel bags to collect the valuables within. Victims rarely notice that they have been robbed until the culprit is long gone. Snatchers are typically spry teenage boys who run past their targets and use their momentum to pry away the purse. If this type of attack occurs, don't engage the thief; they typically carry pocket knives. Yell at the top of your lungs to draw the attention of passersby.

Group thieves, usually several women wearing long garb with one or several children, target people doting on the kids while a juvenile accomplice pilfers a bag from behind. Once taken, the loot disappears under the voluminous clothing of one of the perpetrators.

Shoeshine polishers have been known to drop their brush in front of people in the hope someone will pick it up. They then offer a polish to the helpful bystander only to demand payment after. Ignore dropped brushes and keep walking.

ATM thieves have been known to loiter near ATMs waiting to "assist" with transactions, purporting that the machine is only in Turkish. All ATMs have an option for English instructions. Avoid ATMs when banks are closed, and if someone does approach, do not enter any details into the machine. Press *sil* (delete) or, *iptal* (cancel) to get your card back. *Onay* (confirm/yes) and *giriş* (enter) may be the other options on the screen in this situation.

Cons

Lone male and 20-something travelers are targets of a variety of scams that ultimately result in robbery. One of these is restricted to the tourist areas of Beyoğlu and Aksaray near Sultanahmet, both in Istanbul. The first scenario involves a well-dressed man who strikes up a conversation in impeccable English, then suggests going to a hip bar or nightclub that he knows. The lounge owner or staff are in on the scam, and once seated, several strangers join the party. Once the tab arrives, the traveler is expected to pay the full amount, which always greatly exceeds the amount of cash he is carrying. Unable to pay the exorbitant total, the victim is forcefully coerced to hand over his credit card. Victims of this con have reported the theft of all of their cash, brutal beatings, and even being forced to a nearby ATM to withdraw the daily limit on their credit cards.

Similar attacks can occur at any time in bars or restaurants in tourist areas. Once again, a conversation will be started, then a change of venue will be suggested. The victim who takes the bait is robbed of his wallet and possessions on the way to the "happening" or "scenic" spot and dropped to the nearest curb. Another scam is the "traveling companion," in which a new acquaintance enthusiastically pleads to show you the sights of his beautiful country personally.

To prevent being conned, be aware of the individual sitting across from you. Be in the moment, and use common sense. Order your own drinks, and pay for them on the spot. Adamantly refusing to change location or informing the con artist that a couple of your friends are on the way will most likely deter him. If your new pal doesn't want to accompany you to a bar of your choosing, that's a good indication that he is not to be trusted. If all else fails, just excuse yourself and leave.

Drugging

Drugging isn't common but still occurs in evening entertainment areas. In this scenario, individuals spike alcoholic drinks and then rob their victims of their personal belongings after transporting them to a seedy location. Keep your drink with you at all times and watch orders at the bar.

Terrorism

Terrorism is an ongoing issue in Turkey; foreign governments habitually warn their citizens traveling to the country, particularly Istanbul, to be wary of potential terrorist activity. That means avoiding demonstrations and large gatherings, as even peaceful protests can turn confrontational and even violent. That said, the risk of harm from any sort of political incident or violence is possible, though rare. If you sense trouble on the streets, get out of the district you're in to a safer location.

There are several active domestic and international terrorist groups in Turkey. They're more prevalent in the southeastern parts of the country bordering Syria, although threats to other Turkish regions do occur. These militant parties vehemently and violently oppose each other or the state on a variety of political, religious, or ethnic issues. The best-known include Al-Qaeda and the PKK (Kurdistan Workers Party). The PKK, however, agreed to a ceasefire in March 2013 as part of an ongoing peace process with the Turkish state. They have been responsible for a number attacks on Turkish security forces, government offices, and towns opposing the party since 1984. Led by imprisoned Abdullah Öcalan, the group was formed to restore rights and self-determination to the Kurdish people of Turkey and northern Iraq.

Attacks by terrorist groups usually involve car bombs, armed attacks, and suicide bombings. These have occurred as recently as 2013 when several events reminded Turkey of the ever-present threat outside southeastern Turkey with attacks on a police compound in Ankara, and a suicide bomber outside the U.S. Embassy in Ankara. Have you wondered why there are no garbage bins in Turkey? They've proved to be a convenient drop-off for bombs. Again, vigilance is advised when visiting public areas anywhere in Turkey or anywhere else in the world.

Information and Services

MONEY

The currency used in Turkey is the *Türk lirası* (Turkish lira; TL). One lira consists of 100 *kuruş*. Coins come in denominations of 1, 5, 10, 25, and 50 *kuruş* and 1 and 2 liras. Bank notes come in 5, 10, 20, 50, 100, and 200-lira denominations. The *yeni Türk lirası* (new Turkish lira) was introduced in 2005, deleting six zeroes from the old currency. Up until then, goods were touted in the millions, a price some traditional businessmen still operate with in rural areas. In 2012, a new Turkish lira symbol (₺) was adopted; however, locals have been reluctant to use it due to its resemblance to the euro and other symbols, and prices are still most often listed in TL or TRY. Turkish lira and euros are used interchangeably to price hotels and tours. Always confirm the currency quoted to avoid confusion.

It is wise to travel with a combination of payment options—credit cards and cash. But since there's no currency inspection at customs, and U.S. dollars, euros, and British pounds can be exchanged, wait to buy a small amount of Turkish currency (about 100TL) at the exchange booth near the luggage carousel in the arrivals hall; exchange rates are far more favorable within Turkey than abroad.

Banks are notorious for handing out large denominations that shop owners and small restaurateurs will glare at if presented because it means they lose valuable change. Try to keep as many smaller-denomination bank notes as possible, and use larger bills for big-item purchases or out on the town.

Note that the 2014 drop in the value of the lira amid corruption claims against the government may see the prices and rates listed in this book differ from those you'll see during your travels.

ATMs, Banks, Currency Exchange, and Credit Cards

Banks and automatic teller machines (ATMs) with English menus are widespread in Turkey, with some ATMs able to dispense euros and U.S. dollars in addition to liras from cards bearing the Cirrus, Maestro, Visa, and MasterCard logos. The maximum daily withdrawal is 1,000TL.

Credit cards are widely accepted in Turkey. Rare is the *pansiyon* or village eatery owner who has not yet added this payment option. While the acceptance of American Express and Diner's Club is limited to chain hotels, cards with the Visa or MasterCard/Access logos are welcomed by most hotels, shops, bars, and restaurants. Cash can be obtained on these credit cards at ATMs and banks nationwide, and miles or points can be accrued and redeemed at participating hotels.

To withdraw cash, use ATMs attached to banks during banking hours (9am-noon and 1pm-5pm Mon.-Fri.), so if something goes wrong—like your card being swallowed—personnel are close by to help. As in any big city, ATM scams do occur and are more prevalent after-hours and on weekends. Be wary of anyone loitering near ATMs. If anyone randomly tries to help you, stop what you are doing immediately—do not touch any keys that might give away your PIN. If a credit card receipt is misplaced, there's no need to worry; only the last four digits of your account number are displayed, as is customary in other parts of the world. Pay in cash for greater bargaining power.

Banks in Turkey are reliable. **Türkiye İş Bank, Garanti Bank,** and **HSBC** are among the country's most reputable banking establishments. Services extended to travelers are currency exchange (rates are typically higher than at exchange kiosks), cashing traveler's checks (although reluctantly), and cash withdrawals on credit or debit cards.

In a country where most hotel rates are listed in euros, changing currency is common practice. Currency exchange bureaus charge little, if any, commission to compete for both travelers' and locals' funds. To exchange foreign paper currency, head to a **döviz bürosu** (9am-7pm daily, later during high season), found along major thoroughfares. Also, exchange kiosks open 24-7 can be found at airports. Bank and hotel exchange rates are so steep in comparison that even with a small cut or a slightly higher exchange rate, you'll lose. As a rule, the more touristy the area, the greater the commission will be.

For wire transfers (money transfers), **Western Union** operates through many financial institutions in Turkey, among which are Ziraat Bank, Finansbank, ING Bank, Garanti Bank, Fortis Bank, Deniz Bank, and all PTT post offices (www.ptt.gov.tr). Respecting the banking hours (9am-5pm Mon.-Fri.), although some PTT offices are open Saturday, services at any of one of these firms' branches should be easy. Using branches closer to tourist areas will increase your chances of finding English-speaking staff.

PTT post offices throughout Turkey will undertake all kinds of the money management services, often at a fee. Ask your hotel for the branch near you.

Tipping

Tips are what make the services world go round in Turkey. Staff often rely on gratuities on top of mediocre wages, and it's customary to reward good service. A restaurant bill normally has some charges added to the total. One is VAT (sales tax) and another maybe a *servis ücreti* (service charge). If the service charge is not added, a 10 percent tip is polite.

The etiquette for tipping hotel staff varies. Two to five liras is the going rate for bellboys, who not only lug bags around but also provide quick tours of rooms and their gadgets. A 10 percent extra charge for a meal ordered is standard. Upon checkout, an additional tip of 10-50TL is ideal for housekeeping and general hospitality, depending on the quality of the hotel.

Tips for transportation services vary. Unless you really appreciated the service, there is no need to tip taxi drivers, coach drivers and their assistants, and *dolmuş* drivers. On Blue Cruises, however, the going rate for tipping is about 5TL per crewmember per day.

Masseurs and tour guides expect an additional financial reward over prices quoted for their services. The rule of thumb is no more than 10 per cent for more expensive treatments and tours. Street musicians can be waved on at no fee but will sing graciously if 5-10TL is slipped into the strings of their instrument.

Traveler's Checks

Traveler's checks are becoming a thing of the past and are more of a hassle and certainly more expensive to convert when traveling through Turkey. Few banks honor traveler's checks, and they may send you on a wild goose chase to find a bank that does. Don't be surprised if a fee of up to US$20, or as much as 20 percent of the check, is requested. In the end, credit cards are more efficient and have lower fees.

Still, should you plan to carry traveler's checks, purchase them at a bank or though American Express, Visa, and MasterCard in your hometown. They're issued in various dominations. Retain copies of all the checks at home; these serve as proof of purchase and ensure a refund if they are lost. Once in Turkey, it is best to cash them at PTT post offices, who take a smaller fee than banks and hotels. Ask your hotel for the nearest branch.

COMMUNICATIONS AND MEDIA
Mail

At the **PTT post offices** (444-1788, www.ptt.gov.tr) conveniently located around the country, you can purchase stamps (*posta pulu*), send letters under two kilograms, conduct money management services, purchase and add value to HGS highway toll cards, and receive telegrams. These offices are identified by a yellow rectangular sign with the blue PTT logo. Visit PTT online or ask your hotel concierge for the nearest location. Most are open

9am-5pm Monday-Friday, with a few open for longer hours and on Saturday. Packages over two kilograms are regarded as cargo and can be sent via **PTT Kargo** (www.ptt.gov.tr), often beside the post office, or **DHL** (444-0040, www.dhl.com.tr) or **FedEx** (444-0606, www.fedex.com/tr). Most businesses will also arrange door-to-door delivery from their shop with DHL, saving you the task of sending a package yourself.

As of 2014 the international postage (*yurtdışı*) rate was 2.20TL for a 20-gram letter up to 28TL for a two-kilogram registered parcel; sending a postcard abroad costs 2.20TL, and cargo up to 30 kilograms can be shipped at a cost calculated when you ship it based on the contents of the package. If you are shipping important cargo, consider sending by registered mail (*taahhütlü posta*) at a charge 7.25TL for a 250-gram package up to 28TL for a two-kilogram registered parcel. Do not seal the package until after postage costs are determined. The Turkish mail system is efficient but it can take up to three weeks or more for mail to arrive overseas. Express mail services will incur an extra charge, but can be worth it.

Telephones

Calling internationally to and from Turkey can be easy. While in Turkey, it's recommended to use a smartphone, laptop, or tablet to connect to Wi-Fi and use accounts like Skype to make domestic and international calls. Skype also allows you to set up a Skype number, where friends back home can contact you directly (if you're within Wi-Fi range) for the cost of a local call. Another option is to purchase a **Türk Telekom** (444-1444, www.turktelekom.com.tr) prepaid card, which allows you to make calls from any landline in the world using a private password. These can be purchased by phone or online through the company, or at most newspaper stands and corner grocery stores (*bakkals*) displaying the Türk Telekom sign.

When making calls from landlines or cell phones, the general format for Turkish domestic phone numbers is 0XXX/YYY-YYYY, where X is the area code or mobile phone company's code (starting with 05), and Y is the individual number. The country code for Turkey is +90.

To dial Turkey from overseas, dial your international call prefix (011 in the United States) followed by 90XXX/YYY-ZZZZ—dropping the initial zero from the area code. Phone numbers with the format 444-YYYY can be dialed from outside Turkey by dialing the international calling prefix and then 90444-YYYY. To call overseas from Turkey, dial 00 + country code + area code + number.

To call within Turkey on a landline, dial the area code, including the initial zero, followed by the seven-digit phone number. Calling 444-YYYY numbers do not require any area code and are charged at the cost of a local call.

Cell Phones

Bringing a cell phone purchased overseas to Turkey can be a headache. You can use your existing phone and SIM card on international roaming in Turkey with no problem, but if you buy a Turkish prepaid SIM card and place it in your "foreign" phone, the SIM card will become blocked within days and you'll be unable to make calls. To remedy this, don't buy a Turkish SIM card in the first place, and use your smartphone with Wi-Fi to make calls using apps and software like Skype or Viber. If you want to buy a Turkish SIM card, you'll need to register your foreign phone with the government for 120TL, payable to Iş Bank or a tax office (Vergi Dairesi). Alternatively, buying a new or used phone within Turkey from your SIM card dealer removes the need for registration. As a nonresident of Turkey, registering your phone will give you access to your SIM for six months before it is blocked again. Registration is possible for one phone every two years. Once the 120TL is paid, return to your Turkish phone company to complete the registration process. An additional service fee will be charged. **TürkCell** (444-0532, www.turkcell.com) will charge 50TL whereas **Avea** (444-1500, www.avea.com.tr)

charges 35TL. Vodafone (444-0542, www.vodafone.com.tr), another reputable dealer, will also charge a fee. Registration must be done within 30 days of arrival.

Phone companies are located in the lobby of Istanbul's international airport arrivals terminals and can assist you in purchasing a starter pack with a SIM card and prepaid units to get you connected right away. Deals vary, so it pays to scout for the best bundle for calling, texting, and data services.

Internet Access

The majority of cafés and restaurants have free Wi-Fi access for guests. Most hotels provide free Internet connections or Wi-Fi either in rooms or in public areas. The larger ones have in-room wired connections whose use may require a password or a fee. Hotels and *pansiyon* inns may also have a PC for complimentary guest use, or can point you to an internet café that charges around 2-5TL per hour to access the Internet.

English-Language Publications

Larger hotels stock daily copies of **Hürriyet Daily News** (www.hurriyetdailynews.com) and **Today's Zaman** (www.todayszaman.com), Turkish English-language newspapers for guests. Most newspaper kiosks in tourist areas will also have them for sale. These kiosks and some bookstores sell English-language lifestyle magazines produced locally, including the bimonthly **The Guide** (www.theguideistanbul.com, 10TL), **Time Out Istanbul** (6.50TL), which appears monthly, and the quarterly connoisseur guide *Cornucopia* (www.cornucopia.net, 39TL). International newspapers such as the **International New York Times** (http://international.nytimes.com) and newsmagazines like the **Economist** (www.economist.com) are readily available at larger bookstores throughout Istanbul.

MAPS AND VISITOR INFORMATION
Tourism Offices and Websites

In planning your trip, make sure to visit the websites of the **Ministry of Culture and Tourism** (www.goturkey.com, www.kultur.gov.tr). These resources are geared for the tastes and sensibilities of international visitors, with everything you need to know about Turkey's various destinations, attractions, and the best times to visit, along with a trip planner. Similar sites are maintained in English and Turkish by some of Turkey's *belidiyeler* (municipalities), for example, Istanbul (www.ibb.gov.tr), Ankara (www.ankara.gov.tr), İzmir (www.izmir.bel.tr), Bodrum (www.bodrum.bel.tr), and Çeşme (www.cesmebelediyesi.com).

Maps

Tourism offices around the country provide detailed maps for free or at low cost. Souvenir shops and bookstores also offer commercial maps ranging in coverage from municipal to national levels at a cost of 10-30TL. **Google Maps** (http://maps.google.com) makes it simple to find an address, but the exact location of businesses on a street is not always correct. Other map sites include **Yahoo! Local Maps** (http://maps.yahoo.com) and **Via Michelin** (www.viamichelin.com).

For a no-nonsense national highway map that lists all turn-offs, distances, and points in Turkey down to the scale of remote villages, get MepMedya's ***Türkiye Karayolları Haritası,*** available at most gas stations and bookstores, including DK and Remzi. Visit the **Directorate of Highways** (www.kgm.gov.tr) for maps and the location of toll roads. A long list of maps of Turkey, its cities, and its roads exists in paper or downloadable form at **Omnimap** (www.omnimap.com); these can be ordered before your departure or downloaded for a fee.

WEIGHTS AND MEASURES

Turkey uses the metric system. Distances are calculated in centimeters (1 cm = 0.39 inches), meters (1 m = 3.28 feet or 1.09 yards), and kilometers (1 km = 0.62 miles); weight is measured in grams (100 g = 3.5 ounces) and kilograms (1 kg = 2.2 pounds); land area is in hectares (1 ha = 2.47 acres); volume is in liters (1 L = 2.11 U.S. pints, 33.8 U.S. ounces, or 1.05 quarts); and temperature is in degrees Celsius (20°C = 68°F). Time in Turkey is stated using the 24-hour clock (17:00 = 5pm).

Resources

Glossary

açık: open
Anatolia: Asian subcontinent of Turkey
araba: car
arasta: row of shops
Avrupa: Europe
Asya: Asia
ayran: yogurt drink
bahçe: garden
balık: fish
bay, bayan: male, female
bedesten: covered marketplace
belediye: municipality
börek: filled pastry
bulvarı: boulevard
caddesi: road
caïque rowboat
cami/camii: mosque/mosque of
çay: tea
çiğer: liver
çıkışı: exit
çorba: soup
darbuka: drum
deniz: sea
deniz mahsulleri: shellfish and crustaceans
dolmuş/dolmuşlar: communal taxi/taxis
dünya: world
dürüm: lavash bread filled with roasted meat
et: meat
ezan: Islamic call to prayer
fasıl: traditional Turkish music
fez: Ottoman felt hat
fırın: bakery
fıstık: nut
fünıküler: funicular railroad, cable car
gar/garı: train station/train station of
gazete: newspaper
giriş: entrance
göl: lake
gözleme: Turkish pancake
gület/gületler: wooden motorized sailboat/sailboats
güveç: stew
hamam: Turkish bath
han: inn
haremlik: part of palace or home for women
hijab: veil worn by Islamic women
hısar: fortress
hükümet: government
imam: worship leader of the mosque
indirim: discount
iskele/iskelesi: port/port of
jeton: token for public transportation
kahve: coffee
kale: castle
kapalı: closed
kek: tea cake
kilise/kilisesi: church/church of
kıtabevi: bookstore
kıtap: book
köfte: grilled meat patties
köfteci/köfteciler: small eatery/eateries for grilled meat patties
kokteyl: cocktail, mixed drink
koltuk: seat
konak/konaklar: residence/residences
köşk: mansion
külliye/külliyesi: mosque complex/complex of
kuzu: lamb

lahmacun: Turkish pizza with ground lamb
liman: port
limon: lemon
lokanta/lokantalar: canteen style restaurant/restaurants
lokum: Turkish delight
mahallesi (mah.): neighborhood
mahfililer: a raised dais where the Koran is read
medrese/medreseler: Ottoman Islamic school/schools
metro: subway/metro
meydan/meydanı: town square/town square of
meyhane/meyhaneler: Turkish tavern/taverns
meyve: fruit
mezeler: starters before a main course
meze/mezeler: small appetizer/appetizers
mihrab: niche indicating the direction of mecca
minbar: where the imam leads prayers and sermons
müezzin/müezzinler: singer/singers appointed by the mosque to lead the call to prayer
müze/müzesi: museum/museum of
narghile: water pipe or hookah
numara: number
otel: hotel
otogar/otogarlar/otogarı: bus station/bus stations/bus station of
otoyol: motorway
pansiyon: inn (pension)
pasaj: passage, arcade
pasta: cake (moist)
patlıcan: eggplant
pazar: market
postal kodu: postal code
radyo: radio
rakı: aniseed-flavored aperitif
salata: salad
şarap: wine
şaraphane/şaraphaneler: wine bar/bars
şehir: city
selamlık: part of palace or home for men
servis: free shuttle service by a coach company
seyahat: trip
simit: circular baked bread with sesame seeds
sinema: movie theater
şiş: skewered meat
sokak: street
soyad: surname
su: milk
televizyon: television
tiyatro: theater
tramvay: tramway
türbe/türbeler: tomb/tombs
turizm: tourism
Türk kahvesi: Turkish coffee
tuvaletler: toilets
uçak: airplane
ülke: country
yeni: new
yolu: highway
zeytin: olive
zeytinyağ: olive oil

Turkish Phrasebook

Outside popular tourist spots and the big cities of Istanbul, İzmir, and Ankara, few people in Turkey speak or understand English (although their sense of hospitality inevitably coerces them to practice their repertory). To get the most out of your trip, learn the basics of the Turkish language, including pronunciation and basic sentence structure. The use of a few well-placed Turkish words will be appreciated. Refrain from speaking English with strangers without at least breaking the ice by saying *merhaba* (MEHR-hah-bah), meaning "hello," or *affedersiniz* (af-feh-DEHR-see-neez), "excuse me." The most important phrase to learn is *Pardon, Türkçe konuşmıyorum* (pahr-DOHN Tur-K-che KO-nush-ME-yorum), "I'm sorry, but I don't speak Turkish."

The Turkish alphabet contains 29 letters, including 23 of the letters used in English, without X, Q, and W, plus six modified letters: ç, ğ, ş, ı, ö, and ü.

PRONUNCIATION

The majority of Turkish letters are pronounced as they would sound in English, but there are a few easy-to-remember exceptions. The three golden rules to speaking Turkish are: 1. Each letter is pronounced; 2. Each letter has only one sound; and 3. Letters are never combined to produce other sounds (as ph produces "f" in English). Letters to be emphasized are capitalized.

Vowels

a as 'a' in "tar": *baba* bah-bah (father), *anne* AHN-ne (mother)
e as 'e' in "bed": *sen* (you), *yer yehr* (place)
i as 'ee' in "see": *iyi* ee-yee (good), *sinema* SEE-neh-MAH (movies).
ı as 'e' in "open": *sıcak* suh-JAHK (hot), *kız kuhz* (girl)
o as 'o' in "often": *kol* kohl (arm), *yok* yohk (no)
ö as 'i' in British "bird": *ölüm* UH-luhm (death), *söz* suhz (word)
u as 'ou' in "you": *uzun* oo-ZOON (long), *uçak* oo-CHAHK (airplane)
ü as 'u' "cube": *üzüm* Ü-züm (grapes), *yüksek* yük-sek (high)

Consonants

b, d, f, k, l, m, n, p, r, t, v, and **z** have almost the same pronunciation as in English.
c as 'j' in "jar": *cam* jahm (glass), *bacak* bah-JAHK (leg)
ç as 'ch' in "chat": *çöp* chuhp (trash), *çim* cheem (grass)
g as 'g' in "golf": *garson* gahr-SOHN (waiter), *göl* guhl (lake)
ğ is not pronounced. This 'g' is crowned by a silencing breve that lengthens the sound of the vowel that precedes it, as in *dağ* daah (mountain) and *değil* DEH-eel (not).
h as 'h' in "hat": *hava* HAH-vah (air or weather), *her* hehr (every)
j as 's' in "vision": *jandarma* zhan-DAHR-mah (national guard)
ş as 'sh' in "sham": *şair* SHA-eer (poet), *eş* esh (spouse)

Although **w** and **x** are not officially used in the alphabet, they do appear in foreign words that have come into the Turkish vocabulary. Likewise, **â**, which dates back to Ottoman Turkish, is used rarely to lengthen the 'a' sound.

BASIC EXPRESSIONS

Turks are polite and use formalities profusely. Use greetings appropriate to the time of day and the situation.

Hello Merhaba
Good morning İyi günler
Good evening İyi akşamlar
Good night İyi geceler
How are you? Nasılsınız?
I'm very well, thank you. İyiyim, teşekkür ederim.
I'm not well. İyi değilim.
Thank you Teşekkürler, Sağ ol, or Mersi
Thank you very much Çok teşekkür ederim
You're welcome. Bir şey değil.
Please Lütfen
Pardon me Affedersiniz or pardon
Yes Evet
No Hayır
Welcome Hoş geldin
Pleased to meet you Memnun oldum
See you later Görüşürüz
Good-bye Allaha ısmarladık
I don't know. Bilmiyorum.
My name is . . . Adım …
Just a moment, please. Bir dakika, lütfen.
Excuse me (to get attention) Bakar mısınız
Sorry (when you have done something wrong) Özür dilerim
Do you speak English? Siz İngilizce konuşur musunuz?

I want.../I don't want . . . ...istiyorum/... istemiyorum
I don't know Turkish. Türkçe bilmiyorum.
I don't understand. Anlamıyorum.
Would you like . . . ...istiyormusunuz?
good/beautiful güzel
a lot/many çok
a little az
all hepsi
every her
big büyük
small küçük
hot sıcak
cold soğuk
now şimdi
later sonra
this/these bu/bunlar
that/those şu/şunlar
who kim
what ne
when ne zaman
where nerede
why neden
how nasıl
do you have . . . ? ...var mı?

TERMS OF ADDRESS

Strangers should be addressed using the formal pronoun *siz* (you). Once individuals become familiar, using *sen* (you) is appropriate. In general, women are referred to by their first name followed by *hanım efendi* (lady), while *bey efendi* (Mr., sir) is used for men.

I ben
you (formal) siz
you (familiar) sen
he, him; she, her; it o
we, us biz
they, them onlar
Mr., sir Bey
Mrs., Miss, Madam Hanım
wife karı
husband koca
friend arkadaş
boyfriend; girlfriend erkek arkadaş; kız arkadaş, sevgili
son; daughter oğul; kız
brother; sister erkek kardeş; kız kardeş
older brother abi
father; mother baba; anne
grandfather; grandmother dede; büyük anne, babaanne (**father's mother**), anneanne (**mother's mother**)

TRANSPORTATION AND DIRECTIONS

Where is . . . ? ...nerede?
How far is it to...(İzmir)? (İzmir)...ne kadar uzakta?
from (İzmir) to (Istanbul) (İzmir)'den (İstanbul)'a
Where (how) do I (we) go . . . ? Nereye (nasıl) giderim (gideriz) . . . ?
bus; bus station otobüs; otogar
bus stop otobüs durağı
Where is the bus going? Otobüs nereye gidiyor?
taxi; taxi stand taksi; taksi durağı
communal taxi; communal taxi stop dolmuş, dolmuş durağı
train; train station tren; tren istasyonu
port iskele
boat; steamboat; sailboat bot, gemi; vapur; tekne
airport havalimanı, havaalanı
plane uçak
bicycle bisiklet
Can I buy a ticket to . . . ? ...bir bilet satın alabilir miyim?
first (second) class birinci (ikinci) sınıf
round-trip gidiş-dönüş
one-way tek yön
reservation rezervasyon
baggage bagaj
Stop here, please. buraya durun, lütfen.
entrance (to enter); exit (to exit) giriş (girmek); çıkış (çıkmak)
open; closed açık; kapalı
ticket office; booth bilet gişesi
(very) near; far (çok) yakın; uzak
to (to Istanbul, to the supermarket); toward -a (İstanbul'a), -e (market'e)
by (position, by the door) yan, kapının yanında
by (method, by train) 'ile, tren'ile

through (inside of, among) *içinden, arasından*
from (America) *-den, -dan (Amerika'dan)*
right; left *sağ; sol*
straight ahead *dümdüz*
ahead *ilerde*
front; in front of *ön; önde*
beside *yanında*
in the back of; located behind *arkada*
corner *köşe*
stoplight *trafik ışığı; trafik lambası*
turn; to turn *sapış; sapmak*
street; avenue; boulevard *sokak; cadde; bulvar*
highway *otoyol, karayolu, ekspress yol*
bridge *köprü*
toll *geçiş ücreti*
address *adres*
directions; give directions *tarife; tarife vermek*
north; south *kuzey; güney*
east; west *doğu; batı*

ACCOMMODATIONS
hotel *otel*
Is there a room? *Oda var mı?*
May I (we) see it? *Ben (biz) onu görebilir miyim (miyiz)?*
What is the (daily, weekly) rate? *(gündüz, haftalık) tarifesi ne kadar?*
Is that your best rate? *O en iyi tarifeniz mi?*
Can the rate be lowered, if paying by cash? *Nakit ödeyerek, tarife inebilir mi?*
Is there something cheaper? *Daha ucuz bir şey var?*
single room *tek kişilik oda*
double room *iki kişilik oda*
family room *aile odası*
double beds *iki kişilik yatak*
twin bed *tek kişilik yatak*
crib *bebek karyolası*
with private bath *oda içi banyo'ila*
hot water *sıcak su*
air conditioning *klima*
shower *duş*
towel *havlu*
soap *savun*
toilet paper *tuvalet kağıdı*

blanket *battaniye*
bed sheet *yatak çarşafı*
fan *fan, vantilatör*
key *anahtar*
manager *yönetici, manajer*
owner (hotel) *sahip (otel sahibi)*
housekeeping *oda hizmeti*

FOOD
I'm (we're) hungry; I'm (we're) thirsty. *acıktım (acıktık); susadım (susadık).*
Enjoy your meal *Afiyet olsun.*
menu *menü, yemek listesi*
order; to order *sipariş; sipariş etmek*
glass *bardak*
fork *çatal*
knife *bıcak*
spoon *kaşık*
napkin *peçete*
soft drink *kola, soda*
coffee *kahve*
tea *çay*
bottled water *su şişesi*
tap water *musluk suyu*
bottled carbonated water *soda, gazoz*
beer *bira*
white wine; red wine *beyaz şarap; kırmızı şarap*
milk *süt*
juice *meyve suyu*
cream *krema*
sugar *şeker*
salt *tuz*
cheese *peynir*
snack *ara öğün, çerez*
breakfast *kahvaltı*
lunch *öğle yemeği*
daily special *günlük yemeği menüsü*
dinner *akşam yemeği*
check, bill *adisyon, hesap*
egg *yumurta*
bread *ekmek*
salad *salata*
fruit *meyve*
vegetables *sebze*
soup *çorba*
dessert *tatlı*
ice cream *dondurma*

appetizer (hot appetizer) *mezze (ara sıcak)*
main meal *ana yemek*

SHOPPING
Can I exchange dollars (traveler's checks)? *Dolar bozdurabilir miyim?*
Can I purchase Turkish liras? *Türk lirası satın alabilir miyim?*
What is the exchange rate? *Döviz kuru ne kadar?*
How much is the commission? *Komisyon ücreti ne kadar?*
Do you accept credit cards? *Kredi kartları kabul ediyor musunuz?*
How much does it cost? *Bu ne kadar?*
Anything else? *başka bir şey?*
money *para*
money order *para havalesi*
currency exchange bureau *döviz bürosu*
expensive *pahalı*
cheap *uçuz*
more, too much *daha, fazla*
less *az*
a little *biraz*
too much *çok fazla*
coat *palto*
cotton *pamuk*
dress *elbise*
pants *pantalon*
scarf *eşarp*
shirt *gömlek*
shoes *ayakabı*
socks *çorap*

HEALTH AND SAFETY
Help me please. *Bana yardım edin lütfen.*
I am ill. *Hastayım.*
Call a doctor. *Bir doktor çağırabilir misiniz?*
Take me to...(doctor) *Beni...(doktor'a) götür*
ambulance *ambülans*
emergency *açil*
doctor *doktor*
dentist *diş hekimi*
hospital *hastane*
police station *karakol*
burn (sunburn) *yanık (güneş yanığı)*
cramp *kramp*

fever *ateş*
headache *baş ağrısı*
nausea *bulantı*
pain *acı, ağrı*
stomachache *mide ağrısı*
toothache *diş ağrısı*
vomiting *kusma*
antibiotic *antibiotik*
aspirin *aspirin*
birth control pills *doğum kontrol hapı*
condoms *prezervatif*
contraceptive foam *kontraseptif köpük*
diaper *bebek bezi*
medicine *ilaç*
ointment; cream *melhem; krem*
pharmacy *eczane*
pill; syrup *hap; şurup*
sanitary napkin *hijyenik ped*
toothbrush *diş fırçası*
toothpaste *diş macunu*
arm *kol*
ear *kulak*
eye *göz*
face *yüz*
finger *parmak*
foot *ayak*
hand *el*
head *baş*
hip *kalça*
knee *diz*
leg *bacak*
mouth *ağız*
neck *boyun*
nose *burun*
stomach *mide*
toe *ayak parmağı*

COMMUNICATIONS
long-distance (international) telephone call *şehirlerarası (uluslararası) telefon konuşması*
May I call...? *...çağırabilir miyim*
collect call *karşı ödemeli*
station-to-station call *santral aracılığıyla konuşma*
person-to-person call *ihbarlı konuşma*
credit card *kredi kartı*
post office *postane*

general delivery *genel dağıtım*
postcard *kartpostal*
stamp *posta pulu*
letter *mektup*
envelope *zarf*
air mail *hava yolu ile*
registered/certified *taahhütlü*
money order *posta havalesi*
package; box *paket; kutu*
string; tape *ip; teyp*

AT THE BORDER

border *sınır*
customs *gümrük*
immigration *göçmen*
immigration booth *göçmen gişesi*
visa *vize*
passport *pasaport*
inspection; control *denetim; kontrol*
border guard *gümrük görevlisi*
profession *meslek*
marital status *medeni dürümu*
single *bekar*
married; divorced *evli; boşanmış*
widowed *dul*
insurance *sigorta*
title *mülkiyet*
driver's license *ehliyet*

AT THE GAS STATION

gas station *benzin istasyonu*
gasoline *benzin*
unleaded *kurşunsuz*
Fill it up, please. *Depoyu doldur, lütfen.*
car tire *araba lastiği*
air *hava*
water *su*
oil (change) *yağ değişimi*
grease *makine yağı*
My...doesn't work. *...çalışmaz.*
battery *akü*
radiator *radyatör*
alternator *alternatör*
generator *dinamo*
windshield *ön cam*
tow truck *çekici*
repair shop *tamirhane*

USING THE INTERNET

computer *bilgisayar*
home page *anasayfa*
about us *hakkımızda*
our menu *menümüz*
photo gallery *galeri*
getting there *ulaşım*
contact *iletişim*
email *e-posta*
telephone *telefon*
price/prices *fıyat/fıyatları*
password *şifre*

VERBS

Turkish has two classes of verbs: those that end in *-mak* and those that end in *-mek*. When conjugating, these suffixes are replaced by the verb ending for the subject. Because these endings convey a pronoun, most Turks omit the pronoun altogether when speaking. For example, the verb *gelmek* (to come) in first-person singular in the present tense becomes *gelerim* (I come). Learn to conjugate one verb from each group and you'll have learned Turkish conjugation. It's fairly easy once you get the hang of it. Turkish primarily uses the present continuous tense to speak about the now.

to eat *yemek*
I, you eat; he (she, it) eats *ben yerim, sen yersin, o yer*
we, you, they eat *biz yeriz, siz yersiniz; onlar yer*
to climb *tırmanmak*
I, you climb; he (she, it) climbs *ben tırmanarım, sen tırmanarsin, o tırmanar*
we, you, they climb *biz tırmanarız, siz tırmanarsınız, onlar tırmanar*
to do *yapmak*
I, you do; he (she, it) does *ben yapırım, sen yapırsın, o yapır*
we, you, they do *biz yapırız, siz yapırsınız, onlar yapır*
to be *olmak*
I, you are; he (she, it) is *ben olurum, sen olursun, o olur*

we, you, they are *biz oluruz, siz olursunuz, onlar olur*
to buy *satın almak*
I, you buy; he (she, it) buys *ben satın alırım, sen satın alırsın; o satın alır*
we, you, they buy *biz alırız, siz satın alırsınız, onlar satın alır*
to go *gitmek*
I, you go; he (she, it) goes *ben giderim, sen gidersin. o gider*
we, you, they go *biz gideriz, siz gidersiniz, onlar gider*
to walk *yürümek*
to love; to like *sevmek; beğenmek*
to work *calışmak*
to want *istemek*
to eat *yemek*
to swim *yüzmek*
to tour; to travel *dolaşmak; gezmek*
to write *yazmak*
to repair *tamir etmek*
to stop *durmak*
to get off (the bus) *inmek*
to get on (the bus); to ride *binmek*
to stay *kalmak*
to drink *içmek*
to leave *ayrılmak*
to look at *bakmak*
to look for *aramak*
to have (own) *sahip olmak*
to give *vermek*
to carry *taşımak*
to come *gelmek*

NUMBERS

zero *sıfır*
1 *bir*
2 *iki*
3 *üç*
4 *dört*
5 *beş*
6 *altı*
7 *yedi*
8 *sekiz*
9 *dokuz*
10 *on*
11 *on bir*
12 *on iki*
13 *on üç*
14 *on dört*
15 *on beş*
16 *on altı*
17 *on yedi*
18 *on sekiz*
19 *on dokuz*
20 *yirmi*
30 *otuz*
40 *kırk*
50 *elli*
60 *altmış*
70 *yetmiş*
80 *seksen*
90 *doksan*
100 *yüz*
101 *yüz bir*
200 *iki yüz*
500 *beş yüz*
1,000 *bin*
10,000 *on bin*
100,000 *yüz bin*
1,000,000 *bir milyon*
one-half *yarım*
one-third *üçte bir*
one-fourth *dörtte bir*

TIME

What time is it? *Saat kaç?*
It's one o'clock. *Saat bir.*
It's two in the afternoon. *Saat on dört.*
It's 1pm *Saat one üç.*
five-thirty *saat beş buçuk*
a quarter till 10 *ona çeyrek var*
a quarter past three *üçü çeyrek geçiyor*
an hour *bir saat*
minute *dakika*
today *bugün*
yesterday *dün*
tomorrow *yarın*
morning *sabah*
noon *oğle*
afternoon *oğleden sonra*
evening *akşam*
night *gece*

DAYS AND MONTHS

Monday *Pazartesi*

Tuesday Salı	**after** sonra
Wednesday Çarşamba	**before** önce
Thursday Perşembe	**January** Ocak
Friday Cuma	**February** Şubat
Saturday Cumartesi	**March** Mart
Sunday Pazar	**April** Nisan
today bugün	**May** Mayıs
tomorrow yarın	**June** Haziran
yesterday dün	**July** Temmuz
a week bir hafata	**August** Ağustos
a day bir gün	**September** Eylul
a month bir ay	**October** Ekim
a year (time) bir sene	**November** Kasım
year (age) bir yaş	**December** Aralık

Suggested Reading

MODERN TURKEY

Finkel, Andrew. *Turkey: What Everyone Needs to Know*. New York: Oxford University Press, 2012. Finkel, a witty columnist in the Turkish media, presents 50 questions and answers about Turkey's people, politics, culture, and religion in 224 pages of essential reading for any traveler or expatriate in Turkey.

Gordon, Philip H. *Winning Turkey: How America, Europe, and Turkey Can Revive a Fading Partnership*. Washington DC: Brookings Institution Press, 2008. In this 115-page report, the former director for European Affairs at the National Security Council discusses Turkey's crucial geopolitical importance in the world and its increasing role as a regional economic leader.

Kinzer, Stephen. *Crescent and Star: Turkey between Two Worlds*. New York: Farrar, Straus and Giroux, 2002. Former Istanbul *New York Times* bureau chief and passionate observer of Turkey's path toward Westernization and economic transformation, Kinzer gives a concise introduction to the country: Atatürk's post-World War I foundation of a modern secular Turkish state and the peculiar constitution of contemporary society.

Mango, Andrew. *The Turks Today*. London: Overlook TP, 2006. The fifth of seven titles by this Istanbul-born, UK-based author, this book conveys why this globally unique, Western-looking Muslim country—and its citizens, which Mango knows so well—are so different from its neighbors to the east and south.

Pope, Nicole, and Hugh Pope. *Turkey Unveiled*. London: Overlook TP, 2004. Longtime Istanbul residents, the Popes are a writer-journalist team who attempt to demystify a conflicted country that continues to evade categorization and present a historical recital of Turkey's arduous political twists and turns since the disintegration of the Ottoman Empire.

White, Jenny. *Muslim Nationalism and the New Turks*. Princeton, NJ: Princeton University Press, 2012. Voted one of ForeignAffairs.com's Best

International Relations Books in the Best Books on the Middle East category for 2012, this book explores the changing face of Turkish nationalism amid the recent friction between Islamic and secular society.

HISTORY

Faroqhi, Suraiya. *Subjects of the Sultan: Culture and Daily Life in the Ottoman Empire*. London: I. B. Tauris, 2005. An Ottoman scholar by trade and an international lecturer, the German-born Faroqhi is a master of Ottoman culture and language. No other book describes the sultans' court's day-to-day living practices—even commonplace rituals such as bathing, shopping, loving, and grieving—and its evolution over the six centuries until the sultanate was finally exiled.

Lloyd, Seton. *Ancient Turkey: A Traveler's History*. Berkeley, CA: University of California Press, 1999. Neither a textbook nor an archaeological guide, this work attempts to bridge the past and the present through a look at the Turks and their ancestors, their land, and the surviving monuments that connect them.

Lord Kinross. *Ottoman Centuries: The Rise and Fall of a Nation*. New York: Harper Perennial, 1979. Kinross packs the more than 600 centuries of grand conquest and ultimate demise of the Ottomans into as many pages. This magnificent book has been considered the essential text for Ottoman scholars for the last 30 years.

Moorhead, Alan. *Gallipoli*. Sydney: Cornstalk, 1992. A movie starring Mel Gibson was adapted from this hard-to-find book, in which Winston Churchill's catastrophic World War I campaign to gain Istanbul is recounted in sometime tear-rending detail.

MEMOIRS AND TRAVELOGUES

Ashman, Anastasia M., and Jennifer Eaton Gökmen. *Tales from the Expat Harem: Foreign Women in Modern Turkey*. Berkeley, CA: Seal Press, 2006. Eaton and Ashman, comrades in quills and U.S. expatriates, ingenuously assembled 30 personal memoirs of women from four different countries living in Turkey.

Brosnahan, Tom. *Turkey—Bright Sun, Strong Tea: On the Road with a Travel Writer*. Concord, MA: Travel Info Exchange, 2005. Turkey expert Tom Brosnahan humorously relates his travels through the country from his first foray as a bushy-tailed U.S. Peace Corps volunteer and his first Turkish tea almost 50 years ago.

Revolinski, Kevin. *The Yogurt Man Cometh: Tales of an American Teacher in Turkey*. Eden, SD: Citlembik/Nettleberry, 2006. Revolinski recounts his yearlong adventures in Turkey while working as a teacher in Ankara. Travel tales, memories, and humor add up to a delightful tale of cultural hopscotch.

Schneider, Dux. *Bolkar: Travels with a Donkey in the Taurus Mountains*. Bloomington, IN: Xlibris, 1978. Enrapt by the southeastern Anatolian range, Schneider's book is a rare window into the daily lives of Turkey's nearly extinct nomadic cultures.

Settle, Mary Lee. *Turkish Reflections*. St. Petersburg, FL: Touchstone, 1992. Settle recounts her experiences with traveling through Turkey from slumbering coastal villages to noisy and frantic Istanbul, which she describes as "as polite and friendly as a country village."

LITERATURE

Kemal, Yaşar. *Memed, My Hawk*. New York: NYRB Classics, 2005. An epic of grand scale, *Memed* is the story of any small town in Anatolia in the days of the omnipotent a☒a (landlord). Seeking a way out of a life of arduous work, young Memed escapes and becomes a bandit in the hope of freeing his people from the clutches of their master. In the process, he becomes as violent and ruthless as he is kind in his adventurous crusade that spans history and politics.

Pamuk, Orhan. *Istanbul: Memories of a City*. New York: Knopf, 2005. This sweeping novel offers a glimpse into the soul of one of the world's greatest cities told by its most renowned writer, Orhan Pamuk, recipient of the 2006 Nobel Prize for literature. Of the dozen titles penned by Pamuk, these are also highly recommended: *The Black Book* (New York: Vintage, 2006), *My Name Is Red* (New York: Vintage, 2002), *The New Life* (New York: Vintage, 1998), and *Snow* (New York: Vintage, 2005).

Şafak, Elif. *The Bastard of Istanbul*. New York: Penguin, 2008. This is one of award-winning novelist and women's studies professor Elif Şafak's forays into fiction. The novel deals with issues of Turkish national identity and the Armenian "question" through a zany cast of female characters and a plot that extends to North America. For this, Şafak was indicted for "public denigration of Turkishness," charges that were later dropped. Also by this author: *The Forty Rules of Love: A Novel by Rûmî* (New York: Viking, 2010), *The Flea Palace* (London: Marion Boyars, 2007), and *The Saint of Incipient Insanities* (New York: Farrar, Straus & Giroux, 2004).

Internet Resources

Tourism Turkey
www.goturkey.com
The official website of Turkey's Culture and Tourism Ministry covers officialdom, region-specific activities, destinations, museums, and history. A convenient trip planner lets you peruse hotels, holiday resorts, and B&Bs.

Turkey Travel Planner
www.turkeytravelplanner.com
Operated by travel writer Tom Brosnahan, this website is filled with tips and recommendations for hotels, restaurants, books, and maps.

Istanbul
http://english.istanbul.com
Packed with lodging and dining options, tour operators and tour ideas, articles on the city's shopping meccas, and an updated events calendar.

All About Turkey
www.allaboutturkey.com
Tour guide Burak Sanal's award-winning website is packed with historical details about every civilization that has walked across Anatolia. It's truly exhaustive.

MyMerhaba
www.mymerhaba.com
The essential online guide for expatriates includes a calendar, cultural articles, restaurants, and "survival basics" that are a great tool for travelers.

Binnur's Turkish Cookbook
www.turkishcookbook.com
Turkish cook Binnur manages this website full of homegrown Turkish recipes.

Yabangee
www.yabangee.com
Find dining and entertainment listings as well as articles on Turkish cuisine, culture, and trends on this site intended for expats.

InsideOutIstanbul
http://insideoutinistanbul.wordpress.com
Expat Lisa Marrow's beautifully written narrative describes life and customs in Turkey.

MUST-HAVE APPS
Burası Orayı
www.buradanoraya.com
Plot your travel with timetables for all public transit in Istanbul with one of the few apps available in English. It can tell you which buses, trains, trams, airport shuttles, and ferries can transport you from point A to point B.

Foursquare
www.foursquare.com
Bars and restaurants come and go, so putting Foursquare on your smartphone will help you find the current best places for dining and nightlife.

Sesli Sözlük
www.seslisozluk.net
The app most bilingual people use to translate Turkish words into English includes handy audio recordings of words so you can perfect your pronunciation.

Booking.com
www.booking.com
Pick hotels from your smartphone in a couple of easy steps. The app has all the features of its Web-based partner.

XE Currency Converter
www.xe.com
The easiest currency converter app, which can convert prices in Turkish lira to multiple currencies on one screen.

Index

A

Abasiyanik, Sait Faik: 80
Abdalonymos, King: 52
Abdülaziz, Sultan: 61, 67
Abide Memorial: 151
accommodations: 24, 423, 429
Acropolis of Bergama: 156, 187
Acropolis of Kaunos: 275
Acropolis of Xanthos: 295
Adalar (Princes' Islands): 12, 17, 79-81, 100, 108-109
Aegean Sea: 382
Ağaçaltı Kilisesi (Church under the Tree): 354
Agora of Kadifekale: 194
Agora of Kaunos: 275
agriculture: 407
Ahmet Piristina Museum of Metropolitan History and Archive: 196
air travel: 415, 417
Akaretler: 61
Akbank Arts Foundation: 85
Akvaryum Koyu: 173
Akyaka: 271
Akyarlar: 20, 260
Alabey Mosque: 171
Alaçatı: 12, 20, 156, 206
Alâeddin Camii (Alaeddin Mosque): 314, 359
Alexander Sarcophagus: 52
Alexander the Great: 388
Alexandria Troas: 176
Alibey: 180 ş
Ali Muhiddin Hacı Bekir: 16, 88
Ali Paşa Çarşısı: 143
Altar of Zeus: 187
Altınkum Beach: 20, 207
Altın Portakal Film Festivalı: 319
Altıyol: 70
Amadeus: 172
Anadolu Medeniyetleri Müzesi (Museum of Anatolian Civilizations): 370
Anatolia: 16, 53, 179
Anatolia and Troy through the Ages: 53
Ancient Orient Museum: 53
Ancient Phocaea: 189
Andriake: 308
animals: 385-386
Anıtkabir (Atatürk Mausoleum): 27, 330, 368
Ankara: 13, 24, 27, 365-377
Ankara Citadel: 369
Anker Travel: 215
Antalya: 13, 22, 23, 24, 312-327
Antalya Aquarium: 320
Antalya Müzesi (Antalya Museum): 23, 315-316

Antiphellos Ruins: 302
Anzac Commemorative Site: 150
Anzac Cove: 149
Anzac Day: 147, 162
Aperlai: 306
Aphrodisias: 244-245
Apollonia: 306
Apollo Smintheus Temple: 176
apse mosaic: 39
Aquadream waterpark: 267
Aqua Fantasy: 233
Aqualand: 320
aquariums: 320
Arcadian Way: 219
archaeological sites: general discussion 19; Anadolu Medeniyetleri Müzesi (Museum of Anatolian Civilizations) 370; ancient cities itinerary 18-23; Ankara 369, 371; Antalya Müzesi (Antalya Museum) 315-316; Aphrodisias 244-245; Arkeoloji Müzesi (Archaeological Museum), Bursa 128; Arkeoloji Müzesi (Archaeological Museum), Çanakkale 162; Arkeoloji Müzesi (Archaeological Museum), Konya 362; Aspendos, Perge, and Side 316; Assos 176, 177-178; Bergama (Pergamum) 184-187; Biga Yarımadası 176; Bodrum 253-255; Bozcaada diving to 173; Cappadocia cave dwellings 335, 341, 342, 347, 351, 354; Cappadocia underground cities 351-353; Efes (Ephesus) 215-221; Fethiye 281, 282; Foça 189; Hattuşaş (Boğazkale) 377-380; Hippodrome (At Meydanı) 43-44; Istanbul Archaeological Museums: 52; İzmir Archaeological Museum: 195; Iznik 134, 136-137; Kadifekale 194-195; Kaş 302; Kaunos 274; Kekova Adası (Kekova Island) 306; Kekova Bay 306, 308; Library of Celsus 19; Lycian rock tombs 275; Macedonian Clock Tower: 143; Olympos 310; Pamukkale 238, 239-242; Patara 296; Priene, Miletus, and Didyma 236-238; Sarayiçi 145; Sart (Sardis) 202-204; Seven Churches of the Revelation 27-28; Termessos 318; Tlos 293; Troy 165-170; underwater 253, 259; Xanthos 295
architecture: Atatürk Mausoleum (Anıtkabir) 368; Ayasofya (Saint Sophia Church) 35, 38; Beylerbeyi Imperial Palace 67; Blue Mosque (Sultanahmet Camii) 40-41; Cırağan Palace 65; Dolmabahçe Palace 61-62; Edirne bridges 145; Fatih Camii (Fatih Mosque) 73; French Street (Fransız Sokak) 59; Gothic 76; Green Mosque (Yeşil Cami) 121; Haydarpaşa Train

Station 70; Istanbul Gar (Istanbul Train Station) 53; Istanbul Museum for History of Science and Technology in Islam 53; İzmir 194; Knidos 272; Küçüksu Kasrı (Küçüksu Palace) 66; Malta Köşkü 63; Marmara University 71; Mausoleum of Halicarnassus 254; Mevlânâ Museum 358-359; Miniatürk 17, 78; Mosque of Süleyman the Magnificent 47-49; Muğlan 271; Nuruosmaniye Mosque 47; overview of Ottoman 48; Taksim 12; Topkapı Palace 41; *yalılar* (waterside mansions) 65; Yivli Minare (Fluted Minaret) 314;Yıldız Park 63; *see also* mosques
Arıburnu cemetery: 150
Arkeoloji Müzesi (Archaeological Museum), Bergama: 185
Arkeoloji Müzesi (Archaeological Museum), Bursa: 128
Arkeoloji Müzesi (Archaeological Museum), Çanakkale: 162
Arkeoloji Müzesi (Archaeological Museum), Konya: 362
Armory and Council Hall: 42
army, Turkish: 405
Arpanu Travel: 57
art: Bozcaada 171; Istanbul Biennial 85; Istanbul Modern Müzesi 61; İzmir museums 196; Museum of Turkish and Islamic Arts, Istanbul 44; Pera Museum 59; Sakıp Sabancı Museum 61; Tophane 58; Turkish and Islamic Arts Museum, Edirne 142; Türk Islam Eserleri Müzesi (Turkish and Islamic Arts Museum), Bursa 125; *see also* crafts; mosaics
Artemis: 229
Artemision (Temple of Artemis): 223
Aşağı Düden Şelalesi (Lower Duden Falls): 320
Asansör (elevator): 194
Asclepeion (Temple of Healing Arts): 186
Ashkenazi Synagogue: 56
Asian Shore (Istanbul): 12; accommodations 99-100; food 107-108; sights 67-72
Askeri Müze ve Kültür Sitesi Komutanlığı (Military Museum): 60
Asmalı Mescit: 58
Aspendos: 248, 316, 317
Aspendos Theater: 317
Assos: 19, 156, 176-180
Ataol Şarapçılık: 172
Atatürk, Colonel Mustafa Kemal: 60, 149, 397-399
Atatürk Evi (Atatürk House): 128, 139
Atatürk Evi (House of Ataturk): 196
Atatürk Kültür Merkezi (Atatürk Cultural Center): 59-60
Atatürk Mausoleum (Anıtkabir): 330, 368
Atlantis: 181
At Meydanı (Hippodrome): 43
ATMs: 437

authors: Abasiyanik, Sait Faik 80; Christie, Agatha 53, 58; Day of the Poets and Homer Readings 172; Greene, Graham 53; Hemingway, Ernest 58; literature 411-412; Loti, Pierre 76, 78; Pamuk, Orhan 58, 80; Rûmî 360; Varol, Mehmet 275
Avanos: 26, 343
Ayana: 173
Aya Nicola Kilisesi (Church of St. Nicholas): 23, 307
Ayasofya (Saint Sophia Church): 12, 15, 19, 30, 35, 38
Ayasofya Camii (Mosque of Ayasofya): 136
Ayasofya cat: 19
Ayasofya Hürrem Sultan Hamam (Baths of Roxelana): 43, 93
Aya Triada Manastırı (Monastery of the Holy Trinity): 59, 80
Aya Yorgi Kililesi ve Manastırı (Aya Yorgi or St. George Monastery): 18, 80, 81
Ayazma beach: 173
Ayazma Festival: 172
Aydınlık beach: 236
Ayışığı Manastırı (Moonlight Monastery): 181
Aynalı Çarşı (Mirrored Bazaar): 161
Ayvali: 351
Ayvalık: 19, 24, 180-184
Azize Barbara Kilisesi (St. Barbara Chapel): 335
Azize Katarina Kilisesi (St. Catherine Chapel): 336

B

Babadağ (Father Mountain): 290
Babakale: 176
Bağdat Caddesi: 68, 72
Bağla: 260
Bahattin'in Samanlığı Kilisesi (Bahattin's Granary Church): 355
baklava: 16, 56
Balat: 76
Balık Pazarı (Fish Market): 59
ballet: 257, 373
Balyan family: Beylerbeyi Sarayı (Beylerbeyi Imperial Palace) 67; Çırağan Palace 65; Dolmabahçe Sarayı (Dolmabahçe Palace) 62; Empire Period work 48; Florence Nightingale Museum 71; Küçüksu Kasrı (Küçüksu Palace) 66; Ortaköy Camii (Ortaköy Mosque) 64; Yıldız Parkı 63
banks: 437
Barbarossa: 230
Bardakcı: 260
Baris Towers: 369
Baroque Period: 48
Basilica Cistern (Yerebatan Sarayı): 15, 30, 43
Basilica of St. John: 18, 224
Basilica of St. Nicholas: 307
baths, Turkish: general discussion 93; Ayasofya

INDEX

Hürrem Sultan Hamam (Baths of Roxelana) 43; Bursa 128; Çeşme Peninsula 204; Hierapolis 241; Kuşadası 230; Marmaris 267; Termal 138-139
Baths of Faustina: 237
Baths of Roxelana (Ayasofya Hürrem Sultan Hamam): 43
Batık Şehir (Sunken City): 307
Bay of Göcek: 279
Bazaar Gate (Çarşı Kapısı): 46
Bazaar Quarters: 45-51
bazaars and markets: Ali Paşa Çarşısı 143; Beyazıt Meydanı (Beyazıt Square) flea market 47; Bodrum 255; Bursa 126; Çanakkale 161; Eyüp 76; Fethiye 21; fish markets 23, 59; Grand Bazaar (Kapalı Çarşı) 46; Güneşli Bahçe Sokak 17; Kadıköy 69; Kadıköy Çarşısı 70; Kemeralti Bazaa: 194; *see also* farmers markets
Beach cemetery: 149
beaches: general discussion 20; Antalya 319; Bodrum 260; Bozcaada 170, 173; Çeşme Peninsula 204, 207; Çıralı Plajı (Çıralı Beach) 310; Dilek Milli Parkı 236; Faralya 292; Fethiye 282-283; Hısarönü Yarımadası (Hısarönü Peninsula) 271; Istanbul 90; Iztuzu Beach 276; Kalkan 298; Kaputaş 301; Kaş 302; Kuşadası 232; Marmaris 267; Ölüdeniz 290; Patara Beach 296; Seddülbahir 151
Beach Park: 320
bedesten (marketplace): 126
Before Lunch Boast Cruises: 284
Belcekiz Plajı (Belcekiz Beach): 283, 290
Belgrade Forest: 90
Bergama (Pergamum): 184-191
Beşkapılar (Five Gates): 190
Bet Israel Synagogue: 196
Bet Nissim Synagogue: 68
Bet Yaakov Synagogue: 68
beverages: 425
Bey, Osman: 126
Beyazıt II Mosque: 126
Beyazıt Meydanı (Beyazıt Square): 47
Beyazıt Mosque: 47
Beyg: 94-96
Beylerbeyi Sarayı (Beylerbeyi Imperial Palace): 67
Beyoğlu: 17; accommodations 96-97; food 104-106; map 55; sights 54-60
Biga Yarımadası: 176
Big Bus tours: 57
biking: Bodrum Bicycle Festival 258; Bozcaada 172; Demre 22; Fethiye 280; Istanbul 90
Bird Paradise National Park (Kuşcenneti Milli Parkı): 124
Birds of Paradise: 197
bird-watching: 124, 133, 197
Bitez: 20, 260
blacksmiths: 126

black tea *(çay)*: 16, 56
Blue Cave: 301
Blue Cruise: 13, 15, 18-23, 258
Blue Lagoon: 21, 22, 290
Blue Mosque (Sultanahmet Camii): 12, 30, 40
boating: Antalya 321; Ayvalık 182; Blue Cruise 258; Bodrum 257, 259; Bosphorus cruise 64-67; Bozcaada 173; *caïque* (imperial rowboat) 57; Çeşme Peninsula 208; Fethiye 283; Foça 190; Gemiler Adası (Boat Island) 283; *gületler* accommodations 24; International Çakabey Optimist Yacht Race 204; International Sailing Week of Istanbul 92; Istanbul 90, 92; Kaş 303; Marmaris 267
boat travel: 415
Bodrum: 13, 20, 22, 249-264
Bodrum Antik Tiyatrosu (Bodrum Antique Theater): 254
Bodrum Bicycle Festival: 258
Bodrum Castle: 253
Bodrum Deniz Müzesi (Bodrum Maritime Museum): 255
Bodrum Life: 251
Bodrum Sualtı Arkeoloji Müzesi (Museum of Underwater Archaeology): 253
Bodrum Yacht Festival: 257
bodysurfing: 290
Boğazkale: 377-380
Boğazköy Museum: 377
Bonjour Pansiyon: 24, 182
Book Bazaar: 47
books: 86
Bosphorus: 97-99, 106-107
Bosphorus Bridge: 65
Bosphorus Cross-Continental Race: 92
Bosphorus cruise: 17, 19, 30, 64-67
Bouleterion-Odeon.: 217
Bouleuterion (Senate), Patara: 296
Bouleuterion (Senate), Troy: 169
Bozcaada: 12, 19, 24, 156, 170-176
Bozcaada Lezzet Festivali (Local Tastes Festival): 172
Bozcaada Sanat Galerisi (Bozcaada Art Gallery): 171
Bozcaada Uçurtma Festivali (Kite Festival): 172
Bozcaada Vintage Festival: 172
Bozdoğan Kemeri (Valens Aqueduct): 73
bridges: 145, 178
brothel, Ephesus: 218
Burgazada (Fort Island): 80
Burning Rock: 311
Burn Kiteboard World Cup: 92
Bursa: 12, 22, 120-132
Bursa Bazaar: 125
Bursa Kent Müzesi (Bursa City Museum): 125
bus tours: 57
bus travel: 418
butterflies: 292

Butterfly Valley: 23
Büyükada: 18, 80, 90
Büyük Çakıl Plajı (Big Pebble Beach): 302
Büyükkale (Great Fortress): 378
Büyük Saray Mozaik Müzesi (Great Palace Mosaics Museum): 45
Büyük Tapınak (Great Temple): 378
Büyük Valide Han: 51
Byzantine aqueducts: 18
Byzantine Basilica: 295
Byzantine Fortress of the Knights of St. John: 306
Byzantine Gate: 241
Byzantine palace: 75
Byzantine shops: 203

C

cable cars: 17, 58
Caddebostan: 91
Çadır Köşkü (Tent Pavilion): 63
Caferağa Medresesi: 51
Café Turco: 225
Cağaloğlu Hamamı: 93
caïque (imperial rowboat): 57
Çalış: 282
calligraphy slates: 39
Camel Wrestling Festival: 225
Camlica Hill: 68
Çanakkale: 22, 159-184
Çanakkale Deniz Zaferi (Çanakkale Naval Victory): 162
Çanakkale Destanı Tantıtım Merkezi: 149
Çanakkale Kent Müzesi: 161
Çandır Kültür Evi: 275
Canterbury: 150
Cape Helles: 151
Cape Helles Memorial Center: 151
Cappadocia: 332-356
Cappadocia and Central Anatolia: 13, 328-380; Ankara 365-377; Cappadocia 332-356; geography 383; Hattuşaş (Boğazkale) 377-380; highlights 330; itinerary 25-27; Konya 356-365; map 331; photo-ops 19; recreation 22, 26; tours 332-334; unique accommodations 24
caravanserais: 266, 344, 356
Çarıklı Kilise (Church with Sandals): 336
carpets: Büyük Valide Han 51; Hereke 66; Istanbul shopping 88-89; Vakıflar Halı ve Kilim Müzesi (Vakıflar Carpet Museum) 45; see also specific place
carriage rides: 80, 81
Çarşı Caddesi: 161
Çarşı Kapısı (Bazaar Gate): 46
car travel: 68, 416, 417
Castle Bar & Restaurant: 23, 266
Castle of St. Peter: 253
cave-dwellings, Göreme Acık Hava Müzesi: 335
Cave of Zeus: 236
Çavuşin: 25, 341-342
çay (black tea): 16, 56
Çayağzı (Andriake): 308
Çekirge: 118, 128
Cemberlitaş Hamamı: 93
Çengelhan Rahmi M. Koç Müzesi (Rahmi M. Koç Museum): 369
Çengelköy Iskele Restaurant: 16, 107
ceramics: Avanos 343; Il Murat Hamamı 137; Istanbul 87
Çeşme: 12, 204
Çeşme Fortress: 204
Çeşme Müzesi (Çeşme Museum): 204
Çeşme Peninsula: 20, 204-209
Chamber A, Hattuşaş: 380
Chamber B, Hattuşaş: 380
Changing of the Guard: 369
Chevalier Island (Şövaliye Adası): 283
Chez Galip: 343
children, traveling with: 428
children's activities: Antalya Aquarium 320; Aqua Fantasy waterpark 233; Aqualand and DolphinLand 320; Blue Lagoon 290; Children's Museum 52; Istanbul Dolphinarium 79; Istanbul Forum 86; İzmir Doğal Yaşam Parkı (İzmir Wildlife Park) 196-197; Oyun ve Oyuncak Müzesi (Toys and Games Museum) 196; Rahmi Koç Müzesi (Rahmi Koç Museum) 78; Santralistanbul Museum 79; Termal baths 139; Tünel Funicular 58
Children's Museum: 52
Chimera: 248, 311
Chora Museum (Kariye Müzesi): 17, 30, 73
Christianization: 389-390
Christie, Agatha: 53, 58
Christ Pantocrator: 39
Chunuk Bair: 151
churches: Aya Nicola Kilisesi (Church of St. Nicholas) 307; Ayasofya (Saint Sophia Church) 35, 38; Aya Triada Manastırı (Monastery of the Holy Trinity) 59, 80; Çavuşin 342; Chora Museum (Kariye Müzesi) 74; Church of Agios Haralambos 205; Church of Koimesis 137; Church of St. John the Baptist 229, 342; Church of St Stephen of the Bulgars 76; Fener Rum Patrikhanesi (Church of Saint George and the Greek Patriarchate) 75; Göreme 335, 336; Ihlara Valley 354; Istiklal Caddesi 59; Kılıç Ali Paşa Hamamı 93; Meryem Ana Kilisesi (Church of Mary) 171; Mustafapaşa 350; Ortahisar (Middle Castle) 347; Red Basilica (Kızıl Avlu) 185; Saint Antoine 59; Sarıca Kilisesi (Sarıca Church) 348; Sart (Sardis) 203; St. Jean Anıtı (Basilica of St. John) 224; St. Panteleimon 68; Surp Krikor Kilesi 68; Surp Takavor Ermeni Kilisesi 70;

457

INDEX

Taksiyarhis Kilisesi (Church of the Archangel) 180, 181
Çiçek Pasajı (Flower Passage): 59
Çiçek Pazarı (Flower Market): 126
Çimenlik Fortress: 161
Çınarlı Cami: 181
Cırağan Palace: 65
Çıralı: 310
Çıralı Plajı (Çıralı Beach): 310
Circular Building: 275
cisterns: 43
Citadel, Ankara: 13, 19, 369
City's: 60, 86
City Walls: Istanbul 74; Iznik 118, 135; Kuşadası 230
civilizations, ancient: 387-389
Çiya Sofrası: 16, 17, 108
Classical Period: 48
climate: 383
clinics: 433
Clock Room: 62
clock towers: Antalya 314; Bursa 127; Çanakkale 161; İzmir 194; Makedonya Kulesi (Macedonian Clock Tower) 143; Saatli Cami (Mosque with a Clock) 180
clothing: 427
coffee: French Street (Fransız Sokak) 59; Mecca-style 66; Turkish 16, 426
Column of Constantine: 47
Column of Julian: 371
Commercial Agora: 219
cons: 435
Constantine and Helen Church: 350
Constantine VII Porphyrogenitus, Emperor: 75
consulates: 421
Çöp(M)adam: 181
Çorlulu Ali Paşa Medresesi: 51
coronation square: 39
Corvus Vineyards: 172
crafts: Avanos pottery 343; Ayvalık 181; Çöp(M)adam 181; *gullet* building 282; Hüsnü Züber Evi (Hüsnü Züber House) 128; Irgandi Bridge 124; İzmir museums 196; Iznik Foundation 137; Museum of Woodwork and Masonry 361; puppetry 126; Selçuk/Efes Festival 225; Şirince 229;Vakıflar Halı ve Kilim Müzesi (Vakıflar Carpet Museum) 45; Yörük (nomadic herders) tribe 179
credit cards: 437
crime: 435
cruises: *see* boating
Crusader Fortress: 21, 281
Crystal Palace: 62
Çukurcuma: 58, 85
Culture Museum & Restaurant-Cafe: 347
Cumhürriyet Müzesi (Museum of the Republic): 372
Cunda: 180, 181
Curetes Way: 217
currency exchange: 437
customs: 422
Cybele Open Air Temple: 190

D

Dalaman River: 22, 259
Dalyan: 13, 21, 274-280
Dalyan-Bostancı: 90
dance: general discussion 413; Ankara 373; Hidrellez (Coming of Spring Festival) 145; International Ballet Festival 257; International Golden Karagöz Dance Competition 129; Kaş Lycia Festival 302
Dardanelles Strait: 12, 160-161
Datça: 272
Datça-Marmaris region: 267
Day of the Poets and Homer Readings: 172
Deësis mosaic: 40
Demirciler Çarşısı (blacksmiths bazaar): 126
demography: 409
Demre: 13, 22, 23, 307-309
Deniz Müzesi (Museum of Naval History): 62
Deniz Restaurant: 16, 199
Derinkuyu Yeraltı Şehir (Derinkuyu Underground City): 352
desserts: 88
diarrhea, travelers': 434
Didyma: 212, 236-238
Dilek Milli Parkı: 236
Dilim Pastanesi: 69
directions: 429
disabilities, access for travelers with: 427
Dış Kale (External Castle): 190
Divan Çukurhan: 24, 374
diving: *see* scuba diving
Diving Festival: 258
Dolmabahçe Sarayı (Dolmabahçe Palace): 17, 30, 61-62
dolmuş (communal taxi): 419
DolphinLand: 320
dolphins: 79
Domed Church: 275
Domitian Gate: 241
Domitian Square: 217
Domitian Temple: 217
Dorians: 272
Double Church: 219
dress: 431
drink: 425
driving: 68, 416, 417
drugging: 436
Düden Şelalesi (Duden Waterfalls): 319

E

early antiquity: 387
East Gate, Troy: 169
economy: 402, 406-408
Edirne: 12, 140-147
Edirne Müzesi (Edirne Museum): 140
Efes (Ephesus): 212, 215-221
Efes Müzesi (Ephesus Museum): 221
Eğritaş Kilisesi (Church with the Crooked Stone): 354
Egyptian Spice Bazaar (Mısır Çarşısı): 17, 49
Ekmekçizade Ahmet Paşa Köprüsü: 145
Eleven: 320
Elmalı Kilise (Apple Church): 335
El Nazar Kilise (Church of the Evil Eye): 336
Embarkation Pier: 150
embassies: 421
emergency services: 110
Emirgan: 60-64
Emirgan Park: 61
Emir Han: 125
Emir Sultan Camii (Emir Sultan Mosque): 124
Empire Period: 48
environmental issues: 384
Ephesus: 12, 18, 22, 27, 212, 215-221
Ephesus Museum: 21, 221
Ephesus Region: 214-238
Erciyes Dağı: 344
Eşfrezade Abdullah Rûmî Tomb: 137
Eski Aynalı Çarşı (Old Mirrored Market): 126
Eski Cami (Old Mosque): 140
Eski Datça (Old Datça): 272
Eski Foça: 189
Eski Kaplıca (Old Baths): 128
etiquette, social: 431
Etnografya Müzesi (Ethnography Museum), Ankara: 27, 372
Etnografya Müzesi (Ethnographic Museum), İzmir: 196
Etnografya Müzesi (Ethnography Museum), Konya: 362
European Fortress (Rumeli Hisarı): 65
e-visas: 14
exotharnex: 39
Eyüp: 76
Eyüp Camii (Mosque of Eyüp): 17, 77

F

Faralya: 292
farmers markets: Bodrum: 255; Cunda: 180; Kadıköy Çarşısı: 70; Ortaköy: 63
Fatih: 72
Fatih Camii (Fatih Mosque): 73
Fatih Köprüsü: 145
Fatih Sultan Mehmet Bridge: 65
fauna: 385-386
Feast of Sacrifice (Kurban Bayramı): 38
Fenerbahçe: 68, 72
Fenerbahçe Parkı: 72
Fener neighborhood: 76
Fener Rum Patrikhanesi (Church of Saint George and the Greek Patriarchate): 75
ferries: Asian Shore (Istanbul) 68; Bodrum 264; Bozcaada 170; Çanakkale 165; Fethiye 287; İzmir 201; Kuşadası 235; Marmaris 270; Princes' Islands (Adalar) 81
Festival of Somewhere: 76
festivals: 85
Fethiye: 13, 21, 280-297
Fethiye Camii (Victory Mosque): 74
Fethiye Museum: 282
film festivals: Altın Portakal Film Festivalı 319; International Film Festival, Ankara 373; International Film Festival, Bodrum 258; Istanbul International Film Festival 85; Short Film Festival 198
First Bridge (Bosphorus Bridge): 65
First Courtyard: 41
fish: 16
fishing: 258
flora: 385
Florence Nightingale Museum: 71
Flower Market (Çiçek Pazarı): 126
Flower Passage (Çiçek Pasajı): 59
Foça: 156, 189-191
folk traditions: Camel Wrestling Festival 225; Culture Museum & Restaurant-Cafe 347; Etnografya Müzesi (Ethnography Museum), Ankara 372; Etnografya Müzesi (Ethnographic Museum), İzmir 196; Festival of Somewhere 76; Kaş Lycia Festival 302; Selçuk/Efes Festival 225; Turkish Night 17
food: general discussion 424-425; Ali Usta Dondurmacı (Ali the Ice Cream Master) 71; Bozcaada Lezzet Festivali (Local Tastes Festival) 172; cooking classes 180; Dilim Pastanesi 69; Festival of Somewhere 76; Kadıköy Çarşısı 70; Kanlıca yogurt 66; Pierre Loti Café 77; regional specialties 16; restaurants 426-427; sweets 88; *see also specific place*
fortress, Pigeon Island: 230
Fortress of Bozcaada: 171
Fortress of the Knights of St. John: 23, 306
Fortress of the Seven Towers (Yedikule): 76
Fountain of Trajan: 217
fountains: Fountain of Kaiser Wilhelm II 44; Nymphaeum 240; Patriça Doğa Parkı (Patrica Natural Reserve) 181; Polio Fountain 217; Sacred Fountain 186; Üç Şerefeli Cami (Mosque with Three Galleries) 140; Ulu Cami (Great Mosque) 125

1453 Panorama Museum: 73
Fransız Sokak (French Street): 59
French Street (Fransız Sokak): 59
French War Memorial and Cemetery: 151
Fun Beach: 208

G

Galata: 56
Galata Köprüsü (Galata Bridge): 17, 19, 50
Galata Mevlevihanesi (Galata Mevlevi Monastery): 57
Galatasaray Lisesi: 59
Galata Tower (Galata Kulesi): 17, 56
Galata Tower bell: 52
Gallipoli National Park: 12, 22, 118, 147-153
Gallipoli Peninsula (Gelibolu Yarımadası): 147-153
Garajistanbul: 85
gardens: Atatürk Evi (Atatürk House) 128; Ayasofya Camii (Mosque of Ayasofya) 136; Bozcaada Sanat Galerisi (Bozcaada Art Gallery) 171; Gülhane Parkı (Gülhane Park) 51; Topkapı Palace 42; Tulip Festival 61, 85; Yıldız Parkı (Yıldız Park) 63
gay nightlife: 84
gay travelers: 432
Gazı, Orhan: 126
Gelibolu Yarımadası (Gallipoli Peninsula): 147-153
Gelibolu Yarımadası Tarihi Milli Parkı (Gallipoli National Park): 118, 147-153
Gemiler Adası (Boat Island): 283
Gemiler Beach: 283
geography: 382-383
ghost towns: 288
Göcek: 279
Gökova: 271
Golden Horn: 50
golf: 259, 321
Göl Kapıları (Lake Gate): 135-136
Göltürkbükü: 260
Göreme: 335-341
Göreme Acık Hava Müzesi (Göreme Open-Air Museum): 330, 335
government: 403-406
Grand Bazaar (Istanbul): 12, 15, 30, 46, 85
Grand Bazaar (Kuşadası): 232
Grand Theater: 219
gratuities: 438
Greater Istanbul: 17, 72-81
Great Mosque (Ulu Cami): 125
Great Mountain (Uludağ): 132-133
Great Palace Mosaics Museum (Büyük Saray Mozaik Müzesi): 45
Great Synagogue: 143
Greek culture: 170, 172
Green Beach Club: 91
Greene, Graham: 53
Green Mosque (Yeşil Cami): 118, 124
Green Tomb (Yeşil Türbe): 121
Grotto of the Seven Sleepers: 220
guides: 427
Gülerada Şarapcılık: 172
gületler (motorized wooden sailboats): 24, 258, 267
Gulf of İzmir: 196
Gülhane Parkı (Gülhane Park): 51, 90
Güllük Dağı Milli Parki (Güllük Mountain National Park): 318
Gülpınar: 176
Gümüşlük: 20, 260
Güvercin Adası (Pigeon Island): 230
Gymnasium of Vedius: 220

H

Habbele: 173
Haci Bayram Camii (Haci Bayram Mosque): 371
Haci Bayram Türbesi (Haci Bayram Mausoleum): 371
Hacı Özbek Camii: 137
Hadrianus Kapısı (Hadrian's Gate): 314
Hafize Sultan Caravanserai: 266
Hagia Eirene: 40
Halicarnassus: 254
Hall of Honor: 368
hamam: see baths, Turkish
Hamid II, Sultan Abdul: 63, 394
hans (inns): Bursa Bazaar 125; Büyük Valide Han 51; Dibekli Han 256; Emir Han 125; Hafize Sultan Caravanserai 266; Kızlarağası Han 194; Koza Han (Cocoon Market) 126; Öküz Mehmet Paşa Kervanserai 204, 230; Yalı Han 161; Zincirli Han 47
Harbor Baths 219
harem, Topkapı Palace: 42
Harpies' Tomb: 295
Hattuşaş (Boğazkale): 13, 377-380
Haydarpaşa Train Station: 70
Hayta Meyhane: 23, 305
Head of Medusa: 237
health: 140, 432-436
heatstroke: 434
helicopter tours: 57
Hellenic and Roman Temples: 275
Hercules Gate: 217
Heybeliada: 80
Hich Hotel: 26, 363
Hidirlik Kulesi: 315
Hidrellez (Coming of Spring Festival): 145
Hierapolis: 13, 21, 212, 238, 239-242
Hieroglyphic Chamber 2: 378
hiking: Antalya 321-322; Bodrum 258; Cappadocia 22; Fethiye 280; Göreme 335, 336, 337; Ihlara Valley 354; Istanbul 90; Kabak Koyu (Kabak Cove) 292; Kelebek Vadisi (Butterfly Valley) 292; Lycian Way 22, 296, 322; Pedesa 256; Saklıkent Gorge 293, 294; Uludağ Milli Parkı 133

Hippodrome (At Meydanı): 15, 43, 52
Hisar Camii: 194
Hısarönü Yarımadası (Hısarönü Peninsula): 271
history: 387-403
History of Science and Technology Museum: 53
Hittite Empire: 377, 387
Homer: 166, 172
Hopkins, Tara: 181
horseback riding: Bodrum 258, 259; Cappadocia 22; Fethiye 284; Göreme 336, 338; Marmaris 267
horse-drawn carriage rides: 80, 81
hospitals: 433
hot-air ballooning: Cappadocia 22, 26; Göreme 336; İzmir Hot Air Balloon Fiesta 225
Hotel Armagrandi: 24, 174
hot springs: Çeşme Peninsula 208; Pamukkale 238, 241; Sultaniye Kaplıcaları (Sultaniye Hot Springs) 277
House of the Virgin Mary: 18, 225
Hüdavendigar Camii: 177
Hüdavendigâr I Murat Camii: 129
Hüdavendigar Köprüsü: 178
Hüsnü Züber Evi (Hüsnü Züber House): 128

I

Iakovidis, Spyros: 167
Iç Bedesten (Inner Bazaar): 47
Ice cream: 71
Içmeler: 267, 271
Içmeler Köyü: 236
IDO ferries: 68, 81
Ihlara Vadısı (Ihlara Valley): 25, 330, 353-355
Ihlara Vadisi Turistik Tesisleri (Ihlara Valley Touristic Facility): 354
II Murat Hamamı: 137
Ikinci Beyazit Külliyesi: 140
Ilıca: 20, 208
Imperial Courtyard: 42
Imperial Gate: 41
Imperial Loge: 121
Ince Minare: 360
industry: 408
Inner Bazaar (Iç Bedesten): 47
inner narthex: 39
insect bites: 433
insurance, health: 432
International Ballet Festival: 257
International Film Festival, Ankara: 373
International Film Festival, Bodrum: 258
International Golden Karagöz Dance Competition: 129
International Istanbul Theater Festival: 85
International İzmir Festival: 221
International Music Festival: 373
International Sailing Week of Istanbul: 92
International Troy Festival: 162

Internet access: 110, 440
Iplikçi Mosque: 359
Irgandi Bridge: 124
Isabey Camii (Mosque of Jesus): 18, 224
islands: Adalar (Princes' Islands) 12, 17, 79-81; Bozcaada 170; Chevalier Island (Şövaliye Adası) 283; Chios 204; Gemiler Adası (Boat Island) 283; Güvercin Adası (Pigeon Island) 230; Kameriye 271; Kekova Adası (Kekova Island) 306; Mediterranean 12-island tour 21, 283; off Ayvalık 180; Samos 236; Tavşan Adası (Rabbit Island) 256
İsmet İnönü: 369
Istanbul: 19, 29-115; accommodations 94-101; best-of itinerary 15-18; entertainment 81-85; food 101-109; highlights 30; history 33; information and services 109-110; maps 32, 36-37, 55; planning tips 12, 33; recreation and sports 90-93; shopping 58, 60, 72, 85-89; sights 34-81; site closure days 38; tours 57; transportation 110-115
Istanbul Arkeoloji Müzesi (Istanbul Archaeological Museums): 52
Istanbul Biennial: 85
Istanbul Dolphinarium: 79
Istanbul Forum: 86
Istanbul Gar (Istanbul Train Station): 53
Istanbul Gate: 135
Istanbul International Art and Culture Festival: 85
Istanbul International Film Festival: 85
Istanbulkart: 34
Istanbul Marathon: 92
Istanbul Modern Müzesi: 61
Istanbul Museum for History of Science and Technology in Islam: 53
Istanbul Music Festival: 85
Istanbul's International Jazz Festival: 85
Istanbul Surları (Istanbul City Walls): 74
Istanbul through the Ages: 52
Istanbul University: 47
Istiklal Caddesi: 17, 30, 58
Istiniye Park: 86
Italian Synagogue: 56
itineraries: 14
İzmir: 12, 191-209
İzmir Arkeoloj i Müzes i (İzmir Archaeological Museum): 195
İzmir Avrupa Caz Festival (İzmir European Jazz Festival): 198
İzmir Doğal Yaşam Parkı (İzmir Wildlife Park): 196-197
İzmir Hot Air Balloon Fiesta: 225
İzmir International Fair: 197
İzmir International Festival: 198
İzmir Mask Museum: 196
İzmir Museum of History and Art: 196

Iznik: 12, 133-138
Iznik Arkeoloji Müzesi (Iznik Archaeological Museum): 136-137
Iznik Foundation: 137
Iznik Şehir Surları (City Walls): 118, 135
Iztuzu Beach: 20, 274, 276
Izzet Paşa Köşkü Mansion: 81

JK

Jade Beach Club: 232
jazz, European: 198
Jeep safaris: 258, 284
jewelry collections: Arkeoloji Müzesi (Archaeological Museum, Bursa) 128; Topkapı Palace 42; Ulumay Museum 127
jewelry shopping: 87
Jewish culture: İzmir 196; Kuzguncuk 68; *see also* synagogues
Johnston's Jolly: 150
John the Apostle: 224
Kabak Koyu (Kabak Cove): 292
Kabatepe: 149
Kadifekale: 194-195
Kadıköy: 68, 69
Kadıköy Çarşısı: 70
Kadınlar Plajı (Women's Beach): 232
Kadir's Treehouses: 24, 310
Kaleiçi (Old Town) Antalya: 19, 23, 24, 311
Kaleiçi (Old Town) Edirne: 143
Kaleiçi Müzesi (Kaleiçi Museum): 23, 315
Kale Kapısı Meydanı (Fortress Gate Square): 314
Kaleköy: 13, 23, 306
Kalın Burun: 173
Kalkan: 13, 297-301
Kalpakçılar Caddesi: 47
Kameriye: 271
Kanlıca: 66
Kanyon: 236
Kapalı Çarşı (Grand Bazaar): 30, 46, 126
Kaptan June Sea Turtle Conservation Foundation: 276, 277
Kaputaş: 20, 301
Karagöz Antiques: 126
Karagöz-Hacıvat puppets: 129
Karagözler: 282
Karagöz Museum: 129
Karaincir: 260
Karaköy: 56
Karaköy Güllüoğlu: 16, 56
Karanlık Kilise (Dark Church): 336
Karasu Burun: 236
Karatay Müzesi (Karatay Museum): 359
Kariye Müzesi (Chora Museum): 30, 73
Kaş: 13, 22, 23, 301-309
Kaş Lycia Festival: 302
Kaunos: 274

Kavaklı beach: 236
Kayakapı Premium Caves: 24, 349
Kayaköy: 13, 19, 21, 280, 288
Kayalar Cami (Mosque of the Rocks): 190
Kaymaklı Yeraltı Şehir (Kaymaklı Underground City): 352
Kekova: 23, 284
Kekova Adası (Kekova Island): 23, 306
Kekova Bay: 248, 306
Kelebek Vadisi (Butterfly Valley): 292
Kemal Erol: 89
Kemeralti Bazaar: 194
kepenek (felt coats for shepherds): 126
Kesik Minare Kulliyesi (Broken Minaret Mosque): 315
Kılıç Ali Paşa Hamamı: 93
Kınaliada: 80
Kırımızı Okul (Red School): 76
Kırk Damaltı Kilisesi (Forty Checkered Church): 355
Kırkpnar Yağı Güreşleri (Kırkpınar Oil Wrestling Festival): 118, 143
Kitchen and Porcelain Collection: 42
kiteboarding: 92
Kite Festival: 172
kitesurfing: 173, 260
Kızıl Avlu (Red Basilica): 185
Knidos: 272
Kocabağ: 345
Koca Çalış: 283
Kocatepe Mosque: 372
Kokar Kilisesi: 354
Konak Meydanı (Mansion Square): 193
Konak Pier: 194
Konya: 13, 26, 356-365
Konya Il Kültür & Turizm Müdürlüğü: 362
Konyalı Topkapı Sarayı Lokantası: 16, 17, 102
Kordon: 195
Korfmann, Manfred: 166
Koyunoğlu Şehir Müzesi (Koyunoğlu City Museum): 362
Koza Han (Cocoon Market): 126
Kral Kapı (King's Gate): 379
Krupp Fortress Gun: 162
Küçük Çakıl Plajı (Small Pebble Beach): 302
Küçüksu Kasrı (Küçüksu Palace): 66
Kuleli Military High School: 66
Kültürpark in İzmir: 195
Kültür Parkı (Culture Park), Bursa: 128
Kurban Bayramı (Feast of Sacrifice): 38, 410
Kurşunlu Banyo: 139
Kurtuluş Camii (Liberation Mosque): 186
Kurtuluş Savaşı Müzesi (Museum of the War of Independence): 372
Kurukahveci Mehmet Efendi: 426
Kuşadası: 13, 230-236
Kuşcenneti Milli Parkı (Bird Paradise National Park): 124

Kuştur and Pygale Beaches: 232
Kuyumcular Çarşısı (Jewelers Market): 126
Kuzguncuk: 67, 68

L

Lake Gate (Göl Kapıları): 135-136
landscape: 382
language: 411
Lara Beach: 320
Lara Sandland: 319
late antiquity: 388
Late Period: 48
latrine, Ephesus: 218
leather: 88, 194
Lefke Gate: 136
lesbian nightlife: 84
lesbian travelers: 432
Leymona Beach and Restaurant: 303
libraries: Ayasofya 39; Aya Triada Manastırı (Monastery of the Holy Trinity) 80; Dolmabahçe Sarayı (Dolmabahçe Palace) 62; Fener Rum Patrikhanesi (Church of Saint George and the Greek Patriarchate) 75; İstanbul Arkeoloji Müzesi (Istanbul Archaeological Museums) 52; Istanbul Modern Müzesi 61; Library of Celsus 19, 218; Pergamum 187; Sevim & Necdet Kent Library and Nostalji Café 181; Topkapı Palace 42
lighthouses: 72, 171
Limanağızı: 303
Lion's Gate: 379
Lions Tomb: 302
literature: 411-412
Lone Pine: 150
Loti, Pierre: 76, 78
Love Valley: 25, 337
Lower Agora: 187
luggage storage: 109
Luke the Evangelist: 216
Lycian Tomb: 295
Lycian tombs: 19, 21, 274, 275
Lycian Way: 22, 292, 322
Lydian Empire: 202

M

Mahmud II, Sultan: 67
Maiden's Tower (Kız Kulesi): 67, 68
mail: 110, 438
Makedonya Kulesi (Macedonian Clock Tower): 143
Maki 29 Beach: 260
malls: 87
Malta Köşkü: 63
Manavgat Waterfalls: 318
Mansion Square (Konak Meydanı)
maps: 86, 440

marathons: 92, 172
Marble Court: 203
marble jar: 39
Marmara Denizi (Sea of Marmara): 120-139, 382
Marmara University: 71
Marmaray train: 68
Marmaris: 22, 265-273
Marmaris Castle: 265
Martyrium of St. Philip the Apostle: 240
masks: 196
Mausoleum of Halicarnassus: 52, 254
Mausolus: 254
Mavi Mağara (Blue Cave): 301
Mavi Yoculuk (Blue Cruise): 258
May Day: 38
media: 440
medical care: 433
medicine, ancient: 186
Medieval era: 390
Mediterranean coast: 20
Mehmet, Fatih Sultan: 65, 73
Mehmet Çavuş Monument: 151
Mehmet I, Sultan: 121
Mehmet II, Sultan: 73, 392
Mehmet III, Sultan: 50
Memerli Plajı (Marble Beach): 321
Memmius Monument: 217
Merkez Plajı (Downtown Beach): 232
Mermer Burnu (Marble Cape): 173
Meryemana (House of the Virgin Mary): 12, 225
Meryem Ana Kilisesi (Church of Mary): 171
metric system: 441
Mevlânâ Culture Center: 26, 356
Mevlânâ Festival: 362
Mevlânâ Müzesi (Mevlânâ Museum): 26, 330, 358
Mevlânâ Shrine: 13, 358
Mevlevi Order: 360-361
Mevlevi Sofrası: 26, 363
Mevlevi Tekke (Whirling Dervish Monastery): 315
Middle City: 187
Miletus: 212, 236-238
Military Museum (Askeri Müze ve Kültür Sitesi Komutanlığı): 60
Military Museum and Çimenlik Fortress: 161
military sights: Anzac Day 162; Bergama (Pergamum) 187; Çanakkale Deniz Zaferi (Çanakkale Naval Victory) 162; Deniz Müzesi (Museum of Naval History) 62; Fortress of Bozcaada 171; Gallipoli National Park 147-153; Krupp Fortress Gun 162; Kuleli Military High School 66; Kurtuluş Savaşı Müzesi (Museum of the War of Independence) 372; Military Museum (Askeri Müze ve Kültür Sitesi Komutanlığı) 60; Military Museum and Çimenlik Fortress 161; Museum of Atatürk and the War of Independence 369; *Nusrat*

minelayer ship 161; Rahmi Koç Müzesi (Rahmi Koç Museum) 78; Selimiye Kislasi (Selimiye Barracks) 71; Turkish Naval Academy 80
minbar: 39
Miniatürk (Miniature Park of Turkey): 17, 78
Miracle Beach Club: 232
Mısır Çarşısı (Egyptian Spice Bazaar): 49
Moda: 68, 71
Moda Çay Bahçe (Moda Tea Garden): 71
money: 109, 437-438
Moonlight Monastery: 181
mosaics: Ayasofya 35, 39, 40; Ayasofya Camii (Mosque of Ayasofya) 136; brothel, Ephesus 218; Curetes Way 217; Fener Rum Patrikhanesi (Church of Saint George and the Greek Patriarchate) 75; Fethiye Camii (Victory Mosque) 74; Great Palace Mosaics Museum (Büyük Saray Mozaik Müzesi) 45; Kariye Müzesi (Chora Museum) 74; Rüstem Paşa Camii (Mosque of Rüstem Paşa) 49
Mosque of Süleyman the Magnificent (Süleymaniye Camii): 47-49
mosques: Antalya 314, 315; Ayasofya Camii (Mosque of Ayasofya) 136; Ayvalık 180, 181; Beyazıt II Mosque 126; Beyazıt Mosque 47; Blue Mosque (Sultanahmet Camii) 30, 40; Bozcaada 171; Çimenlik Fortress 161; Edirne 140, 142; Emir Sultan Camii (Emir Sultan Mosque) 124; Eyüp 76, 77; Fatih Camii (Fatih Mosque) 73; Fethiye Camii (Victory Mosque) 74; Foça 190; Green Mosque (Yeşıl Cami) 118, 121, 124; Haci Bayram Camii (Haci Bayram Mosque) 371; Hüdavendigar Camii in Assos 177; Hüdavendigâr I Murat Camii 129; Isabey Camii (Mosque of Jesus) 224; İzmir 194; Iznik 136, 137; Kanlıca 66; Kocatepe Mosque 372; Kurtuluş Camii (Liberation Mosque) 186; Kuşadası 230; Mevlânâ Müzesi (Mevlânâ Museum) 359; Mosque of Süleyman the Magnificent (Süleymaniye Camii) 47-49; New Mosque (Yeni Cami) 50; Nuruosmaniye Mosque 47; Orhan Gazı Camii (Orhan Gazı Mosque) 126; Ortaköy Camii (Ortaköy Mosque) 64; Osmanağa Camii (Mosque of Osman the Landowner) 70; Rüstem Paşa Camii (Mosque of Rüstem Paşa) 49; Selimiye Camii (Selimiye Mosque) 118, 140; tips for visiting 429; Ulu Cami (Great Mosque) 125; Üryanizade Mescid Camii 68
mud baths: 21, 274, 277
Muradiye Camii: 140
Muradiye Kü lliyesi (Muradiye Complex): 127
Murat I, Sultan: 177
Murat II, Sultan: 127, 128
Murder on the Orient Express: 53
Museum at Aphrodisias: 245
Museum of Anatolian Civilizations: 13, 27, 370
Museum of Atatürk and the War of Independence: 369
Museum of Innocence: 58
Museum of Turkish and Islamic Arts (Türk ve Islam Eserleri Müzesi): 44
Museum of Victory: 78
Museum of Woodwork and Masonry: 361
Museum Pass: 34
music: Ankara 373; Askeri Müze ve Kültür Sitesi Komutanlığı (Military Museum) 60; Atatürk Kültür Merkezi (Atatürk Cultural Center) 59-60; Hidrellez (Coming of Spring Festival) 145; International İzmir Festival 221; International Music Festival 373; Istanbul 83, 85; İzmir Avrupa Caz Festivali (İzmir European Jazz Festival) 198; shopping for 86; Süreyya Operası (Süreyya Opera and Culture Center) 70
Mustafa, Prince: 49
Mustafapaşa: 350
Mycenae: 167
My Local Guide Istanbul: 76
Myndos: 256
Myra ruins: 23, 308

N

Nakibey: 91
naval history museum: 62, 78
Necropolis at Hierapolis: 241
Necropolis at Xanthos: 295
Nek, the: 151
Nereids Monument: 295
Neve Shalom Synagogue: 56
Nevizade Street: 59
New Balance Half Marathon and 10K Run: 172
New Mosque (Yeni Cami): 50
New Thermal Spring (Yeni Kaplıca): 128
Nicene Creed: 216
Nicephorus Phocas: 342
Nicholas, Saint: 296
Nightingale, Florence: 71
nightlife: *see* specific place
Nike: 217
Nişantaş (Marked Rock): 378
Nişantaşı: 60
No. 2 Outpost: 150
Noah's Ark Carpets And Kilims: 89
nomadic herders: 179
Northern Aegean Coast: 154-209; beaches 20; Bergama (Pergamum) 184-191; Çanakkale and Troy 159-184; highlights 156; history 158; İzmir 191-209; maps 157; planning tips 12, 158; unique accommodations 24
Nuruosmaniye Kapısı (Nuruosmaniye Gate): 47
Nuruosmaniye Mosque: 47
Nusrat minelayer ship: 161
Nymphaeum: 240

O

Obelisk at Theodosius: 44
Obelisk at Xanthos: 295
Odion (Theatre), Troy: 169
Oil Wrestling Festival: 118, 143
Öküz Mehmet Paşa Kervanserai: 204, 230
Old Book Bazaar (Sahaflar Çarşısı): 47
Old Greek House: 350
Olimpos Beydağları Sahil Milli Parkı (Olympos Bey Mountains Coastal National Park): 309
olive oil: 407
Ölüdeniz: 13, 20, 21, 22, 23, 248, 283, 290
Ölüdeniz Tabiat Parkı (Ölüdeniz National Park): 290
Olympos: 19, 23, 24, 310
Open-Air Museum: 25, 335
Orhan Gazı Camii (Orhan Gazı Mosque): 126
Orhaniye: 271
Orient Express Restaurant: 53
Orient Express terminus: 53
Original Acropolis: 295
Original Yaka Parkı: 293
Ortahisar (Middle Castle): 347
Ortahisar Castle: 347
Ortakent: 260
Ortaköy: 63
Ortaköy Camii (Ortaköy Mosque): 64
Osmanağa Camii (Mosque of Osman the Landowner): 70
Osman and Orhan Türbeleri (Tombs of Osman and Orhan): 126
Osmanlı Evi Müzesi (Ottoman House Museum): 127
Ottoman architecture: 24, 48
Ottoman cuisine: 16
Ottoman era: 391-397
outdoor adventures: 22
Oyun ve Oyuncak Müzesi (Toys and Games Museum): 196
Özkonak Underground City: 353

P

packing: 427
Palace of Attalid I: 187
Palace of Eumenes II: 187
Palace of Porphyrogenitus (Tekfur Sarayı): 75
Palace of Priam: 169
Palaestra Terrace: 275
Palm Beach Club: 298
Pamphylia: 316
Pamuk, Orhan: 58, 80
Pamukkale: 13, 21, 238-245
Pamukkale Arkeoloji Müzesi: 241
Papaz Hammamı Beach Club: 232
paragliding: Blue Lagoon 22, 284, 290; Fethiye 280
parks: Bird Paradise National Park (Kuşcenneti Milli Parkı) 124; Dilek Milli Parkı 236; Emirgan Park 61; Fenerbahçe Parkı 72; Gallipoli National Park 118, 147; Gülhane Parkı (Gülhane Park) 51; Güllük Dağı Milli Parki (Güllük Mountain National Park) 318; İzmir 195; Kordon 195; Kültür Parkı (Culture Park) 128; Ölüdeniz Tabiat Parkı (Ölüdeniz National Park) 290; Olimpos Beydağları Sahil Milli Parkı (Olympos Bey Mountains Coastal National Park) 309; Patriça Doğa Parkı (Patrica Natural Reserve) 181; Uludağ Milli Parkı 132; Yıldız Parkı (Yıldız Park) 63
Paşabağları: 26, 342
Paşa, Barbaros Hayrettin: 63
Paşa, Rüstem: 49
passports: 14
Patara: 248, 296
Patara Beach: 20, 296
Patriça Doğa Parkı (Patrica Natural Reserve): 181
Pedesa: 256
Pera Müzesi (Pera Museum): 58
performing arts: Ankara 372-373; Istanbul 85; İzmir International Festival 198; Uluslararası Festival 129
Pergamum: 12, 27, 184-191
Perge: 316
Persian Mausoleum: 189
pharmacies: 433
phone services: 439
photo-ops: 19, 76
Pierre Loti Café: 16, 17, 77
Pigeon Valley: 25, 337
pirates: 230
Pırlanta Beach: 20, 207
planning tips: 12-14
plants: 385
Plateia: 241
Plutonion: 240
poetry: 172, 360
police: 422
Polio Fountain: 217
politics: 403-406
pools: 91-92
porphyry columns: 39
postal services: 438
Priam's Treasure: 168
Priene, Miletus, and Didyma: 212, 236-238
Princes' Islands (Adalar): 12, 17, 79-81, 100, 108-109
Professional Windsurfers Association's World Cup: 204
Prytaneion: 217
puppetry: 126, 129
Pürenli Seki Kilisesi (Church with the Heather Terrace): 354
Pygale Beach: 232

Q R

Quinn's Post: 150
rafting, white-water: 22, 259
Rahmi Koç Müzesi (Rahmi Koç Museum): 17, 78, 369
Ramadan: 13, 38
Red Basilica (Kızıl Avlu): 185
Red Bull Aegean Cross: 204
Red School (Kırımızı Okul): 76
Red Tower: 315
Red Valley: 337
religion: 409-411
Rengigül Art Gallery: 171
Republic Monument: 60
Reşadiye Yarımadası (Reşadiye Peninsula): 272
residency visas: 421
restaurants: 426-427
Rock 'n Coke: 85
Roman Amphitheater (Fethiye): 281
Roman Amphitheater (Hierapolis): 240
Roman Amphitheater (Kaş): 302
Roman Amphitheater (Miletus): 237
Roman Baths (Dalyan): 275
Roman Baths (Pergamum): 187
Roman era: 389-390
Roman Pillar Tomb: 295
Roman residence: 203
Roman Road: 203
Roman Theater at Iznik: 137
Roman Theater at Side: 318
Roman Theater at Termessos: 318
Roman Theater at Xanthos: 295
Rose and Honey Valleys: 25, 337
Roxelana: 49
Ruins of Sardis: 203
Rumeli Hisarı (European Fortress): 61, 65
Rûmî: 330, 358, 360
Rüstem Paşa Camii (Mosque of Rüstem Paşa): 49

S

Saatli Cami (Mosque with a Clock): 180
Sacred Fountain: 186
Sacred Pool: 21, 240, 241
Sacred Relics: 42
Sacred Way: 218
Safiye: 50
Sağlık Müzesi (Health Museum): 140
Şahabettin Paşa Köprüsü: 145
Sahaflar Çarşısı (Old Book Bazaar): 47
Şahin, Belgin: 171
Sahip Ata Vakıf Müzesi (Foundation Museum): 362
sailboarding: 208
Saint Antoine: 59
Saint Sophia Church (Ayasofya): 30, 35, 38
Sait Faik Abasiyanik Müzesi (Sait Faik Abasiyanik Museum): 80
Sakıp Sabancı Museum: 61
Saklıkent Gorge: 21, 22, 294
Şale Pavilion: 63
Salı Pazarı (Tuesday Farmers Market): 70
Salt Market (Tuz Pazarı): 126
Samos: 236
Sanctuary of Trajan: 187
Sandal Bedesten (Silk Bazaar): 47
sand sculpture: 319
Santa Claus: 307, 308
Santa Claus Island: 23, 283
Santralistanbul Museum: 79
Saray Gate: 137
Sarayiçi: 144
Saray Köprüsü: 145
Sarcophagus of Fethiye: 281
Sarcophagus of the Mourning Women: 52
Sarıca Kilisesi (Sarıca Church): 348
Sart (Sardis): 12, 27, 156, 202-204
Saruhan: 26, 344
Schliemann, Heinrich: 166, 168
Schliemann's First Trench: 169
science museums: 53
scuba diving: Ayvalık 181; best bets 22; Bodrum 258, 259; Bozcaada 173; Çeşme Peninsula 208; Diving Festival 258; Fethiye 280, 284; Marmaris 267
seafood: 16
sea kayaking: 280, 284
Sea of Marmara: 120-139, 382
seasons, best travel: 13
Sea Turtle Conservation Foundation: 277
Second Courtyard: 41
secularization: 398
Seddülbahir: 151,
Şehir Hatlari: 64, 68, 73, 77
Şehzade Ahmet Türbesi: 127
Şeker Bayramı (Sugar Holiday): 38
Selçuk: 13, 18, 221-228
Selçuk/Efes Festival: 225
Selimiye: 271
Selimiye Camii (Selimiye Mosque) in Edirne: 140
Selimiye Camii (Selimiye Mosque) in Iznik: 118
Selimiye Camii (Selimiye Mosque) in Konya: 359
Selimiye Kislasi (Selimiye Barracks): 71
Selim the Sot: 49-50, 140
Semazens (whirling dervishes): *see* whirling dervishes
Şems-i Tebrizi Mosque and Mausoleum: 359
senior travelers: 430
seraphim: 39
Serpent Column: 44, 52
Seven Churches of the Revelation: 27-28
Seven Sleepers: 220
Sevim & Necdet Kent Library and Nostalji Café: 181

Şeytanın Kahvesi: 181
Şeytan Sofrası (Satan's Table): 181
shadow puppets: 129
Shell Green cemetery: 149
Short Film Festival: 198
Shrapnel Valley cemetery: 149
Side: 316, 317
Side Museum: 318
Sifne Bay: 20, 208
silk: 125, 126
Silk Bazaar (Sandal Bedesten): 47
Silk Road: 121
Sinan, Mimar: Ayasofya (Saint Sophia Church) 38; Baths of Roxelana (Ayasofya Hürrem Sultan Hamam) 43; Bazaar Quarters 45; Classical Period work 48; Edirne bridges 145; Mosque of Süleyman the Magnificent (Süleymaniye Camii) 47-49; Selimiye Camii (Selimiye Mosque) 140
Sinasoss Church: 350
Şirince: 18, 19, 212, 228-230
Sirkeci: 51-54
Şişli: 54-60
Skaian Gate (South Gate): 169
skydiving: 22, 221
smoking: 435
Smyrna: 27
snakebites: 433
snorkeling: 173, 267
snow sports: 22, 133, 382
soccer: 68, 72
social customs: 431
social issues: 129
Soğukçeşme Sokak: 40
Solar Beach: 91
Southern Aegean Coast: 210-245; Ephesus Region 214-238; highlights 212; maps 213; Pamukkale 238-245; planning tips 12, 214; tours 214
South Gate, Troy: 169
Şövaliye Adası (Chevalier Island): 283
Sphinx Gate: 379
Spice Bazaar: 19, 49, 85
spices: 17, 19, 49
Spoonmaker's Diamond: 42
sports: 92-93
Stadium of Aphrodisias: 244
State Agora: 217
St. Basil's Church: 335
Stele of Saint Gregory Thaumaturgus: 40
St. George Monastery: 81
St. Jean Anıtı (Basilica of St. John): 224
St. Nicholas Monastery: 283
stone ramp, Troy: 169
St. Panteleimon: 68
St. Philip the Apostle: 240
student visas: 421
Suadiye: 91
Suburban Theater: 241
Sugar Holiday: 38
Süleymaniye Camii (Mosque of Süleyman the Magnificent): 47-49
Süleymaniye Hamamı: 93
Süleyman Paşa Medresesi: 137
Süleyman the Magnificent: 47-49, 393
Sultanahmet: 12, 15; accommodations 94-96; food 102-104; map 36-37; sights 35-45
Sultanahmet Camii (Blue Mosque): 30, 40
Sultan Banyo: 139
Sultaniye Kaplıcaları (Sultaniye Hot Springs): 277
Sultan Kayıkları: 57
Sultan Murat II: 127
sultan's loge: 39
Sulu Bahçe (Water Garden): 173
Suma Beach: 91
Sümbüllü Kilisesi (Hyacinth Church): 355
Sunan-İnan Kıraç Kaleiçi Müzesi: 315-316
Sunset Point: 25, 335
sunstroke: 434
Sunu mosaic: 40
Süreyya Operası (Süreyya Opera and Culture Center): 70
surfing: 284
Surp Krikor Kilesi: 68
sweets: 88
swimming pools: 91-92
swim races: 92
Sword Valley: 337
Symbols Cafe: 16, 426
synagogues: Ashkenazi Synagogue 56; Bet Nissim Synagogue 68; Bet Yaakov Synagogue 68; Great Synagogue, Edirne 143; Istiklal Caddesi 59; Italian Synagogue 56; İzmir 196; Neve Shalom Synagogue 56; Sart (Sardis) 203; Zülfaris Synagogue 56

T

Tahtakale: 85
Taksim: 12, 17, 59-60, 96-97
Taksiyarhis Kilisesi (Church of the Archangel): 180
Talay Şarapcılık (Talay Winery): 172
Tarihi Galatasaray Hamamı: 93
Tarlakusu Gurmeko Kafe: 180
Tavşan Adası (Rabbit Island): 256
taxis: 420
technology museums: 53
Tekeli Mehmet Paşa Camii: 314
Tekfur Sarayı (Palace of Porphyrogenitus): 75
telephones: 439
Temenni Hill: 347
Temple of Aphrodite: 244

Temple of Apollo (Didyma): 237
Temple of Apollo (Hierapolis): 240
Temple of Apollo (Side): 317
Temple of Artemis (Epheus): 12, 216
Temple of Artemis (Sardis): 203
Temple of Artemis (Selçuk): 223
Temple of Athena (Assos): 176, 177
Temple of Athena (Bergama): 187
Temple of Athena (Foça): 190
Temple of Athena (Priene): 237
Temple of Athena (Side): 317
Temple of Athena (Troy): 169
Temple of Augustus and Rome: 371
Temple of Cybele: 240
Temple of Demetre: 187
Temple of Dionysus: 187
Temple of Hadrian: 217
Temple of Healing Arts: 186
Temple of Telesphorus: 186
Temple of Zeus Asclepius: 186
Tenedos: 170
tennis: 92
Tenodos Museum: 171
Tent Pavilion (Çadır Köşkü): 63
Tepebaşı: 58
Termal: 138-139
Termessos: 318
Terrace Houses: 217
terrorism: 436
Tetrapylion: 244
textiles: 88, 194
Theater Gymnasium: 219
Theater of Aphrodisias: 244
Theater of Kaunos: 275
theft: 435
Third Courtyard: 42
Thrace and the Sea of Marmara 116-153; Edirne 140-147; Gelibolu Yarımadası (Gallipoli Peninsula) 147-153; geography 382; highlights 118; maps 119; planning tips 12, 120; Sea of Marmara 120-139
Thyatira: 27
Tiled Kiosk: 53
tipping: 438
Tlos: 21, 293
Tokalı Kilisesi (Church with Clasp): 336
Tomb of King Amyntas: 21, 281
Tomb of Saint Luke: 216
Tombs of Osman and Orhan (Osman and Orhan Türbeleri): 126
Tophane: 58, 60-64
Topkapı Sarayı (Topkapı Palace): 12, 15, 30, 41
tourism: 408
Tourism Development Cooperative: 290
tourist information: 440
toy museum: 196
traffic safety: 429
train travel: general discussion 415; Haydarpaşa Train Station 70; Istanbul Gar (Istanbul Train Station) 53; Marmaray train 68; Venice Simplon Orient Express 53
trams: 58
transportation: 415-420
traveler's checks: 438
travel tips: 429
Travertines: 21, 212, 238, 239
Treasury: 42
Treaty of Kadesh: 53
tree houses: 19, 24, 310
Triumphal Gate of Modestus: 296
Troad: 176
Trojan Horse: 162, 168
Trotsky, Leo: 81
Troy: general discussion 12, 165-170; *Anatolia and Troy through the Ages* 53; as a highlight 156; International Troy Festival 162
Troy I: 168, 169
Troy II: 168, 169
Troy III-V: 168
Troy IX: 168
Troy VIIb1 and Troy VIIb2: 168
Troy VIII: 168
Troy VIa: 168
True Blue Beach Club: 91
tufa formations: 342
Tulip Festival: 61, 85
Tulip Period: 48
Tunca River: 145
Tünel: 85
Tünel Funicular: 58
Tünel Pasajı: 58
Turasan Şarapevi (Turasan Winery): 348
Turgutköy: 271
Turkey's for Life: 280
Turkey Tour Center: 57
Turkish 57th Regiment Memorial: 151
Turkish and Islamic Arts Museum, Edirne: 142
Turkish coffee: 16, 426
Turkish delight: 16
Turkish Naval Academy: 80
Turkish Night: 17, 84
Turkish Railroad Museum: 54
Türk Islam Eserleri Müzesi (Turkish and Islamic Arts Museum in Bursa): 125
Türk ve Islam Eserleri Müzesi (Museum of Turkish and Islamic Arts in Istanbul): 44
Turquoise Coast: 246-327; Antalya 312-327; beaches 20; Bodrum 249-264; Dalyan 274-280; Fethiye 280-297; highlights 248; Kalkan 297-301; map 250; Marmaris 265-273; Olimpos, Çıralı, and Chimera 309-311; planning tips 13, 249; unique accommodations 24

turtles, loggerhead: 21, 22, 274, 276, 277
Turunç: 267, 271
Tutku Tours: 196
Tuvana Hotel: 24, 323
Tuzburnu: 173
Tuz Pazarı (Salt Market): 126
12-Island Tour: 283
23 Nisan: 369

U

Üçağız: 306
Uçhisar: 344
Uçhisar Kalesi (Uçhisar Castle): 26, 344
Üç Şerefeli Cami (Mosque with Three Galleries): 140
Ulu Cami (Great Mosque): 125
Uludağ (Great Mountain): 22, 132-133
Uludağ Milli Parkı: 132
Ulumay Museum: 127
Uluslararası Festival: 129
underground cities: 330, 351-353
UNESCO sites: Hattuşaş (Boğazkale) 377; Istanbul Gar (Istanbul Train Station) 54; Istanbul Surları (Istanbul City Walls) 75; Pamukkale 238; Sultanahmet 35; Troy 165-170; Ürgüp caves 24; Zelve Open-Air Museum 342
Unison Travel: 90
Unknown Soldier Monument: 150
Ürgüp: 24, 26, 330, 347
Ürgüp Museum: 348
Üryanizade Mescid Camii: 60
Üsküdar: 68
Üsküdar Çinili Hamamı: 93
Uzun Plajı (Long Beach): 232

V

vaccinations: 433
Vakıflar Halı ve Kilim Müzesi (Vakıflar Carpet Museum): 45
Valens Aqueduct (Bozdoğan Kemeri): 73
Valide Banyo: 139
Varol, Mehmet: 275
V Beach: 151
Venice Simplon Orient Express: 53
V-GO: 283
Victory Day: 373
vintage car tours: 57
Virgin Mary: 225
visas: 14, 421

W

Walled Obelisk: 44
War Museum: 151
War of Independence: 369, 372, 396-397

waterfalls: Aşağı Düden Şelalesi (Lower Duden Falls) 320; Düden Şelalesi (Duden Waterfalls) 319; Manavgat Waterfalls: 318; Turgutköy 271; Yukarı Düden Şelalesi (Upper Duden Falls) 321
water parks: 233
water safety: 433
wealth distribution: 408
weather: 383
Westernization Period: 48
Western Mediterranean: 382
whirling dervish: general discussion 361; Galata Mevlevihanesi (Galata Mevlevi Monastery) 57; Konya Il Kültür & Turizm Müdürlüğü 362; at Mevlânâ Museum 26, 358, 359; Mevlevi Tekke (Whirling Dervish Monastery) 315
White Valley: 337
wildlife viewing: Bosphorus cruise 64; Dilek Milli Parkı 236; Uludağ Milli Parkı 133
Wilhelm II, Kaiser: 44
windsurfing: Bodrum 260; Çeşme Peninsula 208; Fethiye 285; Professional Windsurfers Association's World Cup 204
wineries: Bozcaada: 24, 171; Cappadocia: 345, 348
Wines of Turkey: 345
women travelers, tips for: 430, 431
Wooden Yacht Regatta: 257
work visas: 421
World Tennis Association's Istanbul Tennis Cup: 92
World War I: Gelibolu Yarımadası (Gallipoli Peninsula) 147-153; history of 395-396; Museum of Atatürk and the War of Independence 369; Nusrat minelayer ship 161; Tenodos Museum 171
wreck dives: 22, 208, 284
wrestling, oil: 118, 143

XYZ

Xanthos: 248, 295
Xanthos Gate: 295
Xuma Beach: 260
yachting: 257
Yakaköy: 293
Yali Beach Club: 298
Yalı Han: 161
yalılar (waterside mansions): 65
Yalı Mosque: 171
Yazılıkaya (Inscribed Rock): 379
Yedikule (Fortress of the Seven Towers): 76
Yeni Cami (New Mosque): 50
Yeni Foça: 189
Yeni Kaplıca (New Thermal Spring): 128
Yeni Köprü: 145
Yenişehir Gate: 136
Yerebatan Sarayı (Basilica Cistern): 30, 43
Yerkapi (Earth Gate): 379

Yeşil Cami (Green Mosque), Bursa: 118, 121, 124
Yeşil Cami (Green Mosque), Iznik: 137
Yeşil Türbe (Green Tomb): 121
Yılan Kilisesi (Snake Church): 336, 354
Yıldız Parkı (Yıldız Park): 63
Yivli Minare (Fluted Minaret): 314
yogurt: 66
Yörük (nomadic herders) tribe: 179, 275
Yoruk Ali Beach: 91
Yukarı Düden Şelalesi (Upper Duden Falls): 321
Yunatçılar Şarapçılık: 172
Zafer Tower: 369
Zelve: 342
Zelve Open-Air Museum: 26, 342
Zemi Valley: 337
Zincirli Han: 47
zoos: 196-197
Zülfaris Synagogue: 56

List of Maps

Front maps
Istanbul & the Turkish Coast: 2-3
European and Asian Istanbul: 4-5

Discover Istanbul & the Turkish Coast
chapter divisions map: 13

Istanbul
Istanbul: 32
Sultanahmet and Vicinity: 36-37
Beyoğlu: 55

Thrace and the Sea of Marmara
Thrace and the Sea of Marmara: 119
Bursa: 122-123
Iznik: 134
Edirne: 141

The Northern Aegean Coast
The Northern Aegean Coast: 157
Çanakkale: 160
Ayvalık: 180
İzmir: 192
Çeşme Peninsula: 205

The Southern Aegean Coast
The Southern Aegean Coast: 213
Selçuk: 222
Kuşadası: 231

The Turquoise Coast
The Turquoise Coast: 250-251
Bodrum: 252
Around the Bodrum Peninsula: 255
Fethiye: 281
Antalya: 313

Cappadocia and Central Anatolia
Cappadocia and Central Anatolia: 331
The Cappadocia Region: 333
Konya: 357
Ankara: 366-367

Photo Credits

Title page: the Blue Mosque, © Jeremy Reddington/123RF.
All other photos © Leeann Murphy except the following, sourced from 123RF.com:
pg. 7 © DBA Jurin; pg. 8 (top left) © Boris Breytman; pg. 8 (top right) © Tomas1111; pg. 9 (bottom left) © Mariusz Prusaczyk; pg. 10 (top) © Luciano Mortula; pg. 10 (bottom right) © Asta Plechaviciute; pg. 14 © Pavol Kmeto; pg. 19 © Evren Kalinbacak; pg. 20 © Sanai Aksoy; pg. 21 (top left) © Alberto Loyo; pg. 21 (top right) © Viacheslav Khmelnitskiy; pg. 22 © Kevin Richardson; pg. 25 © Mikhail Markovskiy; pg. 26 © Anton Kudelin; pg. 28 © Multitel; pg. 29 © Alex Popov; pg. 31 © Michael Spring; pg. 79 © Igor Simanovsky; pg. 82 © Ozgur Guvenc; pg. 86 © Luciano Mortula; pg. 91 © Halil Erdogan; pg. 106 © Ozgur Guvenc; pg. 114 © Al Ariturk; pg. 116 © Engin Korkmaz; pg. 117 © Ufuk Zivana; pg. 136 © Valery Shanin; pg. 143 © Elkin Yalgin; pg. 154 © Desert Snowflake; pg. 155 © Burak Akmak; pg. 159 © Homeros; pg. 169 © Alexander Trofimov; pg. 186 © Stockbksts; pg. 195 © Silver John; pg. 203 © Omer Genc; pg. 212 © Alexander Shadrin; pg. 220 © Julius Fekete; pg. 237 © Fotoworld; pg. 246 © Cobalt; pg. 247 © Tatiana Popova; pg. 290 © Tsarskaya; pg. 295 © Valery Shanin; pg. 306 © Romasph; pg. 314 © Tatiana Popova; pg. 317 © Tatiana Popova; pg. 320 © Luch Shen; pg. 328 © Alexander Tasefskyi; pg. 329 © Transnirvana; pg. 334 © Mesut Dogan; pg. 343 © Alexander Donchev; pg. 352 © Ozgur Guvenc; pg. 379 © Ollirg; pg. 381 © Ariturk; pg. 414 (top) © Roberto Giobbi; pg. 414 (bottom) © Alexander Donchev.

MAP SYMBOLS

══ Expressway	○ City/Town	✈ Airport	⛳ Golf Course
── Primary Road	⦿ State Capital	✗ Airfield	🅿 Parking Area
── Secondary Road	⊛ National Capital	▲ Mountain	Archaeological Site
┈┈ Unpaved Road	★ Point of Interest	✦ Unique Natural Feature	⛪ Church
┄┄ Trail	• Accommodation	Waterfall	⛽ Gas Station
┈┈ Ferry	▼ Restaurant/Bar	♨ Park	Glacier
┉┉ Railroad	■ Other Location	⬛ Trailhead	Mangrove
Pedestrian Walkway	△ Campground	⛷ Skiing Area	Reef
⊞⊞ Stairs			Swamp

CONVERSION TABLES

°C = (°F - 32) / 1.8
°F = (°C x 1.8) + 32
1 inch = 2.54 centimeters (cm)
1 foot = 0.304 meters (m)
1 yard = 0.914 meters
1 mile = 1.6093 kilometers (km)
1 km = 0.6214 miles
1 fathom = 1.8288 m
1 chain = 20.1168 m
1 furlong = 201.168 m
1 acre = 0.4047 hectares
1 sq km = 100 hectares
1 sq mile = 2.59 square km
1 ounce = 28.35 grams
1 pound = 0.4536 kilograms
1 short ton = 0.90718 metric ton
1 short ton = 2,000 pounds
1 long ton = 1.016 metric tons
1 long ton = 2,240 pounds
1 metric ton = 1,000 kilograms
1 quart = 0.94635 liters
1 US gallon = 3.7854 liters
1 Imperial gallon = 4.5459 liters
1 nautical mile = 1.852 km

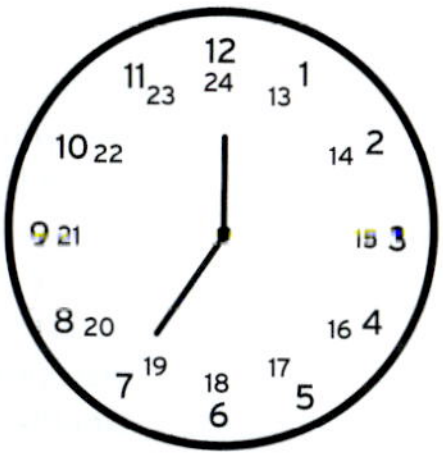

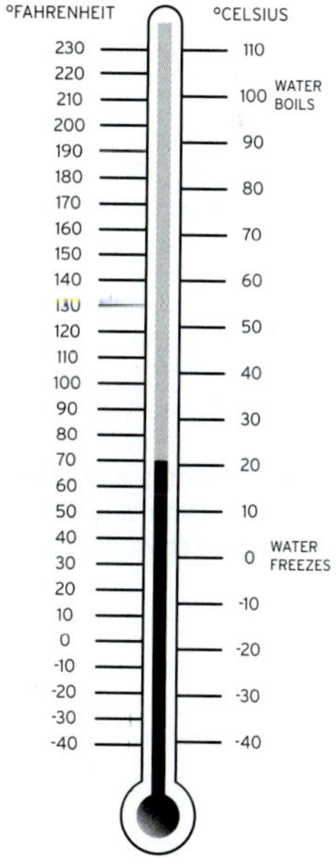

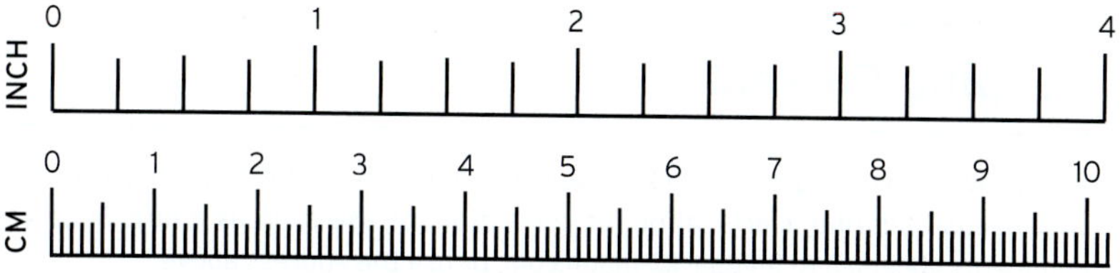

MOON ISTANBUL & THE TURKISH COAST
Avalon Travel
a member of the Perseus Books Group
1700 Fourth Street
Berkeley, CA 94710, USA
www.moon.com

Editor: Nikki Ioakimedes
Series Manager: Kathryn Ettinger
Copy Editor: Christopher Church
Graphics and Production Coordinator: Domini Dragoone
Cover Design: Faceout Studios, Charles Brock
Moon Logo: Tim McGrath
Map Editor: Kat Bennett
Cartographer: Stephanie Poulain
Indexer: Rachel Kuhn

ISBN-13: 978-1-61238-613-3
ISSN: 2155-157X

Printing History
1st Edition – 2010
2nd Edition – December 2014
5 4 3 2 1

Text © 2014 by Leeann Murphy and Avalon Travel.
Maps © 2014 by Avalon Travel.
All rights reserved.

Some photos and illustrations are used by permission and are the property of the original copyright owners.

Front cover photo: Interior of the Sultanahmet Mosque in Istanbul, © Tetra Images/Getty Images

Printed in China by RR Donnelley

Moon Handbooks and the Moon logo are the property of Avalon Travel. All other marks and logos depicted are the property of the original owners. All rights reserved. No part of this book may be translated or reproduced in any form, except brief extracts by a reviewer for the purpose of a review, without written permission of the copyright owner.

All recommendations, including those for sights, activities, hotels, restaurants, and shops, are based on each author's individual judgment. We do not accept payment for inclusion in our travel guides, and our authors don't accept free goods or services in exchange for positive coverage.

Although every effort was made to ensure that the information was correct at the time of going to press, the author and publisher do not assume and hereby disclaim any liability to any party for any loss or damage caused by errors, omissions, or any potential travel disruption due to labor or financial difficulty, whether such errors or omissions result from negligence, accident, or any other cause.

Keeping Current

If you have a favorite gem you'd like to see included in the next edition, or see anything that needs updating, clarification, or correction, please drop us a line. Send your comments via email to feedback@moon.com, or use the address above.